THE PROGRESS OF WORLD-WIDE MISSIONS

THE PROGRESS OF
WORLD-WIDE MISSIONS

BY REV. ROBERT HALL GLOVER, M.D., F.R.G.S.
*Missionary in China for Eighteen Years; Foreign Missions
Secretary for Eight Years; Director of Missionary Course in
the Moody Bible Institute of Chicago for Five Years; Home
Director for North America of the China Inland Mission for
Thirteen Years*

Revised and Enlarged

BY J. HERBERT KANE, M.A.
Barrington College, Barrington, Rhode Island

HARPER & BROTHERS, PUBLISHERS, NEW YORK

To

MY WIFE

*Truest helpmate through many years of united
missionary life and labor, and through trying
periods of separation entailed by my long
journeys afield in China and my later visits to
other distant mission lands,*

This book is affectionately dedicated.

R.H.G.

CONTENTS

ERRATUM

The author regrets that there was not sufficient time before this edition went to press to make an important correction. On several pages the Church of The Nazarene is wrongly listed as one of several Pentecostal groups. This error of classification will be corrected in subsequent printings.

J.H.K.

PREFACE TO THE
REVISED AND ENLARGED EDITION

The death of Dr. Robert Hall Glover in 1947 robbed the Christian Church of one of the great missionary statesmen of the twentieth century. Recognized as the outstanding leader of the Interdenominational Foreign Mission Association, which now represents 25 per cent of North American missionary personnel, Dr. Glover was in constant demand as a missionary speaker and counselor. His greatest single contribution to the cause of missions, so dear to his heart, was his book, *The Progress of World-Wide Missions*, which grew out of his lectures at Moody Bible Institute in the 1920's.

Through the years this book has been widely used at home and abroad. It has also been translated into several foreign languages. A questionnaire sent out in 1954 revealed the fact that over 90 per cent of all the Bible institutes and colleges in the United States and Canada were then using this book as the main text in their History of Missions courses. And this in spite of the fact that it had not been revised since 1939! With continued demand came the request that the book be revised, and the writer was asked to undertake the task. Having used the book as a student, having known the author personally, and having worked with him in the same mission (China Inland Mission), I consider it a distinct privilege to have a share in the ongoing of so influential a book.

Revision is always difficult; it is doubly so when one is revising the work of another person. One hesitates to remove the old even when it has become obsolete. But significant and far-reaching changes have taken place in the world of missions during the past twenty years, so much so that some authorities refer to a "revolution in missions." It is twenty-one years since Dr. Glover revised this book the last time. What great upheavals the world has witnessed in the intervening years! Some countries, like China, once the largest of all mission fields, are now closed. Others, like Nepal, have opened for the first time. Protestant missionary personnel has increased 50 per cent since 1939. Old, well-established Missions, such as the Southern Baptist Convention and the Lutheran Church-Missouri Synod, have taken on new life and have greatly expanded their overseas commitments. Dozens of new Missions, denominational and undenominational, have been born. Young Missions barely twenty-five years old, such as Wycliffe Bible Translators, already have a staff of several hundred missionaries. Certain fields which before the war had only two or three societies working within their borders, such as Taiwan and Thailand, now have anywhere from twenty to sixty different missionary agencies. In all parts of the mission field the indigenous churches are coming into their own, getting on their feet financially, and even sending their own missionaries to sister churches in other parts of the world. No two decades since the beginning of the modern missionary era have brought about so many changes in missionary history and strategy. Any revision that takes all these factors into consideration must be fairly extensive in scope and nature.

Names have posed another problem. Madagascar is now Malagasy. Ubangi-Shari has become the Central African Republic. But how many readers are aware of this? Two countries unite to form a federation, only to have the federation dissolved six months later in the solvent of revolution. One needs a private line to the United Nations Information Office to keep abreast of the fast-moving events of the twentieth century. Mission names likewise cause difficulty. Churches unite and new names appear in missionary literature, but it takes time to become accustomed to the new ones. One mission has a double-barreled name—one part for home consumption and the other for overseas use. Another society has two names, one for the Orient and the other for the Occident! Some readers will identify a mission by its old name; others will know it only by the new. To use both is cumbersome. To employ a footnote or parenthesis with every mention of a new name is tedious.

In the case of countries I have indicated the official name at the head of the chapter, but I frequently employ the popular name throughout the book. Where missions are concerned it has not been so easy to be consistent. In some instances I have thought it wise to use the old name when speaking of the early history of the mission and the new name when referring to recent events. From time to time throughout the book I have added the old name or the new one in parenthesis for the benefit of the reader. I trust this will not be confusing.

The reviser wishes to express his indebtedness to Dr. Frank W. Price, director of the Missionary Research Library, New York City, and his able assistant, Mr. John T. Ma, for the kind and helpful manner in which they placed the research facilities of the Library at my disposal. A word of appreciation is likewise due the many mission secretaries and executives, both at home and abroad, who answered my questionnaire and furnished annual reports and other materials which greatly aided in the execution of this task. Without their generous co-operation such an undertaking could not have been carried out.

Last, but by no means least, I owe a debt of gratitude to my wife for her patience, understanding, and constructive criticism, and especially for her labor of love in typing the entire manuscript in her "spare" time.

J. HERBERT KANE

Barrington, Rhode Island
May 1960

AUTHOR'S PREFACE

The author did not set out to write a book. The present volume has grown out of outline studies prepared for his own classes in Missions. He has yielded to the repeated requests of his students, and of others who shared the studies in pamphlet form, that they might be made more widely available in permanent book form.

The volume makes no pretense of furnishing a complete account of Christian missions. It merely attempts to sketch in simple outline the development and extension of the missionary enterprise from apostolic times to the present day, with emphasis upon some of the events and characters of outstanding importance and inspiration. It is designed primarily as a textbook for use in institutions and mission study groups, where the object sought is some familiarity with the missionary enterprise in general, without particular reference to any one section of the Church. But it has been the author's aim to give to the book a popular rather than a technical tone, as to its subject matter and style, and thus to make it adaptable and interesting to the individual reader as well.

Book references at the foot of the page and a condensed Bibliography at the end of the book are given to facilitate further research. Outline maps are inserted to aid the student in following the geographical expansion of missions as traced in the successive chapters.

The question of the place statistics should occupy has caused some perplexity, because of the desire on the one hand to satisfy those who seek concrete and detailed information, and the fear on the other hand of making the book heavy with a lot of dry figures and tables. The aim has been to strike a happy medium in this matter.

A uniform summary of mission statistics at the end of each chapter was at first planned, but this was later felt to be unsatisfactory because of the fact that the statistics available for the different fields are far from uniform, whether in their classification, their date, or their interpretation. The latest complete figures, contained in *World Statistics of Christian Missions,* published in 1916, are already in many instances far from accurate because of the marked development of the work as well as the drastic world changes which have taken place since they were compiled.

In the case of such fields as India, China, and Japan, which publish Year Books of their own, brief up-to-date statistical summaries have been given, but in other cases, like Africa and Latin America, where many separate fields are involved, this has been found impracticable.

ix

General figures such as areas, populations, etc., are based upon the latest edition of the *Statesman's Year Book* (1923) except where data from more direct sources may have been available. Round numbers have frequently been substituted for exact ones as being easier to remember.

As regards the geographical scope of the book, obviously some limits have had to be imposed. No attempt, therefore, has been made to deal with the great field for evangelical missions in European countries today, nor yet with the work among Indians, immigrants, and other special classes in the United States and Canada. The Arctic regions, comprising Alaska, Hudson Bay, Labrador, and Greenland, have been omitted because these areas have been already largely evangelized, and the task which remains within them is in the hands of the home churches of America and Denmark. For the same reason Australia and New Zealand have not been included in the chapter on Oceania (Pacific Islands), since the evangelization of the diminishing remnants of the aborigines of Australia and the Maoris of New Zealand is now being cared for by the various churches of those lands. All the above areas and constituencies fall more properly under the head of Home Missions, and together they furnish ample material for a separate volume.

It is hardly necessary to state that much of the material incorporated in the present volume has been drawn from other books, of which the number consulted must have reached to many hundreds. Wherever quotations have been made, acknowledgment is given in footnotes.

The author's heartfelt thanks are due in particular, and are here tendered, to two esteemed friends—to Mr. Delavan L. Pierson, editor of *The Missionary Review of the World*, who has painstakingly read through the manuscript, made corrections, and given valuable counsel, and to the Rev. J. E. Jaderquist of New York, who by his sympathy, suggestions, and practical help in a number of ways has contributed no little to the task of preparing the volume for publication.

If the Lord may be pleased to use this book in some measure to deepen missionary conviction and quicken the pulse of missionary effort in this strategic hour of unprecedented missionary opportunity combined with vast missionary need still existing, the author will be profoundly grateful.

ROBERT H. GLOVER

Chicago
February 1924

PART ONE
RISE AND DEVELOPMENT

PERIODS OF CHRISTIAN MISSIONS

For convenience of study the history of Christian missions may be divided into the following periods:

I. Period of Apostolic Missions. 1st Century.
From the Ascension of Christ to the Death of John (33–100).

II. Period of Early Church Missions. 2nd and 3rd Centuries.
From the Death of John to Constantine (100–313).

III. Period of Early European Missions. 4th to 8th Centuries.
From Constantine to Charlemagne (313–800).

IV. Period of the Middle Ages. 9th to 15th Centuries.
From Charlemagne to Luther (800–1517).

V. Period of the Reformation. 16th and 17th Centuries.
From Luther to the Halle Missionaries (1517–1650).

VI. Period of the Early Missionary Societies. 18th Century.
From the Halle Missionaries to Carey (1650–1792).

VII. Period of Modern Missions. 19th and 20th Centuries.
From Carey to the Present Day (1792–   ).

I

INTRODUCTORY

CHRISTIAN MISSIONS DEFINED. Christian missions have a twofold objective: The proclamation of the gospel to the unconverted everywhere according to the command of Christ, and the establishment of a strong, spiritual, indigenous Church in every country.

"*Missions*" comes from the Latin *mitto*—"I send." A missionary is therefore a "sent one." "Apostle," from the Greek *apostello*—"I send," is a synonym for missionary, and the latter and more familiar word may be substituted for the former throughout the New Testament without altering the sense. For example, the fifth book of the New Testament may be called "The Acts of the Missionaries." The term "missions" implies three essential factors, viz., a sender, one sent, one to whom sent.

Jesus Himself was the great missionary. He constantly spoke of Himself as the Messenger sent by the Father to a lost world. And He said, "As my Father hath sent me, even so send I you" (John 20:21).

The missionary does not go or speak at his own initiative, but as the commissioned agent of the One who sent him. And the more absolutely he represents Him, and the more intelligently and faithfully he conveys His message, the more perfectly does he fulfill his missionary calling.

"*Proclamation*" carries the idea of publicity and also of authority. The missionary's message is no private or commonplace matter to be whispered in the ear, but an official declaration of supreme authority and universal import, to be sounded forth in clarion notes. The missionary is to "cry aloud and spare not."

"*Gospel*" means "good tidings." The very name "gospel" indicates its missionary nature, for "tidings" can be tidings only to those who are ignorant of them, and they can be "good" tidings only to those who hear them. It is therefore the very essence of the gospel (good tidings) that it be proclaimed to all men.

"*Unconverted*" means "not turned to"—Christ, and hence signi-

3

fies a lost condition. Cf. Ezek. 33:11—"Turn ye, turn ye; for why will ye die?" The term embraces equally those who through willfulness reject the gospel, those who through indifference neglect it, and those who through ignorance do not know it—that is, *all men everywhere*. The terms "home" and "foreign," commonly applied to missions, are not scriptural, they are merely human terms of convenience. "Unconverted" men are lost—in America, Africa, or Asia alike. Whether the sinner is such through inexcusable willfulness or through unfortunate ignorance, his condition is alike one of peril, and his only hope is in turning to Christ.

"*According to the command of Christ.*" The missionary enterprise rests upon His command and commission for its authority. Christ did not merely express a wish or offer a suggestion. He gave an order, clear, explicit, peremptory—"Go ye into all the world and preach the gospel to every creature." Such is His final, most imperative, most inclusive command, and it is binding upon His followers everywhere and for all time.

But the task is not completed when the gospel has been preached to every creature. Jesus Christ said, "I will build My Church," and the missionary objective has not been fully reached or realized until the converts to Christianity have been adequately instructed in the truth as it is in Jesus and have been organized into a dedicated, dynamic fellowship called the Christian Church. And this Church should be nurtured and strengthened until it becomes in deed and in truth a self-governing, self-supporting, and self-propagating Church.

MISSIONARY MOTIVES. Having defined Christian missions, it naturally follows to consider what have been and what should still be the principal motives to missionary effort. What considerations mainly prompted the first apostles, the early Church, and the long succession of noble men and women who all through the ensuing years have toiled and sacrificed and hazarded their lives in the missionary enterprise? And what are the motives that should actuate Christians today to similar service and sacrifice?

These motives may be divided into two classes:

1. *Motives based upon external facts, or, motives which spring from a consideration of the condition of the heathen.*[1]

[1] The term "heathen" is here used advisedly, and is not intended to give offense. Webster's definition of "heathen" is a pagan, idolater, Gentile, unenlightened person. The Christian, if he is imbued with the Spirit of Christ, will be the first to recognize that the so-called "heathen" have no monopoly on moral or spiritual degradation. Jeremiah declared that the heart, not of the

(a) *Their Temporal Condition.* Even on mere philanthropic grounds the needs and claims of missionary lands have always been, and still are, tremendous. Their dire poverty, wretched homes, unremitting toil, gross intellectual ignorance, unrelieved physical sufferings, and the utter absence of a thousand features which brighten and bless the homes and communities of Christian lands— all this is a mute and pathetic appeal for help.

(b) *Their Moral Condition.* Heathen lands reek with filthy and degrading habits, abominable practices, unmentionable cruelties and crimes, and every form of moral corruption freely tolerated and indulged. Slavery, witchcraft, caste, and polygamy, furnish notorious illustrations of these things. They call insistently for correction.

(c) *Their Spiritual Condition.* This constitutes a paramount claim, far outweighing the previous two. The heathen are not only temporally unfortunate and morally depraved; they are also spiritually lost, for they are wicked and willful sinners. They are not living up to the light of their own consciences, indeed few of them profess to be.

Scripture describes the heathen as "having their understanding darkened, being alienated from the life of God" (Eph. 4:17–19); "enemies [of God] by wicked works" (Col. 1:21); "children of disobedience" (Eph. 2:2; 5:6); "children of wrath" (Eph. 2:3); "without Christ, having no hope, and without God in the world" (Eph. 2:12).

Scripture likewise unfolds God's mode of dealing with all men on the sin question. It declares that "the wages of sin is death" (Rom. 6:23); that "the wicked shall be turned into hell, and all the nations that forget God" (Psa. 9:17); that "the fearful, and the unbelieving, and the abominable, and murderers, and whore-mongers, and sorcerers, and idolaters, and all liars, shall have their part in the lake which burneth with fire and brimstone" (Rev. 21:8); that the only hope of escape is through Christ, for "neither is there salvation in any other" (Acts 4:12).

The basis of God's judicial dealing with all classes of mankind is

---

heathen, but of *man*, is deceitful above all things and incurably wicked. The unregenerate man is the same the world over, and stands in need of the redeeming grace of God in Jesus Christ. Moreover, it should be remembered that social and moral conditions are not the same in all parts of the non-Christian world. Where the great ethical religions have held sway, conditions have been better than in other parts of the world which have known nothing but animism through the centuries. And even in these parts of the world, education, largely the work of Christian missions, has done much to ameliorate the situation.

most clearly set forth in the Epistle to the Romans. In Chapter I, directly following the Apostle's great statement of missionary obligation and the power of the gospel (vv. 14–17), we find a terrific indictment of the heathen world and an appalling picture of its spiritual wickedness and moral filthiness. The heathen are declared to be without excuse as to their idolatrous rites and abominable practices, because of the measure of light which God has given them, even apart from the gospel, through nature and conscience (vv. 19, 20). In Chapter II the cases of the self-righteous Gentile moralist and Jewish legalist are taken up, and their guilt is shown to be aggravated by reason of their added light and privilege. The absolute fairness of God's judgment of all men, whether the heathen under conscience, the Jew under law, or the hearer of the gospel under grace, is made clear (vv. 6, 12, 14, 15). In Chapter III the argument leads on to a final verdict of guilt against the whole human race (vv. 2, 9–12), culminating with the words, "that every mouth may be stopped, and all the world may become guilty before God" (v. 19).

The world's guilt and need thus established, the Apostle thereupon proceeds at once to introduce God's great plan of salvation through faith in Jesus Christ. When Chapter X is reached, a clear and beautiful summary is given of the equality before God of Jew and Gentile, and of His abounding grace toward all alike, so that "whosoever shall call upon the name of the Lord shall be saved" (vv. 12, 13). But immediately afterwards come those convicting words: "*How* then shall they call on him in whom they have not believed? and *how* shall they believe in him of whom they have not heard? and *how* shall they hear without a preacher? and *how* shall they preach, except they be sent?" (vv. 14, 15). How? How? How? How?—unanswerable questions these, constituting one of the most convincing arguments for missions! What solemn responsibility do they lay upon all those who hold the only remedy for the condemning sin of the heathen world!

Acts 10:34–35 is sometimes cited as proof that the heathen can be saved without the gospel. But the very incident with which the text is connected defeats any such argument. For Cornelius was "accepted" of God only as an approved candidate for fuller light, and it was through the gospel message preached by Peter that he and his family were finally saved.[2]

---

[2] Limits of space forbid fuller discussion here of this solemn subject, but those who experience difficulty in reconciling the condemnation of the heathen with divine justice and love will find a most helpful treatment of the subject in Dr. Dennis' *Foreign Missions After a Century*, pp. 202–214.

2. *Motives based upon internal experience, or, motives which spring from a consideration of Jesus Christ and our relation to Him.*

(a) *Loyalty*—the loyalty of servants to their master, of soldiers to their captain, of subjects to their sovereign. And this not in a mere slavish or legal sense, but with wholehearted allegiance and a supreme desire for the exaltation of Christ. This motive was uppermost in the apostles and the early Church. Jesus Christ, who claimed to be the Son of God and the Saviour of men, had been despised and rejected, shamefully treated and crucified as a condemned criminal. His claims must be vindicated, His honor defended, the beauty and holiness of His character and the divinity of His person and work displayed. He must be recognized, be accepted, be loved and enthroned in the hearts of men as Saviour and Lord. To this end all their preaching and efforts were directed (Acts 2:22–24, 32, 36; 3:6, 13–16; 4:10–12, 26–30).

This should be no less potent a missionary motive today, for Jesus Christ is still despised and hated both by multitudes in nominally Christian lands and by millions under the sway of Satan and his wicked spirits in heathen lands. Having made complete atonement for sin, Christ "sat down on the right hand of God, from henceforth expecting till his enemies be made his footstool." How long His expectation has remained unfulfilled! Much is rightly said of the boon that the Lord's coming will be to Christians and to all suffering humanity, as well as to "the whole creation which groaneth and travaileth in pain." But all too little is said or thought of what it will mean to Himself, who so long has waited to "see of the travail of his soul and be satisfied." Loyalty to Christ, then, and a jealous passion for His exaltation, should be the first compelling motive of missions.

(b) *Gratitude*—for His infinite grace and countless blessings received. Why was I not a heathen, a deluded idolater or demon worshiper? Why was I born in a gospel-lighted land, with Christian parents and churches and an open Bible, and countless uplifting influences? Is there any *inherent* difference between me and a poor pagan in Africa or India? No, the difference is all due to the grace of God. All I am and all I have I owe to Him. And unless I am a base ingrate, I shall measure my responsibility to less favored souls by my own blessings and privileges in Christ. Remembering that in the sovereign arrangement of God the positions of the heathen and myself might have been interchanged, I should resolve to do as much for them as I should wish and expect them to do for me if they were where I am and I where they are.

(c) *Love*—for Him who died for us, and His love within us for all for whom He died. This is the supreme motive. It embraces loyalty and gratitude, but transcends them both. It is God's own and only motive. "God so *loved* the world that he gave his only begotten Son." "Christ *loved* the church and gave Himself for it." "Hereby perceive we the *love of God*, because he laid down his life for us; and *we ought to lay down our lives for the brethren*." "If ye *love* me, ye will keep my commandments." "*Lovest* thou me? Feed my sheep." Love does not merely regard the command, but cherishes the wish behind it. Love is not measured and calculating, but reckless, prodigal. It counts no service too long, no sacrifice too great. Such love has burned like a holy fire in the hearts of missionaries of all ages.

To Thee, O Lord, I offer myself, my wife, my children, and all that I possess.—Raymond Lull.

I have one passion; it is He and He alone.—Zinzendorf.

I wanted to wear out my life in His service, for His glory. I rejoiced in my necessity of self-denial. I cared not where or how I lived or what hardships I went through, so that I could but gain souls for Christ.—David Brainerd.

Only divine love filling the heart and pervading the life is equal to the tests and demands of true missionary service today.

THE MISSIONARY IDEA IN THE OLD TESTAMENT. It should not be overlooked that while Christian missions properly begin only with the New Testament, yet the missionary idea is found all through the Old Testament. The Bible from cover to cover is a missionary book. From the very beginning God revealed His plan and purpose as a world-wide one. He said to Adam, "Be fruitful, and multiply and *replenish the earth*" (Gen. 1:28), indicating a world-wide design for Adam's race. The same charge, identically, was repeated when the race was given a new start under Noah (Gen. 9:1). *Diffusion* was God's thought. Strange indeed, then, yet true, that the history of men, God's creatures, has been one long, persistent effort, either ignorantly or willfully, to evade or thwart this purpose.

As early as Genesis IV we detect this in the worldly family of Cain, who "builded a city and called it after the name of his son." Then in Gen. 11:1–9 we find a people not aiming, as God would have them, to reach the ends of the earth, but saying, "Go to, let us build *us* a city and a tower whose top may reach unto heaven, and let us make *us* a name *lest* we be scattered abroad upon the face of the whole earth." The very thing God wanted was the thing they set to work explicitly to defeat. And more than this. For already it was God's purpose, although not yet revealed, to make the human race a means to the exaltation of His Son, that *His* name should be "above every name, that at the name of Jesus every knee should bow . . ." (Phil. 2:9–11). But *they* said, "Let us make *us* a name." Does not this same spirit of self-love and self-glory still dominate the nations of the world, even those that are nominally Christian, whose chief ambition and whose strenuous effort is not to bring about the universal kingdom of Christ, but rather their own dominion and glory? And so God had to interpose, confound their language and upset their ambitious plans. We read, "So the Lord scattered them abroad from thence *upon the face of the whole earth;* and they left off to build the city."

Next, God chose Abraham and the Jewish people, not to lavish upon them an exclusive love, but with the world-wide purpose, expressed in His own words, that "in thee shall *all the families of the earth* be blessed" (Gen. 12:3; also repeated to Abraham, 22:17, 18; to Isaac, 26:2–4; and to Jacob, 28:12–14). But the Jews stumbled at the divine purpose and selfishly misappropriated His blessings to themselves. Consequently God had to lay that nation aside for the time as a failure.

Suggestions of the world-wide reach of God's plan of grace, and striking examples of missionary spirit and effort are not wanting all through the Old Testament. Abraham begins the long procession of missionaries which has covered four thousand years of time. His divine call (Gen. 12:1) still furnishes a worthy model for that of every modern missionary, while his later discharge of active missionary functions in relation to the raid of Chedorlaomer (Gen. 14:1–16) and sinful, heathen Sodom (Gen. 18:22–33) are fine examples of love and zeal.

Joseph was indeed a God-sent missionary to Egypt and the adjoining countries of his day.

Esther is another beautiful missionary type. Identified by nature with a condemned race, but elevated by grace to a place of royal favor, she rightly interprets her position of privilege as meant not for her own selfish gratification, but as a God-given opportunity to help her afflicted people. And so, with noble self-renunciation and courage she flings herself into the breach, and at the risk of her own life rescues a whole nation from impending doom.

The story of Jonah is a fine illustration of God's concern for the heathen, and His patience in leading them to repentance.

It also gives us an example of a runaway missionary—an example which it is to be feared has been followed all too often since. Yet Jonah was finally a successful missionary, as the results proved.

The missionary aim and spirit pervade such Psalms as the 2nd, 67th, 72nd, and others, and the same world-wide outlook is to be found throughout the prophets, even where the central message relates to Israel. (Compare such passages as Isa. 45:22; 52:10; 55:5; 56:6, 7; Jer. 16:19; Zech. 9:10; Mal. 1:11.) Some of the messages of Isaiah and Amos reached out beyond Israel, while Jeremiah's main "burden" concerned the Gentiles. The Jews of the Captivity and the Dispersion, headed by the royal Daniel himself, were theistic missionaries to the East, as well as to southern Europe and northern Africa, down to the time of Christ.

Beautifully suggestive of the breadth of God's sovereign grace is His placing of Rahab and Ruth, both originally heathen women, in the covenant line of which Christ came. The same spirit breathes in the prayer with which Solomon, the type of Christ in His glorious coming kingdom, dedicated the Temple, making request on behalf of "a stranger that is not of thy people Israel, when he shall come out of a far country for thy name's sake." "Hear thou in heaven, thy dwelling place, and do according to all that the stranger calleth to thee for; that *all peoples of the earth* shall know thy name to fear thee" (1 Kings 8:41, 43). And the divine response was, "I have heard thy prayer and thy supplication that thou hast made before me" (1 Kings 9:3).

By such landmarks is God's missionary design distinctly traceable throughout the Old Testament.

II

PERIOD OF APOSTOLIC MISSIONS
FROM THE ASCENSION OF CHRIST
TO THE DEATH OF JOHN (33–100)

Christian missions, in the strict sense of the term, began with the return of the disciples to Jerusalem from the Mount of Ascension. But the earthly ministry of Jesus is by common consent included in the apostolic period, as being not only in itself pre-eminently missionary but also fundamental to the whole subject and enterprise.

Excellent books, such as Latham's *Pastor Pastorum* and Bruce's *Training of the Twelve,* have traced, in the course which Christ's earthly life and labors took, the distinctive design of the schooling of His disciples for their future work. And it is but an easy step further to conceive of His aim as reaching out beyond the narrow circle of His immediate followers to the larger company of His appointed laborers in every succeeding age. For these His life constitutes not only an abiding inspiration but, as well, a permanent model of service. The same may consistently be said of the record of the apostles, inasmuch as it is continually reiterated that they were filled and controlled by the Holy Spirit in their utterances, counsels, and operations. God evidently intended the inspired record of the first generation of missionary activity to be a sample for every succeeding one. Without therefore disparaging the cry in some quarters for more books on the science of missions, and while fully recognizing the value of collations of opinion and experience, is it not still true that altogether the best, the safest, the most practical textbook on missionary principles and practice for all time is the New Testament? This applies even to methods as well, since in their broad scope they also remain permanent, and we venture to affirm that the actual lines pursued by Christ and the apostles will be found, with reasonable adaptation, still to be the best and most effective today.

Let us first take note of some missionary principles and methods taught or illustrated in the New Testament, and then outline briefly missionary progress during this period.

APOSTOLIC MISSIONARY PRINCIPLES. 1. *The aim of missions to make Jesus Christ known to all men as the only Saviour from sin.*
(a) It is a *distinctive* aim—and that spiritual. Nothing is more apparent in Christ's and His apostles' ministry than this, but it needs strong emphasis today. Our work, like theirs, is neither commercial, political, nor even philanthropic. Our aim is not the reconstruction of the state or of society, even though our message may exert powerful influence along these lines. Let such accessory results follow as they may; it is for us to hold faithfully to our distinctive aim of preaching Jesus Christ.

(b) It is a *unique* aim. It claims that all men are in a condition of desperate need, for which Christ is the only remedy; that all religions, even at their best, fail utterly of providing salvation from sin; that Christ is indispensable; that outside of Him there is no salvation either here or hereafter. Missionary effort that is not rooted in strong conviction on this point can never be what it ought to be. Neither habitual contact with heathen life nor yet the admission of helpful teaching and even fragments of spiritual truth in certain of the ethnic religions should ever be allowed to dim the missionary's realization of this solemn fact.

(c) It is a *determining* aim. It should rule our spirits and control our methods as with a hand of iron. There should be no slipping into vague conceptions of duty or drifting into promiscuous projects. All methods employed should be held insistently to the one supreme end. Alas for too many instances of the miscarriage and failure of missionary enterprises through their becoming absorbed in the method to the losing sight of the original aim, and their ultimate substitution of the means for the end!

2. *The policy of missions is the widest diffusion, in contrast to any narrower delimitation.*
This is everywhere apparent in our Lord's ministry, both in precept and in practice. "The field is the world," "Go ye into all the world," "to all nations," "to every creature," "unto the uttermost part of the earth"—such are His own words. His personal example was no less emphatic. Witness His constant movements from place to place, His journeys from one extreme of Palestine to the other, His three distinct circuits throughout Galilee, His visits to Samaria and the coasts of Tyre and Sidon. When a Sabbath's strenuous work in Capernaum had created for Him a unique opportunity, His deliberate words to His disciples are, "Let us go

into the next towns that I may preach there also, for therefore came I forth." He sends out first the Twelve and later the Seventy, two by two, "into every city and place, whither he himself would come." In despised Samaria He bids His exclusive Jewish disciples lift up their eyes and behold their spiritual harvest field. In the parable of the Good Samaritan He strikes a blow at provincialism by interpreting the term "neighbor" to mean the man who needs help, whoever or wherever he be. He makes the miracle of feeding the five thousand a missionary parable in itself, directing an equal and impartial distribution of bread to near and far alike, until "they were *all* filled."

The same policy is repeatedly illustrated in Acts. The first Pentecost after Christ's death sees representatives of a dozen or more countries gathered providentially at Jerusalem to hear "every man in his own tongue" the new gospel message. A little later God uses persecution to scatter abroad the tardy Church so that they "went everywhere preaching the Word." Philip is divinely called away from the Samaria revival to minister to the Ethiopian eunuch and thus extend the witness of the gospel into Africa. Bigoted Peter is dispatched to Gentile Cornelius at Cæsarea, with results as vital to himself and the other apostles as to Cornelius. Antioch displaces Jerusalem as the Christian center because of its more liberal spirit and wider outreach. The conservative Jewish leaders give place to Paul, the apostle to the Gentiles, and the real foreign missionary movement is launched. Even after this, God has to correct the persistent tendency to narrower vision and effort by halting Paul in his second missionary tour of Asia Minor. A man of Macedonia beckons him to regions yet untouched, and God turns the tide of evangelization westward into Europe, the cradle of modern civilization. Paul himself, in a career that knows no parallel in missionary annals, eventually reaches Italy and even Spain.

Is it not incumbent upon the Church at home and missionaries abroad to examine their policy of work to determine whether it squares with the New Testament in insisting on giving precedence to direct and aggressive evangelism and pressing ever onward and outward to "the regions beyond" so long as there remain anywhere areas and populations still wholly unevangelized? There will always be the excuse of much to do nearer home and apparently too few to do it. Yet this cannot alter the fact of the irreparable loss to those left wholly destitute, nor yet the fact that an impartial and un- delayed offer of salvation to all men is the divine command. The terms of our Lord's commission make the first great task of the

Church to be *the evangelization of all men* rather than the conversion of any one favored section or the education of any one preferred class.

3. *The responsibility of missions rests upon every member of Christ.*

The command "Go ye" did not exhaust itself upon the little group that first heard it from the lips of their risen Lord, but is authoritatively repeated whenever and wherever a new company of believers is formed.

The apostolic age furnishes a fine example on this point. We read of the Christians in Jerusalem that "they were *all* scattered abroad, except the apostles; therefore they went everywhere preaching the Word." Of the Thessalonian converts it is said that "from them sounded forth the Word of God not only in Macedonia and Achaia, but also in every place," so that the apostles "needed not to speak anything." As to missionary giving, the Macedonian churches in deep poverty "abounded unto the riches of their liberality." With such conditions, little wonder that the work moved forward and results were what they were.

It is quite true that the *leadership* was invested then, as now, in a distinctive class, divinely called and qualified by special spiritual gifts. But these official workers exercised their true function, not by monopolizing the work, but by leading and "perfecting the saints [the entire Church] unto the work of ministering" (Eph. 4:11, 12 R.V.). It was a time pre-eminently of individual effort, of general consecration to the task of proclaiming the gospel. Some one aptly terms it the "Laymen's Missionary Movement of the First Century." Of missionaries in the modern sense of the term there were few; of those who devoted their full time and strength to the work of preaching there were few; but of those who made their trade, their profession, their everyday occupation, of whatever sort, the means of extending their faith, there was a multitude."[1]

No principle is of more vital importance today, whether to the Church at home or on the mission field. The success or failure of world evangelization is wrapped up in it, for as long as the spread of the gospel in any land depends solely upon a corps of official workers, however efficient and earnest, the outlook is hopeless. The only hope lies in response to the truth—"every Christian a missionary."

APOSTOLIC MISSIONARY METHODS. Principles are fundamental; methods grow out of them by a natural process. If we have been guided to a right selection of principles these will be productive of fruit-

[1] E. M. Bliss, *The Missionary Enterprise* (New York: Revell, 1908), p. 14.

ful suggestion as to proper methods. Space forbids more than the briefest mention of methods employed in New Testament times. The student can readily and profitably develop for himself the points cited.

1. *Oral Preaching.* This is the supreme method for all time. "He ordained twelve . . . that he might send them forth *to preach*" (Mk. 3:14). "They went forth and *preached everywhere*" (Mk. 16:20). "It pleased God by the *foolishness of preaching* to save them which believed" (1 Cor. 1:21). Is there not a significance in the fact that the Holy Spirit at Pentecost assumed the form of tongues, as betokening the part that preaching was to play in the Church age? The direct and immediate result of Spirit-indited preaching was 3,000 souls saved that day and 5,000 more a little later. (See also Acts 5:42; 8:4, 5, 35, 40; 13:5; 28:31; 1 Tim. 2:7; 2 Tim. 1:11; 4:2; 1 Cor. 1:17.)

There is need for a revival of *the preaching idea,* and for a deeper sense of the glory and dignity of simple gospel preaching. Would that God would give to every mission field, from among her own sons, preachers like Wesley and Whitefield and Spurgeon and Moody—great-souled, impassioned, convincing—and through them show forth the true power of preaching!

Where shall we preach? From Christ's day to ours this question has given little difficulty wherever and whenever the true evangelistic spirit has been present. Jesus Himself preached in the Jewish synagogue, on the mountainside, by the Lake of Galilee, at Samaria's well. The apostles preached in the Temple and synagogue, in house, market place, amphitheater, in the courts of prisons, and in the audience hall of a Roman governor. Later evangelists and missionaries have preached in English barns and meadows, in Welsh mines and workshops, in American theaters and city slums, in Chinese teashops and temple squares, in Indian bazaars and at Tibetan fairs, in accustomed and unaccustomed places—in a word, everywhere.

Especially would we emphasize *open-air preaching,* a method adopted by Jesus, and valuable not only for His own time and conditions but for every age and land. It is a bad sign when any church abandons it, no matter how good its chapel equipment may be.

2. *Strategic Centers.* Such centers as Jerusalem, Capernaum, Antioch, Ephesus, Corinth, and Rome stand out far too plainly in New Testament missions for us to escape the lesson of the importance of similar centers today, with their vast populations and powerful radiating influences.

3. *Itineration.* Witness Jesus' successive Galilean circuits and

Paul's missionary tours. Such work still demands its full share of attention along with the centers, and must be systematic and sustained to yield the full results. It has two ends in view: (*a*) the proclaiming of the gospel to the unsaved, and (*b*) the visitation of groups of converts for teaching and oversight (Cf. Acts 8:14, 25; 11:22–26; 15:36).

4. *Personal Work and Social Intercourse.* Looking again at the Master's ministry, one has only to think of Nicodemus, the woman at Sychar's well, Zacchæus, the rich young ruler, the wedding feast at Cana, Simon the Pharisee's dinner, and the home at Bethany, to be impressed with the prominent place these methods hold in missions. (See also Acts 10:24; 16:13–15; 18:2, 3, 26; 28:23, 30, 31.) Nowhere do conditions and customs lend themselves more happily to such measures than on the mission fields today. But these social opportunities need to be seized and held faithfully to the spiritual ends in view, or they may easily become profitless and even a snare.

5. *Literature and Letter Writing.* What are the four Gospels but written accounts of the gospel message designed to supplement verbal preaching when the wide extension of the field of missionary operations required such added means? What were the New Testament epistles originally but letters from missionaries to mission churches and individual converts at a distance? These records took permanent form as the New Testament Scriptures and led the way to the vast output of printed Scriptures, and later on of tracts and other literature, which constitute so effective and indispensable a factor in the missionary enterprise today. Nor would it be easy to estimate the value of the ministry of personal letter writing on the part of the missionary as a means of help and blessing, both to believers and unbelievers.

6. *Training of National Workers.* John the Baptist began such work. Our Lord made it His own greatest ministry, as we have already seen. Paul selected and trained younger men, notably Timothy and Titus, and urged them in turn to do the same (2 Tim. 2:2). This is to be regarded as the crowning missionary method, inasmuch as the missionary's true aim should not be to make himself indispensable, but rather the very reverse, by raising up nationals to take his place. The missionary who successfully does this may be said to work by multiplication instead of mere addition. It should be noted, too, that our Lord's method as a trainer was to maintain the closest connection between class studies and the actual work. Didactic instruction should always be interspersed liberally with practice in chapel preaching, personal work, and

itineration, and preferably under the leadership of the teacher himself.

APOSTOLIC MISSIONARY PROGRESS. The authentic record of missionary progress during this period is to be found in the New Testament itself, to which record secular history adds its corroborative testimony.

1. *Extent of Propagation.* The countries mentioned in Acts as represented by the company assembled in Jerusalem on the occasion of the first Pentecost after Christ's ascension indicate something of the extent of gospel witness-bearing even thus early in the period. We read of "Parthians and Medes, and Elamites, and the dwellers in Mesopotamia, and in Judæa, and Cappadocia, in Pontus, and Asia, Phrygia, and Pamphylia, in Egypt, and in the parts of Libya about Cyrene, and strangers of Rome, Jews and proselytes, Cretes and Arabians" (Acts 2:9–11). A glance at the map shows the territory here mentioned to include the entire area now known as the Near East, from Persia on the east to the Mediterranean on the west and Arabia and Egypt on the south, with the addition of Rome far to the west in Europe.

Other passages attest the extension of the field of missionary operations still farther, for we read of Barnabas of Cyprus (Acts 4:36), Nicolas of Antioch (Acts 6:5), the Ethiopian eunuch (Acts 8:27), and Ananias of Damascus (Acts 9:2, 10).

Then we have the record in Acts of the missionary activities of Peter in Judea and Philip in Samaria, and the much more extensive journeys of the Apostle Paul. These journeys are summed up by Paul himself in Romans 15:19 in one comprehensive statement— "from Jerusalem, and round about unto Illyricum"—which makes them cover Palestine, Syria, Asia Minor, Greece, Macedonia, and the territory on the eastern shore of the Adriatic Sea. Subsequently this great missionary's career extended to Italy, and there is good reason to believe that he even lived to see the fulfillment of his desire to visit Spain, at the western confines of Europe (Rom. 15:24). Some authorities take 1 Peter 5:13 as evidence that the Apostle Peter labored at Babylon in Mesopotamia.

So wonderfully effective was the missionary propaganda of this brief period that before the death of the apostles, churches had been planted in all influential centers of Asia Minor and Greece, and in Rome itself, and few parts of the vast Roman Empire had not at least heard of the new faith. "By the end of the first century Christ had been preached from Babylon to Spain (3,000 miles), from Alexandria to Rome, by a Greek-speaking Church.

It was a *witnessing* church. The word 'witness' occurs in the New Testament 175 times."

The great centers of missionary propagation during this period were, in turn, Jerusalem, Antioch, Ephesus, and Alexandria. The greatest missionary was the Apostle Paul. The first Christian martyr was Stephen.

2. *Number of Converts.* Not only the extent of propagation but also the results achieved must be taken into account in appraising missionary work. While the New Testament furnishes no complete numerical summary of the missionary results of this period, it bears abundant testimony to the fruitful character of the work done. Acts 2:41 tells of 3,000 souls being won to Christ on the day of Pentecost, and Acts 4:4 tells of 5,000 more very soon afterwards. The subsequent chapters of Acts make frequent mention of other conversions, and the repeated use of the word "multitudes" is evidence of large accessions to the Church. (Cf. Acts 5:14; 6:1, 7; 8:6, 12; 10:44, 48; 11:21, 24; 12:24 et al.)

The various epistles of the New Testament were written to organized congregations of Christians scattered over the wide area above outlined. On the basis of all the data available it has been estimated that by the close of the apostolic period the total number of Christian disciples had reached half a million.

3. *Quality of Converts.* This is another important feature which enters into the appraisal of missionary results. The Book of Acts and the New Testament epistles throw clear light upon the character of the Christian converts and churches of the apostolic age. On the one hand, they bear witness to the mighty power of the Holy Spirit upon individuals and assemblies, to the varied gifts and graces of the Spirit in exercise among them, to keen discernment of spiritual truth, to fervent praying, sacrificial giving, and heroic enduring of persecution for Christ's sake. On the other hand, they reveal moral weaknesses and lapses into sin, doctrinal errors and subtle heresies, painful discord and schism among the brethren.

All this goes to show the admixture of true and false professors, robust and feeble Christians in the missionary churches from the very beginning. The Holy Spirit has given a faithful record of both the bright and the dark side of the early Church, for the comfort and encouragement of missionaries in later times.

III

PERIOD OF EARLY CHURCH MISSIONS
FROM THE DEATH OF JOHN TO CONSTANTINE (100–313)

While the first century of missions must ever stand in a class by itself because of the personal life and ministry of our blessed Master and His immediate disciples as its very center and inspiration, yet, when due allowance has been made for this unique fact, it may be said that the general lines and features of the work during this earliest period continued largely unchanged throughout the two centuries which followed, which we have designated the Period of the Early Church. Among the features to be noted are:

EXTENSION. It would be erroneous to draw the conclusion from Acts and other New Testament references to missionary operations of the time that only the few apostles and others mentioned had an active share in the extension of the gospel. Mark tells us that "they went forth and preached everywhere," and Luke says that "they that were scattered abroad went everywhere preaching the word." The record of Acts serves merely as a sample. We have already noted the wide scope of the gospel testimony in the apostolic period as indicated by the list of countries represented in Jerusalem at Pentecost. Persia, Arabia, Mesopotamia, Asia Minor, Greece, Italy, and Egypt and other parts of North Africa all received the message. Nor should we conclude that this first Pentecost was the only one from which seeds were scattered into many distant parts to spring up and bear fruit.

The period following the death of the apostles was not one of great leaders so much as of many leaders. The whole Church was imbued with the spirit of witnessing, and in the course of ordinary social intercourse, travel, and commerce, rather than by any extensive organized movement, the gospel spread far and wide, and little companies of believers sprang up in many lands.

From Ephesus the work extended through Asia Minor, and the seven Churches mentioned in the Apocalypse were established and became self-supporting and self-propagating. The well-known letter of Pliny, Governor of Pontus in Asia Minor, to the Emperor Trajan bears impressive testimony to both the number and the character of Christians in that province. Connected with Syria during this period are such famous names as *Ignatius*, the writer of epistles and martyr under Trajan; *Justin Martyr*, the philosopher; *Eusebius*, the early Church historian; and a little later, *Jerome*, the great scholar who produced the Latin version of the Scriptures called the Vulgate.

In Egypt and North Africa Christianity became strongly entrenched in such centers as Alexandria and Carthage, and there is a touching story of its introduction into the court of the queen of Abyssinia by two young Tyrian captives, and the beginning therefrom of the Abyssinian Church which even Islam failed to overcome.

Whatever of truth there may be in the tradition that Thaddeus and Peter became missionaries to Persia, certain it is that at Edessa, the modern Urfa, there was a strong Christian community in the middle of the second century, and that the king, Abgar, himself became a zealous Christian and is claimed by the Armenians as their first leader in the faith. There are notices of churches in Arabia in the early part of the third century. It is authentic history that *Pantænus* of Alexandria went to India about A.D. 190, in response to messengers sent with an appeal for Christian teachers, and that he found Christians there who possessed a Hebrew Gospel of St. Matthew. Just after the close of this period there existed there about three hundred and fifty flourishing churches.

Athens and Corinth early became strong Christian centers in Greece, while Tacitus, the Roman historian, records that multitudes of Christians abode in Rome. From that city they spread northward through Italy into Gaul, where such noted men as *Irenæus* and *Pothinus*, friends and disciples of Polycarp, the disciple of John, introduced Christianity among the Franks and founded churches in Lyons, Vienne, and Paris. Others crossed the Rhine to the Germanic tribes, and some went even to the British Isles.

Clement and Irenæus, in the first and second centuries respectively, speak of the evangelization of Spain. In the middle of the third century Cyprian of North Africa addressed a letter to a church in Spain, and so great was the advance there that a gathering of nineteen bishops in A.D. 306 is mentioned.

MISSIONARY CENTERS. Jerusalem, Antioch, Ephesus, Alexandria, and Carthage were successively, along with Rome, the great missionary centers of the first three centuries.

Jerusalem, ever to be remembered as the starting point of world-wide missions, retained its broad missionary character only a short time, and then became merely the center of the Church of the Circumcision, with the Apostle James as its first Bishop.

Antioch, much more cosmopolitan, soon succeeded Jerusalem as the home base of missions, from which Paul started on his three missionary tours. It became the patriarchate of all the East till eclipsed by Constantinople, and shed its light far and wide over Asia. It sent missionaries overland through Persia to India and even remote China, and promised to conquer central and eastern Asia for Christ till overwhelmed by Saracen and Tartar. Antioch, once a city of half a million, is now a mere squalid village.

Ephesus won distinction as a missionary center through the successive labors of Paul and John. In the fifth century a council was held there to settle a bitter theological controversy led by rival archbishops, Cyril of Alexandria and Nestorius of Constantinople, the result of which was that Nestorius became an exile and founded the Nestorian Church, which for five centuries was notable for its missionary zeal and its devoted and successful efforts throughout Asia.

Alexandria in turn eclipsed the cities already mentioned and became the intellectual center of the world and the most aggressive and influential center of Christendom, with *Carthage* as a second great center in Africa. They produced the ablest teachers and writers of this period, the best known being *Clement, Origen, Tertullian, Cyprian,* and *Augustine.* Specially worthy of mention here is the great *Catechumens' School of Pantænus* in Alexandria, which served the combined purpose of the defense of the orthodox faith against current heresy and of a training school for missionaries—the first of its kind—who went forth not only into northwestern and eastern Africa, but also to Arabia, India, and Ceylon. Pantænus himself, its president, as already noted, went to India about A.D. 180–190.

GROWTH AND INFLUENCE. The following quotations will serve to impress the fact of the remarkable progress of the gospel during this period, and of the widespread and profound influence exerted by its devoted adherents.

There is no people, Greek or Barbarian, or any other race, by whatsoever appellation or manner they may be distinguished, however ignorant of art and agriculture, whether they dwell in tents or wander about in covered wagons, among whom prayers and thanksgivings are not offered, in the name of the crucified Jesus, to the Father and creator of all things.—Justin Martyr (103–165).

We are but of yesterday, and yet we already fill your cities, islands, camps, your palace, senate, and forum. We have left you only your temples.—Tertullian (160–240).

In all Greece and in all barbarous races within our world, there are tens of thousands who have left their national laws and customary gods for the law of Moses and the Word of Jesus Christ; though to adhere to that Law is to incur the hatred of idolaters and to have embraced that Word is to incur the risk of death as well. And considering how, in a few years and with no great store of teachers, in spite of the attacks which have cost us life and property, the preaching of that Word has found its way into every part of the world, so that Greeks and Barbarians, wise and unwise, adhere to the religion of Jesus—doubtless it is a work greater than any work of man.—Origen (185–251).

There flourished at that time many successors of the apostles, who reared the edifice on the foundations which they laid, continuing the work of preaching the gospel, and scattering abundantly over the whole earth the wholesome seed of the heavenly kingdom. For a very large number of disciples, carried away by fervent love of the truth, which the divine Word had revealed to them, fulfilled the command of the Saviour to divide their goods among the poor. Then, taking leave of their country, they filled the office of evangelists, coveting eagerly to preach Christ and to carry the glad tidings of God to those who had not heard the word of faith. And after laying the foundations of the faith in some remote and barbarous countries, establishing pastors among them and confiding to them the care of those young settlements, without stopping longer they hastened on to other nations, attended by the grace and virtue of God.—Eusebius (266–340).

Accurate statements of the actual number of Christians at the close of this period are obviously impossible. Estimates by various authorities range from one-tenth to one-twentieth of the entire population of the Roman Empire. In A.D. 240, when Gregory Thaumaturgus went as Bishop to Neo-Cæsarea, chief town of Pontus, he found there only seventeen Christians, and when he left in A.D. 265, he left only seventeen non-Christians.

About the same time Cornelius, Bishop of Rome, gives the number of Roman Christians as fifty thousand, or one-twentieth of the total population of a million.

"By the opening of the fourth century Christian Missions had so covered the then known world, that when Constantine came to the throne, he found Christianity if not numerically, at least intellectually and morally, so potent a factor that it must be considered and deferred to. It could not be ignored."[1]

[1] E. M. Bliss, *The Missionary Enterprise* (New York: Revell, 1908), p. 20.

PERSECUTIONS. From the time of the first martyr, Stephen, the early Christian Church was destined to suffer persecution as it faced the mighty political power of Rome, and the deeply entrenched opposition of heathen nations to which it carried the gospel.

Rome, at first inclined to regard the Christians as harmless fanatics, soon changed her attitude, and despite their loyalty and exemplary conduct treated them with suspicion and dislike. As the new cult grew and spread rapidly the rulers became alarmed lest it should weaken the imperial grasp upon great provinces. Prohibition of the faith and persecution of those who embraced it set in and became more and more severe. So unpopular were Christians that for centuries parts of Rome were undermined to form catacombs, where Christians held their meetings in days of persecution, and where the bodies of the dead were laid away. Hundreds of thousands of martyrs sealed their testimony with their blood, among the earlier and most noted of whom were Paul, Ignatius, Polycarp, and Justin Martyr.

Ten distinct persecutions are usually recognized, ranging at intervals from A.D. 64, under Nero, to A.D. 303, under Diocletian. The first of these, planned and carried out by Nero, serves as a sample of all. To cover up his own crime of having wantonly set fire to the city of Rome, and to escape the fury of the populace, Nero deliberately charged the Christians with the crime. The following sentences are taken from a full and vivid description of the horrible orgy by the historian Tacitus:

First those were seized who confessed they were Christians; next, on their information, a vast multitude were convicted, not so much on the charge of burning the city as of hating the human race. And in their deaths they were also made the subject of sport, for they were covered with the hides of wild beasts, and worried to death by dogs, or nailed to crosses, or set fire to, and when day declined, were burned to serve for nocturnal lights. Nero offered his own gardens for that spectacle, and exhibited a Circensian game, indiscriminately mingling with the common people in the habit of a charioteer.

In the catacombs of St. Sebastian in Rome rest the bodies of tens of thousands of Christians, many of them martyrs; nor were these by any means all who loved their Master even unto death. Needless to say, all such efforts to quench the vital spark of divine truth, far from succeeding, only fanned it into a flame and scattered it the more widely. The blood of the martyrs proved then, as it has proved ever since, to be the seed of the Church.

IV

PERIOD OF EARLY EUROPEAN MISSIONS
FROM CONSTANTINE TO CHARLEMAGNE (313–800)

THE CHURCH AT HOME AND MISSIONARY EFFORT ABROAD. Constantine's professed conversion on the eve of his becoming Emperor of Rome was the beginning of a mighty change in the outward standing of the Christian Church and also in its inward character. The story is well known of his seeing a wonderful cross in the sky with the words "*In hoc signo vince!*" (By this sign conquer!) At once adopting the cross as his standard, he led his armies on to victory and then, in his famous Edict of 313, proclaimed Christianity the State religion. Viewed from without this seemed a glorious triumph for the faith, and it is true that it meant new safety of profession and liberty to preach. But in reality it wrought grievous injury to the true cause of Christ through the influx into the Church of a great number of persons who were Christian in name only. The foes which had previously threatened the Church from without now began to attack it from within. Purity of faith and simplicity of worship gradually were lost, and spiritual declension set in. Missionary zeal and activity at once began to wane. The Church leaders were compelled to divert their energies from propagating the gospel to defending the faith. "From a purely missionary point of view, it began the system of compromise with error—of nationalism instead of individualism in conversion—which in the East made the Church an easy prey to Islam, and in the West produced Jesuit Missions."[1]

From A.D. 328, when Constantine removed the capital from Rome to Byzantium (now Istanbul), the history of the Church, like that of the Empire, was divided into Eastern and Western. The *Eastern Church* became engrossed in theological controversies, to the sad loss of its spiritual life and hence also of its missionary

[1] George Smith, *Short History of Christian Missions* (Edinburgh: T. and T. Clark, 1880), p. 57.

24

vision. It fell into a deep sleep from which it was not aroused for many centuries. The *Western Church* was less disposed to discussion than to action. Moreover, the sweeping down upon its territory of great hordes of barbarians from northern Europe compelled attention. Alas, that the Church employed worldly tactics, and sought to attract these pagan tribes by the glitter of religious paraphernalia and elaborate ceremonial rather than by the power of the gospel. As a protest and reaction against this state of affairs many devout men withdrew into solitude, thus laying the foundations of monasticism. A few, more discerning of the real need, and the only way to meet it, heroically gave themselves up to the task of penetrating these distant wilds with the message of the cross. The missionary work of the several centuries which follow, however, stands out in contrast to that of the early Church in being the effort of a few individuals and not of the Church as a whole.

Among the most prominent missionaries of this period were the following:

Ulfilas (311–388), whose name means "the little wolf," was the apostle to the *Goths* north of the Danube River. His parents were among the Christian captives carried off by a band of warlike Goths on one of their incursions into Asia Minor. When about twenty years old he was taken by Alaric, king of the Goths, on an embassy to Constantinople, where he remained ten years and became a Christian scholar. He then returned as a missionary to the Goths and labored until the whole nation accepted the new faith. He was revered and hailed by his converts as a second Moses.

He added to his work as a missionary by giving the letterless Goths the Bible, to do which he had to invent for them an alphabet. He translated the whole Bible, except the books of Samuel and Kings, which he omitted lest their contents should prove too stirring to this warlike people. This Bible is of great value because of its being the oldest form of the Teutonic speech, and more than half of the Gospels is still preserved in the University of Uppsala, Sweden. It is known as the "silver Bible" because of its being written in silver letters on a purple ground.

Martin, Bishop of Tours (316–396), was the pioneer missionary of *Gaul* (France) after the Franks and other northern tribes had invaded this region, where Christianity had earlier been brought by Irenæus and others. Martin was a soldier, and adopted military methods which would be strange and inconsistent in our day. From Tours as a center he led his army of monks through the land, destroying idol temples and groves, and proclaiming the gospel. He is still held as the patron saint of France.

Patrick (396–493), the first great missionary to *Ireland,* and its immortal patron saint, was, contrary to common repute, not an Irishman but a Scotsman. As a boy he was carried captive from his Christian father's home near the present Glasgow, and sold as a slave to a chieftain in northern Ireland, who used him to herd his sheep. There he reflected on his early teaching, and, like the prodigal son, "came to himself." Later he escaped, was retaken, and again escaped. He spent some time in one of the monastic schools of France, and then returning to his father's home he had a night vision like Paul, and heard voices from the Irish coast crying, "We beseech thee, child of God, come and again walk among us." Unheeding the entreaties of his parents and friends, he set out for Ireland, where he spent more than a third of a century in widespread and vigorous evangelism. He was undaunted by the opposition of the pagan chieftains of the Druids. Everywhere he gathered the people about him in the open field and preached Christ to them. His burning zeal and deep sincerity, coupled with a kindly gentleness of manner, completely won the hearts of the peasants and nobility alike. He planted hundreds of churches and baptized thousands of converts. He also founded monastic schools, which became centers of learning and devotion, and whose influence was felt throughout the Middle Ages and in distant parts of the world.

Altogether Patrick imparted a stronger impulse than any other man to medieval missions. A mass of grotesque and unreliable legends clings about his name. It is significant that despite the claims of the Roman Catholic Church upon St. Patrick, his message and methods were more distinctly those of Protestantism than were those of his contemporaries. He had no connection with the Pope, his grandfather was a married priest, and in the reliable accounts of his career there is no reference to such Romish practices as auricular confession, extreme unction, or the worship of Mary.

Columba (521–596). It was fitting that Ireland, indebted for her evangelization to a Scotsman, should in return give to *Scotland* her apostle. Columba was of royal birth, liberal gifts, and high education. He was distinguished for his piety and zeal, and, like Patrick, was a man of constant prayer. After founding several monastic communities in Ireland, he crossed the Irish Channel with twelve companions in 563, and on the small Island of Iona, the most famous center of the Druid superstition, established a center which became one of the most noted missionary schools in history. Not only were all northern Scotland and the adjacent Hebrides, Orkney, and Shetland Islands evangelized by Columba and his immediate followers, but "for two centuries or more Iona was the place in all the world whence the greatest amount of evangelistic influence went forth, and on which, therefore, the greatest amount of blessing from on high rested."[2]

Augustine (505?–605) was the great missionary pioneer to *England*. Gregory the Great, while an abbot, saw three Anglo-Saxon youths exposed for sale in the market at Rome. Attracted by their fair complexion and hair, he asked of what race they were, and when told they were Angles, he wittily replied, "Not 'Angles' but 'angels.'" He desired to go to England as a missionary, but was not permitted by the Pope. When later he himself became Pope he dispatched Augustine with forty Benedictine monks. Hearing tales of the savagery of the Saxons, Augustine at first, like Jonah, turned back. But sternly ordered forward by Gregory the company landed at Kent. They were kindly received by King Ethelbert, who already had some knowledge of the truth through his Frankish wife, Bertha, herself a Christian. Within a year Ethelbert was baptized, and soon after, in accord with the times, his parliament adopted the faith, and in a single day ten thousand of his people were immersed. Canterbury Cathedral was founded and Augustine became its first Archbishop.

Columbanus (543–615), a scholarly Irish monk, whose heart became fired with missionary zeal, set out with twelve companions for Germany. Landing in *Burgundy*, he won the disfavor of the king by his simple austerity and fearless censure of evil living, and pressed onward beyond the Rhine, even reaching the wild Suevi, ancestors of the modern *Swiss*. Like Martin of Tours he waged war against paganism with fiery zeal, smashing idols and burning temples and establishing monasteries in their place. His last effort was to establish work in Italy. He succeeded in founding a monastery across the Alps at Bobbio, where he soon died at an advanced age.

Willibrord (657–739), an Englishman educated and deeply influenced by the Irish Church, was the first missionary to *Holland* and *Denmark*. He faced great pioneer hardships in a rough land and among wild people, but battled on courageously against much opposition, and though finally rejected, he planted the gospel among a people destined centuries later to be among the boldest defenders of the Christian faith.

Boniface (680–755), the great missionary of central Europe, was the apostle especially of *Germany*. He was of noble birth and fine

---

[2] Thomas Smith, *Medieval Missions* (Edinburgh: T. and T. Clark, 1880), pp. 50, 51.

scholarship, but roused by the tales of Willibrord's sufferings, he turned his back upon attractive prospects at home and set out for Holland to join that then aged missionary. Later, declining to succeed Willibrord as Bishop of Utrecht, he pressed on into Hessia and Saxony. He found among the Germanic tribes a chaotic condition of paganism interwoven with some Christian ideas received from earlier Roman, and perhaps also Irish, missionaries. With heroic courage he undertook perilous pioneer journeys in many directions. On one occasion, finding that many of his converts had returned to their old Thor worship, he seized an ax and in the presence of thousands of enraged heathen and trembling half-Christians cut down a sacred oak of Thor. When the mighty tree crashed to the ground and Boniface was not, as they expected, stricken by a bolt from heaven, the people shouted his praise and came in thousands to be baptized.

During twenty years he is said actually to have baptized one hundred thousand converts, though this statement is likely an exaggeration. He was as great an organizer as an evangelist, founded monasteries, schools, and even convents, and welded together these raw heathen into a strong church, although it must be admitted that his methods were not above question, judged by present standards. In his old age Boniface yearned over the land of his first love and returned to Holland. On the shores of the Zuyder Zee, at the age of seventy-five, pillowing his head upon a volume of the Gospels, he received the death stroke at the hands of the pagan ancestors of the Dutch and became a martyr for Christ. His disciple, Gregory of Utrecht, founded there the great missionary college of the time—a fitting memorial of Boniface.

THE RISE AND SPREAD OF ISLAM. While the gospel was thus being carried to the countries of western Europe, there suddenly arose in the East a new religion, destined to have a vital bearing upon world evangelization as one of its most powerful antagonists. This was Islam. Its founder, *Mohammed*, was born in Mecca about A.D. 570. His early life was passed in obscurity, but his marriage at the age of twenty-eight to a wealthy widow, Kadijah, freed him from temporal cares and afforded him leisure for contemplation. He had opportunity to observe not only the paganism of the Arabs, but also Judaism and Christianity, both of which had entered Arabia and were all too sadly tainted in doctrine and enervated in spiritual power. When about forty years of age, Mohammed began to have "visions." His own temperament, together with the persuasions of his wife, who was ambitious for his advancement, led him to interpret these as revelations from God and a call to take up the task of a spiritual reformer. He began to preach, his message being that "there is no God but Allah, and Mohammed is His Prophet." He called his doctrine *Islam*—meaning submission to the divine will. Believers slowly gathered round him, but his claims for himself, as well as his bitter opposition to idolatry, aroused the rulers and townsfolk of Mecca, and in A.D. 622 he was forced to flee for his life to Medina. From this flight, known as the *Hegira*, the Muslim calendar is dated. His career soon changed from that of a mere preacher to that of a political leader and warrior. At first his aims seemed to be confined to exterminating idolatry from his own land of Arabia, but his signal military successes at the head of a small band of followers whetted his ambition. He came to aspire to be the leader of a fierce world-wide crusade against idolatry, and to restore the pure religion which had been revealed by God to the prophets, of which he claimed to be the last and greatest. Meeting with opposition from the Jews, on whose support he had counted, he became fired with a bitter hatred toward them. There was in him a strange mingling of lofty devotion to the will of God and craft and cruelty in carrying out his own ambitions.

His biographers differ widely in their estimates of his character. Some earlier writers extol him as a virtuous man, a pure patriot, and a sincere philanthropist. Later ones swing to the opposite extreme and brand him as a monster of iniquity. Rejecting both of these extreme views one author says:

> He was an Oriental, and became an Oriental potentate. He had the Oriental idea that the privilege of a potentate included indulgence in sensuality. He was not only an Asiatic, but an Arab, an Ishmaelite, nurtured in the faith that his hand must be against every man, strength against strength, stratagem against stratagem, force and fraud against fraud and force. That he believed throughout in his own divine commission no judicious biographer maintains. That he was earnest and honest in his desire to put a stop to the profanities and corruptions of Asiatic heathenism I think should be frankly admitted.[3]

His Arabian armies were possessed by a wild fanaticism and a thirst for plunder and conquest. The prophet's injunction to them was to exterminate all heathen and apostates, and to offer to Jews and Christians the choice of the Koran, tribute, or death. The Eastern provinces of the Roman Empire fell an easy prey before their furious advance. Syria, Mesopotamia, Persia, Asia Minor, and Egypt and North Africa, with their great cities, all fell into

[3] *Ibid.*, p. 164.

the hands of the Muslims. They even swept westward through Europe, and in eight years completed the conquest of Spain. From there they crossed the Pyrenees into southern Gaul, and the Muslim power threatened to encircle Christendom and wipe out the Christian Church. Such a calamity was averted by the crushing defeat dealt the Muslim army by *Charles Martel* and his Frankish soldiers in A.D. 732 at Tours. The tide was stemmed and Europe saved from being overrun by the Arab hordes. The terrible blight of Islam remained, however, and steadily extended over the Levant, North Africa, and western Asia including Persia.

The doctrines and rites of Islam are to be found in the *Koran,* which professes to be a divine revelation to the prophet and is accepted by his followers as the Word of God. Somewhat smaller than the New Testament in size, it is a strange jumble of facts and fables, laws and legends, full of historical errors and superstitions, and is unintelligible without a commentary. While the Muslim doctrine of God is monotheism, its deity, far from being the loving and beneficent God of the Christian Bible, is an unfeeling despot, infinitely removed from His creatures, and with no mediator between. It depicts a hell of fearful torments and a heaven of grossest sensual delights. It sanctions slavery, polygamy, and the degradation of woman. Its only real philosophy is a blind fatalism, which has stamped itself upon every Muslim country and subject, and paralyzed all progress. Its prayers are merely the "vain repetitions" of a formula, its fastings are a farce, its almsgivings are but a pittance. Its pilgrimages to Mecca constitute a strong bond of union among its widely scattered adherents.

As to the bearing of the religion of Islam upon Christian missions, past or present, we cannot do better than quote the following words written by Sir William Muir, which express not only our own personal conviction but also, we believe, that of the body of evangelical missionaries at large:

They labor under a miserable delusion who suppose that Islam paves the way for a purer faith. No system could have been devised with more consummate skill for shutting out the nations over which it has sway from the Christian faith; for there is in it just so much truth— truth borrowed from previous Revelations, yet cast in another mold—as to divert attention from the need of more. *Idolatrous* Arabia (judging from the analogy of other nations) might have been aroused to spiritual life, and the adoption of the faith of Jesus; while *Muslim* Arabia is, to the human eye, sealed against the divine influences of the gospel. Many a flourishing land in Africa and in Asia, which once rejoiced in the light and liberty of Christianity, is now crushed and overspread by darkness. It is as if their day of grace had come and gone, and there remained to them "No more sacrifice for sins." That a brighter morn will yet dawn on these countries we may not doubt; but the history of the past, and the condition of the present, is not the less true and sad. The sword of Mohammed, and the Koran, are the most stubborn enemies of Civilization, Liberty, and Truth which the world has yet known.

V

PERIOD OF THE MIDDLE AGES
FROM CHARLEMAGNE TO LUTHER (800–1517)

The features of this period to be noted as bearing upon the course of Missions may be summed up under three heads: 1. Direct Missionary Operations. 2. The Crusades. 3. The Monastic Orders.

DIRECT MISSIONARY OPERATIONS. The succession of pioneer efforts to evangelize the countries of northern Europe, which we have already noted in the previous period, extended into the earlier portion of this period. Among the leaders and movements deserving mention were the following:

Ansgar (800?–865). A monk of Corvey, a French convent, he was sent back to *Denmark* by the Emperor Louis the Pious, along with King Harold, who had been converted to Christianity. It was a mission of danger that called for a heroic spirit. He opened a Christian school in Denmark, but its success was limited by the unfriendly attitude of the people. Later he made two visits to *Sweden*, on the first of which his ship and all his belongings were seized by pirates. He established his center at Hamburg, on the border between Denmark and Germany, from which convenient point he paid visits in turn to Denmark and Sweden. An attack by heathen Danes, however, completely destroyed his church, school, and library, and his work suffered many vicissitudes. But he was a man of piety, courage, and prayer, and finally succeeded in breaking down the opposition of King Olaf of Sweden, and even of King Horic of Denmark, the bitterest foe of Christianity. Freedom for Christian worship and the building of churches followed, and thus the way of the gospel was prepared in both of these northern kingdoms, where Ansgar is now venerated as "the ideal missionary" and the Apostle of the North.

Norway, Iceland, and Greenland. Norway received Christianity from England in the tenth century. Three valiant and patriotic

Norman princes—Haakon and the two Olafs—tried to introduce it by force, and their zeal and violent measures for the extermination of the worship of Odin and Thor were worthy of Mohammed himself. The final triumph came when the sacred image of Thor fell in fragments under the blows of a Christian soldier, and out of it crept a multitude of mice, snakes, and lizards.

Iceland was colonized in the ninth and tenth centuries by noble families of Norsemen, who took with them their gods Odin and Thor. An Icelander, having been converted in Saxony, took home with him a priest who endeavored to start a mission there in 981, but after seven years he was banished. The precious seed, however, had been planted. King Olaf of Norway himself continued to send missionaries, and finally paganism was completely stamped out and Iceland won to Christianity.

Greenland was in turn evangelized from Iceland, the main instrument being *Leif the Lucky,* son of the Norseman, Eric the Red, the reputed colonizer of Greenland. On his voyage Leif is said to have been driven south by storms and to have landed on the coast of New England four hundred years before Columbus made his voyage of discovery.

Otto, Bishop of Bamberg. Otto carried the gospel in the twelfth century to the *Pomeranians,* who had come under the sway of Poland. In contrast to the first missionaries, who were men of shabby dress and ascetic habits, he went in great episcopal pomp, supported by the King of Poland, and attended by a richly robed retinue whose splendor profoundly impressed this pleasure-loving people. But more than this, Otto's many Christ-like deeds and his spirit of unselfish devotion won their hearts. Thousands accepted baptism; Slavic idols and temples were destroyed; and finally, after thirty years, their most famous idol, of gigantic size, whose worship was supported by taxes, war spoils, and votive offerings, was dethroned in its temple on the island of Rügen and committed to the flames.

Cyril and Methodius (815?–885). These two brothers, who were Greek priests, were sent from Constantinople to the *Bulgarians* in response to a call from a Bulgarian prince whose sister had been converted while a captive on the Bosporus. Cyril was a philosopher and Methodius an artist. The interesting story is recorded of the conversion of Bogoris, the savage king of the Bulgarians, by the drawing by Methodius of the Scene of the Last Judgment upon the wall of the palace. The king led his subjects in being baptized and Christianity was established. From Bulgaria these brother-missionaries extended their labors into *Moravia* and *Bohemia,* and thus their good work became prophetic of that later brotherhood known by the name Moravian, which became one of the foremost agencies in carrying the gospel to the very confines of the heathen world.

In addition to their evangelistic work, Cyril and Methodius did for the Slavs what Ulfilas had done for the Goths, by reducing their language to writing and translating the Bible and Liturgy into Slavonian. The language of this Bible is today to the Russian what Gothic is to the German. A far-reaching effect of this provision of the written character has been to bind the Slavic peoples together, and thus raise an impassable barrier between them and Latin Christianity.

Conversion of the Russians. A century later the Eastern Slavs were turned in a body to Christianity, after the fashion of the early Franks and English, by the baptism of King Vladimir in 988. A princess of his house, Olga, had been led into the Christian faith by a visit to Constantinople in 955 and had been baptized. Vladimir, her grandson, was a thorough pagan, but after investigating through envoys the various religions—Christian, Jewish, and Muslim—he finally became Christian, and cemented his profession of the new faith by marriage with the sister of the Greek Emperor. This marriage laid the foundation for Russia's claim to the inheritance of the Byzantine Empire.

One more missionary name belonging to this period remains to be mentioned and his career sketched, and that the greatest of all —Raymond Lull. But the account of his life much more appropriately follows that of the Crusades, not merely from the standpoint of the order of events, but even more because of the bearing of the Crusades and Lull's career upon each other.

THE CRUSADES. The remarkable series of expeditions known as the Crusades, termed by some the "missions militant" of the Church, cannot, strictly speaking, be regarded as a missionary movement, but so great and widespread were the influences exerted by them, directly or indirectly, upon the religious, intellectual, and social life of the whole civilized world that they cannot be passed by without mention.

Seven Crusades are usually reckoned, occurring at intervals between 1095 and 1272. Their immediate object was to avenge the oppression and cruelties practiced by the fanatical Muslims against the Christians of Syria and particularly the pilgrims to Jerusalem, and to deliver the Holy Land from the power of Islam. Peter the Hermit, an enthusiast, was sent by Pope Urban II through northern

Italy and France to preach a Crusade. Urban himself lent his strong influence to the movement. At the close of a memorable speech of his the whole assembly, swept by a tide of emotion, cried out as one man *"Deus Vult"* ("God wills it") and this expression became the war cry of the advancing hosts. A flame of fanatical zeal spread over all Western Christendom. King and subject, noble and peasant, clergy and laity, old and young, saint and sinner became bound together under the spell of this new inspiration, and willingly sacrificing home, possessions, and even life, flung themselves into the holy war.

Their motives differed widely. Every passion of the human heart was appealed to by the Pope. Penitents were promised absolution from all sins; debtors were made immune from the hand of the law; those who died in action were assured of eternal blessedness and reward. Love of adventure, desire for military renown, and even greed for loot, all had their place along with religious zeal as incentives to spur on these promiscuous multitudes, which numbered many hundreds of thousands.

Among the more important leaders, besides Pope Urban and Peter the Hermit, were Godfrey of Bouillon, Bernard of Clairvaux, King Louis VII of France, Emperor Conrad III of Germany, and Richard the Lion-Hearted of England. The sufferings and losses sustained by the Crusaders were terrible indeed. Many succumbed to the hardships of the journey, others perished in shipwrecks, while vast numbers fell in battle or were taken captive by their Saracen foes. The military successes won were few and short-lived. True, Constantinople, Nicæa, and Antioch were in turn occupied, and Jerusalem was captured in 1099 by Godfrey, who was elected its Christian king. But the repeated attacks of surrounding Muslims upon Palestine could not long be withstood, and finally in 1187 the Holy City itself was retaken, to remain until 1917 in Muslim hands.

As time went on the religious fervor which had at first dominated the Crusades cooled, worldly motives prevailed, political and religious rivalries sprang up among the various leaders, and failure to realize the ends hoped for at length led to the abandonment of the enterprise. But if the immediate objects of the Crusades were not achieved, yet the effects were manifold and far-reaching. The following may be mentioned:

1. A better acquaintance and understanding came about between the people of the West and East. The old spirit of prejudice and even hatred, which had prevailed in the West toward the East, and notably toward all Muslims, gave way to a larger spirit of

appreciation and sympathy—a change distinctly favorable to missionary progress.

2. The Crusaders came in contact with the older and more advanced civilizations of the Greeks and Saracens, and Eastern arts, sciences, and inventions were introduced into Europe.

3. Commerce, especially maritime, greatly expanded, bringing new wealth to Europe and causing great cities to spring up. Along with these changes, the fact also that so many nobles impoverished themselves in preparation for the Crusades tended to an equalizing of the social classes.

4. The closer relations into which the Crusades brought laymen with the clergy served to give to the former a truer knowledge of the latter. Much of the traditional spirit of veneration for the papal court and clergy was lost and freedom of opinion fostered—a change which became a real factor in preparing the way for the Reformation of a century later.

5. While, as already remarked, the Crusades were not in any true sense a missionary movement, yet they did contribute to the spread of Christianity in regions where it was little known. Also, while their aims and efforts were for the punishment and overthrow of the Muslims, rather than their Christianization, yet there were a few souls in that age who, in contrast to the prevailing spirit, showed a genuine concern for the spiritual welfare of Muslims, and set on foot the earliest plans for missionary work among them. Such, for example, was Peter the Venerable, Abbot of Cluny in France, who studied the Muslim creed with sympathy and prepared translations of the Scriptures and other works with a view to influencing them.

But the one whose name will forever stand out in this connection with incomparable luster is Raymond Lull, the first and still the greatest missionary to the Muslims. After the Crusades had proved a failure, it was he who inaugurated the gospel method of conquering the false faith. He seemed to be raised up by God to prove by his example what the Crusades might have become, and might have done for the world, had they fought for the Cross with spiritual instead of carnal weapons, and approached the Saracens with the Word of Truth rather than with force of arms.

Raymond Lull (1235–1315) was born of a noble Spanish family, on the island of Majorca. His father took part in one of the Crusades. The story of Lull's life reads like a romance. He was a brilliant student, a skilled musician, and a gay courtier. In the midst of a profligate career he was arrested by a vision of Christ on the cross, experienced an agony of repentance, and then, turning his back on all his former life and associates, gave himself up in full consecration to Christ and to preparations and plans for the conversion of the Saracens. Convinced of the need of a thorough knowledge of the language of any people for a successful approach to them, he himself mastered Arabic and used his wealth in seeking to establish schools in which others might study various languages and fit themselves for missionary work.

In vain, however, did he appeal to both Church and State for help, and at length, failing to induce others to join him, he went alone to the fanatical Muslim center of Tunis, North Africa. There he was so successful in his arguments with the Muslim doctors that he was thrown into prison and shortly afterwards sent from the country. Returning a second time to Africa, he was again imprisoned, though the Muslims spared his life in recognition of his splendid courage. When a third time he persisted in going to Africa in spite of threats against his life, he was set upon while preaching at Bugia and was stoned to death at the age of eighty. "In an age of violence he was the apostle of heavenly love. Let this motto from his own great book be adopted by all of his true successors: *"He who loves not, lives not; he who lives by the Life cannot die."*"[1]

"He is the one connecting link in Missions between the apostles of Northern Europe and the leaders who, following the Reformation, carried the Gospel to every part of the rapidly increasing world."[2]

THE MONASTIC ORDERS. Christian monasticism (a word signifying the "lonely" life) had its rise in Egypt in the third century, when Paul the Hermit and other Christians withdrew into the desert to avoid the Decian persecution.

During the period after Constantine made Christianity the state religion the monastic movement grew apace. Devout men, grieved and disgusted by the formalism and corruption of the Church and the shocking moral evils of the age, but lacking courage or conviction actively to oppose these things, retired to lonely retreats with the idea of preserving their own sanctity. Some went to fanatical lengths of asceticism in their unnatural life of solitude and idleness, and became a prey to the very evils and excesses which they had sought to escape. Others, more moderate, formed themselves into cloisters or communities, supporting themselves by various industries, and extending hospitality to strangers and help to the poor. And not a few of these communities became centers

[1] George Smith, *Short History of Christian Missions* (Edinburgh: T. and T. Clark, 1880), p. 108.

[2] E. M. Bliss, *The Missionary Enterprise* (New York: Revell, 1908), p. 33.

of missionary training and propagation. "Monachism on its good side was the missionary organization through which Christendom worked up to Wycliffe, Huss and Luther."[3] Such centers were Iona in Scotland and those founded by Martin in France, Patrick in Ireland, and Boniface in Germany. In fact all the missionary pioneers cited in this and the preceding periods were monks and monastic leaders.

Later, mainly during this medieval period, there sprang up the various monastic sects which have since become so famous as constituting the Missionary Orders of the Church of Rome. The most prominent of these are:

The Benedictines. This sect was the earliest in the West and was founded by *Benedict of Nursia* (480–543), who was regarded as the ideal monk. His great monastery was at Monte Cassino, near Naples, but the order rapidly extended so that at one time there are said to have been as many as thirty-seven thousand monasteries, the majority in France, though not a few also in Italy, Sicily, Spain, and other countries. They promoted education and literature during those intellectually sterile centuries, and thus while not actually missionary they contributed materially to the development of religious life and Christian civilization. Because of their long black gown and cowl they were sometimes called "Black Monks."

The Franciscans. This sect owed its existence to *Francis of Assisi* (1182–1226). He was the son of a rich merchant, and, like Lull, was suddenly converted from a life of sin and pleasure, and devoted himself to preaching repentance and caring for the sick. He drew to himself a band of followers whom he called "Fratres Minores" ("Little Brothers"), otherwise known from their garb as "Gray Friars." Francis took upon himself and imposed upon them the threefold vow of celibacy, poverty, and obedience, and sent them out, two by two, to preach in several countries, observing literally Christ's injunction to take neither shoes, scrip, nor staves.

Francis himself took part in one of the Crusades, evidently with a genuine purpose for the evangelization of the Saracens. In Egypt, where a price was upon every Christian's head, he fearlessly marched alone into the Muslim army and approached the Sultan with the words, "I am not sent of man, but of God, to shew thee the way of salvation." So touched was the Sultan's heart by this display of zeal and courage that he dismissed Francis with honor, allowed him to preach the gospel to the Muslims, and even manifested some spiritual concern himself.

The Franciscan order produced some of the great theologians

[3] George Smith, *op. cit.*, p. 146.

of the period. It has sent out more missionaries than any other Roman Catholic sect except the Jesuits, and is still an active force along these lines. The mention of Monte Corvino and other Franciscan missionaries to China and the Far East, who belonged to this period, is reserved for a later section.

The Dominicans. This order was founded by a Spanish priest named *Dominic* (1170–1221) about the same time as the Franciscans. Its members were called Preaching Friars, and it spread rapidly as a theological and missionary body within the Roman Church. Aside from their far-reaching missionary efforts the Dominicans became notorious mainly as being the agents of the Pope in carrying on a relentless and bloody campaign with the object of uprooting the Albigenses of southern France and other sects who, because of their determined resistance to the claims of the Roman Catholic priesthood and the abuses of the Papacy, were branded as heretics. Thus began the inhuman Inquisition, which will forever remain an indelible stain upon Rome.

The Jesuits. By far the most renowned of all the monastic orders is that known as the Jesuits, or the Society of Jesus. It was founded by *Ignatius Loyola* (1491–1556), a Spaniard of noble birth, together with several others of like mind, among whom was *Francis Xavier,* destined to become the greatest of Jesuit missionaries. Their initial object was to devote their lives to the care of Christians and the conversion of Saracens in the Holy Land, but the organization soon extended its aims and became the greatest of all Roman Catholic foreign missionary agencies.

To the three vows of the other orders was added a fourth vow, by which every Jesuit bound himself to go in unquestioning obedience to any part of the world and to undertake any task at the command of his superior. The binding nature of this Jesuit vow, the secret machinations of the Society, and its persistent ambition for both ecclesiastical and political power have brought it into frequent conflict with Church and State.

As a missionary society its operations extended principally to India, China, Japan, the Philippine Islands, Africa, South America, Mexico, California, and Canada. Two strong institutions established at Rome and heavily endowed by rich patrons of the Society have supplied most of its missionaries. One in every seven Roman Catholic missionaries throughout the world is a Jesuit. They labor in 71 missions where they operate 6,640 stations, 4,000 schools, 350 hospitals, and 16 leprosaria. Second to missions the Jesuits emphasize education, then retreats. It is the largest order in the Church, having a total membership of 32,000.

VI

PERIOD OF THE REFORMATION
FROM LUTHER TO THE HALLE MISSIONARIES (1517–1650)

RELATION OF THE REFORMATION TO MISSIONS. Mighty as were the changes wrought, and far-reaching as were the influences exerted by the Reformation, it is to be borne in mind that that movement was not missionary in its character. It was a battle against ecclesiastical abuses, moral corruption, and veritable heathenism within existing Christendom; and so absorbed were the reformers with the struggle for freedom from the Papacy, and with the task also of establishing new communities in the faith and developing the church life of these, that the needs of the outside world were forgotten. Indeed, there is all too abundant evidence that most of the leaders of the Reformation, including *Luther, Melancthon, Calvin, Zwingli,* and *Knox,* seem to have had no serious sense of responsibility for direct missionary efforts in behalf of heathen or Muslim. Despite their clear conceptions and statements of the fundamental doctrines of evangelical faith, they showed a remarkable ignorance of the scope of the divine plan and of Christian duty in relation to the gospel. Great mission fields lay round about them, especially in North Africa and western Asia, while large communities of Jews were scattered among them. Yet for these they did nothing and apparently cared nothing.

Hence we have the remarkable spectacle for many years of a live Protestant Church without mission interest, while the church which had been left because it lacked life was carrying on extensive missions in the Orient, and a little later in America.[1]

Indirectly, the Reformation was perhaps responsible for this effort on the part of the Latin Church, inasmuch as it was the loss of so much territory in the Old World that stirred up the papal power to seek fresh conquests in the New.

[1] Louise M. Hodgkins, *Via Christi* (New York: Macmillan, 1901), p. 161.

Having been themselves emancipated from the superstitions and slavery of a false doctrine and a harsh ecclesiastical government, it would be thought most natural that the reformers and those who followed them should promptly turn their attention to spreading these glad tidings among non-Christian peoples, but here a strange anomaly is found in the fact that there has been hardly any period in the entire history of the Christian Church so destitute of any concerted effort to spread the gospel in heathen lands than just this period of the Reformation.[2]

At the same time it must be recognized that by the Reformation new and better foundations were laid for greater work which was to follow. There was an insistent call for a return to the teachings of the Bible, and the Bible plainly taught the duty of the evangelization of the world. Moreover, the reformers applied themselves to the task of translating the whole Bible into the principal European languages.

The vernacular Bible became a missionary book to Christendom itself; and when Christians had mastered it somewhat during two centuries they began to send it to the rest of the world, with missionaries to translate and to preach it.[3]

It was a slow process and it took no little time to restore the sense of personal responsibility for the salvation of non-Christians, which has always been an underlying principle of missionary activity but which during ten or more centuries of doctrinal corruption and spiritual darkness had practically disappeared. But here and there noble souls arose to lead the way in discerning and responding to this long-lost-sight-of Christian duty.

ACTIVE MISSIONARY EFFORTS. Up to the Reformation the missionary work of the Christian Church was undivided, but from the Reformation onward it became separated into two very distinct and often-times antagonistic forces—Roman Catholicism and Protestantism. It is scarcely necessary to say that the scope of this course of study does not extend, in the main, beyond the missionary work of the evangelical section of the Christian Church known by the name Protestant. The false doctrines, unscrupulous methods, and questionable results of Roman Catholic missions in some areas of the world forbid their recognition in the same class with Protestant missionary work. It will be essential, however, to the completeness of the outline of Christian missionary effort in most of the great mis-

[2] Alfred De W. Mason, *Outlines of Missionary History* (New York: George H. Doran, 1912), p. 53.
[3] George Smith, *Short History of Christian Missions* (Edinburgh: T. and T. Clark, 1880), p. 122.

sion fields to mention Roman Catholic operations, as in many instances antedating Protestant efforts. And it is to be acknowledged that, despite the condemnable features of papal propaganda just referred to, the lives and labors of some of its missionaries, particularly the early pioneers, have displayed a spirit of self-sacrificing devotion, fortitude, and zeal that compels appreciation and admiration. Foremost among such is one who belonged to the Reformation period and who must ever be ranked among the greatest characters of missionary annals. He was:

Francis Xavier (1506–1552). Xavier was the disciple and associate of Loyola, founder of the Jesuits, and commenced the great foreign missionary work of that order. In 1540 he was sent by the Pope to Goa, the Portuguese colony on the west coast of Hindustan, and thence shortly to the pearl fisheries extending from Cape Comorin to Madras along the east coast. Later he labored at Travancore, where he baptized thousands of natives. After three years in southern India his restless spirit impelled him onward to the Malay Peninsula and adjoining islands, where he spent another three years. There he came in contact with a young Japanese, an escaped murderer, whom he made a convert; and learning through him of the Japanese nation Xavier's soul became fired with zeal to visit and evangelize Japan. With this Japanese convert, Hanjiro, as his guide the great missionary landed in Japan in 1549.

The picture is drawn of him "trudging bare-footed, carrying his box containing everything necessary for celebrating the Holy Sacrament up and down the hills of Kioto or along the shore of Oita, calling the nation that alternately gave him welcome and rebuff, and which he termed 'the delight of my soul.' " His journeys in Japan occupied two and a half years, and although unable to speak the language and laboring under other great disadvantages he claimed and baptized many thousands of converts.

His last efforts, after revisiting Goa, were to enter China, but they were unavailing, and in 1552 he died of fever on the little island of Sancian (St. John), off the southeast coast of China. His despairing cry, "*O rock! rock! when wilt thou open to my Master?*", uttered as he faced the impassable wall of Chinese exclusion, has found an echo in the hearts of many hundreds of later missionaries, whose fervent prayers and faithful labors, along with Xavier's, have been God's instrumentality in breaching the wall and forcing open the door into the most populous nation of the world.

In Francis Xavier perhaps more strikingly than in any other Romish missionary we have an example of that strange and paradoxical combination of depth of genuine love and devotion to

Christ and holy passion for souls along with doctrines woefully unsound and policies of work utterly unworthy.

In attempting to sum up his character and career we cannot do better than to quote from Dr. Arthur T. Pierson's rarely fine appreciation of Xavier, expressed in his inimitable style. Referring to him as the Romish Apostle to the Indies, Dr. Pierson writes:

He was misguided, no doubt; but no other life, since Paul's, has shewn such ardor and fervor, such absorbing zeal for the greater glory of God, such self-forgetting, self-denying passion for the souls of men, as that of the young Saint of Navarre, whose withered relics are still adored in the Church of Bom Jesus at Goa.

To the doctrine of free grace, unconsciously imbibed in boyhood, he owed his genuine experience of faith in Christ, his strong hold upon Him, and the inspiration of an unselfish purpose. To his Papal and Jesuit training we trace that admixture of confidence in outward rites and good works which alloyed and vitiated his otherwise superb service. To sprinkle holy water in baptism, to recite the creed and a few prayers, limited his methods and measured his success. His preaching practically knew nothing of the purging away of sin by intelligent faith in the atoning blood. He said, *"feci christianos"*—"I make Christians"; and it is not strange if the disciples he made often shocked their "maker" by glaring vices and flagrant sins.

He mastered no Oriental language, and was often without an interpreter. . . . His was the gospel of sacraments and ceremonies, preached in mute action, but with what lofty enthusiasm! To baptize a new-born babe would save a soul; to mumble a few prayers would deliver from purgatory; and so he went on with wild passion for numbers, carrying the counting of converts to the last extreme of error and absurdity. It was the lasting warning against that mechanical theory which gauges the success of missions by numerical results. . . .

Yet, notwithstanding all these drawbacks, this Jesuit fanatic puts to shame all who read the story of his life, by the utter self-abnegation he exhibited. . . . The man who could cheerfully forsake the paths of indulgence and scholarship for one perpetual pilgrimage amid the sickening sights and stifling air of Oriental heathenism; who could on God's altar lay himself, with his brilliant mind and prospects of preferment, with youth, wealth, worldly ambition, all tempting him to self-seeking—and know only the glory of God—such a man cannot be simply set aside as a fool or a fanatic.[4]

During a brief but intense missionary career of only ten years this remarkable man is said to have planted the Cross "in fifty-two different kingdoms, preached through nine thousand miles of territory, and baptized over one million persons."

[4] Arthur T. Pierson, *The New Acts of the Apostles* (New York: Baker and Taylor, 1894), pp. 67, 68.

"In visions of the night when he saw the world conquered for Christ, he would spring up shouting, 'Yet more, O my God, yet more!' and his whole life was a commentary on his own motto: 'Ad Majorem Dei Gloriam' ('To the greater glory of God')."[5]

Of missionary efforts on the part of the Reformation Church there is sadly little to record. It is true that, following out the idea advanced by Calvin and others of the reform leaders that the duty of extending the gospel into non-Christian lands rested with the State rather than the Church, some Protestant governments, notably those of Geneva and Holland, and later England also, did make attempts to found Christian colonies in heathen lands. In the charters granted to both the Dutch and the English East India Companies it was stipulated that measures should be taken for the planting of the Church and the conversion of the heathen, and chaplains were sent out for this purpose with the early colonizing and trading expeditions to the Far East and the New World. But mission interests were always secondary to colonial interests, and whenever the two clashed mission work had to yield.

Weird interest attaches to an expedition of French Huguenots sent to Brazil by Calvin and Coligny, but which ended disastrously through the treachery of its leader Villegagnon.

But the truth is that neither the new Church itself, nor yet its leaders, were ready for a missionary movement, and it was not until the middle of the seventeenth century that the agitations and efforts of the few individuals who were ahead of their times in discerning the Church's true mission in the world gathered sufficient momentum to set in motion missionary plans once more.

[5] *Ibid.*, p. 69.

VII

PERIOD OF THE EARLY MISSIONARY SOCIETIES
FROM THE HALLE MISSIONARIES TO CAREY (1650–1792)

The roots of modern missions reach back to the Reformation in the very real sense that a revival of apostolic faith was the necessary precursor of a revival of apostolic life and work. Yet, as already remarked, the reform leaders and the Reformation Church as a whole were for at least a full century almost completely devoid of missionary spirit or effort. Indeed, the Reformation movement ran into a serious new danger from its rigid preoccupation with matters of doctrine alone. As Dr. George Smith expresses it, the seeds of controversy sown by Lutheran orthodoxy began to bear a harvest which would have been fatal to the spirituality of the Church but for the Pietist movement, which by example and preaching gradually aroused the Church to a deeper spiritual life and, as a natural consequence, to renewed missionary zeal and action.

Here and there one man was reached and roused, his eyes opening to the fact that millions were dying without the gospel; his ears opening to the cry of want and woe which, like the moan and sob of waves on the seashore, tells of storm and wreck. Now and then a man went forth, while as yet the church as a whole seemed locked in icy indifference and insensibility.[1]

It remains to trace the course of this stream from its fountainhead of quickened spiritual life and missionary conviction, through the rivulet stage of feeble individual effort, until, fed from every side, it steadily grows into a river which has continued to flow on and out, with ever-deepening current and widening reach, unto the ends of the earth.

The subject matter of this period does not call for any particular classification. It will suffice to sketch briefly in order the individuals

[1] Arthur T. Pierson, *The New Acts of the Apostles* (New York: Baker and Taylor, 1894), p. 74.

and groups who were the most prominent factors in leading the way to the formation of the early missionary societies which were, in turn, forerunners of the greater and more highly organized missionary enterprise of the modern period.

VON WELZ, THE MISSIONARY AGITATOR. To this Austrian baron, singular as the fact is, belongs the credit of sounding, about 1664, the first general and vigorous missionary appeal to the Church. He was the first of that succession of godly pioneers of this period who, to use Dr. Pierson's words, "formed the mold in which modern missions took shape." In a series of three pamphlets he boldly set forth the missionary duty of the Church, and called for the formation of an association for the extension of the gospel among the heathen, and for the establishment of a college to train missionaries. He put the following three searching questions before the slumbering conscience of the Church: (1) "Is it right that we, evangelical Christians, hold the gospel for ourselves alone, and do not seek to spread it?" (2) "Is it right that in all places we have so many students of theology, and do not induce them to labor elsewhere in the spiritual vineyard of Jesus Christ?" (3) "Is it right that we spend so much on all sorts of dress, delicacies in eating and drinking, etc., but have hitherto thought of no means for the spread of the gospel?"

His manifesto was an anticipation of Carey's epoch-making *Inquiry into the Obligation of Christians* more than a century later, and it met with a similar or even worse reception. It is a commentary upon the religious condition of the times that one of the leading and best men among the clergy met Von Welz' appeal with a bitter rebuke, denouncing him as a dreamer, fanatic, hypocrite, and heretic, and arguing that it was absurd, even wicked, to cast the pearls of the gospel before the heathen.

Meeting thus with rebuff and ridicule, and failing to move others to action, Von Welz heroically resolved to be true to his own convictions. He proceeded to Holland, was there ordained by a poor priest as "an apostle to the Gentiles," and taking with him 36,000 marks set sail for *Dutch Guiana*. There he soon became a victim to an inhospitable climate and bad conditions and filled a martyr missionary's grave. But in vain? A thousand times, no! He was a grain of wheat which, cast into the ground to die, brought forth abundant and abiding fruit. "Such men are God's agitators, sent to marshal the conscience of the church, to mold the law of its life and the methods of its work in conformity with His Word and will."[2]

[2] *Ibid.*, p. 76.

THE PIETIST LEADERS AND TRAINING SCHOOL. The emphasis laid by the Reformation leaders upon justification by faith, vital as was that doctrine, was at the expense of the equally vital truth of sanctification, and a trend toward moral degeneration in the new Church set in. The Pietist movement, led by *Philip Spener* (1635–1705), who has since been called "the German Wesley," and his even more distinguished follower, *August Francke* (1663–1727), was a revolt against barren orthodoxy and dead formalism, and an earnest effort to raise the standards of Christian life. Spener's bold protest against wickedness in high places naturally called forth bitter opposition. Nevertheless the revival movement sowed seed in some hearts which eventually bore a great harvest. It led to the founding, in 1698, of the *University of Halle,* which became a center of the strongest missionary influence and the birthplace of the first organized foreign missionary effort.

THE DANISH-HALLE MISSION TO INDIA. This was the first foreign mission to be the direct product of Reformed Christianity. It was brought about through the influence of Dr. Lütkens, a chaplain of the Danish court and the bosom friend of Francke. He laid before King Frederik IV of Denmark the duty of providing Christian education for the people of the Danish colonies. The good king cordially responded with both sympathy and financial help. Lütkens proceeded to found at Copenhagen a college for the preparation of missionaries, but in the meantime secured through Francke at Halle the first two missionaries for the project.

These were *Bartholomew Ziegenbalg* and *Henry Plütschau,* who, sent forth in November, 1705, reached *Tranquebar,* 150 miles south of Madras, on the east coast of India, only in July, 1706. Touching on their way at the Cape they saw the pitiable condition of the Hottentots under the blighting rule of the Dutch, and it was the appeal sent home by these two men that moved the Moravians to undertake the first mission to South Africa.

Upon their arrival in India they at once encountered severe trials and difficulties. Strangely and sadly enough, the greatest of these came not, as might have been expected, from the heathen, but from the Danish authorities. In spite of the fact that the mission had the sanction and support of the King of Denmark, the Danish East India Company dared to send to the Danish Governor at Tranquebar, by the same ship on which Ziegenbalg and Plütschau sailed, secret instructions to block their way by every possible means, and that official obeyed his instructions with a will.

Picture, then, these first two Protestant missionaries to tread the soil of India standing unsheltered on the shore the first night after they landed, left by the Governor to shift for themselves. Being finally allowed to occupy a house upon the city wall, close by the heathen quarters, with dauntless courage they began to study the Tamil language within six days of their arrival, at first sitting down with the native children and writing in the sand with their fingers. Such remarkable progress did Ziegenbalg make that in eight months he could talk fluently in Tamil, and in his third year he completed the first translation of the New Testament into any of the native languages of India.

On the 12th of May, 1707, ten months after their arrival, they publicly baptized five adult heathen slaves of Danish masters, and a few months later nine Hindus, as the first fruits of their labors. Next year Ziegenbalg made his first preaching tour into the kingdom of Tanjore. The publication at home of his letters to his former instructors, Lange and Francke, and particularly his accounts of friendly conferences held by him with the Brahmans, aroused widespread interest in Europe. One result was that help, financial and otherwise, was given to the mission by two English societies, one "for Promoting Christian Knowledge" formed in 1699, the other "for the Propagation of the Gospel" in 1701. Both of these originally had colonial rather than foreign missionary work in view.

Ill health took Plütschau from the field in 1711. Ziegenbalg continued his labors arduously, though weakened as a result of hardships endured, for which the cruel treatment of the Danish Governor was in part responsible. In 1719, at the early age of thirty-six, and after twelve short but momentous years of foreign service, this noble pioneer passed from earthly toil and suffering to heavenly rest and reward. The following word picture of his deathbed is given by Dr. Pierson:

> When about to depart, so intense was the glory that smote him, that he suddenly put his hands to his eyes, exclaiming, "How is it so bright, as if the sun shone full in my face!" Soon after, he asked that his favorite hymn might be sung, "Jesus, my confidence," and on the wings of sacred song he took his flight, leaving behind over three hundred and fifty converts, catechumens and pupils, a missionary seminary and a Tamil lexicon, but best of all the Tamil Bible.[3]

Who can estimate the worth to God of such lives in relation to His purpose of grace toward a great land like India, comprising one-fifth of the entire living human family? But such lives belong not alone to one land, however great. They are a priceless benedic-

[3] *Ibid.*, p. 80.

tion and heritage to Christians of every land and age. And may that benediction and heritage be made secure to those who read these lines, through the yielding of their hearts to be freshly filled with that divine love and grace which alone inspired those saintly men to the sacrifice they endured and the service they rendered!

Still another name connected with this same Mission and also Halle University stands out with deserved prominence and claims mention here. It is that of *Christian Frederic Schwartz* (1726–1798), whom Dr. Pierson calls "the founder of the native Christian church in India." It was while a pupil under Francke at Halle that his missionary interest was first awakened by seeing the Bible in strange Tamil characters, as it was being put through the press for the Tranquebar Mission; although long before this his godly mother, dying in his infancy, dedicated her child, as did Hannah, to the Lord for His peculiar service.

Schwartz's missionary career in India, which began in 1750 and lasted forty-eight years, was as remarkable as it was long. Coupled with singular piety and the zeal of love were extraordinary linguistic gifts and a magnetic force of character that won all hearts and held their unbounded confidence. He mastered not only Tamil but also Persian, Hindustani, English, and Hindu Portuguese, and versed himself in Hindustani literature and mythology, thereby extending his ministry and influence beyond the masses to the greatest Muslim princes, the educated Brahmans, and the various European classes. He preached everywhere and incessantly, covering the whole eastern coast and opening many chapels and schools.

In addition to such direct missionary work, "on account of his perfect integrity, fluency in the language and knowledge of public affairs, he became the chief medium of communication between the native princes and the British Government. So loved and trusted was he on both sides that, when the fiercest enmity prevailed between a native province and the government, 'Father Schwartz' was at liberty to go in either camp at his will."[4]

A striking instance of this was afforded when an insurrection was raised by Hyder Ali, a Muslim. Schwartz was the only man through whom that proud tyrant would consent to treat with the British. "Send me the Christian; he will not deceive me," he demanded. All unsought, this humble missionary wielded the power of a foreign ambassador as well as of a magistrate within the native state. Nor did these high honors or offices affect in the least his essential missionary spirit or ministry. To the end he lived in the most unassuming and frugal manner, uniformly refusing the

[4] Louise M. Hodgkins, *Via Christi* (New York: Macmillan, 1901), p. 205.

princely gifts repeatedly pressed upon him in return for valued services rendered, and even declining to accept a large legacy left him by a military officer.

His career was indeed unique and remarkable. When at last he died, in 1798, noble monuments were erected to his memory by the prince of Tanjore and the East India Company, while a granite tablet was placed by the foreigners in his chapel. But a more precious and abiding monument than all of these is the rare record of fruitful service to multitudes and the fragrant memory of a life that magnified Christ his Master before men.

Perhaps no closing testimony to this great missionary could be more impressive than the following. At his funeral

the Rajah's heir, Serjofee, could not be kept, even by Hindu custom, from taking his place as a chief mourner; and three years later, at his own cost, built him a superb marble monument, executed by Flaxman. The epitaph he himself wrote, the first English verse ever known to be written by a native Hindu:

> "Firm wast Thou, humble and wise,
> Honest and pure, free from disguise;
> Father of orphans, the widow's support;
> Comfort in sorrow of every sort.
> To the benighted, dispenser of light,
> Doing, and pointing to that which is right.
> Blessing to princes, to people, to me,
> May I, my Father, be worthy of Thee,
> Wisheth and prayeth thy Sarabojee."[5]

HANS EGEDE, THE APOSTLE TO GREENLAND. Turning from the hot tropics to the frozen polar regions, we have another example of one who was called and thrust out by God to carry the gospel to that inhospitable clime. The story of Hans Egede (1686–1758) and his equally heroic wife, Elizabeth, and their mission to Greenland is full of impressive features. Egede was educated at Copenhagen College and had settled in a pastorate in Norway when he heard the tale of the early colonizing and evangelizing work under Leif the Lucky in Greenland, and of the misfortunes through which communications with that remote region had been broken off, with the result that after nearly three centuries of neglect the poor inhabitants had relapsed into heathenism. His impression at the time was that these people were the descendants of the old Norsemen colonists and hence in a double sense his brethren. His heart was strangely moved and he could not shake off the conviction that God was

[5] Pierson, op. cit., p. 93.

calling him to Greenland. His proposal to go met with strong opposition from both his wife and his parish, which it took several years to overcome. Meanwhile God wrought a deeper conviction and preparation in Egede's own heart, and then so completely changed his wife's attitude that she became perhaps the stronger of the two.

In 1721 they set sail from Bergen with a company of forty-six persons, to find at the end of their perilous voyage not the Norwegian descendants they looked for, but instead a race of untutored Eskimos. The outlook was most discouraging, but they threw themselves undaunted into the hard task, learning the unwritten language and framing new words where necessary for the expression of the new ideas which they brought. They suffered the severest hardships, their support from home became more and more reduced and uncertain, and finally the new Danish king recalled the European colonists.

But the heroic Egedes persuaded a few to remain with them, and through many fresh trials and vicissitudes they succeeded in laying the foundation of the modern colony of Christian Greenlanders, of which Godthaab (good hope) is the capital. During an awful scourge of smallpox, which decimated the people, Egede and his wife were veritable angels of life in their devoted ministry to both the bodies and the souls of the dying Eskimos. They were the sole means of bringing salvation to hundreds of precious souls. A unique and impressive feature of Egede's missionary work was that in a time of deep distress of soul because of the apathy of the people he asked and received from God, as a token of the divine presence and power, the supernatural gift of healing, and exercised it in scores of cases.

ZINZENDORF AND THE MORAVIANS. It was from the Pietist movement that the Moravian Church received its missionary call. The sect now generally called Moravian is among themselves known as the United Brethren. Zinzendorf was not its founder but rather its reviver and the progenitor of its missionary work. The sect itself dates back to the pre-Reformation period, when, in 1467, the persecuted Bohemian followers of John Huss, with certain Waldenses and Moravians, joined together under the name *Unitas Fratrum* (United Brotherhood). Bitterly persecuted though they were by their enemies they numbered 400 churches when the Reformation awoke. Later, in the seventeenth century, they again suffered at the hands of the Jesuits and were well-nigh exterminated. In 1722, Christian David, a humble but zealous convert from Romanism, gathered together the remnant and led them into Saxony, where in a most providential way they came upon one of the estates of Count Zinzendorf. That good Christian nobleman gave them refuge and land, and a settlement was built called *Herrnhut* ("the Lord's Watch"), which to this day remains the center and headquarters of the Moravian Church.

Count von Zinzendorf (1700–1760) himself was grandson of an Austrian nobleman who for conscience' sake gave up all his estates. Young Zinzendorf was brought up by a godly grandmother and aunt, who were Pietists, and almost from infancy he evinced spiritual traits of rare depth. He was first educated as a boy under Francke at Halle, afterwards at the University of Wittenberg, where he was noted for his fervent spiritual character. Although later exposed to the strongest temptations in the way of worldly allurements and honors at Paris and Dresden, he withstood them all, and finally he felt constrained, against the wishes of his guardian and friends, to resign the high position he had been given at Dresden and to devote his life wholly to evangelistic work.

His chosen life-motto was, *"I have one passion; it is He, and He alone."* At the marriage altar he and his young bride, also of noble birth, covenanted together and with the Lord to renounce their rank and to devote all their property as well as themselves to the service of Christ. In 1727 he became the spiritual superintendent of the Herrnhut colony, and in 1737 was ordained Bishop of the Moravian Church.

Meanwhile an incident occurred which exerted a deep and lasting influence upon Zinzendorf, and through him turned the tide of the whole Moravian movement in a missionary direction. It was in 1731 that the Count was called upon to represent the Saxon court at the coronation in Copenhagen of Christian VI of Denmark. While there he saw two Eskimos who had been baptized by Hans Egede, and learned with deep regret of the decision to give up the mission in Greenland. His attendants also met a Negro, Anthony, who told them of the cruel lot of the slaves in the Danish West Indian colonies. Zinzendorf's sympathies were profoundly stirred, as in turn were those of the Brotherhood when he narrated to them the incidents upon his return home. It was promptly resolved to take up the work in Greenland, while two devoted men were found and almost immediately sent out to St. Thomas in the West Indies. Thus in God's own simple but wonderful way began the renowned foreign missionary work of the Moravians, which rapidly extended farther to Central and South America, Labrador, the Indians of the United States and Alaska, to South Africa and

Australia, and even to the snow-bound passes of the Himalayan mountains on the remote borders of Tibet.

Some of their missionary efforts seem not to have been fully successful, and, measured by the size of their work or the number of converts in any particular field, their undertakings may perhaps appear to some minds to have fallen short of the most satisfactory results. Notwithstanding, the Moravians have set and maintained a standard of missionary devotion never yet approached by any other church body.

While the Protestant churches at large are sending, at the very highest estimate, one member in two or three thousand, the Moravian Church sends *one in every ninety-two*. They furnish the unique spectacle of having three times as many members in their foreign missions as in their home churches.

Such a report on the part of a community so weak in numbers and in wealth constitutes one of the marvels of modern missions. Without a doubt it is traceable in large measure to the mighty spiritual impulse imparted by that remarkable man who, as their leader, set before them an example of such unqualified consecration of every talent, faculty, and resource he possessed to the Christ whom he adored. The Brotherhood caught and perpetuated the spirit of their leader. Their seal is a lamb on a crimson ground, with the cross of resurrection and a banner of triumph, with the motto: *"Vicit agnus noster, eum sequamur"* ("Our Lamb has conquered; let us follow Him"). They have presented to the Church of Christ a splendid object lesson of the great fundamental missionary principles as taught in the Scriptures. They have recognized themselves in debt to the world as trustees of the gospel, and have been taught frugality of habits, readiness to sacrifice, and prompt obedience to the call of God to go anywhere, and with an emphasis upon the worst and hardest of fields as having the first claim. And no missionaries of the Cross have been bolder as pioneers, more patient or persistent under difficulties, more heroic in suffering, or more entirely devoted to Christ and the soul needs of men than those of the Moravian Brotherhood.

MISSIONS TO NORTH AMERICAN INDIANS. Highhanded policy on the part of English sovereigns, and in particular religious intolerance, led to an ever-increasing stream of emigration to America, beginning early in the seventeenth century. The first company of these Puritans, known even since in history as *"the Pilgrim Fathers,"* sailed in the *Mayflower* in 1620, and landed at New Plymouth on the Massachusetts coast. While the dominating motive of these new colonists was religious freedom for themselves rather than the carrying of the gospel to others, yet the fact of their religious character and of the price they had paid for their convictions naturally prompted to efforts in behalf of the Indians around them, and it is claimed that the various accounts sent back to England of the extension of the gospel among the Indians contributed much to the interest aroused in the new continent.

Among those who devoted themselves to the spiritual needs of the Indians, mention here can be made of only a few of the most prominent.

Roger Williams (1606–1683), the founder of Rhode Island, while filling a pastoral charge among the whites devoted his best energy to working among the Indians. He learned their language, published a helpful Indian-English handbook, and was for forty years the staunch friend of the tribesmen, laboring for their material and spiritual welfare and frequently standing boldly in defense of their rights against the aggressions of the white man.

John Eliot (1604–1690) occupies the first place in the list, because of the great length and signal value of his service, and has been called the Apostle to the North American Indians. A distinguished student at Cambridge, England, and a master of the original languages of the Scriptures, young Eliot himself traced his conversion and deepest spiritual blessing to the holy influences of the home of Thomas Hooker, the Puritan exile, under whom he was for a time a teacher and whom he followed to the New World in 1630.

Eliot began work as a minister at Roxbury, Mass., but his heart was soon drawn out intensely toward the Indians, and taking up the study of the language of the Pequot tribe of Iroquois Indians he gave the remaining fifty-eight years of his life to the work of their evangelization. In 1646, in the wigwam of one of the chiefs, he preached the first sermon ever known in their language. It proved a memorable service indeed, for the spirit of religious inquiry began to burn, and from that starting point souls in ever-increasing numbers came under conviction of sin and were saved. He threw himself unreservedly into the work with all his splendid gifts and energies, fearlessly facing perils and cheerfully bearing privations for Christ's sake. He naturally incurred the bitter hatred and opposition of the Indian priests, and plots were laid against his life, but in vain. As the influence of his preaching spread farther and farther afield his labors grew both in intensity and in variety. He became in turn evangelist, pastor, teacher, statesman, translator, and trainer of an Indian ministry.

Facing the great difficulty of maintaining proper standards of

Christian living among his converts in their old heathen setting, he gathered them together and organized a number of centers which became known as "Praying Towns," the first of which was at Natick, near Boston. "Here the Christian Indian could go to a church where an Indian pastor preached, and to a school where an Indian teacher taught, and could live a Christian life free from the persecutions of the non-Christian Indians about them. The Indians who came to this town made a covenant as follows: 'The grace of Christ helping us, we do give ourselves and our children to God to be His people. He shall rule over us in all our affairs, not only in our religion and the affairs of the church, but also in all our works and affairs of this world.' "[6]

By 1671 Eliot had gathered some 3,600 converted Indians into fourteen settlements. But perhaps an even greater legacy which he left behind him consisted of twenty-four carefully trained Indian preachers, and the "Moheecan Bible," a complete translation of the Word of God into an Indian language, which he effected during the years 1661–1663—*the first Bible ever printed in America.* The fact that that famous Bible has no longer one living reader in no way detracts from the value of Eliot's gifted and consecrated labor upon it. But it does constitute a lasting monument to the shameful and indefensible treatment by which Eliot's Christian community and the Indians in general were basely destroyed before the insatiate greed and unscrupulous measures of the "civilized" white settlers, whose acts of violence were too often unrestrained and even condoned by those in authority. The national period of the United States government's relation to the Indian has been fitly called a "century of dishonor," and must always remain a disgraceful stain upon the pages of American history.

Even in Eliot's day there were not a few among his own countrymen who "not content to withhold aid, pitilessly pelted him with the hail of ridicule, or hurled at him the mud clods of aspersion." Yet long before his death his work had compelled recognition in Britain. "It was largely because of the interest excited in England by Eliot's work that 'the Society for the Propagation of the Gospel in New England' was organized in England (1649), 148 years before the Society inspired by William Carey. Its work, with a greatly increased scope, was later taken over by 'the Society for the Propagation of the Gospel in Foreign Parts' (1701)."[7]

[6] Mary T. Gardner, *Winners of the World* (Boston: Old Corner Book Store, 1909), p. 90.

[7] L. C. Barnes, *Two Thousand Years Before Carey* (Chicago: Christian Culture Press, 1900), p. 409.

In addition to the translation of the Bible, Eliot produced several valuable original works in one of the Indian languages, and it was at the end of his Indian Grammar that he appended his famous motto, so fittingly applicable to all true missions: *"Prayer and pains, through faith in Jesus Christ, will do anything."*

The Mayhews. The record of this family, like that of the well-known Scudder family later in India, is unique in that the missionary spirit was carried down through five consecutive generations, their continuous service extending 160 years. Thomas Mayhew, Sr., an English merchant, in 1641 became the Crown patentee of the islands now known as Martha's Vineyard, Nantucket, and the Elizabeth Isles, off the coast of Massachusetts, and the Governor of the colony which was formed thereon. His son was pastor of the Colonists' Church, but soon took up work for the Indian tribes living on the islands. With deep devotion the five generations of Mayhews undertook and accomplished the evangelization of these Indians, some thousands of whom became Christians and were organized into churches. Zechariah Mayhew, of the fifth generation, continued his work as pastor to the tribes until his death in 1806.

David Brainerd (1718–1747), under the auspices of the Scottish Propagation Society, began work among the Indians near Stockbridge, Mass., but his main field of labor was among the aborigines of the Delaware River region. His missionary career was a brief one of only three or four years. Then, broken down by the hardships and exposures to which he had unfalteringly subjected himself in his long and perilous journeys and self-sacrificing labors for the Indians, he died of tuberculosis at the home of his warm friend, Jonathan Edwards, the famous preacher. But his short life of twenty-nine years has left behind it an influence seldom equaled in its powerful effect upon others. The memory of David Brainerd has been cherished by the most spiritual of each succeeding generation of Christians, and today is still as fresh and fragrant as ever—not because of his work but because of the rare depth of his spiritual life and his saintliness of character. Like Enoch, he walked with God, and the memoirs left of his inner life of communion and prayer lead the reader into the very "holiest of all."

It was Brainerd's holy life that influenced Henry Martyn to become a missionary and was a prime factor in William Carey's inspiration. Carey in turn moved Adoniram Judson. And so we trace the spiritual lineage from step to step—Huss, Wycliffe, Francke, Zinzendorf, the Wesleys and Whitefield, Brainerd, Edwards, Carey, Judson, and ever onward in the true apostolic succession of spiritual grace and power and world-wide ministry.

Roman Catholic Efforts. Mention may be made of Roman Catholic missions of this period to the Indians of the United States and Canada, but particularly Quebec. These missions were happily of a distinctly higher order than those carried on in South and Central America. The Franciscans began work among the Hurons near Quebec in 1615, followed by the Jesuits among the Iroquois south of Montreal in 1669. Among the names of these early laborers stand such as *Brebœuf, Marquette, La Salle,* and others—hardy pioneers who penetrated the forests and braved the greatest hardships without a murmur. Not a few fell victims to the passions of the cruel savages; others gave their strength and life for their Indian converts. The work of these worthy men is commemorated by beautiful paintings of the scenes of their labors still to be seen in the Roman Catholic Cathedral of St. James in Montreal. The bitter wars which followed between the French and English sadly interfered with this work, and finally most of the missions disappeared entirely.

VIII

THE BIRTH OF MODERN MISSIONS

The foregoing records bring us to the dawn of the modern missionary era, which by common consent and for substantial reasons is said to have begun with Carey. "The gathering at Kettering marks the beginning of the associate organization, which has been at the basis of the most successful missionary enterprises. Individual responsibility and mutual action took the place of the pure individualism of the apostolic and medieval ages, the ecclesiastical order of Roman Catholicism, and the State missions of the early Protestant era."[1]

PREPARATORY FORCES. Changes in the world at large as well as within the Church now witnessed that a new epoch had been reached. Geographically, a new hemisphere had been discovered, while knowledge of the old had vastly increased. Commercial and colonizing schemes had brought the ends of the earth into new contact. The great East India Companies, Dutch and English, had—without intention or desire, it is true—paved the way for the missionary by making travel to, and residence in, Eastern countries more practicable and safe. New inventions and scientific discoveries began to contribute their help. But a far greater factor still was what is known as the *Renaissance*, which had freed the intellectual and religious world from the tyranny and blight of medieval systems and traditions. On every hand there was the awakening of new life.

The developments in the religious world were by no means the least notable. The effects of the Reformation and Pietist movements have already been traced. It must be confessed that rationalism had brought evangelical religion to a low ebb in Germany and Holland, and formalism was sadly in evidence in the Established Church of England. But meanwhile the evangelistic movement

[1] E. M. Bliss, *The Missionary Enterprise* (New York: Revell, 1908), p. 66.

under the Wesleys and Whitefield had begun, and the visit of John Wesley to America and his later contact with Zinzendorf and the Moravian center at Herrnhut exerted a distinct missionary influence upon the great leaders of Methodism.

Last of all to be mentioned, but surely not least in effect, was a marked revival of prayer for the heathen world among the more spiritual Christians of the Old and the New Worlds. Robert Millar, of Paisley, published in 1723 a *History of the Progagation of Christianity, and the Overthrow of Heathenism,* in which he powerfully urged prayer as the first of nine means for the conversion of the heathen. The effect was great. Similar appeals by other leaders followed at intervals. In 1744, as a result of a refreshing revival, a call was issued widely for a sustained concert of prayer "that God's kingdom may come," and in 1746 a memorial was sent to America inviting all Christians there to unite in the same petition. It met with a hearty response from Jonathan Edwards, and a sermon by him which followed was one of the influences that stirred the heart of William Carey. To this new volume of prayer, the fruit of spiritual revival, are to be traced the beginnings of the modern missionary enterprise.

THE FATHER OF MODERN MISSIONS. William Carey has been justly called "the father of modern missions." His career constituted an epoch indeed. It brought about a veritable revolution in missionary planning and thinking. Hitherto missionary undertakings had been mere isolated and spasmodic efforts on the part of individuals or little groups, while the mass of the churches, ministers and members alike, remained utterly indifferent and apathetic toward the condition of the pagan world. It was through Carey that there came an outburst of general missionary zeal and effort such as had not been since the days of the apostles, inaugurating a new era of united, organized, and systematic operations which have continued without abatement and with ever-widening reach and increasing force to the present day.

More than one missionary writer refers to the year 1792 as *"annus mirabilis,"* the famous date from which missionary annals are to be reckoned backward and forward. Dr. D. L. Leonard places this year along with A.D. 44, when the Holy Ghost said, "Separate me Barnabas and Saul for the work whereunto I have called them," and A.D. 53, when by a vision Paul was bidden to lay the foundations of the gospel in Europe. He adds: "We may speak of the 'Carey epoch' with every whit as much propriety as of the Luther Reformation. We may as fitly term him the apostle of Modern Missions as Paul the apostle to the Gentiles, of Augustine apostle to the Britons, or Boniface apostle to the Germans."[2]

William Carey (1793–1834).[3] This Nestor of modern missions was born of poor parents in a village of Northamptonshire, England, in 1761. As a boy he evinced a taste for learning, and was a diligent pupil of the village school. At the age of fourteen William was apprenticed to a shoemaker at Hackleton. Brought up as a Churchman, he early experienced a real change of heart, joined the humble Baptist Church, and at eighteen began to preach. To supplement his meager support as a pastor he continued his work as a cobbler. Resolved to fit himself for higher service, he utilized every available moment for classical study and wide reading, and by dogged perseverance, perhaps even more than by brilliancy of intellect, he mastered Latin, Greek, Hebrew, French, and Dutch, and gained a good knowledge of botany and zoölogy.

A copy of Cook's *Voyages Around the World,* which fell into his hands, made a deep impression upon him, leading his thoughts and sympathies out to distant lands, and a profound conviction laid hold upon him of the greater duty and task of the Church to carry the gospel to the heathen world. Before him in his cobbler's stall hung a large map of the world, with such statistics and other information written upon it as he was able to collect respecting every country.

At a ministerial meeting in Nottingham, when invited by the moderator to suggest a subject for discussion, young Carey proposed "The duty of Christians to attempt the spread of the gospel among heathen nations." As revealing something of the weight of cold indifference and even stubborn opposition to missions which Carey had to overcome singlehanded, the venerable moderator rose and in an agitated voice said: "Young man, sit down. When God pleases to convert the heathen, He will do it without your aid or mine." Soon after this Carey published *An Enquiry into the Obligation of Christians to use means for the Conversion of the Heathen,* which still holds high rank among missionary treatises.

But May 31, 1792, is the date which will always remain memorable as the birthday of the new world-wide era of missions, for on that day Carey preached his famous sermon from Isaiah 54:2, 3, giving out the great missionary maxims, *"Expect great things from God,"* *"Attempt great things for God."* So profound was the impression

[2] Delavan L. Leonard, *A Hundred Years of Missions* (New York: Funk and Wagnalls, 1913), p. 71.

[3] The dates following names of missionaries, hereafter given, are those of their missionary service.

made that soon afterwards, at *Kettering,* a company of twelve ministers formed the first *Baptist Missionary Society,* subscribing for its expenses £13. 2s. 6d. Carey offered himself as the first missionary, and after overcoming further severe opposition and tests of faith, and being refused passage in an English ship because of the hostility of the East India Company to missionary work, he finally, with his wife and a companion, sailed in June, 1793, in a Danish vessel, and five months later landed at Calcutta. His parting message to the friends at home was terse and impressive. "Yonder in India," said he, "is a gold mine. I will descend and dig, but you at home must hold the ropes."

The founding of the *Baptist Missionary Society* marked the beginning of a new era in the history of the Protestant Church. Other societies followed in quick succession. The famous *London Missionary Society,* at first interdenominational but now mostly Congregational, was founded in 1795. Two years later the *Netherlands Missionary Society* was organized on the Continent. The great *Church Missionary Society,* the missionary arm of the Church of England, came into existence in 1799. The *British and Foreign Bible Society* was founded in 1804.

THE GENESIS OF AMERICAN MISSIONS. About this time there was a quiet but far-reaching movement of the Spirit of God on this side of the Atlantic. The call to preach the gospel to all nations came to *Samuel J. Mills* while he was following the plow on his farm in Connecticut one day in 1802. Four years later, in obedience to the heavenly vision, he entered Williams College at Williamstown, Mass., to prepare for the Christian ministry. There he kindled a fire whose sparks were destined to be carried to the ends of the earth. Samuel J. Mills may be termed the counterpart in America of William Carey in England; and the now famous *"Haystack Prayer Meeting"* at Williamstown was the birthplace of modern American missions, just as the Kettering Assembly was of English missions.

The story is too familiar to require recounting in detail of how Mills, in whose soul the missionary passion had begun to burn from the very hour of his conversion, gathered around him at Williams College a little company of kindred spirits—James Richards, Francis Robbins, Harvey Loomis, Gordon Hall, Luther Rice, and Byron Green—now known as *"the Haystack group,"* to pray, ponder, and plan for some mission to the heathen. Later, at Andover Seminary, three others—Adoniram Judson, Samuel Newell, and Samuel Nott—joined the infant Society, and it was directly due to the prayers and efforts of this consecrated company that, in 1810, the *American*

Board of Commissioners for Foreign Missions came into being as the first Society of its kind on this side of the Atlantic.

On February 19, 1812, Messrs. *Judson* and *Newell* and their wives embarked for India, followed only nine days later by *Gordon Hall, Luther Rice,* and *Mr. and Mrs. Nott* bound for the same field. The first band of missionaries sent to Ceylon established a Mission on the Jaffna Peninsula in 1816. *Dr. John Scudder,* the first missionary physician ever sent abroad, joined the Ceylon Mission in 1819. In 1820 *Levi Parsons* and *Pliny Fiske* arrived in the Near East and established the Palestine Mission. Twelve years later the Cape Palmas Mission was founded on the west coast of Africa.

The decided change in the character and scope of the missionary enterprise from this point onward calls for a change in the manner of setting forth the facts. Hitherto the point of vision has been Christendom, as we have sought to trace the development of conviction and zeal for the world's evangelization within the home churches, and the outreach of efforts in behalf of the unevangelized. Now we must transfer the point of vision to non-Christian lands, and present in order the general facts and features of the different missionary lands and the beginnings and progress of gospel work within them. The facts connected with the ushering in of this new period make India our natural starting point.

PART TWO
WORLD-WIDE EXTENSION

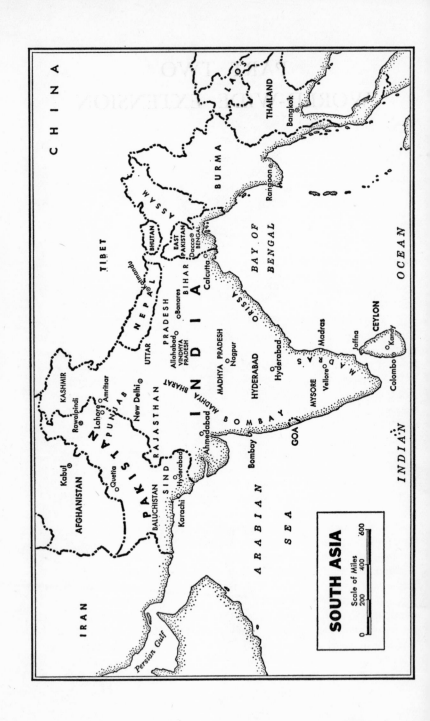

IX

SOUTH ASIA

INDIA

Area:	1,270,000 sq. mi.	Population:	400,000,000
Capital:	New Delhi	Religion:	Hinduism
			Islam

THE LAND. India extends from Pakistan on the west to Burma on the east, from the Himalayas on the north to Cape Comorin on the south. It is a great peninsula, triangular in shape and divided physically into three distinct sections: the mountainous Himalayan region in the north; the fertile river plains of the Ganges, Indus, and Brahmaputra in the center; and the plateau known as the Deccan in the south, girt about by the Vindhya Mountains on the north, and the Eastern and Western Ghats on either side.

POLITICAL HISTORY. Only the briefest outline of Indian history can be given here, and that for the purpose of supplying the connection between India and the outside world. The first Europeans to reach India were the Portuguese, about 1500. Their sole object was trade and they established their center at Goa on the west coast, an enclave which they hold to this day. In 1616 the Danish East India Company founded settlements at Tranquebar and Serampore. The Dutch opened a factory near Calcutta in 1651.

England's contact with India began in 1614 through the British East India Company, which a short time later established trading posts at Madras, Calcutta, and Bombay. By the middle of the eighteenth century the British East India Company had outmaneuvered its rival companies and established its supremacy in the subcontinent. Following the Sepoy Mutiny in 1857 the British government stepped in and assumed political control. On January 1, 1877, Queen Victoria was proclaimed Empress of India. After half a century of nationalist agitation led by Mahatma Gandhi and Jawaharlal Nehru,

India finally gained its independence on August 15, 1947, and achieved Dominion status within the Commonwealth of Nations. On January 26, 1950, it became a sovereign democratic republic. By special arrangement it remained a full member of the Commonwealth. India is a charter member of the United Nations, where it wields considerable influence as leader of the neutral bloc in the cold war.

THE PEOPLE. With almost 400,000,000 people, India is the second largest nation in the world, second only to its colossal neighbor to the northeast, China. Racially the population may be classified in five main divisions: (1) Aryans or Hindus, the predominating race; (2) Dravidians (known as Telugus, Tamils, Kanarese, etc.), mainly in the south; (3) aboriginal hill tribes, such as the Santals, Khonds, Bhils, Khols, Karens, etc.; (4) tribes of Indo-Chinese origin, found chiefly on the southern slopes of the Himalayas and in Assam and Burma; (5) descendants of the early Muslim conquerors of Arab, Afghan, Mongol, and Persian origin. According to the Indian Constitution Hindi and English are to be the official languages until 1965, after which only Hindi will be recognized. With 14 major language groups it is difficult for any government to fix on one language and declare it to be the national tongue. Actually there are about 180 languages and dialects spoken in various parts of the country.

THE RELIGION. Hinduism is the dominant religion of India. It has 340,000,000 adherents. Muslims, though outnumbered more than eight to one, are not an inconsiderable group with 40,000,000 followers. There are 9,000,000 Christians, divided almost equally between Catholics and Protestants; and 7,000,000 Sikhs, 200,000 Buddhists, 120,000 Parsees and some 25,000 Jews.

The Constitution guarantees freedom of religion, and the government has made a noble effort to uphold the Constitution. Popular sentiment among the Hindu people, however, is definitely against conversion, or "proselytizing" as they call it. In the fall of 1956 the Indian press carried a violent denunciation of missionary activities in India, particularly in Madhya Pradesh. As a result the Central Government appointed a Committee of Enquiry into Christian Missionary Activities in that state. The Report did much to allay fear and the situation improved thereafter; but certain restrictions have been placed on missionary activity by the Central Government. It will no longer admit foreign missionaries into frontier provinces and primitive tribal areas. Government permission must be obtained before opening new mission centers. Missionaries from Commonwealth countries are admitted freely; but those from the United States are carefully screened and only a small percentage of them are permitted to enter the country. Returning missionaries can obtain permits to re-enter "if their residence in India did not give cause for serious misgivings." Doubtless some of these restrictions are dictated by considerations growing out of India's expressed desire to remain neutral in the cold war. The fact that 80 per cent of the money used by Christian missions in India comes from the United States does not help the situation. Before any foreigner is admitted to India the sponsoring agency, whether secular or religious, must be able to prove that the position cannot be filled by an Indian national. This is not always easy to do.

Hinduism. This religion of 85 per cent of the people of India is one of the oldest religions in the world. Originating in Brahmanism, it has passed through three distinct phases identified as the nature worship of the Vedas, the metaphysical speculation of the Upanishads, and the personal devotion of the Gita. Like most other religions, Hinduism has had its periods of revival and decline. In its more popular forms it degenerated into a huge system of animal sacrifice and idol worship.

Krishna, one of its most popular deities, is reputed to have had some 16,000 wives and, in the minds of his millions of devotees, is the incarnation of sensual lust. Little wonder that for centuries temple prostitution was a regular part of Hindu worship. The temple carvings in Benares, the sacred city of the Hindus, are mute testimony to the depths to which religion can be degraded.

Here as elsewhere there have been noble exceptions, Gandhi being the most outstanding example so far as Hinduism is concerned. Though he lived and died a devout Hindu, Gandhi greatly admired the character of Jesus Christ, accepted many of His principles, and was particularly fond of the Sermon on the Mount. He actively opposed the caste system and devoted much time and strength to championing the cause of the outcastes—now known as the scheduled classes—whom he called Harijans, the children of God.

Reform Movements. Modern Hinduism, which began about 1800, has witnessed three great reform movements which have had considerable influence on Christian missions. The first of these was the *Brahmo Samaj* founded by *Ram Mohun Roy* (1772–1833), friend and admirer of Alexander Duff. He realized that if Hinduism were to hold its own against Christianity it would have to undergo certain drastic reforms. With this in mind he agitated for the abolition of suttee, denounced idol worship and the caste system, and encouraged scientific education. Following his death the Brahmo Samaj split three ways and, as a result, lost a good deal of its influence.

The second such movement was the *Arya Samaj* founded by *Swami Dayananda* (1824–1883). This school took its stand on the Vedas and refused to recognize any later developments. Like the Brahmo Samaj it denounced idol worship and caste; but it paid little or no attention to the metaphysics of the Upanishads. In time it degenerated into a nationalistic party fanatically opposed to everything foreign, whether Muslim, Christian, or pagan.

These two movements, while progressive in spirit and aiming at social reform, are strongly rationalistic and pantheistic in their tendencies. These mere "halfway houses between Hinduism and Christianity" cannot be regarded as helpful, any more than can Islam with its boasted monotheism. Because of their philosophical approach and concern for social reform, the new prophets of Hinduism exercise a powerful influence over the student body. Their movements may, therefore, be classed among the serious opposing forces to missionary work.

The greatest challenge to Christianity, however, comes from the third and latest reform movement introduced by *Ramakrishna* (1836–1886), and popularized not only in India but throughout the world by his favorite disciple, *Swami Vivekananda* (1863–1902). Known as the *Ramakrishna Mission* or the *Vedanta Society*, it engages extensively in social, medical, and educational work as well as in religious activities. In recent decades the Vedanta philosophy has spread to the West, and mission centers have been established in North and South America, England, and France. Their religion tends to be eclectic. One religion is as good as another and all roads lead to God. Religions are many but Truth is one. In their meeting rooms are texts taken from the various scriptures of the world, also pictures of Ramakrishna, Jesus, Buddha, and others.

In order to render Hinduism more palatable to the twentieth century man every effort is made to present it in the very best light in terms of present-day progress. Vedanta literature is replete with such terms as harmony, tolerance, science, democracy, the modern mind, etc. There is little doubt that the leaders of the Ramakrishna movement believe that the new religion which they espouse is the faith of the future. Christian leaders in India are far from sure that Hinduism is dead. In fact, they are rightly concerned over the renaissance through which it is now passing. Rather than believing that Christianity will compete successfully with Hinduism in the foreseeable future, they are afraid that in India Christianity may be swallowed up by the "mother of all religions." Hindus themselves think their religion is not only the most ancient in the world but also the most modern and the best suited to resolve the problem of the world's many conflicting faiths.

EARLY PIONEERS. Mention has already been made of the earliest recorded efforts by Pantænus; of the early Roman Catholic missions under *Francis Xavier;* and of the devoted and fruitful labors of *Ziegenbalg, Plütschau,* and *Schwartz,* all of the *Danish-Halle Mission,* who hold the distinction of being the first Protestant missionaries to India. Lutheran missionaries under the *Society for Promoting Christian Knowledge* worked in the Tamil country of South India in the eighteen century and many thousands of converts were baptized; but after the death of Schwartz their missions languished and at length only a few Christians remained. In 1793 *Carey* went to India and had to take refuge in the Danish settlement of Serampore because no missionaries at that time were allowed to reside in the British dominions. *Henry Martyn* landed in Calcutta in 1806 as a chaplain of the East India Company. He and his fellow chaplains, *Brown, Buchanan, Corrie,* and *Thomason,* did much to prepare the way for the future missionaries. With a change in the East India Company's charter in 1813 it became possible for missionaries to live and work in British territories of the India subcontinent. This important development marked a turning point in the history of Christian missions in the country. Thereafter missionary societies in ever-increasing numbers took up work in India.

William Carey (1793–1834). Carey's first years in India were years of severe trial, the opposition of the civil authorities, the ill health of his family, and financial need being added to the many formidable difficulties of a pioneer missionary career in that early period. But with heroic courage and a firm faith in God he faced and overcame them all. For five years he supported himself as superintendent of an indigo factory, while mastering several languages, holding daily religious services for the factory employees, itinerating among the villages, and working at the translation of the Scriptures.

In 1799 he was joined by *Marshman* and *Ward,* the three forming the famous "Serampore Triad." Together they laid strong foundations for subsequent missionary activities by establishing schools, colleges, and printing presses, in addition to their evangelistic and pastoral work. Later, Carey's rare linguistic gifts were recognized by the Governor General, who invited him to accept the post of teacher of Bengali, Marathi, and Sanskrit in the new Fort William College at Calcutta. With the liberal salary of £1500 received for this service Carey supported himself and his two colleagues on a frugal scale, devoting the larger portion to the promotion of his beloved work.

Carey's monumental work was that of translator and author. By himself or under his supervision translations of the Scriptures, in whole or in part, were made in no fewer than 35 languages or dialects. In addition to these he compiled and published grammars in the Sanskrit, Bengali, Marathi, Telugu, and Sikh languages, and dictionaries in Bengali and Marathi, besides editing numerous works in both English and the native languages. The magnitude of his literary accomplishments is truly astonishing, and well earned for him the title of "The Wycliffe of the East."

Withal, he believed in preaching, practised his belief uncompromisingly everywhere, and labored constantly for the conversion of individuals. He also threw his whole force and influence into efforts to abolish degrading and inhuman heathen practices, and was largely the means of securing the passage, in 1801, of a law prohibiting the throwing of children into the Ganges in sacrifice, and of another law, in 1829, abolishing the horrid suttee rite of burning widows on the funeral pyres of their husbands.

It was when Dr. Carey had corrected the last sheet of the eighth edition of the Bengali New Testament, in 1832, that he uttered the words: "My work is done. I have nothing more to do but to wait the will of God." He did not relinquish his labors, however, until he was compelled to take to his couch. On the ninth of June, 1834, the aged saint and veteran apostle entered into rest, having given to India forty-one years of priceless service, and leaving the whole Christian Church and indeed the entire world his permanent debtors.

Following closely upon Carey and his colleagues we have several other great missionary pioneers of India who call for mention not only on the ground of their personal merits, but even more because of the representative character of their work. Each was, so to speak, a mold after which some one of the various lines of approved missionary policy and activity for the future was shaped.

Henry Martyn (1806–1812). Born in southern England in 1781, this "saint and scholar" distinguished himself as a student at Cambridge, and expected to follow the legal profession. But out of a deepened spiritual experience, due in large measure to reading David Brainerd's life, he was impelled to dedicate himself to God for missionary service. He applied to the newly formed Society of the Church of England to be sent to India, but since, under the rule of the East India Company, this was impossible, he accepted a chaplaincy as the only means to his end in view.

Landing in Calcutta in 1806, he enjoyed a brief season of fellowship with Dr. Carey and his co-laborers, and this connection proved
a providential link in the chain of God's leading, by which Martyn's
rare literary gifts were applied to the work of translation. While
faithfully performing his chaplain's duties in several successive military posts, his spirit reached out to a wider ministry of preaching,
holding discussions, and opening schools among Hindus and Muslims;
but particularly did he devote himself to the study of Arabic and
Persian, as well as to Hindustani and Sanskrit. By arrangement with
the Serampore missionaries the Persian translation of the New Testament was committed to Mr. Martyn. The heat of the Indian plains
proved too severe a test to his delicate constitution, a change became
imperative, and an ocean voyage was recommended. This plan was
taken advantage of by this devoted servant of God to attempt to
verify the accuracy and utility of his Persian version of the New
Testament by a visit to Arabia and Persia for intercourse with learned
nationals of these lands.

Two days after his arrival in India, Henry Martyn had written:
"Now let me burn out for God," and no words could more fitly
express the spirit and record of that life "whose devotion, fervid zeal,
and deep spirituality have led as many to become missionaries as
David Brainerd's flaming life."[1]

Alexander Duff (1829–1863). This hardy Scotsman and great missionary was a pioneer in two senses, as being the first missionary of
the Church of Scotland to India, and as leading the way to higher
educational missions in that land. Dr. Pierson ranks him with Carey
and Livingstone as "one of the great missionary triad of the new
age."

Reaching Calcutta in 1830, at the age of twenty-four, after a
memorable voyage on which he twice suffered shipwreck, Duff
threw himself energetically into his appointed task. He began a new
chapter in Indian missions by introducing the policy of making
English rather than the vernacular the medium of higher education,
and also by insisting upon giving the Bible an essential place in the
daily school curriculum. His plan was novel, and it was greeted
with mistrust by missionary leaders and with opposition by Indian
Brahmans. But the aged Carey gave his approval and sympathy, and
the friendship of an educated and enlightened Brahman of great
influence, Ram Mohun Roy by name, proved a timely help.

With unflinching courage the young missionary educator opened
his school, and on the very first day faced the issue by bidding his

[1] Harlan P. Beach, *India and Christian Opportunity* (New York: SVM,
1904), p. 167.

pupils repeat after him the Lord's Prayer in Bengali, and then putting into the hands of each one a copy of the Gospels and calling upon a pupil to read. An ominous silence ensued, after which one of the number said: "This is the Christian Master. We are not Christians. How then can we read it?" Whereupon Ram Mohun Roy, who was present, quietly rose and replied: "Christians have read the Hindu Shasters and have not become Hindus. I have read the whole Bible, and you know that I am not a Christian. Read the book and judge for yourselves." The day was won, and the school became so popular that increased accommodation was soon necessary and many had to be turned away. Duff followed up his advantage by arranging a course of lectures for educated men on natural and revealed religion. These lectures aroused great excitement and no little antagonism, but a spirit of inquiry was awakened, and Duff was rewarded by seeing a number of gifted men renounce Hinduism and accept Christ. Some of these later became prominent in the gospel ministry.

Ill health twice compelled Dr. Duff to return home, in 1834 and 1849, but the loss to India was perhaps more than compensated by the missionary impulse he imparted to the home churches, not only of Great Britain, but also of the United States, which he toured in 1854. Dr. A. T. Pierson calls him "the most eloquent missionary orator of the century," and writes: "He made the very pulse of missions to beat quicker, shaping missionary effort and moving hundreds to *go*, as well as tens of thousands to *give* . . . and gave such impetus to work in other lands as no man since has ever equaled."[2]

Dr. Duff's home church conferred upon him high degrees and honors, and after failing health required his taking final leave of India he accepted, in 1863, a Missionary Professorship, in which position he delivered lectures each winter in the colleges of Aberdeen, Edinburgh, and Glasgow. By this and every other means, until death removed him in 1878, he labored to strengthen and extend the cause of missions, on whose altar his own gifts and powers had been unreservedly laid.

Reginald Heber (1822–1826). This early missionary of the Church of England became the second Bishop of Calcutta. His career was cut short by death, but his name will ever be remembered and honored in connection with his immortal missionary and devotional hymns. The best known of these are: "From Greenland's Icy Mountains," "The Son of God Goes Forth to War," and "Holy, Holy, Holy, Lord God Almighty." He "united the zeal and piety of the Christian with the accomplishments of the scholar and the gentleman. Few men have ever won in equal measure the general esteem of society in India."[3]

John Scudder, M.D. (1819–1855). To this man belongs the honor of being the first medical missionary to India. Picking up Gordon Hall's tract entitled *The Conversion of the World*, the heart of the young physician of New York City was stirred, and in 1819 he sailed for India under the American Board. Later the *Reformed Church in America*, of which he was a member, organized its own separate work on the field. Dr. Scudder labored in Ceylon and afterwards established a work of great value at Madras.

"No stronger, more versatile, or more successful missionary pioneer ever evangelized a people as healer, preacher, teacher, and translator, in season and out of season. He lived in praying and working till, although he knew it not, he realized his ambition even in this world, 'to be one of the inner circle around Jesus.' There was not a town in southeastern India which had not heard the gospel from his lips, while his descendants worked by his side and took up his mantle."[4] Not only did Dr. and Mrs. Scudder's whole family follow their parents' example of devoting their lives to missionary service, but also their children's children after them, and now the fourth generation of this illustrious family is in the work.

BRITISH SOCIETIES. As might be expected, much of the pioneer missionary work in India was undertaken by British societies. The earliest mission was, of course, the society under which William Carey first went out in 1793. At that time its name was the *Particular Baptist Missionary Society for Propagating the Gospel Among the Heathen*. Now known simply as the *Baptist Missionary Society*, it includes three other societies: the *General Baptist Missionary Society*, formed in 1816; the *Bible Translation Society*, formed in 1840; and the *Baptist Zenana Mission*, formed in 1867. Following their arrival in 1793 Carey and his associates settled in Serampore in west Bengal. Calcutta was opened in 1801 and Howrah in 1821. During the second decade of the nineteenth century the Mission moved into North India and opened three stations, Agra (1811), Patna (1816), and Delhi (1818). In the third decade they extended their sphere of operation into Orissa and established stations at Cuttack (1822), Berhampur (1825), and Puri (1825). The one station in Assam was not opened until 1903. Today India, with 504 churches and 36,756 members served by 138 missionaries and 505 full-time national

---

[3] Caroline Mason, *Lux Christi* (New York: Macmillan, 1902), p. 146.
[4] George Smith, *Conversion of India* (New York: Revell, n.d.), pp. 164–65.

workers, is the largest of the seven mission fields of the Baptist Missionary Society.

The *London Missionary Society*, founded in 1795, sent its first worker to India in 1798. *Nathaniel Forsyth* settled in Calcutta, where he became self-supporting, and immediately gave himself unstintingly to the work. He died in 1816, exhausted from his labors; but he had been joined by reinforcements in 1812. In the meantime another group of London Missionary Society workers, under the leadership of Ringeltaube, reached Tranquebar on a Danish ship and established a station in Madras in 1805. Work in the southern part of Travancore got under way in 1818, and from there it was extended to the central and northern districts. Following the revision of the East India Company's charter in 1813 the Mission rapidly enlarged its staff in India, consolidating existing centers and opening new ones.

The first worker of the *Church Missionary Society* in India was stationed in the United Province. He was an Indian, *Abdul Masih,* Henry Martyn's sole convert from Islam. He was placed at Agra in 1813. Ten years later he was ordained by Bishop Heber and thus became the first Indian clergyman of the Church of England. Meerut was entered in 1815, Benares in 1817, Lucknow in 1858, and Allahabad in 1859. The educational work of the Society at the present time centers in Meerut, where there are a college, two high schools, and two middle schools. C. M. S. work in the northeast began in Calcutta in 1816. Four other main stations were opened in this area during the first century of work. Also in 1816 the C. M. S. began its work in Travancore and Cochin in the southwest. For the first twenty years the Mission sought to assist the ancient Syrian Church of Malabar, which claims to have been founded by St. Thomas; but ever since 1837 it has given itself to the evangelization of non-Christians, thousands of whom have been baptized. The oldest C. M. S. station in the Telugu-speaking country on the east coast is at Masulipatan. It was opened by the famous *Robert T. Noble* in 1841 and became the spiritual birthplace of many Brahmans. It was in this district that the first Indian bishop, *Rev. V. S. Azariah* of Dornaval, was consecrated in 1912. The ministry of this remarkable man lasted until 1945.

Three Scottish societies took up work in India during the second quarter of the nineteenth century. The first of these was the *Scottish Missionary Society*, whose first party of workers reached Bombay in 1823. One of their outstanding leaders in those early days was *John Wilson*, who arrived in 1829. Later he transferred to the Church of Scotland and still later to the Free Church of Scotland. A great linguist, he labored for thirty-five years in Bombay whence he was able to make fruitful contact with Hindus, Muslims, and Parsees, many of whom he led to Christ. The *Church of Scotland* entered India with the arrival of its illustrious missionary, *Alexander Duff*, whose school work in Calcutta became the model for missions all over India and even in other parts of the world. From Calcutta the Mission expanded its work to Bombay and Madras. Its work was mainly along the educational lines laid down by Duff. With the formation of the *Free Church of Scotland* in 1843, Duff and his colleagues transferred their affiliations to the new Church, thus introducing a third Scottish society into the country.

In 1826 the *Society for Promoting Christian Knowledge* turned over its work to the *Society for the Propagation of the Gospel in Foreign Parts;* but it was not until the 1840's that the latter began to reap a harvest in the Tinnevelly district once worked by the Danish-Halle Mission. By 1846 the Society for the Propagation of the Gospel had several hundred converts in its Bengal field. That same year it opened work among the Gond tribe in what is now the Central Provinces.

The *Wesleyan Methodist Missionary Society*, a local body formed in 1819 in Madras, opened centers in that city, Bangalore, and Negapatam. At first its work was mostly among the Europeans; it was not until reinforcements arrived that it was able, in 1857, to establish a strong work among the Indian population. The *General Baptists* arrived in 1821 and, after consulting their Baptist brethren at Serampore, decided to open work in Orissa. The *Irish Presbyterians* entered India in 1841 and on the advice of John Wilson established a mission at Kathiawar. A group of Plymouth Brethren missionaries inaugurated the work of *Christian Missions in Many Lands* in Madras in 1836. Brethren Assemblies, several hundred strong, are to be found in all parts of India.

It is impossible to enumerate all the British societies in India, but one more group is worthy of mention, the *Salvation Army*. India was the Army's first overseas mission field. *Mr. F. de Lautour Tucker*, a member of the Indian Civil Service, read a copy of the *War Cry* and became a Salvationist. He took the Indian name of *Fakir Singh* and began the Salvation Army work in Bombay in 1882. In an all-out effort to ingratiate themselves with the common people, especially those in the villages, the early missionaries adopted Indian food, dress, names, and customs, even to the extent of going barefooted. In addition to evangelistic work, various forms of social work were undertaken for the amelioration of suffering caused by famine, flood, and epidemic. Educational facilities were provided for the depressed classes: elementary, secondary, and industrial schools; cottage industries; peasant settlements; etc. Medical work originated at Nagercoil in 1896. Work among the Criminal Tribes began in 1908. Salvation Army officers continue today to give loving, sacrificial service to the poor and needy in some 4,825 centers of work. Evangelistic work is an integral part of their program and many of their converts join the Army and become missionaries to their own people. Medical services are offered without discrimination to all classes and communities in 24 Army hospitals and dispensaries in all parts of the country.

AMERICAN SOCIETIES. As time passed Protestant missionaries multiplied. They came from more and more countries and from more and more denominations. The largest number of missionaries came from the British Isles. The second largest contingent was from the United States of America. The *American Board of Commissioners for Foreign Missions*, the first board to be formed in this country, was the first American society to enter India. The initial group of missionaries landed in Calcutta in 1812. Meeting with determined opposition on the part of the East India Company, they moved to Bombay and established permanent work in that city on the west coast in 1813. It was under the American Board that *Dr. John Scudder* sailed for Ceylon in 1819.

From Ceylon a thrust was made into South India, and in 1835 a station was opened at Madura, a stronghold of Hinduism. The following year Dr. Scudder moved to Madras. In 1947 the Madura Mission of the American Board became part of the *Diocese of Madura and Ramnad of the Church of South India*. The work in this area is heavily institutionalized with two colleges, three high schools, four normal training schools, a trade school for men, an industrial school for women, and about ninety village schools. There is also a hospital. The Marathi Mission in the Bombay area continues with 22 missionaries and 562 paid Indian workers.

The *American Presbyterian Mission* has been in India since 1834, when it opened its first station in the Punjab. Two years later it organized its North India Mission. The Mutiny of 1857 cost the Presbyterians the lives of 14 missionaries and of their wives and two of their children, as well as the lives of several Indian Christians. During the period of rapid expansion which followed the Mutiny the Presbyterians entered their third field when in 1870 they took over an independent work which had been maintained for some years at Kolhapur by *Royal G. Wilder*. The Presbyterian Mission is now integrated with the *United Church of Northern India* and its 146 fraternal workers are under the supervision of that body.

The work of the *Reformed Church in America* in India dates from the year 1857, when it first organized its foreign mission board. Dr. John Scudder, who had served for many years in Madras under the American Board, immediately transferred to his own Mission and became its first missionary to India. Also transferred to the new Mission at that time was the Arcot Mission of the American Board, inaugurated in 1853 by two of Dr. Scudder's sons. In 1956 the Telugu work of the Arcot Mission was completely integrated with the *Rayalaseema Diocese of the Church of South India,* which now has 460 congregations and 10,930 communicants. The Tamil work is in process of integration.

Dr. Nathan Brown pioneered the work of the *American Baptist Convention* in India. Three major fields were opened in 1836. These were Assam, Bengal-Orissa, and South India. The ministry has been exceedingly fruitful, especially in Assam and South India where the combined church membership on January 1, 1959, was 308,000. The latest *Report* expresses concern at the "alarming decrease in missionary staff," due in part to health factors. The missionary staff in 1955 numbered 151; at the close of 1958 it had dropped to 109— and new converts are being gathered in at the rate of 20,000 a year.

American Lutherans began work in India in the 1840's. Their first field was in the Telugu country in South India, where they collaborated with the American Board. With the passing of the decades other Lutheran missions, both American and Continental, joined the work. In 1911 Lutheran membership had climbed to 216,842. By 1949 the figure had more than doubled and stood at 567,334. According to the 1959 *Christian Handbook of India* there are now ten Lutheran Churches in the country supported by 11 missionary societies. Three of the Churches are fully autonomous.

The India Mission of the *Methodist Episcopal Church* owed its inception, in part at least, to the visit of Alexander Duff to America in 1854. The first missionary appointee was *Dr. William Butler* who, with his wife, reached Calcutta in 1856. After many difficulties occasioned by the Sepoy Mutiny of 1857 the first permanent station was opened at Naini Tal in 1858. Lucknow was occupied later in the same year. The first appointees of the *Woman's Foreign Missionary Society* to any country were *Miss Isabella Thoburn* and *Dr. Clara A. Swain,* who arrived in Bombay in 1870. Within three months Miss Thoburn had started in Lucknow India's first Christian college for women; it is now called the *Isabella Thoburn College.* Dr. Swain proceeded to Bareilly and there, in 1874, she founded the first hospital for women in Asia. Under the leadership of two missionary bishops, *James M. Thoburn* and *William Taylor,* Methodist missions in India and other parts of southern Asia prospered greatly. No other Church in India covers so wide an area or maintains a larger number of institutions. After a century of work Methodist churches are to be found all over India—north, east, west, and south. The Methodist Church in India is divided into ten annual conferences representing 180,000 full members and 215,000 preparatory members. If baptized children were included the total membership would be well over 600,000. Its many hospitals, schools, and colleges are among the finest institutions in the land.

Prominent among several societies from Continental Europe are the *Basel Mission* (1834), the *German Evangelical Lutheran Mission* (1841), and *Gossner's Society* (1845). World War I struck a sad blow at these missions through the necessary withdrawal of their German workers from British territory. Every possible effort was made by the British and American societies of similar church order to care for the churches and activities thus left without oversight; but in spite of this the work suffered a severe setback.

Around the turn of the century India attracted the attention of several interdenominational faith missions. The first of these was the *Christian and Missionary Alliance,* whose pioneer workers reached India in 1887. In 1892 this Mission merged with the *North Berar Faith Mission,* which had been founded ten years earlier by *Rev. and Mrs. Mark B. Fuller.* Today the Christian and Missionary Alliance has 7 stations north of Bombay and 12 stations east of Bombay on the railway to Nagpur. After a year's work in Ceylon the *Ceylon and India General Mission* transferred several of its workers to South India. Working out from Bangalore, which later became its headquarters, it initiated work among the Tamils and later among the Telugus. In 1937 the Mission decided to close its Ceylon field and concentrate on India, and its Ceylon staff was transferred to North India. *The Evangelical Alliance Mission* entered India in 1905. *Rev. and Mrs. O. A. Dahlgren,* its first missionaries, settled at Navapur in the Khandesh district in the Bombay Presidency. The five years from 1945 to 1949 saw the greatest increase in the Mission's staff in India. During that time 41 new workers arrived on the field. Today the Mission has 45 churches in India. *International Missions, Inc.* (formerly the India Mission) came into being in 1930 in response to a great need in Hyderabad State which no existing society was able at the time to meet. The district proved to be one of the most fruitful in the entire country, being in a mass movement area. The Mission has had its largest growth since 1945. In 1959 it reported over 400 churches with a membership of 18,000. Its 78 missionaries, assisted by 110 nationals, are working in three language areas: Telugu, Kanarese, and Marathi.

EVANGELISM. The preaching of the gospel has always been an integral part of the missionary program in all places and in all ages. India, with its 700,000 villages, has been no exception. The early missionaries, following Carey's lead, gave themselves unremittingly to the preaching of the gospel. Even those engaged primarily in education and medicine did not neglect this most important phase of missionary endeavor. In season and out of season they took advantage of every opportunity to preach Christ. Not only in churches and chapels but on the streets, in the temples, in the market places, on the threshing floors, at the religious fairs and festivals, and by the sacred rivers, they called upon the multitudes of India to "turn to God from idols to serve the living and true God." Tracts, gospel posters, and Scripture portions were used extensively to supplement the oral preaching. It was feared that with the coming of Independence evangelism might fall on evil days. To some extent it has. Spokesmen for the Government of India have on more than one occasion stated that evangelistic missionaries are not welcome in the new India, and of course "proselytizing" is anathema; but the Constitution guarantees freedom of religion and the gospel continues to be preached in India.

MEDICAL MISSIONS. In spite of the fact that the British ruled India for almost a century, very little in the way of medical facilities was provided for the people. Consequently there was as great a need for medical missions in India as in other parts of Asia and Africa. Especially urgent was the need for women doctors to minister to the secluded womenfolk of India who in the early days would sooner die than accept the professional aid of a male physician. As a young girl in her teens *Ida Scudder* received her call to be a medical missionary to the women of India when in the course of a single night three women—the wife of a Brahman, the wife of a Hindu, and the wife of a Muslim—all died in childbirth rather than consent to have her father attend them. Returning to India after a period of training in the United States, Dr. Ida Scudder opened a medical school for women in Vellore, South India. Using a deserted shed for a dissecting room, she opened her first class in anatomy with one microscope, two books, and a few bones. Fourteen of her original eighteen pupils passed their final exams with flying colors to become the first graduating class of what later grew to be the *Vellore Medical College*. From those humble beginnings Vellore has become in the last forty years the outstanding college of its kind in India. It draws its support from 40 different denominations, 20 of which are in the United States. It has a staff of 182, of whom 21 are foreigners. There are 331 medical students and 253 nurses; 90 per cent of these are Christians. A similar though smaller institute in North India is *Ludhiana Medical College*. To enumerate the many medical institutions maintained by Christian missions in India would be impossible; suffice it to say that according to the *Christian Handbook of India* for 1959 there are 238 hospitals, 60 dispensaries, 13 tuberculosis sanatoria, and 52 leper colonies being operated under Christian auspices. With singular appropriateness the Church of India can sing:

> The healing of His seamless dress
> Is by our beds of pain;
> We touch Him in life's throng and press
> And we are whole again.

EDUCATIONAL MISSIONS. Education on all levels has been the concern of Christian missions in India ever since William Carey's day. Encouraged by the example of Alexander Duff, missionary bodies early came to see the value of higher education as a means of reaching the intelligentsia of the country. This was especially true of Scottish societies, which established and maintained large and influential colleges in various parts of the country. Others, such as the Basel Mission, have emphasized industrial work. The need and opportunity for this, as well as for orphanages, grew largely out of successive years of dire famine and plague, and from caste difficulties. Almost every mission provides educational facilities for its own converts if not for non-Christians. Elementary schools are numbered by the thousands. Christian institutions of higher education include at the present time 47 colleges, 315 high schools, 65 normal schools, and 43 industrial schools. The clamor for higher education continues unabated. In the past ten years the number of students has increased from 230,000 to 720,000. To accommodate them the government has established 16 new universities. So great is the demand for Christian education that some institutions, such as Ludhiana Medical College, can accept only one out of ten applicants. Alas, just when the opportunities are the greatest there is a dearth of Christian teachers, and the National Christian Council has issued a call to all churches to present to their students and young people the challenge of the teaching profession.

The education of the women of India was no easy task. None but the most aggressive and optimistic of missionaries could have overcome the apathy and prejudice of the early years. One Brahman, when asked by a lady missionary for the privilege of educating his daughter, replied, "Next you will want to take away my cow and educate her." Even some of the missionaries were skeptical. Alexander Duff, the great missionary who pioneered in male education in India, said on one occasion, "You might as well try to scale a wall fifty feet high as to educate the women of India." Some of the missionaries had the courage and skill to scale the wall, among them Isabella Thoburn, who opened the first college for women in India. When one of her graduates, *Miss Lilavati Singh,* toured the United States she amazed her audiences with her brilliant and eloquent addresses, some of which were "beyond the depth of the average preacher." When President Harrison heard Miss Singh address the Ecumenical Missionary Conference in New York in 1900 he remarked: "If I had given a million dollars to foreign missions, I should count it wisely invested if it had led only to the conversion of that one woman."

The best known and most worthy of all, however, was Pandita Ramabai, universally acknowledged to be the most distinguished Indian woman of her day. Her education was so thorough and her intellectual ability so great that the highest title possible for a native woman was conferred upon her. Forsaking idolatry she turned to Christ, and then consecrated herself with a love and devotion truly wonderful to the emancipation of child-wives and child-widows from their terrible bondage. In the famines and pestilences of 1897 and later years her ministry expanded far beyond her original design, as she threw herself into the desperate situation and rescued thousands of girls and women from death, destitution, and the base designs of wicked men. Never will the writer forget the privilege he enjoyed of being the guest of this remarkable woman in her great Christian settlement known as *"Mukti"* (salvation), and addressing her "family" of many hundred sweet-faced little child-widows. Her schools, orphange, and rescue home have witnessed some wonderful outpourings of the Holy Spirit and the conversion of great numbers of souls.

After more than thirty years of prodigious labor, this great "scholar, saint and servant," as one of her biographers designates her, fell asleep in Jesus on the 5th of April, 1922. Her death was noted in both the secular and the religious press the world around, and a host of her friends of every race deeply mourned her loss. But she "being dead yet speaketh" through thousands of lives touched and changed by her direct ministry, and other thousands inspired by her noble example.

THEOLOGICAL EDUCATION. There is no more important work than that of training future leaders of the Christian Church. Failure to produce an adequate number of fully trained national leaders has been the greatest single weakness of the missionary movement. With 36 theological seminaries and more than 50 Bible schools, India is in a better position than many mission fields; but even this number is barely sufficient to provide a steady stream of preachers and teachers for an ever-increasing Protestant community of over 4,000,000. The administration of these schools is largely in the hands of Indian nationals; but there is a high percentage of Western teachers, and heavy subsidies from the West are still required. There is also a paucity of theological texts in regional languages. Outstanding among the many theological institutions is Serampore. It has 19 colleges affiliated with it in different parts of the country; 5 of them prepare students for the B.D. degree and 14 for the L.Th. diploma.

CHRISTIAN LITERATURE. Few fields in the world are better supplied with Christian literature than India. Here, too, we can trace the influence of William Carey whose first companion and colleague at Serampore was William Ward, a printer by trade. In spite of the fact that less than 20 per cent of the population can read, there is a considerable variety of literature available, both in English and in the vernacular. A total of 38 Christian presses are operating full time turning out a veritable Niagara of Christian literature. In most mission fields the bottleneck is distribution: in India there are no fewer than 107 centers for the distribution of Christian literature. Available to the Christian public of India are 231 periodicals, 116 in English and 115 in 18 Indian languages. Bible correspondence courses are offered in more than a score of languages, including English. The courses with the largest coverage are the *Emmaus Home Studies, Voice of Prophecy,* and *Light of Life.* The last one, prepared originally by *Rev. Donald Hillis* of The Evangelical Alliance Mission, now appears in 22 Indian languages, with regional schools and offices conducted by at least 12 different missions. One of these offices, known simply as Box 66, Vellore, has enrolled over 100,000 students in the past six years; 85 per cent of them were not Christians.

One must not conclude, however, that all literature needs have been met. In spite of all that has been done along this line there are still areas of great need, as the following paragraph from the *East and West Review*, October, 1956, reveals:

In 1918 there were published surveys of the literature which was available in the main languages of India, together with estimates of what were regarded as the most outstanding needs. It is a chastening experience to look through those reports, almost 40 years later, and to realize that for the most part those needs remain unfulfilled. Not only that, but in most categories of literature in the North Indian languages there is actually less available now than there was then.[5]

The largest and most important of the agencies concerned with literature is, of course, the *Christian Literature Society*. The *National Christian Council* has established five regional literature councils for the promotion of its literature program. Other agencies are the *Evangelical Literature Fellowship*, the *Society for Promoting Christian Knowledge*, etc.

BIBLE TRANSLATION. William Carey, with almost 40 translations to his credit, was the Bible translator *par excellence*. Today the complete Bible is available in 26 languages, the New Testament in 21 additional languages, and individual books in another 39 languages or dialects, which means that some portion of the Word of God has been published in 86 languages of India. Revision of old versions is going on constantly. At present, New Testament revision is in progress in 7 languages, including Bengali, Marathi, and Hindi. The work of Scripture publication is the responsibility of the independent *Bible Society of India and Ceylon*, which maintains 71 branches in the two countries. This Society is trying to secure local support by a membership scheme in the churches. By 1957 it had secured 15,280 members. The Society, though independent, still receives funds and Scripture supplies from both the British and the American Bible Societies. A new project sponsored by the Bible Society is the publication of the Four Gospels in serial form in the newspapers of the main regional languages. In 1957 it distributed 1,124,775 copies of the Scriptures.

ZENANA WORK. The peculiar seclusion of India's women and the distressing conditions attending their life by reason of such things as child-marriage, widowhood, and, formerly, suttee made it necessary for the early missionaries to adopt special methods of work

[5] James Stuart, "Christian Literature in India and Pakistan," *East and West Review*, Oct., 1956.

in order to reach the womenfolk of India with the gospel. The wives of the earliest missionaries—*Mrs. Marshman, Mrs. Sarah (Boardman) Judson* and others—began direct work for women. *Miss M. A. Cooke*, sent out by the *Church Missionary Society* in 1820, was the first single woman missionary to India. She opened many schools for girls. At least three societies worked exclusively among women: the *Zenana Bible and Medical Mission*, the *Church of England Zenana Missionary Society*, and the *Woman's Union Missionary Society*. Their work involved visiting the women in the seclusion of their own apartments (zenana) and sharing with them in a personal way the good news of the gospel.

In this close, heart-to-heart encounter the Christian missionary learns the needs and sorrows of India's oppressed wives and mothers. Here, in the very deepest heart of it, absolutely closed to men missionaries, the family life in all its multiform misery can be reached with the healing and purifying touch of Christianity.[6]

With the emancipation of woman in modern India this type of work has necessarily undergone considerable modification, so much so that the Zenana Bible and Medical Mission has recently changed its name to the *Bible and Medical Missionary Fellowship*. There is also the possibility that it may merge with the Woman's Union Missionary Society.

CHILDREN'S WORK. The children as well as the women of India had special needs calling for special treatment. Two classes in particular, child-widows and temple girls, had a claim on the love and devotion of the followers of the One who said, "Suffer the little children to come unto Me." Through the years a vast amount of time, energy, and money have been spent in a noble effort to provide food, clothes, shelter, and education for the many unfortunate children. The *1959 Handbook* lists 85 orphanages. Some of these are for boys, some for girls, and some take in both. In addition there are 87 social and welfare organizations, most of which are hostels ministering exclusively to children. Space permits the mention of only one such institution, the *Dohnavur Fellowship* in the Tinnevelly District, maintained by the well-known and saintly *Amy Carmichael* and her devoted colleagues, both Indian and Western.

Prostitution, "the oldest profession in the world," is by no means the monopoly of India; but in that land it not only had the sanction of religion but was definitely linked with it. Parents gave or

[6] Mason, *op. cit.*, p. 203.

sold the girl to the nearest temple while she was still a baby. When eight or nine years of age she was taken to the temple and "married to the gods," after which one of the temple priests became her "husband." After she had learned to sing and dance she was ready to satisfy the sensual passions of any male Hindu who frequented the temple. For fifty years Miss Carmichael fought this iniquitous traffic, and during that time she rescued thousands of children from a life of shame. The law regarding temple prostitution has been reformed, but the practice has not been entirely stamped out. Miss Carmichael went to her reward in 1951, but Dohnavur still shelters almost 1,000 children. As late as 1945 one who knows both India and Dohnavur well wrote:

I know of no greater moral contrast in India than to pass from the dark recesses of the Madura Hindu temple, with its life-sized obscene carvings in stone and its neighborhood of temple prostitution, to Miss Carmichael's radiant Christian institutions where one sees hundreds of beautiful little children who have been rescued from the very jaws of hell, now the very flowers of God. They were rescued when too young to know the infamy from which they were spared, the dark pit from which they were lifted.[7]

MASS MOVEMENTS. No treatment of missionary history in India is complete without some reference, however brief, to the mass movements which, according to Sherwood Eddy, have accounted for 80 per cent of the Christians in India. These movements invariably took place among the outcastes, more euphemistically known as depressed, or scheduled classes. The movements began in South India and were experienced by the London Missionary Society in Travancore, the Church Missionary Society in Tinnevelly and Madras, and the American Baptist Mission in the Telugu country. The last one furnishes one of the most wonderful instances of the miracle-working power of God in modern times. The *Lone Star Mission* at Ongole, after 28 years of seed-sowing, had reaped a meager harvest of only 30 souls. Three times the Mission had been on the verge of closing; but the divine restraint was felt. With the arrival of *Dr. and Mrs. John E. Clough* in 1865 the Mission took on new life; and shortly afterwards revival broke out with the conversion of *Yerraguntla Periah,* an outcaste Madiga. In a single day, July 3, 1878, Dr. Clough baptized 2,222 outcaste believers. By the end of the year 9,606 persons had been received into the Church. Since that time more than a million outcaste Malas and

[7] Sherwood Eddy, *Pathfinders of the World Missionary Crusade* (New York: Abingdon-Cokesbury Press, 1945), p. 127.

Madigas have been won to Christ in this area. A similar movement took place in North India under the leadership of *Bishop Thoburn*. When he arrived in India in 1859 the Methodist Church there had only 13 members. When he retired in 1908 there were some 200,000.

It is recognized that such mass movements are not without their serious resultant problems. Unworthy motives are usually to be found on the part of some in seasons of what may be termed "wholesale conversions"; others are apt to get wrong or superficial ideas of what Christianity really is; others again mistake Christian liberty for license and are tempted to lay aside courtesy for their neighbors and due respect for their superiors. These and other dangers call for much prayer and watchfulness, and for careful Bible instruction and discipline. Alas, too often the missionary staff is painfully insufficient for the added strain.

INTERCHURCH CO-OPERATION. In no other country has interchurch collaboration progressed so far as in India. This is seen in all phases of Church life and work. In the realm of education, the Madras Christian College and the theological seminaries at Bangalore and Serampore are shining examples. In the medical field, mention could be made of the union medical colleges at Vellore and Ludhiana. The Baptists, the most diverse denominational group in India, have organized themselves into various regional councils, unions, and conventions, most of which are members of the all-embracing *Baptist Union of India, Pakistan, Burma, and Ceylon*. Ten Lutheran Churches have banded together under the *Federation of Evangelical Lutheran Churches in India*. This large group represents a baptized membership of 550,000. The *Evangelical Fellowship of India* is a member of the World Evangelical Fellowship. The largest and most influential of all co-operative agencies is the *National Christian Council*, which was organized in 1914 and now comprises 13 regional councils. The National Christian Council of India is one of the strongest and most effective in all Asia. Its official organ is the *National Christian Council Review*.

CHURCH UNION. Church union has proceeded farther in South India than perhaps any other mission field in the world. As early as 1901 the mission churches brought into existence by the United Free Church of Scotland and the Reformed Church in America merged to form the *South India United Church (Presbyterian Synod)*. Four years later the London Missionary Society and the American Board joined to form the *Congregational General Union of South*

India. In 1908 these two bodies merged to form the *United Church of South India* with a combined membership of 145,000. In September, 1947, after twenty-eight years of patient and painstaking negotiations, the United Church of South India joined with the Anglican and Methodist Churches of South India to form the largest, most comprehensive non-Roman church union since the Reformation, the *Church of South India.* This new Church comprises 14 dioceses; present membership is about 350,000. The Christian community numbers 1,000,000. In spite of its numerical strength and the high caliber of its clergy, three elements of weakness appear in this great Church: (1) it is too dependent on funds from abroad; (2) only half of its 14 bishops are Indian nationals; (3) it suffers from a continuing shortage of rural clergy.

The Church of South India has extended an invitation to other Churches to join the union. The Lutherans and the Baptists responded to the call and a series of exploratory discussions began. Later on the Baptists withdrew. The Lutherans found the Church of South India's rigid stand on the historic episcopate difficult to accept and at present negotiations are at a standstill. The Church of South India is in friendly relations with the four non-Roman Syrian Churches in South India, which claim descent from St. Thomas, but it has no official connection with any of them. The Mar Thoma Church has indicated its desire to join the Church of South India, but to date it has refrained from doing so on the grounds that it wishes first to see the Syrian Churches themselves achieve unity.

At the other end of India a second union of Protestant Churches has been effected. This is the *United Church of Northern India,* which resulted from the coming together of twelve Churches brought into existence by missionary societies from six foreign countries. As now constituted the United Church includes elements from four denominational groups, Presbyterian, Congregational, Reformed, and Moravian. The United Church, with a membership of 150,000, is divided into seven synods. The Christian community is just under the half-million mark. Negotiations are now under way with the Anglican, Methodist, and Baptist Churches, looking forward to an even larger union, possibly in 1960.

A third union of Churches is contemplated in western India. Representatives of the Basel Mission, the Church of India, Pakistan, Burma and Ceylon, and the Methodist Church of Southern Asia have met informally to discuss the possibility of church union in western India.

NATIONAL MISSIONARY SOCIETY. Of the many organized efforts on the part of the Indian Christians to take the gospel to their own people only one can be mentioned here, the *National Missionary Society* founded at Serampore in 1905. The two men who did most to promote its interests in the early years were *K. T. Paul* and *Bishop Azariah.* Working in about 50 centers in eight states, it has become a leading factor in the Indianizing of Christianity. Its leaders felt that they had much to learn from India's ancient religions, and consequently have sought to emphasize renunciation and self-sacrifice rather than organization and activity. They have tried to make Christianity truly indigenous by rooting it in the life and soil of the East. As a result their program has included ashrams and brotherhoods as well as hospitals and schools. One of its more fruitful endeavors is a triennial all-India conference to quicken the spiritual life of the churches and challenge young people to missionary service. It operates its own press and has published the *National Missionary Intelligencer* for more than half a century; it also publishes five vernacular missionary journals.

PAKISTAN

Area:	365,000 sq. mi.	Population:	85,000,000
Capital:	Rawalpindi	Religion:	Islam

THE LAND. Pakistan, situated in the northern part of the subcontinent of India, is divided into two parts, East Pakistan and West Pakistan. Between these two sections of Pakistan lie 1,200 miles of Indian territory. West Pakistan has a population of 38,000,000. It comprises the four provinces of West Punjab, the North West Frontier, Sind, and Baluchistan. East Pakistan was carved out of the eastern part of Bengal and the Sylhet district of Assam, where the Muslims predominated. Its population is 47,000,000.

POLITICAL HISTORY. Fearing that as a minority group they would be reduced to the status of second-class citizens in an independent India, the Muslims insisted on their right to establish a separate state in the subcontinent of India. Their leader was Mohammed Ali Jinnah, head of the Muslim League. Accordingly, when India was granted independence in August, 1947, the new state of Pakistan came into being. The first few weeks of independence witnessed one of the greatest upheavals of history, when nearly 6,000,000 Muslims entered Pakistan from India, and about 4,000,000 Hindus fled to India. It was all over in about two weeks, but the soil of both countries ran red with blood. The impartial ministry of the Christian Church to Muslim and Hindu alike during those dreadful days made a very favorable impression. The present Constitution was adopted in March, 1956, at which time Pakistan became an Islamic republic. It continues its full membership in the Commonwealth of Nations. It is solidly lined up with the West in the cold war, being a full member of both the Baghdad Pact (now called the Central Treaty Organization) and the Southeast Asia Treaty Organization.

THE PEOPLE. Pakistan has only a meager supply of natural resources, insufficient rainfall, and an undeveloped economy. Consequently the people are extremely poor even by Asian standards. The official languages are Urdu in the West, and Bengali in the East. For all practical purposes English is to remain the official language until 1967. About 85 per cent of the populace is illiterate. In the North West Frontier Province live the freedom-loving Pathans. The Sikhs live in the Punjab. They are a martial people whose men were the best troops in the Indian army.

THE RELIGION. The people of Pakistan are Muslims. Those in West Pakistan are much more devout than those in East Pakistan. The latter have never been very orthodox because they are largely of low-caste Hindu origin. Only since Partition have these Muslims become more orthodox. Signs of revival are seen in the growing adoption of Muslim dress, attendance at Friday prayers, and the erection of new mosques. There are about 500,000 Christians, the largest religious minority in the country. In no other Muslim country does the Christian missionary enjoy so much freedom to carry on religious work. Open-air preaching is a common practice and it is never difficult to attract an attentive and orderly crowd. Most mission hospitals have a planned program of personal evangelism in the wards and regular preaching services among the outpatients. In the winter of 1957 a campaign in seven large cities placed a Gospel of Matthew in every Muslim home where someone could read. Mission schools and colleges continue to exert a wholesome Christian influence among the intelligentsia. At one time the government ordered that Islamic teaching be provided for all Muslim pupils; but a united protest averted the problem, for the time being at least. The Constitution guarantees religious freedom but does not permit religious instruction other than that of the religion of the student. The government, however, has appealed for missionary teachers in government colleges.

MISSIONS. Owing to the fact that what is now Pakistan was until recently India, and also that when Partition took place most missions and churches in the northern part of the subcontinent found their fields cut right in half, it is not easy to trace either the beginnings of Christian missions or their later developments. The situation is further complicated by the division of Pakistan into East and West. Only one or possibly two missions have work in both areas. It will be necessary, therefore, to deal with them separately, and we shall take West Pakistan first.

The oldest and largest mission in the area is the *American Presbyterian Mission,* which has been in Pakistan since it opened its first station in Lahore in 1849. The pioneer missionary was *Charles W. Forman,* who gave forty years of outstanding service, mostly in educational work. Other stations were entered in the following order: Sialkot, 1855; Gujranwala, 1863; Zafarwal, 1880; Pasrur, 1884; and Kasur, 1913. Experience has proved that education is the best method of evangelism in a Muslim community. In West Pakistan the *United Presbyterian Mission* has built up an unusually fine system of Christian schools, ranging from primary school to college. Besides scores of elementary schools at the village level there are middle schools, high schools, technical schools, and an industrial home. The center of their educational work is Lahore, where they maintain four institutions of higher learning. *Rang Mahal High School* for boys, opened in 1849, has an enrollment of 2,000 students; 90 per cent of them are Muslims. *Forman High School* for girls, now in its 106th year, provides much-needed education for 500 Muslim girls of Lahore city. *Forman Christian College,* a liberal arts college affiliated with the University of the Punjab, is the oldest college in Pakistan, having been founded in 1864. Now a union institution, *Kinnaird College for Women* was founded by the Presbyterians in 1913 and was a pioneer in higher education for women. Today it holds a very high place in this field, attracting Muslim girls from East Pakistan, Afghanistan, and other foreign countries. Equally famous is *Gordon College* in Rawalpindi. Best known for its work in chemistry, botany, and physics, it is a liberal arts institution affiliated with the Punjab University. Present enrollment is around 1,000. Medical work centers in four hospitals, one of which is a union institution established in 1947. Now supported by eight missions, the *United Christian Hospital* in Lahore is widely known for its excellence, drawing patients from such distant places as Calcutta, Bombay, Singapore, and Kabul. In addition to Bible schools for the training of evangelists and Biblewomen, the Presbyterians established the *Gujranwala Theo-*

logical Seminary in 1877. It is now a union institution and the only theological seminary in West Pakistan. It trains students for the Presbyterians, Methodists, and Anglicans.

The United Presbyterians have the largest number of Christians in West Pakistan. On January 1, 1957, the Presbyterian Mission was integrated with the Church and its missionaries are now fraternal workers under the *United Church in Pakistan*.

The *Church Missionary Society* entered this field in the middle of the nineteenth century. The first station to be opened was Karachi in 1850. Peshawar was occupied in 1854, Multan in 1856, Narowal in 1859, Bannu in 1865, Lahore in 1867, and Quetta in 1886. The Diocese of Lahore was founded in 1877. By the turn of the century the Mission had a score of main centers in what is now West Pakistan. At Quetta, its only station in Baluchistan, there are a new hospital and a large congregation. In the North West Frontier Province hospitals are maintained in two centers, Peshawar and Bannu. They serve many members of the frontier tribes, including the Afghans. Nine stations are operated in the Punjab. The work in Karachi is under the *New Zealand Church Missionary Society*. Much of the women's work in these parts is carried on by the *Church of England Zenana Missionary Society*. Educational work goes hand in hand with church work. The Church Missionary Society schools in West Pakistan are chiefly for children from Christian homes.

The *American Methodists* entered West Pakistan in the latter half of the nineteenth century. The first station was Karachi, opened in 1873. Methodist work in Lahore was started in 1881 in the wake of revivals under *Bishop William Taylor*. The converts were mostly English-speaking Anglo-Indians. They began self-supporting churches in various cities in the Punjab. In 1900 this work was turned over to the *British Methodists* and thereafter the Americans devoted their efforts to work among indigenous groups. In no time at all a mass movement began among the Chuhras (Hindu outcastes) of the Central Punjab. There were only 1,200 Christians in 1902; by 1915 they had increased to 15,000, and the movement continued for another ten years. Methodist work in West Pakistan today is divided into four districts with a superintendent in charge of each. There are main centers with resident missionaries at Karachi, Quetta, Lahore, Raewind, and Stuntzabad. In each of these places there is a well-rounded program of evangelistic, medical, and educational work. Total Methodist membership is around 35,000, and there are 50 missionaries, and 32 ordained and 47 unordained national preachers.

The *Salvation Army* has been in West Pakistan since 1883, when it opened its first station in Lahore. Later the work was expanded to Karachi. A recent report indicates a following of 22,000 Christians meeting in 600 places of worship. The *Associate Reformed Presbyterian Church* has about 5,000 members. The *Woman's Union Missionary Society* of America has long had a hospital at Multan. Several American missions have entered West Pakistan since World War II. *The Evangelical Alliance Mission* established headquarters in Abbottabad and already they have 53 missionaries on the field. The *Conservative Baptists,* who entered the country in 1954, have 28 missionaries engaged in village evangelism, literature, and medical work in three districts in the province of Sind. The Ceylon and India General Mission, known in Pakistan as the *Pakistan Christian Fellowship,* has three stations in West Pakistan and two in East Pakistan. *International Missions, Inc.,* reports a good beginning with 27 missionaries. Barely under way, they have been able to organize one congregation of 30 members.

East Pakistan, with a larger population than that of West Pakistan, has been a much neglected area so far as Protestant missions are concerned. Until very recently East Pakistan had fewer than 100 missionaries compared with almost 600 in West Pakistan. In East Pakistan the ratio of missionaries to the total population has been about one to 700,000.

The first society to take up work in East Pakistan was the *Baptist Missionary Society* of England. Work was started at Dinajpur in 1795. Jessore was occupied in 1805, Dacca in 1816, Barisal in 1828, Khulna in 1860, Chittagong in 1881, and Rangpur in 1891. Two other centers were opened in 1901. These nine stations are still manned by the Baptist Missionary Society. Because Islam is so strong, Christianity has not made very much headway in these parts. After 160 years of work the Society reports 124 congregations with a membership of 5,000. Educational work is confined to 85 primary schools. Another long-established society is the *Australian Baptist Mission* whose 120 churches represent another 7,000 baptized believers.

In the postwar period several new missions, most of them American, have taken up work in this needy field. The *Southern Baptists* entered East Pakistan in 1956 and now have three missionary couples in the Dacca area. No churches have as yet been organized. The year 1956 also witnessed the arrival of the first contingent of the *Association of Baptists for World Evangelism.* Working out from Chittagong they have made themselves responsible for 6,000,-000 primitive people belonging to the tribes of the Matamahari Valley in the extreme southeast corner of the country. The *Church of God* is represented in East Pakistan by seven missionaries. Since their first station was opened several years ago at Lalmanihat they have made gratifying progress. Several additional stations have been established and Christian congregations are growing up in each of them. Other missions in East Pakistan are the *Assemblies of God,* the *Seventh Day Adventists,* and the *Worldwide Evangelization Crusade.*

The Christian Church in Pakistan is predominantly a rural church. Its half million Christians are mostly converts or descendants of converts from the outcastes of Hinduism. They came with little or no wealth, property, or education. Even today the Christian Church is 85 per cent illiterate and desperately poor, living at a level of existence which affords barely enough to keep body and soul together.

There is a Christian Council in both East and West Pakistan. The West Pakistan Council carries on a vigorous program of evangelism, literature, and building of churches. It is sponsoring a special Forward Movement in evangelism with a view to rousing the slothful in the churches and to intensifying efforts to spread the gospel among the Muslims. A pledge card to be signed by church members reads, "I promise to try at least once a week to make the Lord Jesus Christ known to non-Christians during this year." Here, as in other Muslim lands, converts from Islam are pitifully few. Almost invariably the convert is called upon to suffer the loss of all things, including wife and children, and he does well if he holds his job. Some evangelistic work has been done among the few Hindus who stayed behind at Partition in 1947. Not a few of them have manifested an interest in the gospel, but paucity of workers has hindered the full exploitation of this situation.

CEYLON

Area:	25,332 sq. mi.	Population:	8,700,000
Capital:	Colombo	Religion:	Buddhism
			Hinduism

THE LAND. Ceylon is an island in the Indian Ocean off the southeast coast of India. This is the land of the "spicy breezes" referred to in the well-known missionary hymn, "From Greenland's Icy Mountains."

POLITICAL HISTORY. Like most of the countries in that part of the

world, Ceylon has an ancient history extending back before the
Christian era. Since 1505 three European colonial powers have ruled
it, each for about 150 years. They were the Portuguese, the Dutch,
and the British; and each brought its own language and religion.
At one time, about the turn of the nineteenth century, more than
half of the population of Ceylon was Christian, at least in name.
It achieved full independence within the British Commonwealth
of Nations on February 4, 1948.

THE PEOPLE. In Ceylon there are four main communities: the Sinhalese, the Tamils, the Moors and Malays, and the Burghers. There
are 6,000,000 Sinhalese and 2,000,000 Tamils. The Moors and Malays
account for another 600,000, and there are about 50,000 Burghers.
In addition there are smaller groups, among them the Beddahs who
are the aborigines, living now in the jungle fringes. Following
independence the Sinhalese attempted to impose their culture on
the whole island. Sinhala was made the national language and
there was some agitation to declare Buddhism the state religion.
The Tamils rebelled and community riots broke out. In May, 1958,
a state of emergency was declared. The Premier, Mr. Bandaranaike,
was assassinated in September, 1959. Had the assassin been a
Hindu instead of a Buddhist the entire island might have been
plunged into a bloodbath.

THE RELIGION. Buddhism was introduced into Ceylon from India
by the great Buddhist emperor, Asoka, in the third century B.C.
The Sinhalese are Buddhists, the Tamils are Hindus, and the Moors
and Malays are Muslims. There are about 900,000 Christians, nine-
tenths of whom are Roman Catholics.

With the coming of independence the Christian Church in
Ceylon fell on evil days. A concerted attempt has been made to
identify Buddhism with nationalism and to accuse the former
colonial powers of deliberately suppressing Buddhism in favor of
Christianity. A Buddhist Commission was appointed by the government to document these ugly "facts," and its report, "The Betrayal
of Buddhism," caused quite a stir throughout the country. This
report, though full of distortions, contained enough truth to make
the charges stick, at least in the minds of the patriotic Buddhists.
This anti-Christian movement was further stimulated by the international celebration in 1954 of *Buddha Javanti,* the 2,500th anniversary of the enlightenment of Gautama Buddha. The movement
has distinct "messianic" overtones, with suggestions that Ceylon
is the Promised Land for Sinhalese Buddhists and that all others

should be deprived of the rights of citizenship. Buddhism is definitely undergoing a resurgence in Ceylon, and many prominent Christians have under pressure returned to the Buddhist fold. The most conspicuous of these was the former premier, Mr. Bandaranaike, who was originally an Episcopalian.

In spite of the official coolness on the part of the government, however, there is still considerable latitude for evangelism. The exceptions, of course, are in the schools and on the air. The churches are free to preach the gospel even out-of-doors, and the individual is legally free to change his religion if he so desires.

MISSIONS. Christianity was first introduced into Ceylon by the Portuguese, and during their rule Roman Catholicism flourished. When the Dutch assumed control they did their best to suppress Catholicism and introduce Protestantism. They were more successful in the latter than in the former, for when the British took over in 1796 there were about a third of a million Protestants and an even larger number of Catholics. During the first decade of British rule tens of thousands of Protestants returned to Catholicism and not a few of them reverted to Buddhism or Hinduism.

Being a British possession, Ceylon naturally attracted societies from that country. The first in the field was the *London Missionary Society*, which was founded in 1795. Its venture in Ceylon was short-lived, beginning in 1804 and ending fourteen years later in 1818. The first continuing work was that of the *Baptist Missionary Society*, which had been at work in India since William Carey's arrival in 1793. Its pioneer missionary to Ceylon was *James Chater*, who was transferred to that field when war forced his evacuation from Burma in 1812. Following Chater's death in 1830 *Ebenezer Daniel* became leader of this mission. The work extended from Colombo to other centers, but converts were slow in coming. After a century of work the Baptist community numbered only between 3,000 and 4,000. In 1958 they had 74 baptisms. At the same time the Report acknowledged that the Pentecostal groups had made great headway during the past twenty years and have at the present time about 5,000 adherents, many of whom had been Baptists. Following the death of two old and experienced ministers, the Baptist Missionary Society admitted a "ministerial crisis."[8]

In 1814 the *English Methodists* began work in Ceylon. The leader of the first group was *Thomas Coke*, who had previously labored in the United States and the West Indies. Coke died en route to Ceylon, but his colleagues carried on and succeeded in establish-

[8] *Baptist Missionary Society 1958 Report*, p. 17.

ing a lasting work which included schools as well as churches. The gospel was preached and converts were made among the Burghers, the Sinhalese, and the Tamils. In 1958 they reported a church membership of 11,800 and a Christian community of 23,511. In the 1958 communal riots the Christians exemplified the healing and reconciling power of the gospel.

During the period of communal tension our members belonging to the various races have lived together as one family. Wherever home guards were formed to guard each road or peace committees were formed, our members were in the forefront. . . . Christian influence prevailed in the area and our members took opportunity to advise people not to throw acid or hurl bombs in self-defense. All our homes were refugee camps and were able to entertain, irrespective of caste and creed.[9]

The *American Board of Commissioners* took up work in the island in 1815. Its workers located on the Jaffna Peninsula in a small area 20 by 40 miles, close to the district worked by the Wesleyan Methodists and later by the Anglicans. In 1947 the Christians connected with the Ceylon Mission formed the *Ceylon Diocese of the Church of South India*. Its 28 churches have a membership of 3,142. The 1957 Report lists 10 missionaries and 860 Ceylonese workers on the staff. The missionaries are all engaged in institutional work at Jaffna College and two hospitals.

The island of Ceylon was one of the first fields to engage the attention of the *Church Missionary Society*. It was not until 1818, however, that the Mission actually got under way in the island. Work among the Sinhalese was begun at Kandy in 1818, at Baddegama in 1819, at Kotte in 1822, and at Kurunegala in 1880. In the Tamil area, Jaffna was occupied in 1818 and Colombo in 1850. The *Tamil Coolie Mission* (now the *Tamil Church Mission*) was begun in 1855. Educational institutions include four colleges for men and two colleges and two middle schools for girls. There are two teacher training schools, one for Sinhalese and one for Tamils. In both of these the Methodists co-operate with the Church Missionary Society. The Anglicans, whose main strength is in the capital city of Colombo, are the largest non-Roman group in the island. They have about 25,000 members.

The first party of twelve missionaries forming the *Ceylon and India General Mission* sailed from Scotland in October, 1893. The following year several members of the original party were transferred to India, where the Mission was destined to do most of its work. It continued to work both fields until 1937, when its

[9] *The Burning Word,* 1958 (English Methodist Report), p. 6.

Ceylon staff was transferred to the United Provinces in North India. The reason for the transfer was the fact that the Mission in Ceylon had a very small territory in a well-occupied area with no opportunity for contiguous expansion. It still retains its full name even though its work has been confined to India for over twenty years.

The *Salvation Army* has been working in Ceylon since 1883. In 1957 it reported 175 churches. The *Seventh Day Adventists* have two schools and five churches with a membership of 575. Other missions include the *Dutch Reformed Church,* the *Christian Reformed Board of Missions,* and the *Assemblies of God.* Pentecostal adherents are estimated at 5,000. The *Lutheran Church-Missouri Synod* opened a mission in Ceylon in 1958 and the *Conservative Baptists* in 1959.

CHURCH UNION. Negotiations for church union have been going on for some years. Participating in these negotiations are the Anglicans, Methodists, Presbyterians, and Baptists. Considerable progress has been made but certain major problems must be solved before union can become a reality. The *National Christian Council,* founded in 1912 as the All-Ceylon Conference, is a member of the International Missionary Council. The *Evangelical Fellowship of Ceylon* is affiliated with the World Evangelical Fellowship.

LITERATURE. Because English was for many years the official language of Ceylon and is still the lingua franca of the educated class, there is today a great dearth of Christian literature in Sinhala. There is, moreover, a shortage of Sinhalese Christian writers, so there is little prospect that the need for literature in this tongue will be met in the near future.

NEPAL

Area:	54,000 sq. mi.	Population:	8,500,000
Capital:	Katmandu	Religion:	Hinduism
			Buddhism

THE LAND. Nepal is a tiny country, 550 miles long and 150 miles wide, located in the Himalaya Mountains between India on the south and Tibet on the north. Mount Everest, the highest peak in the world, is in Nepal. The life of the country is concentrated in the rich valley of Katmandu. Gautama Buddha was born near the border of Nepal in the sixth century B.C.

POLITICAL HISTORY. From 1846 to 1951 Nepal was ruled by the Rana family, a member of which always held office as prime minister. In 1951 it became a constitutional monarchy. For centuries Nepal was isolated from the remainder of the world; it is only in the last decade that it has opened its doors to outside influences. In 1955 it was admitted to the United Nations, and in 1956 it exchanged ambassadors with the United States. More recently it has established diplomatic relations with Russia, China, Japan, France, and other countries. It has received a good deal of economic and technical assistance from both the United Nations and the United States. Democracy is trying to come to birth in this ancient kingdom, but the process is slow and painful.

THE PEOPLE. The Nepalese are Mongolian in origin with an admixture of Indian blood. The people are divided into various hill tribes. The Gurkhas are the dominant race; they came originally from India and are known throughout the world for their bravery and prowess in war. Ninety-seven per cent of the population is illiterate.

THE RELIGION. For centuries the Hindus of Nepal have tried to preserve the integrity of their religion from all contamination from without. As recently as 1956 reactionary elements within the government proposed that the people should not disturb the Sanatana (Eternal) Hindu religion, which has been handed down from time immemorial in this land, by practising or preaching Christianity or Islam, etc., that are not their religions; and that one should not convert any Hindu; if someone does convert a Hindu, both shall be liable to punishment of three years in prison.

Fortunately, the legislation was defeated and the concept of freedom of religion was upheld by the prime minister in a broadcast in which he said: "We shall grant absolute religious freedom to all; but in no case will we tolerate injustice, tyranny, and immorality in the name of religion." In practice, religious freedom is anything but "absolute." According to government regulation no Nepalese citizen may be baptized, and evangelistic work is not permitted.

MISSIONS. After being closed to Christian missionaries for two centuries Nepal opened its doors ever so cautiously in 1950. Immediately the *United Mission to Nepal* took advantage of the situation and Christian missions entered the tiny kingdom of Nepal for the first time. The United Mission to Nepal is an international, interdenominational mission with headquarters in India, where it maintains close contact with the National Christian Council.

Its present staff numbers 75 workers drawn from 8 countries and 13 church and mission groups. The Mission, which recently completed the first five-year contract with the Nepalese government, is now negotiating a second agreement. The first one provided only for educational and medical work. It is hoped that when the national Constitution is completed it will make some provision for religious liberty, including missionary work. It may be possible under the second contract to move the Mission Headquarters to Katmandu.

The largest project to date is the 50-bed *Abode of Peace Hospital* in the capital. In 1956 it cared for 600 in-patients and 7,600 out-patients, and 153 operations were performed. Some 17,000 patients were cared for in rural centers served by the hospital doctors and nurses; and nurses, midwives, and laboratory technicians are being trained. A language and orientation center has been established in Katmandu. A revised edition of the Nepali New Testament and the Psalms has been issued, and work is now proceeding on the revision of the Old Testament.

Recently the *Mission to Lepers,* not a member of the United Mission, was granted permission to locate a leprosarium at Bhangahan.

TIBET

Area:	470,000 sq. mi.	Population:	3,000,000
Capital:	Lhasa	Religion:	Lamaism

THE LAND. Often referred to as the "Roof of the World," Tibet lies to the west of China, north of India, east of Afghanistan, and south of Russia.

POLITICAL HISTORY. Tibet became a powerful nation in the seventh century A.D. and by the the eighth century was exacting tribute from China. A thousand years later the Manchu Empire sent an army to Lhasa and took control of Tibet. It has always chafed under Chinese domination and has taken advantage of every opportunity to throw off, however temporarily, the Chinese yoke. The Chinese People's Liberation Army invaded Tibet in 1950, and in May, 1951, Tibet was declared an autonomous region, with Red China responsible for defense and foreign affairs. Chinese oppression became unbearable and the Dalai Lama fled to India in 1959, leaving the Panchen Lama the sole puppet of the Chinese Communists in Tibet.

THE PEOPLE. The Tibetans are of Mongolian origin, but through the years they have had much closer ties with the Burmese than with the Mongols. Many Tibetans are to be found in west and northwest China. Trade between Tibet and India has been carried on for years, and small communities of Tibetans are located in North India.

THE RELIGION. Lamaism is a form of Buddhism, the most corrupt form to be found anywhere in the world. The country abounds in lamaseries, some of them large and ornate and housing as many as 20,000 priests. Nearly every family provides one son for the priesthood. The Chinese Communists have done their best to break the power of Lamaism and convert Tibet into a secular state; but to date they have not made much progress. The war on Lamaism has been intensified since the flight of the Dalai Lama.

MISSIONS. Inner Tibet has never been open to the gospel, though one or two intrepid missionaries have managed to make extensive journeys into the outlying areas. Even in prewar days the only contact that missionaries had with Tibetans was in the border areas. There are few Christians among the Tibetans, and no church. Workers of the *Central Asia Mission* stationed at Chaman in Baluchistan continue to make contact with people traveling to Quetta; and the *Mission to Lepers* maintains a leprosarium at Kalimpong in North India. It is impossible to accommodate all the Tibetans who seek admission. The *Moravian Church* has carried on work in the Nubra Valley, and the publication of the monthly magazine, *Snangsal*, has been resumed. The *Mar Thoma Church of India* has supported two missionaries on the Tibetan border since 1954. From their base at Mansiari they have been working among the border communities, particularly the Bhotyas.

In December, 1955, two Tibetans were ordained to the ministry of the Moravian Church in Leh on the border of Tibet. The Leh Church is a member of the *United Church of North India. The Evangelical Alliance Mission* has two primary schools, two high schools, two boys' schools, and a hospital on the frontier.

The complete Bible has been available in the Tibetan language for some years. The 1954 Report of the British and Foreign Bible Society states:

We know that practically the whole of the first edition of a thousand copies of the Tibetan Bible published in 1948, has gone into Tibet, and that many have found their way into the monasteries, where they are being studied by the monks.[10]

In this part of the world there are several countries to which the Christian missionary has not yet been given access. These are Bhutan, Sikkim, and Afghanistan. Bhutan, an independent state, and Sikkim, a protectorate of India, are both Buddhist countries, and to date no missionary work has been permitted within their borders.

Afghanistan, a Muslim state, is one of the most backward countries in the world. Only in this postwar period has it permitted foreigners in any numbers to reside in the country. At present there is quite a colony of Point Four personnel, teachers and technicians, under government contract. Among them are several keen Christian laymen who are desirous of introducing Jesus Christ to the Afghans. Preaching, proselytizing, and even personal witnessing among the Afghans are strictly prohibited; but in recent years the government has permitted the American colony to hold religious services for its own community on the understanding that Afghans not be present. More recently, a still further concession has been made, permitting Afghans to attend funeral services for American personnel. There are several missions working on the borders of Afghanistan and from time to time they have opportunity to contact Afghans and give them the gospel. There are also several hundred Afghan students and trainees in the United States, some of whom have had fruitful contacts with the Christian Church.

[10] *Trumpets of Jubilee*, p. 51.

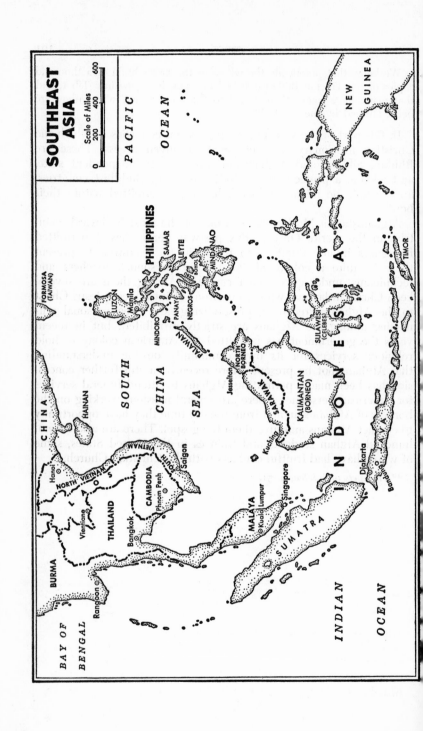

X

SOUTHEAST ASIA

BURMA

Area: 260,000 sq. mi.
Capital: Rangoon

Population: 20,100,000
Religion: Buddhism

THE LAND. Burma, the most westerly of the countries of Southeast Asia, is separated by high mountain ranges and vast jungle areas from India on the west and China on the east. In size Burma is somewhat smaller than the state of Texas. The northern and western parts are mountainous. On the east is a large plateau. In the center is the fertile basin of the Irrawaddy River. Located in the tropics, Burma's climate is hot most of the year. The rainy season, lasting from May to October, is always a welcome relief.

POLITICAL HISTORY. After 120 years of British rule, Burma gained her independence in January, 1948, and is today an independent republic. Unlike her two neighbors, India and Ceylon, Burma elected to sever all ties with the British Commonwealth. The first decade of independence has been a struggle against insurrection, lawlessness, and inflation. Considerable progress has been made, but the new country is still a long way from the political stability necessary for the smooth functioning of parliamentary democracy. In October, 1958, Dr. U Nu, premier of Burma since Independence, resigned in favor of a military general with emergency powers. The government reverted to civilian control early in 1960. Burma is a member of the United Nations. In the cold war she has maintained a position of strict neutrality.

THE PEOPLE. The Burmese, who are Mongolian in race and supposed originally to have migrated from the borders of Tibet, constitute three-fourths of the population. These Burmese people, 15 million of them, occupy central Burma from the Irrawaddy Delta to Mandalay. They are surrounded by mountain tribes of varied ethnic origin and of primitive social organization. In temperament they are complacent and fond of pleasure.

Largest of the three principal tribes is the Kachin tribe, numbering about three million. They are located for the most part in northern Burma in the Bhamo and Myitkyina districts. Like the other tribes in Burma, the Kachins are animists. Protestant Christians among them number about 25,000.

A second group, the Chins, known as the Hill (north) and the Plain (west) Chins, number about 200,000. The response to the gospel has been greater among the Hill Chins, where present church membership stands at 33,000. In 1957, 58 village churches were under construction in the Chin Hills. Of the Chins who live on the plain only 2,000 have embraced Christianity.

The third group, the Karen tribe, is located in east Burma on the border of Thailand. Linguistically the Karens are divided into two groups, the Pwo and the Sgaw. The Government Information Department estimates that the various Karen and Kayal language groups total about two million.

It is among the Karens that Christianity has made the most progress. There is a strong self-supporting and self-propagating church among them. Karen Christians now number about 100,000. So numerous are they that the Burmese Buddhists refer to Christianity as "the Karen religion."

The Karens are supposed to have cherished certain old traditions which, strangely enough, seem to point to some earlier knowledge of the biblical narrative. This gave them a vague expectancy of some kind of emancipation that would come to them through white teachers from the West. They were thus remarkably prepared for the coming of the missionary and gave heed to his message; and from the beginning they evinced a spiritual receptivity which has few parallels in missionary annals. This in part may explain the phenomenal success of Christianity among the Karens.[1]

THE RELIGION. Burma has been described as the "Land of the Pagodas." The conical spires of the white and gold pagodas dominate the landscape in all parts of Burma. These shrines to the memory of Gautama Buddha are a mute reminder that the Burmese people are wholly given over to Buddhism. The lofty Shwe Dagon Pagoda at Rangoon, covered with gold leaf at a cost of a million dollars, is one of the most famous shrines in the world. As elsewhere in Southeast Asia, Buddhism in Burma is mixed with animism.

[1] The Karen tradition, it is only right to say, is doubted by many historians.

Though not strictly speaking a state religion, Buddhism in Burma enjoys special privileges not granted to other religions. In keeping with the modern trend encouraged by the Declaration of Human Rights sponsored by the United Nations, the Constitution of Burma guarantees freedom of religion. At the same time the government, through its Sasana Council, is lending active support to the resurgence of Buddhism now taking place. Pagodas are being rebuilt, centers for study and meditation are being established, and Buddhist missionaries are being sent into the hill country to convert the animists there to Buddhism. Buddhist missionaries are also going abroad, some to Western countries, with the message of Buddha. A recent announcement that the Prime Minister plans to make Burma a Buddhist state has caused concern in Christian circles.

The Sixth Great Buddhist Council, commemorating the 2,500th anniversary of the enlightenment of Buddha, was held in Rangoon from May, 1954, to May, 1956, and attracted Buddhist leaders from all parts of the world. One outcome of the Council was a new version of the Tripitaka (the Buddhist Scriptures) and the translation of the same into several modern languages.

It cannot be said that Christianity has made any great impact on Buddhism in Burma. Only a very small number of Buddhists have been won to Christ. A generous estimate places the figure at 12,000.[2]

MISSIONS. Burma was the first, and to this day remains the largest and most successful, of the foreign mission fields of the *American Baptist Convention.* The beginnings of Protestant work in Burma will forever be associated with the illustrious name of *Adoniram Judson,* America's first and greatest missionary. Judson was one of a group of missionary volunteers, graduates of Andover Theological Seminary, who were instrumental in the organization of the first American foreign missionary society, the *American Board of Commissioners for Foreign Missions.* It was under this Congregational Board that Adoniram Judson and Samuel Newell and their wives sailed for India in 1812 to join the famous Serampore Trio. During the ocean voyage Judson changed his views on baptism and upon arriving in India he and his wife were immersed by Carey's associate, Rev. William Ward. With characteristic honesty Judson resigned from the Congregational Board and offered his services to the Baptists in America. This providentially led to the formation

[2] Rajah B. Manikam, *Christianity and the Asian Revolution* (Madras and New York: Friendship Press, 1949), p. 248.

of the *Baptist Society for the Propagation of the Gospel in India and Other Foreign Parts.* Judson became its first missionary.

Ordered out of India in 1814 by the East India Company, Judson and his wife made their way in a "crazy old vessel" to Rangoon. Here Judson applied himself with "terrific concentration" to the learning of the Burmese language, in which he became very proficient. Missionary life in those early days was beset with all kinds of privations, persecutions, and frustrations. It took five long years of toil and tears to win the first convert. Just when the work was becoming established and a second station had been opened at Ava, war broke out between England and Burma, and Judson was imprisoned as a spy. His body already weakened by malaria, he spent 21 months in filthy jails under indescribable conditions. Five pairs of heavy fetters inflicted scars which he carried to his dying day. Meanwhile, Mrs. Judson gave birth to a child, lay at death's door for a month with smallpox, and almost succumbed to a siege of spotted fever.

Upon his release from prison Judson retired to Rangoon, where his wife died in 1826. Shortly thereafter he transferred his headquarters north to Moulmein. By 1834 he had completed the translation of the entire Bible into Burmese. That same year he married Sarah Hall Boardman, widow of a colleague who had died after four years of service in Burma.

During twenty years of interrupted work, Judson completed his translation of the entire Bible, published tracts, prepared a grammar, and almost completed his monumental English-Burmese dictionary. At the time of his death, the Burmese church had a membership of seven thousand, and Judson had the oversight of 163 missionaries, Burmese pastors, and assistants. Like Paul, Judson was in a unique way called to suffer for Christ. He had lost two gifted wives and several children in different parts of the world. As he himself lay dying, while taking a sea voyage as his only hope of recovery, he exclaimed: "Oh, no man ever left the world with more inviting prospects, with brighter hopes, with warmer feelings." He died at sea without a friend, and his wasted body was buried without a prayer; but his triumphant and unconquered spirit had entered the abundant life beyond.[3]

Judson's work was mostly among the Burmese. The first non-Burmese group to be reached with the gospel was the Karen people. The pioneer missionary to this group was *George Dana Boardman,* who in 1828 opened a station at Tavoy. Associated with Boardman was an early Karen convert, *Ko Tha Byu,* who became a

[3] Sherwood Eddy, *Pathfinders of the World Missionary Crusade* (New York: Abingdon-Cokesbury Press, 1945), p. 33.

flaming evangelist and initiated a mass movement towards Christianity among his own people. Cut down in 1831 in the prime of life, Boardman was able to do little more than lay the foundation.

The Karen movement toward Christianity in which Judson, Boardman, and Ko Tha Byu had been pioneers continued. Wade reduced the Karen language to writing. Literature was prepared, including translations of the Bible into the tongues of various branches of the Karens. In 1856, 11,878 church members were reported. In 1914 the total was 47,530 and there were 192 ordained and 541 unordained preachers and 883 teachers. Schools were organized. Clergy were trained. The Karens undertook the financial support of their churches and schools and became more nearly independent of subsidies from the outside than almost any other group of Christians in southern and eastern Asia.[4]

According to the 1957 Report there are among the Karens 316 schools, and 1,061 organized churches with a total membership of 103,904 under the care of 1,719 national workers.[5]

The first missionary to the Kachins in the 1870's was a Karen evangelist, but there were no baptized converts until 1882. The Kachin church has the New Testament and most of the Old Testament, and Kachin Christians number 29,134. They have 416 churches and chapels and 366 other centers of worship.[6]

In the Chin district there are 424 organized churches with a membership of 31,555.[7]

All three of the above mentioned groups have their own autonomous Baptist Convention. The Baptists also have a thriving work among the Lahu, Wa, and other tribes. Total Baptist statistics for Burma include 1,811 churches with 196,041 members. Its 620 schools give instruction to 43,819 pupils. It operates 3 hospitals and 18 dispensaries, 3 theological seminaries and 11 Bible schools. Some idea of the vast extent of its indigenization may be seen from the fact that 87 per cent of its organized churches are entirely self-supporting and its missionary staff numbers only 61—greatly reduced since World War II.[8]

Though they are the oldest and largest, the Baptists are not the only mission in Burma. The *Anglican Church in Burma,* which celebrated its 100th anniversary in 1959, is represented by two independent organizations within the Church of England: the

[4] Kenneth Scott Latourette, *A History of the Expansion of Christianity* (New York: Harper & Brothers), Vol. VI, p. 231.

[5] *Along Kingdom Highways, 1957,* pp. 190, 198.

[6] *Along Kingdom Highways, 1958,* p. 188.

[7] *Along Kingdom Highways, 1957,* p. 190.

[8] *Ibid.*

Society for the Propagation of the Gospel and the *Bible Church-men's Missionary Society.*

The *Society for the Propagation of the Gospel* was launched in Burma by the educational work of *John Ebenezer Marks,* a Hebrew Christian, whose notable missionary career spanned forty years. Dr. Marks founded *St. John's College* in Rangoon, and later established the Royal School at Mandalay, to which King Mindon sent his four sons for a modern education. The S.P.G. today is working among the Burmese, the Karens, and the Chins. Church members, mostly Karens, number 12,000. They have 47 ordained nationals in charge of 68 congregations in 27 towns. They operate one primary school, one middle school, and six high schools. There are five missionaries under the S.P.G. in Burma.

The *Bible Churchmen's Missionary Society* opened work in Upper Burma in 1924. Just before World War II they expanded their work among the Khumis in the Arakan Hills in western Burma. This is their most rapidly growing field, the number of Christians increasing from 100 to 500 between 1952 and 1957. Four of their 24 national workers are ordained. Sixty-six churches have a combined membership of 860 under the leadership of 24 nationals. They maintain three hospitals and five dispensaries. Missionaries number 23.

The *Methodist* work in Burma is divided between two groups, the *American Methodists* in the south and the *English Methodists* in the north.

The *American Methodist* work in Burma began with a "Macedonian call" from a group of Indian Methodists lately come to Rangoon from Calcutta. In 1879 *Rev. and Mrs. R. E. Carter* were dispatched from India to begin work in Rangoon. A church was soon organized among the European and Eurasian community, and later on the work expanded to include the Pegu and Hanthawaddy districts nearby. Present personnel includes 12 missionaries, 16 pastors, and 173 school teachers. Sixteen churches represent a membership of 1,258. Educational institutions include one primary school, two middle schools, and four high schools.

The annexation of Upper Burma by the British in 1886 confronted the English Methodists with the obligation of taking the gospel to that neglected part of the world. As a result this group entered Upper Burma in 1887 and established headquarters in Mandalay. Working almost exclusively among the Burmese Buddhists, they have not met with the same numerical success as the Baptists. Their missionary staff, 14 in number, is not large. They have 10 pastors for 59 churches, with a membership of about

3,800. They have no high schools but do maintain one Bible school and a seminary.

Other societies in Burma include the *Salvation Army*, the *Seventh Day Adventists*, and three *Pentecostal* groups.

POSTWAR DEVELOPMENTS. The Christian Church suffered greatly during the war. From the Irrawaddy Delta to northern Burma churches were damaged or destroyed, many Christians suffered for their faith and nearly all records were lost. In the early postwar years a good deal of rehabilitation was necessary to get the churches back on their feet.

Since Independence, state schools have been increasing rapidly in number in almost every section of the country. Hundreds of primary schools formerly under Baptist auspices have now been incorporated into the state educational system and all higher education is now in the hands of the government. There are still many Christian primary schools in the frontier areas managed mostly by local Christians with some mission help. In spite of government competition Christian schools and hostels continue to attract more students than can possibly be accommodated. In one instance registration had to be closed seven months before the opening of school.

Teacher training is a problem. At present, government training institutions will accept only candidates who promise to work for the government. The government will not train teachers for private schools, nor does it give encouragement or recognition to the training programs conducted by the churches and missions. Doubtless this has something to do with the fact that of the 160 teachers employed by the S.P.G. schools, 60 are listed as non-Christians.

The Christian Church faces competition from another area. With the coming of Independence, Buddhism has taken a new lease on life. A Burma Hill Tracts Buddhist Mission was organized in 1946 and it now has 14 centers, 13 monasteries, and one missionary training school from which 65 Buddhist missionaries have gone out to the hill tracts.[9]

In 1958 there were 379 students enrolled in the dozen or more Bible schools and theological seminaries. Outstanding among the latter is the *Burma Divinity School* at Insein, a co-operative effort in which the Methodists and Anglicans now have a part.

The complete Bible now exists in six of the main languages of Burma. Translation work continues in several languages. Most

[9] Manikam, *op. cit.*, p. 249.

recent is the New Testament in Khumi-Chin, which was completed by missionaries of the Bible Churchmen's Missionary Society in 1958. Work continues on the translation of the Old Testament into Haka Chin. Revision of the Lahu New Testament proceeds, as does the translation of the New Testament into Pa-O, or Taungthu. The Bible Society in Rangoon is distributing the Scriptures in 21 languages of Burma. Since the war 20,000 Bibles and 10,000 New Testaments have been sold in the Karen language alone.

INTERCHURCH MOVEMENTS. The Baptist work in Burma is extremely well organized. Besides the autonomous conventions among the various tribes, there is the all-inclusive *Burma Baptist Convention.* Its 89th Annual Meeting at Mandalay in October, 1957, was attended by nearly 5,000 people, representing practically all of the races of Burma. Other organizations include the *Burma Baptist Christian Endeavor Union,* the *Federation of Burma Baptist Women's Societies,* and the *Burma Baptist Ministers' Council.* The American Baptist Mission has for some time been completely integrated with the Burma Baptist Convention and its missionaries are now fraternal workers under the direction of the Convention.

Wider still in its affiliations is the *Burma Christian Council,* which has membership in the International Missionary Council.

MALAYA

Area: 50,600 sq. mi.	Population: 6,275,000
Capital: Kuala Lumpur	Religion: Islam
	Buddhism

THE LAND. This long, finger-like peninsula, extending southward almost to the equator, forms the extreme tip of the continent of Asia. Malaya is almost equidistant from the great population masses of India and China. It is right in the center of Southeast Asia. Moreover, it is astride the main sea and air routes to Australia and across the Pacific to the United States. Its stategic importance is apparent to all. Most of Malaya is jungle country, whence come half of the world's rubber and one-third of its tin.

POLITICAL HISTORY. On August 31, 1957, the Federation of Malaya joined the host of free nations and became a new member of the British Commonwealth of Nations after 175 years of British rule. Like the other newly independent nations of the postwar period, Malaya is not without serious internal problems. Three years is hardly long enough to test the mettle of the new state, but so far it has managed its affairs with considerable success.

THE PEOPLE. Malaya is a multiracial country. The Malays, with a population of 3,080,000, are the dominant race. The Chinese, many of whom have been in the country for several generations, are second with a total of 2,350,000. There are approximately 750,000 Indians. Eurasians (13,000), Europeans (17,000), and others (65,000) make up the remainder of Malaya's 6,275,000 people. Each major race has its own language and religion. The Malays are Muslims and, of course, speak Malay. The Chinese are Buddhists and speak four main Chinese dialects: Hokkien, Hakka, Teochow, and Cantonese. The Indians are Hindus and speak mostly Tamil. In addition to these three languages there is English. Malay has been declared the official language of the country, but for all practical purposes English remains the lingua franca for the time being.

An important development took place in June, 1948, when the Communists took to the jungles to carry on their shooting war with the Malayan government and the British High Commissioner, Sir Henry Gurney, decided to resettle the people in New Villages. Altogether 582 New Villages were carved out of the jungle, surrounded with barbed wire and reinforced by military patrols; and almost 1,000,000 people, mostly Chinese from the rubber and tin plantations, were forcibly removed from their scattered habitations and established in these New Villages. This gigantic transfer of population was costly in terms of human freedom, but as a military measure it was eminently successful, and today the Communists are no longer a problem. Though the Communist menace is past, the New Villages remain as a large-scale social experiment, involving about 15 per cent of the population. These Villages have providentially provided the Christian Church with a unique evangelistic opportunity.

THE RELIGION. As already intimated, Malaya has three main races and each race has its own religion. The Malays, being both the dominant and the indigenous race, are the masters of the country. They are Muslims, and Islam is the state religion. This is not new; it stems from the British occupation.

When the British government made its treaties with the Malay States in the nineteenth century, the agreement was that each State would accept the advice of a British officer in all matters of administration except those relating to the Muslim religion and the

Malay customs. This policy was designed "to preserve the Malay way of life." Under British rule it was not, therefore, permissible for missionaries to work among the Malays. Their efforts were confined to the non-Muslim minorities, the Chinese and the Indians.

The new Constitution provides that "subject to the requirements of public order, public health and morality, every person has the right to profess, practice, and propagate his religion." But it goes on to state that this does not apply to the aborigines, and that no person under eighteen may choose his own religion. Despite the progressive *tone* of the new Constitution, the government still frowns upon "proselytizing," and missionaries are barred from 140 of the New Villages which are wholly or predominantly Muslim.

EARLY MISSIONS. Christianity was first introduced into Malaya by the Portuguese, who captured Malacca in 1511. *Francis Xavier*, the greatest Roman Catholic missionary of all time, spent three years in Malaya in the 1540's, and was buried there. Later his remains were removed to Goa, where they have become an object of great veneration. As a result the Roman Catholics, with 86,000 members, are twice as strong today as the Protestants. In 1641 the Dutch captured Malacca and brought with them Reformed Christianity, but they did little to propagate it among the people. The British arrived on the scene in 1786 and occupied Penang. In 1824 Great Britain seized Malacca from the Dutch, and Malaya became a British possession.

Dr. William Milne of the *London Missionary Society* was the first Protestant missionary to Malaya. He settled in Malacca, where he opened the *Anglo-Chinese College* with a view to training Chinese to become missionaries to their own country, which at that time was closed to Western missionaries. He also set up a printing press to produce Christian literature to be smuggled into China. A few years later he was joined by *Mr. G. H. Thomson*, who concentrated on work among the Malays.

When China was opened to missionary work by the Treaty of Nanking in 1842, the London Missionary Society transferred the Anglo-Chinese College to Hong Kong and only one man, *Rev. S. D. Keasberry*, elected to remain in Malaya. He supported himself by teaching and operating a printing press.

In 1848 the first *Anglican* missionary arrived in Malaya. He was sent out by the *Society for the Propagation of the Gospel* to work among the Chinese and Indians.

The *Presbyterian Church of England* opened work in Penang in 1851. In 1885 the *American Methodists* entered Malaya and branched out from there to the Philippines, Sarawak, Borneo, Java, and Sumatra. With ample resources of both men and money, they soon became the largest of the Protestant Churches. They have concentrated largely on schools for the Chinese and Indians, and have established a worthy reputation in that field. In 1958 they reported 62 schools, primary and secondary, with 53,089 students, only 15 per cent of whom were Christians. Sixty of the 62 schools have national principals. Enrollment has trebled since 1940.[10] The greatest weakness of this fine system of schools is the fact that only 60 per cent of the 1,815 teachers are Christians. Qualified Christian teachers are difficult to secure in a country where Christians are a minority and there is no Christian college. Indeed, the only post-high educational institution is the University of Malaya, a state institution in Kuala Lumpur which has a very limited enrollment. To relieve this shortage the *Malay Christian Council* is making plans to open a Christian college on an ecumenical basis. In the meantime the Methodist Church has eight hostels providing Christian nurture for 350 Malayan students. It has 12,000 members and a community of 22,000.[11]

The *Anglican Church*, a century old, has 6,000 members and a following estimated at 16,000. The English Presbyterians number approximately 8,000.[12]

POSTWAR DEVELOPMENTS. The Japanese overran the peninsula of Malaya in their lightning thrust south to the "impregnable" bastion of Singapore. They met with little more than token resistance; consequently the war damage in Malaya was not nearly so great as elsewhere. With the coming of peace the missionaries returned to the land and picked up the threads of their work. When the China field closed in 1949 a number of missions transferred some of their China missionary staff to Malaya. This was just in time to take advantage of the unique evangelistic challenge of the New Villages established as a result of the emergency between 1950 and 1953. The largest group of the ex-China missionaries belonged to the *Overseas Missionary Fellowship* (China Inland Mission). This Mission now has 119 workers in Malaya, most of them in the New Villages.

Some of the 582 Villages have been closed, and others have been absorbed by nearby communities. Because of their Muslim popula-

[10] *Mission and Witness, 1958,* p. 65.

[11] Missionary Research Library, *Protestant Churches of Asia, the Middle East, Africa, Latin America, and the Pacific Area, 1959,* p. 64.

[12] Manikam, *op. cit.,* p. 249.

tion, 140 Villages have been declared "out-of-bounds" to the Christian messenger. Out of 410 Chinese and Indian Villages in August, 1958, there was Christian work in 212, and resident workers in 79. This means that half of them are still without any Christian witness. Efforts have been made to interest the Christians in the larger towns in this new venture, but there has been little response.

Owing principally to lack of privacy, life in these Villages has not been easy. Most of the work has been carried on in the open air, homes, shops, and improvised quarters. At first the adult population was both sullen and suspicious; but gradually, through children's classes and Sunday School work, prejudice has been broken down and some progress has been made. Other forms of work include reading classes, medical work, mobile clinics, and films. Altogether there are 14 missions working in the New Villages. The largest of these are: *Christian Missions in Many Lands,* with 35 places of worship; *Mar Thoma Syrian Church,* with 24; *Southern Baptist,* with 19; and *United Lutheran,* with 10.[13]

There are three Bible schools and one seminary. Established in Singapore in 1948 *Trinity College,* with an enrollment at present of over 100, is supported by Presbyterians, Anglicans, and Methodists. Parallel courses are taught in Chinese and English.

Christian literature, always a problem on the mission field, is in especially short supply in Malaya. Christian literature in the Chinese language has become a major problem since China closed in 1949. To meet this problem the *Council on Christian Literature for Overseas Chinese* was formed with headquarters in Hong Kong. Since its founding in 1951 the Council has published 571 books, which it is distributing through bookstores in all parts of Southeast Asia. The greatest difficulty of all is finding Christian writers. Of the 65 titles published by C.C.L.O.C. in 1956 only four were original Chinese manuscripts.

Since Malay has been declared the official language of the Federation, the problem of Christian literature is bound to become increasingly serious. So far as is known no Christian author is writing in Malay, nor is anyone being trained.

INTERCHURCH RELATIONS. In 1948 the *Malayan Christian Council* came into existence, with headquarters at Singapore and regional councils at Penang, Ipoh, and Kuala Lumpur. It has been greatly strengthened recently by the appointment of a full-time secretary. Sponsored originally by the Presbyterians, Anglicans, and Methodists, the Council now includes 12 different churches, missions, and

[13] *World Christian Handbook, 1957,* p. 53.

agencies. With the coming of Independence there has naturally been a strong desire for Christian unity. To study this matter the M.C.C. has appointed a Faith and Order Committee to deal with four important items: the Scriptures, the Creeds, the Sacraments, and the Ministry. The M.C.C. is a member of the International Missionary Council.

NOTE: The facts and figures given in this section on Malaya include Singapore. The reason for this is that mission boards have always regarded the island of Singapore at the tip of the Malay Peninsula as part of their work in the larger geographical area of Malaya. Actually, a good deal of their work is in Singapore, with its huge population of 1,238,000, of whom 947,000 are Chinese. In June, 1959, Singapore was granted full independence and is now a sovereign state within the British Commonwealth of Nations. It has a thriving Christian community which includes almost 50 Protestant churches of many denominations. Many of the missions working in Malaya have their field headquarters in Singapore. The recent change in the status of the island may alter the picture in the near future.

THAILAND

Area: 200,000 sq. mi.   Population: 23,000,000
Capital: Bangkok   Religion: Buddhism

THE LAND. Thailand lies between Burma on the north and west, Laos and Cambodia on the east, and Malaya on the south, with a long coastline on the Gulf of Siam and the Indian Ocean. In area it is about equal to Spain, or four times the size of New York State. It is mountainous in the north and south. Between the two lies the great central plain with its abundant rainfall and luxuriant vegetation, crisscrossed by a network of rivers and canals along which, in leisurely fashion, passes much of the trade of the country.

POLITICAL HISTORY. Siam has the distinction of being the only country in Southeast Asia that did not fall prey to Western colonialism in modern times. An absolute monarchy for many centuries, Siam underwent a bloodless revolution in 1932. Since then the country has been plagued with political instability. In little more than twenty-five years, it has had thirteen coups or attempted coups, often accompanied by assassination. The latest coup took place on October 20, 1958, when Field Marshal Sarit Thanarat dissolved the National Assembly, scrapped the Constitution, banned all political parties, and declared martial law because of "pressure of internal and external forces, especially the Communists." King Aduldet proclaimed an interim constitution January 28, 1959, and named Marshal Thanarat premier on February 9. In 1949 the government changed the English name from Siam to Thailand. Thailand is a member of the Southeast Asia Treaty Organization.

THE PEOPLE. The population of Thailand is far from homogeneous. The natives belong to the Thai race, who came originally from China. The Siamese proper are one of three subdivisions of the Thai. They live in southern Thailand and are the dominant element in the land. The other subdivisions are called Eastern and Western Shan, or Thai. Then come the Laos, of whom there are well over one million in northern Thailand. These are divided into thirty or more tribal groups, each speaking a different dialect. The Chinese constitute a third important class, even more numerous than the Laos; they are to be found chiefly in the Bangkok area, though large numbers are scattered through the country. They are the strongest and wealthiest group in Thailand and almost completely control the trade. Their free intermarriage with the Thais has had the effect of improving the quality of the latter race.

In addition to these main racial elements the population includes many people of the adjacent countries: Malays, Cambodians, Vietnamese, Karens, etc. The Thai people have been described as "tolerant but conservative, gracious but sensitive, proud but shy." Tuberculosis is very prevalent, and leprosy is the major health problem of the country, there being 200,000 persons with this disease.

ADVANCED CONDITIONS. Although the Thais, like the Burmese, are inclined to be easygoing, Thailand is one of the most advanced countries in Asia. It possesses excellent roads; modern postal, telegraph, and police systems; well-equipped schools; and many other features of Western civilization. Bangkok, the capital, has its trolley cars, electric light, automobiles, radio and television, modern hotels, and up-to-date manufacturing plants. Consequently, the standard of living is high. Indeed, material prosperity is one of the reasons why the Christian message has not been accorded a better reception.

THE RELIGION. While other countries such as Burma and Ceylon have been completely Buddhist for many centuries, Thailand is the only country in Southeast Asia where Buddhism is the state religion. Consequently Buddhism dominates every aspect of the life of the people. Scattered throughout all parts of the country are 20,000 monasteries and temples housing 170,000 mendicant monks who, in their brilliant saffron robes, go from door to door every morning to receive the meritorious alms gladly given by the grateful populace. Every male citizen is expected to enter the Sangha (Buddhist Order) for three months, and men in civil service or government employ are paid during their stay in the Sangha. Being a state religion, Buddhism is identified with patriotism. To be 100 per cent Thai, one must be a Buddhist. The people are open and friendly, and in theory there is a form of religious tolerance; but in practice complete ostracism and severe persecution are the portion of any Thai person who dares to make an open confession of Jesus Christ. To change one's religion is to be a traitor to one's country.

EARLY MISSIONS. Protestant work in Thailand began with the famous *Dr. Karl F. A. Gutzlaff* of the *Netherlands Missionary Society,* who landed in Bangkok on August 23, 1828. Working day and night he and Mrs. Gutzlaff translated the whole Bible into Siamese and a considerable portion thereof into Lao and Cambodian. They also prepared a dictionary and a grammar of the Siamese and Cambodian languages. Following the death of his wife in childbirth, Gutzlaff left Thailand for China after a short stay of only three years.

In response to Gutzlaff's appeal, *Rev. David Abeel,* M.D., of the *American Board of Commissioners for Foreign Missions,* became the first American missionary to Thailand. He arrived on June 30, 1831; but ill health forced him to withdraw. His place was soon taken by *Dan Beach Bradley,* who was destined to play a very important role in the early evangelization of Thailand.

Baptist work in Thailand began in March, 1833. The first missionaries were *Rev. and Mrs. John Taylor Jones.* They were sent over by the *Baptist Mission* in Burma, which at that time could ill afford to spare one of its six couples. Thus Thailand became the second field to be entered by the *American Baptist Board.* Although appointed to work among the Thai, Mr. Jones was especially interested in the Chinese in the Bangkok area. Six months after his arrival he had the joy of baptizing his first converts—three Chinese. Two years later he was joined by *Rev. William Dean,* who took over the Chinese work.

The early history of the Baptist Mission in Thailand centered around these two men. Jones, working with the Thai people, concentrated on the translation, production, and distribution of Christian literature. A brilliant linguist, he is reputed to have been more eloquent in Thai than in English. His greatest work was the translation of the New Testament, completed in 1843. The Chinese church founded by Dean in Bangkok in 1837, with 11 charter members, was the first Protestant church organized in the Far East.

The *Presbyterian Board of Foreign Missions* was established in 1837 and three years later its first missionaries to Thailand, *Rev. and Mrs. William P. Buell,* arrived in Bangkok. At that time there were 24 Congregational and Baptist missionaries in Thailand. Ten years later, after 18 years of hard pioneer work, the American Board gave up its Thailand mission without baptizing a single Thai convert. Lack of reinforcements and a series of misfortunes forced the Baptist Mission to terminate its work in 1869, leaving the entire field to the Presbyterians.

The early years were filled with hardship and trial, owing mainly to the bitter opposition of the antiforeign king and Buddhist priests. The missionaries were prevented from renting or buying property, and on one occasion were ordered out of their premises to find shelter as best they could. Their few converts were fiercely persecuted and their helpers imprisoned. But when the prospect seemed hopeless the hostile king suddenly died. The enlightened and friendly prince succeeded to the throne, and all was changed. Since then the missionaries have enjoyed the marked favor of the government and their work has had unhindered course. Some of them were placed in charge of royal hospitals and given official position. Several lady missionaries were invited to teach the women of the royal household.

It was nineteen years before the Presbyterians baptized their first convert, *Nai Chune.* Undaunted by the hardships and lack of results, they persevered through the decades and today are the largest and most influential Christian group in Thailand, with 72 missionaries in ten major cities and covering one-third of the country. Besides their church and evangelistic work, they operate 8 hospitals and 29 schools. Their most important station is Chiengmai, the largest city in north Thailand, where, besides a church, they have *Prince's Royal College* (boys), *Dara Academy* (girls), *McGilvary Theological Seminary, McCormick Hospital* and the famous *McKean Leprosy Colony,* regarded by some as the finest in the world.

An important milestone was reached in 1934 when the churches of the Presbyterian Mission organized to form the *Church of Christ in Thailand*. Complete integration between Church and Mission took place in 1957 when the Presbyterian Mission turned over all its property to the Church of Christ in Thailand and its missionaries became fraternal workers under the direction and discipline of the Church. This Church, by far the largest in the country, now has 119 organized churches with a total membership of 17,241. Fifty-seven of its ministers are ordained.

The *Seventh Day Adventists* have been in Thailand since 1918. They have specialized in medical work and literature. They have a well-equipped hospital in Bangkok. Most of their converts have been from the Chinese business community in the Bangkok area.

The *Christian and Missionary Alliance,* occupying the eastern sector of Thailand, began work in 1929. Over the years they have labored diligently to build up a strong indigenous Church. Today they have resident missionaries in 15 of the 19 provinces for which they were originally responsible. Working out from their headquarters at Karat, they operate 2 Bible schools and 40 leprosy clinics.

POSTWAR PROGRESS. During World War II, Christian work was almost completely suspended because of the Japanese occupation and Buddhist pressure. Membership in the Church of Christ fell from 10,000 in 1939 to 6,000 in 1946. Rehabilitation in the immediate postwar years taxed the resources of both Church and Mission; but the tide turned, and between 1950 and 1958 church membership doubled and giving quadrupled.

About a dozen new missions have entered Thailand since the closing of the China field in 1949. The largest of these, from a personnel point of view, is the *Overseas Missionary Fellowship* (China Inland Mission), which now has 150 missionaries working in three main areas: the tribal people in the north, the Thai people in the central plain, and the Muslims in the south.

A thrilling chapter in modern missions is being written in north Thailand, whose precipitous mountains are the home of some 30 primitive tribes living in almost complete isolation from the rest of the country. It is only in the last few years that Christian missions have penetrated these inaccessible regions. The burden of this difficult pioneer work rests at present on the Overseas Missionary Fellowship, which has 42 missionaries living in seven different tribal areas. Already they have suffered one casualty. Miss Lillian Hamer was shot and killed in Lisu territory in April, 1959. Other missions have 15 workers in the tribal country of north Thailand. The two great obstacles to the progress of the gospel are demon worship and opium planting. The latter was prohibited by government action in 1959. It remains to be seen how effective this order will be.

Other missions now working in Thailand include the *American Baptist Mission, Southern Baptist Mission, Pentecostal Mission, New Tribes Mission, Worldwide Evangelization Crusade, Oriental Boat Mission,* and the *International Child Evangelism Fellowship. Jehovah's Witnesses* have more than a score of missionaries in Thailand. Including the *Y.M.C.A.* and the *American Bible Society,* there are 17 mission boards working in Thailand with 420 missionaries.

The American Bible Society, now known as the *Thailand Bible House,* has been in the country since 1837. The complete Bible has been available in the Thai language since 1896, and Scripture portions have been translated into all the major dialects. A revision committee, under the leadership of *Rev. H. G. Grether,* is working on a new version of the Bible in modern Thai. It is to be based on the Hebrew and the Greek, and will contain a number of Pali words which will help to make it more intelligible to the Theravada Buddhists of Thailand.

After 130 years of missionary labor there are only some 20,000 Protestant Christians, or one-tenth of one per cent of the population. "Perhaps it is true to say that of all the major countries in East Asia, it is in Thailand that the Christian community exerts the least influence in the life of the nation."[14]

VIETNAM

Area:	65,700 sq. mi.	Population:	12,000,000
Capital:	Saigon	Religion:	Buddhism

THE LAND. The Republic of Vietnam, sometimes referred to as South Vietnam in contrast to North Vietnam which is Communist, is the most southeasterly of all the countries of Asia. On the west it is bounded by Laos and Cambodia, once part of Indo-China; on the east and south it is washed by the South China Sea. Its northern border is the 17th parallel, which is the dividing line between Communist and Free Vietnam.

POLITICAL HISTORY. After 175 years of colonial rule the three states of the former French Indo-China—Vietnam, Laos, and Cambodia—

[14] Manikam, *op. cit.,* p. 240.

gained their independence within the French Union at the close of World War II.

Under the leadership of Ho Chi Minh the Communists in the north part of the country, who had fought the Japanese during the occupation, now turned their attention to the French and the non-Communist nationals. A devastating civil war dragged on until France, cornered and conquered at Dienbienphu, sued for peace at the Geneva Conference in July, 1954. It was there that the country was bisected at the 17th parallel, the industrial north with approximately 13 million people going to the Communists and the agricultural south with close to 12 million remaining free.

Only the most confirmed optimists believed that the government of Vietnam in 1954 had much chance of withstanding Communist pressure from without and political corruption from within. But under the strong, authoritative leadership of a devout and dedicated Roman Catholic the country gradually recovered from the effects of the civil strife. Surrounded by innumerable foes and facing insuperable difficulties, Premier Ngo Dinh Diem, a man of rare courage and integrity, has brought his nation through its first five turbulent years; and today Vietnam is well on the way to political and economic stability.

THE PEOPLE. The population is made up of two major groups: the Annamese, who occupy the fertile plains, and the many tribes, numbering about one million, which inhabit the mountainous regions. The Annamese are an extremely ancient people. They are descended from a tribe belonging to the Mongolian race which, between 2,000 and 3,000 years before the Christian era, occupied the southern part of China. For more than one thousand years (111 B.C.–A.D. 968) they were ruled by a Chinese dynasty, thus becoming strongly influenced by Chinese civilization. The literary and moral code of Confucius gave definite shape to Annamese thought and religion, with results distinctly seen even to this day; for the prevailing religion of the Annamese is a Chinese mixture of Confucianism, Buddhism, and Taoism, with the worship of ancestors and genii as the outstanding feature.

THE RELIGION. The dominant religion of the Annamese is Buddhism, though here, as everywhere else in Southeast Asia, it is inextricably bound up with animism. Coming as it did from China, it has been considerably diluted by both Confucianism and Taoism. "A logical extension of the eclectic spirit of the Vietnamese is the new cult of Cao Dai. Caodaism is a syncretic religion that combines elements from Buddhism, Confucianism and Taoism, as well as from Roman Catholicism and Islam. It now claims to have a membership of three million."[15]

Introduced during French rule, Roman Catholicism has registered large gains in Vietnam. The ministry of this Church in the areas of education, medical work, and rural uplift is to be greatly commended. There are many Roman Catholic Christians holding high government posts. Before Partition in 1954 it was estimated that there were 2,500,000 Catholics in Indo-China.

MISSIONS. The *Christian and Missionary Alliance,* which entered Indo-China from its South China field in 1911, was the first, and for 40 years remained the only Protestant work in the part of Indo-China now known as Vietnam. In the early years the Mission suffered a good deal of opposition from the French (Catholic) authorities, but gradually the missionaries won their way, and the work became firmly established on a sound indigenous basis. In 1927 the *Vietnam Alliance Church* was organized with its own administrative set-up. On January 1, 1959, it had 201 organized churches with 235 national ministers and a baptized adult membership of 15,766, or a Christian community of about 40,000. These figures do not include some 30 churches, with their pastors and members, north of the 17th parallel in Communist territory.

Following the peace settlement in 1954 C. & M.A. missionaries in central Vietnam served largely in the rehabilitation of suffering congregations and the restoration of destroyed chapels. In the south they ministered in government refugee camps. In Saigon the *John Olsen Memorial Studio* records gospel broadcasts for the Far East Broadcasting Corporation in Manila; and in 1953 the *Alliance Press* published 12,500,000 pages of gospel literature in eight languages. The *Central Bible School,* with 75 students, is located at Tourane not far from Communist territory. The entire Bible has been available in Vietnamese for many years. In 1959 the Mission had 125 missionaries in Vietnam.

Somewhat more recent, but equally fruitful, has been the Mission's work among the many tribes of Vietnam. Here a small number of missionaries assisted by 116 national workers are active in 60 organized churches and over 100 outstations. The Vietnamese Church has dispatched nine couples to work among the tribes.[16] An Intertribal Church has already come into existence, and in 1957

[15] *Ibid.,* p. 239.
[16] A. C. Snead, "Progress and Peril in Indo-China," *World Dominion,* Sept.–Oct., 1954.

the first tribal preachers ever to be called to the ministry were ordained.

To furnish these many tribes with the Word of God and Christian literature is a major task before the Mission. Portions of the Old Testament, several Epistles, and two Gospels are available in Raday. The Church now possesses several Epistles, a hymnal, and a catechism in Koho. Only the Gospel of Mark and some booklets are available in Chru. A hymnal has been published in Jarai. There are two Bible schools in the tribal area, one at Dalat and the other at Banmethuot.

The *Seventh Day Adventists* have been in Vietnam for a number of years. Besides six churches, they have two hospitals, one in Cholon and the other in Saigon. The *Worldwide Evangelization Crusade* began work in Vietnam in 1958, and *Wycliffe Bible Translators* followed them in 1959.

LAOS

Area: 236,800 sq. mi.	Population: 2,000,000
Capital: Vientiane	Religion: Buddhism

THE LAND. One of the most inaccessible and least known countries of Asia, Laos lies between Thailand on the west and Vietnam on the east. To the south is the sister kingdom of Cambodia. The country is mountainous and in places densely forested. Communications are poor; in 1954 there were only 1,150 miles of all-weather roads in the country.

POLITICAL HISTORY. Once an integral part of French Indo-China, Laos became an independent sovereign state within the French Union in July, 1949. It is now a constitutional monarchy. The king is not only head of the state but also the supreme authority in religious affairs. It is a member of the United Nations and is receiving a good deal of technical and economic assistance from the United States.

THE PEOPLE. The people of Laos are divided into two main groups, the Laotians and the aborigines, who are known as "mountain people." Principal minority groups are the Chinese (12,000) and the Vietnamese (15,000). The Laotians form the largest segment of the population. There were only 35,042 children in primary school in 1954.[17]

[17] *Statesman's Year Book, 1958*, p. 1211.

THE RELIGION. The Laotians are Buddhist in culture and religion. The Buddhism of Laos is much purer than that found in Vietnam. Consequently, missionary work has been much more difficult and converts have been fewer. The mountain people, of course, are animists.

MISSIONS. The first work in Indo-China was begun in 1902 by Swiss members of *Christian Missions in Many Lands*. They located in three stations in the southern part of what is now the Kingdom of Laos. This Mission operates a leprosarium and has about 1,000 church members. The New Testament in Lao appeared in 1926 and the entire Bible six years later.

The largest program of Christian work is carried on by the *Christian and Missionary Alliance*, which is working in the northern part of the country among both Laotians and aborigines. Among these sturdy mountaineers there began in 1950 a mass movement resulting in 4,000 conversions. Interrupted by the Red invasion of the early 1950's, the work resumed in 1955 with almost miraculous results. In one year 172 families threw away their fetishes. Almost 1,000 baptized believers are to be found in 63 organized churches, while 52 preaching places account for many Christians who have not yet joined the Church. A recent mid-winter conference attracted 1,500 delegates. The Mission has no educational or medical work in Laos. Their one Bible school is at Xieng Khouang. So far, results among the Laotians have been negligible. In 1958 the *Overseas Missionary Fellowship* (China Inland Mission) entered the country from their Thailand field. They now have 20 workers located in five centers.

CAMBODIA

Area: 67,500 sq. mi.   Population: 4,400,000
Capital: Pnom-penh   Religion: Buddhism

THE LAND. Cambodia, with a recorded history that goes back to the beginning of the Christian era, lies south of Laos, east of Thailand, and west of Vietnam.

POLITICAL HISTORY. Like her two neighbors to the north and east, Cambodia was for many decades a part of French Indo-China. In 1949 Cambodia was granted independence as an Associate State of the French Union. November 9, 1953, which marked the transfer of French military powers to the Cambodian government, is considered Independence Day. It was not until January, 1955, that Cambodia became financially and economically independent of both France and the other former Associate States of French Indo-China, Vietnam and Laos. In June, 1952, King Sihanouk assumed the premiership. Seven months later he dissolved Parliament and replaced it with a Consultative Assembly. In March, 1955, he abdicated in favor of his father in order to form a strong political party, the Popular Socialist Community, which in recent years has completely dominated the politics of the country. Known now as Prince Sihanouk, he is immensely popular with the people. Cambodia is a member of the United Nations.

THE PEOPLE. The Cambodians form the backbone of the populace, estimated at 4,400,000. In the forests of the northeast live various primitive tribes. Foreign minorities include 250,000 Vietnamese, 215,000 Chinese, 85,000 Chams, and 3,000 Europeans.[18]

THE RELIGION. Theravada Buddhism is the religion of the Cambodians. The king is the supreme religious authority. The hill tribes are animists. It is estimated that there are 20,000 Roman Catholics, mostly Vietnamese and Europeans.

MISSIONS. The *Christian and Missionary Alliance* is the only mission in Cambodia. At present they have fourteen couples among the Cambodians and one among the Chinese. Their work includes the *Alliance Press* and a Bible school. Missionary work has been very difficult. In about thirty years only 400 people have been baptized, and about an equal number attend services. The entire Bible in Cambodian was published in 1956. The *British and Foreign Bible Society* has one full-time colporteur in the country. He speaks three languages and sold 12,000 copies of the Scriptures in 1957.[19] Seven of Cambodia's 14 provinces are still without any Christian witness.

The *Far Eastern Gospel Crusade* has recently announced its intention to enter Cambodia as soon as workers are available.

INDONESIA

Area: 575,000 sq. mi.   Population: 84,000,000
Capital: Djakarta   Religion: Islam

THE LAND. Indonesia consists of four large islands—Sumatra, Java, Borneo (Kalimantan), and Celebes (Sulawesi)—and about 3,000

[18] *Statesman's Year Book, 1958*, p. 876.
[19] *Worlds Apart*, p. 87.

small ones. This vast archipelago forms a broken bridge between Asia and Australia, and stretches for some 3,000 miles from east to west. Sumatra alone is 1,150 miles long. Borneo, twice the size of England, Scotland, and Wales, is 570 miles wide at the equator. Only Java has a complete railway system. Sumatra boasts three widely separated sections of track; the other islands have yet to see a train. Tropical forests cover 77 per cent of Borneo, 62 per cent of Sumatra, and 17 per cent of Java.[20]

POLITICAL HISTORY. The Republic of Indonesia was proclaimed on August 17, 1945. It was not until December 28, 1949, however, that the Dutch, after 350 years of colonial rule, reluctantly relinquished their hold on this wealthy country and turned over the reins of government to the United States of Indonesia. The Indonesian ship of state has experienced some rough sailing in the first decade following Independence. A short-lived civil war in 1956–57 threatened to overthrow the central government. Indonesia's President Sukarno has declared that the parliamentary form of democracy practised in the West is not suited to the political climate of the East. He is a strong advocate of "guided democracy"—another term for benign dictatorship! In December, 1957, he ordered the expulsion, by stages, of the 60,000 Dutch nationals then in the country.

The Constitution provides for freedom of religion, and the government has set up a Bureau of Religious Affairs to care for all matters relating to church and mission business. It is not easy, however, for missionaries to enter the country. To obtain a permanent visa it is necessary to be sponsored by some local organization which is registered with the government. In the case of new missionaries such sponsorship is often difficult to secure.

In 1956 there were 35 Christians in Parliament.

THE PEOPLE. With 84 million people, Indonesia is the sixth largest nation in the world. Its people are Malay-Polynesian in origin. They speak over 250 dialects and 25 major languages. The official language is Bahasa Indonesian, which is based on Malay. The main foreign languages are Dutch, English, and Chinese.

The population of Indonesia is by no means evenly distributed throughout the islands. Java, the smallest of the four large islands, has a teeming population of almost 50 million. With about 1,040 persons to the square mile, Java is one of the most densely populated

[20] D. Bentley-Taylor, *Indonesia* (pamphlet), pp. 7, 11.

places in the world. Borneo, which is much larger than Java, is mostly jungle land and has only 3 million people. Sumatra has 12 million. Some of the principal races are the Bataks and Minangkabaus in Sumatra, the Javanese and Sundanese in Java, the Menadonese and Buginese in Celebes, and the Dayaks in Borneo. The small Japanese colony was expatriated after World War II. The Chinese form the largest and by far the most influential foreign minority. Much of the retail trade is in their hands, and their prosperous firms are found all over the islands. They have a higher standard of living than the Indonesians, with whom they are not popular. Their numbers have been variously estimated at from two to five million. A government decree, effective January 1, 1960, prohibited aliens from retail trading in rural areas and has forced thousands of Chinese merchants to return to Communist China.

THE RELIGION. In the course of their history the people of Indonesia have embraced and practised three different religions: Hinduism, Buddhism, and Islam. Buddhism has died out except among the Chinese. Hinduism flourishes on the island of Bali. Islam is the religion of 90 per cent of the people, which makes Indonesia the largest Muslim country in the world. The Muslims of Indonesia are not nearly so fanatical as their co-religionists in the Near East. In Java alone some 100,000 Muslims have been converted to Christianity—a record matched by no other mission field in the world. There are about one million Roman Catholics and approximately 3,200,000 Protestants in the country. Together they comprise about 5 per cent of the population. With the exception of the Jacobite Churches of South India, Indonesia has the oldest Protestant settlements in Asia.

MISSIONS. The Portuguese and the Spaniards first landed in Indonesia at the end of the fifteenth century, and Christian missionaries accompanied the traders. When the Portuguese were driven out of the Moluccas by the Dutch about the beginning of the seventeenth century many of the 80,000 Roman Catholic converts embraced the Protestant faith. Thus Protestantism dates its origin back to 1607 in the Moluccas and to 1612 in Timor.

During the seventeenth century, missionary work, what little there was, was sponsored by the United East India Company. Although organized for commercial purposes, this company held itself responsible for the propagation of Christianity in the East Indies. This plan, commendable as it was, had several weaknesses, the principal one being that missionary work came to be regarded

as the responsibility of the government rather than the Church.
In time it became difficult to obtain recruits. By 1776 Dutch
ministers in the East Indies had dropped to 22, only five of whom
could speak the vernacular.

Not until the missionary awakening spearheaded by Carey and
Judson reached the continent of Europe and sending societies were
founded in the Netherlands and the Rhineland were missions on
a large scale begun in the Dutch East Indies. With the location of
Dutch and German missionaries in Sumatra, Borneo, Celebes, Timor,
etc., great religious changes took place among the animistic peoples of those areas. Missionary giants such as Nommensen among
the Bataks, and Kruyt and Adriani among the Toradjas were
instrumental in leading thousands to Christ.

Under Dutch colonial law Christian workers were denied access
to certain parts of the country lest they stir up unrest among the
Muslims. Also, the colonial government permitted only one society
to work in a given area. Thus there developed regional churches,
each with its own language and culture.

Sumatra. The *Basel Evangelical Missionary Society* began work
in western Sumatra in 1858. The largest and most successful work
was that of the *Rhenish Missionary Society,* whose outstanding
leader, *Ludwig Nommensen,* is remembered with affection to this
day. They began about 100 years ago among the Bataks in the Lake
Toba region. The Batak Church, with 650,000 adherents, and the
Nias Church, with 170,000, are the fruit of the Rhenish Mission
in Sumatra. Only four generations ago these Bataks were cannibals,
and the first missionaries, *Munson* and *Lyman* of the *American
Board,* were killed and eaten by them. This Church today is self-
governing and practically self-propagating and self-supporting.

Java. Although Protestant work in Java covers nine-tenths of
the island, Christians constitute only one-quarter of one per cent
of the population. The outstanding society there has been the
Netherlands Missionary Society, which began work about the
middle of the nineteenth century. The Christian community on
Java now numbers about 105,000 and is divided into three independent Churches: the Church of West Java, the Church of Mid-
Java, and the Church of East Java. The Churches in Mid- and West
Java are small. Most of the 100,000 Muslim converts in Indonesia
are to be found in East Java. The 22,000 Chinese Christians in Java
are organized into four independent Church groups, all of them
members of the National Christian Council.

Celebes. The pioneer society here was the *Netherlands
Missionary Society,* which entered the northeastern peninsula in

1822. Today in that area the Church of Minahasa has 350,000 members. It is said that nine out of ten persons in Minahasa today are professing Christians. In 1890 the Mission began work among the Toradjas. Around 1910 a mass movement towards Christianity began and today the 175,000 Christians are organized into two large independent Churches. The *Christian and Missionary Alliance* entered the Celebes in 1928 and located in the capital city of Makassar.

Besides the three Churches mentioned above, there are four others whose membership brings the total Christian community in Celebes to 650,000.

Borneo. The *Rhenish Missionary Society,* pioneer in Dutch Borneo, began work among the Dayaks in the southeastern part of the island in 1835. Their work, however, showed little fruit and in 1925 the field was turned over to the *Basel Evangelical Missionary Society.* This society has a thriving work in the southern part of the island, where the Kalimantan Evangelical Church has 32,000 members. The *Christian and Missionary Alliance* has been working among the headhunters of Borneo for thirty years with amazing results. The Mission entered East Borneo in 1929 and West Borneo four years later.

Other Islands. The *Protestant Church of the Moluccas,* the fruit of the work of the *Netherlands Missionary Society,* has 400 full-time workers and a Christian community of 275,000. One-half of the population of Timor is now Christian. The Church there has a membership of 300,000. In Bali, where the Hindus predominate, the Christian community, numbering 2,700, is both small and weak. In the islands northeast of Celebes the *Christian Evangelical Church of Sangihe Talaud* has 120,000 members. The *Methodist Church of Australia* reports a Christian community of 280,000.[21]

Altogether 31 ecclesiastical bodies with a total membership of 2,600,000 now constitute the *Indonesian Council of Churches.* Under the inspiration of *Dr. H. Kramer* and *Professor J. H. Bavinck* the indigenization of the Indonesian Churches progressed considerably. Between 1930 and 1940 eight Churches, headed by the Batak Church, gained their independence; and today they are actively promoting self-government and self-support. The latter has not been easy to achieve, owing to a tradition of state aid under the colonial system of government. The state continues to help church-operated schools and hospitals. Some of the Churches still receive subsidies from abroad for certain aspects of their program, especially theological education. Many local ministers supplement their salary

[21] *World Christian Handbook, 1957,* p. 41.

by teaching religion in the schools (for which they are paid by the government), by working their own farms, or by operating shops.

POSTWAR DEVELOPMENTS. Until World War II the Protestant missionary situation in Indonesia was fairly homogeneous, most missionaries coming from the Netherlands and being of the Reformed faith. A large influx of new missions after World War II changed the picture somewhat, but it is still correct to say that in nearly every Church the form of organization is Presbyterian. There is no Episcopal work in Indonesia. The Baptists were among those who entered the field after the war.

During the Japanese occupation, missionaries were interned, funds were cut off, churches were bombed, theological schools were closed, and pastors were killed. In the Protestant Church of the Moluccas alone, 90 leaders met a violent death. After the war many Europeans did not return. The Batak Church, which at one time had 60 foreign workers, now has only 12.

The missions entering the field after the war were mostly from the United States. Among these are: *Overseas Missionary Fellowship* (China Inland Mission), working among the established churches; *Unevangelized Fields Mission, Worldwide Evangelization Crusade, Baptist Mid-Missions,* and *New Tribes Mission,* all working among the animistic tribes in the outlying islands; and the *Southern Baptist Convention,* which has five centers, including a theological seminary, on Java and is now looking to Sumatra. The *Seventh Day Adventists* report 271 places of worship and the *Assemblies of God,* 19.[22]

THEOLOGICAL EDUCATION. In a land with over thirty separate regional Churches, theological education is a major problem. There are about 5,000 local congregations but only some 500 ordained ministers. There are two theological schools on a university level: the *Djakarta Theological College,* founded in 1934; and the *Faculty of Theology* of Nommensen (H.K.B.P.) University, established in 1954. In addition there are six such schools on the junior college level. The Christian and Missionary Alliance maintains three Bible schools, two in Borneo and one in Celebes.

NOTE: It should be remembered that the figures for church membership in this chapter are not restricted to baptized adults but include children and adherents as well. In other words, the statistics represent the extent of the Christian community rather than the actual membership of the Christian Church.

[22] *Ibid,* p. 42.

Sarawak and North Borneo. These two British territories are situated in the northern part of Borneo, one of the four large islands of Indonesia. Hence the reason for including them in the section on Indonesia.

British interest in Sarawak dates back to 1841 when Sir James Brooke obtained it from the Sultan of Brunei. In 1888 it was placed under British protection. After liberation from the Japanese it was ceded to the British Crown in July, 1946. The land area is about 47,000 square miles. The population in 1956 was estimated at 626,000. Of these 197,000 are Sea Dayaks, 186,000 are Chinese, 153,000 are Malays and Melanaus, 48,000 are Land Dayaks, and 40,000 belong to other indigenous tribes. The capital is Kuching, 18 miles up the Sarawak River.

North Borneo, with a coastline of 900 miles, was administered by the British North Borneo Company under royal charter from 1881 to 1946, at which time it was transferred to the British Crown. It has a land area of 29,000 square miles and forms the extreme northeastern tip of the island of Borneo. Its capital, Jesselton, is a small town of 12,000 people. Like Sarawak it suffered considerable damage from the Japanese occupation. Estimated population in 1956 was 390,000, of whom 90,000 were Chinese.

MISSIONS. The *Church Missionary Society* has maintained churches and schools in these parts from the beginning of the work under *Francis McDougall* in 1848. Their numerous schools range from meagerly equipped village schools in the Sarawak jungle to the two large secondary schools in Kuching, from which graduates, mostly Chinese, have gone out to assume positions of leadership throughout Sarawak and North Borneo. In North Borneo the principal Anglican schools are at Jesselton and Sandakan. Altogether the Anglicans have 38 primary and 6 secondary schools in Sarawak, and 62 schools in North Borneo. The most pressing need is for more and better teachers.

The *American Methodist* work in Sarawak began in 1901, when a Chinese pastor from Fukien visited the country in search of a new home for the band of Christians who accompanied him. Two years later *Rev. James Hoover* came from Malaya to minister to the spiritual needs of this group. The Methodist work has centered in the Rejang River district. Its chief concern has been for the Chinese, among whom there are now 62 churches. Their workers are trained at their theological school at Sibu. Following the disruption occasioned by World War II the *Sarawak Provisional Annual Conference* was organized on December 1, 1952, with 59 churches represented. There are now 16 ordained pastors and a similar number of supply preachers to shepherd the flock of 5,000 members and 9,000 prospective members. One of the first acts of the Conference was the establishment of a Bible school. The many Methodist schools, once a vital part of Christian witness in Sarawak, have one by one passed under the control of local boards and are now used "for educational purposes only."

Work among the Dayaks was begun in 1938 by a Batak pastor from Sumatra who remained during the war. At Christmas time in 1949 the first converts were baptized, and by 1953 church membership had reached 15,000. One of the most notable features of the Dayak Church is the zeal with which its lay members propagate the faith in the course of their daily occupations. A mass movement among the Dayaks is quite possible.

Borneo today is a country in which "civilization" is coming in rapidly, and this could leave the Dayak world largely at the feet of an alert Church, for the old taboos are breaking down, and there is a readiness to turn to the Christian Faith which is almost overwhelming, straining to the uttermost the resources of the Church.[23]

The *Basel Evangelical Missionary Society*, which has been in North Borneo since before the first World War, now has a self-supporting Church of over 3,000 members. Since 1952, when they began work among the Dusun people, they have increased their staff from two to ten.

The *Conservative Baptist Foreign Mission Society* decided in the fall of 1959 to open a new field in North Borneo.

PHILIPPINE ISLANDS

Area: 115,707 sq. mi.   Population: 22,700,000
Capital: Quezon City   Religion: Roman Catholicism

THE LAND. Slightly smaller than Japan, the Philippines are the largest group of islands in the Malay Archipelago. There are 7,083 islands in the group, but only 10 per cent of them are inhabited. Eleven large islands constitute 90 per cent of the land area and account for 90 per cent of the population. The islands extend more than 1,000 miles from north to south and about 600 miles from east to west. They form a sort of triangle reaching from Borneo in the south to Formosa in the north. There are both coral and volcanic islands

[23] *The Moving Spirit,* 1958, p. 26.

in the group, among them 12 active volcanoes. The whole country, with the single exception of Samar, is quite mountainous, some peaks rising to 8,000 and 10,000 feet. Much of the land is impenetrable jungle.

POLITICAL HISTORY. The Philippine Islands were discovered by Magellan in 1521 and conquered by Spain in 1565. In 1898 they were ceded to the United States as a result of the Spanish-American War. During World War II they fell to the Japanese. Heavy damage was sustained, principally from Allied bombings. At the close of the war, after almost half a century of tutelage, the Filipino people received their independence; the Republic of the Philippines came into existence on July 4, 1946. In the early postwar years it was on the verge of destruction; the Communist Huks were in possession of the northern island of Luzon and were banging on the gates of Manila. In addition, the government was riddled with corruption. The man who saved the day was Ramon Magsaysay. As Minister of Defense he defeated the Huks; and later as President he gave the country honest, efficient government.

THE PEOPLE. The people of the Philippines may be divided into three main families, the Negritos, the Indonesians, and the Malayans. The Negritos are probably the original inhabitants who were gradually driven back into the hills and jungles by successive waves of invaders. Today there are about 30,000 of these black-skinned, curly-haired pygmies, who are exceedingly primitive in life and habits. They are found in Luzon and Negros, and in smaller numbers in Panay, Palawan, and Mindanao. The Indonesians invaded the Philippines and drove the aborigines into the forests and mountains. They were tall, brown-skinned, and straight-haired, and possessed a superior form of civilization. Later on, the Malayans came to the Islands. They, too, were brown-skinned, but short in stature and with curly hair. They were of a higher order than the Indonesians and in time overran the Islands, introducing rice-growing, weaving, pottery, and woodwork. They built bamboo houses on stilts and thatched them with nipa palm. These people eventually came to dominate the country and today the Filipinos are regarded as the descendants of these Malay invaders.

These three main groups are divided into smaller groups speaking 130 different languages and dialects. Eight trade languages are understood by about 90 per cent of the population. Tagalog, Visayan, and Ilocano are the principal trade languages; but English is the most widely spoken language, for obvious reasons. Tagalog has been the national language ever since Independence in 1946.

THE RELIGION. The Philippines is the only nominally Christian country in the Orient. The great majority of the Filipino people are members of the Roman Catholic Church, which has been in the Islands ever since Magellan's fateful voyage around the world in 1520. This means that the social, economic, and political institutions of the country have been profoundly influenced by Christian concepts. Roman Catholicism in the Philippines is basically Spanish and resembles the type found in Spain, Mexico, and South America rather than the more enlightened, tolerant kind practised in the United States; but it must be acknowledged that the Catholic Church stemmed the tide of Islam, elevated womanhood, and inculcated in society the ethical standards of Christianity, in theory at least. About 83 per cent of the people are Roman Catholics, organized into 6 archbishoprics, 14 bishoprics, 1 apostolic prefecture, and 5 prelatures. The *Philippine Independent Church,* formed in 1902 and comprising about 10 per cent of the population, is Roman Catholic in background but denies the spiritual authority of the Roman Pontiff. The formal introduction of Protestantism coincided with the American occupation that followed the Spanish-American War. Today there are 800,000 Protestants in the country. Non-Christian groups include 800,000 Muslims, 350,000 pagans, and 50,000 Buddhists, as well as some others. The Constitution of the Philippine Republic recognizes the principle of the separation of Church and State; but the Protestants have expressed great concern regarding the rapid increase in the number of Roman Catholics in control of education and social welfare and within the political parties. The Vatican has a papal nuncio in the Philippines, and recently a Filipino Ambassador was appointed to the Vatican.

MISSIONS. In 1873 an English businessman in Manila succeeded in distributing several copies of the New Testament to various parts of the Islands by disguising the covers. One of them fell into the hands of a Dominican friar, *Alfonso Lallave,* whose life and teachings were so changed that he was brought to trial in Manila, defrocked, and exiled to Spain. There he translated Luke into the Pangasinan dialect. In 1896 *Don Pacual Pabete,* a journalist who was a political exile to Spain, in co-operation with the *British and Foreign Bible Society,* translated the Synoptics and Acts into Tagalog. With unusual foresight the Bible Society had Filipino exiles in Spain translate portions of the Scriptures into many other dialects, thus preparing for the American missionary occupation. Protestantism, then, began as an underground movement in the Philippines, within the shadow and under the ban of the Spanish regime. By the time the American missionaries arrived there were 35 tiny congregations with a total membership of 400 Christians.

With the American occupation came an influx of Protestant societies from the United States. The first on the field was the *Presbyterian Mission,* whose pioneer missionary, *Rev. James B. Rodgers,* arrived in April, 1899. In 1907 the Presbyterians and the Methodists opened the *Union Theological Seminary* in Manila. The Filipino Mission is today the third largest of the 23 fields of the Presbyterian Church in the U.S.A. In 1947 the Mission became integrated with the Church in the Philippines and now its 67 missionaries are fraternal workers under the United Church. There are 836 organized churches and 136 unorganized churches, with a total of 99,146 communicants.

The second mission to send its representatives was the *Methodist Episcopal Church. Bishop James M. Thoburn* visited Manila in March, 1899, and made preparations for Methodist work in the country. Pending the arrival of the first missionaries, *Rev. Nicolas Zamora,* an early convert, was given charge of the Filipino work. The first Methodist missionaries were five women belonging to the Woman's Foreign Missionary Society. They reached Manila in February, 1900. *Rev. Thomas H. Martin* arrived a month later, and the following year *Dr. Homer C. Stuntz* (later Bishop) arrived to take over the superintendency of the work. The first Bible school for women was opened by *Miss Winifred Spaulding* in 1903. The first Mission Conference was organized in 1905 and the Annual Conference followed in 1908. The Methodist Church work has grown considerably in the past 50 years and today it is the largest Protestant group in the Islands, having four Annual Conferences, a membership of 65,000, and a Christian community many times that number. In 1957 forty-five nationals were ordained to the Methodist ministry and many more were in training. The fifty Methodist missionaries in the Philippines are appointed to their tasks by the Filipino Bishop and one of the Annual Conferences. The medical work includes three clinics in various parts of Luzon and a 130-bed hospital and a nurses' training school in Manila. Both of these institutions are administered entirely by Filipinos.

Until 1952 the Methodists were confined to the island of Luzon in the north; but in that year a visit by *Bishop Jose L. Valencia* to the southern island of Mindanao resulted in the formation of

17 Methodist congregations there. Most of the 800,000 Muslims (Moros) in the Philippines are located on this island, and it is to them as well as to the many immigrants from the crowded north that the Methodist Church is directing this new evangelistic thrust. There are two Methodist-related colleges in the Philippines: *Philippine Christian College,* an interdenominational college in Manila, and *Philippine Wesleyan College,* which has four departments, at Cabanatuan.

In the past quadrennium, 1952–56, the significant advances of the church in the Philippines were made in its rural outreach, the development of national leadership, and in student work and medical evangelism. . . . Increase in church membership has prompted the construction of many new chapels, made largely of native materials, in the smaller barrios. Thousands of dollars have gone into this building program since the war. Parsonages for district superintendents are being built in each of the fifteen active districts, with partial aid from the churches of America.[24]

The *American Baptists* arrived on the field in 1900 and concentrated their efforts on the islands of Panay and Negros. The first mission hospital in the Islands was opened in Iloilo by *Dr. J. Andrew Hall.* Later *Emmanuel Hospital* was opened in Roxas City. The *Convention of the Philippine Baptist Churches,* formed in 1935, now comprises 251 churches, all self-supporting, with an aggregate membership of 20,000. Their educational program centers in three institutions of higher learning: *Central Philippine University* and the *College of Theology,* both in Iloilo, and *Filamer Christian Institute* in Roxas City.

The *Protestant Episcopal Mission* began work in 1902. It has always conceived its first responsibility to be to the Anglo-American communities in Manila and elsewhere throughout the country. The Mission also maintains a strong, self-supporting work among the Chinese in Manila. Other areas of interest are a well-established work among the Igorots of Mountain Province in Luzon and among the indigenous peoples of southern Mindanao. Its work in all of these areas is evangelistic, educational, and medical, and there is a definite striving towards full self-support. The medical work centers in *St. Luke's Hospital* and *School of Nursing. St. Andrew's Theological Seminary,* one of nine in the Islands, is maintained by the Anglican Church. By special agreement the clergy of the Philippine Independent Church receive their training at St. Andrew's. At present they represent about half of the student body. The first

[24] *Methodist Overseas Missions, 1956, p. 132.*

Filipino Bishop, *Benito C. Cabanban,* was consecrated in February, 1959. The Episcopal Church has 51,000 members, 36 ordained Filipino priests, 17 American priests, and 3 Chinese priests.

The *Disciples of Christ* made their appearance in 1901. Avoiding Manila, they went to northern Luzon and established a station at Laoag. Between 1901 and 1954, 70 missionaries of this Board saw service in the Philippine Islands. They now have 136 congregations and a membership of about 10,000.

In 1902 the *Christian and Missionary Alliance* began work on the island of Mindanao. A year later it was suddenly suspended when the only missionary died of cholera. For several years after the work was resumed in 1908 the Mission had only two couples on the field; but beginning with 1923 reinforcements began to arrive and by the time of the Pearl Harbor attack there were 30 workers in the Islands, all of whom survived the horrors of the Japanese occupation. When the China field closed in 1949 some of the Christian and Missionary Alliance workers were transferred to the Philippines. More recently they have extended their work to the Sulu Archipelago. In 1957 they reported 313 churches and 10,000 members.

The *American Board of Commissioners* took up work on the island of Mindanao in 1903. According to its latest report it still maintains five centers on that island. Five of its missionaries are teaching at *Silliman University* in Dumaguete on Negros Island. Most of its work is medical and educational, and its members work closely with the United Church in the Philippines.

The *Seventh Day Adventists* initiated missionary work in the Philippines in 1910. Here as elsewhere they developed strong institutions, including 118 elementary schools, 2 high schools, 2 colleges, and 3 hospitals. They are working in three main geographical areas: Luzon, Mindanao, and Visayas. Their 773 organized churches represent a membership of almost 60,000 believers.

The *Association of Baptists for World Evangelism* sent its first workers to the Philippines in 1928. Through the years it has made steady progress and today, with 93 missionaries, it is one of the largest missions in the Philippines. It has work in Luzon, Mindanao, Palawan, and Visayas.

The *Philippine Independent Church,* a body of some 2,000,000 members, sought freedom from Rome at the turn of the century, and after long "wandering in the wilderness" its bishops received consecration at the hands of the American Episcopate in 1947. Referring to this historic transaction the American Episcopal Mission has stated:

Seldom in history has a young and comparatively small mission, such as ours in the Philippines, been called on to give valid orders and sacraments to an independent, indigenous Church fifty times its size. Our relationship to the Philippine Independent Church is unique. It took a good deal of humility and hope on the part of the Philippine Independent Church to approach this Church asking for Holy Orders in the Apostolic Succession, for permission to use our Prayer Book in its Spanish translation, and that we train their candidates for Holy Orders in our Seminary in Manila. It took some faith and charity for us to accept such a challenge. It is one of the great ventures in faith in the mission field in our time, and one which bids fair to end happily. While our mission has made its greatest effort in Manila, the Mountain Province and Mindanao, the Philippine Independent Church has made its appeal to the Ilocano and Tagalog people on Luzon and the Visayans of the Southern Islands. Should the day come, and we pray and believe that it will, when our mission in the Philippines shall join forces with the Philippine Independent Church to form one indigenous Church in the Islands, the two groups would complement each other.[25]

The Philippine Independent Church is sometimes referred to as the *Aglipayan Church* after the priest *Aglipay* who led the revolt against Rome in 1902 and later organized the new Church.

WAR DAMAGE. It is estimated that during World War II, 80 per cent of all church properties were destroyed, mostly by American planes and guns. Following the war the Philippines was in ruins and the people were destitute of everything but the bare necessities. The United States government inaugurated an extensive program of rehabilitation, as did also the various mission boards, aided by the Church World Service. More recently large sums of money have been allocated from the United States government's War Claims Fund. The Methodist Mission received $270,000 in war claims in 1958. Damaged buildings have been repaired and enlarged and new buildings, with the latest equipment, have been erected. So far as physical plant and equipment are concerned, many churches and institutions are better off today than they were before the war.

THE UNITED CHURCH OF CHRIST. In 1948 three denominations joined to form the *United Church of Christ in the Philippines*. These were the *United Evangelical Church* (Presbyterian and Congregational), the *Evangelical Church* (United Brethren and Disciples), and the *Philippine Independent Methodist Church*. In 1956 the United Church had an adult membership of 105,000, with some 35,000 children under its care. The Department of Christian Education

[25] *Our Overseas Missions* (March, 1958), p. 25.

maintains 3 Bible schools, 2 high schools, and 5 colleges. The Department of Public Welfare operates 5 hospitals and 6 dispensaries under the supervision of 22 doctors and 47 nurses. Its Board of Missions has made itself responsible for the tribespeople in Mountain Province on Luzon and the long-neglected tribespeople of southern Mindanao. The spearhead of its work among the Moros of Mindanao is *Dansalan Junior College*. This college opened in 1950 with 28 students, only four of whom were Moros (Muslims). In 1957 there were 310 students, of whom 233 were Moros. Some idea of its missionary vision may be gained from the fact that the United Church in recent years has sent its own missionaries to Thailand, Indonesia, Okinawa, and Hawaii. As might be expected the United Church, though independent, is not yet fully self-supporting. The General Assembly budget for administration, promotion, theological education, etc., still requires foreign funds from the co-operating mission boards. Recently the Executive Committee has taken action looking forward to full self-support in eight years. In the meantime four mission boards are supporting 70 missionaries and fraternal workers assigned to the United Church. In 1957 they made a grant of $180,000 towards the educational, medical, and administrative work. The United Church of Christ is a member of the World Council of Churches.

CHRISTIAN UNIVERSITIES. Not many mission fields the size of the Philippines can boast one, much less two, Christian universities; but this is the case in the Philippines. *Silliman University* is located in Dumaguete City in the province of Negros Oriental. Founded in 1901 by the Presbyterians as an institute, it is now a full-fledged university comprising eleven schools and colleges. Enrollment in 1956 was 2,995. There were 177 faculty members, of whom 36 were missionaries and fraternal workers furnished by the four co-operating mission boards. The first Filipino president, *Dr. Leopoldo T. Ruiz*, was appointed in 1953. Along with high academic standards there is a strong evangelical witness. Sunday morning chapel service attracts approximately one-third of the student body. In 1955 no fewer than 196 students registered their decisions to become Christians. *Central Philippine University*, an American Baptist institution, began as a small industrial school for boys in Iloilo in 1905. From a humble beginning it has grown to become one of the most advanced institutions of higher learning in the Philippines. Bible instruction is offered to all students through grade school, high school, and college. The aggregate enrollment in its ten colleges in 1958 was 2,861.

THEOLOGICAL EDUCATION. There are nine centers of theological training in the Philippines. Foremost among them is *Union Theological Seminary* in Manila. It was started in 1907 as a joint effort by the Presbyterians and the Methodists. In 1919 they were joined by the United Brethren. Today the seminary trains ministers for the United Church and the Methodists. Enrollment in 1957 was 121. There are 9 faculty members and 22 part-time instructors. Second to Union Seminary in point of numbers is *St. Andrew's Theological Seminary* in Manila, established by the Anglicans in 1947. As already noted, the Philippine Independent Church sends its clergy to St. Andrew's for training. Other seminaries include the *College of Theology* at Silliman University, *College of Theology* at Central Philippine University, *Lutheran Seminary* (Manila), *Philippines Baptist Theological Seminary* (Southern Baptist, Baguio), *Laoag College of Theology* (Disciples, Laoag), *Baptist Bible Seminary* (Association of Baptists for World Evangelism, Manila), and *Far Eastern Bible Institute and Seminary* (Manila). In addition there are almost a score of Bible institutes.

POSTWAR DEVELOPMENTS. The Philippines, like many other fields in the Far East, has seen a large influx of new missions since the war. Some of these, like the *Far Eastern Gospel Crusade* and *Orient Crusades*, were newly organized missions starting work for the first time. Others, like the *Wycliffe Bible Translators, Baptist General Conference, New Tribes Mission*, and the *Southern Baptist Convention*, had previously worked in other parts of the world and were simply adding the Philippines to their list of mission fields. Still others, like the *Overseas Missionary Fellowship* (China Inland Mission), were ex-China missions looking for new fields in which to continue their work. By 1956 there were 30 Protestant societies in the Philippines, and several more have been added since.

The missions with the most rapidly expanding programs are the *Southern Baptists* and the *Overseas Missionary Fellowship*. The former began work among the Chinese in the city of Baguio in 1949. Two years later they opened a seminary. In 1953 they initiated work among the Filipinos, also in Baguio. Later they moved to the southern island of Mindanao, where they opened a hospital at Mati. By 1955 they had three centers on Luzon and three on Mindanao, with work among both the Chinese and the Filipinos in each case. In 1959 they reported 36 churches and 106 Sunday Schools in the care of 24 pastors. Their present missionary staff numbers 50.

The *Overseas Missionary Fellowship* entered the Philippines in 1952 and established work on the island of Mindoro, which up to that time had never had a resident Protestant missionary. Today, after seven years of work, it has 76 missionaries (among them 28 single ladies) in 14 main stations. Already they have contacted seven hitherto unreached tribes. Languages are being reduced to writing and Bible translation work is proceeding apace. Ten infant churches have been organized along indigenous lines, and as many more groups meet regularly for Christian worship. In 1958, 1,500,000 pieces of literature were published for the Philippines.

MISSIONARY RADIO. One of the most amazing developments in postwar missions in the Far East has been the rapidly expanding program of the *Far East Broadcasting Company,* organized by a group of American GI's who served in the Philippines during World War II. Located in Radio City, a twelve-acre piece of land outside Manila, Station DZAS, known as the *Voice of the Orient,* is now using eleven transmitters to broadcast the gospel 20 hours a day in 36 languages to all parts of the Far East. Pre-tuned radios have been placed in *barrios* all over the Islands, and thousands of persons in inaccessible regions hear the Christian message every day. Follow-up work is done by means of Bible correspondence courses in English, Chinese, and the major languages of the Philippines. Since the beginning over 300,000 have enrolled in the "Bible School of the Air," and by 1958 some 40,000 persons had completed the course. Their latest venture is the erection of a 100,000-watt station on Okinawa by which it will be possible to beam the gospel to all parts of Asia, including Siberia and Tibet.

A second station, DYSR, the *Voice of Christian Brotherhood,* is sponsored by the *Philippine Federation of Christian Churches* in co-operation with Silliman University. In addition to daily broadcasts for local consumption the station helps to train radio technicians from all parts of Southeast Asia.

BIBLE TRANSLATION. *Wycliffe Bible Translators,* a group of highly trained specialists in linguistics, have recently sent a staff of workers into the Philippines to engage exclusively in translation work, including both the Scriptures and related books. The next ten years should see a major break-through in the problem of Christian literature in the vernacular. The *American Bible Society* reports that the entire Bible is available in eight major languages. Various books of the Bible have been translated into ten additional languages.

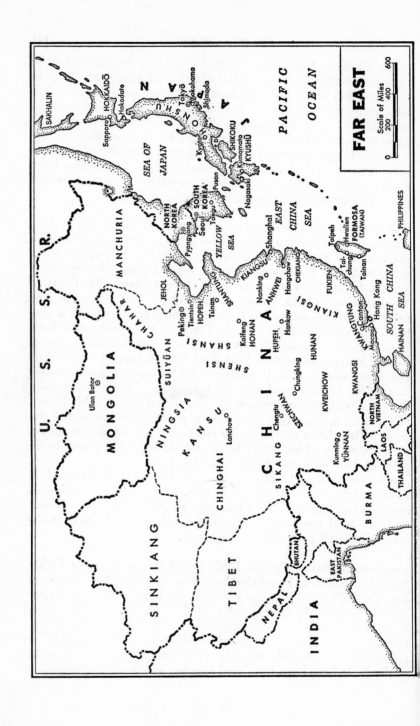

XI

FAR EAST

CHINA

Area:	3,750,000 sq. mi.	Population:	650,000,000
Capital:	Peking	Religion:	Confucianism, Taoism, Buddhism, and Islam

THE LAND. Variously known as the Middle Kingdom, the Celestial Empire, and the Land of Sinim (Is. 49:12), China is the oldest of the existing nations. Its legendary history goes back to about thirty centuries before the Christian era; its true historical period is conceded by Western scholars to date from 2200 B.C. to 2000 B.C. In other words, China's history began 1,500 years before the founding of Rome, 700 years before the Exodus, and 300 years before the call of Abraham. Imagine a nation which has seen the rise, wane, and final extinction of the greatest world empires of history—Assyria, Babylon, Greece, and Rome—and yet lives on, the same compact race, unimpaired in vitality and increasing steadily in numbers!

It is fitting that the world's largest nation should be located on the world's largest continent. Situated in eastern Asia, China has a coastline of 2,200 miles on the east and south. On the west it is hemmed in by the world's highest mountains, the Himalayas. Its isolation from the rest of the ancient world was complete when it built the Great Wall to keep out the "barbarians" from the north. Included in the land area of China are two huge territories, Manchuria in the northeast and Tibet in the west. Outer Mongolia, which used to be part of China, is now an independent Communist state.

POLITICAL HISTORY. The history of modern China may be said to have begun with the Opium War of 1839–1842 which resulted in the

143

opening of five treaty ports to foreign commerce and Christianity. Slowly and with considerable reluctance China adopted Western ways. From time to time political reforms were introduced, but in each case it was "too little and too late," with the result that China in the nineteenth century became the victim of Western imperialism which reduced it to colonial status without granting it colonial benefits. The Revolution of 1911, which overthrew the Manchu government and established the Republic of China, was followed by a period of political instability which played into the hands of the Communists. Under the tutelage of the Kuomintang, China tried valiantly to become a modern democratic nation and doubtless would have succeeded had it not been for the Sino-Japanese War. Weakened by eight years of war, wracked by inflation, and honeycombed with corruption, the Nationalist government fell easy prey to the Communists who came to power in 1949. Whether we like it or not, the Red regime in Peking is here to stay. During the last ten years unprecedented progress has been made in science, industry, agriculture, and education, albeit at terrific cost in terms of human freedom.

THE PEOPLE. Without a census it was impossible to know exactly what China's population really was. Published estimates ranged all the way from 250 million to 485 million; but it was not until the Communists came to power that a scientific census was taken, in 1953, which revealed an astounding population of 580 million in continental China. It is reckoned that the population of China is increasing at the rate of 12 million each year. If this be so, its population today cannot possibly be less than 650 million; and if the present trend continues China will have a population of one billion by the year 2000. It is a solemn fact that fully one-fourth of the entire human family lives in China. The Chinese themselves have always spoken of five "races" in their country: Chinese, Manchu, Mongol, Muslim, and Tibetan. In addition to these there are many tribal groups, the aborigines living in the west and south-west, who did not have a written script until the missionaries gave it to them. The Chinese are physically strong and possess great powers of endurance and adaptability. They are proverbially patient and frugal, and, as a rule, peace-loving. Among the indisputable marks of a worthy and venerable civilization are their elaborate system of patriarchal government; their remarkable written language and literature; their world-famed discoveries, such as the mariner's compass, gunpowder, and the art of block printing; their unique manufacture of silks, porcelain, lacquerware, etc.; and their vast store of valuable empirical knowledge along every line.

THE RELIGION. It is usually stated that there are three chief religions in China—Confucianism, Taoism, and Buddhism. This does not mean, however, as might be inferred, that the people are divided into three different sects each with its separate faith. Most of the Chinese profess all three religions, and practise one or other as occasion prompts them.

Confucianism, derived from the teachings of the great Chinese philosopher, Confucius, who lived in the sixth century B.C., is, strictly speaking, not so much a religion as a system of political and social ethics. The instructions of Confucius are confined to the duties and relations of society and the state. While he mentioned the Supreme Ruler, under the term "heaven," he gave no clear account of such a being, did not define man's duties toward him, and was silent regarding a future life. Yet the system embodies the worship of nature and of departed spirits, ancestors in particular. "Thus sanctioned by the sage, ancestral worship has remained the heart and soul of Chinese religion."[1]

Confucius became an object of special worship, all cities being provided with temples in his honor. The mandarins performed official worship to the sage twice a year. No images or priests were connected with this worship, and Confucianism in theory was opposed to idolatry. Yet in popular practice the worship of idols, as well as nature worship (the deities of the hills, the rivers, the wind, the rain, etc.), went on along with ancestral worship, all enjoying together the official sanction of the state.[2]

Taoism claims as its founder Lao-tzu, a great philosopher born fifty years before Confucius, but the system has long since departed from the theories of its reputed founder, and is today grossly materialistic and full of all kinds of grotesque superstition. It has brought the Chinese into bondage to innumerable demons and evil spirits, and is responsible for a great variety of absurd beliefs and harmful practices.

Buddhism was imported into China from India in A.D. 67 by

---

[1] Arthur H. Smith, *The Uplift of China* (Young People's Missionary Movement, 1907), p. 92.

[2] In Communist China, Confucius is regarded as the personification of feudalism, and consequently has been completely debunked. He has been dropped from the textbooks, and his birthday passes unnoticed by people and press alike.

the Emperor Ming Ti, who was dissatisfied with the materialistic trend of Confucianism and Taoism, and welcomed a religion which by its doctrines of the transmigration of souls and future punishment professed to shed some light upon the fate of the dead. It met with much opposition, and even today "its position is that of an officially proscribed, though actually tolerated, heresy."[3] Yet it has gained general recognition and a multitude of followers, and has filled China with its temples and shrines.

There are also scattered through China, mainly in the western provinces, Muslims estimated at 20 million in number. They are much less zealous in their religious practices than the Muslims of India and the Near East, but maintain their forms of faith, abstain rigidly from eating pork, and do not intermarry with the Chinese. They are, as a rule, stronger in their resistance to Christianity than any other of the religious sects, and thus far very few have become Christians.

THE NESTORIANS. The earliest known introduction of the Christian faith into China was by the Nestorians, who early in the sixth century came overland from the west, resolutely pushing their way across vast deserts and lofty mountains. These Syrian priests appear to have been kindly received by the Emperor, and to have made a large number of disciples. Strange indeed is it that after being propagated for some eight centuries the Nestorian faith lost its influence to the extent that every trace of the movement disappeared and its very existence in the Empire was forgotten. Only in 1625 was a buried marble tablet discovered by accident in Sian, a province of Shensi, bearing the date A.D. 781 and recording in Chinese and Syriac characters the arrival of the missionaries and the success of their work. This famous *Nestorian Tablet* is still on exhibit in the city of Sian.

EARLY ROMANIST EFFORTS. An Italian monk, *John de Monte Corvino*, reached China by the overland route from India about 1294. Like the Nestorians, he was well received by the Mongol Emperor, the great Kublai Khan, and his work was at least outwardly very successful. A church was built and an orphan asylum conducted at Peking, thousands were baptized, and the New Testament and Psalms were translated into Chinese. But in 1368 the Mongol dynasty gave place to the Ming dynasty, and the new rulers viewed the "foreign religion" with disfavor. A period of bitter persecution broke

[3] Smith, *op. cit.*, p. 105.

out, and a blank of nearly 200 years followed in the history of Christianity in China.

LATER ROMANIST ACTIVITIES. Next came the effort of the great Jesuit missionary, *Francis Xavier,* to enter China—an effort cut short by his death in 1552. The actual entrance was effected by the distinguished monk, *Matteo Ricci,* and a companion, who were sent from Macao in 1580 and traveled through the country disguised as Buddhist priests. After encountering many trials and difficulties, the labors of these men and their successors met with pronounced success, churches were built and Christian communities formed. The priests' scientific knowledge won for them no little prestige and favor at Peking. But then the inherent proclivity of Romanism to internal dissension and political intrigue asserted itself. Bitter disputes arose among the various orders—Jesuits, Franciscans, and Dominicans—with respect to the consistency of Christians practising Confucian rites. Their persistent meddling in political affairs, moreover, was strongly resented by the Chinese authorities. The result was a growing disfavor, and in the early eighteenth century outbreaks of violent persecution all but annihilated the Roman Catholic Church in China. At last, in 1724, Christianity was proscribed by edict and the missionaries were banished from the Empire.

PROTESTANT MISSIONS. Protestant missionary work began with Morrison's arrival in 1807, and may be divided into the following periods:

(1) 1807–1842—to the Opium War.
(2) 1842–1860—to the Treaty of Tientsin.
(3) 1860–1895—to the Sino-Japanese War.
(4) 1895–1911—to the Chinese Revolution.
(5) 1911–1950—to the Evacuation.

First Period (1807–1842). *Robert Morrison* (1807–1834), the noble Protestant missionary pioneer to the Chinese nation, was sent out by the *London Missionary Society* in 1807. Like Carey, he was of humble parentage and occupation—a shoe-last maker—and acquired a good education and several languages by dint of persevering application. Like Carey, too, he was refused passage by the East India Company, so reached Canton via the United States in an American ship. His famous retort to a sneering question put to him by a shipowner in New York reveals something of the Christian character of the young pioneer. "So then, Mr. Morrison, you really expect to make an impression on the idolatry of the great Chinese Empire?" asked the skeptic. Quickly and with emphasis came the reply, "No, sir, but I expect God will."

None but a man prepared by God would have been equal to the task Morrison faced. He was unwelcome alike to the Chinese, the East India Company, and the Jesuit missionaries at Macao. Trials and discouragements thickly beset him; he met with opposition at every turn. At first he dwelt in a room of an American warehouse in Canton, dressed in Chinese garb, and was obliged to conceal himself indoors while pressing his task of Chinese language study. Soon he was compelled to withdraw to Macao, a coast port 90 miles south, which had been in the possession of Portugal since 1557. At the end of two years his linguistic attainments won for him the position of translator for the East India Company. God's hand was unmistakably in this, for it not only provided Morrison with a liberal salary, but, what was far more, it secured him the safest and perhaps the only means of remaining in China.

In addition to his official duties he applied himself assiduously to the task of thoroughly mastering the language and translating the Scriptures, while also embracing the limited opportunities presented to him for evangelistic work. In 1813 the translation of the New Testament was completed, and that of the entire Bible in 1818, with some help from Dr. Milne. Besides the Bible, Morrison ultimately published more than a score of different works, including a Chinese grammar and his monumental dictionary of six volumes and 4,500 pages. In 1814, after seven long years of patient toil, he baptized in Macao the first known Chinese Christian convert, Tsai A-ko. In 1824 Morrison visited England and was received with honor by the churches and also by the King. He returned to China in 1826 and died there in 1834.

The missionary life of Dr. Morrison covered but twenty-seven years, yet in view of the circumstances and the difficulties of the time, his achievements are almost incredible. Although his actual converts were less than a dozen, and although he was excluded from all but a corner of the land to which he devoted his life, yet by his literary labors he laid the foundations for all future work, and by giving the Chinese the Christian Scriptures in their own language he captured a commanding position in the very heart of the land to be possessed. "By the Chinese Bible," he said himself, "when dead, I shall yet speak."[4]

William Milne, Morrison's first associate, arrived in 1813. He

4 *Ibid.,* p. 141.

attempted to join him in Macao, but was compelled to withdraw, and finally settled at Malacca. There he established an Anglo-Chinese college and a printing press. He was joined in 1816 by *Walter Medhurst*, and together these two pioneers, undaunted by the fact of being denied residence in China, carried on in Malacca, Batavia, and other points in Malaysia and the Dutch East Indies, to which many Chinese had emigrated, a vigorous work of preaching, teaching, translation, and publication, the influence of which was mightily felt within the Empire itself, despite the best efforts of her rulers to counteract it.

Dr. Karl Gutzlaff, of the *Netherlands Missionary Society*, deserves mention along with the above named trio of the London Missionary Society as an able and effective pioneer of this early period. Despite the rigid prohibitions of the Chinese government against missionaries and Christian literature, Gutzlaff contrived, as surgeon or interpreter, to make several voyages in trading vessels up and down the coast. Stoned by angry mobs, hounded by the police, haled before the mandarins, he yet succeeding in distributing large quantities of Scripture portions and tracts, and the accounts of his adventures stirred up new interest at home in Chinese missions.

AMERICAN PIONEERS. The earliest American missionaries to China were *Rev. E. C. Bridgman* and *Rev. David Abeel*, sent out by the *American Board* in 1829. Bridgman's most valuable contribution to Chinese missions was his literary works. His name ranks high among Bible translators and revisers. He began the publication of the *Chinese Repository*, a storehouse of valuable information about China, which continued to be issued for twenty years.

In 1833 *Dr. S. Wells Williams* joined the little group as missionary printer, but was destined to distinction later on as sinologue, historian, and diplomat. His *Middle Kingdom* is still the standard authority on the Chinese Empire.

Dr. Peter Parker was the first medical missionary to China, sent out by the *American Board* in 1834. He established a hospital at Canton, which laid just claim to being the first institution in non-Christian lands with distinctive aims of its kind. It had a marvelous career under the direction of a long line of distinguished missionary physicians. Dr. Parker was singularly successful in overcoming by his skill the animosity of the Chinese, and has been said to have "opened China at the point of the lancet." In no mission field has medical work met with a more imperative call of need or found a vaster field of service; in none has such work been more signally used in disarming bitter prejudice, in opening the door for the gospel, and thus in ministering healing to sinful souls as well as to diseased bodies.

Second Period (*1842–1860*). This period dates from the end of the Opium War in 1842 to the ratification of the Treaty of Tientsin in 1860, at the close of what is known as the Arrow War. Some knowledge of the course of development of political and commercial relations between China and other nations during these early years is essential to a proper appreciation of the conditions attending the efforts of pioneers in introducing missionary work.

The immediate occasion of the Opium War was the attempt of British vessels to import a consignment of Indian opium at Canton. This act of forcing upon China a destructive drug which has proved her greatest national curse and the ruin of countless millions of her people, body and soul, can never in itself be justly defended, but must be regarded as an indelible blot upon the fair name of Britain. Yet it must be recognized that opium was not the real *cause*, but only the *occasion* of the war. The true cause lay in the conceited arrogance of the Chinese government, its utter contempt for treaty obligations entered into, the outrageous restrictions placed upon commerce, and the insulting and intolerable treatment of foreigners. The war clearly had to come, but it is ever to be regretted that an unrighteous and indefensible incident was the occasion of it.

God, however, turned the unhappy event to China's spiritual blessing, for by the Treaty of Nanking the five ports of Canton, Amoy, Fuchow, Ningpo, and Shanghai were opened to foreign residence and trade, and Hong Kong was ceded to Great Britain. At once there followed an inrush of missionary forces and activities such as has probably never been paralleled in any other land in the same time. In addition to the London Missionary Society (1807), the American Board (1830), and the Protestant Episcopal Church of America (1835), which were already on the ground, or, more properly speaking, waiting at the doors, other societies entered the field in the following order:

> 1842. American Baptist Missionary Union
> American Presbyterian Mission
> American Reformed Church Mission
> 1843. American Southern Baptist Mission
> 1844. Church Missionary Society
> 1846. Basel Missionary Society

1847. American Methodist Episcopal Mission
English Presbyterian Mission
Rhenish Mission
1848. American Southern Methodist Mission
1852. English Wesleyan Missionary Society
1859. English Baptist Missionary Society

Not a few memorable names occur in the list of the missionaries of this period. Among the best known are *Dr. Legge,* whose translations of the Chinese Classics, and commentary thereupon, have become famous; *Drs. Lockhart, Hobson,* and *Kerr,* medical pioneers; *Dr. William Ashmore,* best remembered as a staunch champion of the principle of a self-supporting and self-propagating national church; *Rev. William C. Burns,* translator of Bunyon's *Pilgrim's Progress* and many helpful hymns, whose saintly character as well as distinctive methods of getting close to the Chinese exerted a powerful influence.

A few sentences may well be quoted from Dr. A. H. Smith's general summary of the above two periods of Protestant Missions in China. Referring to the missionary movement in military terms, he writes:

To this Christian invasion there was almost everywhere opposed on the part of the Chinese a steady and a powerful resistance. . . . The missionaries were everywhere watched, suspected, despised, insulted, and, as opportunity offered, plundered. They were denied a spot for the sole of their foot to rest upon, were repeatedly driven out only to return again, and when at last a habitation or a chapel had been laboriously secured, it was perhaps torn down, and the weary process had to be begun anew. It is not strange that amid insanitary surroundings, with unwholesome food, and incessant anxieties and toils, many men and women utterly broke down. Out of a total of 214 male missionaries previous to 1860, 44 had died. . . . The foundations of all the subsequent mission work in China were by them laid deep, and strong, and well. The average missionary life of this handful of men was but seven years, and but one attained to forty years. But in view of the Bible translations and repeated revisions, "commentaries on the Scripture written, grammars and dictionaries of the language prepared, tracts printed, converts made, churches formed, native preachers employed, Christian schools organized," the way hewn out of obstinate rock, and China in spite of the Chinese themselves opened, it was impossible for those then living not to exclaim in devout thanksgiving and praise, "What hath God wrought?" . . . Let us learn from the records of the past how vast are the results which God can accomplish with but a handful of human laborers, and from a contemplation of the yet greater task remaining, what a trumpet-call is sounding for men and women of like spirit with those who have gone before to enter into and complete their labors.[5]

Third Period (*1860–1895*). The Opium War had not after all settled the matters at issue between China and foreign nations, and the ground had all to be wearily gone over again. Another war broke out in 1856, known as the Arrow War. Canton was captured by the British and French; treaties were made at Tientsin in 1858, only to be set at nought by China; and it was only in 1860, when Peking was taken by a foreign force, that the treaties were finally ratified. The Treaty of Tientsin stipulated that ten more cities should be opened to trade and the whole Empire opened to missionaries, and that Christian converts should be free from persecution.

As a result of this second "opening of China" there was at once an exodus of missionaries from the few centers already occupied to the new treaty ports, and efforts soon followed to penetrate the interior. But despite all treaties signed and promises made by China's rulers, the actual opening up of China, whether to missionary work or to foreign intercourse, was destined to be in the teeth of bitter opposition from the authorities and frequent antiforeign uprisings of the people, throughout this entire period and even beyond it. Missionary progress up to the very end of the nineteenth century was punctuated by insult, riot, and bloodshed.

Serious outbreaks occurred in 1870 at Tientsin and Hankow, when over a score of foreigners were brutally killed and much property was destroyed. Another virulent antiforeign demonstration took the form of vile anti-Christian placards and pamphlets issued from the capital of Hunan province in 1890. These were followed by riots in the Yangtze valley and the murder of missionaries in Hupeh province in 1891 and 1893. In 1895 took place the memorable Kucheng massacre in Fukien province, when ten members of the Church Missionary Society were murdered. In all, 26 Protestant martyrs are recorded previous to the Boxer massacre of 1900, while many Roman Catholics and other foreigners suffered a like fate.

During this period missionary work expanded at a rapid pace. Wherever missionaries went churches, schools, and hospitals sprang up. In addition to the 3 major Bible societies—the British and Foreign Bible Society, the American Bible Society, and the National Bible Society of Scotland—11 tract societies were organized and 11 mission presses were established in various parts of the country.

The first All-China Missionary Conference was held in Shanghai

[5] *Ibid.,* pp. 151–53.

in 1877. In 1890 a second Conference, meeting in the same city, issued an appeal for 1,000 men to be sent to China within five years to speed up the "evangelization of China in this generation." By the time of the Centenary Celebration in 1907 Protestant forces comprised a total of 94 societies with a combined membership of 3,445 missionaries occupying 632 stations.

SOME PROMINENT MISSIONARIES. Among the many worthy names connected with this third period only a few can be mentioned:

Dr. Griffith John (1855–1912), of the London Missionary Society, was the pioneer worker at Hankow, where for half a century he remained the central missionary figure. He was a fearless itinerant and an indefatigable preacher, and the great number of splendid gospel tracts which came from his pen have carried conviction to multitudes, and made Dr. John's name a beloved household word all over China.

Dr. W. A. P. Martin (1850–1916) was noted as a Christian educator and writer. His best-known work, entitled *Evidences of Christianity*, became a missionary classic and had an enormous circulation. He was signally honored by the Chinese government in being made president of several high government institutions, including the Imperial University at Peking.

James Gilmour (1870–1891), known as "Gilmour of Mongolia," labored heroically for the wild, roving Mongols of that vast, elevated northern plain. He cheerfully endured hardships and privation, spending long periods afield among them, sharing their black skin tents and unpalatable food, and suffering the rigor of their bitterly cold winters, as he relieved their sick bodies and ministered the gospel to their dark souls steeped in the superstitions and vices of a degraded Lamaism.

Others of this period were *Dr. J. L. Nevius* (1854–1893), strong in his advocacy of missionary methods making for a self-propagating national church; *Dr. Ernest Faber* (1865–1899), one of the ablest and most voluminous writers in Chinese, whose books exerted a deep and lasting influence; *Rev. David Hill* (1865–1896), of the Wesleyan Mission at Hankow, saintly in character and rich in good works, who during his relief work in the great famine of 1877–78 first influenced Mr. Hsi, afterwards a distinguished pastor of the China Inland Mission; *Bishop Moule* (1858–1918), of the Church Mission at Hangchow; *Dr. Y. J. Allen* (1860–1907), and *Dr. Timothy Richard* (1869–1919), able contributors to Chinese Christian literature; *Dr. J. C. Gibson* (1874–1919) of Swatow, one of the two Chairmen of the great China Centenary Conference in 1907;

Rev. F. W. Baller (1873–1922), of the China Inland Mission, whose Chinese dictionary, language primer, and other textbooks have assisted hundreds of missionaries in acquiring Chinese. But a host of other missionary leaders of almost or quite equal prominence with these could be mentioned.

China Inland Mission (1865). One outstanding figure of this period we have reserved for separate mention in connection with the Society of which he was the founder. This is *Rev. J. Hudson Taylor* (1853–1905), whom God chose and prepared for a role of unique importance in the task of evangelizing the millions of China. Mr. Taylor first went to China in 1853. His early intimate relations with Rev. William Burns exercised a strong influence upon his life and subsequent service. Compelled soon to return home because of ill-health, he became overwhelmed with the thought of the spiritual needs of the vast interior of China, still scarcely touched with the gospel. Before long he became convinced that God was calling him to undertake a forward movement in this direction. The result was the formation in 1865 of the China Inland Mission, and in the following year Hudson Taylor, with a party of fifteen, sailed for China to begin that work.

The China Inland Mission was the first and, until 1950, largest of a number of missionary movements to which the name "faith mission" has been applied, because of their principle of making no direct solicitation of funds for their work. The workers are guaranteed no fixed salary, but trust the Lord to supply their needs through the voluntary offerings of His people in answer to prayer. This Mission is international and interdenominational, candidates from different countries and various evangelical sects all working together harmoniously. The missionaries include laymen as well as ordained ministers and both single and married women as well as men receive official appointment; the women constituting more than half of the missionary staff.

The policy of the work is strongly evangelistic, the great objective being the widest possible witnessing of the gospel to those who have never heard it, to the end that all may have the opportunity of salvation, and that the task of world-wide evangelization committed by Christ to His Church may speedily be completed in preparation for the Lord's return.

The whole history of this Mission has been attended by the rich blessing of God. Besides being the largest of the many missions which worked in China, the China Inland Mission stands out before the whole world as one of the strongest witnesses to the faithfulness of God in supplying the needs of so great a company of His workers over many years, in answer to simple faith and prayer.

Christian and Missionary Alliance (1888). This Society, patterned largely after the China Inland Mission in its principles and practice, had a worthy share in the pioneer work of several of the last provinces of China to be entered with the gospel.

Fourth Period (*1895–1911*). SINO-JAPANESE WAR (1894–1895). This war broke out over a dispute between China and Japan regarding their respective rights in Korea. Within a few months the Chinese troops were everywhere defeated, the Chinese navy destroyed, several important ports captured, and Manchuria occupied. China's defeat at the hands of a small nation like Japan was a keen humiliation, and rudely awakened her more thoughtful leaders to the first realization of her national impotence. The conviction grew upon them that drastic reforms must be carried out and modern institutions and methods no longer scouted but adopted, if China was not to be hopelessly doomed. Thereupon began a bitter struggle between the progressive and reactionary parties in Chinese officialdom, in which struggle the young Emperor, Kuang Hsu, openly aligned himself with the reformers, while his aunt, the notorious Empress Dowager, as strongly sided with the opposing faction. By a skillful stroke of diplomacy the Empress Dowager and her party gained the upper hand, the Emperor was made virtually a prisoner, and the newly initiated program of reform was suddenly laid in the dust.

BOXER UPRISING (1900). The triumph of the Empress Dowager and the reactionary party at Peking swiftly culminated in the memorable Boxer uprising of 1900. Numerous points of friction with foreign governments and with foreigners in China, and growing alarm at the steady gain of foreign ideas and influence within the Empire, united to precipitate a crisis. An elaborate plot was hatched to murder or drive out every "foreign devil" and to stamp out every seed of hated foreignism from the country. The blow fell most heavily upon the missionaries, because of their being scattered far in the interior in every part of the realm. Volumes have been written of the fearful sufferings endured by the missionary body and the national church, especially in the north, but the full story can never be told. Altogether 189 Protestant missionaries and their children were put to a cruel death. The two missions which lost most heavily were the China Inland Mission, with 79 martyrs, and the Christian and Missionary Alliance, with 36. How many

Chinese Christians suffered martyrdom will never be accurately known, but the number certainly reaches into thousands. Many of these Christians refused the offer of life at the price of renouncing allegiance to the Saviour, calmly laid their heads upon the block and sealed their testimony with their blood. Such a record will ever constitute an enriching heritage to the Church of Christ in China and the whole world.

As to the effect upon missions, never did a storm cloud more truly have a silver lining. Never did a malicious blow of Satan hurled against the Church of the living God more signally fail of its object and rebound to his own hurt. Once again was it demonstrated that "the blood of the martyrs is the seed of the Church." The Boxer uprising not only put missionary work upon a safer basis, through the new conditions insisted upon by the great Powers, but it imparted to the movement the mightiest spiritual impetus up to that time.

If statistics are any criterion, more real progress was made in the first ten years of the twentieth century than in the previous one hundred years. By 1915 there were 170,000 students enrolled in mission schools. In ten years the Bible societies had stepped up their output of Scripture portions from 2,519,758 to 6,148,546. Church membership approximated 270,000.

Fifth Period (*1911–1950*). CHINESE REVOLUTION. The Revolution which broke out with startling suddenness on October 9, 1911, was the final outburst of smoldering fires of discontent which had existed under the surface for years. In an incredibly short time the imperial forces were defeated, the revolutionists were in control, the baby Emperor and Prince Regent were forced to abdicate, and the whole world stood aghast at the spectacle of the oldest despotic monarchy suddenly turned into the youngest republic.

This Revolution was in no sense antiforeign. Indeed, some of its leaders had been pupils in mission schools or otherwise in touch with missionary propaganda; and it may be said that far as that propaganda was, and always is, from advocating political revolution, yet the great ideas of righteousness, justice, and liberty which Christianity inculcates had begun to exercise their inevitable influence in China, as they earlier had done in Western lands, so that many who were not prepared to give their personal allegiance to Christ were nevertheless made impatient of conditions to which they formerly submitted with feelings either of indifference or of helplessness. From this viewpoint Christian missions may be regarded as having been the *efficient* cause of the Chinese Revolution.

The year 1922 was a memorable one from many points of view. It was in that year that the great Protestant Conference was held in Shanghai. Almost without exception every mission and church was represented on that historic occasion. For the first time in missionary history the Chinese delegates outnumbered the foreign missionaries. One writer described it as follows:

It was an impressive gathering, not only by the actual numbers there and the feeling it gave of an ecumenical Christianity over-leaping all national as well as denominational barriers, but also because it represented 402,599 baptized Christians with some 400,000 others under instruction, ordained clergy numbering 1,745, and a missionary body of some 6,000 men and women.[6]

Perhaps the most notable achievement of the 1922 Conference was the creation of the National Christian Council. Provision was made for a permanent staff of a Chinese General Secretary and Chinese and foreign assistant secretaries on equal footing. Another outcome of the Conference was the formation of a Home Missionary Society, controlled and supported by the Chinese Churches.

Missionary personnel reached its peak in 1926 at which time there were in China 8,325 Protestant missionaries representing 157 societies. This made China with its teeming population the largest mission field in the world. After the evacuation of 1927, occasioned by the antiforeign sentiment which culminated in the "Nanking Incident," missionary personnel never again exceeded 6,500. By 1935 there were 270 mission hospitals in all parts of China. This is hardly a large number for a country the size of China; but when compared with only 60 government hospitals and 80 public hospitals the figure is significant.

From the numerical point of view the number of Christian converts was small. Never at any time were there more than four million Christians, of whom three million were Roman Catholics. This is a disappointingly small figure when one considers that it represents less than one per cent of the population. On the other hand, it must be acknowledged that the influence of this minority group was out of all proportion to its numerical strength. In the early 1930's, 35 per cent of those listed in *Who's Who in China* had at one time or another been connected with Protestant schools. In 1931 about nine-tenths of all nurses in China were Christians. In line with this is the testimony of a non-Christian foreign news-paper correspondent with opportunities for wide observation that Christianity had produced a special type of human being in China,

[6] E. R. Hughes, *The Invasion of China by the Western World*, p. 92.

more alert, more modern, and more committed to the public welfare.[7] It is a matter of record that most of the moral and social reforms of the last one hundred years can be traced, either directly or indirectly, to the influence of Christian missions.

Protestant missions suffered a major setback during the Sino-Japanese War of 1937–1945. Church and mission work was disrupted and property damage was extensive. By opening their compounds and even their homes to refugees, the missionaries were able to save tens of thousands of Chinese women and girls from the lust and atrocities of the Japanese soldiery. After Pearl Harbor the missionaries in occupied China were placed in concentration camps. Those in Free China tried to keep one jump ahead of the advancing Japanese armies until ultimately about three-quarters of the country was evacuated.

Immediately after the war the missionaries returned to begin the work of rehabilitation. They were barely back on their stations when the Red armies from the north pushed south, crossed the Yangtze River and overran the whole of continental China. The People's Democratic Republic of China was established in Peking on October 1, 1949. Almost to a man the 4,062 Protestant missionaries in China at that time elected to stay on, hoping that some kind of *modus vivendi* could be found whereby they might be able to carry on a modified form of Christian witness. Alas! All such hopes proved to be vain.

While paying lip service to the concept of freedom of religion, the Chinese Communists made it quite clear that they regarded religion as "the opiate of the people" and missionaries as the spearhead of a "cultural aggression" against China. They verily believed that the missionaries were wolves in sheep's clothing, unscrupulous, treacherous, and dangerous, and accused them of being political agents working hand-in-hand with their respective governments, all the while using religion and philanthropy as a cloak for their real intentions—intrigue and espionage. In spite of the accusations made against them and the many restrictions placed on their work and movements, they remained at their posts until their presence became a source of embarrassment, to say nothing of danger, to their Chinese colleagues. When that stage was reached there was nothing for them to do but to withdraw quietly from the China scene, hoping that the Church would then be better able to cope with the pressures and problems created by the totalitarian regime.

[7] George E. Sokolsky, *The Tinder Box of Asia* (New York: Doubleday, Doran, 1932), pp. 21–22.

Accordingly, in the early part of 1951 a general and progressive evacuation got under way. By 1953 only a handful of Protestant missionaries were left in China and they were either in prison or under house arrest. As a result of the Geneva Conference of 1955 these remaining missionaries were released one by one and permitted to leave the country. The last Protestant missionary to leave China was Miss Helen Willis of the Plymouth Brethren. She left in April, 1959. That some 4,000 missionaries from all parts of the country should have finally made good their escape from Communist China, with only half a dozen casualties, is a miracle of God's care and protection. When one remembers the nature of the charges made against them, the ruthlessness of the Communist cadres, the age and infirmity of the older missionaries, and the gravity of the international situation at the time, it is a wonder that so many of them got out alive.

THE CHURCH UNDER COMMUNISM. The Constitution of Red China guarantees religious liberty. The Christian Church, therefore, has not gone underground. It continues to function as a recognized legal body, but its work and witness have been severely curtailed. There has been no open, organized persecution of the Church. The Communist government prefers to control it rather than to obliterate it. In this way it avoids making martyrs, and at the same time it can use the influence of the Church and its leaders to promote the cause of socialism.

When the Communists first came to power there was a period of uncertainty which witnessed a considerable falling away of church members. After a year or two some of the less timid believers returned to the fold. From time to time the government has carried out purges on one pretext or another, and these have not been without their effect on the Church.

While the Church as such has not been forced to close its doors, not a few of its strongest leaders have been liquidated by the Communists, usually on trumped-up charges having a moral or political complexion. Others have been brainwashed, after which they are of little use to either the Church or the State. Mission schools were incorporated into the public school system and the colleges and universities, some 13 in all, passed into government hands. The 300 mission hospitals were taken over by the Department of Health. The government has permitted the churches to retain possession of all mission property formerly used for church purposes including, in many instances, missionary residences. The churches are free to rent to outside organizations all surplus buildings and to use the proceeds to subsidize their programs. Without this concession it is doubtful whether the paid ministry of the Protestant churches could have been maintained.

Christian literature is produced in Shanghai and sent through the mail to churches in all parts of China. The Bible House continues to operate, mostly on stocks left over from pre-Liberation days. *Tien Feng,* the most influential church magazine, continues publication every fortnight. While it contains some church news and religious articles of real value, it is plainly a propaganda medium whereby government directives and the Communist party line are communicated to the Christian community in a subtle and effective form. Four theological schools are functioning, one each in Peking, Nanking, Canton, and Chungking. The People's Communes introduced in the summer of 1958 have gravely affected the work of the Church. Shanghai's 120 churches have been reduced to about 20, and only 4 remain in the city of Tientsin. Pastors and evangelists of the closed churches have been sent into productive work on farms and in factories. Rural churches have been especially hard hit and many of them have ceased to exist. But God has not left Himself without a witness, nor has Jesus Christ forsaken His Church. He who is able to make the wrath of man to praise Him is working all things after the council of His own will, and He will yet perfect that which concerns His people. The Church may be smaller, but it is stronger. Much of the deadwood has been swept away and what remains is built on a sure foundation. The Christians may be less vocal, but they are not less virile than they were in better days.

It should be stated that the Church in China is not a persecuted Church, at least not in the accepted sense of that term. Rather is it a controlled Church, and the instrument used for this purpose is the Three-Self Patriotic Movement which is organized on the national, provincial, and local levels. The leaders of the Movement are all church personnel, most of whom were ardent leftists even before "Liberation." Chairman of the Movement, *Dr. Wu Yao-tsung,* is the most powerful Protestant leader in China. The method of control is both simple and effective. The Religious Affairs Bureau of the government passes on to the Patriotic Movement the directives and "suggestions" of the Party, and the Movement conveys these to the churches at all levels. All churches and church leaders are expected to join the Three-Self Patriotic Movement. This is the price of survival. Deviationism in this matter is not tolerated. Those who have refused to join have been brainwashed, liquidated, or purged as rightists.

TAIWAN

Area: 13,900 sq. mi.   Population: 9,200,000
Capital: Taipei   Religion: Buddhism

THE LAND. Formosa, meaning "beautiful," is the name that was given
by the Portuguese to a cucumber-shaped island lying about 90 miles
off the east coast of China. It is 250 miles from north to south
and about 60 miles wide. A mountain range running the entire
length of the island, with peaks reaching to 12,000 feet, forms
the main topographical feature of the country. The Chinese name
of the island is Taiwan, meaning "terraced bay." A plentiful rainfall ensures luxuriant crops sufficient for domestic consumption
with something left over for exporting. The climate is hot and
very humid most of the year.

POLITICAL HISTORY. Formosa was returned to China at the close of
World War II after being in Japanese hands for exactly 50 years.
When the Chinese Communists overran the mainland in 1950
Generalissimo Chiang Kai-shek transferred the Nationalist government and the remnants of his once mighty army to Formosa, where
they have remained ever since. The Communists have many times
declared their intention of "liberating" Formosa, and doubtless
would have done so had it not been for the presence of the
United States Seventh Fleet in the Formosa Strait. Formosa is all
that remains of Nationalist China. With strong and stubborn American support it has been able to cling to its tenuous position in the
United Nations, including its permanent seat on the Security
Council, which grew out of its wartime status as one of the "Big
Five." Both the Generalissimo and Madame Chiang are practising
Christians, as are also other members of the central government.
There is complete freedom of religion, and missionary work has
been greatly accelerated since the war.

THE PEOPLE. There are four distinct groups on Formosa. (1) *The
Aborigines.* Altogether there are nine different hill tribes with a
total population of 150,000. Four of these tribes are fairly large: Amis
(45,000), Paiwans (40,000), Taiyals (33,000), and Bununs (20,000).
The origin of these tribes is obscure. Two or three of them may be
Malayan; others, more fair-skinned, are Polynesian. They live in the
mountain areas and are to be found in all parts of the island
except the western coastal plain. (2) *The Hakkas.* These people,

700,000 strong, came originally from South Fukien and North Kwangtung on the mainland. They are located in the foothills in south and central Formosa. They speak Hakka, which is similar to Cantonese. (3) *The Taiwanese.* With 6,000,000 people, the Taiwanese form the main section of the population and are the backbone of the island's life and economy. They inhabit the fertile plain along the west coast. They migrated in the seventeenth century from the Amoy district of Fukien and speak the Amoy dialect. (4) *The Mainlanders.* These are the Chinese who fled the mainland with the Nationalist government in 1949–50. Reliable estimates place their number at approximately 2,000,000. This includes the 400,000 soldiers who came with the army. These people represented for the most part the wealthy, educated elite who preferred exile to "liberation." They speak Mandarin, the national language of China, which is now the official language of Formosa.

THE RELIGION. Buddhism is the religion of Formosa and it has a very strong hold on the people. There are some 4,000 Buddhist temples on the island, most of them kept in good repair. The hill tribes are animists.

EARLY MISSIONS. From 1865 to 1950 the Presbyterians were the only denomination in Formosa. The *English Presbyterians* were the first to enter the field. Their work in the south of the island began in 1865, and by the end of the first decade they had 22 churches with 1,000 members. The *Canadian Presbyterians* began their work in the north in 1872. After ten years they could report 20 organized churches.

The career of the Canadian missionary, *George Leslie Mackay,* who was known as the "Black-bearded Barbarian," constitutes one of the most thrilling narratives in modern missions. With a fearless faith in God he faced all sorts of dangers and difficulties in the early years of his labors, including repeated attempts on his life. Overcoming hatred and hostility he gradually won over his worst enemies, endeared himself to the people by his sacrificial devotion to their physical and spiritual needs, and lived to see a large work firmly established in 60 stations, which included schools, a hospital, and *Oxford College* for the training of Christian workers. Dr. Mackay married a Chinese woman. He was among the strongest advocates of a self-supporting and self-propagating Church.

In 1885, after twenty years of labor, there were 29 national workers in the Church of South Formosa. In the following year this Church began its own outreach by opening three stations in the

Pescadores. During the first decade of Japanese occupation (1895–1905) church membership doubled. Significantly enough, the greatest gains in Formosa coincided with periods of stress and strain during the two World Wars.

The first presbytery was organized in the south in 1896, and in the north in 1904. In 1912 these presbyteries united to form one synod for the whole island. The General Assembly was constituted in March, 1951, and that same year the Church joined the *World Presbyterian Alliance*. The following year it became a member of the World Council of Churches. Church and Mission are now completely integrated and the missionaries are fraternal workers under the Church. According to the latest annual report (1957) the Presbyterian Church of Formosa now has 183 organized churches, 426 chapels, and 43,700 members.[8]

POSTWAR DEVELOPMENTS. Two of these call for special mention: the mighty moving of the Spirit of God among the hitherto unreached mountain tribes, referred to as "Pentecost in the Hills," and the large influx of new missions.

Owing to Japanese opposition no work was attempted among the wild mountain tribes prior to World War II. During the war a remarkable work was begun by a Taiyal tribeswoman, Chi-oang by name, who had previously received some Christian instruction at the Presbyterian Bible School in Tamsui back in 1930 when she was fifty-eight years of age! After the war the missionaries returned to find a Christian community of 4,000 Taiyals, meeting in 12 churches which they themselves had built! From the Taiyals the work spread to the Amis, Bununs, Paiwans, and Yamis. Since the close of the war more than 160 churches have been built with their own hands and at their own expense. Baptized church members increased from 3,000 in 1953, to 16,400 in 1956. Incorporated into the Presbyterian Church in Formosa, these tribal churches now have their own elders and deacons. More than 100 leaders have being trained in the Bible school in Hwalien. Bible translation is going forward in Paiwan, Taiyal, and other tribal tongues. Two dialects, Ami and Bunun, now have at least one whole New Testament book.

The other postwar development was the influx of new missions, mostly from the United States. With the closing of the China mainland many missions transferred some of their personnel to Formosa. In contrast to prewar days, when there were only two

---

[8] Missionary Research Library, *Protestant Churches of Asia, the Middle East, Africa, Latin America, and the Pacific Area* (1959), p. 68.

missions in Formosa, in 1956 there were 63 missionary societies and 11 other groups (agencies) with overseas connections. Sixteen of these had fewer than ten workers in Formosa. The vast majority of the new missionaries speak only Mandarin; consequently, they can make little contribution to the evangelization of the 6,000,000 Taiwanese who constitute the largest segment of the population. Eighty per cent of the 480 missionaries now on the island are from the United States.

New missions in the postwar period include: *Assemblies of God, Oriental Missionary Society, Overseas Missionary Fellowship* (China Inland Mission), *Southern Baptist, Conservative Baptist, Free Methodist, Mennonite,* and half a dozen *Lutheran* missions.

INTERCHURCH CO-OPERATION. Six different missionary societies are co-operating with the Presbyterian Church of Formosa. The Lutherans have achieved a notable union in the *Taiwan Lutheran Mission,* composed of seven participating missions. There is no National Christian Council. A degree of inter-mission co-operation is brought about by the *Taiwan Missionary Fellowship,* which sponsors an annual missionary conference.

INDIGENOUS MOVEMENTS. No account of Christian work in Formosa would be complete without mention of two indigenous Churches with considerable numerical strength. The *Little Flock,* with a membership estimated at 20,000, originated on the mainland and has only recently spread to Formosa. It has a good deal in common with the Plymouth Brethren though in no way affiliated with them. The *True Jesus Church* is a Pentecostal group founded in 1926 by a former Presbyterian Taiwanese. This church now numbers 16,000, including 8,500 tribal members.

EDUCATION. For its size Formosa is fairly well supplied with educational facilities. There are two Christian universities, the *Tunghai University* (Union) in Taichung and *Soochow University* (Methodist) in Taipei. In addition there are two colleges, one junior college, and three middle schools. Five seminaries and seven Bible schools furnish pastors and evangelists for the churches.

MEDICAL WORK. The Presbyterians have two hospitals and the Happy Mount Leprosarium. The Seventh Day Adventists and the Mennonites each maintain a hospital. There are ten clinics, five of them in tribal territory.

OTHER WORK. Radio has been more widely used in Formosa than in any other country on the mission field. Taking a leading role in this new field of endeavor is *The Evangelical Alliance Mission* which is devoting a good deal of time and thought to this work. At present they have 147 programs each week over 15 commercial stations in the seven leading cities. Four languages are used: Mandarin, Taiwanese, Hakka, and Russian.

The *Orient Crusades* Bible correspondence course had by 1957 enrolled 210,418 students. The *Pocket Testament League* distributed over a million Gospels of John, many of them among the servicemen. The Protestant community in Formosa now numbers approximately 150,000.[9]

JAPAN

Area: 143,000 sq. mi.
Capital: Tokyo

Population: 92,000,000
Religion: Shinto
            Buddhism

THE LAND. Japan, or Nippon, otherwise known as the Land of the Rising Sun, consists of four main islands, Honshu, Kyushu, Shikoku, and Hokkaido, which lie off the northeast coast of Asia. Its nearest neighbors are Korea and Russia. These islands form a chain over 2,000 miles long, but averaging only 100 miles in width. If placed on the east coast of the United States they would extend from Maine to Cuba with Tokyo, the capital, lying off Cape Hatteras. Japan is of volcanic origin and very mountainous. Peerless Fuji, the highest volcano, rises 12,365 feet above sea level. It is the pride of the nation and the subject of its poetry, legend, and art.

POLITICAL HISTORY. According to Japanese mythology both the land and the people are of divine origin. The first emperor, Jimmu Tenno, was founder of the present dynasty. He is reputed to have lived about 660 B.C.; but it is now conceded that all records prior to A.D. 461 are unreliable and that genuine history begins only from that date. Civilization entered Japan from China via Korea about the middle of the sixth century of the Christian era. For almost 700 years—from 1190 to 1868—it was ruled by the Shogunate. Japan's first contact with the West came when the Portuguese landed there in 1543. Later on the Portuguese were driven out and complete isolation enveloped the country for 230 years, until it was forced to open its doors to foreign commerce by Commodore

[9] Missionary Research Library, *loc. cit.*

Perry of the United States in 1853. With the Meiji Restoration in 1868 Japan forever abandoned its isolation and decided to pattern all of its institutions, military, educational, and political, after the West. In 1889 it became a constitutional monarchy. It defeated China in 1895 and ten years later wiped the Russian navy off the Pacific, thus becoming a first-rate world power. Japanese lust for power led it from one conquest to another. In 1931 it seized Manchuria. Six years later it invaded China. On December 7, 1941, it bombed Pearl Harbor and within a matter of months had chased the white man out of the Far East; the Japanese flag could be seen everywhere, from Sakkalin to Singapore. Its victories, however, were short-lived. When at the close of World War II Japan was stripped of all its overseas possessions it lost 44 per cent of its territory. Today its 92,000,000 people must live in an area about the size of California, and only one-fifth of it is arable.

THE PEOPLE. The origin of the Japanese people is shrouded in mystery. Their own historians acknowledge this, at the same time stating that undoubtedly some of their ancestors came from northern Asia, others from Korea, and still others from Malaysia. "They are, at any rate, a mixed race, as anyone can see from their different facial types. Some are flat-faced and heavily bearded; others are oval-faced with high brows, more prominent noses, and with scanty beards."[10] In the northern island of Hokkaido live the Ainu, survivors of an ancient and aboriginal race, now reduced to 18,000 in number. They are evidently distinct from the Japanese and are thought by some to be a fragment of the Aryan race. The Japanese possess not a few attractive traits. They are clean and neat in person and habits, esthetic in their tastes, quick-witted and apt to learn, so polite that they have been dubbed "the Frenchmen of the Orient" and enterprising and ambitious to a degree. Two of their outstanding characteristics are filial piety and national patriotism. Soldier and statesman alike will commit hara-kiri rather than bring disgrace on emperor or country.

THE RELIGION. The oldest and indigenous religion is Shinto, "The Way of the Gods," evidence of which is still everywhere to be seen in the shrines and the artistic torii or gateways to the shrines. Shinto was a system of ancestral and nature worship which no doubt exercised some moral influence in the early history of the people. But it developed a grotesque pantheon of 8,000,000 gods and

[10] J. H. De Forest, Sunrise in the Sunrise Kingdom (New York: Eaton and Mains, 1904), p. 40.

goddesses and bred all sorts of degrading superstitions and licen-
tious rites. Until recently there were two schools of Shinto, State
Shinto and Sect Shinto. Sect Shinto included some 20,000,000 devotees. State Shinto, in theory at least, embraced all Japanese and
included obligatory emperor worship at Shinto shrines throughout
the country. Part of the democratization of Japan after World War
II was the separation of Church and State, as a result of which
State Shinto was disestablished on December 12, 1945. A second
blow was dealt to State Shinto when Emperor Hirohito on January
1, 1946, issued an Imperial Rescript in which he renounced his
claim to divinity. Since the signing of the peace treaty in 1953
nationalism has been showing signs of resurgence, and there are
reports that the populace as well as government officials are once
again visiting Shinto shrines. There is no indication that Shinto is
on the wane; the 115,000 shrines which dot the landscape continue
to enjoy the prosperity characteristic of the national economy. The
proposed nationalization of the huge Yasukumi Shrine, sacred to
the war dead; coercive methods used by Shinto organizations to
raise funds for community shrines; the effort to revive the observance of "Kigensetsu," the anniversary of the founding of the Japanese Empire by the mythological Emperor Jimmu Tenno—these and
other trends indicate that Shintoistic nationalism is far from dead.

Buddhism was introduced from China by way of Korea in A.D.
552. It was several centuries in fighting its way to acceptance, and
in doing so it did not scruple to compromise its original moral and
ethical standards, and underwent such tremendous evolution of
doctrine that Japanese Buddhism has been regarded by Buddhists
of continental Asia as heretical. But it met the longing for light
on the great questions of the origin and destiny of life, upon which
the national cult was silent, and finally it took complete possession
of the field. Buddhism has exerted a powerful influence in Japan,
and it still has great life and power. It boasts 88,000 temples,
many of them of imposing style and proportions, and it is today
naïvely copying Christian methods of work such as schools, Sunday
preaching, Young Men's Associations, and the like.

Buddhism is on the march in Japan as in other parts of the
Far East. An estimated 1,200,000 persons participated in the
Oeshiki festival at Honmoji Temple in Tokyo on October 12 and
13, 1958, to commemorate the 677th anniversary of the death of
Saint Nichiren, the founder of Nichiren Buddhism. Japanese scholars
have taken special interest in the revision of the Buddhist Scriptures. Through the writings of Suzuki and others Zen Buddhism is
attracting the attention of scholars in all parts of the world,

especially the United States of America. In 1957 the first American was ordained to the Buddhist priesthood in Japan, and a wealthy widow has established an institute for the study of Zen Buddhism.

EARLY ROMANIST EFFORTS. The first contact with Japan by Europeans was probably in 1542, when Mendez Pinto, a Portuguese navigator, following in the track of Vasco da Gama, reached the islands. Other adventurers followed and were well received, and with them came the Jesuits and the first introduction of Christianity.

To *Francis Xavier,* the great Jesuit, belongs the honor of being the first missionary to Japan. The story has already been told of his meeting with a Japanese refugee named Hanjiro in Malacca, his landing in Japan in 1549, and his subsequent labors there. Xavier himself remained in Japan only two and a half years, and never fully mastered the Japanese or any other foreign tongue. Yet his earnest efforts were wonderfully blessed, and his example inspired scores of other Jesuits to follow him to Japan.

The chaotic political conditions prevailing at the time, together with a decadent Shintoism and a degenerate Buddhism, created a most favorable opportunity for the new propaganda, which bore rapid and abundant fruit. By 1581 there were 200 churches and 150,000 professed Christians. The converts represented all classes, including Buddhist priests, scholars, and noblemen as well as the common people. Two Daimios embraced Christianity and ordered their subjects to take the same step or go into exile. Even Nobunaga, the Minister of the Mikado, who hated the Buddhists, gave the new movement his powerful support, though apparently only for political reasons. So loyal to the Church were the native converts that they sent an embassy of four young nobles to Rome to pay their respects to the Pope. This embassy was received with high honors, and on its return brought seventeen more Jesuit fathers. The new religion grew apace, its leaders and supporters showing no scruples against the use of coercion and persecution to effect converts. Accessions to the Church are said to have reached 600,000 and even a million in number.

Those were palmy days indeed, and high hopes were entertained that Japan would become wholly Christian. But suddenly dark clouds began to gather on the horizon. Nobunaga, the protector of the Christians, was assassinated, and his successors, Hideyoshi and Iyeyasu, two of Japan's greatest men, were turned against Christianity by the fear that the foreign priests had political designs. Nor were their fears entirely groundless, for one of the weaknesses of Roman Catholicism has always been to become entangled in politics, and its emissaries in Japan were no exception to the rule. Added to this, dissensions arose between the Portuguese Jesuits and the Spanish Dominicans and Franciscans, who had come in large numbers from the Philippines, and methods and practices altogether unworthy of true Christianity contributed to bring about disaster to the cause.

PERSECUTION OF CHRISTIANS. Systematic persecutions began, culminating in the famous edicts of 1606 and 1614, which prohibited Christianity and aimed at utterly exterminating it from the realm. Foreign priests and friars were banished and sentence of death was pronounced upon every convert who refused to renounce his faith. The persecutions which followed were of the most horrible kind. Christians were burned, crucified, buried alive, subjected to every form of torture that barbaric cruelty could devise. Their heroic fortitude in bearing suffering and calmly facing martyrdom is said by Dr. William E. Griffis, that eminent authority on Japan and Korea, to have equaled that of the martyrs of bloody Roman arenas in the early Christian centuries.

Finally, in 1638, some 37,000 native Christians, driven to desperation, seized and fortified the old castle of Shimabara and made a brave stand for their lives. A veteran army was sent against them, and after four months the castle was taken and all were slaughtered. Further resistance was futile, and the sword, fire, and banishment did their work so completely that it appeared as if every trace of Christianity was swept away. Yet Christians remained, worship was carried on in secret and 230 years later when the country was re-opened whole villages of professed Christians were found who had retained the faith, albeit in a corrupt form.

The only means of communication with the outside world during this long period of exclusion was through a small colony of Dutch traders, who were allowed to remain under strict surveillance on the tiny island of Desima in Nagasaki harbor. Ships were permitted to visit them occasionally, but Bibles and Christian books were rigidly prohibited. Yet it was an object lesson of another civilization which was not without effect upon the Japanese mind and helped to prepare the way for the open door.

FIRST PROTESTANT CONTACTS. In the summer of 1837 the American ship, *Morrison*, sailed from Macao into Yedo Bay. The purpose of the voyage was to return seven Japanese shipwrecked sailors to their homeland, and through this humanitarian gesture to effect, if possible, friendly commercial relations between the United States and Japan. On board ship were three missionaries: *Karl Gutzlaff,* official interpreter of the British government in China; *Peter Parker,* medical missionary of the *American Board of Commissioners;* and S. *Wells Williams,* of the same Board and stationed at Macao. The *Morrison* attempted a landing on Kyushu but was fired on by the powerful Satsuma Clan and returned to Macao without accomplishing its mission. Gutzlaff had already translated John's Gospel and First Epistle into Japanese. They had been printed on the American Mission Press in Singapore in May, 1837, but it was just too late for the precious cargo to go on the *Morrison.*

THE DOOR REOPENED. The steady increase of trade on the Pacific, the cruel treatment of foreign sailors and fishermen from time to time stranded on the Japanese coast, the danger attending well-meaning efforts to return shipwrecked Japanese to their own land —these and other considerations called more and more insistently for the opening of Japan, and it was the United States which took the first definite steps to effect this end.

A fleet of four warships was despatched under *Commodore Perry,* and on July 8, 1853, dropped anchor in Yedo Bay, and an interview with the government was demanded. After a lot of parleying, an official of high rank was sent out and received from the Commodore a letter from the President of the United States addressed to the Emperor of Japan. Perry thereupon sailed away, but returned eight months later with a larger squadron to effect under pressure the signing of a treaty on March 31, 1854, by which the two ports of Shimoda and Hakodate were opened to American trade. Other nations were quick to claim similar advantages, but met with strong opposition. In 1858 *Townsend Harris,* representing the United States, negotiated a new and more liberal treaty, as did also Lord Elgin for Great Britain a few weeks later. These treaties secured for the first time the right of citizens of the nations concerned to reside in certain Japanese ports, and thus reopened the long closed door to missionaries as well as merchants.

It was some time, however, before these rights were enjoyed with safety. Intense antiforeign feeling prevailed, and a succession of outrages upon foreign residents extended over several years. Severe reprisals were carried out by British and Allied fleets in the form of bombardments of two Japanese ports. These actions not only made a lively impression upon the Japanese, but led to friction among the powerful rival clans and factions, and finally to the overthrow of the Shogunate and the restoration of sovereign power to the Mikado, or Emperor, in 1868. The Emperor himself ratified the foreign treaties, the seclusion of centuries was over, and Japan emerged into a new national day.

THE PROTESTANT VANGUARD. The Church at home had been eagerly watching for the door to open, and was not slow to enter it. Indeed, the advance guard had already been partially prepared for the task by service in the neighboring land of China. The first missionary to arrive was *Rev. J. Liggins* of the *Protestant Episcopal Church* of America, on May 2, 1859, two months before the time stipulated by the treaties. One month later he was joined by *Rev. C. M. Williams* (afterwards Bishop) of the same Church. In October, *J. C. Hepburn*, M.D., and wife, of the *American Presbyterian Board*, landed; in November, *Rev. S. R. Brown* and *D. B. Simmons*, M.D., of the *Reformed Church of America;* and only a week later *Rev. Guido F. Verbeck*, also of that Church. Early in 1860, *Rev. J. Goble*, who had been with Perry's expedition, arrived under the *American Baptist Free Missionary Society*. Thus, within four months from the opening of the treaty ports to foreign residents, seven American missionaries were on the ground, and within a year four American societies had begun work.

An interval of nine years elapsed before other organizations added their forces. The *Church Missionary Society* of England and the *American Board* both sent their first missionaries to Japan in 1869.

The *Woman's Union Missionary Society* opened the *Doremus School for Girls* in Yokohama in 1871, the first school of its kind in Japan. *Nathan Brown* of the *American Baptist Convention* began work in 1872. The *Society for the Propagation of the Gospel* and the *American Methodist Episcopal Church* entered in 1873.

The first Missionary Conference was held September 20 to 25, 1872, in Yokohama. The three problems before the Conference were the organization of Japanese churches along non-denominational lines, theological education, and Bible translation. The first theological school, really only a class, was opened by *Rev. S. R. Brown* in Yokohama. In that first class were men of outstanding ability who later became leaders of the Japanese Church. In 1877 three theological schools united to form the *Union Theological Seminary* in Tokyo. As for Bible translation, the New Testament was completed in 1874 and published in 1879. The Old Testament was completed in 1887. A completely new revision called the Kogotai Bible came out in 1955.

NOBLE PIONEERS. "It was a noble band of men, exceptional even among those whose names have become famous in missionary annals. Not one but has left his stamp upon new Japan. Of great intellectual ability, they were gifted with marvelous tact in dealing with a people that had for half a century been an enigma to the Occidental. Patient, persevering, seeking the best in those with whom they came in contact, they won a personal place such as it has seldom been the fortune of missionaries to win in the first years of their life in a new land."[11] Only meager mention can here be made of the three most outstanding figures of this early group.

Dr. James C. Hepburn was a typical pioneer and medical missionary, who had seen service in Singapore and China before entering Japan in 1859. His medical skill and success, coupled with a gentle and tactful manner, did much to dispel prejudice against Christianity and to win the confidence and esteem of multitudes during his thirty-three years of unremitting labor for Japan. In addition to being a medical missionary he was an educator of the first rank, whose services the Japanese government tried in vain to secure at high prices. But his even greater distinction was as a translator. He prepared a Japanese-English Dictionary and a Bible Dictionary in Japanese, and was the chief translator of the Holy Scriptures among a small group of able men, including Doctors Brown and Verbeck.

"No more sublime hour has been reached in the history of this awakening people than when, after nearly thirty years of patient toil, he [Hepburn] formally presented the Japanese Bible to the nation. Before a great audience, he lifted up the five superb volumes and formally presented to the Sunrise Kingdom the complete Word of God in the tongue of Japan."[12] "Taking in one hand the New Testament and in the other the Old, he said: 'A complete Bible! What more precious gift—more precious than mountains of silver and gold—could the Christian nations of the West offer to this nation! May this sacred Book become to the Japanese what it has come to be for the people of the West—a source of life, a messenger of joy and peace, the foundation of a true civilization, and of social and political prosperity and greatness.' "[13]

Dr. Samuel R. Brown, of the Dutch Reformed Church, left a deep and lasting mark upon the Japanese nation as the pioneer of missionary education. He opened at Yokohama the first English

[11] E. M. Bliss, *The Missionary Enterprise* (New York: Revell, 1908), p. 299.

[12] Arthur T. Pierson, *The New Acts of the Apostles* (New York: Baker and Taylor, 1894), p. 339.

[13] Arthur T. Pierson, *The Modern Missionary Century* (New York: Baker and Taylor, 1901), p. 116.

school in Japan, and won great influence by his rare gifts and abilities as well as the deep love which he showed for the people. He insisted upon the Bible as the secret and center of the progress of England and America, aroused enthusiasm in the young men of Japan for Western learning and ways, and it was largely due to his influence that the government decided to send the first Japanese students to study in England and America. Dr. Griffis, the biographer of Dr. Brown, calls him "A Maker of the New Orient," and bears testimony that "in this twentieth century Japanese college presidents, editors, pastors, translators, authors, statesmen, men of affairs, and leaders in commerce and literature by the score are 'images of his own life,' while in other countries hundreds gladly acknowledged the inspiration gained under him as their teacher."

Dr. Guido F. Verbeck, the remaining member of this famous triumvirate of early leaders in Japan, became the most distinguished of all, and his influence even outran that of the other two as a molder of New Japan. A rare linguist, he acquired the Japanese vernacular so perfectly that he could not be detected as a foreigner, and charmed his audiences by his fluent speech. In him was combined a great variety of eminent gifts in a degree that is most unusual. He was at once educator and evangelist, orator and translator, brilliant statesman and humble personal worker. In 1868, after the Revolution in Japan, he was invited to take a leading part in organizing the great Imperial University at Tokyo and planning a new system of national education. It was largely under his influence and guidance that in 1871 an Imperial Embassy was sent to visit Western countries, while in 1874 he was called into the service of the Senate to aid in framing a new Constitution for the Empire. "A man without a country," as he styled himself, having actually no rights of citizenship either in Holland, the land of his birth, or in the United States, where he had been educated, he was accorded by the Japanese government a "special passport" never granted to any other foreigner before or since, received the high decoration of "The Rising Sun," and at his death was given a state funeral.

Such are some of the men whom God raised up and used in the mighty task of laying the foundations of missions in this little but wonderful Land of the Rising Sun, a land destined to extend her influence all over the Orient.

EARLY DIFFICULTIES. It was in the face of difficulties neither few nor small that the early Protestant missionaries pursued their work. The political intrigues of the earlier Romanists had left a deep-seated hatred of Christianity. In every town and village the old anti-

Christian edicts of the period of exclusion were still posted publicly, and as late as 1868 an edict was issued which read thus: "The wicked sect called Christian is strictly prohibited. Suspected persons are to be reported to the respective officials, and rewards will be given." The missionaries were viewed with suspicion by the government, and with mingled hostility and fear by the people. Spies were constantly sent to watch them, and threatening letters were written them. Their earliest converts, and even some of those merely employed to teach them the language, were secretly arrested and thrown into prison. Twelve foreigners were killed in the one year of 1870. With the removal of the anti-Christian edicts in 1873 many more missionaries poured into the country. In 1884 new regulations secured larger religious toleration; but it was not until 1889 that all restrictions were removed and the missionaries were free to travel in all parts of the interior.

ENGLISH SCHOOLS. Owing to official opposition the missionary effort in the early years was confined largely to educational and medical work, chiefly the former. Among the enthusiastic young men who flocked to the English schools were not a few Samurai who later on became leaders in government and Church. The diary of one student read:

Many Samurai are studying language with the foreigners and many of the young men use the free time between lectures to listen to Ballagh speak of Christianity. Their young minds are deeply impressed by Ballagh's teaching, and this has been the motivation in forming a prayer meeting. Prayers come one after the other. . . . Some started to cry they were so deeply moved, and others began to shout although they never prayed before. It seemed to me that there was a great revival before my eyes.

THE THREE BANDS. Protestant Christianity in Japan developed along three distinct lines identified as the *Sapporo Band*, the *Yokohama Band*, and the *Kumamoto Band*. The Sapporo Band, under the leadership of *Dr. W. S. Clark*, represented Puritanism or orthodoxy; it was concerned with cultural relationships and stressed indigenous Christianity. The Yokohama Band included such stalwart leaders as *Hepburn, Ballagh, Verbeck, Samuel Brown*, and *Nathan Brown*. This group manifested a strong tendency to union. They represented Reformed Theology, emphasized educational work, and were characterized by social concern. The Kumamoto Band was headed by *Captain L. L. Janes*. It represented Congregationalism, was liberal in theology, and maintained an ethical emphasis.

One incident connected with the Kumamoto Band should be mentioned here since in the providence of God it was destined to bear vitally upon the whole subsequent spiritual history of the realm.

In 1872, *Captain L. L. Janes,* an American army officer from West Point, was engaged by a feudal prince of the southern island of Kyushu to found a military school in the interior city of Kumamoto. Although not a missionary, Captain Janes was an earnest Christian, filled with a strong desire to lead to Christ the hundred young men thus placed under his care. His wife was a daughter of the well-known Dr. Scudder, early missionary to India, and she supported her husband's efforts with much prayer.

Having won the love and loyalty of his pupils by his rare teaching gifts and attractive personality, Captain Janes by and by invited them to Bible readings in his home, and a little later to a preaching service on Sunday mornings. Before long a deep work of grace began in many hearts, and finally a revival swept through the school, and more than half of the students made a clean-cut decision for Christ. The climax came when one evening, early in 1876, forty students climbed a hill overlooking the city, and after prayer drew up and signed a "declaration" solemnly covenanting to renounce all worldly ambition and dedicate their lives to the high task of preaching the gospel throughout the Empire.

It is not surprising that this action met with loud protest and strong opposition, both in the school and among the relatives of the boys. Bitter persecution broke out, fathers threatening their sons with the death penalty, mothers threatening to commit suicide in order to atone for the disgrace brought by their offspring upon the family name. Some of the boys were imprisoned, others were banished from their homes, while a plot was laid, fortunately without success, to kill the whole company.

Captain Janes himself was forced out of the school, but not before he had providentially learned through an American newspaper that a Christian school had recently been opened by Neesima in Kyoto. Thereupon thirty members of this Kumamoto Band, driven from their homes and native province, made their way five hundred miles overland to Kyoto and, together with the handful of students already gathered there, formed the nucleus of the first Christian college in Japan, which was to grow into the great Doshisha University.

Joseph Hardy Neesima. It is fitting to introduce at this point some account of Neesima, that most illustrious of all Christian converts and native apostles of Japan, because of the relation which his career bears to the Kumamoto Band just mentioned. One would search far to find a more impressive illustration of the power and providence of God in human life than Neesima's history and its interlinking with that of this memorable Band.

Neesima's life story, as told by at least two biographers in full,[14] and by many other writers in brief, is one of peculiarly fascinating interest. He was born in Yedo in 1843, and as a mere boy he renounced idolatry. Later, a stray copy of an abridged Chinese Bible falling into his hands, he was struck with the opening words, "In the beginning, God created the heavens and the earth." His youthful mind reached out in a quest for the true God, and he prayed, "Oh, if you have eyes, look upon me; if you have ears, listen for me." He chanced also to catch a glimpse of an atlas of the United States, and filled with a great desire to see the Western world he contrived in 1864 to get to Hakodate and to smuggle himself on board an American schooner for Shanghai. Thence he worked his way to Boston, employing his spare time on the long voyage in studying English and reading a Chinese New Testament bought in Hong Kong. It was without doubt of God's ordering that the ship on which Neesima sailed was owned by the *Hon. Alpheus Hardy*, a prominent Christian man of Boston. Hearing from the ship's captain about the interesting Japanese runaway, Mr. Hardy befriended him, named him "Joseph Hardy," and gave him a good education at Amherst College and Andover Seminary.

In 1871 the Japanese embassy on its visit to America heard of Neesima and engaged him as interpreter. Here was another unmistakable mark of God's guiding hand, for the favor of these distinguished men secured for the young Christian a pardon for the "crime" of having left his own land without permission, enabled him to visit the best educational institutions in America and Europe, and won for him on his return to Japan the friendship and influence of some of the foremost governing leaders. Indeed, every effort was made to pursuade Neesima to enter government service, but no attraction of office or wealth could turn him aside from his God-given purpose to devote himself to gospel work. He became at once a bold and earnest witness among his people, and was the pioneer of public gospel preaching in the interior.

Neesima's great life work was the founding of the *Doshisha*, designed as a collegiate and theological school to train Christian workers for Japan. It was a daring scheme for him to choose as a

[14] J. D. Davis, *A Sketch of the Life of Rev. Joseph Hardy Neesima* (New York: Revell, 1894).

Arthur S. Hardy, *Life and Letters of Joseph Hardy Neesima* (Boston: Houghton Mifflin, 1892).

place for such a school the ancient capital and sacred city of Kyoto, with its 3,500 temples and 8,000 Buddhist priests, but, nothing daunted, he opened his school there in a small room in November, 1875, with eight pupils. When, in 1890, death overtook this great man of God in the midst of his active labors, the Doshisha had grown into a great and well-equipped institution of nearly 700 students. It gave the needed impulse to Christian education in Japan, and many among its thousands of graduates have held high places in their country's history.

GROWTH AND DEVELOPMENT. We are ever thus being reminded in missions that the gospel is a living seed of irresistible power. The records of missionary labor and results furnish the most glorious evidences of Christianity in all the world, and Japan has been no exception to the rule.

The first convert was baptized after five years (1864), the next two—one of them, Wakasa by name, being an official of high rank—two years later. The first Japanese church was organized at Yokohama on March 10, 1872, by *Rev. J. H. Ballagh* of the Reformed Church, with eleven members. The years from 1859 to 1872 have been called the *Period of Preparation*. Next came the *Period of Popularity*, from 1873 to 1888, during which Christianity grew steadily in favor. Old customs and ideas were rapidly giving way before the influence of the West, and the missionaries were much sought, not only for spiritual ends but as well because of the useful knowledge they possessed on many lines. It became easy to get large audiences to preach to, and Christian schools became crowded with pupils. There were large accessions to the Church, yet among them were undoubtedly not a few in whose hearts no real saving work of grace had been wrought, but who were mere intellectual converts, eager to recognize and embrace the external benefits of the Christian religion.

By 1888 this tide of favor had reached its height, and reaction now began to set in. This was due in part to the strenuous opposition of the Buddhists, who saw their power waning, and realizing the need of new tactics to save their cult from downfall, they began to imitate the methods of their Christian antagonists by opening schools and preaching halls, organizing young men's associations, women's prayer meetings, temperance societies, and the like. But a greater factor than Buddhism in bringing about reaction was the rise of strong nationalistic sentiment, fed by friction with foreign powers over the revision of treaties and other matters. Conservatives seized the opportunity to stir up antiforeign spirit under the guise of an appeal to national loyalty. This sentiment affected even Christians, causing free criticism of the missionaries, and leading on to the advocacy of a Japanese form of Christianity, a modification of certain doctrinal beliefs, and an "independent" church movement.

These influences, although for a time apparently checking the progress and diminishing the numbers of the Christian Church, were not without their real advantages. A sifting process took place by which nominal converts disappeared but real Christians remained, with their faith and convictions strengthened. The spiritual life of the Church was purified and deepened, and the Lord continued in His own way to "add to the church daily such as were being saved."

Statistics compiled in 1900, after four decades of missionary activity, showed "a total of 42,451 Protestant Christians, 538 churches, of which about 100 were self-supporting, and 348 groups of Christians not yet organized into churches."[15]

LOYALTY OF CHRISTIANS. For many years the notion that Christianity was something inherently "foreign" persisted in the Japanese public mind, and the loyalty of the Christians to their own nation was constantly called in question. Opposition to Christianity on this score manifested itself particularly in the schools, and Christian teachers and students were discriminated against in spite of the Constitution's plain declaration of religious liberty and equality.

The war with China in 1894–95 afforded an excellent opportunity to put such charges and imputations squarely to the test, and it was clearly demonstrated that Christian Japanese could fight no less bravely than their Buddhist compatriots. Later, in 1904–05, came the more serious war with Russia. "This was Christianity's opportunity. In the camps, at home, on the battlefield, Christian men were in the van. With a Christian admiral to lead her fleets, a Christian American missionary to lead in prayer to the God of battles, Christian women to care for wounded and sorrowing, it became evident that a Christian Japan might not be less Japanese than the old dreams of the *samurai*."[16] As a result, Christianity in Japan vindicated itself, and missionary work won new recognition and influence, numbering among its converts persons of high standing and even national distinction, and enjoying ever-increasing opportunities and returns right up to the present.

NATIONAL CHURCHES. The desire for church union has been strong

[15] De Forest, *op. cit.*, p. 116.
[16] Bliss, *op. cit.*, p. 311.

in Japan from the beginning. In 1877 three missions, the *Presbyterian Church in U.S.A.*, the *Presbyterian Church of Scotland* and the *Dutch Reformed Church*, united to form the *United Church of Christ in Japan*. In 1890 the word "united" was dropped. Thereafter the official name was the *Church of Christ in Japan*, or the "Nikki." In February, 1887, the *Church Missionary Society*, the *Society for the Propagation of the Gospel*, and the *Protestant Episcopal Church of America* united to form the *Japan Episcopal Church*. By 1894 the denominational organization was firmly rooted. The first Japanese bishops were appointed in 1923. Today the Anglican Church has ten dioceses all over Japan and is the second largest Church in the country.

The Methodist denomination took shape more slowly. The *Japan Methodist Church* resulted from a union in 1907 of three groups, the *Methodist Episcopal Church, North*, the *Methodist Church of Canada*, and the *Southern Methodist Episcopal Church*.

The *Holiness Church* developed rapidly during the late twenties and early thirties. In 1927 it had 165 churches; by 1932 the number had risen to 439, with 19,523 members and 428 ministers—a threefold increase in five years. The evangelistic work of this Church extended to Manchuria, Korea, China, Formosa, Singapore, the Celebes, and Brazil. In 1932 the Church divided; and following the war it split again, this time into six groups.

[In 1892 the United Lutheran Church began work at Saga on Kyushu. A second center was established in Kumamoto in 1898. Ten years later there were three missionary families and two single men on the field, and church membership stood at 300. By 1921 sixteen additional missionaries had come and the work was expanded in a dozen cities.] Ten new Lutheran Missions entered Japan after the war. Negotiations are now going on among eleven groups and the expectation is that one great Lutheran Church of Japan will emerge in the near future. The Lutherans are now the third largest denominational group in the country.

In 1903 *Barclay F. Buxton* and *Paget Wilkes*, both formerly in Japan under the Church Missionary Society, teamed up and formed the *Japan Evangelistic Band*. Through the years the Band has concentrated on village evangelism and Bible school work. Its leaders, with a "deeper life" ministry of the Keswick type, have had a wholesome influence far beyond their own Mission. The *Oriental Missionary Society*, founded by *Charles E. Cowman*, took up work in Japan in 1898. Associated with Cowman were *E. A. Kilbourne* and two Japanese brethren, *Sasao* and *Nakada*. The new Mission emphasized four truths: a new life, sanctification, divine healing, and the Second Coming of Christ.

During the fifteen-year period from 1912 to 1926, when the political climate of Japan was favorable to the spread of democratic ideas, Christianity made substantial progress. Through the influence of John R. Mott, who visited Japan in 1913, an all-Japan evangelistic campaign was launched during which 4,788 meetings were held. These were attended by 777,119 persons, of whom 27,350 registered their desire to learn more. About the same time the "Kingdom of God Movement" was inaugurated, its goal set at a million souls. The National Christian Council was formed in 1923. During this period church membership increased from 79,000 to 166,000, an increase of 110 per cent in 15 years.

This was followed by a period of stagnation during the years when militarism was rampant. From the Mukden Incident in 1931 to the end of World War II the churches were at a veritable standstill. The situation was further complicated by the passing in 1939 of the Religious Bodies Law which brought all religion under state control. According to this law all Christian churches were to be lumped together and treated as a mere "kyodan"—a religious association. In July of that year thirty *Salvation Army* leaders were arrested as spies. Four years later the Army was dissolved altogether. The same fate befell the *Seventh Day Adventists*. The *Anglican Church* disbanded and went underground. Three hundred pastors of the *Holiness Church* went to jail when they insisted that Jesus Christ would return to judge the world—including Japan. Towards the end of World War II the militarists organized the *Japan War-Time Religious-Patriotic Association*, which forced the Shintoists, the Buddhists, and the Christians into one body.

POSTWAR DEVELOPMENTS. During the immediate postwar period, from 1946 to 1950, Christian missions had a golden opportunity in Japan. The disestablishment of State Shinto, the denial of his deity by the Emperor, and the call of General Douglas MacArthur for more missionaries, together with the utter disillusionment of the Japanese people, presented the Christian Church with an unprecedented opportunity to win Japan for Jesus Christ. The younger generation, seeking in Christianity a foundation for national reconstruction, crowded into the churches to learn what the religion of the conquerors had to offer. It looked for a time as if Japan might become a Christian nation.

As soon as the Occupation Authorities gave them the green light Protestant missions, old and new, moved into Japan to fill the spiritual vacuum occasioned by the total collapse of militarism and the temporary eclipse of Shinto. All the old missions returned and began at once the colossal task of rehabilitation. Almost without exception these missions increased their personnel and greatly expanded their prewar programs. At the end of the war the *Southern Baptists* had 8 men in three stations; today they have 113 missionaries, 67 organized churches, and 95 preaching places. *The Evangelical Alliance Mission,* one of the smaller missions in prewar days, has grown by leaps and bounds to become the largest Protestant society in the country with well over 200 missionaries and an aggressive program of evangelism, Bible school work, radio broadcasting, and literature. With the coming of the ten new missions the *Lutherans* now have 295 missionaries, 181 Japanese ministers, 159 churches, and 10,869 baptized members.

Scores of new missions entered Japan for the first time after World War II. Some of these were newly organized missions, such as the *Far Eastern Gospel Crusade,* the *Conservative Baptist Foreign Mission Society, World Vision, Inc., Japan Evangelical Mission, Free Christian Mission,* etc. Still other missions, while new to Japan, were not new to the Orient. Many of them had had work in China, in some cases for many decades, and simply transferred their workers to Japan when the China field closed in 1950. Included in this category are the *Overseas Missionary Fellowship* (China Inland Mission), the *Advent Christian Mission, Liebenzeller Mission,* and others. Additional missions to enter Japan in recent years are the *Association of Baptists for World Evangelism, Baptist General Conference of America, Baptist Mid-Missions, Independent Board for Presbyterian Foreign Missions, New Tribes Mission, American Soul Clinic,* etc. Not all the new missions were from the United States. Some 15 or 20 European societies have entered Japan during this period, most of them coming from Norway and Sweden.

A glance at the *Japan Christian Yearbook* reveals the proliferation of missions and agencies in present-day Japan. The 1957 edition lists no fewer than 144. Many of these groups have little more than a skeleton staff on the field. Fifty-two of them have fewer than six workers, while another twenty-four have between six and ten workers each. Another striking feature is the large concentration of missionaries in the urban areas. Missionaries the world over have a tendency to settle down in the big cities with their large populations, to the neglect of the peasants in the rural districts. Nowhere is this tendency more marked than in Japan; in 1955 ten large cities accounted for 1,261 of the 1,427 missionaries then in the country. Tokyo headed the list with 655! This no doubt accounts for the fact that 90 per cent of the 3,000 organized Protestant churches are found in the cities. There are only 7,000 Christians in the whole of rural Japan.

NEW RELIGIONS. One of the most significant religious phenomena of the postwar period has been the resurgence of the indigenous religions. These religions originated in the unstable decades before Commodore Perry's visit in the 1850's. They were revived in the 1880's and thrived for a time until they were suppressed between the two World Wars. Since the second World War these religious sects have again come to the fore. Estimates of their number have run as high as 700, but this seems to be a greatly inflated figure; many have already ceased to exist. On January 1, 1958, according to one authority the new religions numbered 126.[17] They range all the way from the *Religious Sightseeing Organization* to *Tenrikyo*, which boasts its own capital city, university, and 2,000,000 adherents. None of their founders has had a university education, yet their leaders today, including many women, are energetic, magnetic personalities. Usually their power is derived from a state of trance when they are possessed by a spirit. They claim to have supernatural revelations, and appeal especially to peasants, workers, and the simple middle-class people. Their teaching is syncretistic rather than original. A Shinto-animistic basis is evident with many; others have originated from the nationalistic Nichiren Buddhism; and all are closely tied up with ancestor worship and Confucian ethics. Naturally, they stress their Japanese origin and character. They seek to meet the people on their own level and minister to their personal and social needs. They avoid theological jargon and employ plain talk. They organize discussion groups where family problems can be thrashed out; and they do a great deal of personal counselling. Their meetings are marked by an evangelistic atmosphere, with testimonies, faith healings, exorcism of demons, and other supernatural phenomena. Festivals and pilgrimages foster fellowship. Christianity no longer has a monopoly on such terms as "God," "faith," "love," and "salvation," all of which are borrowed unblushingly and used indiscriminately by practically all of the new religions.

THE UNITED CHURCH OF CHRIST IN JAPAN—KYODAN. In its original form the Kyodan was a political maneuver on the part of the Japanese government to organize one great Protestant Church

[17] *International Review of Missions* (July, 1959), p. 282.

which could be controlled more easily than dozens of smaller groups. The inaugural assembly took place in June, 1941. At first eleven blocs composed of 32 affiliating groups were organized, with each bloc retaining a measure of autonomy. At the second assembly in November, 1942, the bloc system was abolished and government control was rendered complete. Several denominations refused to co-operate and immediately became the objects of attack. Among the dissenters were the *Salvation Army*, the *Seventh Day Adventists*, the *Holiness Church*, and the *Episcopal Church*, all of which either were dissolved or went underground for the duration of the war.

With the abolition of the Religious Bodies Law in November, 1945, the churches were free to determine their own affiliations, either within or without the Kyodan. Some influential groups, such as the Anglicans, Lutherans, Southern Baptists, and the Salvation Army, elected to go their separate ways and to this day are not members of the Kyodan. But the Kyodan did not fall apart. Cleansed of the political contamination which attached to it as a war-time "religious party," its remaining church groups closed ranks and there emerged the *United Church of Christ in Japan.* It has three main elements: Presbyterian, Congregational, and Methodist. Post-war progress has been most gratifying and today the Kyodan is by far the largest and strongest Protestant group in Japan. According to the 1959 *Japan Christian Yearbook* it has 1,229 organized churches and 307 preaching centers. Ministers, ordained and un-ordained, number 2,168 and the total membership is 175,506. It is organized into 14 presbyteries; missionaries are welcomed as specialists in pioneer evangelism, social work, literature, audio-visual aids, and especially as teachers. At the present time there are 371 foreign missionaries serving in various capacities. Between 60 and 70 per cent of the churches are financially independent; the preaching places are almost wholly dependent. Central funds supply the means for pioneer projects and for building purposes when the initial costs are high. In 1952, 48.5 per cent of the total funds for the United Church were received from abroad. This had dropped to 39.2 per cent by 1956. Between 40 and 50 per cent of the churches and preaching places are the result of postwar work. Young people make up almost 70 per cent of the membership, and most of the members come from the middle-class urban population. A *Home Missions Society* was set up in 1953. The northern island of Hokkaido has figured largely in postwar effort; a five-year plan called for the establishment of 100 new churches there in preparation for the centennial year of 1959. In 1956 the General Assembly of the Kyodan created a *Board of Overseas Missions* to send missionaries to Southeast Asia and Brazil, where Japanese live in considerable numbers.

SCRIPTURE DISTRIBUTION. In 1949 General Douglas MacArthur appealed for 10,000,000 Scriptures for Japan. With characteristic efficiency the *Pocket Testament League,* under the leadership of *Glenn Wagner,* volunteered its services and in two short years completed the project. The *American Bible Society* contributed 2,500,000 copies of the Scriptures to the people of Japan, and the *Gideons* of Japan placed 300,000 Bibles in public places. The publication of the Colloquial Bible in 1955 was an epochal event in Japanese Christian history. Since that time the *Japan Bible House* has been pushing the distribution of the Scriptures through secular bookstores, a Bible van, and 40 full-time colporteurs. The National Library Association placed the new Bible on its list of recommended books, which goes to 3,000 libraries throughout the country, and the Mainichi Newspapers awarded a special prize to the Bible Society for the production of such a fine and accurate translation in modern Japanese. As a result Scripture distribution soared to an all-time high of 1,901,737 copies in 1958. The General Secretary in his 1958 Report writes: "The Bible is becoming the Book of the people. At least the attitude to the Bible as a foreign book is disappearing. The Bible has, moreover, been placed by the newspapers at the head of our classical literature."[18] One authority writes: "It would seem that almost every family in Japan has at least once possessed some Christian Scripture, and almost every individual has had access to a copy."[19] The Braille edition of the Colloquial Bible, in 32 volumes, appeared in August, 1956, and circulation in the first 18 months reached 8,786 copies. There are 140,000 blind persons in Japan, about 3,000 of whom are Christians.

MASS EVANGELISM. The spiritual bankruptcy of the Japanese people at the close of the war provided the Christian Church with a unique opportunity for mass evangelism on an unprecedented scale. Both the old-line denominations and the newer missions made a concerted effort to capitalize on the heart hunger of the defeated nation. The *Oriental Missionary Society* through its "Every Creature Crusade" has been going from one prefecture to another, holding tent meetings in a central city for four to six weeks and visiting, as far as possible, every home in every city, town, and village. Their

[18] *Worlds Apart,* p. 98.
[19] Charles W. Iglehart, *Cross and Crisis in Japan* (New York: Friendship Press, 1957), p. 61.

plan calls for the establishment of 200 self-supporting churches in five years. The *United Church of Christ* sponsors several evangelists-at-large. One of them, *Dr. William Axling,* a veteran Baptist missionary, reported over 16,000 first-time decisions and 12,000 rededications from his meetings. Sponsored by the National Christian Council, *Dr. E. Stanley Jones* has been conducting evangelistic campaigns in Japan every other year since 1949. The meetings attracted vast audiences in all parts of the country and tens of thousands registered their decision for Christ. On his third visit he preached in 72 cities in all four islands and non-Christians signed 27,000 decision cards. Beginning with 1954 the *Lacour Special Evangelism Crusade,* a Methodist-sponsored program, has visited Japan each summer for an intensive evangelistic campaign. The 1957 Crusade Team comprised 30 American preachers assisted by Japanese pastors and interpreters. Each summer the Crusade concentrates on a certain number of "centers" and aims to leave behind in each place the nucleus of a church which will in time become strong and self-supporting. The Crusade seeks to combine three main factors: preaching the gospel, cultivating the spiritual life of the converts, and organizing churches. Other noted evangelists, Japanese as well as Western, have conducted nationwide campaigns. Among them should be mentioned *Dr. Toyohiko Kagawa, Trevor Morris, Frederick R. Levett* (sponsored by *World Dominion*), *Bob Pierce* of *World Vision,* and others. *Youth for Christ International* held a World Congress on Evangelism in Tokyo in August, 1953. Delegates from 35 countries met with 1,000 missionaries and an equal number of Japanese colleagues. Following the Congress, 60 teams toured Japan for a two-week mission and reported 20,000 decisions. A small but enterprising group known as the *Navigators* specializes in follow-up work, giving the new converts much-needed instruction in dynamic Christian living based on Bible study, the memorizing of Scripture, and personal witnessing. Stanley Jones has described Japan as "the ripest evangelistic field in the world."

No greater mistake could be made than to conclude, as many have apparently done from a merely superficial acquaintance with Japan, and from foolishly placing a wrong estimate upon her adoption of so many advanced features of modern civilization, that this fair Sunrise Kingdom no longer needs the same missionary attention as other Eastern lands. Japan is a beautiful land, her people are clever and attractive, her education has been modernized, her commerce has expanded, her science and technology are advanced—in a word, she has been *civilized.* But Japan is still to be *Christianized.* After one hundred years of missionary effort the

Protestant Church numbers only about 375,000, or a little more than one-third of one per cent of the population!

MEDICAL MISSIONS. Compared with other mission fields little medical work has been attempted in Japan. The reason is that shortly after the Meiji Restoration in 1868 Japan wholeheartedly accepted Western civilization, including medical science; and through the years it has made great strides in this branch of humanitarian endeavor. Christian medical institutions, therefore, are few and far between in Japan. The *Anglican Church* has for many years maintained two hospitals, one in Tokyo and the other in Osaka. Postwar hospitals include a 100-bed hospital in Kyoto (*Southern Baptist*) and a 120-bed hospital in Osaka (*Southern Presbyterian*). The *Seventh Day Adventists* have enlarged their hospital and sanitarium in Tokyo. The *United Church* has a hospital near Yokosuka and the *Salvation Army* has reopened its hospital. Twenty or so clinics are operated by other missions. Japan has a fair share of Christian doctors, 400 of whom belong to the *National Christian Medical Association*. Many of these doctors have their own private hospitals in which a Christian witness is given.

EDUCATIONAL MISSIONS. Compulsory and universal education has long been a feature of modern Japan, with the result that Japan is one of the most literate countries in the world. This being the case there has been little need for Christian missions to enter the educational field. Consequently, it is not surprising to learn that there are only 12 mission schools on the elementary level. There are 65 junior high schools, 74 senior high schools, 34 junior colleges, 16 colleges, and 6 graduate schools. Total enrollment is around 133,000. Most of the high schools are for girls. The largest girls' school in Japan is the Southern Presbyterian school, *Kinjo Gakuin*, in Nagoya. It has over 5,000 students in six departments. The average percentage of baptized Christians in these schools is rarely more than 10 per cent—usually from 2 to 3 per cent in the freshman class and 5 to 10 per cent in the graduating class. Competent Christian teachers are difficult to obtain. On an average only six out of ten teachers are Christian. This greatly weakens the Christian testimony.

The outstanding postwar venture in higher education was the opening in 1953 of the *International Christian University* in Tokyo. Sponsored in 1948 by the Federal Council of the Churches of Christ in America and the Foreign Missions Conference of North America, it is now supported by 15 co-operating denominations in the United

States and Canada. They have raised the major share of the $6,000,-000 used to date in the establishment and maintenance of this united Protestant enterprise. Total enrollment in September, 1958, was 732; 42 per cent were women, the highest percentage of all co-educational colleges in the country. It was hoped that the university would attract many students from abroad and thus be truly international; but there are only 81 non-Japanese students, and 46 of these are Americans. Of the 160 faculty members, all but 30 are Japanese. Emil Brunner, the famous Swiss theologian, spent three years on the faculty and did not a little to enhance the prestige of the institution in its infancy.

In the area of theological education *Japan Harvest* for April, 1959, lists 29 evangelical Bible institutes, seminaries, and colleges with an aggregate enrollment of 1,700. In the past ten years these institutions have graduated 2,084 theological students. If the more liberal institutions were included the figures would be much higher. There are five theological seminaries which confer the B.D. degree, three of which also grant the degree of Doctor of Theology.

RADIO MINISTRY. There are as yet no Christian broadcasting stations in Japan. There are, however, several Christian programs on commercial stations. In 1956 the total was 50 such programs each Sunday in various parts of the country. The *Lutheran Hour* was heard over 20 stations, *Light of the World* over 7, *Glad Tidings* over 8, and the *Voice of Prophecy* over 6. These, of course, are in English, and consequently have a limited audience. *AVACO*, the voice of the National Christian Council, broadcasts almost every day from Tokyo or some other city. The *Pacific Broadcasting Association*, sponsored by The Evangelical Alliance Mission and the Japanese Evangelical Mission, maintains a weekly program on five stations, including a 50,000-watt station in Tokyo. The *Far East Broadcasting Company* is erecting a 100,000-watt Christian radio station on Okinawa which should be in operation early in 1960.

NEWSPAPER EVANGELISM. This unique missionary method was introduced by *Dr. Albertus Pieters* in 1910 and has been used rather extensively in Japan ever since. In the beginning its plan was to use paid space in the daily press for presenting Christian truth through a series of short expositions of Scripture texts. An offer to supply Christian literature and to answer questions by interview or by mail on application to a certain office was appended. Newspaper evangelism was resumed after the war but the form was somewhat changed. The exposition of Scripture is no longer used, the cost being prohibitive. In its place an advertisement is placed in the newspaper offering to put the interested person in touch with "Christian Pen Pals," either in Japan or abroad, correspondence to be carried on in either Japanese or English. Three such advertisements placed in three metropolitan dailies as an experiment brought 5,000 applications.

SOME JAPANESE CHRISTIAN LEADERS. Besides Joseph Hardy Neesima, mentioned earlier in connection with the Kumamoto Band, there have been other sons of Japan deserving of mention as valiant apostles in the Christian Church. Some of these received their earliest inspiration from Neesima's example and took their training in the institution which he founded. A few of the best known and most representative leaders may here be mentioned.

There is *Paul Kanamori,* who was one of the leaders of that famous Kumamoto Band and a member of the first theological class in the Doshisha University. Known the world over for his great "Three-Hour Sermon," he preached to multitudes throughout Japan, Formosa, and Korea, and guided tens of thousands into the Christian faith.

There is *Kimura,* the "Moody of Japan," who in huge evangelistic campaigns conducted in the great cities of Japan, and in tours among his nationals in Manchuria, Korea, Hawaii, and the South Sea Islands, preached to more than a million people.

There is *Colonel Gumpei Yamamuro,* the "General Booth of Japan" and former distinguished head of the Salvation Army, a great social evangelist of prewar Japan, a speaker of tremendous power, and a stirring writer whose *Gospel for the Common People* has sold more than 1,000,000 copies and now, after a generation, is being reissued by his son.

Most famous of all Japanese Christian leaders is *Toyohiko Kagawa,* called the "St. Francis of Japan" because of his sacrificial service to the poor and oppressed. He is at once scholar, scientist, mystic, poet, novelist, preacher, and social reformer. He is the author of 190 books, several of which have had enormous sales. After spending sixteen years in the slums of Kobe, Kagawa decided to attack the cause of human suffering—exploitation—rather than to alleviate its symptoms. Accordingly he organized the first strike and helped to form the first labor union in Japan. He pioneered in such diverse operations as co-operative medical service, group insurance, agricultural co-operatives, etc. He organized Christian centers in the cities and gospel schools in the rural districts. In addition to all this social and humanitarian work he has devoted a good part of his life to evangelism. During his lifetime 240,000 persons have signed decision cards. At the age of seventy-one he is still going strong.

THE NON-CHURCH MOVEMENT. Peculiar to Japan is the *Non-Church Christian Movement* (Mukyokai) founded by *Uchimura Kanzo* (1861–1930), one of the outstanding Christian leaders of the last generation. Like Martin Luther he believed that Christianity, whatever else it is, must be biblical in content. Himself a great Bible student, he built his entire Movement around the study of the Bible. In an attempt to return to a primitive New Testament form of Christianity, he deliberately shunned the ecclesiastical paraphernalia of Western Christianity and sought to establish vital, spiritual "churches" without organizational structure or official membership. They have no church buildings of their own, preferring to use lecture halls for their Bible talks. Their appeal is mostly to the intellectual class, so much so that some critics have labelled the Movement rationalistic rather than biblical. They observe neither baptism nor the Lord's Supper, nor do they have any official connection with the ecumenical movement. Firm believers in pacifism, they refused to compromise with the militarists even during the war. Somehow they managed to come out on top. The Movement was greatly strengthened by the commendation of the famous Swiss theologian, Emil Brunner, during his three years in Japan in the mid-1950's. He described these people as the "cream of Japanese Christianity, vital and Biblical in the very best sense." The numerical strength of the group is not known; but informed estimates range from 50,000 to 75,000.

MISSIONARY ASSOCIATIONS. Protestant missionaries in Japan are divided into three groups for purposes of fellowship, consultation, and co-operation. These are the *Fellowship of Christian Missionaries,* the *Evangelical Missionary Association of Japan,* and the *Japan Bible Christian Council.* The first mentioned has no statement of faith and includes in its membership both liberals and conservatives, the liberals predominating. Each of the other two groups has a well-defined statement of faith, and membership is limited to conservatives. The Japan Bible Christian Council includes nationals as well as missionaries in its membership. The combined membership of the Evangelical Missionary Association of Japan and the Japan Bible Christian Council is three times as large as that of the Fellowship of Christian Missionaries. Of course, there are individual missionaries who do not belong to any of these three associations.

THE NATIONAL CHRISTIAN COUNCIL. The National Christian Council was dissolved during the war but with the coming of peace it was revived. Its membership includes the Kyodan, the Anglicans, the Lutherans, and the Baptist Convention. Some Presbyterians cooperate with it, as do also the Salvation Army and the Nazarenes. It represents four-fifths of all the Protestants in the country. Like its counterpart in other countries, the National Christian Council in Japan is far from self-supporting. A good share of its budget still comes from abroad. Until 1957 there were only six Churches in the Council. Its official organ is the *Japan Quarterly*, now in its twenty-fifth year. The Evangelical Missionary Association of Japan issues the *Japan Harvest*, a monthly magazine.

KOREA[20]

Area:	38,450 sq. mi.	Population:	23,150,000
Capital:	Seoul	Religion:	Shamanism
			Buddhism

THE LAND. The earliest name for Korea, conferred by her Chinese civilizer in the twelfth century before Christ, was *Cho-sen*, or Morning Calm, and this is still the name used by the people today. The word *Korea* comes from *Korai*, the name of the northernmost of three states which were joined into a united Korea a millennium ago. Korea's centuries of deep seclusion have also won for her the name of the Hermit Nation.

Korea lies on the east coast of Asia. The entire peninsula is about 600 miles long and 135 miles broad, with a coastline of 1,750 miles, and an area, including numerous small islands which cluster along its western and southern shores, estimated at nearly 90,000 square miles. Its size is thus almost that of New York and Pennsylvania combined, or slightly larger than England, Scotland, and Wales. The Yellow Sea on the west and the Japan Sea on the east separate her respectively from China and Japan, while her territory joins that of China and Russia on the north. She thus occupies a striking position as a buffer state between three great political powers, among which she has been a continual bone of contention.

[20] This section deals with the Republic of Korea, commonly referred to as South Korea. If Communist North Korea were included the figures for area and population would be considerably higher.

POLITICAL HISTORY. Like its two greater neighbors, China and Japan, Korea has a history reaching back into antiquity. The first authentic date is 1122 B.C., when a Chinese noble called Kija, having incurred the anger of the Chinese emperor, migrated with 5,000 retainers to Korea and organized a new state. The intervening centuries, right down to recent times, have been marked by frequent intertribal warfare punctuated by repeated invasions from China, Mongolia, and Japan. The Hermit Nation was able to preserve its isolation until 1876 when Japan, itself just emerging from 230 years of isolation, forced a treaty upon it. Six years later China did the same; and the United States, Great Britain, and other Western powers soon followed suit. As a result of these treaties, Seoul and the ports of Chemulpo, Pusan, and Wonsan were opened to foreign commerce. By defeating China in 1895 and Russia in 1905 Japan established itself as the paramount power in Korea and for two years maintained a protectorate over it. Then in 1910 it formally annexed the country, which it held until the close of World War II. The Koreans should have been granted complete independence at that time, but owing to Russian obstructionism the country was divided at the 38th parallel, where the American and Russian armies met at the time of liberation. The Republic of Korea (South Korea) came into being in August, 1948. A month later the North Koreans formed their own government and called the new state the People's Democratic Republic. The country is still divided between the communist North and the democratic South.

THE PEOPLE. Korea seems originally to have been peopled from the mainland, but an admixture at some time is believed to have considerably modified both the physical characteristics and the language of the race. Just as Korea lies geographically between China and Japan, so its people come midway between their two neighbors in physical and intellectual qualities. The Korean resembles the Mongolian in general appearance, is larger in stature than the Japanese, but smaller than the northern Chinese, has good physique and quite average strength and endurance. The woeful absence of all knowledge of hygiene and attention to sanitation and quarantine, however, has caused disease of almost every kind to work dreadful havoc. Ague, smallpox, typhus, and Asiatic cholera especially abound. The mortality among little children is appalling.

In temperament, Dr. Horace G. Underwood describes the Koreans as being "not as phlegmatic as the Chinese nor as volatile as the Japanese," and adds: "They are not as slavishly bound by superstition, not as devoted to their old religions, not as faithful, perhaps, to the traditions of the past, as the Chinese; nor as initiative and ambitious as the Japanese."[21]

Dr. George Heber Jones writes in a leaflet: "Whereas in China the cast of mind is commercial, giving us a nation of merchants, and in Japan it is military, giving us a nation of warriors, in Korea it is literary, giving us a nation of scholars."

By other writers more initiative is claimed for the Koreans than either of these other two races possesses, and they are credited, in common with the Chinese, with real ability, in contrast to the mere genius of imitation and adaptation in which the Japanese excel.

THE RELIGION. It is sometimes said that the Koreans are without any religion. Compared with the peoples of other non-Christian lands they have certainly not been strongly held by any religious system, and certain influences have tended to weaken their faith in their old religions. Temples and shrines are few, and priests are relegated to a very low place in the social scale.

Shamanism is the oldest of Korea's faiths, and today still exerts a stronger influence upon the people than any other. It teaches a great array of spirits, good and evil, of which the good ones are to be invoked, and the evil ones, which predominate, propitiated. The system has gathered into itself a mass of grotesque superstitions.

Buddhism entered Korea in the fourth century, and through her was later introduced into Japan. In Korea it gradually gained considerable power, and during a certain dynasty became the national religion. Later on, partly because of its meddling in politics, it came under the ban, and large numbers of its temples were demolished. Stringent laws enacted against Buddhism were not repealed until after the Sino-Japanese War (1895), when the pro-Japanese party came into power. Buddhism has all along maintained large and well-endowed monasteries throughout the country; and among the common people, and especially the women, it still holds its own.

Confucianism came over from China in earliest times, along with her literature, and has done much to mold the thought and life of the nation. But as elsewhere it is to be regarded as a system of ethics rather than a religion. Its adherents are mainly the educated classes, although its chief rite of ancestral worship is universally observed throughout Korea.

ROMAN CATHOLIC MISSIONS. Late in the eighteenth century some members of the Korean Embassy at Peking came in contact with

[21] Horace G. Underwood, *The Call of Korea* (New York: Revell, 1908), pp. 45–46.

Roman Catholic missionaries and brought back that faith to Korea. Supplying, as it did, what the existing religions lacked, it was well received and grew rapidly. In 1835 two Romanist missionaries secretly entered the country, and others soon followed. Persecution broke out, however, from time to time, incited by the corrupt Buddhist priests, and many converts suffered martyrdom along with the missionaries. In 1864, under a new regent who hated foreigners, and Romanists in particular, a violent storm of persecution burst, the Roman Catholic bishop and eight of his associates were seized and killed, and a veritable inquisition was instituted, under which at least 10,000 converts were put to death. Roman Catholic Christianity in Korea was threatened with extermination and has never fully rallied from the blow. The effect of the persecution upon the Koreans was to create a great dread of all foreign religions, and this has proved a drawback to subsequent missionary effort, both Protestant and Romanist.

PROTESTANT BEGINNINGS. The first Protestant efforts in behalf of Korea were put forth by Rev. *John Ross*, a Scottish Presbyterian missionary at Mukden, in Manchuria, whose interest was aroused by his contact with Koreans on the border. He took up the study of their language, translated the entire New Testament into Korean, and sent Korean colporteurs across the border to distribute it. These efforts were so blessed that "when Protestant missionaries came to Korea later they found whole communities in the north professing Christianity, studying the Bible among themselves, and only waiting for someone to come and teach them."[22]

The signing of the treaty between Korea and the United States in 1882 afforded a new "open door" for missionary work which the churches of America promptly prepared to enter. The *Northern Presbyterian Board* in 1884 appointed *Rev. J. W. Heron*, M.D., to Korea, but his departure was delayed, and meanwhile *Dr. H. N. Allen* of the same Society, who was already in China, was transferred to Korea and thus became the first Protestant missionary to the Hermit Nation. His medical skill, and particularly his success in treating surgically the wounds of a high official who was a cousin of the queen, were providentially used to win the favor of the court and smooth the way for the missionaries who soon followed, even though Dr. Allen himself did not continue in mission work but entered the diplomatic service.

In 1885 *Rev. Horace G. Underwood* of the Northern Presbyterian Board, and *Rev. H. G. Appenzeller* and *Dr. W. B. Scranton* of the

[22] *Encyclopedia of Missions,* Vol. I, p. 534.

Methodist Episcopal Board, arrived on the field. In 1888 the *Y.M.C.A.* of the University of Toronto sent out *Rev. James S. Gale,* who later joined the Presbyterian Mission and has become well known for his interesting books on Korea. Other societies followed, the *Australian Presbyterian* entering in 1889, the *English Episcopalian* (S.P.G.) in 1890, the *Southern Presbyterian* in 1892, the *Southern Methodist* in 1896, and the *Canadian Presbyterian* in 1898.

POLICIES AND METHODS. The consideration of policies and methods of work assumes much more than ordinary interest and importance in the case of Korea by reason of the unusual results which so early attended missionary efforts here. On this point we cannot do better than quote from Dr. H. G. Underwood, one of the earliest pioneers and foremost missionary leaders in Korea for many years. He writes: "Very early in the history of the work, almost at its beginning, God in His Providence led us to adopt methods that have been said by some to have been unique, but in reality are simply those that have been adopted by numbers of missionaries in different parts of the world. The only unique feature has been the almost unanimity with which these have been followed by the whole missionary body in this land."[23]

This writer cites the visit to Korea, in 1890, of *Dr. John L. Nevius,* of Chefoo, China, well known throughout the entire missionary world for his advocacy of methods making for a self-supporting and self-propagating national church, and speaks of the influence exerted upon Korean mission policies by the several conferences held by Dr. Nevius with the Korean missionaries. Continuing, Dr. Underwood writes: "After careful and prayerful consideration, we were led in the main to adopt the 'Nevius method,' and it has been the policy of the Mission:

"*First,* to let each man 'abide in the calling wherein he was found,' teaching that each was to be an individual worker for Christ, and to live Christ in his own neighborhood, supporting himself by his trade;

"*Second,* to develop church methods and machinery only so far as the native church was able to take care of and manage the same;

"*Third,* as far as the church itself was able to provide the men and the means, to set aside those who seemed the better qualified, to do evangelistic work among their neighbors;

"*Fourth,* to let the natives provide their own church buildings,

[23] Underwood, *op. cit.,* p. 5.

which were to be native in architecture, and of such style as the local church could afford to put up."[24]

Following this line of policy, the first Christians in the place generally became the teachers of others, themselves meeting in classes for Bible study and instruction as to their duties. As one and another evinced special fitness for Bible teaching and Christian service these would be given supervision of districts, their support being undertaken by the groups ministered to. Graded classes for these leaders were formed, which in time developed into schools for systematic theological training.

BIBLE CLASSES. Another prominent feature was the holding of large popular Bible classes in each district, for several weeks during the season of the year most convenient for the Christian community. The attendance at such gatherings gradually grew and varied, from 200 in the south to 1,300 in the north. Those who thus gathered returned home to assist in holding local classes under the direction of the missionaries and district leaders, and thus systematic Bible instruction was carried on throughout the entire field occupied. In 1927 there were 541 classes with an attendance of 7,754 men and 11,325 women in the Pyeng Yang station.

SCHOOL WORK. The need of educational work has not been lost sight of, although it has been held secondary to evangelism both in proportion and in order. The principle adhered to has been to provide Christian education primarily for the children of the churches rather than to conduct schools for the heathen as an evangelistic agency. Each local church was encouraged to open and support its own primary school under a Christian teacher, and so heartily have the churches responded to their duty on this line that one mission alone, in 1907, reported 337 such primary schools, all but three of which were entirely self-supported.

It became necessary for the missions to take the initiative to some extent in the matter of schools of higher academic instruction, so that in the main they have provided the buildings, equipment, and teaching staff. But even in these the students have been expected to meet their own support and the running expenses of the school, and the national churches have shown a noble spirit in making earnest efforts to share even the cost of these school plants for the education of their sons.

All this stands in striking contrast to the prevailing policies and

[24] *Ibid.*, pp. 109–10.

methods in most other mission fields, and to their results as well. It is impossible to account for the difference by assuming greater material prosperity on the part of the Koreans, for they are certainly as poor as any Eastern race. These developments are rather an impressive testimony to the splendid results attainable by the adoption and maintenance from the very beginning of true scriptural principles and methods of missionary work, while at the same time they afford a beautiful example of what the Spirit of grace can accomplish in the hearts of converts but recently saved from heathenism.

GROWTH AND EXPANSION. Mission work in Korea does not fall into any well-marked periods. Dr. Underwood suggests a possible division into the periods of preparation, expansion, beginning of large harvests, and greater ingatherings, but says: "From the very beginning we have been permitted to see results, and the work has been steadily progressing with an ever-increasing momentum up to the present time."[25]

From the first there were many who gave a willing ear to the missionary's message, and the books he offered were purchased eagerly. The north especially seemed to have been prepared by the wide seed-sowing that had been done earlier from China, and for this reason missionary trips and efforts were at first mainly directed thither. The first three converts were baptized in 1886. In 1890, after only five years, and those necessarily given largely to preliminary itineration, procuring property, language study, translation work, etc., there were over 100 converts.

This receptivity on the part of the Koreans was recognized as a call for reinforcements from home, and the existing missions steadily enlarged their staffs and expanded their work, while other societies entered the field. Then, following the Sino-Japanese War of 1894–95, the period of large harvests began, with ever-increasing numbers of inquirers and converts. But even these great results were in turn completely eclipsed by those of the first few years of the new century, which far exceeded the highest hopes of the most optimistic missionaries, and led to Korea's becoming known as "the missionary marvel of the age." By 1907 there were actually over 1,000 self-supporting churches with some 30,000 members and over 120,000 adherents, and these churches contributed that year nearly $80,000 in U. S. money.

The following figures speak eloquently of the growth of one station within a period of four short years. In 1895 there were in

[25] *Ibid.*, p. 134.

the city of Pyeng Yang twenty church members, and in the province adjacent seventy-three baptized persons. In 1899 there were 1,182 church members and 7,433 adherents, meeting in 153 self-supporting churches, and that year the Christian community built thirty-eight new church buildings and gave $1,891 in U. S. money. The 1938 report of the Presbyterian Mission for Pyeng Yang listed 24 Presbyterian churches within the city and its environs, and there were as many more churches of other connections. In the Pyeng Yang station district there were 400 Presbyterian churches, with 20,000 members and 5,000 catechumens. All of the 70 Korean pastors, as well as 50 other workers, were supported entirely by the Korean Christians.

That was twenty years ago. After ten years of Communist rule things have greatly changed. Little is known of the present condition of the Church in North Korea; but it is safe to assume that war, persecution, and destitution have all taken their toll.

THE GREAT REVIVAL. This marvelous visitation of the Spirit of God, of which the whole Christian world has heard, centered in Pyeng Yang. Like all other revivals it began with prayer—earnest, united, persevering prayer by missionaries and national Christians alike, born of a deep Spirit-given soul hunger for a richer, fuller experience of divine grace and power. For months, beginning in the late summer of 1906, groups met day after day to pray, and although no manifestation came, their prayers knew no cessation.

Then 1907 dawned, and from all points of the north country Christians gathered, 700 strong, for the customary Bible study classes at the central station. It was in the course of those meetings, on January 14, that the Spirit fell upon the whole assembly with deep heart-searching and conviction. It is not easy to describe the wonderful scenes that followed, the intense, conscious presence of God, the pungent conviction, burning tears, and agonizing confessions, and the new and marvelous sense of peace and joy and liberty which followed. Old and young, educated and ignorant, missionary, national worker, and young convert—all came under this divine influence and power. Sinners were converted; backsliders were reclaimed; Christians got a new vision of God; confessed their sins, failures, and shortcomings; adjusted their differences; made apologies and restitution; and were filled with new love for Christ and souls and new power for service. For two weeks schoolwork and all other ordinary activities were laid aside and everything gave place to prayer.

The wave of revival soon spread to Seoul and all parts of the land, and here and there similar manifestations occurred. Beyond

Korea, too, the movement extended. The churches of Mukden, Manchuria, heard of the revival and sent two elders to investigate. Rev. Jonathan Goforth also came from China. As these messengers carried back reports of what they had seen and heard in Korea the Holy Spirit was poured out in like manner and measure, first in Manchuria and later in center after center in China, with wonderful results which are felt to this day. Thus hath it pleased God to manifest His grace and power through poor, humbled Korea unto the purifying and enriching of the life of the Church in the vast empire of China, whence the first rays of gospel light had, a generation before, penetrated the gross darkness of the little Hermit Nation.

KOREAN CHRISTIANS. While rightly attributing this wonderful revival and the phenomenal progress of missions as a whole in Korea to the sovereign hand of God, we cannot overlook the fact that certain qualities in the Christian converts of Korea have played an important part in bringing about such results, by providing God with means to work through. We should sadly miss much of the lesson the Lord would teach the entire Christian Church through what has taken place in Korea if we failed to observe and ponder some of the traits and graces exhibited in marked degree by the Christians of that land. Among these are to be noted:

A High Conception of Discipleship. "From the early days of the mission there has prevailed among the Korean converts a very high conception of the privileges and responsibilities of church membership. A Korean Christian is always more than a mere church-member; he is a worker giving his services freely and gladly to extend the knowledge of Christ among his neighbors. It has not been an unusual thing for a pastor of a local church to have not less than one-third of the entire membership of his church on the streets on a Sunday afternoon, engaged in house-to-house visitation and personal work among their unconverted neighbors."[26]

Love for God's Word. This is most marked. Practically all Korean Christians are Bible students. Old as well as young make up the Sunday School enrollment. Sunday Schools in the large city churches vary in attendance from 2,000 to 3,000. Whole chapters of Scripture are commonly memorized even by the illiterate and the aged. A unique feature of mission work in Korea already noted is the system of Bible study classes of all grades, held in the centers for periods ranging from four days to a month. Not only the national workers and more advanced Christians, but the rank and file of the members

[26] James S. Gale, Korea in Transition (New York: Young People's Missionary Movement), pp. 192-93.

as well, attend these gatherings, saving and sacrificing to be able to come, and traveling long distances from every part of the district.

Spirit of Prayer. The Korean Church has always been known as a praying Church. Prayer meetings are held not once a week but once a day, usually at daybreak. Postwar visitors to Korea have reported almost unanimously on the huge gatherings for prayer in the early hours of the morning in burned-out churches and unheated buildings. In the larger cities it is not uncommon to find prayer meetings which attract a thousand earnest Christians every morning of the week.

Self-Propagation and Self-Support. It is a question whether any other mission field has furnished an example of zeal and devotion on these lines, or a record of results achieved, to equal those of Korea. It is quite true that striking instances of these traits in individual converts are not wanting in other fields. But the unique feature about Korea is that these features dominate the Church as a whole. Let us quote a few testimonies from among many which are at hand.

From the first the Koreans were made to believe that the spread of the gospel and growth of the church was their work rather than ours. We are here to start them and guide them in their efforts, but it is theirs to do the work.—Dr. Sharrocks.

The Korean is a preacher of the gospel by a kind of spiritual instinct; he knows and does this one thing only; he provides for his church schools without a cent from the homelands; he gives of his means a tenth or more; sometimes he gives all he has over a bare living.—Dr. James S. Gale.

Not only in prayers, but in works as well, are the rank and file of the Korean Christians instant in season and out. I dare say there is no land in the world where there is so much personal and unpaid—in money—hand to hand, and heart to heart, evangelistic work done as in Korea.—Rev. J. Z. Moore.

The Koreans themselves established Christianity in distant communities where no white man had ever been.—F. A. McKenzie.

The progress of Christianity is unprecedentedly rapid. Native churches, instead of depending on foreign aid, are becoming self-supporting, self-governing, self-propagating. An astonishing revival spirit and evangelistic zeal prevail, and converts are gathering by scores and hundreds. Self-denying giving is manifested in a unique fashion.—Dr. A. T. Pierson.

Sacrificial Giving. Many touching instances of keen sacrifice in the giving of the Korean Christians "for Christ's sake and the gospel's" could be cited. Dr. George Heber Jones reports that "Korean men have been known to mortgage their houses that mortgages might be removed from the houses of God; to sell their crops of good rice, intended for family consumption, purchasing inferior millet to live upon through the winter, and giving the difference in cost for the support of the workers to preach among their own countrymen. Korean women have given their wedding rings, and even cut off their hair that it might be sold and the amount devoted to the spread of the Gospel."

The same missionary told of the leader of a little village group of Christians, who, when all other resources had been exhausted to meet the cost of a new chapel, sold his only ox, and the next spring he and his brother hitched themselves in place of the ox and dragged the plow through the fields that year.

Subscriptions not only of money, but also of time, to be given to evangelistic work and manual labor in the erection of churches, are quite the order of the day, thousands of Christians contributing from a week to a month of time, and many still longer periods.

PERSECUTION. The Koreans have a proverb: "He that is born in the fire will not faint in the sun." This has certainly been true of the Korean Church, which has had more than its share of persecution, first under the Japanese, then during World War II, and more recently under the Communists. A large number of Christians took part in the independence uprising in March, 1919. Thereafter the Christian Church was always suspect in the eyes of the Japanese authorities. By October of that year the Presbyterian Mission reported that 336 pastors, elders, and helpers had been arrested as well as 2,125 male and 531 female members. Forty-one had been shot and killed and 6 beaten to death, while 1,642 were still in prison. Other denominations suffered proportionately.

A change in the Japanese administration gave the Koreans a breathing spell in the 1920's; but with the rise of Japanese militarism in the following decade the Korean nation once again became the victim of Japanese oppression. Particularly offensive to the Christians was the matter of emperor worship. Those who failed to comply were sent to prison. Even the missionaries were suspected of subversive activities and their movements were under constant surveillance, especially after Japan's invasion of China in 1937. In 1939 the Japanese ordered all missionaries to leave Korea. After Pearl Harbor the Protestant Church, regarded as a potential Fifth Column because of its former close ties with the United States, went underground. When the war was over the State Department permitted a limited number of missionaries to return, but they were confined to

South Korea. None of them was permitted by the Communists to enter North Korea.

AFTERMATH OF THE KOREAN WAR. Far more devastating than World War II was the war between North Korea and South Korea which broke out June 25, 1950, and ended with the armistice signed on July 27, 1953. Compared with World War II, the Korean War was sometimes referred to as a "pocket war," but the people of Korea did not so regard it. The physical destruction and material losses ran into hundreds of millions of dollars. Worse than this was the indescribable human misery represented by four million refugees, tens of thousands of orphans and widows, and an estimated 20,000 amputees, mostly civilian.

The Christian Church, along with every other institution, suffered staggering losses. One-third of all church buildings were damaged or destroyed. In Seoul alone no fewer than 200 churches were damaged. The Bible House was destroyed three times in three successive years and its secretary wrote: "All my effort these last three years has fallen to zero. I am lonely and tired. . . . The five families of our staff have only the clothes they stand up in."[27]

When the war was over the main task of both the churches and the missions was that of rehabilitation. The *American Methodist Mission* allocated $840,000 to rebuild Methodist churches and $275,000 for schools and hospitals. Korean Christians added $350,000 of their own. The *Presbyterian Mission* paid 25 per cent of all rehabilitation costs for the Korean Presbyterian churches. The *Friends' Foreign Service Unit* at Kunsan Hospital not only treated the sick but also conducted an excellent medical training program. The *Mission to Lepers* entered Korea in 1956, and today maintains seven out-patient clinics in the country districts. *World Vision, Inc.*, has taken a special interest in the many war orphans and has provided thousands of them with food, clothing, shelter, education, and Christian instruction.

According to the *Korean Christian Handbook* there are 1,500,000 Protestant Christians in Korea. Roman Catholics total only 242,000. The three largest denominations are the Presbyterian, Methodist, and Holiness. The Presbyterians are the largest group in Korea; they account for 66 per cent of the 5,281 churches. In recent years there has been a division in the Presbyterian ranks, with the result that there are now three groups: the Presbyterian Church of Korea, with 550,000 members; the Presbyterian Church in the Republic of

[27] *Trumpets of Jubilee*, p. 26.

Korea, with 175,000 members; and the Head Presbyterian Church of Korea, with 140,000 members.[28] There are more Presbyterian churches in Seoul and Taegu than in any other two cities in the world, and the Presbyterian Theological Seminary in Seoul, which had an enrollment of 660 in 1957, is the largest seminary of that denomination anywhere in the world. Of the 350 Christian chaplains in the armed forces of the Republic of Korea, 308 are Protestants, most of them Presbyterian or Methodist. In 1953, 244,016 copies of the Scriptures were distributed through these chaplains to the men in the services.

The *Korean Methodists* are organized into three annual conferences with 27 districts comprising 639 organized pastoral charges and 379 meeting places. This represents an overall increase of 90 per cent over the 1952 figure of 540. Three hundred and thirty-six of these churches are fully self-supporting and another 295 have reached the halfway mark.

Working along indigenous lines the *Oriental Missionary Society,* known in Korea as the *Holiness Church,* has made steady progress through the years. When the missionaries evacuated in 1939 they left 6,000 baptized members in 250 churches. Today with only nine missionaries on the field they have almost 500 churches and 200 preaching places, every one of which is self-supporting. Total membership is 115,000. After the Korean War the Holiness Church took on 50 major projects, among them 20 orphanages for which the Church has assumed full responsibility. There is not a single missionary in any of these. Besides the theological seminary with over 300 students it maintains 12 Bible schools for the training of lay evangelists. These also are self-supporting. In 1956 the churches reported 82,000 decisions for Christ in evangelistic campaigns.

Other denominations, with their churches, include the *Seventh Day Adventists* (251), *Southern Baptists* (155), *Salvation Army* (104), *Church of Christ* (61), *Assemblies of God* (44), *Anglicans* (18), *Nazarene* (16), *Church of God* (8), and *Jesus Church* (5). *Jehovah's Witnesses* report 20 churches. The 1957 *Korean Christian Yearbook* lists 41 missions and agencies at work in the country; about half of them are newcomers since World War II. Included in this category are the *Southern Baptist Convention, The Evangelical Alliance Mission, Independent Board for Presbyterian Foreign Mis-*

---

[28] The Presbyterian Church of Korea at its 44th General Assembly in September, 1959, was rent asunder when the anti-ecumenical minority broke away over the issue of membership in the World Council of Churches. Happily the schism was healed five months later when a Special Assembly decided, in the interest of local unity, to withdraw from the W.C.C.

*sions. Orthodox Presbyterian Church, International Child Evange-
lism Fellowship,* and other smaller missions.

CHRISTIAN LITERATURE. At the close of World War II there was no
Christian literature in process of publication. A good beginning was
made, only to be interrupted when the Communists took Seoul in
1950 and destroyed everything. Rehabilitation in this realm has been
slow. Of the 700 publishing firms formerly in Korea only 50 were
in operation in 1957. The *Korean Bible Society,* in spite of crippling
material losses, reported in 1957 the highest circulation of the Scriptures in ten years. A Federation of Bookstores comprising 13
bookshops has been formed. The Bible House, autonomous
now for several years, still requires and receives financial aid from
abroad.

HIGHER EDUCATION. As might be expected in a country like Korea,
the various missions have through the years made a substantial
contribution to higher education. Besides the theological seminaries
maintained by all the larger missions there are several mission-
sponsored colleges and universities. The Presbyterian Mission has
three colleges, *Soong Sil* in Seoul for refugees from the north,
Keimyung in Taegu, and a new college which opened in Taejon in
1956 with an enrollment of 82. Located in the capital are the great
Methodist *Ewha Women's University,* the *United Christian College,*
and *Yonsei University.* Yonsei grew out of the merger in 1955 of
two union schools, *Chosun Christian University* and *Severance
Union Medical College.* Its present student body is over 4,000. That
these institutions of higher learning continue to exert a strong
Christian influence and maintain a clear Christian witness is seen in
the fact that following a recent preaching mission by Dr. Harry
Denman more than 700 faculty members and students of Ewha
University asked for Christian baptism.

CHRISTIAN RADIO. In the last few years three radio stations have been
erected in Korea for the purpose of broadcasting the gospel. Station
HLKY in Seoul went on the air on December 15, 1954. This small
station sponsored by RAVEMCCO is designed to reach South Korea
and beam the gospel into North Korea. Station HLKX, a 20,000-watt,
short-wave station operated by The Evangelical Alliance Mission
is located on the seashore at Inchon. It is broadcasting the gospel
daily in five languages, including Chinese and Russian. Letters from
China indicate that the programs are being heard behind the
Bamboo Curtain. A third station began broadcasting in March, 1959.
It is Station HLKT in Taegu. It is sponsored by the local churches
in Taegu with some assistance from RAVEMCCO.

OVERSEAS MISSIONARY ENDEAVOR. No indigenous church has really come of age until it has learned to share the Christian message with non-Christian peoples in neighboring countries. In addition to all that the Korean churches are doing towards the support of the work and the spread of the gospel in their own land, they have again set an example for other mission fields to follow by launching missions among their own countrymen in foreign lands such as China, Hawaii, Mexico, and the Pacific coast of the United States; and the Presbyterian Church of Korea has sent four missionaries to work with the Church of Christ in Thailand. They hope to send another worker in the near future to serve with the Presbyterian Church in Formosa.

THE FUTURE OUTLOOK. What has been written in these pages pertains only to South Korea. The picture in Communist North Korea is obscure. There is no missionary work at all and doubtless very little freedom for church work. Both North and South Korea want one united country, but each wants it on its own terms. If the country is united on Communist terms the future decline of the Church is not difficult to imagine. If the union takes place under a democratic form of government there is every reason to believe that all Korea will be evangelized. This is its desperate need as expressed by former President Syngman Rhee, himself a devout Methodist, when he stated on one occasion: "Korea must be united; Korea must be free; Korea must be democratic; but as the foundation for all this, Korea must be a Christian nation."[29]

[29] *Methodist Annual Report, 1953*, p. 106.

XII

INTRODUCTION TO THE MIDDLE EAST

THE AREA. The term "Middle East" or "Near East" is a convenient designation given to a not-too-well defined geographical area stretching from the eastern part of the Mediterranean basin to the Indus River. Scholars differ as to exactly which countries fall within this area. Some would include Greece as well as Libya and other North African countries in the west; others would include Pakistan and Afghanistan in the east. For the purpose of this study we shall include the following eight countries: Turkey, Iran, Iraq, United Arab Republic (Egypt and Syria), Jordan, Lebanon, Saudi Arabia, and Israel, in all of which there is some form of Christian work and witness.

Oil in tremendous quantities is found in three of these countries: Iran, Iraq, and Saudi Arabia. Together they produce 3,500,000 barrels a day, nearly all of which goes to Europe via the Suez Canal and pipelines running through Syria. President Nasser of the United Arab Republic, therefore, though he has no oil of his own, can control its distribution; and at any time, on whatever pretext, he can stop its flow and in a matter of weeks cripple the entire economy of Europe.

STRATEGIC IMPORTANCE. A glance at the map will reveal at once the strategic position of this area. Constituting as it does a bridge between the three great continents of the Old World—"Asia the continent of the past, Europe the continent of the present, and Africa the continent of the future"—it has well been called the "Crossroads of the World." This area is of particular interest to the student of missions for the following reasons:

1. *It was the cradle of the human race.* Mount Ararat in Armenia, lifting its snow-crowned head 17,000 feet high, stands as a mighty

monument to our earliest ancestors, for it is the traditional resting place of the ark and the site whence Noah and his family replenished the earth. Somewhere in this region to the south, perhaps in the Euphrates Valley, the Garden of Eden is thought to have been located. The territory upon which this lofty mountain looks down was the home of the early races of mankind.

2. *It was the site of the world's greatest ancient empires.* Here in the Near East, Egypt, Assyria, Babylon, Medo-Persia and Greece, the mighty kingdoms of the hoary past, all in succession took their rise, flourished, and waned. No other region in the world compares with the Near East in its wealth of monuments, ruins, and landmarks of ancient civilization; and archeological research has here found its largest field and richest rewards.

3. *It was the homeland of three of the world's great religions,* all of them monotheistic: Christianity, Judaism, and Islam. Hundreds of thousands of pilgrims converge on this area every year. Mecca, Meshed, Jerusalem, and Kerbala are names to conjure with. The piled ruins of civilization upon civilization, of crusade upon crusade, of conquest after conquest, mark this area; and here, in closer proximity than in most other places in the world, scores of religious sects assiduously propagate their own doctrines while at the same time jealously guarding their own devotees from the proselytizing activities of others. The religious hopes and fears, beliefs and prejudices of all the world's continents focus in the Middle East.

4. *It was the land of the Bible and the Saviour.* All the scenes and events of the Old Testament Scriptures lay here, and—what will ever make the Near East of transcendent interest to Christian hearts —the Holy Land is here, the land where our blessed Saviour lived and died and rose again, from which also He ascended to heaven, and to which He will some day return to reign.

THE PEOPLE. The total population of these eight countries, according to the most reliable estimates, is about 68,000,000. The bulk of this population is found in three countries: United Arab Republic (27,000,000), Turkey (24,000,000), and Iran (20,000,000). Lebanon, Jordan, and Israel have fewer than 2,000,000 people each.

Nowhere within a similar area is there to be found a greater diversity of races, a fact which adds great complexity to the missionary task in the Middle East. This makes some mention of the different races essential to a proper understanding of the situation, from whatever viewpoint it is to be regarded.

Turks. The real Turks are Mongolian in origin. They pushed their way westward from the vast plains of Turkistan eight or nine centuries ago. Thus they are newcomers as compared with most of the other races. By faith they are Muslims. They have earned a world-wide reputation for cruelty by their brutal treatment of their Christian neighbors in days gone by. In war they are fierce and courageous fighters, as evidenced by the contingent of 1,200 Turkish soldiers who fought in Korea under the United Nations.

Armenians. The Armenians are a very ancient people with a well-attested national history of 2,500 years. The kingdom of Armenia once reached from the Mediterranean to the Caspian Sea. They are a hardy, industrious, and intelligent people who have set a high value on education. They maintain their own system of schools and were among the first to embrace the higher educational advantages introduced by the Western missionaries. They were the first nation to adopt Christianity; and through centuries of persecution and repeated massacres they have held tenaciously to their Christian faith. The wholesale massacres of these people by the Turks during the first World War stand out among the most heinous national crimes in history.

Greeks. Up to a rather recent date the coast of Asia Minor was peopled by this race, the direct descendants of the ancient Greeks who lived there. Most of the Greeks now live in Greece, a country that lies outside the purview of this study; but not a few are to be found in other parts of the Middle East. Most of them are merchants. Religiously they belong to the Greek Orthodox Church, of which the seven churches of Asia mentioned in the Book of The Revelation were the forerunners. They are an intelligent people. A fair proportion of them are well educated and, like the Armenians, they maintain a system of good schools, including many of higher grade.

Kurds. These hardy, semi-nomadic tribesmen, of whom there are three or four million, inhabit the region known as Kurdistan located in eastern Turkey, western Iran, and northern Iraq. They are a pastoral people, dwelling in tents and villages, and ruled by feudal chieftains. The Kurds are of Eastern ancestry. Their language is Aryan at its base, though mixed with Turkish, Arabic, and Persian. They are classed as Muslims but they are not zealous as such. Their worship is a strange mixture, including elements of paganism and also some rites resembling those of Christianity.

Arabs. The Arabs are an ancient and interesting people of Semitic stock. At least the tribes of northern Arabia are held to be descendants of Ishmael, thus making the Arab a cousin to the Jew. Bursting the bounds of their original peninsular home, they have repeatedly swept over Syria, Mesopotamia, and Egypt, leaving a permanent impress on these lands. A striking evidence of this is the fact that

Arabic, a sister tongue to Hebrew, is the lingua franca of the Middle East. The Arabs possess a strong religious instinct. Most of them are Muslims and propagate with ardent zeal the faith of their prophet Mohammed. They are fine specimens of physical development and as a race are above average intellectually. In appearance and customs they differ widely according to their environment. Without doubt they are the most important element in the Middle East today; and Nasser's pan-Arabism is not likely to diminish their evident sense of destiny, which is the most significant factor in the political pattern now evolving in that part of the world.

Assyrians. This race, dwelling mostly in Syria, Lebanon, and northern Iraq, is chiefly Semitic in stock, with Greek, Roman, and Crusader blood intermixed. They are bright in intellect and keen for education. They make industrious farmers and shrewd merchants. As to religion, most of them are Christians. The formerly great Nestorian Church is now largely among these Syriac-speaking people.

Jews. More than any other group, the Jewish people have been scattered to the four corners of the earth. The Balfour Declaration of 1917 opened Palestine to Jewish immigration; but it was not until Hitler's rise to power in the 1930's that there was anything like a mass exodus of Jews from Europe. Following World War II another exodus took place, from Eastern Europe. The Palestinian War of 1948 precipitated a third great exodus, this time from the Arab countries of the Middle East. Today there are few Jews in the Middle East outside of Israel where, at the close of the first decade of independence, the Jewish population stands at 1,680,000. The Jews now in Israel are divided into three groups: the Orthodox Jews, who want to build the new state on the Torah; the Zionists, whose aspirations are more economic and political than religious; and the new generation of young people who, lacking the religious convictions of the first group and the idealism of the second group, are in danger of drifting into indifference if not frustration. Most of them rally to nationalism.

Persians. The Persians of today are of the same old Iranian stock that inhabited the land in the days of Nehemiah and Queen Esther. The Arab conquerors of the seventh century forced their Muslim faith on Persia, and nine-tenths of the present populace is Muslim. The Iranian Muslims, however, are more tolerant and approachable than their co-religionists found in other parts of the Middle East. The Persians fall into two classes, tent dwellers, or nomads, and town dwellers. The former constitute one-fifth of the total. Like the Bedouin Arabs they lead a nomadic life, tending their flocks and herds on the steep mountainsides. The townspeople cultivate the fertile valleys, raising grain and luscious fruits. They also spin and weave wool and mohair, and make vegetable dyes. Others are skilled craftsmen engaged in the manufacture of the world-famous Persian rugs and shawls of beautiful design, exquisite enamel work on metal, and mosaic work in bone and ivory. They have been leaders in art and architecture since prehistoric times. Much of Islamic architecture is of Persian origin.

Egyptians. While the streets of Cairo, Egypt's splendid capital and Africa's greatest city, present a never-ending pageant of Oriental life—Copts, Turks, Syrians, Nubians, Sudanese Negroes, Bedouins, and many others—for practical purposes the population of Egypt may be said to consist of two classes. First there are the Arab Muslims, originally from Arabia, who have settled in the rich corn lands of the delta of the Nile and now comprise nine-tenths of the population. Secondly, there are the Copts, who are the true Egyptians, "the direct descendants of the men who built the pyramids and who, when the rest of the world was asleep, developed a civilization which has been the wonder of the ages."[1]

POLITICAL SITUATION. No area in the world has undergone such rapid and radical changes in the twentieth century as has the Middle East. The postwar period has been particularly turbulent. Country after country has staggered from one crisis to another, and the end is not yet. Three events, among others, have contributed to this state of affairs: the decline of British influence, the rise of nationalism, and the birth of Israel. Within the last few years a fourth factor has been introduced—pan-Arabism. Its champion is Gamal Abdel Nasser, president of the United Arab Republic, which was created by the federal union of Egypt and Syria on February 1, 1958.

Without doubt the greatest single cause of tension in the Middle East was the creation of the state of Israel in May, 1948. To this day the Arab countries adamantly refuse to recognize the existence of the Jewish state and are determined to drive the Israelis into the sea, if it is the last thing they do. All United Nations' efforts at conciliation have failed to produce a final solution; and Arab intransigence refuses to permit a settlement of the refugee problem except on Arab terms. Only the presence of the United Nations Emergency Force in the Sinai Peninsula has prevented further bloodshed.

In addition to all this the Arabs are not united among themselves.

[1] Cornelius H. Patton, *The Lure of Africa* (New York: Missionary Education Movement, 1917), p. 45.

For some time now Egypt has been carrying on a war of words and threats with Jordan and, more recently, with Iraq. King Hussein has been the target of several abortive coups engineered from abroad. Doubtless Egypt would have swallowed up Jordan long ago had it not been for the knowledge that such a move would supply Israel with the coveted pretext for grabbing the Jordanian enclave west of the Jordan River. In an attempt to match Nasser's growing strength, King Feisal of Iraq and King Hussein of Jordan announced the Arab Federation of Iraq and Jordan two weeks after the merger of Egypt and Syria. Six months later the Federation was dissolved as a result of the military coup of July 14, 1958, when King Feisal was assassinated and a new republic was created under Premier Abdul Karim el-Kassem.

The Middle East situation is further complicated by the ever-present threat of Communism. The shadow of the great Russian bear falls ominously across this entire region. The Baghdad Pact and the Eisenhower Doctrine represent the most successful and concerted efforts of the West to deter Soviet aggression in the Middle East. The former was considerably weakened by the withdrawal of Iraq in 1959. The latter suffered its severest test in the summer of 1958 when President Chamoun of Lebanon requested and received speedy and effective military aid from the United States to stave off an imminent revolution which threatened the status quo throughout the entire Middle East. For a time it looked as if Syria was about to be sucked into the Soviet orbit, and was saved only by Nasser's timely annexation of that country.

Turkey, a member of the North Atlantic Treaty Organization and the Central Treaty Organization, is the Western world's staunchest ally in the Middle East. Israel is the only genuine democracy in this part of the world and religiously, politically, and psychologically it is oriented towards the West; but it has been reluctant to take an open stand in the cold war. Nasser and his United Arab Republic seem determined to follow an independent course described as "dynamic neutrality." Little Lebanon, once regarded as the most modern and prosperous country in the Middle East, was badly shaken by the events of the summer of 1958. Arabia, still a feudal state, is the most backward politically of all the Middle East countries. For a time, during the crisis in the oil industry in 1951–1952, it looked as if Iran might completely break with the West; but it weathered the storm, resisted Soviet pressure, and today is lined up with the United States. Jordan continues to maintain its precarious existence as an independent state, threatened by Nasser's pan-Arabism on the one hand and by Communist infiltration on the other. During his first year in office Premier Kassem of Iraq successfully withstood several attempts to bring down his regime.

Time and again in the past four years the world has been on the brink of war because of events in the Middle East. The nationalization of the Suez Canal, Israel's "preventive" war in the Sinai Peninsula, the Franco-British invasion of Egypt, the swift and bloody revolution in Iraq, the landing of United States Marines in Lebanon —any one of these might have precipitated World War III. Politically the Middle East is the most unsettled, unpredictable area in the world of the mid-twentieth century.

THE RELIGION OF ISLAM. Islam, commonly referred to as Mohammedanism, is, along with Judaism and Christianity, one of the great monotheistic religions of the world. It has more in common with Christianity than any other religion except Judaism. Like Christianity, it is definitely missionary in its outreach and truly universal in scope. It has one sacred Scripture, the Koran, which every devout Muslim believes was created by God and revealed to Mohammed by the angel Gabriel. At the same time Islam has always been Christianity's greatest foe and threatens to become its greatest rival. It regards all Christians as blasphemers, and converts to Christianity are considered to be both apostates and traitors and are treated accordingly.

Islam first appeared in the seventh century of the Christian era in the western part of the Arabian Peninsula, subsequently known as the Hijaz, or Holy Land. Spreading rapidly north through the Levant and west through Egypt and across North Africa, it offered to both Christian and pagan alike a choice between the Koran and the sword. Most people preferred the former, with the result that the Christian Church all but disappeared from North Africa; and today the entire region known as the Middle East is dominated by the Crescent, not by the Cross.

While Islam has extended to all parts of the world, and two of its largest nations—Pakistan and Indonesia—are Muslim countries, the Middle East remains to this day the religious and cultural center of the Muslim world. Though chased from one place to another— Arabia, Damascus, Baghdad, Cairo—by the fortunes of war, the Caliphate has always remained in the Middle East. The Pilgrimage, one of the Five Pillars of Islam, has through the centuries brought untold millions from the ends of the earth to such holy cities as Mecca (Arabia), Meshed (Iran), and Kerbala (Iraq). Al Azhar University, the oldest university in the world and the fountainhead of Muslim culture the world over, is located in Cairo. Converts to

Islam are to be found in all parts of the world, but its theologians and reformers have come almost invariably from the heartland of Islam. While mosques and minarets may be seen in all five continents, the inner citadel of Islam is located in the Middle East. If one would probe to the soul of this great religion, he must know the Arab world.

Islam, like Buddhism, is divided into two schools or sects, the orthodox Sunni Sect and the Shiah Sect. The schism originated with a dispute regarding the fourth successor to the Prophet as Caliph, or Leader of Islam. The Prophet's son-in-law, Ali, was defeated by his rival, Muawiya; and Ali's son, Hussein, was afterwards killed at the Battle of Kerbala in Iraq in A.D. 681. The Shiahs still consider that Ali was the rightful head and have never acknowledged the Caliphs, but have given their allegiance to the descendants of Ali, known as the "Imams." They believe he will one day reappear. Kerbala, not Mecca, is their chief place of pilgrimage. They are less fanatical than the Sunnis, and many of them have followed the mystic path of Sufism. Egypt, Jordan, and Syria are Sunni. Iran, on the other hand, is Shiah, which accounts in part for the fact that it is the only country in the Middle East where a Muslim may profess Christianity without precipitating a communal riot.

Like most other religions, Islam has had its periods of decline and revival. In recent decades, and especially since World War II, it has been undergoing a resurgence which is causing real concern in Christian missionary circles. Always a missionary religion, it has taken on new life, adopted new methods, and almost certainly bids fair to increase in both strength and numbers in the years ahead. It is winning converts in Africa many times faster than Christianity. From a Church Missionary Society missionary in Kenya comes this statement:

The Muslims are making Africa the continent of their greatest missionary activity, and new mosques may be seen in many towns, even far inland. The most active sect of Muslims here are followers of the Aga Khan. . . . This sect is very wealthy, organized on an all-Africa basis, and is very strong on all kinds of social service for their people. They have many fine schools, some hospitals and clinics and clubs, and are very public spirited.[2]

From Uganda comes this report:

There has undoubtedly been a big increase in Muslim adherents during the past five years. In 1949 there were nine aided Muslim

[2] *Churchnews* (July, 1957).

schools in Bugishu-Bukedi; there are now (1956) over fifty. Mostly small, it is true, but all eager to expand as soon as teachers are available.[3]

Islam is on the march and, incredible as it may seem, its leaders have their eyes on the United States of America. The head of the Ahmadiyya Movement, in a speech in Karachi, said:

We need men to take it upon themselves to spread the message of Islam everywhere. Do you think that if you pay contribution here the people of America will become Muslims themselves? It is not possible. Somebody has to go to them and preach. The number of the missionaries that are already in the field is not enough. I am thinking of asking every Ahmadi family to dedicate one member of their family for the service of Islam.[4]

FREEDOM OF RELIGION. In every Muslim country freedom of religion is a matter of grave concern to the Christian Church and the Western missionary. Surprisingly enough, the Koran (Surah 2:257) teaches that "there is no compulsion in religion." It also says: "He that can believe, shall believe; he who cannot believe shall disbelieve. The only sin is to be a hypocrite." Just how the Muslims reconcile these statements with their long history of coercion and persecution it is difficult to say. Perhaps they have done with them what some Christians have done with certain passages of the New Testament—ignored them! Be that as it may, it is a known fact that wherever Islam holds sway, religious liberty, certainly as we in the West understand it, simply does not exist; and this is true in spite of the fact that all of these eight countries except Saudi Arabia have signed the *Universal Declaration of Human Rights* sponsored by the United Nations, Article XVIII of which reads:

Everyone has the right of freedom of thought, conscience and religion; this right includes freedom to change his religion or belief, and freedom, either alone or in community with others, and in public or private, to manifest his religion or belief in teaching, practice, worship and observance.

No state in the latter half of the twentieth century can be considered modern and democratic unless it makes provision for personal liberty on the part of the individual citizen. Accordingly the Middle East nations are obliged to pay lip service to freedom of religion, but in every case the freedom is circumscribed in the interest of "public order and good morals," a convenient phrase which readily lends itself to almost any kind of interpretation.

[3] *Ibid.*
[4] *Ibid.*

In most of these countries freedom of religion means that each minority non-Muslim group is permitted to minister to the spiritual needs of its members within the precincts of its own churches; but it does not include permission to do evangelistic work designed to win outsiders to Jesus Christ. This they term "proselytizing," and that is anathema in most Muslim countries. No matter what the Constitution may say, no Muslim is allowed *by the community* to change his religion. To do so is to become an apostate to the faith and a traitor to the country. For a converted Muslim to accept Christian baptism is to court certain persecution, often death.

So confined is the Muslim that in some countries of the Middle East a follower of Islam who changed his religion would in effect be tearing up his birth certificate, citizenship papers or passport, voting registration and work permit, and would become like a man without a country.[5]

So entrenched is the opposition to conversion that almost all the ancient Churches and many of the younger ones hesitate to encourage it. They have come to the place where they no longer *expect* Muslims to identify themselves openly with the Christian Church. Doubtless there are many secret believers among the Muslims, whose faith is known only to themselves and God. This fact must be borne in mind when we attempt to appraise the meager results of 140 years of missionary work in the Middle East.

ANCIENT EASTERN CHURCHES. The Ancient Churches of the Middle East are old as Pentecost, for it was in Jerusalem that the First Church Council was established, and in Antioch that the followers of The Way were first called Christians. Never since its founding in the first century have Palestine, Lebanon, Syria, and Egypt been without the Christian Church. An estimated 7,000,000 Christians are to be found today in the Eastern Churches located in the Middle East. These Ancient Churches may be divided as follows:

I. EASTERN ORTHODOX.

1. *Greek Orthodox.* This is the original national Church of the Eastern Roman, or Byzantine, Empire. Various branches are self-governing, but they are in communion with one another. The Patriarchate of Constantinople is the chief one. The Church of Greece is under its authority, as are also the patriarchates of Antioch, Alexandria, and Jerusalem, and the Metropolitan Church of Cy-

[5] R. Park Johnson, *Middle East Pilgrimage* (New York: Friendship Press, 1958), p. 142.

prus. The Russian and Balkan Orthodox Churches are additional branches.

2. *Nestorian* (Assyrian). This was a great Church in the Middle Ages, extending across Persia to India and Central Asia as far as China. Only a small group of so-called Assyrians, mainly in Iran, Iraq, and Syria, remains of this once mighty missionary Church.

3. *Syrian Orthodox,* known as "Jacobite" after one of its early missionaries, Jacob Bardaeus, who died in A.D. 578. Its Monophysitic doctrine opposed the main orthodox church of the Byzantine Empire.

4. *Coptic.* This is the old national Church of Egypt. It is the largest of all the Ancient Churches in the Middle East. It, too, is Monophysite in doctrine.

5. *Armenian* (Gregorian). This is the National Armenian Church. The Armenians have the distinction of being the first nation to become Christian. It is Monophysite in doctrine. Since the Turkish massacres the largest concentration is in the Soviet Union, though many are found throughout the Middle East.

II. ROMAN CATHOLIC. The final split between the Eastern and Western Churches came in A.D. 1054.

1. *Regular Catholics.* There are a few Regular Catholics, or "Latins," in Palestine, Syria, and Lebanon.

2. *Maronite.* It began as a Syrian nationalist protest against the Byzantine Church and adopted the Monophysite heresy. It was named for the legendary St. Marun. In 1181 it disavowed its heresy and submitted to Rome. This arrangement was confirmed in 1516. The Maronite Church uses its own Syriac liturgy. It is the major Christian group in Lebanon.

3. *Uniate Churches.* These are Eastern Orthodox Churches which have broken away from the parent organization and have joined the Roman Catholic Church. The two requirements were the acceptance of Roman Catholic doctrine and the acknowledgment of the Pope. Autonomy was granted in liturgy, language, and government. Several Uniate Churches have married clergy. These Churches resulted from splits, as follows: the *Chaldean* from the Nestorian Church, partial in 1551, complete in 1681; the *Greek Catholic* from the Greek Orthodox Church in 1724; the *Coptic Catholic* from the Coptic Church in 1732; the *Syrian Catholic* from the Syrian Orthodox (Jacobite) Church in 1783; and the *Armenian Catholic* from the Armenian Orthodox (Gregorian) Church, some groups as early as 1439 but mostly in the eighteenth century.

Alas, these Churches have completely lost their missionary vision and are content to perpetuate their own nominal existence from generation to generation without any thought of growth or expansion. Time will tell whether they will adopt sufficient reform to render outside assistance unnecessary or whether the Protestants, now numbering about 100,000, will become so virile that they will win the day and assume Christian leadership in the Middle East.

EARLY SOCIETIES. Malta came into the possession of the British in 1799. British and American missions immediately established a beachhead on this strategic island. By 1815 the *London Missionary Society* and the *British and Foreign Bible Society* as well as the *American Board of Commissioners for Foreign Missions* had entrenched themselves at Malta. Four other missions were there: the *Church Missionary Society*, which established a missionary college; the *Society for the Promotion of Christian Knowledge;* the *Society for the Propagation of the Gospel in Foreign Parts;* and the *London Jews' Society.*[6]

The first work was that of exploration. *Rev. William Jowett,* a priest of the *Church of England,* visited Egypt and Palestine in 1818. *Rev. Joseph Wolff* of the *London Jews' Society* made important journeys in 1821. *Pliny Fiske* and *Levi Parsons* of the *American Board* arrived in 1819 and traveled extensively in Palestine and Syria. The missionary career of these two pioneers lasted only a few years. Fiske lies buried at Beirut, and Parsons at Alexandria.

The first twenty years of this century of missions was spent largely in spying out the lands. The accounts of the travels, exploits and adventures of these intrepid explorers are most fascinating and exciting. The story of *Eli Smith* and of *H. G. O. Dwight* in their journey from Constantinople to Tabriz, Persia, traveling 2,500 miles on horseback and 1,000 miles by water through a wild country beset with robbers and perils of every kind rivals any tale of travel or adventure ever written.[7]

Little did these earliest missionaries or the churches which sent them out realize the magnitude of the task they were undertaking. The Middle East at that time was largely an unknown quantity. It was a stunning problem in all its aspects—this vast sweep of territory then known as the Turkish Empire, covering the full extent of Bible lands and embracing forty or more millions of diverse peoples thrown together physically and yet separated by irreconcilable dif-

[6] The full name of the society was the *London Society for Promoting Christianity Among the Jews.* Its present name is *Church Missions to Jews.*

[7] William H. Hall, *The Near East: Crossroads of the World* (Interchurch World Movement, 1920), p. 118.

ferences of race and religion. There were backward material conditions of every kind, prevailing ignorance and illiteracy, outlawry, crime, and cruelty—and all under the oppressive hand of a despot at Constantinople, who as Sultan was supreme political ruler and as Caliph was the exalted head of the Muslim world.

In the course of time settled work was begun in the various countries. At first there was no attempt to convert the Muslims. Indeed, the only pretext under which Western missionaries at the beginning of the nineteenth century could gain admission to the Ottoman or Iranian Empires was that of ministering to Christians and Jews. Nor was there any thought of establishing separate Protestant communities. The original aim was to revive the Ancient Churches, which had lost both vision and vitality, and through them to reach out to the great world of Islam which for thirteen centuries had "defied the armies of the Living God." The American Board in its instructions to *Rev. Justin Perkins,* pioneer missionary to Iran in 1834, stated: "Your main object will be to enable the Nestorian Church, through the grace of God, to exert a commanding influence in the spiritual regeneration of Asia."[8] To this end co-operation, not competition, was the order of the day.

But the futility of such hopes and efforts soon became apparent. While at first the missionaries received a friendly welcome in certain quarters, the ecclesiastical leaders of the Eastern Churches soon began to manifest disfavor and, before long, open hostility. Finally a storm of persecution broke out and all evangelicals were branded as heretics and excommunicated from the Church.

This contingency at once created the necessity for a new organization, inasmuch as according to Turkish law persons not connected with some recognized religious sect were denied all civil status, could collect no debts, could be neither married nor buried—in short, they had no longer any part or lot in their own nation. Consequently, the Armenian Evangelical Church (Istanbul) was organized in 1846, and an official firman was secured from the Sultan in 1847 recognizing the first Protestant sect in the Middle East.

The result was that one by one the Western missions were obliged to form their own churches, which are now known as Evangelical Churches. In 140 years of effort comparatively few Muslims have been won to Christ. The Evangelical Churches of the Middle East, therefore, have drawn most of their converts from the Ancient Churches, the largest number coming from the Coptic, Gregorian, and Orthodox Churches. Thus the very thing the Eastern Churches

[8] *A Century of Mission Work in Iran 1834–1934* (Board of Foreign Missions, Presbyterian Church in the U.S.A.), p. 18.

feared has come to pass and they have lost many of their members to the Protestant Churches.

OCCUPATION OF THE FIELD. From the beginning, mission comity has been happily observed by the various societies working in the Middle East. The *American Board* was responsible for the Armenians in Turkey and the Nestorians in Iran. The *Presbyterian Church (U.S.A.)* worked among the Maronites in Lebanon, and also in Iran where in 1870 they took over the enterprise of the American Board. The *United Presbyterians* have been in Egypt since 1854 and are now the largest mission in that country. The *Reformed Church of America* chose the hardest field of all, Arabia. The *Church of England*, with six dioceses in the Middle East, has no great single missionary organization. Its work is carried on by private missionary organizations such as the *Church Missionary Society*, the *Bible Churchmen's Missionary Society*, the *Society for the Propagation of the Gospel*, the *Society for the Promotion of Christian Knowledge*, and the *Church Missions to Jews* (formerly the London Jews' Society). The Church Missionary Society, with work in Iran, Egypt, Jordan, Lebanon, and Syria, has the widest spread of all the missions in the Middle East. The Church Missions to Jews is working among the Jewish people in Israel and Iran. Non-denominational missions with a long history in the Middle East are the *British and Syrian Mission* (Lebanon and Syria), now known as the *Lebanon Evangelical Mission*, *Christian and Missionary Alliance* (Palestine), and the *Egypt General Mission* (Egypt), now known as the *Middle East General Mission*.

EDUCATIONAL MISSIONS. Owing to the fanatical character of Islam in the Middle East it has seldom been possible for the Christian missionary to engage in direct evangelism. Of necessity he has been obliged to adopt a cautious approach in order to avoid giving the impression that he is there to make converts. It is not surprising, therefore, to learn that medical and educational work have been given top priority by all missions operating in this area.

Primary schools were begun everywhere, and at one time the Presbyterians had 220 schools in Egypt alone. Secondary schools followed, and finally colleges. Added to these are schools for Bible training and a variety of technical subjects including medicine, dentistry, commerce, and engineering. The whole system finds its capstone in three great institutions which have achieved international fame: *Robert College* at Istanbul, founded in 1863 by Dr. Cyrus Hamlin; the *Syrian Protestant College* at Beirut, founded in

1866 by Dr. Daniel Bliss; and the *American College for Girls* at Istanbul. The Syrian Protestant College became the *American University of Beirut* in 1920. These three institutions are now independently incorporated and endowed and are no longer, strictly speaking, missionary enterprises. Their influence on the Middle East cannot well be overstated.

Most famous of the three is the American University of Beirut which began almost 100 years ago with 16 students in a rented house. Its graduates now number in the thousands and are to be found occupying high positions in all parts of the Middle East as lawyers, doctors, teachers, editors, engineers, statesmen, and preachers. At the founding session of the United Nations in San Francisco in 1945 there were more graduates from the American University of Beirut than from any other institution in the world. Lowell Thomas has described it as "Uncle Sam's best single investment overseas." Emir Feisal called its founder, Dr. Daniel Bliss, the "grandfather of Syria," and his son, Howard Bliss, the "father of Syria." And he added, "Without the education this college has given, the struggle for freedom would never have been won. The Arabs owe everything to these men."

Other missionary institutions of higher learning include three colleges in Turkey under the American Board and four Presbyterian colleges, two in Egypt, one in Lebanon, and the other in Syria. In every instance these institutions were pioneers in the realm of higher education, especially for women; and to this day they continue to offer to the keenest minds of the Middle East the finest in Christian education. Their halls are filled to capacity and every year students are turned away for lack of room.

MEDICAL WORK. The fact that the two American pioneers in the Middle East, Levi Parsons and Pliny Fiske, were stricken down with fever in their first term of service pointed up the need for medical missionaries. Shortly after the death of his colleague, Fiske wrote to his Board: "May we not hope that the churches of our Lord which have sent us to this land will ere long send to our aid a skillful physician who will watch over our bodily health and also assist us in our spiritual labors."[9]

Before the American churches could respond to the call, however, the first medical missionary to the Arabs, *Dr. Edward Dalton* of the London Jews' Society (Church Missions to Jews) had arrived in Beirut on January 6, 1825. Barely eight years later the first American

[9] James Batal, *Assignment Near East* (New York: Friendship Press, 1950), p. 72.

doctor, *Asa Dodge*, arrived in the same city, followed in 1834 by Dr. *Asahel Grant*, who went to Iran and settled in Urmia, now known as Rizaiyeh.

These men formed the vanguard of a long and illustrious line of medical missionaries who were destined to write one of the most glorious chapters in the annals of missionary work. Others who followed in their train included *Paul W. Harrison*, who blazed the trail in Arabia; *D. R. Johnston*, who launched the medical work of the United Presbyterians in Egypt; and two women doctors, *Anna Watson* and *Caroline Lawrence*, who founded the *American Mission Hospital* in Tanta, Egypt.

The first Christian hospital in the Middle East was established in Jerusalem in 1844 by the Church Missions to Jews. Medical work in Egypt got under way in 1869. Two years later the American Presbyterians commenced their healing ministry in Lebanon. Today their famous *Kennedy Memorial Hospital* in Tripoli treats 4,000 patients a year. The same Mission has six hospitals in Iran, two in Lebanon, and one in Syria. The Reformed Church in America has eight hospitals in Arabia. Altogether there are some 40 church-related hospitals in the Middle East. The vast majority of the patients treated in these institutions are Muslims.

CHRISTIAN LITERATURE. From the beginning missionaries in the Middle East realized the importance of Christian literature. Levi Parsons wrote to the home Board: "A missionary should have on hand a large supply of tracts in Greek, Russian, Armenian, Turkish, and Syriac. All are willing to read, and to all God can impart His blessings." When the first printing press, donated by the members of the Old South Church in Boston, arrived in Malta with *Rev. Daniel Temple* in 1822, Mr. Pliny Fiske wrote: "I think the printing will go on tolerably well, but there will be continual difficulties, hindrances and perplexities until we have a missionary printer—an able, faithful, and pious man." *Homan Hallock*, who landed in Malta in 1826, proved to be such a person. After twelve fruitful years in Malta, the Arabic part of the press was moved to Beirut. Now called the *American Mission Press*, it occupies its own two-story building and with modern machinery can turn out 3,000 pages an hour.

The religious and educational impact of the Mission Press has not been confined to Lebanon. It has flowed across the Euphrates River into Iraq, aiding the missionary stations in Mosul, Kirkuk, Baghdad, Amarah, and Basrah. Through translations in the Persian language, its influence has continued on into Iran, carrying the Christian message to such Moslem-entrenched centers as Teheran, Tabriz, Muhammara, Bushire, and

Isfahan. Its publications found their way wherever Moslems could read in Arabic, the language in which every orthodox Muslim reads his Koran—to China, New Zealand, the Philippines, Australia, Indonesia, Zanzibar, and Dar es Salaam in eastern Africa.[10]

Its ministry has been literally worldwide in scope. Its books are eagerly bought by Arabic readers in all parts of the Western Hemisphere. At one time the only Arabic publications to be found in the United States came from Beirut.[11]

Its greatest achievement was the printing of the Arabic Bible. The monumental task of translation was begun in 1846 by *Rev. Eli Smith*. After his death seven years later it was continued and finally completed by his colleague, *Dr. Cornelius V. A. VanDyck*, in 1864. Since that time the Mission Press has printed the Arabic Bible in 72 different forms and more than 2,300,000 volumes. In addition it has printed a billion and a half pages of biblical commentaries, hymnbooks, tracts, and religious stories. Today its catalog lists more than 500 different book titles.[12]

Other presses at work in the Middle East include the *Nile Mission Press*, for many years located in Egypt but recently moved to Beirut, and the *American Board Press* in Istanbul.

CHRISTIAN BROADCASTING. For some years now the Near East Christian Council has been laying plans for the erection of a 100,000-watt radio station that will broadcast the gospel to all parts of the Middle East. The plans call for an initial outlay of some $250,000. Twenty-five per cent of the personnel in this new venture are to be Americans. Their principal contribution will be the training of Christian nationals in the technique of radio broadcasting. Failing to secure permission for such a station from any of the Arab countries, the Council appealed to Ethiopia. Authorization was readily granted, the franchise going to the *Lutheran World Federation*. The Near East Christian Council will participate in half the program time and will be responsible for all broadcasts in the languages of the Middle East. Plans call for an eventual 50,000-watt transmitter—both medium and short wave—capable of reaching all Africa and the Middle East. Operations will get under way in early 1962.

In the meantime the Audio-Visual Committee of the Near East Christian Council has begun the preparation of programs to be broadcast over commercial stations as outlets become available. In January, 1959, they began a series of weekly programs entitled

[10] *Ibid.*, pp. 32–33.
[11] *Ibid.*, p. 33.
[12] *Ibid.*, pp. 34–45.

In the Procession of Light over the Lebanon Broadcasting Station. The programs, with their popular appeal, were an immediate success; and the Station requested that two be presented each week instead of one, saying that they were their most popular programs. A leading Beirut daily acclaimed the series as the "most successful radio program in many years." Another program, known as *From the World of Spirit,* is heard over Radio Lebanon every Sunday afternoon.

INTER-MISSION CO-OPERATION. Where the Protestant minority is so pathetically weak and the opposition of Islam so deeply entrenched, it is essential that evangelical groups achieve with all possible haste the highest degree of inter-mission co-operation. Some progress has been made; no doubt more will come in time. One example is the *United Mission in Iraq,* which combines the resources of four American boards in that region. The *Near East School of Theology* in Beirut is sponsored by five different bodies. In *Aleppo College* (Syria) two American missions, Congregational and Presbyterian, work side by side. Attempting to co-ordinate the work in all parts of the area is the *Near East Christian Council,* which was formed in 1929. Originally designed for missionary co-operation, it has encouraged the Evangelical and the Ancient Churches to become members. In 1955 the largest Protestant body in the area, the Coptic Evangelical Church, joined. The Council looks forward to the day when the Eastern Churches will also join in the common cause.

XIII

MIDDLE EAST

TURKEY

Area: 301,380 sq. mi.   Population: 24,122,000
Capital: Ankara   Religion: Islam

THE LAND. Turkey is all that is left of the great Ottoman Empire which ruled the Middle East for many centuries. It occupies the peninsula of Asia Minor, which juts westward from the continent of Asia. It is bounded on three sides by three different seas: the Mediterranean on the south, the Aegean on the west, and the Black Sea on the north. It extends eastward to Iran and Russia. Its southern neighbors are Syria (United Arab Republic) and Iraq. A tiny portion of it lies beyond the Bosporus in Europe.

POLITICAL HISTORY. Modern Turkey dates from 1923, when the great nationalist and patriot, Mustafa Kemal, became the first president of the Republic of Turkey. The new Constitution, based on the Western democratic pattern, introduced sweeping reforms in all areas of life, public and private. Freedom of conscience and free compulsory education on the primary level were among the more important innovations. Religious property was confiscated, religious garb was prohibited, polygamy was outlawed, and many mosques and shrines were closed. Divested of his office by the Grand National Assembly, the Sultan went into exile. With the abolition of the Turkish Caliphate came complete separation of Church and State. In short, Turkey became, almost overnight, a thoroughly secular state.

EARLY MISSIONS. With the British occupation of Malta in 1799 and the subsequent buildup of missionary societies on that strategic island, Turkey became the natural gateway to the Christianization of the Middle East. Mention has already been made of the explora-

223

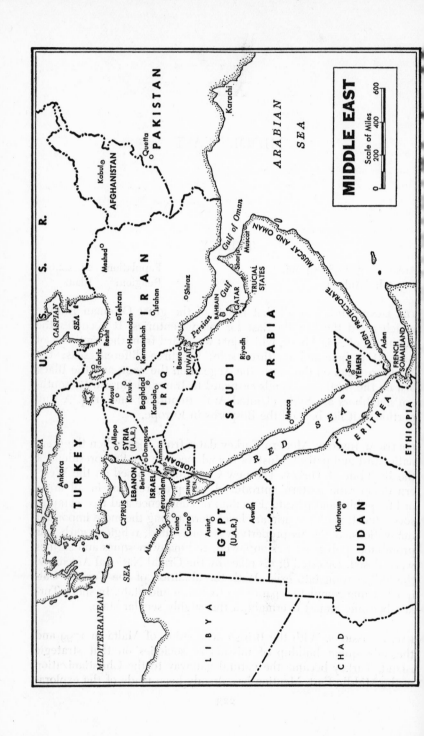

tory nature of the first two decades of missionary work in that part of the world. Landing in Smyrna (Izmir) in 1820, *Pliny Fiske* and *Levi Parsons,* pioneers of the *American Board of Commissioners for Foreign Missions,* set out to explore the possibilities of missionary work in Asia Minor. Ten years later *Eli Smith* and *H. G. O. Dwight* undertook a long and dangerous journey from Malta through Asia Minor, Armenia, and far-away Persia, and then back to Malta. Permanent work in Turkey began with *Rev. William Goodell* of the American Board, who established his residence in Constantinople (Istanbul) in June, 1831. From Constantinople the work spread to other centers in Asia Minor and Armenia. Goodell's long career was devoted to evangelistic work, his outstanding contribution being the translation of the Bible into Armeno-Turkish. Converts came almost exclusively from the Armenian Church, which proceeded to persecute and ultimately to excommunicate the "heretics" who had thus fallen away. The new believers had no other choice than to form a new ecclesiastical structure. The first evangelical church in the Middle East was organized in Constantinople in 1846 and the new Protestant sect received legal status as a religious community in 1850.

In the meantime other societies had entered the field. The *Basel Evangelical Missionary Society* entered Turkey in the 1820's and began a work among the German settlers in the Caucasus region. Later on their work extended to include Muslims and Armenians. *Karl Pfander* was one of their outstanding leaders in that period. During the following decade the great *Church Missionary Society* opened a station in Smyrna from which its workers made extensive journeys throughout Asia Minor. Following the Crimean War this Society and the *Society for the Propagation of the Gospel in Foreign Parts,* also an Anglican mission, opened work in Constantinople, where they ministered directly to the Muslims. They had the famous Karl Pfander head up this delicate and dangerous venture. Violent persecution accompanied conversion, and in the 1870's the work in the capital was discontinued. Insufficient funds was a contributing factor in this decision.

Other societies, both British and American, entered Turkey and remained for longer or shorter periods. The list includes the *American Baptists,* the *Disciples of Christ,* the *Church of the Brethren,* the *English Quakers,* and the *London Jews' Society.* But one by one they all pulled out and today the American Board of Commissioners bears almost sole responsibility for the Protestant cause in Turkey. The *Seventh Day Adventists* report one church of 60 members and three full-time workers in Turkey.

In 1957 the American Board had 89 workers in the country.[1] Their major work is education. They maintain four schools, two for girls and two for boys, one of which is located in the home town of Saul of Tarsus. Their medical work includes a hospital and two clinics. Church work centers in Istanbul, where there are four Armenian Protestant churches, a Greek church, and an English-speaking church in the Dutch Chapel. The publication department of the Mission is also located in Istanbul. An additional twenty-five short-term teachers sailed for Turkey in August, 1958.[2]

Space has already been given to the two world-famous schools in Turkey: *Robert College*,[3] founded in 1863 by Dr. Cyrus Hamlin, and the *American College for Girls*, opened in 1871. Both are located in Istanbul. Through the years these two institutions have had a profound influence on Turkey, Bulgaria, and the entire Middle East.

The American Board reports that after thirty years of secularization Islam is beginning to make a comeback. New mosques are being built and Muslim religious publications are again flowing from the press. Even the Koran, regarded by most Muslims as too sacred to be translated, has now appeared in a Turkish edition. Most significant of all is the fact that in 1956 the Ministry of Education issued an order making compulsory the teaching of Islam in the junior high schools throughout the country.

EGYPT

Area: 385,000 sq. mi.	Population: 23,435,000 [4]
Capital: Cairo	Religion: Islam

THE LAND. No country outside of Palestine is better known to Bible students than "the land of Egypt," which looms so large on the pages of the Old Testament and in the history of Israel. On the north it is bounded by the Mediterranean Sea, on the east by Israel and the Red Sea, on the south by the Sudan, and on the west by Libya. More than 95 per cent of Egypt is desert land, which means that its large population of more than 23 million are concentrated in the 13,500 square miles of the Nile Delta and Valley, one of the most

---

[1] *American Board of Commissioners for Foreign Missions 146th Annual Report, Spring 1957*, p. 28.

[2] *American Board, 148th Report, Fall 1958*, p. 6.

[3] An interesting article on Robert College appeared in *The National Geographic* (September, 1957).

[4] Figures for the entire United Arab Republic are: 437,300 sq. mi. and 27,435,000 population.

densely populated areas of the world. Being a one-crop (cotton) agricultural economy, Egypt has found it difficult to improve its standard of living even with Nasser's many reforms. It has no oil, which is one reason for Nasser's passionate dedication to pan-Arabism.

POLITICAL HISTORY. Great Britain ruled Egypt from 1882 to 1922, when it became an independent state, though British military occupation did not end until 1936. In July, 1952, the army staged a revolution which resulted in the abdication and exile of King Farouk and the establishment of the Republic of Egypt. Gamal Abdel Nasser, one of the principal instigators of the revolution, became president of the Republic in 1956. On February 1, 1958, Egypt and Syria merged to form the United Arab Republic. The United Arab Republic is a member of the Arab League, which has its headquarters in Cairo.

THE PEOPLE. The population of Egypt may be said to consist of two classes, the Arab Muslims and the Copts. The Arab Muslims, originally from Arabia, have settled in the fertile Delta of the Nile and now comprise nine-tenths of the entire population. The Copts are the true Egyptians, the direct descendants of the men who built the pyramids.

THE RELIGION. Muslims comprise 91 per cent of the population, the remainder being made up of various Christian groups. The 1947 census showed 1,186,353 Orthodox Copts, 86,918 Protestant Copts, 72,764 Roman Catholic Copts, 89,062 other Orthodox, 50,200 other Roman Catholics, and 16,338 Protestants. Jews at that time numbered 65,639.[5] Most of them have since fled to Israel.

The Coptic Church of Egypt with a million and a half members is numerically the strongest church in the Middle East. The Copts are recognized as full citizens and they have special representation in parliament. They took to Western education earlier than the Muslims and until recently provided half of all the teachers in the country. At the present time about 30 per cent of the teachers are Copts. They also hold a majority of the posts in certain government departments.

Islam is the state religion of Egypt. Article XII of the Education Act passed in March, 1948, states: "No school may teach pupils, boys or girls, whatever their age, a religion other than their own even with the consent of the parents."

[5] *Statesman's Yearbook 1958*, p. 961.

EARLY MISSIONS. For a time during the eighteenth century the *Moravians* maintained a mission among the Copts in Egypt, but later they withdrew. In 1815 *William Jowett* visited Egypt on behalf of the *Church Missionary Society*. He was cordially received by the Coptic Patriarch but no work was established at that time. In 1821 *Joseph Wolff* of the *London Jews' Society* visited Alexandria and Cairo; and in 1847 resident missionaries were placed in Cairo but they did not remain long.

Modern missions in Egypt may be said to have begun with the Church Missionary Society in 1818. As elsewhere in the Middle East, the aim of the C.M.S. was to co-operate with the existing Eastern Churches (in Egypt the Coptic Church) and through them seek to reach the Jews and Muslims. Co-operation, however, proved impossible and the C.M.S. gave up its work in 1862, returning twenty years later when the British took control of Egypt. From that time the C.M.S directed its work to the conversion of the Muslims. Medical work was begun in Old Cairo in 1899. Menouf, Ashmoun, and Shubra Zanga were occupied in 1910. Ten years later Egypt and the Sudan were separated from the See of Jerusalem; and in 1945 a separate diocese was set up in the Sudan. Anglican work in Egypt was greatly influenced by the godly *Temple Gairdner*. In 1908 he founded the movement known as the "Friends of the Bible." It established fifty parochial branches which met weekly for Bible study, and out of this grew the Coptic Sunday School movement which is now so active. The Arabic-speaking Anglican Church has five parishes, four in Cairo and one in Menouf. Communicants number about one thousand. The Mission has two hospitals and two girls' schools.

By far the largest and most successful mission in Egypt is the *United Presbyterian Mission,* known simply as the *American Mission,* which commenced its great work in 1854. Unlike the Church Missionary Society, this Mission sought and won thousands of converts from among the Copts. Consequently, it was able to build up a large and well-organized Church which became fully autonomous in March, 1958. Known as the *Coptic Evangelical Church in the Nile Valley,* it comprises six presbyteries and has 30,000 members and 300 ministers. It is the largest Protestant Church in the Middle East. It has its own missionary organization, the *Egypt Evangelical Mission,* which supports one missionary working with the Upper Nile Mission in South Sudan. Through the years the United Presbyterian Mission has maintained strong educational and medical institutions in eight large centers. These include, in addition to over 220 primary schools, 2 hospitals, 2 colleges, 4 secondary schools, and 5 preparatory schools. These vastly influential institutions are now under the direction of the Coptic Evangelical Church, in which 111 Presbyterian missionaries are serving as fraternal workers. While referring to the work of the United Presbyterians, mention should be made of the *American University* at Cairo, now an independent institution, which was founded in 1921 by Dr. Charles R. Watson, at one time a member of that Mission.

The *Egypt General Mission,* an independent faith work of British origin, began evangelistic work in Alexandria in 1898. It came into being as the result of the prayers of Miss Annie Van Sommer and was originally known as the Egypt Mission Band. Its first group of seven young men were greatly burdened for the evangelization of the hundreds of Muslim villages in the Nile Delta. As men and funds permitted stations were opened. After fifty years of work the Mission had 45 missionaries and 10 stations, all in the Delta region. The largest center was Shebeen-el-Kanater, where the Mission's only hospital was located. Here three doctors and five nurses ministered to the physical and spiritual needs of more than 50,000 patients in 1955. The Free Schools Law passed in 1948 dealt a severe blow to the modest educational program and its two schools were closed. The production of Christian literature and the distribution of the Scriptures played a large part in the work of this Mission. In 1957 its five churches had a combined membership of 150.

The *Nile Mission Press* (now known as *Arabic Christian Publishers*), which for half a century served not only Egypt but all parts of the Middle East, was also an indirect outcome of the faith and prayers of Miss Van Sommer.

The *Assemblies of God Mission* began work in Assiut in 1908. Three years later a second station was opened at Alexandria. Later still they established an Evangelistic Center in Cairo where 3,000 copies of *The Morning Star* were published each year. By 1929 there were 12 stations and 41 national workers. Most of their converts were from among the Copts. In November, 1931, a *District Council of the Assemblies of God* was organized, composed of both Egyptian and Western personnel. In 1959 there were 118 churches, most of them in the charge of ordained Egyptian ministers assisted by ten missionaries. Weekly attendance averaged 12,000. The outstanding project of this Mission is without doubt the *American Orphanage* at Assiut. It was opened in 1911 by *Lillian Trasher,* who is known as "Nile Mother." For almost half a century the orphanage has been a work of faith and a labor of love, supported entirely by free-will offerings from Egypt and abroad. It has grown to a large institution with twelve major buildings. Since its inception it has accepted and cared for more than 7,000 orphans and widows. Miss Trasher is still in charge and has the personal care of all orphans under three years of age. The orphanage family now numbers 1,200.

Other Pentecostal groups in Egypt include the *Church of God* with 16 congregations and the *Pentecost Faith Mission*. The *Seventh Day Adventists* have 25 churches with a total membership of 770.

The English branch of the Plymouth Brethren, known as *Christian Missions in Many Lands*, has had a very fruitful ministry in Egypt. Without hospitals or schools it has managed to build up 165 assemblies with an estimated membership of 6,500, making it, so far as numbers go, the second largest Church in Egypt. This work is largely indigenous and has had few foreign workers.

RECENT DEVELOPMENTS. The British and French intervention in the Suez Crisis in 1956 dealt a body blow to British missions in Egypt. The sudden expulsion of all British missionaries brought to an end the missionary work of the Church Missionary Society, the Church Missions to Jews, the Egypt General Mission, and Christian Missions in Many Lands. Schools and hospitals were taken over and all property was sequestered by the government. American missionaries did what they could to fill the gap left by the departure of their British colleagues; but the damage was irreparable. Diplomatic relations between Egypt and Great Britain were resumed on the lower level in the fall of 1959. British missionaries may be permitted to return to Egypt in the near future. In the meantime the Nile Mission Press has located at Beirut. The Egypt General Mission changed its name to the *Middle East General Mission* and transferred its workers to Lebanon and, more recently, to Eritrea. Four of its non-British members remained at Herz in Egypt; but in June, 1959, they reported: "We are still in the dark as to what to do or where to go."[6] It is gratifying to know that the schools and hospitals belonging to these missions are continuing their ministry. Some are under Egyptian Christian leadership now; others, Muslim. The Christian staff is reported to be serving at the former *English Mission College* under the Muslim headmaster. Voluntary prayers are conducted and the Christian Union Classes meet once a week. The Shebeen Hospital continues to function under a Muslim superintendent who has permitted the resumption of Bible lessons in the women's wards and weekly evangelistic meetings in the hospital chapel. The Bible-women of the Egypt General Mission continue their village visitation at such main centers as Suez, Ismailia, and Zeitoun. Indeed, one of the bright spots in the Egyptian picture is the admirable way in

[6] *Vision and Commission* (June, 1959), p. 12.

which the Egyptian Christians have assumed responsibilities thrust upon them by the Suez Crisis. The government has permitted the *American Bible Society* to take over the property and direct the ministry of the British and Foreign Bible Society in Cairo.

SYRIA AND LEBANON

THE LAND. As stated in a previous section, Syria merged with Egypt on February 1, 1958, to form the United Arab Republic. From a missionary point of view, however, Syria has no connections with Egypt, whereas it has been intimately linked with Lebanon. Hence the reason for putting these two countries together and treating them as a single unit. Syria is much larger than Lebanon, but Lebanon has a much greater concentration of Christian work. The land area of Syria is 72,000 square miles. Its capital was the ancient city of Damascus. The estimated population is about four million, and the religion is Islam. Lebanon, the smallest of the Middle East states, is located at the southwestern tip of Syria and borders on the Mediterranean Sea. In the matter of religion Lebanon is unique in the Middle East in that it is equally divided between Muslims and Christians, the latter being for the most part Roman Catholic Maronites. The land area of Lebanon is only 4,015 square miles and its population is a mere 1,450,000. Beirut is the capital. After twenty years of French mandatory rule Lebanon gained its independence in 1944. The landing of U.S. Marines in Lebanon in July, 1958, doubtless saved the country from further bloodshed and possible revolution. Lebanon is a member of the Arab League.

POLITICAL HISTORY. Syria is a very ancient country, having been conquered by the Persians, the Greeks, and the Romans in the preChristian era. In Christian times it was once part of the Byzantine Empire and later, for 400 years, it formed part of the Ottoman Empire. Following the breakup of the latter after the first World War, France was given a mandate over Syria. It was not until January 1, 1944, that it realized its full independence. On February 1, 1958, it was annexed by Egypt and is now part of the United Arab Republic.

THE RELIGION. "Syria and Cilicia" are frequently mentioned in the New Testament as regions of extensive missionary activity in the apostolic era. Even before the fall of Jerusalem in A.D. 70 Antioch had become the headquarters of the Gentile branch of the Christian Church. It was there that the epithet "Christian" was first applied to the followers of the Christ. In the seventh century the Muslim Arabs took possession of the country, and from that time Syria has been a Muslim state. Various branches of the Christian Church have managed to survive and today the following groups are found in this region: Greek Orthodox, Jacobites, Nestorians, Armenians, and Maronites.

EARLY MISSIONS. Here again we meet with *Rev. Joseph Wolff*, the much-traveled representative of the *London Jews' Society*. He visited Syria in 1822 and 1823 in search of Jewish communities to whom he might minister the Word of Life. It will be remembered that *Parsons* and *Fiske* of the *American Board* arrived in the Middle East in 1819 and traveled extensively in Palestine and Syria. Fiske's arrival in Beirut in 1823 marked the beginning of the American Board's work in that part of the Middle East. He died there in 1825, but the work which he inaugurated was not allowed to languish. Reinforcements arrived and schools were opened. In 1824 *Mrs. Bird* and *Mrs. Goodell* took girls into their own homes to educate them. Ten years later the first *Girls' School* in the Ottoman Empire was opened in Beirut. Little by little confidence was established and converts were won, mostly from the existing Christian groups. That same year the Malta press was moved to Beirut, where it has done yeoman service for more than a century. In Beirut the *Syrian Protestant College* was opened. In 1920 it became the *American University in Beirut*, which has already been described. In 1870 the American Board relinquished much of its work in the Middle East to the *American Presbyterians*, who had entered Syria in 1835. Today the American Board's work in Syria and Lebanon is confined to two union educational institutions: the *Near East School of Theology* in Beirut, where they provide two staff members; and *Aleppo College* in northwestern Syria, where they have six missionaries.

Through the years the American Presbyterians have been by far the largest mission in Syria and Lebanon. Through their hospitals and schools they have made a significant contribution to the building up of the Evangelical Church, which now numbers about 4,000 communicant members. Educational institutions include two boys' schools (Tripoli and Sidon); four girls' schools (Tripoli, Sidon, Beirut, and Nabatiyeh); and three colleges. These are the *Beirut College for Women*, the *Near East College of Theology* in Beirut, and *Aleppo College* in Aleppo, Syria. These institutions absorb 60 of the 74 Presbyterian missionaries working today in the Syria-Lebanon area.[7]

[7] *121st Annual Report of the Board of Foreign Missions of the Presbyterian Church, U.S.A.*, p. 140.

Three outstanding medical institutions serve this region: *Kennedy Memorial Hospital* in Tripoli; *Hamlin Memorial Sanatorium* near Beirut, the leading center for the care and cure of tuberculosis in the Middle East; and the *Deir-Ez-Zor Hospital* in Syria.

The *British Syrian Mission*, operating on the field as the *Lebanon and Syria General Mission*,[8] is an independent faith mission which has been working in Syria and Lebanon since its founding in 1860. It has no medical work apart from one or two small dispensaries. Its main emphasis through the years has been educational evangelism definitely geared to win converts to Jesus Christ. Its largest institution is the *Training College for Girls* in Beirut, which now has an enrollment of 650 students from some 20 countries. The *Lebanon Bible Institute* in Shemlan is the only Bible school of its kind in the Middle East and trains evangelists and Biblewomen for many missions besides its own. A primary school of 260 boys and girls is the center of the evangelistic work in Tyre, and there is evangelistic work in Baalbek, Hasbeiya, and Ainzahalta. Three other schools are maintained: a boys' school and a school for the blind in Beirut and a primary school in Baalbek. The last named was closed temporarily in July, 1958.

The Mission's only station in Syria is located in Damascus, where there is a primary school for boys and *St. Paul's Middle School* for girls. This work in Damascus was turned over to the local national church in September, 1959. Only four of the Mission's 34 workers are men.

The *Church of God* (Anderson, Indiana) began work in Lebanon before the first World War. Today it has a fairly large, completely indigenous church in Beirut and several evangelists working in Syria. Missionaries stationed in Egypt pay periodic visits to this field. Recent newcomers to Lebanon include *The Evangelical Alliance Mission*, the *Southern Baptists*, and the *Disciples of Christ*. The *House of Onesiphorus*, formerly in Shantung, China, is now located in Lebanon. The *Reformed Presbyterian Church of Scotland* withdrew from Idlib, Syria, in 1952 because of Muslim opposition and transferred its workers to Zahleh in Lebanon. The *Seventh Day Adventists* have eight churches, a college, and a press. The *Danish Church* has an active mission in the desert between Damascus and Palmyra.

Though Lebanon is the smallest of the Middle East countries, its capital city of Beirut is the largest and most important Christian center in that part of the world. It has more educational institutions

[8] On October 1, 1959, the name was officially changed to the *Lebanon Evangelical Mission*.

than any other city in the Middle East. It is the home of two vastly influential Christian presses, the American Press and the Nile Mission Press. Moreover, it is the Middle East headquarters of the British and Foreign Bible Society, where it not only publishes the Scriptures in 30 languages and the Arabic edition of *The Bible in the World,* which is despatched quarterly to all Arabic-speaking countries, but trains colporteurs as well. Scripture distribution in Syria and Lebanon increased 20 per cent in 1956.

IRAN

Area: 630,000 sq. mi.   Population: 20,082,000
Capital: Tehran   Religion: Islam

THE LAND. Iran, with a land area second only to that of Arabia, is one of the most strategically located countries in the Middle East. Extending the entire length of her northern border is the Soviet Union. On the south are the Persian Gulf and the Gulf of Oman. To the west are Turkey and Iraq. Her eastern neighbors are Afghanistan and Pakistan. A large portion of the country is desert. Until quite recently Iran was economically and socially one of the most backward countries in the world. Its greatest source of income is oil, which is found in abundance in the southeast, the refinery at Abadan being the largest in the world.

POLITICAL HISTORY. Reza Shah, an able soldier, seized power in 1925 and set himself to Westernize the country, as Kemal Ataturk had done in Turkey. In an attempt to break the power of Islam, he abolished the veil and introduced other reforms designed to make Iran a modern state. In 1940 the political climate began to change and the government took over all mission schools. The following year Reza Shah was deposed and a reactionary movement developed which came to a climax with the nationalization of the oil industry by Prime Minister Moussadeq, in 1951. During this unsettled period anti-British sentiment ran high and the Church Missionary Society suffered a severe setback. Their hospitals at Isfahan and Shiraz were closed, and two of their three ordained missionaries were expelled. One of them was Bishop Thompson, who had given forty years of devoted service to Iran. The pendulum has since swung the other way, and in 1955 Iran joined the Baghdad Pact. Today it is definitely committed to the West in the cold war. The American Point Four program has widespread operations all over the country and the government is emphasizing education. New colleges have been opened at Isfahan, Shiraz, and Meshed.

THE PEOPLE. The Iranians are the direct descendants of the ancient Persian people of Old Testament times. They have been in possession of their land almost from the dawn of recorded history. They are exceedingly poor and, according to a 1956 estimate, 60 per cent of them are illiterate. Through the centuries they have survived wave after wave of foreign invaders. They are Aryans, not Arabs, by race, and they have never adopted the Arabic language. They have a wonderful literature, and their language, Persian, is a beautiful, poetic tongue.

THE RELIGION. Iran has been the home of three successive religions. The first, Zoroastrianism, was introduced by the prophet Zoroaster in the seventh century before Christ. The second one was Christianity, which was firmly planted in Iran in the third century by Syriac-speaking Christians of Mesopotamia, later known as Nestoria. Four centuries later Islam swept over that part of the world and Iran became a Muslim country. The Church survived as a small remnant, near the Turkish border for the most part. There are 50,000 Armenians, 20,000 Nestorians, 40,000 Jews, and 10,000 Zoroastrians.

The Muslims of Iran belong to the Shiah Sect and are much more tolerant than their brethren in other parts of the Middle East. The government officially recognizes four religions: Islam, Judaism, Zoroastrianism, and Christianity. The law favors religious freedom and extends full freedom of worship to all recognized minorities, including the Bahais. The Evangelical Churches have complete freedom to hold evangelistic services in their own buildings. Converts from Islam are more numerous in Iran than in any other country of the Middle East and their public confession by baptism occasions little comment. The teaching of Islam is compulsory in all schools; but Christian schools under the control of Iranian nationals may give instruction in ethics and may observe Sunday as a day of rest. Meshed, one of the three sacred cities of Islam, is located in Iran.

EARLY MISSIONS. *Henry Martyn* was the first modern missionary to Iran in the beginning of the nineteenth century. After spending four or five years in India as a chaplain of the East India Company he went to Persia to regain his health and to complete his translation of the New Testament. Leaving Calcutta in January, 1811, and touching at Bombay and Muscat, he reached Persia in May, when the heat was at its height. The remainder of the pathetic but thrilling story cannot be told in detail: Martyn's long desert marches, attended by bitter hardships; his loneliness of spirit; the completion and revision of his Persian translation amid physical weakness and suffering; his work of witnessing to the many Mullahs and students who sought him out. He prepared two beautiful gift copies of the Persian New Testament for the Shah and his son; but before the volumes could be presented his growing ill health compelled him to start for Constantinople with the hope of reaching England. The long and desperately hard journey overland proved too much for his frail body, and after enduring the most acute suffering he breathed his last on October 16, 1812, at Tacat in Turkey, where his remains still lie. Though his entire missionary career lasted only six years he completed the monumental task of translating the New Testament into three languages, Urdu, Persian, and Arabic.

Nine years after Martyn's death *Joseph Wolff* of the *London Jews' Society* visited the Jewish communities in Iran. Swiss missionaries of the *Basel Mission* settled in Tabriz in 1831. Most famous of their missionaries was *Karl G. Pfander,* whose long and arduous missionary career took him to Baghdad, Isfahan, Russia, India, and finally to Constantinople. *Rev. Horatio Southgate* of the *American Episcopal Church* made an exploratory trip to Iran in 1836, with a view to strengthening the hands of the Nestorians and Armenians.

In the meantime the first permanent work was established in Iran by the arrival in 1834 of *Rev. and Mrs. Justin Perkins* of the *American Board of Commissioners.* Opened in 1835, Urmia became their central station. With the coming of reinforcements educational and medical work was begun, and in time converts were made. In 1870, after 35 years of effort, the American Board pulled out of Iran and turned its work over to the *American Presbyterian Board.* At that time there were about 3,000 converts, mostly from among the Nestorians.

The *Church Missionary Society* began working in Iran in 1869, almost by accident, when *Rev. Robert Bruce* passed through on his way to India. A devastating famine led him to settle down in Isfahan to give relief. Encouraged when nine Muslims asked for baptism, he decided to remain for a while and ended up by staying there indefinitely, and translating the Old Testament into Persian and revising Henry Martyn's New Testament.

LATER DEVELOPMENTS. For many decades following 1870, Iran was divided between two great missions, the Church Missionary Society in the south and the Presbyterian Church (U.S.A.) in the north. The former sent out its first medical missionary in 1879. Women joined the work in 1891. Kermanshah was occupied in 1897, Yezd in 1898, and Shiraz in 1900. A fifth station was opened later at Abadan. The first bishop of Iran was consecrated in 1912. At one time the C.M.S. had three hospitals in Iran; but all three have been closed in recent years due principally, though not entirely, to lack of staff. Today it has missionaries in Isfahan, Shiraz, and Abadan. The Anglican Church has concentrated on the evangelization of the Muslims and Jews. It has not tried to proselytize the Ancient Churches but has sought instead to strengthen and revitalize them. To this end it has contributed much to the training of their clergy. Its membership, therefore, is not large—between 400 and 500; but, though small, it is described as "truly native and strongly missionary."

The American Presbyterian Mission has developed a strong missionary program along educational and medical lines. It has hospitals in Tehran, Tabriz, Hamadan, Resht, Kermanshah, and Meshed. Robbed of its many fine schools by government action in 1940, it now maintains three community centers in the capital, one in Meshed, and another in Resht. A unique project is the Community School in Tehran for the children of foreign diplomats and Point Four personnel. Classes extend all the way from nursery through high school. Regular Bible classes are held throughout the school and there are chapels for three graded groups every day. Twenty-six nationalities are represented in its cosmopolitan student body of 400.

In 1958 this Mission had 94 missionaries in Iran, including 14 short-term workers. This makes Iran, from a personnel point of view, the second largest of the 22 fields of the Presbyterian Mission, the largest being the Camerouns in Africa. The Church established by the Mission is known as the *Evangelical Church of Iran* and is a member of the World Council of Churches. It has 21 organized churches, 14 ordained ministers, and 2,694 communicants.[9] It operates two high schools, four city elementary schools, and a number of village schools. One of its greatest problems is self-support, which has not yet been achieved.

The *Iran Interior Mission* was founded in 1923 by *Rev. F. M. Stead* as the Faraman Industrial School and Orphanage at Kermanshah. The first reinforcements did not arrive until 1945; and more workers joined them in 1950. Five years later this work was taken over by *International Missions, Inc.*, an independent faith mission which had been at work in India since 1930 under the original name of The India Mission. As yet there are no organized churches. The Mission does not have any medical work nor any educational work apart from that pertaining to the orphanages. Its missionary staff numbers sixteen.

[9] *121st Annual Report of the Board of Foreign Missions of the Presbyterian Church, U.S.A.*, pp. 53, 140.

Other missions in Iran are the *Assemblies of God* with about 600 members and the *Seventh Day Adventists* with 250 members in seven churches.

The *British and Foreign Bible Society* agent in Iran reported in 1957:

We enjoyed full liberty in the task of the distribution of the Scriptures. The total circulation for the year was 32,750 copies compared with 32,596 in 1956 and 26,857 in 1955. These sales have taken place in some 32 languages, in which Persian naturally predominated with a circulation of some 25,000 copies.[10]

The *Church Missions to Jews* have a church and two schools in Tehran.

IRAQ

Area: 172,000 sq. mi.   Population: 6,500,000
Capital: Baghdad   Religion: Islam

THE LAND. Iraq occupies the valleys of two great rivers, the Tigris and the Euphrates. Known from time immemorial as Mesopotamia, it was the cradle of civilization and the home of Abraham, the father of both the Jew and the Arab. It lies between Iran on the east and Syria (United Arab Republic) on the west. It borders Turkey on the north and Arabia on the south. The southern part of the country is desert. Oil, found in the north, is the mainstay of the economy. Seventy per cent of the oil revenues goes to the National Development Board, which plans to restore to the valley of the two great rivers something of its former greatness.

POLITICAL HISTORY. Iraq was freed from the Turks in World War I. A constitutional monarchy was established in 1921 by Great Britain, the Mandatory Power; and in 1932, when the mandate expired, Iraq became a sovereign state and a member of the League of Nations. In 1955 it threw in its lot with the West and joined the Baghdad Pact. In February, 1958, it was united with Jordan in the Arab Federation. Five months later a military coup took the life of King Feisal and Prime Minister Nuri al Said, and brought the present premier, Abdul el Kassem, to power. The revolution, of course, resulted in a new political orientation. The Arab Federation fell apart, and in 1959 Iraq withdrew from the Baghdad Pact. Today it is trying desperately to steer a middle course between Nasserism and.

[10] *Worlds Apart*, p. 54.

Communism. For a time anti-Western sentiment ran high and many foreigners, including missionaries, were expelled from the country. There are increasing signs that Premier Kassem intends to maintain a position of neutrality in the cold war.

THE PEOPLE. Most of the people are Arabs, descendants of the Arabs who migrated centuries ago from Arabia. In the northern part of the country there is a large number of Kurds, some of whom would like to establish their own state of Kurdistan. Communist influence among them is strong. Prior to the Palestinian War there were 120,000 Jews in Iraq; but since the mass exodus in 1950–51 only 5,000 remain.

THE RELIGION. Islam is the state religion of Iraq. In 1940 the Iraqi government passed a law forbidding Iraqis to attend foreign primary schools. It is virtually impossible for a Muslim to change his religion here. Religious minorities include 150,000 Christians, most of whom belong to the Ancient Eastern Churches; 32,500 Yezedees; and 5,000 Jews.

EARLY MISSIONS. Between 1820 and 1850 sporadic efforts were made by various societies to establish Christian work in Iraq. In the 1820's *Joseph Wolff* of the *London Jews' Society* paid a visit to Iraq to contact the large Jewish colonies, at one time numbering over 100,000, in that country. Twenty years later *Henry A. Stern* of the same mission made several visits to Baghdad. For about fifteen years this Society carried on a Jewish work in Iraq and was able to report a number of conversions. The first continuing Protestant work was launched by the *American Board of Commissioners* from their existing base of operations in Armenia. Entering from the north they established a station at Mosul in the 1850's. Here, as in Iran, the American Board did not remain long. The *Church Missionary Society* entered Iraq in 1882 and made Baghdad its headquarters.

LATER DEVELOPMENTS. The *Lutheran Orient Mission,* founded in 1911, has been working all these years among the Kurds in the north. Never a large group, this Mission now has only one missionary, Miss Mary Nienhuis, in Iraq. The Church Missionary Society was unable to continue its work after the first World War; the three small Anglican churches in the country today are under the care of the *Jerusalem and the East Mission* and belong to the Archbishopric of Jerusalem. The *Presbyterian Church (U.S.A.)* entered in 1924 and joined forces with the *Reformed Church in America* and the *Evangelical and Reformed Church* to form the *United Mission in*

Iraq. In 1957 the *Presbyterian Church in the United States* joined the United Mission, but to date its contribution has been made in money rather than in personnel. The largest single project of the United Mission is the School for Girls in Baghdad, which has 250 students. It draws women from the best families in the country, including many Muslims. The first Protestant ordination in Iraq took place on December 19, 1958, when *Rev. Elias Hammo* was ordained in the Arab Evangelical Church in Baghdad. Up to the present the United Mission has no synod or presbytery, there being only six organized but unrelated congregations.

The United Mission has responsibility for the central and northern parts of the country; and the *Arabian Mission,* working from its base in Arabia, is responsible for Amarah and Basrah in the south. *The Evangelical Alliance Mission* entered the field in 1958. Other missions include the *Seventh Day Adventists,* which has four churches; and the *Assemblies of God.* Bible sales were up 50 per cent in 1957.

Since the revolution in 1958 missionary work has been seriously curtailed. Tension has been running high. Evangelistic work has been impossible because no one wants to be associated with the "American imperialists." The Seventh Day Adventist Hospital in Baghdad was closed and fourteen American missionaries were expelled from the country in the spring of 1959. Only three missionaries of the United Mission in Iraq remained; they are connected with the Girls' School in Baghdad. *Rev. and Mrs. Morton Taylor* have recently been permitted to return.

JORDAN

Area:	37,300 sq. mi.	Population:	1,471,000
Capital:	Amman	Religion:	Islam

THE LAND. Jordan is a hatchet-shaped country arbitrarily carved out of the desert east of Palestine, with little or no regard for geography, economics, or history. On the west it is bounded by Israel, on the south by Arabia, on the east by Arabia and Iraq, and on the north by Syria. The small salient west of the Jordan River in what used to be Palestine was incorporated into Jordan in April, 1950. Such well-known biblical cities as Bethlehem, Hebron, Jericho, and the old part of Jerusalem are now in Jordanian territory. The western part of the country is a high plateau; the eastern section is desert. The Haifa-Baghdad road runs through Jordan, as does also the Trans-Arabian pipeline which pumps oil from the Persian Gulf to Beirut. Jordan has no oil of its own. It is politically weak and economically poor.

POLITICAL HISTORY. It is quite impossible here to trace the political fortunes of Transjordan between the two World Wars. Suffice it to say that for many years it was under mandate to Great Britain and had close ties with that country. Soon after World War II, on March 22, 1946, Transjordan became an independent kingdom. In April, 1949, its name was changed to the Hashemite Kingdom of Jordan. Its first monarch, King Abdullah, was assassinated on July 20, 1951, and the present ruler, King Hussein, came to the throne on August 11, 1952. In February, 1958, Jordan and Iraq united to form the short-lived Arab Federation, which fell apart following the Iraqi revolution in July of the same year. Several plots against the life of the King have been made, some of them by his own officers, but each time the plot was discovered in time for effective action. More than once in recent years the country has been in danger of being swallowed up by external aggression.

THE PEOPLE. Before the Palestinian War the population of Transjordan was about 400,000. Since the creation of Jordan this number has been increased by the 400,000 people living in the salient west of the Jordan River. To this figure must be added some 536,000 refugees from Israel, most of whom are still on United Nations relief. This means that the population of the country has trebled in the past decade.

THE RELIGION. Except for a small minority of Arab Christians—about 8 per cent of the population, most of whom live in Jerusalem—the people of Jordan are Muslims. The government recognizes the Christian minority but is trying increasingly to bring them under national control. Since Jordan is a Muslim state, religious education for Christian children who attend government schools poses a problem, for they attend school on Sunday and have Friday off. Severe restrictions are placed on missionary work among the Muslims.

MISSIONS. For well over a century the *Church of England* has had work in various parts of the Middle East, particularly in Palestine. The war of 1948 greatly reduced their staff and curtailed their work. Of seven hospitals in Jordan, Syria, and Lebanon before the war only one remains—the Old Hospital at Nablus, now maintained by the *Arab Episcopal Community*. The *Church Missionary Society* has a girls' school in Amman and extensive relief work in Zerka and Salt. Its hospital in Salt is now operated by the United Nations Relief and Works Agency. The *Jerusalem and the East Mission* has two fine schools which over the years have established an excellent reputation: the *Bishop's School for Boys* in Amman and *St. George's School* in Jerusalem. About 80 per cent of the students are Muslims.

The *Southern Baptists* began work in Jordan in 1952 when they took over the Gilead Hospital in Ajloun from an independent British mission. From Ajloun as a center an expanding program of medical care, education, and evangelism has been projected into neighboring towns and villages. Their educational work includes three kindergartens, four elementary schools, two secondary schools, and a theological seminary. The medical work centers around a hospital and two dispensaries. They have three churches and three chapels.

The *Seventh Day Adventists* have three churches and three schools. The *Christian and Missionary Alliance* has work in Jerusalem and Hebron dating back to the 1890's. The *Independent Board for Presbyterian Foreign Missions* has a church in the "little town of Bethlehem" and *Baraka Sanatorium* at Ain Arroub, ten miles to the south. The *American Friends* conduct two fine schools, one for boys and one for girls, in Ramallah. The eight churches belonging to the *Church of the Nazarene* and the six churches belonging to the *Assemblies of God* are at present under the care of national Christians.

ARABIA

Arabia here refers not to the country but to the peninsula which juts southeastward from Palestine and is bounded on the west by the Red Sea, the south by the Arabian Sea, and the east by the Persian Gulf. It includes several political subdivisions of which Saudi Arabia, with a land area of 618,000 square miles and an estimated population of seven million, is the largest. The only other independent state is Yemen, which has a population of five million. Other territories in the peninsula (together with their populations) include Aden (800,000), Muscat and Oman (550,000), Qatar (40,000), Bahrain (125,000), Kuwait (200,000), and the Trucial States (80,000).

The people in this vast area are all Arabs by race and Muslims by religion. Yemen and Saudi Arabia, in some respects the most backward and feudalistic countries in the world, are completely closed to the gospel. Though both are members of the United Nations neither of them has signed the *Universal Declaration of Human Rights*. Slavery is not only tolerated, it is legalized. Mecca, the most sacred city of Islam, is situated in Saudi Arabia. On its flag are inscribed the words of the Islamic Creed: "There is no God but Allah, and Mohammed is His Prophet." The government of Saudi Arabia will not even permit the Arabian American Oil Company to engage its own chaplains to care for the spiritual needs of its American personnel in Arabia!

EARLY MISSIONS. The Acts of the Apostles makes no mention of any effort to take the gospel to this part of the world though it does refer to the presence of "Cretes and Arabians" in Jerusalem on the Day of Pentecost (Acts 2:11). The Apostle Paul informs us that following his conversion in Damascus he spent "three years" in Arabia (Gal. 1:17-18). Exactly where he was or what he did while there we do not know. We do know that by the end of the fourth century there was a Christian settlement in Hirah. According to Church tradition it was the Apostle Bartholomew who first took the gospel to Arabia. It seems fairly certain that by A.D. 525 Christianity was firmly established there. But the rise and spread of Islam in the seventh century soon obliterated the Christian Church in the Prophet's native land.

MODERN MISSIONS. Modern missionary work in Arabia may be said to have begun with *Ion Keith-Falconer*, the man whose pioneer efforts were used of God to call attention to that ignored peninsula. This young Scottish nobleman, a brilliant Cambridge scholar, gave up fame and fortune and with his equally devoted wife set out in 1885, at his own expense, to reach the destitute Muslims of Arabia and adjacent parts with the gospel. He made his headquarters at Sheikh-Othman, near the British port of Aden, and began a survey of the surrounding territory. But repeated fevers sapped his strength and within two years, at the age of thirty, he died. His work was taken up and is being successfully carried on by the *Church of Scotland*.

When news of Keith-Falconer's death reached the theological seminary of the Dutch Reformed Church in America at New Brunswick, N.J., three young men immediately offered themselves for missionary service in Arabia. When funds were not forthcoming from their denomination they proceeded to organize their own independent mission, the *American Arabian Mission. Rev. James Cantine,* the first missionary, went to Beirut to study Arabic in 1889, followed by *Rev. Samuel M. Zwemer* a year later. In 1894 the *Reformed Church in America* decided to support the project and expanded the work by opening hospitals in Bahrain, Kuwait, Muscat, and Basrah, all on the Persian Gulf. One of the doctors sent out at that time was

Paul W. Harrison, whose fame soon spread far and wide. One day he was summoned to the royal palace of King Adb El Aziz Ibn Saud in Riyadh, in the very heart of the Arabian desert, to stem an epidemic raging in the capital. That call, the first of many that were to follow in the ensuing years, proved to be a turning point in the fortunes of the Arabian Mission; for having secured the royal favor, the missionaries found it much easier to prosecute their work in a hostile climate.

Most illustrious of all the members of the Arabian Mission, and one of the greatest missionaries of all time, was Samuel Zwemer. For sixty years he gave himself indefatigably to the evangelization of the Muslim people, whom he loved with all his heart. A world traveler, a prolific writer, a dynamic speaker, a brilliant scholar, and a great personal worker, Dr. Zwemer was known the world around as "the Apostle to Islam." He founded and for many years was editor of the *Muslim World.* Following "retirement" he taught missions at Princeton Theological Seminary and died in harness at eighty-five. Dr. Zwemer had the mind of a scholar and the heart of an evangelist —a rare combination even in missionary circles.

RECENT DEVELOPMENTS. The Reformed Church in America continues to be the largest mission in this part of the world. Six of its seven hospitals, each with an evangelist, remain strategic centers of Christian witness. Over the years hundreds of thousands of Arabs have been given a personal demonstration of the love of Christ and many of them have been deeply impressed; but few, very few, have openly embraced the Christian faith. There are 48 missionaries, who reside in four centers and continue their healing and teaching ministry. For the first time in thirty years there is no missionary in Amarah where the government expropriated the four residences, the church, and the hospital in March, 1959.

In the spring of 1959 four small congregations of Arab Christians in Muscat, Matrah, Kuwait, and Bahrain got together and laid the foundations for the organization of a synodical Church of Christ in this part of the Middle East. Altogether there are 14 places of Christian worship in the Persian Gulf area.

The *Keith-Falconer Mission* of the Church of Scotland, the second largest mission in Arabia, continues its fine work at Sheikh-Othman, where 15 missionaries are located. After sixty years of blood, sweat, and tears the little church there does not yet have ten members! But the indomitable missionaries refuse to give up.

Since 1945 the *Sudan Interior Mission* has maintained a station in Aden, which they use as a beachhead to contact the half million

Somalis in British and French Somaliland. The *Independent Board for Presbyterian Foreign Missions* has six workers at Sharjah on the Trucial Coast. A newcomer to this part of the world is the *Red Sea Mission Team,* an independent faith mission with headquarters in London, England. Founded in 1951 it now has two stations in Aden Protectorate, one at Sheikh-Othman, and the other at Mukheiras. *The Danish Mission* operates a bookshop in Aden which sustains a steady sale of Scriptures supplied by the *British and Foreign Bible Society.* Aden is the only place in the Arabian Peninsula where the Scriptures may be circulated. Arabia, which has more missionary graves than Christian converts, stands as a constant challenge to the faith and prayers of the Christian Church.

ISRAEL

Area: 7,992 sq. mi.   Population: 1,825,000
Capital: Jerusalem   Religion: Judaism

THE LAND. No country in all the world is so dear to the heart of the Christian as Palestine, whose soil has been rendered forever sacred by the footsteps of the Son of God in the days of His incarnation. Here is the most famous lake in the world—the Sea of Galilee. Here is the town in which our Lord spent thirty years of His earthly life—Nazareth. Here are the "green hill" on which He died, the tomb in which He lay, and the mountain from which He ascended into heaven.

The portion of Palestine now occupied by the Jewish people is not as large as the Palestine of Jesus' day. A large part of Judea and most of Samaria belong to Jordan. Israel has access to only the southern half of the Dead Sea and the upper reaches of the River Jordan. It is surrounded by four Arab nations bent on its destruction: Egypt in the west, Jordan and Syria in the east, and Lebanon in the north. Its Mediterranean coast runs from Haifa in the north to the Gaza strip in the south. No point in Israel is more than 25 miles from the nearest border. In 1955 oil was discovered in the Negeb.

POLITICAL HISTORY. The *Balfour Declaration* of 1917 paved the way for the return of the Jews to Palestine, where they were authorized to establish a "national homeland." The first mass exodus of Jews from Europe did not occur until Hitler came to power. In 1935 about 60,000 Jewish immigrants entered Palestine. The Arabs reacted violently, and for many years Palestine was the scene of strife and bloodshed. Unable to maintain peace between these two factions, Great Britain referred the problem to the United Nations. On November 29, 1947, the General Assembly voted to partition Palestine between the Jews and the Arabs. On May 14, 1948, Great Britain prematurely terminated its mandate; and on the same day the National Council proclaimed the Jewish state of Israel. Soon afterwards war broke out between Israel and her five Arab neighbors. The United Nations intervened and an armistice was signed in July, 1949. Israel insisted on retaining the territory it had gained by the war, which left approximately three-quarters of Palestine in its possession. To date no peace treaty has been signed; consequently, the Arab states are still technically at war with Israel. Without the moral, political, and financial help of the West, particularly the United States, Israel would not have been able to survive as a sovereign independent state. The creation of the Jewish state against the wishes of the Arab world has been the chief cause of tension in the Middle East.

THE PEOPLE. At the beginning of the Palestinian War there were 1,320,000 Arabs and 640,000 Jews in Palestine; but the establishment of the State of Israel resulted in the displacement of almost 70 per cent of the Arab population. As a consequence approximately 950,000 refugees are still living in huge concentration camps in Jordan, Gaza, Lebanon, Syria, and Egypt. There are 175,000 Arabs in Israel, most of them in Galilee. Israel is willing to extend only second-class citizenship to them. The Jews that now comprise Israel came from seventy countries of the world and many of them still speak a foreign tongue. Hebrew is the official language.

THE RELIGION. About 90 per cent of the population are Jews. Of these not more than 25 per cent belong to the Orthodox group, but their influence is greater than their numbers would suggest. The great majority of the 175,000 Arabs are Muslims. Christians make up about 2.5 per cent of the population and belong in the main to the Roman Catholic and the Orthodox Churches. The role of the Christian Church as a spiritual force among the Jewish population is negligible; Christianity in its ecclesiastical form does not attract them.

It is a matter of great regret that so many Hebrew Christians left Palestine, not to return, when Great Britain gave up the mandate in 1948. Those who remained certainly do not number more than 200.[11]

[11] Gote Hedenquist, *The Church and the Jewish People* (London: Edinburgh House Press, 1954), p. 88.

The Constitution provides for religious liberty, but in practice it is greatly restricted. The Ancient Churches—Roman Catholic and Greek Orthodox—are recognized by Israel as religious communities and are able to conduct marriages for their own members. Members of other churches must be married in the synagogue or arrange for the marriage to take place outside the country. Not even the Anglican community is recognized in Israel. It tolerates Gentile Christians, who are free to worship as they please; but it adamantly refuses to recognize the existence of Christian Jews.

Missionaries engaged in purely humanitarian work are welcomed, but any attempt to win the Jewish people to faith in Christ is met with opposition. There is a *League to Combat Apostasy* whose aim it is to obstruct missionary work in every possible way and ultimately to get all missionaries out of the country. Those who show interest in the gospel are under constant surveillance; and pressure is brought to bear when it becomes apparent that a person is preparing to ask for Christian baptism. Perhaps the Israelis are not to be blamed for their intolerance. Hitlerism, the Crusades, and modern anti-Semitism are all too often synonymous with Christianity in the minds of the Jews. The fact that Israel is surrounded on three sides by implacable foes whose avowed intention it is to exterminate her partly explains her attitude towards Western missionaries. In any event, missionary work must be done with the utmost tact and caution.

EARLY MISSIONS. *Anglican* work in Jerusalem began in 1820 when the *London Jews' Society* started working among the Jews in the Holy City. Medical work was begun in 1824. Historic Christ Church, built on the ruins of Herod's palace, had its beginning in 1833. The Anglican Bishopric of Jerusalem was founded in 1940. In 1848 the *Jerusalem Hospital* of the London Jews' Society was opened. After exactly 100 years of Christian witness it was closed during the war of 1948 and has not been reopened. The *Church Missionary Society* took up work in Jerusalem in 1851. Later it opened hospitals at Jaffa and Lydda and an orphanage at Nazareth. Through the years this Mission has worked exclusively with the Arabs in Palestine. A third Anglican mission, the *Jerusalem and the East Mission,* was organized in 1888 to assist various enterprises connected with the diocese. For many years the *Edinburgh Medical Missionary Society* has maintained a hospital in Nazareth. A truly ecumenical project, its present eighteen-member missionary staff comes from five different countries and represents eight denominations. A medical enterprise in Hebron launched by the *Mildmay Mission to the Jews* was later turned over to the *United Free Church of Scotland.* The *Chris-*

tian and Missionary Alliance began work in the 1890's, and by 1914 had work in Jerusalem, Hebron, and Jaffa.

RECENT DEVELOPMENTS. The Arab-Israeli War of 1948 played havoc with Christian missions in Palestine. Damage was extensive. Some properties were destroyed and others were taken over by the military or the government. A good deal of property has not yet been recovered, and much of what was retrieved had to undergo extensive repairs. In a few instances the Israeli government made substantial contributions to repair bills.

The heaviest losses were sustained by the Church Missionary Society, whose responsibility has always been for work among the Arabs. The departure of the Arabs from Israel in 1948 led to the closing of its work in Jaffa and Lydda. Nazareth remained an Arab enclave so the orphanage there was continued. In 1951 these three stations were turned over to the Jerusalem and the East Mission. The *Bishop Gobat School* (Jerusalem), being on the Israeli side of the armistice line, was closed. The *Gaza Hospital* was turned over to the *Southern Baptists* in 1954. They now have work in Jerusalem, Tel Aviv, Haifa, and Nazareth. The *Church Missions to Jews* (formerly the London Jews' Society) continue their good work in Jerusalem, Tel Aviv, and Lydda. Other missions include *Christian Missions in Many Lands, Wesleyan Methodist Missionary Society,* the *Seventh Day Adventists, Assemblies of God, Mennonites,* and the *Church of the Nazarene.* Missionary work in Israel seems to be confined almost exclusively to seven centers: Jerusalem, Jaffa, Tel Aviv, Haifa, Lydda, Nazareth, and Tiberias. Very little has been done in the small towns and villages.

The *British and Foreign Bible Society* and the *American Bible Society* have a Joint Agency in Haifa. In the Israeli army every soldier receives a copy of the Old Testament. It is also a standard textbook in all the schools. This is, of course, the work and policy of the government. The Bible Society is making every effort to offer the *whole* Bible to the people. Sometimes it is of more value to present it in the language of the recipient's birth rather than in Hebrew, which he is still trying to learn. In recent years the Scriptures have been circulated in some 40 different languages in Israel. The circulation for 1958 amounted to 16,256 copies, which included 6,539 complete Bibles.[12]

[12] *The Kingdoms Are Moved,* p. 60.

XIV

INTRODUCTION TO AFRICA

AFRICA

Area: 11,500,000 sq. mi.   Population: 240,000,000

THE LAND. The word "Africa" is said to have come from *Afarik*, the name of a Berber tribe which dwelt in a corner of Tunis in the days before the greater portion of the continent was known, or its vast extent even suspected.

Stanley called Africa the "Dark Continent." The term is fitting from several points of view. Africa is the one continent populated almost wholly by dark-skinned peoples. Also its vast interior lay until recent times in unpenetrated darkness. And finally its native religions are devoid of sacred writings and defined system, and have left their followers in the "blackness of darkness" morally and spiritually.

Africa is the second continent in size, Asia alone being larger. Its area is variously given as from 11,500,000 to 12,000,000 square miles. But figures of such dimensions are hard to grasp, and comparisons are better. Africa is three times the size of Europe, about half again as large as either North or South America, and contains nearly one-fourth the total land area of the globe.

THE PEOPLE. The fact that 523 distinct languages and 320 dialects have been identified in Africa bears impressive testimony to the bewildering array of races and tribes which inhabit the "Dark Continent." Authorities pretty well agree in a general classification of the present native population under five heads:

1. *Berbers*—the aborigines of the Mediterranean states and the Sahara, mainly Caucasian in origin and of very fine physical type.

2. *Arabs*—from Western Asia, constituting the great bulk of the population of Egypt and scattered widely over North Africa.

3. *Negroes*—mainly in the great Sudan, from the Nile to the Atlantic, the purest type being found in the Guinea Coast region.

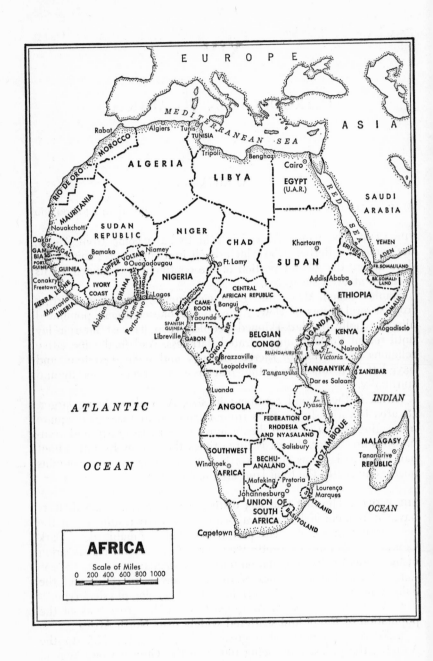

They have receding foreheads, high cheek bones, broad, flat noses, thick lips, woolly hair, and coal-black skin. This region furnished a large majority of the slaves taken to America.

4. *Bantu*—comprising almost all the tribes south of the equator—Kaffirs, Zulus, Basutos, Bechuanas, Matabeles, and others. They closely resemble the Negroes proper in many respects, but have more regular features, are not generally so black or thick-lipped, and speak an entirely distinct group of languages. It is among these people that missionary work has achieved its greatest results.

5. *Pygmies, Bushmen, Hottentots*—scattered through the Bantu section of the continent, dwarfed in stature, primitive and nomadic in habits, and lowest in the scale of African humanity.

EARLY HISTORY. Africa is a paradox in the puzzling contrasts and contradictions its history furnishes. North Africa cradled one of the oldest civilizations of the world. Egypt led the nations in science, art, and literature. Her philosophies dominated the thought of the East. Next to Palestine, Africa was the land most closely connected with Hebrew history. Egypt and Ethiopia figure prominently in both Old and New Testament records. Alexandria for several centuries was the greatest stronghold of early Christianity, with Carthage as a second center. Within two hundred years after Pentecost 900 churches were numbered in North Africa. The first missionary training school was founded in Alexandria in the second century, and from it missionaries carried the gospel to lands near and far. Had the North African Christianity of those early days retained its spiritual life and missionary zeal, the subsequent history of the whole continent might have been very different. Alas, the Church fell a victim to theological controversy, became divided into factions, lost its spiritual vitality and missionary vision, and thus enfeebled, it was unable to stand before the aggressive Muslim invasion of the seventh century. As Roman government in North Africa fell before the Arab conquerors, so Christianity was all but wiped out by the incoming hordes of fanatical Muslims. "For more than 1,500 years Christianity in Africa, except as expressed by the corrupt Coptic and Abyssinian churches, was almost dead, and the 'Dark Continent' throughout its enormous length and breadth remained silent in the shadow of death, waiting for the dawning of a new day."[1]

THE RELIGION. It is difficult, if not impossible, to obtain accurate

[1] Alfred DeW. Mason, *Outline of Missionary History* (New York: Hodder and Stoughton, 1912), p. 164.

statistics in a great, sprawling, diversified continent such as Africa, but broadly speaking the three major religious groups may be divided as follows: 140 million pagans, 70 million Muslims, and 30 million Christians. The Muslims are located almost entirely in North Africa. The pagans predominate in Central Africa; and most of the Christians are found south of the Sahara Desert. Emory Ross, a leading authority on Christian missions in Africa, has stated that this is a larger group of allied Christians than in all the rest of the non-Christian world put together. Of the 30 million Christians, 14 million are Roman Catholic, 12 million are Protestant, and 4 million are Coptic. These figures are approximate, but they afford a fairly good idea of the extent to which Christianity has penetrated the once "Dark Continent."

Paganism, or *Fetishism,* the native religion of Africa, is a species of animism, or the worship of spirits. It is a religion of gross darkness. Its gods are innumerable malignant demons, which the African conceives of as enveloping him on every side and constantly seeking his injury and death. These demons inhabit every object, animate and inanimate—plants, trees, rocks, rivers, reptiles, birds, animals—and also impersonate deceased relatives. Constantly haunted by fear of such evil spirits, the African resorts to *fetishes,* or charms, consisting usually of a mixture of curious natural objects or carved figures—heads of birds, teeth of a lion, leopard, or serpent, pieces of glass, pebbles, human bones, etc.—which he wears upon his body to procure the protection and aid of spirits.

The African's religious philosophy has given rise to various horrible practices. It has led to human sacrifices to supply the needs, avert the vengeance, and win the favor of the gods. It is responsible for the burial alive of the wives of a chief with his dead body, and even for cannibalism, which is said by careful authorities to have originated as a sacrificial feast. It has produced witchcraft, that fiendish system which has taken a toll of countless lives as victims of the witch doctor's poison cup. "It is estimated that 4,000,000 people are killed annually in the endeavor to discover witches. Whole districts have been depopulated by witch trials."[2]

MISSIONARY OCCUPATION. The spread of the gospel and the penetration of African life and culture by Christianity has been phenomenal. In no other continent has the entire social structure been so greatly influenced by Christian missions. One recent visitor wrote:

[2] Wilson S. Naylor, *Daybreak in the Dark Continent* (New York: Young People's Missionary Movement, 1912), p. 99.

I was completely unprepared for the tremendous coverage of the sub-continent of Africa which has been achieved by the missionary agencies. . . . It was a thrilling experience to go into the bush country . . . and find village upon village with Christian congregations.[3]

The Christian penetration of Africa has not been uniform by any means. Christianity has made practically no headway at all among the Muslims in the north. Its greatest numerical gains have come among the Bantu in South Africa. The largest number of Protestant Christians is found in the Union of South Africa, where 90 per cent of the three million Europeans are church members. Ten per cent of the Bantu there are reckoned to be part of the Christian community. The Belgian Congo, with 2,100 Protestant missionaries, has more missionaries per capita than any other country. Happily, the results have been commensurate with the investment, for today the Christian Church—Roman Catholic and Protestant—claims 42.5 per cent of the population. In Tanganyika, 16 per cent of the people profess Christianity.

Missionary personnel is likewise unevenly distributed. Kenya with a population of six million has 847 missionaries and 4,230 national workers, while Tunisia with four million has only 30 missionaries and 2 national workers, both of whom are women. Excluding the Union of South Africa with its many Europen pastors and their white congregations, there are 15,000 Protestant missionaries in Africa. Twenty-eight per cent of them are in two countries, the Belgian Congo and Nigeria. There are 15 Christian Councils, five of which are affiliated with the International Missionary Council. The Scriptures have been translated into about half of the 800 languages and dialects of Africa. The entire Bible is now available in 59 languages, the New Testament in 114 additional languages, and portions of Scripture in 219 more.

AFRICAN CHRISTIAN CONVERTS. The African is of a deeply religious nature, and gives abundant evidence of ability to apprehend lofty spiritual truth. That some converts backslide, yield to temptation, and fail at some point in their Christian walk is not to be wondered at when one considers the heathen heredity and depths of degradation from which they have emerged. Yet many African Christians have come into a spiritual experience of a very high order. Their openness of mind and simplicity of faith have led some of them to a knowledge of Christ and a likeness to Him in character and walk beyond the generality of believers in Western lands.

[3] Roy G. Ross, "Report on Africa," *National Council Outlook* (May, 1958).

THE MUSLIM MENACE. Dr. Cornelius H. Patton in his *Lure of Africa* devotes a chapter to "Islam on the March." He reveals in startling fashion the magnitude of the Muslim menace throughout the northern half of the continent. And he is only one of many writers who have sounded a loud alarm. Both the World Missionary Conference at Edinburgh in 1910 and the Conference on Muslim Missions held in Lucknow in 1911 characterized the Muslim advance in Africa as perhaps the largest world missionary problem confronting the whole Church at the beginning of the twentieth century.

The facts in brief are these. The Arab slaver of yesterday has become the Arab trader of today. His attitude toward the African has changed from one of arrogance to one of condescension. Closer akin than the European to the black man, he has more readily adapted himself to native conditions, and with shrewd diplomacy and patient persistence has succeeded not only in capturing trade but also in making converts by the wholesale to the Muslim faith. The easygoing morals of Islam make it far simpler to win converts to that religion than to Christianity.

Tribe after tribe has been annexed by these Muslim missionaries, until now by far the larger portion of the great Sudan has been pre-empted for the Prophet, and the Muslim advance is sweeping southward into the Congo region and down the two coasts. Nigeria is 40 per cent Muslim, and Cameroun is said to have 500,000 adherents to Islam. The important Swahili tribe of British East Africa is being rapidly won over, and Muslim influence is being powerfully felt as far south as Uganda, Tanganyika, and Nyasaland.

ROMAN CATHOLIC OPPOSITION. Those who know this religion only as practised in free countries will hardly be prepared to appreciate the situation which Protestant missions face in those large sections of Africa controlled by Roman Catholic states, where Roman Catholicism is actively supported by the government. The whole training of the priests leads them to hate Protestant missionaries and to oppose them in every way. "At the beginning of Congo Missions the College of Propaganda at Rome issued this Encyclical, 'The heretics are to be followed up and their efforts harassed and destroyed.' "[4]

The early Protestant missions to Abyssinia were expelled through Jesuit intrigue. Mackay and his colleagues in Uganda were maligned, persecuted, and plotted against by Roman Catholic missionaries. Any amount of evidence is forthcoming from missionaries laboring

[4] R. D. Bedinger, *Triumphs of the Gospel in the Belgian Congo* (Richmond, Va.: Presbyterian Committee of Publication), p. 176.

in Belgian and Portuguese territory as to the systematic and determined efforts of the priests, often by foul means, to obstruct and destroy Protestant work.

Added to this are the hampering legal restrictions imposed by Roman Catholic governments upon Protestant missions, and the serious hindrance of the compromising policies and corrupt practices of Roman Catholic propagandists.

There is no doubt that the Roman Catholic Church is making an all-out bid for the soul of Africa and is determined to dominate that continent in the near future. It uses a variety of methods, including a sound and vigorous educational program, the competitive multiplication of churches, and the saturation of whole communities. In many parts of Africa the Roman Catholics have a virtual monopoly on higher education and are not averse to using this to lure Protestant students into the fold. In Central Africa north of the Zambezi the number of Roman Catholic converts multiplied 65 *times* between 1900 and 1950.

MODERN TRENDS. Change, drastic and dynamic, is the order of the day in all parts of the great continent. Politically, Africa is the last great area of the world in which the colonial pattern still predominates; but the tide of nationalism is rising with each passing day and threatens to engulf the white man unless he comes to terms with reality while there is time. Already new nations have been born, and others are in the pangs of birth. The first Conference of Independent African States, which convened in Accra, Ghana, in April, 1958, included delegates from eight nations and represented 80 million people. Modern cities are springing up all over Africa and attracting the rural population by the millions into these great urban centers where money is made—and spent—faster. As a result tribal life is rapidly disintegrating. The power of the witch doctor is broken, and paganism is fast losing its hold, especially on the younger generation. Education, once the responsibility of the missions, is now passing under government control. Elementary schools are multiplying and every effort is being made to meet the universal demand for higher education. A new day is dawning in the once "Dark Continent," and Christian missionaries and their African colleagues are making a vital and significant contribution to the new order which is emerging.

EARLY MISSIONS—FIVE AVENUES OF APPROACH. It will give us a clearer picture of the vast enterprise of Christian missions in Africa if, before discussing its progress in the individual countries, we first outline the various avenues along which the missionary pioneers traveled in their advance into the heart of the continent in the early years of the nineteenth century. Broadly speaking there were five separate and distinct areas involved and as many avenues of approach.

1. *From the West.* In 1795 the *Baptist Missionary Society* (England) adopted Sierra Leone as its second mission field. They sent out two men, *Rodway* and *Grigg.* One of them died within a number of months and the other proved to be a disappointment. As a result the venture was abandoned two years later. That same year six missionaries of the newly formed *Glasgow and Edinburgh Societies* arrived in Sierra Leone, but this enterprise likewise was of short duration. The first enduring work was established by the *Church Missionary Society* in 1804. It was followed in 1811 by the *English Wesleyans.* The second center of Christian influence in West Africa was Liberia. Two Negro clergymen were among the first settlers to arrive from the United States in 1821. The first white missionaries entered the country in 1833 when the *American Methodists, Presbyterians,* and *Congregationalists* all began work there. Missionary work in the Gold Coast (now Ghana) began with the arrival of the *Basel Mission* in 1828, followed by the *English Methodists* in 1834. Eight years later *T. B. Freedman* entered Nigeria and established work in the southwest part of the country. *Henry Townsend* was the first *Church Missionary Society* representative; he arrived in 1845. The *Southern Baptists* entered Nigeria in 1850. The greatest numerical success has been achieved in Nigeria and Ghana. The strongest denomination in West Africa is the Wesleyan Methodist, the Anglicans and the Baptists following in that order.

2. *From the South.* Protestant missions among the Hottentots and Bushmen began in 1799 with *John T. Vanderkemp* of the *London Missionary Society.* With the coming of *Robert Moffat* in 1817 they extended their work to the Bantu. Moffat spent most of his long career at Kuruman in Bechuanaland where he translated the Bible into the Bechuana tongue. In 1840 *David Livingstone* joined Moffat at Kuruman, but he did not remain there long. His passion for exploration led him into the very heart of Africa. His first expedition took him across the Kalahari Desert to Lake Ngami. From there he traced the Zambezi to its source and then proceeded to Angola on the west coast. Retracing his steps he followed the Zambezi to its mouth, discovering Victoria Falls on the way. In 1866 he set out on his last expedition, determined to find the source of the Nile. In the course of his journeyings he discovered the great lakes of Central Africa and verified the upper reaches of the

Congo. Sixteen years after Livingstone's death the London Missionary Society was fairly well established on Lake Tanganyika; but the price was high. Of 36 men, 11 had died and 14 had retreated in broken health. Five expeditions costing £40,000 were sent out, leaving behind them a trail of hastily dug graves.

3. *From the North.* The late occupation of North Africa on the part of the Christian Church is one of the strange anomalies of missionary history. Separated from Christian Europe by only the nine miles of the Strait of Gibraltar, it should have been the first mission field to claim the attention of the Church. Actually it was one of the last areas to be entered. Missionary effort in North Africa began in Egypt. The year was 1825. The Mission was the *Church Missionary Society.* The original party consisted of five persons. Three of them remained in Egypt to work among the Copts while the other two proceeded to Ethiopia. This venture proved abortive and Ethiopia had to wait another forty years to receive the gospel from the *Swedish Evangelical Society.* In 1854 the Church Missionary Society in Egypt was joined by the *United Presbyterians.* Unlike the Anglicans, they did not co-operate with the Copts; rather they sought to win them to a more dynamic and evangelical faith. Other parts of North Africa were much later in receiving the gospel. The pioneering society among the Muslim population was the *North Africa Mission,* which entered all four of the Barbary States in the 1880's. The home of some of the most fanatical Muslims in the world, North Africa has proved to be a difficult and unproductive field. Preaching the gospel there has been like sowing seed on rocks. The few seeds which took root and grew were soon withered by the scorching sun of persecution. The missionary body, never large, has sustained more than the usual number of casualties through the years, with the result that this 3,000-mile stretch of territory with approximately 25 million inhabitants is less adequately evangelized today than it was thirty years ago. Many stations occupied then are closed now for lack of workers.

4. *From the East.* The Church Missionary Society workers who had entered Ethiopia from Egypt in the 1820's were forced out in 1838. *John Ludwig Krapf,* a German worker, took refuge in Aden and from there made his way to the island of Zanzibar. In 1844 he established the first mission station on the east coast at Mombasa. Two months later his wife and his only child died. Himself sick to death with fever, the deeply stricken man wrote to the directorate of the Society these prophetic words:

Tell our friends that in a lonely grave on the African coast there rests a member of the Mission. That is a sign that they have begun the struggle with this part of the world; and since the victories of the church lead over the graves of many of her members, they may be more convinced that the hour is approaching when you will be called to convert Africa, beginning from the east coast.[5]

Krapf projected bold plans for a chain of stations across Africa from east to west and from north to south in the form of a cross, each station bearing the name of an apostle. People smiled at his idea as a mere idealistic dream; but now, after a century of advance, the dream has become a reality. *John Rebmann* joined Krapf in 1846 and together they added to their missionary achievements the distinction of discovering the two highest peaks in Africa, Kilimanjaro and Kenya. Reinforcements were slow in coming. Krapf retired in 1853 and Rebmann carried on almost single-handedly until he had to withdraw in 1873.

For some years Zanzibar was the main base of operations for Protestant missions in East Africa. The *Universities' Mission to Central Africa* sent out a group of men under the personal direction of Livingstone to establish a station in Nyasa in 1860. Misfortune dogged the steps of these pioneers and they had to withdraw to Zanzibar. Nothing much came of the enterprise until *Bishop Steere* joined the Mission in 1874 and imparted new vigor and vision to it. In time a chain of stations was established from Zanzibar to Lake Nyasa.

Henry M. Stanley made Zanzibar his base and followed the route taken by Krapf and Rebmann on his first journey to locate Livingstone. As a result of his second journey, the *Church Missionary Society* sent a party of eight to Zanzibar in 1874. Tragedy stalked the Mission for years, but patience and perseverance finally won the day and a series of stations was formed from Zanzibar northwest into Uganda, leading eventually to the evangelization of Kenya.

5. *Via the Congo River.* It was *Henry M. Stanley* who really opened Central Africa to the gospel. His 999-day crossing of Africa from Mombasa to the mouth of the Congo River, at the terrific cost of 200 lives, fired the imagination of the Church at home. The *Baptist Missionary Society* of England accepted the challenge and immediately transferred two experienced missionaries, *George Grenfell* and *Thomas Comber*, from the Cameroons to Congo in 1878. Learning that the Congo River was navigable for hundreds of

[5] G. Warneck, *History of Protestant Missions* (New York: Revell, 1904), p. 258.

miles above the Falls, they put a gospel boat on the river above the rapids and established a line of stations right into the heart of Congo. The *Livingstone Inland Mission* entered Congo that same year and founded seven stations, chiefly on the southern tributary of the Congo River. In 1884 the work was turned over to the *American Baptist Mission.* Other societies, American, British, and Continental, soon followed and today the Belgian Congo is one of the great mission fields of Africa.

XV

WEST AFRICA

SENEGAL[1]

Area: 80,617 sq. mi.
Capital: Dakar

Population: 2,270,000
Religion: Animism
            Islam

THE LAND AND THE PEOPLE. Senegal is located in the extreme western part of Africa on the Atlantic coast. It is bounded on the north by Mauritania, on the south by Guinea, and on the east by the Soudanese Republic. The population includes Moors and allied Berber races, but the majority are Negroes. There are 25 tribes, of which the largest is the Oulof with 832,000 members. Islam has won the most important tribes and the followers of the Prophet are increasing daily.

MISSIONS. Because the paramount power (France) was Roman Catholic, Senegal has been sadly neglected by Protestant missions. The first and for many decades the only Protestant society in Senegal was the *Paris Evangelical Missionary Society,* which began its work in 1862. This work, however, did not spread throughout the

[1] French West Africa is no longer a political entity. A referendum in September, 1958, completely changed the political status of the eight territories which up to that time constituted French West Africa. Seven of the territories, Mauritania, Senegal, Sudan, Voltaic Republic, Niger, Ivory Coast, and Dahomey, voted to become autonomous republics within the French Community. Guinea alone voted to sever all connections with France and become an independent state. Togoland, a French protectorate under United Nations trusteeship, is slated for full independence in 1960. Hence the reason for treating each of these new countries individually. There is no Protestant work in the Islamic Republic of Mauritania; therefore it is not included in this chapter. Two of these countries, Senegal and Sudan, federated in April, 1959, to form the Mali Federation. Dahomey and the Voltaic Republic agreed to join the Federation, but under pressure from the anti-federalist Ivory Coast they decided to withdraw. Doubtless the Mali Federation will attract these and other states into its orbit in the not too distant future.

colony; seventy years elapsed before another Protestant mission, the *Worldwide Evangelization Crusade*, entered this needy field in 1936. In 1949 the *Assemblies of God Mission*, working in Upper Volta, sent a survey team to Senegal to ascertain the needs of the people and the prospects of beginning work there. But it was not until July, 1956, that they were able to establish their first station at Tamba-Counda. Sixteen months later they could report:

When the church in Tamba-Counda was finally completed we had a glorious day of dedication on November 3, 1957. This was the day for which we had hoped, worked, and prayed. Within one year God had enabled us to complete three buildings and dig a 100-foot well. We had fulfilled the requirements of the government. Now we must quickly build other stations in order to occupy the entire area for our Lord.[2]

The government has allotted them two additional stations at Kedougou and Kaolack. Buildings at Kedougou were completed in the spring of 1959, and construction work is proceeding at Kaolack.

GUINEA

Area: 92,640 sq. mi.   Population: 2,530,000
Capital: Conakry   Religion: Islam
                                                         Animism

THE LAND AND THE PEOPLE. Guinea lies on the Atlantic coast between Portuguese Guinea on the northwest and Sierra Leone on the southeast. It extends inland along the northern boundary of Liberia as far as the Ivory Coast. On the north it is bounded by Sudan. Some 23 different tribes inhabit this area, the most important of which are the Fullah, Malinké, and Susu. The Fullahs and the Malinkés are fervent Muslims. In the forest regions are three powerful tribes, the Kissis, Tomas, and Guerzas, who are entirely under the power of fetish priests and sorcerers and so far have proved impervious to Islamic influence. Muslims are said to out-number the pagans five to one.

MISSIONS. The first and largest Protestant mission in Guinea was the *Christian and Missionary Alliance*, whose workers opened a station at the Muslim town of Baro in the Niger Valley in 1918. Four years later the Mission extended its work to Kankan, which has since become the headquarters of the Guinea work. The Mission press, which serves all of West Africa, is also located there. Converts in this center have been won from seven different tribes. The *Guinea*

[2] *Senegal* (pamphlet), p. 9.

Bible School is situated at Telekoro. In 1948 four tribes were represented in the student body of twenty. Today the work goes on in
12 main stations. Among the Muslim tribes the converts are few,
but in pagan areas there are 10 large and thriving churches. The
New Testament has been translated into Fullah. The Bible school
students are being taught to translate some of the simpler New
Testament portions into their own tribal dialects.

The *Society for the Propagation of the Gospel* reports 6 missionaries and 10 nationals working in four churches. The *Open
Bible Standard Churches* have two congregations.

SIERRA LEONE

Area: 27,925 sq. mi.   Population: 2,500,000
Capital: Freetown   Religion: Animism

THE LAND. Sierra Leone is a small British possession on the southwest corner of Africa's bulge. Liberia is its eastern boundary,
Guinea is on the north and west, and the Atlantic Ocean is on
the south.

POLITICAL HISTORY. Sierra Leone comprises two territories, the
Colony and the Protectorate. The former was acquired in 1787 by
a group of British settlers for the purpose of founding a colony for
freed slaves. The administration of the colony passed into the hands
of the British government in 1808. In 1896 the hinterland, a much
larger piece of territory, was proclaimed a Protectorate. The Colony
proper consists of a peninsula about 25 miles long and 10 miles
wide. The British colonial policy of indirect rule has resulted, so far
as the Protectorate is concerned, in the retention of 144 Chiefdoms,
each under the control of a Paramount Chief and Council of
Elders known as the Tribal Authority. They are responsible for
the maintenance of law and order.

THE PEOPLE. Here as elsewhere in Africa there are many tribes, each
with its own area and language. The Mendis are the most numerous and occupy the central part of the Southern Province. They are
described as "hardy, cheerful and industrious." The chief occupation of another tribe, the Bulloms, is fishing. Only the Vei tribe has
a written language. Immigrant tribes include the Temnes, Fullahs,
and Mandingos, most of whom are Muslims.

THE RELIGION. The primitive tribes in the hinterland are animistic.

The invading tribes have introduced Islam, which is spreading rapidly in this particular part of West Africa. The Mendi people are wholly Muslim; indeed, the entire Colony is under the influence of Islam. Being a British Colony, Sierra Leone offers complete freedom to the Christian missionary.

MISSIONS. Sierra Leone has the distinction of being the earliest Protestant mission field in West Africa. The first attempt to plant the Church there was made in 1795 by the *Baptist Missionary Society,* which two years before had sent William Carey to India. *Rodway* and *Grigg* were the two pioneers. One of them died; the other proved unworthy. As a result the mission closed in 1797.

That same year six Scottish missionaries were sent out by the *Glasgow and Edinburgh Societies* which had just been formed. This enterprise likewise came to nothing. The first enduring work was established by the *Church Missionary Society.* Africa was the earliest field entered by this great Mission. Its first two missionaries were sent in 1804 to the Susu tribe on the Rio Pongas. Twelve years later, when the Rio Pongas project proved unfruitful, the Mission was transferred to Sierra Leone. One of the outstanding pioneers of this Society was *William A. B. Johnson,* whose brief missionary career of seven years coincided with a remarkable mass movement to Christianity. Here in this one field the Church Missionary Society lost 53 men and women in the first twenty years. But the intrepid pioneers persevered, and the work was gradually extended to the Bullom and Mendi countries, and later to the Temnes, Yalunkas, and Limbahs. As early as possible the Mission shifted responsibility to the Church, which was organized on an independent basis in 1861. From that time the Church undertook the support of its own work in church and school, aided by a small grant from the Society, which terminated in 1890. In 1876 the Church made itself responsible for missionary work in the Bullom and Mendi countries; and in 1908 it assumed responsibility for all the C.M.S. work in the interior. Today the Anglican Church in Sierra Leone has about 11,000 members, most of whom are English-speaking descendants of the freedmen. The Mission's contribution is now confined to educational work in *Fourah Bay College* in Freetown and *Union College* in Bunumbu.

The *English Wesleyans* entered Sierra Leone in 1811 and after several failures established a continuing work. In spite of many difficulties, progress was made; schools were opened and leaders were trained; and eventually the Church became self-supporting. Other groups of Methodists entered the country and commenced work, including the *United Methodist Church*, the *African Methodist Episcopal Church*, and the *Wesleyan Methodist Church*. In 1958 the Methodist Church reported a membership of 8,323 with an estimated community of 16,000. The Report mentions "the total lack of candidates for the Ministry" and lays it to the fact that the minister nowadays is regarded more as a "poor relation" than as a respected leader.

In the 1840's the *American Missionary Association* began a project in the Mendi country. In 1882, by which time several stations had been opened and a number of churches established, the work was transferred to the *United Brethren in Christ*. The change introduced new life into the Mission and from that time growth was more rapid. In 1959 this Society had 24 missionaries in Sierra Leone, assisted by 33 national workers of whom eleven were ordained. Thirty-eight churches had a membership of 1,125.

The *Christian and Missionary Alliance* sent missionaries to Sierra Leone in 1890 as a stepping-stone to the great Sudan beyond. Having gained entrance to the Sudan, the mission in Sierra Leone was abandoned in 1918. Later on, in 1945, the *Missionary Church Association* assumed responsibility for this work.

Other missions in the country are the *Evangelical United Brethren Church*, *Assemblies of God*, and some *Pentecostal* groups whose adherents number about 10,000.

LIBERIA

Area: 43,000 sq. mi.   Population: 2,500,000
Capital: Monrovia   Religion: Animism

THE LAND. Liberia, Africa's oldest independent republic, is located on the western bulge of the continent, facing the Atlantic Ocean on the south. The Ivory Coast is on the east, Guinea on the north, and Sierra Leone on the west. The low, flat coastline is about 350 miles long. Rubber is the chief export; and the Firestone Rubber Company has two plantations of huge proportions.

POLITICAL HISTORY. The American Colonization Society, founded in 1817, sponsored the establishment of a colony for freed slaves on the west coast of Africa. The first band of immigrants landed in 1822. Twenty-five years later the Republic of Liberia became a sovereign state and adopted a Constitution patterned after that of the United States of America. Their motto reads: "The Love of Liberty Brought Us Here."

THE PEOPLE. The people fall into two major categories, the indigenous population and the ex-slaves who returned from America. These Americo-Liberians, as they are known, are highly civilized, and live for the most part in the capital city of Monrovia. They number about 12,000. The government is largely in their hands and they virtually run the country.

The indigenous population belongs in the main to six principal stocks, the Mandingos, the Gissi, the Gola, the Kpwesi, the Kru, and the Greboes. Altogether there are about 30 different tribes. About 60,000 coastal Negroes may be considered civilized. English is the official language, and all missionary work, including literature, must be done in that language in spite of the fact that few of the indigenous people speak it.

THE RELIGION. Animism is the religion of the indigenous peoples, 95 per cent of whom still retain their tribal customs. The Mandingos are Muslim. The Americo-Liberians are, of course, nominal Christians. There is complete freedom of religion. President William V. S. Tubman, himself a graduate of a Methodist school, is a fine Christian gentleman and looks with favor on the work of Christian missions in his country.

INITIAL DIFFICULTIES. Protestant missionary work in Liberia began with the first settlers from America in 1822. The difficulties encountered in those early days can scarcely be imagined. Staggering losses were sustained by all societies. Of 79 missionaries sent out by the *Church Missionary Society* before 1830, 44 died during their first year! Of 75 sent out by the *American Presbyterian Mission,* 31 died and many more were invalided home. Though Liberia continued to exact a terrific toll in lives, a passion for the lost kept many of the brave and dauntless missionaries at their posts regardless of the cost. *Melville B. Cox,* the first foreign missionary of the *Methodist Church* (American), landed in Liberia in 1833, only to die within four months. But his noble example stirred the Church and his dying appeal, "Let a thousand fall before Africa be given up," was heeded.

EARLY MISSIONS. *Mr. and Mrs. Ephraim Bacon,* who had been in Liberia as agents of the American Colonization Society, were the first missionaries appointed to the country by the newly organized *Domestic and Foreign Missionary Society.* But the American Colonization Society prohibited missionary work in the new Republic and refused entry to the Bacons as missionaries. *Mr. and Mrs. James*

Thompson, a Negro couple already in Liberia, came forward and offered their services. They were appointed teachers in 1835, and opened a school at Cape Palmas with five boys and two girls.

The early settlers in Liberia, those who had any religious affiliations at all, were Baptists and Methodists for the most part. Among them were several pastors belonging to these denominations. Two Baptist ministers, *Lott Carey* and *Colin Teague,* were sent out by the *Richmond African Missionary Convention,* a Negro auxiliary of the *General Baptist Convention of America.* They established the first Baptist church in Monrovia, which is still standing.

The first white missionaries went out from America in 1833 when the Methodists, Presbyterians, and Congregationalists all began work in Liberia. From 1835 to 1856 the *American Baptists* sent out a few white workers, then adopted a policy of sending only Negro missionaries. In 1875 they withdrew from the field. The Southern Baptists also withdrew from Liberia in the 1870's when they decided to concentrate all their forces in the Yoruba country in southwest Nigeria. Two Negro Baptist groups have continued through the years, the *Lott Carey Baptist Foreign Mission Convention,* which was organized in 1897, and the *National Baptist Convention, U.S.A.* In 1955 the latter reported 5 schools, 17 missionaries, 80 national workers, one hospital, and thousands of Christian believers.

The *American Methodist* work began in 1833 with the coming of its first missionary, *Melville B. Cox.* From time to time reinforcements, Negro as well as white, arrived from America. For a time during the second half of the century the work languished, but under the inspiration of Bishops Taylor and Hartzell the Mission revived. Today their work centers primarily around two stations, Gbarnga and Ganta, and the *College of West Africa* in Monrovia, which is the oldest institution in Liberia, dating back to 1839. They also co-operate with the American Episcopal Mission in the *Cuttington College and Divinity School.* Besides church work the Ganta station includes a hospital, a leper colony, and a school. Church membership is around 20,000, and there are four districts in its Annual Conference.

The *American Episcopal Church* made several abortive attempts to start work in Liberia in the 1820's. Their first white missionary was *John Payne.* He arrived in 1835, and in 1851 became the first missionary Bishop of Liberia. Other missionaries followed in rapid succession but the climate took a fearful toll and progress was slow. A fine educational system under the leadership of *Bishop Samuel Ferguson* (1884–1916) was established, including village and church schools. *Cuttington College and Divinity School* is the center of the educational work. They have 122 churches and 7,500 baptized members.

The *United Lutheran Church* began work in 1860 when *Rev. Morris Officer* established the first station twenty-five miles up the St. Paul River and called it Muhlenberg. Many missionaries came, served for a while, and left again. Some of them died in Liberia. After languishing for more than a decade owing to lack of recruits, the moribund Mission took on new life with the coming of *David and Emily Day*. It was not until the end of the century that recruits arrived in sufficient numbers to permit the expansion which got under way with the opening up of Kpoloelle in 1908. Other stations across Liberia were opened in the following order: Bethel in 1912, Sanoyea in 1917, Zorzor in 1923, Bellefanai in 1936, Totota in 1945, and Salayea in 1958. The *Evangelical Lutheran Church in Liberia* was organized in 1948. Latest figures indicate 1,648 baptized Christians in 36 congregations and 85 preaching places. These are ministered to by 58 missionaries and 4 Liberian pastors assisted by 40 evangelists. The Mission operates 16 schools. Medical work includes dispensaries at all main stations in addition to two hospitals. The Mission has had its own airplane since 1953.

RECENT MISSIONS. Since the turn of the century several missions have entered Liberia, and today are making a sizable contribution to the upbuilding of the Church in that land. The first of these was the *Assemblies of God,* which launched its Liberian Mission in 1908 with the coming of *Mr. and Mrs. John M. Perkins* and three other couples. Newaka was the first of 15 stations, all of them in the eastern part of the country, southeast of the River Cess. The oldest and largest school, opened in 1931, is at Feloka. A girls' school is located at Newaka and a coeducational school has been developed in Monrovia. With three Bible schools in operation, the Assemblies of God have led the way in the training of national leaders. Its medical work centers in New Hope Town, a 350-acre leper colony established by *Florence Steidel* in 1947. Assemblies of God missionaries are carrying on an aggressive program of evangelism on the two large Firestone Rubber Plantations. Membership in 94 churches is 2,300. Thirty-three ordained pastors are assisted by 93 lay preachers, all trained in its own Bible schools. The Mission operates its own airplane, named *Speed The Light*.

In 1931 *Baptist Mid-Missions* entered Liberia and took over the work abandoned by a former Baptist group in the Central Province. The present work centers in four stations. Medical work includes rural dispensaries and a leper colony. A three-year Bible Institute is located at Tappi. Mid-Missions operates the only mission press in the country. *Worldwide Evangelization Crusade* began in 1938, and today has 41 missionaries in Liberia.

Other missions working in Liberia include the *United Pentecostal Church,* the *Liberian Inland Mission, Pentecostal Assemblies of Canada, New Tribes Mission,* and the *Seventh Day Adventists.* ELWA, radio broadcasting station of the *Sudan Interior Mission,* which went on the air in January, 1954, is located just outside Monrovia.

THEOLOGICAL EDUCATION. This aspect of missionary work has been neglected in Liberia, with the result that national leadership in the Liberian Church is wholly inadequate. One denomination, after a century of work, has only a dozen pastors for ten times that number of churches. More recently there has been increased emphasis placed on this important phase of the work. Baptist Mid-Missions has two Bible schools, a small one at Yila and the more advanced one opened in 1952 at Tappi. The Assemblies of God Mission has opened two Bible schools in the last five years. The only theological seminary is the *Cuttington College and Divinity School* opened in 1949. This is an Episcopal institution in which the Methodists co-operate.

CHURCH AND BIBLE. The Liberian Church cannot be described as a strong Church. Low standards prevail in most parts of the country, particularly in the coastal regions. The misappropriation of church funds is a common problem. Polygamy is practised on a wide scale. There is a great deal of drinking. One impartial observer has attributed this sad state of affairs to the fact that the Word of God has been neglected. After 130 years of Christian work the Bible is still practically unknown. There are no Bibles in the schools and few in the churches. The reason for this is that the government has decreed that English, as the official language, should be the sole medium of communication in church and school. Because of this there has been practically no Bible translation; and very few missionaries have ever taken the trouble to learn the tribal dialects. Diglot editions of the Scriptures would solve this problem, provided the government would go along.

IVORY COAST

Area: 124,490 sq. mi.

Capital: Abidjan

Population: 2,525,000

Religion: Animism

Islam

THE LAND. The Republic of the Ivory Coast is situated just west of Ghana on the Atlantic Ocean. It has the Voltaic Republic and Sudan to the north, and Guinea and Liberia to the west. It is a land of palm-fringed waterways and dense, luxuriant forests with giant trees 150 feet high. The population comprises many tribes, chief of which are the Agnis, Dioulas, Senufos, and Krumens.

MISSIONS. From the Ivory Coast comes one of the strangest tales in the annals of missionary history. The romantic story centers around a colorful personality known as *Prophet Harris*, a Liberian of the Brebo tribe, whose preaching in the Ivory Coast was attended by phenomenal results. As a young lad he came under the influence of Christian teaching. His uncle had been a pastor of a Methodist church in Liberia, and young Harris at the age of twenty underwent a profound spiritual experience. But his great life's work did not begin until 1913 when, as an old man of sixty, he made a preaching tour of the Ivory Coast. Dressed in a long white gown and an ample white turban and equipped with a well-worn Bible and a calabash of water, he presented a striking appearance. Anticipating modern visual-aid techniques he held aloft a large bamboo cross for all to see, explaining that it was on the Cross that God's Son died for the sins of the world. A hundred thousand persons abandoned their idolatrous paraphernalia, and fetishism all but disappeared along the coast. Eschewing gifts and offerings, he accepted only hospitality from his converts. In village after village, congregations were organized and church buildings were erected. Each local church was supplied with a preacher, and "Twelve Apostles" were appointed to rule the Church. Minor prophets were sent inland to evangelize the primitive tribes of the hinterland. After two years of this kind of preaching, Prophet Harris was arrested by the French authorities and deported to his native Liberia. In an effort to crush a mass movement which might easily get out of hand, the government further ordered the burning of all churches. The movement, however, was too strong to be wiped out by such repressive measures. Bigger and better churches were built in place of the flimsy bamboo structures which had been destroyed. Christianity prevailed and fetishism was dead. It was one of the most complete and astounding victories Christianity has ever scored over the forces of paganism.

In 1924 the Harris churches were taken over by the *English Wesleyans*, though some elected to remain independent. The Methodist Church there continues its witness from six main centers of work; but paganism is on the increase and church membership is down to 11,406. The latest Report expresses regret that "in a district which forty years ago was inflamed by the preaching of Prophet Harris, the Church in these days very greatly needs that kindling fire of the Holy Spirit."[3]

In 1930 the *Christian and Missionary Alliance* entered the Ivory Coast and settled among the unreached tribes of the interior. Bouake, in the Baouli tribe, was occupied in 1930 and became the site of the *Central Bible School*. Six other centers have been established. Organized churches now number 109. Alliance workers have translated the New Testament into Maninka and Sonhrai, and certain New Testament books have been translated into other dialects. Churches are multiplying faster than the missionaries can care for them. The greatest need of the hour is reported to be "intensive evangelism, Scripture translations and Bible teaching."

The *Worldwide Evangelization Crusade* took up work in the Ivory Coast in 1934. Thirty-four missionaries are working out from six main centers. The Church has been planted in three tribes, and translation is proceeding in two languages.

One of the earlier fields of the *Conservative Baptist Foreign Mission Society* was the Ivory Coast, which they first occupied in 1947. Their work is centered in the Senufo tribe in the northwest where they have the entire field to themselves. There are 40 missionaries located in 5 stations. In 1953 a hospital and dispensary were opened at Ferkessedougou.

GHANA

Area: 91,843 sq. mi.   Population: 4,700,000
Capital: Accra   Religion: Animism

THE LAND. Ghana, once a part of British West Africa, is one of the maritime countries on the Gulf of Guinea. On the west it is bounded by the Ivory Coast, on the east by Togoland, and on the north by the Voltaic Republic. The country has traditionally been divided into three distinct regions: the Gold Coast in the south, Ashanti in the center, and the Northern Territories.

POLITICAL HISTORY. The independent State of Ghana came into existence in March, 1957, when the Gold Coast and Togoland, both former British possessions, attained Dominion status within the British Commonwealth. There have been reports of a possible

[3] *The Burning Word, 1958*, p. 25.

federation between Ghana and the former French colony of Guinea, but to date nothing has come of it.

THE PEOPLE. The population is composed of more than fifty tribes. Some of them are very backward. The two principal languages are Twi and Ga. In the north, Dagomba is the official language. The Hausa people have their settlements on all the main routes, and by virtue of their superior intelligence exert an influence out of all proportion to their numbers.

THE RELIGION. Most of the tribes are animistic in their worship. The Hausa people are Muslims. The coming of Independence has in no way interfered with the missionary enterprise. Prime Minister Kwame Nkrumah has said that he will continue to welcome Christian missionaries. Most of Ghana's cabinet ministers attended mission schools. Eighty per cent of the children now in mission schools are registered as Christians.

EARLY MISSIONS. Three unsuccessful attempts at missionary work were made by the *Moravians* on the Gold Coast in the early part of the nineteenth century. In 1828 the first gallant band of *Basel* missionaries from Germany and Switzerland stepped ashore at Christiansborg, near the present city of Accra, the capital; but sun and fever were too much for them and they succumbed. Three more arrived in March, 1832. By June only one of them, *Riis* by name, survived. Two others came to his help later, only to die in a short time. But Riis, in true pioneer fashion, refused to accept defeat. Following an extended furlough he returned in 1843 with a band of Moravian Christians from Jamaica. These people of African descent were better able to stand the rigors of the African climate; consequently, they survived and formed the nucleus of a church. Thereafter progress was steady and sustained, so that in the Jubilee Year of 1878 the Basel Mission could claim 4,000 believers with 6 African pastors and 90 lay workers at 9 main stations and 35 outstations.

A peculiar feature of this work was the segregation into separate villages of Christians and pagans. This has resulted in a strong Christian Church with high moral standards. Following World War I, the work passed into the hands of the *United Free Church of Scotland*. By that time the Christian community had risen to 30,000, of whom 12,000 were church members. Every village of any size had a school, and African church workers outnumbered the missionaries six to one. Today the *Presbyterian Church of Ghana* with 44,000 members is an autonomous body and has membership in the World Council of Churches.

The *Methodist Missionary Society* commenced work in 1831. Outstanding among the pioneers was *Thomas Birch Freeman,* a West Indian Negro half-caste who was educated in England. He arrived in 1838 and blazed the trail in Ashanti. Great stress was laid on the training of African workers, and a strong indigenous Church under national leadership has resulted. The *Methodist Church of Ghana,* which in 1959 reported 56,000 members, is now considering the possibility of becoming completely autonomous.

RECENT MISSIONS. Until recently missionary work had been confined to the south and central parts of the country. Only within the last two decades has work been undertaken in the Northern Territories. The pioneer society was the *Worldwide Evangelization Crusade,* which entered this area in 1940. Within ten years it had opened four stations. Good progress has been made also in their medical and evangelistic work.

Baptist Mid-Missions first entered Ghana in October, 1946, in response to the call of local Baptist Christians, some of whom had come from the Yoruba country for trading purposes. They settled first in the south, where they opened three stations along the coast; but in 1949 they opened a second field in the Northern Territories and now have four stations there.

The *Assemblies of God* have a good work in Ghana. Here as elsewhere they have emphasized the training of national workers, and their 33 missionaries are assisted by 19 ordained pastors and 14 lay preachers, the product of their two Bible schools. Their present outreach includes 80 organized churches and 52 preaching places.

Of equal if not greater importance is the fact that in 1955 the *Presbyterian Church of Ghana* committed itself to a mission field in the Northern Territories. About the same time the *Methodist Church of Ghana* launched its own home mission work in the same area, and within a year it extended from Wa to ten other centers where over 900 people were attending night schools, over 100 of them asking to be trained for church membership.

The most recent newcomer is the *Mennonite Mission,* which sent four workers to Ghana in 1957. Other missions include the *African Methodist Episcopal Church,* the *Salvation Army,* and the *Seventh Day Adventists.*

BIBLE TRANSLATION. The complete Bible is available in three main languages: Ga, Twi, and Fanti.

TOGOLAND

Area: 26,491 sq. mi.   Population: 900,000
Capital: Lome   Religion: Animism
                                                       Islam

THE LAND AND THE PEOPLE. Togoland is a long narrow strip of French
territory on the Gulf of Guinea sandwiched between Ghana on the
west and Dahomey on the east. Its northern neighbor is the Voltaic
Republic. Formerly a French protectorate, Togoland received its
independence in April, 1960. The southern part is inhabited by
about 30 tribes, the most important of which is the Ewe. The pagan
tribes in the north are dominated by the Hamitic tribes, who profess
Islam.

MISSIONS. Missionary work in Togoland dates from 1847, when the
North German Mission began its activities at Peki in the extreme
southwestern part of the Ewe country in what is now Ghana. When
the German missionaries were expelled during World War I, their
work in British territory came under the control of the *United Free
Church of Scotland;* their work in French territory passed into the
hands of the *Paris Evangelical Mission.* The Ewe Church continues
to develop along indigenous lines. A General Synod has been established, and a theological seminary provides a steady supply of
pastors.

The *English Methodists* have a number of churches in the charge
of African pastors. The only mission in the northern part of the country is the *Assemblies of God,* whose first station at Dapango, not far
from the border of the Voltaic Republic, was opened in 1940. By
1948 there were 10 national workers and 14 churches and outstations
in this area. Since then three more stations have been opened. The
one at Bassari already reports 35 outstations in a district which a
few years ago was completely pagan. Chiefs, witch doctors, and
people from seven tribes have been won to Christ, and a large
number of persons have offered themselves for Christian service.

DAHOMEY

Area: 41,302 sq. mi.   Population: 1,750,000
Capital: Porto Novo   Religion: Animism
                                                       Islam

THE LAND AND THE PEOPLE. Dahomey is a small territory on the Gulf
of Guinea. It lies between Nigeria on the east and Togoland on the

west. The Voltaic Republic is to the northwest, and Niger to the northeast. The population of Dahomey consists of many different tribes speaking many different languages. In the south is found the Fan branch of the Ewe-speaking tribes, with over 350,000 members, and in the west are the Voltaic tribes. Wayside shrines, snake temples, and sacred groves dot the landscape. Islam also exercises great influence over the Dahomey people.

MISSIONS. The *English Methodists* began work in Dahomey over one hundred years ago. Their main center of work is in the south along the coast, but in more recent years it has extended as far north as Savalou. There is a seminary at Porto Novo. According to their latest report, churches in three different areas have sprung to new life. People who have no personal knowledge of Jesus Christ are attracted to the Christian faith when they see the power of God in answer to prayer. The nourishing of their faith, says the Report, is an urgent task.[4]

The *Assemblies of God Mission* was the first Protestant organization to undertake work in the far north. The pioneers were *Mr. and Mrs. Arthur E. Wilson*, who entered Dahomey from their Upper Volta field and settled in Natitingu in 1945. At first the people were unfriendly; but the loving ministry of an African Christian doctor during an epidemic of spinal meningitis disarmed all prejudice, and the whole Yowabou tribe, led by its chief, expressed a willingness to learn the ways of God. The Bible school, which opened in 1949 with 5 students, now has over 30 students representing 13 different tribes. Since 1950 three additional stations have been opened. A Mission plane greatly facilitates transportation.

The *Sudan Interior Mission* has been at work in this country since 1946, when Kandi and Nikki were occupied. Since then six more centers have been established in four tribal areas. Institutional work includes two Bible schools, a boys' school, and a girls' school. Thirty-four missionaries are working in this region.

NIGERIA

Area: 373,000 sq. mi.   Population: 33,000,000
Capital: Lagos   Religion: Islam

THE LAND. Nigeria is Britain's largest colony. It is located under the great bulge of Africa on the Gulf of Guinea. It is bounded by Dahomey on the west, Niger on the north, and Cameroon on the east.

[4] *The Burning Word*, 1958, p. 25.

POLITICAL HISTORY. Great Britain established control over the southern part of the country in 1886 and over the northern part in 1900. In 1914 the two territories united to form the Colony of Nigeria. Today the Federation of Nigeria comprises three regions: the Northern Region, the Eastern Region, and the Western Region. A wise colonial policy has prepared the Nigerians for complete independence, slated for October, 1960.

THE PEOPLE. Nigeria, with 33,000,000 people, is the most populous country in Africa. Ibadan, which has a population of 460,000, is reputed to be the largest native city on the continent. There are more than 200 tribes and tribal dialects, but the main tribal groups may be reduced to four: the Yorubas in the southwest, the Ibos in the east, and the Hausa and Fulani people in the north and northwest. Unlike Kenya in the east and Algeria in the north, Nigeria has only a small sprinkling of whites—not more than 12,000.

THE RELIGION. In the matter of religion, the population is split three ways: Muslims, Christians, and pagans. The Muslims predominate in the north where the Hausa people have been followers of the Prophet since the fourteenth century. In the Eastern Region the Muslims are outnumbered by both the Christians and the pagans about fifteen to one. Taking the country as a whole, Islam is the dominant religion. It has 15,000,000 adherents. The Premier of Northern Nigeria, Alhaji Ahmadu, a Muslim, has stated publicly to mission officials that Independence in 1960 will not curtail their work. Today these two great monotheistic religions are contending for the soul of Nigeria. A Church Missionary Society worker wrote:

In Western Nigeria animists still outnumber Christians and Muslims together, but in the course of the next century the majority will almost certainly become adherents of one or other of the two great religions. This fact shows how urgent is the missionary task of the Church in these times.[5]

EARLY MISSIONS. Protestant missions in West Africa have achieved their greatest numerical success in Nigeria, where in 1956 church membership stood at 287,026 and the Christian community was reckoned to be about 1,370,000.

The first to enter Nigeria were the *Wesleyan Methodists*, who established a station at Abeokuta in the Yoruba country in 1842 before the British took over. Steady and sometimes spectacular growth has marked the work of this Mission, and today it has one of the largest Churches in Nigeria, with 43,600 members and a Chris-

[5] *East and West* (October, 1958), p. 25.

tian community of 121,000. The Methodist Church in Nigeria is divided into two districts, the East and the West.

The *Church Missionary Society,* destined to become the largest in the whole country, entered Nigeria in 1845. *Henry Townsend* opened the first station at Badagry in the Yoruba territory. Abeokuta was occupied in 1846, Lagos in 1852, and Ibadan in 1853. It was in this country that the first African, the ex-slave *Samuel Crowther,* was consecrated a bishop of the Church of England. Belonging to the inferior Yoruba tribe on the Niger, as a boy he was carried off by Portuguese slave traders, rescued by a British war vessel, and sent to school in Sierra Leone. He early accepted the Saviour; and he showed such ability and devotion in his studies that he was sent to England to complete his education. From his consecration in 1864 to his death in 1893 his missionary career was one of rare dedication and high distinction. The story of his finding and baptizing his own mother, for whom he had long searched, is full of tender pathos.

Today in this Yoruba district are hundreds of organized congregations and thousands of village churches under the direction of three African bishops and more than 200 ordained clergymen. African lay workers, including teachers and evangelists, number well over 5,000.

The work of the Church Missionary Society in the Niger River district began in 1857 when Bishop Crowther, on his third expedition, established three centers of operation. One of these, Onitsha, remains to this day the headquarters of the work. The greatest gains were made in the Delta Region. By 1892 the churches here were organized under African leadership. Today this district is divided into two dioceses. In 1956 there were 76 ordained African clergymen and 6,447 lay workers—5,321 men and 1,126 women.

A third district in Northern Nigeria was opened by the establishment of a station at Lokoja in 1865. An attempt was made in 1890 to reach the Muslims in the Hausa States, but it proved to be abortive. The Bassa country was opened in 1897. The work in this northern section is in Muslim territory; consequently the results have been much less gratifying than in the other two districts. There are about 100 African workers in this area.

The Anglican Church is by far the largest in Nigeria. In 1957 it reported 2,603 churches with 92,000 members and a Christian community estimated at 433,000. The entire work was organized into seven dioceses.

The third society to enter Nigeria was the *Southern Baptist Convention.* Beginning in 1850, they also settled in the Western Region among the Yoruba people. The work was not easy. After fifty years of effort, during which 45 missionaries had labored and 13 had died on the field, the Mission was able to report but meager results: 6 missionaries, 6 churches, 6 outstations, and 385 members. But their brave missionaries persevered and in 1914 the *Yoruba Baptist Association* was organized. It was later changed to the *Niger Baptist Convention,* which now has its own home and foreign mission board. Of its 340 churches, 319 are completely self-supporting. Chapels number 586, and there are 44,000 baptized church members. Education has always been a major part of Southern Baptist work. In 1959 they had 474 primary schools, 24 secondary schools, and 7 colleges. Their theological seminary at Ogbomosho, which has 144 students, is said to be one of the largest and best in Africa. Their splendid medical work includes 6 hospitals and 27 dispensaries under the supervision of 19 missionary doctors, 28 missionary nurses, and 43 African nurses. With over 200 missionaries and a budget of more than a million dollars, Nigeria is the largest of the 39 Southern Baptist fields.

The *United Free Church of Scotland* was another pioneer in Nigeria. Strangely enough, the first group of workers came not from Scotland but from Jamaica. They arrived in 1846 and began work in the coastal section of Calabar. It was not long before reinforcements from Scotland joined them. One of these was the famous *Mary Slessor,* the "White Queen of Calabar," whose heroism is known to all readers of missionary biography. Her life story rivals in many particulars that of David Livingstone. She served in Africa from 1876 to 1915. From an unlettered factory girl in the homeland she advanced to the foremost rank of missionary pathfinders. Her work was that of a pioneer among the most savage tribes of the Calabar hinterland. Almost single-handedly she tamed and transformed three pagan communities in succession. It is a question whether the career of any other woman missionary has been marked by so many strange adventures, daring feats, signal providences, and wonderful achievements. Since 1954 the work of this Mission has been part of the *Presbyterian Church of Eastern Nigeria,* whose 350 churches include about 15,000 members.

LATER MISSIONS. The *Qua Iboe Mission,* founded in 1887 by Samuel A. Bill, a graduate of H. Grattan Guinness's Bible Institute in London, has concentrated on the training of national leaders. Located in the region of the Qua Iboe River, this Mission now has 812 preaching places, which are largely self-supporting, and 40,000 members.

The *Sudan Interior Mission,* founded as an independent faith

mission by *Rowland V. Bingham*, began work in 1901 at Patigi in
the Nupe tribe, 500 miles up the Niger River. In 1909 the first
station among the Gbaris was opened at Paiko. One of the early
pioneers was A. W. *Banfield*, who translated the Bible into the
difficult Nupe dialect and also compiled a dictionary. Being a
mechanic by trade, he decided in 1910 to set up a printing press.
During the past fifty years it has turned out a veritable Niagara of
Christian propaganda, including portions of the Scriptures in nearly
50 different languages. In one year alone the *Niger-Challenge Press*,
now located at Lagos, printed nine million pages of Christian literature which found its way all over West Africa.

In 1917 *John S. Hall* and *C. G. Beachman* began evangelizing the
Tangales. Eight years later the Mission moved north to the great
city of Kano and there established a work among the Hausa people.
Jos, occupied in 1923, is headquarters for the whole of Nigeria.

From a humble beginning the Sudan Interior Mission has become
the largest mission in Africa, with over 1,200 missionaries working
in almost a dozen countries stretching the full width of the great
continent. Nigeria, where there are more than 650 missionaries, is its
largest field. Ethiopia is second with 280 workers. The S.I.M.
churches in Nigeria became wholly autonomous in 1955, and are
now known as the *Evangelical Churches of West Africa*. They have
organized their own *African Missionary Society* which supports
more than 50 missionaries in various parts of Africa.

In recent years this great Mission has pioneered in two fields,
journalism and radio. Sensing the need for a Christian news magazine with sufficient popular appeal to sell on the newsstands of the
cities and towns of Africa, the S.I.M. launched the English edition
of *African Challenge* in 1951. Now appearing in Yoruba and English, its circulation has climbed to over 180,000 copies per issue.
In 1954 the S.I.M. opened the first Christian broadcasting station
(ELWA) in Africa. Located in Monrovia, Liberia, ELWA is now
broadcasting the Christian message in 25 languages to all parts of
West Africa. A new 50,000-watt transmitter now being installed will
enable ELWA to reach all Africa and the Middle East.

The *Assemblies of God Mission* took up work in Nigeria in answer
to a call from some thirty-two indigenous churches needing outside
assistance. Beginning at Port Harcourt in 1939, the work is now
divided into three districts. Ten thousand converts have been won,
mostly among the pagans, and 293 churches have been organized.

The *Sudan United Mission*, comprising five societies, opened its
first station at Wase in 1904 with British workers. Two years later a
party of Americans arrived on the field. In 1907 a group of students
from Cambridge University volunteered for missionary service and

opened a new station at Panyam. The following year two workers from South Africa joined the Mission. The year 1913 witnessed the arrival of Danish workers and a party from Australia and New Zealand. The first training institute was opened at Wukari in 1915. A second school was begun at Gindiri in 1934 with 36 students in attendance. Their first hospital was opened in 1919; two others have been added since. Their evangelistic work has prospered greatly, resulting in 1,274 congregations in the charge of some 1,800 pastors and evangelists, 99 of whom are ordained.

Other missions in Nigeria include the *United Evangelical Lutheran, Christian Missions in Many Lands, Salvation Army, Church of the Brethren, Seventh Day Adventists,* and *Church of God,* among others.

EDUCATION. As elsewhere in Africa the youth of Nigeria have a consuming thirst for knowledge. Only within recent years has the government begun to assume its rightful responsibility in this matter. Free education for all primary school children was implemented in Western Nigeria in 1955 and in Eastern Nigeria in 1957. Up to that time Christian missions had provided 85 per cent of all education and a good deal of the medical work. By 1957, two-fifths of the five million children of school age were in primary school. The demand for secondary education continues to exceed the facilities available. In 1957, 1,365 boys took the entrance examination for 60 vacancies in the Southern Baptist High School at Port Harcourt.

INTER-MISSION CO-OPERATION. The *Christian Council of Nigeria* was founded in 1930. It includes 14 member churches and missions. This Council is not affiliated with either the *International Missionary Council* or the *World Council of Churches.* A scheme of church union has been published by the Nigerian Christian Council and is under consideration by the Anglican, Methodist, and Presbyterian Churches.

Nigeria was host to the important All-Africa Church Conference convened in Ibadan in 1958.

SUDANESE REPUBLIC

Area: 360,331 sq. mi.	Population: 3,710,000
Capital: Bamako	Religion: Animism
	Islam

THE LAND. Sudan is a plateau situated between Senegal and Mauritania on the west and Niger on the east. It is bounded on the north by Algeria and on the south by the Voltaic Republic.

MISSIONS. Protestant work in Sudan began when the *Gospel Missionary Union* entered in 1919. During the first twenty-five years the Mission was understaffed, and consequently not very effective. Since 1946, thirty-six new missionaries have been sent to this field, bringing the total to 44 workers on 8 stations. Bible translation has been in progress since the inception of the work. The New Testament was published in Bambara, the trade language, in 1937. Several Old Testament books have been printed on the field, and the entire Old Testament is in an advanced stage of preparation.

Another Protestant society at work in Sudan is the *Christian and Missionary Alliance*. Its first station was opened at Sikasso in 1923. The early years saw some converts, but it was not until 1931 that a movement of the Holy Spirit began. Four missionaries stationed there at that time were stricken with yellow fever, and within a week three of them had died. Shortly after the laying down of these three lives, twenty young men stepped out for the Lord and the tide turned in many places in Sudan as well as in other parts of French West Africa. Four stations were opened in the 1920's and seven in the 1930's. The *Sudan Bible School*, established at Ntoroso in 1936, offers a four-year course of study and attracts students within a radius of 500 miles. Medical work is confined to small dispensaries and clinics, in each of which there is a clear Christian witness which is bearing fruit. A strong indigenous Church is emerging. That difficulties still abound is plain from the opening words of the latest Annual Report:

Perhaps as never before in the history of the district have we been faced with so many trials, tribulations, and sickness. Tragedy seemed to follow tragedy with the enemy of our souls pressing in on every hand. Yet, in the midst of these severe tests, we are conscious of divine help and victory.[6]

The *Evangelical Baptist Missions*, an independent mission, has work in two main centers, Gao and Tombouctou, with two couples in each station.

VOLTAIC REPUBLIC
(Republic of the Upper Volta)

Area: 105,946 sq. mi.   Population: 3,400,000
Capital: Ouagadougou   Religion: Animism
                                                           Islam

[6] *Annual Report, 1958*, p. 18.

THE LAND AND THE PEOPLE. The Voltaic Republic is completely land-locked. Its neighbors on the south are Dahomey, Togoland, Ghana, and Ivory Coast. The Sudanese Republic is on the west and north, and the Republic of the Niger on the east. The Mossi tribe, which numbers two million, is the principal tribe of the country and the largest in this part of West Africa. The Mossi tribesmen are said to have migrated from Ghana in the tenth century. Altogether there are about 30 tribes in the Voltaic Republic. Fetish and ancestor worship, with blood sacrifice, is woven into the lives, manners, and customs of the Mossi people. The witch doctors exercise tremendous influence. Their counsel is sought in every phase of life—birth, marriage, sickness, and death. Roman Catholicism is strongly entrenched, and Islam is making rapid headway.

MISSIONS. Here again Protestant missions got off to a late beginning. It was not until 1921 that the first society, the *Assemblies of God,* opened their first station at Ouagadougou. Of those early days Arthur E. Wilson wrote:

> Moré was an unwritten language and we very soon realized that our first task was to learn it and then reduce it to writing. So with notebook in hand we started out. Talk about signs and wonders! We made the signs and the people did the wondering! However, by diligent study we were soon able to preach in the native language.[7]

Since then ten other stations have been opened, all in the Central Province. Surrounding these are 133 outstations. In 1948 French Assemblies of God missionaries joined the work and began a school for the children of Christians, which now has an enrollment of 325. The entire Bible has been translated into Moré. The *Central Bible Institute* on the shores of Lake Nagabageré has 42 students enrolled; most of them are married men who have their individual farms and are self-supporting. In 1949 the Church became autonomous and was officially recognized by the government.

Another Protestant group in the Voltaic Republic is the *Christian and Missionary Alliance.* They began work in 1923 among the Black Bobo. Very conservative, these people were reluctant to accept the new religion. The first break in this tribe came in 1933 when twenty-five adults from one village came to ask for instruction. In the process of time other tribes were contacted and other stations opened. The New Testament in Red Bobo was published in 1954, and in Dogon in 1958. The Old Testament in Bambara is now in the press. The third and latest society to take up work in this country

[7] *Upper Volta* (pamphlet), p. 5.

was the *Sudan Interior Mission.* Its first station was opened in 1930 at Fada N'gourma where a Bible school is now located. Two stations were opened in the 1940's, and Madaga was opened in 1954. Its five stations are in the Gourma country.

NIGER

Area: 463,000 sq. mi.   Population: 2,500,000
Capital: Niamey   Religion: Animism
                                                   Islam

THE LAND AND THE PEOPLE. The Republic of the Niger is the largest of the eight territories which formerly made up French West Africa. On the west it is bounded by Sudan, on the east by Chad, on the south by Nigeria, and on the north by Libya and Algeria. The country is divided into two distinct zones, the richly wooded south and the desert lands of the north. The population is composed of various tribes, the most important of which are the Tuareg, Hausa, Jerma, Sanghai, and Tibbu. The chief language is Hausa. There is reason to believe that in the distant past the Tuareg were influenced by Christianity, for they employ the sign of the cross on swords, shields, saddles, and other articles.

MISSIONS. The main Protestant mission in Niger is the *Sudan Interior Mission,* which has 47 workers in the southern part of the country close to the northern border of Nigeria. Zinder was opened in 1924, and Tsibiri in 1928. The hospital established at Galmi in 1950 is the center of their medical work. A leprosarium is located at Maradi. Other institutions include two girls' schools and a Bible school. Six other stations were opened from time to time, bringing the total to ten. This work is mostly in the Hausa country, though two other tribes have been reached.

Sharing this needy field in the Niger Republic is the *Evangelical Baptist Missions,* a society dedicated to the preaching of the gospel in French lands. Their main station is at Niamey where 19 of their 29 missionaries are located. The other 10 workers are distributed among four other stations: Dosso, Gaya, Tabla, and Tera.

XVI

SOUTH AFRICA

ANGOLA

Area: 480,000 sq. mi.   Population: 4,750,000
Capital: Luanda   Religion: Animism
                                                Roman
                                              Catholicism

THE LAND. Angola, sometimes referred to as Portuguese West Africa, is one of three Portuguese possessions on that continent. With a coastline of 1,000 miles, it is located on the Atlantic Ocean between the Belgian Congo on the north and Southwest Africa on the south. On the east it is contiguous with Northern Rhodesia and Belgian Congo.

POLITICAL HISTORY. The Congo region was discovered by the Portuguese in 1482 and the first settlers arrived in 1491. Luanda was founded in 1575. Except for a short period in the 1640's Angola has been in the hands of the Portuguese for more than 450 years. The Portuguese do not envisage self-government, much less independence, for their possessions. Their colonial policy is one of assimilation. All who accept Portuguese culture and speak the Portuguese language become full citizens with all the rights and privileges attaching thereto. The others—and they are the vast majority—do not count.

THE PEOPLE. The tribes in this part of Africa are mostly of Bantu-Negro stock. The Mushi-Kongo and other divisions of the Ba-Kongo were Christians in the sixteenth and seventeenth centuries. They use crucifixes as charms and every person has a "santu," or Christian name.

THE RELIGION. As one might expect, Roman Catholicism is strongly entrenched in Angola. Catholic missions are subsidized and the priests have the status of state functionaries. All educational activities in the Province until 1908 were under the control of the Church. Before the coming of the Protestant missions the Roman Catholic Church had remained dormant for over a century. Competition has prodded her to increased activity, much of which is directed against Protestant converts. The attitude of the government to evangelical missions, however, is cordial and appreciative, and assurance has been given that religious liberty will be upheld as stipulated in the Treaty of Berlin. As a matter of fact, the Protestant missionaries have much more liberty in Angola than they do in Portugal.

MISSIONS. The *Baptist Missionary Society* blazed the trail for Protestant missions in Catholic Angola. Arriving in 1878 they opened their first station in São Salvador. Other stations followed, all of them in the northern part of the country where they now have 250 places of worship.

In 1880 the *American Board of Commissioners* opened a station at Bihe. Progress was slow at first. It was eight years before the first church was organized, and at the end of 25 years fewer than 300 Christians had been gathered. After 1914 growth became more rapid, and today the Mission has 1,400 places of worship. Thirty thousand church members, by their generous giving, have built up what is described as a "phenomenally strong church." In addition they support several thousand bush schools which are providing sound education for the children of Christians and non-Christians alike. In recent years, however, industrialization has played havoc with economic standards, so that now even the most sacrificial giving is inadequate to meet the growing needs of an expanding Church. A fine paragraph in the 1958 Report deserves a place here:

In Angola, more than in any other place, we must do a total job if we are to present the gospel. This means teaching, preaching, translating, writing, training ministers, training teachers, advising pastors, representing the people before the white government, medical work, agricultural work, village sanitation, leprosy work, tuberculosis work (tuberculosis is the scourge of Angola), family life work. All of these things, and many others, must be attempted with the limited funds and by the grievously overworked staff. To neglect, or at least not to attempt any one of them, would be to deny the gospel and to destroy the great faith that the people have in us. The lepers, the tuberculotics, the malnourished and verminous children, the fathers who still feel that it is all right to sell their daughters and beat their wives, the brilliant children ready to lap up learning from any source, the men and young boys torn from their homes to labor in distant places, raising coffee for America's breakfast tables, are all there and many others must ALL receive loving attention from our missionaries or from those of their own people whom we cannot train fast enough if the gospel is to really mean anything at all in this most difficult of lands.[1]

Methodist work in Angola started with *William Taylor*, who was elected missionary bishop of Africa in 1884. In the autumn of 1885, forty-five missionaries (men, women, and children) set out from the United States to open six stations in Africa, five of them in Angola. The *Angola Mission Conference* was set up in 1920 and the *Provisional Conference* in 1940; the *Annual Conference* followed in 1948. The Methodist work today is divided into two districts, Luanda and Malange. The capstone of their fine educational system, serving 6,000 students, is *Taylor Institute*, which has ten separate departments. It is located at Quessua. The Church has a membership of 29,941 and is served by 139 pastors.

In 1889 the *Plymouth Brethren* (Christian Missions in Many Lands) took up work in Angola. Their leader was the well-known pioneer, *Frederick Stanley Arnot*, who in his lifetime made eight or nine historic trips across various parts of Africa. Reinforcements poured in until at one time the Mission had a larger foreign staff than any other Protestant group. Their field is located in the northeastern part of the country not far from the border of Belgian Congo. Here in this area they have 14,750 believers in 145 recognized assemblies. Preaching places number 350.

It is unusual to find two Canadian societies in one country, but that is true of Angola. The older and larger of the two is the *United Church of Canada* which, since its creation in 1925, has continued the good work begun by the *Canadian Presbyterians* some years before. Latest reports place their membership at 12,200.

The other society is the *Canadian Baptist Mission*, which is a newcomer to Africa, having assumed responsibility for the extreme northwest corner of Angola only in 1954. The first missionaries arrived on the field in 1957. Two years later their number had jumped to 18 with 6 more en route. A new Mission full of young blood, it appears to be poised for dynamic action in a challenging situation.

Mr. A. W. Bailey, with the help of Mr. Arnot, entered Angola in 1914 on behalf of the *South Africa General Mission*. In 1918 he settled in Muie on the Kutsi River where today there are a leper colony, a medical clinic, day schools, and a church. In 1920 a party of ten North American workers sailed for Angola where they helped to open a second station at Catota. The present staff of 15 missionaries

[1] *American Board of Commissioners for Foreign Missions, 148th Annual Report, Fall, 1958.*

maintains a leper colony, a hospital, a Bible institute, schools, and outstation work, with evangelism the emphasis in all of these activities.

FEDERATION OF RHODESIA AND NYASALAND

Area:　　478,000 sq. mi.　　　　　　　Population: 7,675,000
Capital: Salisbury　　　　　　　　　　Religion:　Animism

THE LAND. The Federation comprises Northern and Southern Rhodesia and Nyasaland. It is bounded on the north by Tanganyika and Belgian Congo, on the east by Mozambique, on the south by the Union of South Africa and Bechuanaland, and on the west by Angola and Belgian Congo.

POLITICAL HISTORY. The Federation came into being on August 1, 1953, when the three territories were merged into a new federal state. Southern Rhodesia has been a self-governing colony since 1923. The two northern territories have been protectorates under the administration of the British Colonial Office since 1924 and 1891 respectively. The new Federation is a long step towards total independence. When independence comes, possibly as early as 1960, the Federation will become a fully self-governing dominion within the British Commonwealth. Strangely enough, the 7,000,000 Africans in the Federation, especially those in Northern Rhodesia and Nyasaland, are opposed to the whole scheme on the grounds that it is a last-ditch maneuver on the part of the 300,000 European to perpetuate white supremacy under the guise of dominion status. Continued African opposition could conceivably cause the dissolution of the Federation.

THE PEOPLE. The African population is divided into 100 different tribes, most of them of Bantu stock. Some of the more important tribes are the Matabele, Mashona, Nyanja, Swahili, Ngono, and Yao. The Europeans total approximately 300,000, nearly two-thirds of whom are in Southern Rhodesia.

Southern Rhodesia. Christian missions in Southern Rhodesia have from the beginning enjoyed unusual opportunities free from all opposition and persecution. Most of them, therefore, have been increasing at the rate of nearly 100 per cent each decade since the turn of the century. Working mainly in the rural areas within well-defined and self-imposed boundaries, the missions have avoided overlapping and the problems that accompany it.

Missionary work in Southern Rhodesia began in 1859 with the *London Missionary Society,* whose illustrious pioneer, *Robert Moffat,* had long tried to secure a foothold in Matabeleland. In 1829 and again in 1835 he visited the Matabele; but it was not until 1859 that a mission station was finally planted in the country north of the Limpopo River in what is now Southern Rhodesia. Moffat was invalided home in 1870, and died in England in 1883. Between 1870 and 1890 three different societies made three separate attempts to start work in this part of Africa, but each time the venture failed. For thirty years the London Missionary Society was the only mission in Southern Rhodesia. Its workers labored long and hard, but saw little in the way of fruit.

The tide turned in 1890 when Great Britain extended its control over this part of Africa and began making large grants of land to Protestant missionary societies. In one year, 1891, three new missions took up work in Southern Rhodesia. The first of these was the *Church of England,* whose initial efforts were directed to the spiritual needs of the white settlers. Only later did it take the gospel to the Africans. The blessing of God has rested on their work and today the Anglican Church has two dioceses—Mashonaland and Matabeleland—with 90,000 baptized members. It is the largest Protestant group in the country.

The second mission to enter that year was the *Methodist Missionary Society* of England. Taking advantage of the land grants, it soon established strong central stations surrounded by many outstations. Today the English Methodists have 24,000 church members.

The third mission to begin work in 1891 was the *Dutch Reformed Church,* whose foreign missionary personnel increased until at one time it was the largest mission in the field.

The *American Board of Commissioners* inaugurated work at Mt. Silinda in 1893. Here on a large grant of land it has developed *Mt. Silinda Institute,* which offers secondary education, teacher training, carpentry, and construction. *Pierce Memorial Hospital,* in the same center, has a Nurses' Training School connected with it.

In 1895 the *Seventh Day Adventists* acquired a tract of land and began what has developed into a large work with three colleges, a hospital, and a leper colony. Seventy-one churches report a membership of 17,000.

At the end of the nineteenth century the *American Methodists,* under the leadership of *Bishop Joseph C. Hartzell,* established a station at Umtali on a large tract of land with buildings given to him by Cecil Rhodes. The six districts of the Methodist Church are located in the Umtali and Salisbury areas in the eastern section of the country. The Church has grown through the years until in 1956 there were 280 preaching places with 49 ordained African ministers. In 1958 its 191 primary schools were providing education for 31,000 students, almost half of whom were girls. The *Washburn Memorial Hospital* in Nyadiri is the center of its medical work. It is one of the most modern institutions in Africa. The Mission maintains four large farms as part of its contribution to agricultural missions. The English and American Methodists plan to open a theological college at Salisbury.

In 1900 *Mr. Douglas Wood* of the *South Africa General Mission* was appointed to Southern Rhodesia to pick up the threads of the work left by the death of Mr. Coupland at Chingweke. There he prepared a primer and translated the Gospel of Mark. Because of the prevalence of malaria, Chingweke was later abandoned in favor of Rusitu. In this area today there are 22 bush schools, a hospital, a clinic, and a Bible institute.

Messrs. Danielson and Dunkeld, heading for the Zambezi Valley in 1942, were the first missionaries sent to Southern Rhodesia by *The Evangelical Alliance Mission.* They set up the first station on the banks of the Msengedzi River. Mr. Danielson was stricken with typhoid fever and went to be with the Lord on Thanksgiving Day, 1943. Easter Sunday, 1946, witnessed the baptism of the first seven converts. By the end of 1952 the Mission had 52 missionaries on the field. A Bible institute was established in 1953 and a teacher training college in 1956. There are 1,830 students enrolled in 20 schools. In 1957, fifty regular meeting places produced 123 candidates for baptism.

The *Southern Baptists* moved into Southern Rhodesia in 1950 and took over the work which had been progressing favorably for twenty years or more under the care of *Mr. and Mrs. Clyde Dotson,* independent Baptist missionaries. The Ndau Bible, translated by this couple, was published by the *British and Foreign Bible Society* in 1957. In 1959 the Southern Baptists had 30 missionaries in seven main stations and have already established a hospital and a seminary.

Because of the presence of a large number of white settlers—almost 200,000 of them—racial prejudice runs high in Southern Rhodesia. Repercussions are felt within the Christian Church, and many times the missions find themselves caught between the cross fire of nationalism and colonialism. Churches are divided into three groups, African, European, and Mixed. In 1954 the *Missionary Conference* and the *African Missionary Conference* combined to form the *Christian Conference of Southern Rhodesia* with 19 member bodies.

Protestant Christianity claims 250,000 adherents. The Church is strong and growing.

Northern Rhodesia. Ever in search of new fields, Protestant missions in the last quarter of the nineteenth century were not content to settle down in Southern Rhodesia. They pushed north across the Zambezi River into the territory now known as Northern Rhodesia. The *Paris Evangelical Missionary Society* has the honor of being the first mission to enter this part of Africa. The leader of the band was the famous *François Coillard* who settled in the western part of the country in the 1880's. He and his colleagues witnessed God's wonderful working first among the Basutos and later among the incorrigible Barotse of the upper Zambezi. The French Society was followed by the *London Missionary Society,* whose famous missionary, *David Livingstone,* did more than any other man to open Africa to Christianity and commerce. Perhaps this is the place to relate the exploits of this great missionary, traveler, and philanthropist.

This greatest of all Africa's apostles was the direct successor to the Moffats, having joined them at Kuruman in 1840, and later married their daughter, Mary Moffat. His first few years were spent in regular missionary work among various tribes within a limited radius. He then began to push northward, bent upon getting farther into the heart of Africa. After several preliminary trips, during which his family suffered much from illness, he decided to send them to England for two years, while he gave himself to further exploration with a view to opening up the interior to missionary work. Starting out at the end of 1852, Livingstone entered upon his first great journey, which occupied four years. During this time he traced the Zambezi to its source, proceeded thence to the western coast at St. Paul de Loanda, in Angola, and then recrossed the continent to the Indian Ocean, discovering on the way the famous Victoria Falls. This wonderful journey of 11,000 miles, covered entirely on foot, involved untold hardships, dangers, and physical sufferings. At its close, in 1856, Livingstone returned to England with a mass of invaluable records, and was there received with great honor by all classes.

Among the many impressions which his journey in Africa had made upon him, the thing that stirred his soul to its depths was the revolting slave trade, ghastly evidences of which he had witnessed everywhere. In all his continued labors to open up the Dark Continent he was fired by a passionate determination to crush this cursed traffic in human lives and heal "the open sore of the world."

While it was under the official appointment of the British government and as an agent of the Royal Geographical Society that Livingstone returned to Africa in 1858, his missionary spirit and motive appear in the following words, uttered in reply to a suggestion that he should relinquish missionary work and give himself solely to discovery. Said he, "I would not consent to go simply as a geographer, but as a missionary, and do geography by the way. The opening of the country is a matter for congratulation only so far as it opens up a prospect for the elevation of the inhabitants. I view the geographical exploration as only the beginning of the missionary enterprise."

The remaining fifteen years of his life, except for a second brief visit home in 1864–65, were spent in persistent exploration, during which he discovered the sources of the Nile, located the great lakes of East Central Africa, and verified the upper courses of the mighty Congo. For long periods of time he was cut off in the far interior from communication with the outside world. What his mission cost him few if any will ever fully know. Racked by disease, attacked by wild beasts, threatened by savages, robbed and betrayed by carriers, tortured in spirit by the horrors of the slave hunters, "not one man in a million would have pushed forward as he did in the heart of Africa." It was in 1871 that Henry M. Stanley, at the head of a relief expedition sent out by the *New York Herald*, found Livingstone in an exhausted condition at Ujiji, on Lake Tanganyika. But all Stanley's efforts to persuade Livingstone to accompany him home proved in vain, and so the two men parted, Stanley bearing home Livingstone's precious journals of six years, while Livingstone, renewed in health and spirits by his few months' companionship, set out on a fresh journey of exploration, impelled by a firm conviction that his task was not completed. The remainder of the story until that morning of May 1, 1873, when he was found dead upon his knees in a rude hut in Chitambo's village of Ilala on Lake Bangueolo, has been rehearsed the world around.

Livingstone's remains were embalmed and carried, together with all his papers and instruments, a year's journey to Zanzibar, by Susi and Chuma, his faithful African servants. Thence they were conveyed to England and buried with the nation's noble dead in Westminster Abbey. But his heart lies buried in the remote heart of the great continent whose darkness he lived and died to lighten. The names of Africa and David Livingstone will always suggest each the other.

With 650 places of worship and a Christian community of 25,000, the London Missionary Society is the largest mission in Northern Rhodesia.

This territory is the second largest African field of the *Plymouth Brethren*, whose intrepid pioneer, *Fred S. Arnot*, a hardy Scotsman, crossed and recrossed this part of Africa many times. In 1889 he escorted a group to Northern Rhodesia and inaugurated a fine work which has continued to this day. Of 115 present-day missionaries, 29 are nurses. Assemblies number more than 200, and preaching places many times that number.

The *Universities' Mission to Central Africa* has five dioceses in this part of Africa. One of these is Northern Rhodesia, which was entered in 1910. Its 70 churches are greatly understaffed. The 1954 Report referred to the "dangerous shortage of priests, European and African, at a time when there are such wonderful opportunities for the spiritual growth of the Diocese." Four years later the Mission reported that the number of married priests confirmed had doubled in recent years, but they were still in urgent need of single priests to work in the rural stations where 20,000 communicants require pastoral care.

The Copper Belt of Northern Rhodesia, which has in recent years attracted hundreds of thousands of African youths from the rural districts to five big urban centers, presents the Christian Church with both a challenge and an opportunity. The better to meet that challenge, five mission boards decided to pool their resources and have formed the *United Missions of the Copper Belt*. They are the *Universities' Mission to Central Africa*, the *Methodist Missionary Society*, the *Church of Scotland*, the *United Society for Christian Literature*, and the *London Missionary Society*. The activities include evangelism, education, literature, colportage, women's work, and social and recreational work.

In 1903 the *Seventh Day Adventists* started a station on a 5,000-acre farm purchased from the government. They now have a Church of 8,000 members.

In 1909 *Fred Arnot* helped *Mr. A. W. Bailey* of the *South Africa General Mission* to commence settled work among the Kaonde tribe. Luampa, the site of the Mission's largest leper settlement, was opened in 1922. Its Bible institute is located at Chizera. It has three couples working in the Copper Belt.

The *English Methodists* have a small work in Northern Rhodesia. The *Salvation Army* is one of the largest groups, with almost 300 places of worship. *Jehovah's Witnesses* are reported to have grown enormously since 1948. Because the movement is against both Church and State, it appeals to the nationalistic spirit, and the Africans in the territory have joined it in tens of thousands.

Nyasaland. The name of David Livingstone will ever be associated

with Nyasaland, not only because he was the first European to visit
the area but also because three important missions there today owe
their existence to the inspiration of this great man of God. The first
of these was the *Universities' Mission to Central Africa,* which was
organized in 1858. Two years later the first party of missionaries,
under the leadership of *Bishop Charles F. Mackenzie* and accompanied by Livingstone himself, reached Nyasaland. They established
a station just south of Lake Nyasa. Mackenzie died of fever after
being on the field only two years. A series of misfortunes overtook
the Mission and its headquarters was moved to Zanzibar. A second
entrance was effected in the 1870's and this time the enterprise
prospered. The only Anglican mission in Nyasaland, the U.M.C.A.,
has through the years maintained a well-rounded program of evangelistic, educational, medical, and industrial activities. One of its
outstanding missionaries was *William P. Johnson,* who spent more
than half a century in Nyasaland. He preached; conducted schools;
translated the Bible and the Book of Common Prayer into one
dialect, part of the Bible into another, and did other translating into
three additional tongues. The Cathedral which stands where witches
used to be burned on Likoma Island has a congregation of 2,000
each Sunday morning. African ordinands are trained at the theological college on the island. Two teacher training colleges provide
teachers for 150 elementary schools. There are nine small hospitals
staffed by European nurses with African assistants under the supervision of a European doctor. Forty thousand communicants are
scattered over 260 villages.

The second of these missions was the *Livingstonia Mission* of the
United Free Church of Scotland. The moving spirit behind this venture of faith was *James Stewart,* already a missionary of commanding stature and well known as the founder of the *Lovedale Institute*
in South Africa. He had met Livingstone in Africa, and shortly after
the latter's death Stewart proposed to his church that work be
undertaken in Nyasaland. To obtain funds for the new project
Stewart sold his family plate and most of his patrimony. The first
party arrived in 1875 and claimed the west side of Lake Nyasa as
their field. Headquarters was established at Bandawe, half way up
the lake, but was transferred in 1894 to Livingstonia, at the northern end. The outstanding leader of the mission was *Robert Laws,*
who was chiefly responsible for founding and developing at Livingstonia a central educational institution modeled after Lovedale
Institute in South Africa. The first few decades were made extremely
difficult by the slave traders and tribal warfare. After 15 years there
were only 60 converts. The coming of British rule in 1891 caused the
tide to turn. The resultant peace and stability made life and work

easier for the missionaries, and schools and churches began to multiply. By 1914 there were 900 schools and 57,000 pupils.

The third mission was the *Blantyre Mission* of the *Church of Scotland*, whose first contingent of a medical officer and five artisans arrived in Nyasaland in 1876. They staked out an area on the Shiré Highlands, called it Blantyre, and established their headquarters there. In the *Henry Henderson Institute* at Blantyre, nationals are trained as ministers, teachers, hospital attendants, clerks, printers, gardeners, carpenters, machinists, etc.

The churches brought into being by the latter two missions are now known as the *Church of Central Africa*. With 130,000 members and a community of 400,000 it is the largest church body in Nyasaland.

The *Dutch Reformed Church Mission* entered Nyasaland in 1888, and stations were established throughout the Central Province. In time the Dutch Reformed Mission took over some of the southern stations belonging to the Livingstonia Mission, setting the latter free to push farther north.

Three industrial missions entered Nyasaland about the same time. The *Nyasa Industrial Mission* was organized by the Australian Baptists in the early 1890's. The *Zambezi Industrial Mission,* an independent work organized along similar lines, sought to become self-supporting by means of large coffee and cotton plantations. The third such mission to begin operations in the 1890's was the *Baptist Industrial Mission*, which was supported from Scotland.

In 1900 the *South Africa General Mission* entered the southern tip of Nyasaland in response to the invitation of an independent missionary named Anderson. In their first station, Lulwe, there are now a hospital, a dispensary, a primary school, and a school for the blind. A Bible institute is located at Chididi, their only other station.

The *Seventh Day Adventists*, who commenced work in 1902, report 16,000 church members. The medical work centers around a hospital and a leprosarium. Educational work includes 165 schools and the Missionary Training Institute.

The *National Baptist Convention's* work in Nyasaland is centered in Chiradzulu, where it has the *Providence Industrial Mission* and the *James E. East Memorial Hospital*.

MOZAMBIQUE

Area: 288,000 sq. mi.   Population: 6,600,000
Capital: Lourenço Marques   Religion: Animism
                                                Roman
                                                Catholicism

THE LAND. On the east coast of Africa, facing the island of Madagascar, is located one of Portugal's three African possessions, Mozambique. On the west it is bounded by the Federation of Rhodesia and Nyasaland and the Union of South Africa. On the north it meets Tanganyika. A very narrow strip on the south borders on the Union of South Africa.

POLITICAL HISTORY. After five centuries of Arab domination, Mozambique was discovered by Vasco da Gama in 1498 and colonized in 1505. It has been in Portuguese possession ever since. Throughout the nineteenth century it was the ambition of the Portuguese to unite Mozambique with Angola, but the presence of the British in Rhodesia made this impossible. During the third quarter of that century Mozambique was the center of a lucrative slave trade with Brazil.

THE PEOPLE. The Portuguese are notoriously poor administrators; consequently they have not done as much for their colonies as the other European powers have done for theirs. The people of Mozambique are still living under primitive conditions. Leprosy, malaria, and tuberculosis claim many lives every year. Drunkenness, immorality, and venereal disease abound. In 1955 there were only six secondary schools in the whole country. The tribes of Mozambique belong almost entirely to the Bantu race.

THE RELIGION. All Jesuit missionaries were expelled from Portuguese colonies in 1759. Nevertheless, Protestant missionaries have always found it difficult to work in them. Since Portugal became a republic in 1910 and declared the separation of Church and State, conditions have improved somewhat; but even today missionary work in Mozambique is greatly hampered by anti-Protestant restrictions.

MISSIONS. Permanent Protestant work did not get under way in Mozambique until 1880, although fifty years before the *Methodist Missionary Society* had made an abortive attempt to establish a station at Delagoa Bay. The *American Board of Commissioners* also suffered several failures before finally establishing a work at Inhambane in 1883; but they found the climate intolerable and withdrew to Rhodesia five years later.

Fortunately for the cause of Protestantism, the *American Methodists*, under Bishop William Taylor, arrived just in time to take over the three stations abandoned by the American Board. In spite of the many restrictions imposed by the Portuguese authorities on all phases of missionary work, medical and educational as well as evangelistic, the American Methodists have shown commendable patience and perseverance, and today they have a small but strong Church in Mozambique. Their present field is divided into 5 districts with 45 circuits made up of 774 places of worship. The shepherding of 5,000 full members and 20,000 other Christians is in the competent hands of 30 members of the Conference, 18 supply pastors, and 7 members on probation. The medical program is in jeopardy for lack of qualified personnel; there is only one doctor to care for two hospitals and a leper colony. Concern is also felt for the future leadership of the Church. Only two primary schools are operating at present, one at Cambine and the other at Chicuque. Both of them are filled to capacity. *Central Training School* at Cambine, sometimes called "Tuskegee in Africa," is doing a splendid job in training teachers, evangelists, and technicians. It could do a great deal more if the government would grant permission to open a high school. In the capital city their only property is a parsonage, which they acquired in 1930. They were never allowed to build a church; the Methodist Christians there are using facilities provided by the Nazarenes.

Other missions in Mozambique include the *Swiss Mission, Free Methodists, Scandinavian Baptists,* and *Nazarenes.* These societies are all concentrated in the Lourenço Marques district where only one-fifth of the African population lives. The northern part of the country, with 5,000,000 people, is almost totally unreached with the gospel. The Diocese of Masasi, one of the five dioceses of the *Universities' Mission to Central Africa,* takes in a section of northern Mozambique, but the field has never been worked because the government has refused permission and the Mission lacks personnel.

For forty years the *South Africa General Mission* tried in vain to gain a foothold in the country. In 1936 the Mission formed a separate society, the *Missão Evangelica na Africa Portuguesa,* and after many setbacks and much hardship, succeeded in obtaining permission to open a station at Chiuangumabvu. In 1942 they extended the work to Mihecani. This station was established by the *Church of Scotland* in 1913 and later handed over to the *Nyasa Mission,* which in turn retired from the field in favor of the South Africa General Mission. When the government refused to permit the coming of reinforcements the station at Chiuangumabvu was closed, leaving only one station in an area of 151,000 square miles. Yet a strong indigenous work is proceeding. Christians in various localities number 1,500. They support seven pastors and many volunteers who preach in the villages. Two missionary couples hold the fort in this isolated station. The school there has an enrollment of 1,000.

SOUTH WEST AFRICA

Area: 317,000 sq. mi.   Population: 475,000
Capital: Windhoek   Religion: Animism

THE LAND. South West Africa is on the Atlantic Ocean. Angola lies to the north, Bechuanaland to the east, and the Union of South Africa to the south.

POLITICAL HISTORY. The country was annexed by Germany in 1884. Since World War I, it has been administered as mandated territory by the Union of South Africa.

THE PEOPLE. The population is divided three ways: the whites, the Natives, and the Colored. The principal Native races are the Ovambos, the Hereros, the Bergdamaras, the Namas (Hottentots), and the Bushmen. The Bushmen are the oldest inhabitants of South West Africa. The white population is approximately 50,000. There are 55 government schools for white children. The education of the Colored and the Native children is largely in the hands of the missions.

THE RELIGION. The Native races are animists.

MISSIONS. As early as 1805 the *London Missionary Society* sent missionaries to work among the Hottentots, and for a time the *Methodist Missionary Society* also had work among them. The major and continuing work, however, was established by the *Rhenish Missionary Society* in 1839. One of the more notable pioneers was *Hugo Hahn,* who sought in various ways to establish a self-supporting colony of Christians; but the nomadic instincts of the Native races were too strong to permit them to settle down to an agricultural existence. By the end of the century there were about 10,000 Christians among the Namas and the Hereros. In 1950 the baptized membership stood at 87,300. Sixty primary schools provide education for over 5,000 pupils.

In 1870 the *Finnish Missionary Society* began a work among the Ovambo in the north. In 1950 it reported 81 missionaries assisted by 37 ordained Africans caring for the spiritual needs of 64,000 baptized believers. A fine educational system includes 90 elementary schools and 10 high schools with 530 African teachers. This Mission has 9 hospitals and 11 dispensaries. These two Lutheran groups account for more than 90 per cent of the Protestant work in South West Africa. The *Finnish Congregational Mission* and the *Methodist Church of South Africa* have small enterprises in the country.

BECHUANALAND

Area: 275,000 sq. mi.
Capital: Mafeking

Population: 360,000
Religion: Animism

THE LAND. The Bechuanaland Protectorate comprises the territory lying between the Molopo River on the south and the Zambezi River on the north, and extends from the Transvaal Province and Southern Rhodesia on the east to South West Africa on the west.

POLITICAL HISTORY. British interest in this territory dates from 1885. In 1889 it was included in the sphere of the British South Africa Company. A Resident Commissioner was appointed in 1890, and in 1895 it became a Crown Colony and was annexed to the Cape of Good Hope. Local chiefs rule their own tribes under the protection and authority of the British Crown.

THE PEOPLE. Bechuanaland is very sparsely populated, having only 1.3 persons to the square mile. Europeans and Asiatics number about 4,000. The more important tribes are the Bamangwato, Bakgatla, Bakwena, Bangwaketse, and Batawana.

THE RELIGION. The Africans are animists. The Colonial government has always looked with favor on the missionary enterprise. Indeed, it was one of the missionaries, *John Mackenzie*, who in the 1870's strongly advocated that Great Britain assume control of the territory to avoid rivalry and bloodshed.

MISSIONS. The *London Missionary Society* was the first to enter this part of South Africa. Many of its outstanding missionaries are worthy of attention but space permits a reference to only one or two. *Robert Moffat*, who arrived in South Africa in 1817, made many missionary journeys north into what is now the Protectorate of Bechuanaland; but inasmuch as his life's work centered in Kuruman, his story is told briefly in the section on the Union of South Africa. In 1864, six years before Moffat retired from the field, a young man arrived in Bechuanaland. He was *John Macken-zie*. In addition to his prodigious energy as missionary and ex-plorer, Mackenzie had the mind and vision of a statesman and did not hesitate to make recommendations to the British authorities in South Africa. Convinced that the northward thrust of the Boers into Bechuanaland would lead to plunder and destruction, he pressed for British annexation as the best possible means of pacifying the territory and safeguarding the rights of the Africans. He was offered the post of Commissioner for Bechuanaland at $5,000 a year but refused it because he thought it would interfere with his mis-sionary career.

One of the notable converts of the London Missionary Society was *King Khama*. Yielding his heart and life to Christ, he firmly withstood his father's persuasions to have him succeed his father as sorcerer as well as chief, and he became a veritable "Alfred the Great," waging war alike on heathen customs and the white man's rum and other vices. Fearing no one but God and caring only for the welfare of his people, he conducted his government on Chris-tian principles. Laws were made to be kept, and violators were punished regardless of extenuating circumstances. Even the white man had to obey—or get out! He was at the same time a devout and humble Christian and a firm and sagacious state builder. By precept and example he turned a whole savage tribe into a peaceful and industrious Christian people. "To pass from Bechuanaland before Khama to Bechuanaland with Khama is like passing from Dante's Inferno to his Paradiso."[1] At the present time this Society has workers in seven stations in Bechuanaland.

Four other missions are operating in Bechuanaland. The *Her-mannsburg Evangelical Lutheran Mission* has one station, an ex-tension of its work in Transvaal. The *Dutch Reformed Society* has a work among the Bakgatla tribe. The *United Free Church of Scot-land* co-operates with the London Missionary Society in the hospital at Molepolole. Here as elsewhere the ubiquitous *Seventh Day Ad-ventists* are to be found. Their church work is supplemented by a hospital, but as yet they report no educational work.

UNION OF SOUTH AFRICA

Area: 472,000 sq. mi.   Population: 14,200,000
Capitals: Pretoria and   Religion: Animism
          Capetown   Christianity

[1] Wilson Naylor, *Daybreak in the Dark Continent* (Missionary Education Movement, 1912), p. 261.

THE LAND. The Union of South Africa is the most southerly of all the African countries. Its Cape of Good Hope is the extreme southern tip of the continent. Included in this study of the Union of South Africa are the two small enclaves of Basutoland and Swaziland, which are protectorates of Great Britain.

POLITICAL HISTORY. The Union of South Africa came into being in 1910 when the four self-governing colonies of the Cape of Good Hope, Natal, Transvaal, and the Orange Free State were united to form one country. It is an independent dominion within the British Commonwealth of Nations, but anti-Commonwealth sentiment is quite strong. Its policy of *apartheid* makes it the black sheep of the family.

THE PEOPLE. The population is composed of about 3,000,000 whites and 11,000,000 non-whites. The white population is divided almost equally between the British and the Dutch. Eighty per cent of the land is owned by these two groups of European extraction. The Dutch dominate the government and are responsible for the policy of *apartheid,* which is the burning issue in the Union of South Africa at the present time. The non-white population is divided three ways: the Bantu (9,460,000), the Colored (1,320,000), and the Asiatic (430,000). The two official languages are Afrikaans and English.

THE RELIGION. More than 90 per cent of the whites are church members. The Dutch Reformed Church is the largest; its three branches account for almost half of the total white population. The Church of England claims about 15 per cent. Methodists, Presbyterians, Baptists, Lutherans, and Congregationalists follow in that order. There are about 150,000 Roman Catholics among the whites.

The Dutch Reformed Church also has the largest following among the Colored (Mixed) people; the Church Missionary Society is next. Among the Bantu, the Methodists are first, followed by the Church Missionary Society and the Dutch Reformed Church. Of all the Churches in the Union, the Dutch Reformed is the only one which supports the government policy of *apartheid.* The others are putting up a gallant fight for equal rights for all, regardless of race or color. The Dutch Reformed Church was also the only religious body to support the Bantu Education Act of 1953, which dealt a body blow to the educational work of missions. There are 200,000 Hindus and 125,000 Muslims.

The Group Areas Act, which declares where the various racial groups may live, has created grave problems for the churches. Large numbers of Christians have been uprooted and moved to new housing projects. Sites are available for new buildings; but the subsistence-level incomes of the people do not permit them to build in conformity with the building codes. Under these conditions the churches of South Africa, once self-supporting, are finding it increasingly difficult to meet expenses. To aggravate the situation the London Missionary Society, one of the oldest in South Africa, is itself in dire financial straits and is not able to come to the aid of the churches which it founded and has fostered for many years.

THE PROTESTANT VANGUARD. To the *Moravians* belongs the honor of blazing the Protestant missionary trail in South Africa. Indeed, they were the first Protestant missionaries in this modern era to take up work in any part of the Dark Continent. *George Schmidt* was sent out from Herrnhut in 1737 in response to an appeal, in behalf of the oppressed Hottentots, made by Ziegenbalg and Plütschau on their way round the Cape to India in 1705. But the Dutch, then in control of South Africa, met with derision the attempt to Christianize these primitive people whom they regarded and treated as animals. Schmidt persisted bravely, won the confidence of the Hottentots, and within four years baptized a little company of Christian converts. This aroused the bitter hostility of the Dutch settlers, and in 1743 Schmidt was ordered home to Holland by the authorities and never permitted to return.

In 1792 the Moravians made a second attempt to evangelize South Africa. In the very area where George Schmidt had labored they found an old woman who had been baptized by him fifty years before, and she still possessed a copy of the New Testament which he had given her. A station was established among the Hottentots which they called Genadendal. In 1818 they began work among the Kaffirs in the eastern part of the Cape Colony. Under the energetic leadership of *Bishop Hans Peter Hallbeck* (1784–1840) the Moravian enterprise flourished, and stations were opened right up to the borders of the Orange Free State and Natal. For almost 170 years the Moravians have carried on a continuous work. In 1958 they reported 48,000 Christians in 38 main centers.

MISSIONS. The founding of the *London Missionary Society* coincided with the British occupation of the Cape in 1795. Its first missionary to South Africa, *John Theodore Vanderkemp*, reached the Cape in 1799. His initial project was to establish a mission among the Kaffirs. When this failed because of the enmity existing between them and the Dutch settlers, he turned to the Hottentots and founded a center for runaway slaves on Algoa Bay. Vanderkemp married a seventeen-year-old African girl whom he had bought out of slavery. The union was not without its problems, and his missionary career of only 12 years is said to have been shortened because of it. Some of Vanderkemp's colleagues also married Hottentot women, not always with happy results.

One of the best-known missionaries of all time was *Robert Moffat* of the London Missionary Society. He arrived in South Africa in 1817, eleven years after the British first occupied the Cape Colony. He spent some time in Capetown before obtaining permission to proceed inland. Before he set out he was warned against Africaner, a native chief whose barbarous crimes had made him a terror to that region. But meanwhile the gospel had reached and influenced Africaner. Moffat spent six months in his town, and the chief became a true and humble Christian. When Moffat reappeared at Capetown in 1819, bringing with him this converted savage and outlaw, it caused a great sensation.

In 1820 Moffat, having married Mary Smith, left again for the interior and opened Kuruman, the first station among the Bechuana tribes. Later he pressed into the Matabele country as far as the Zambezi River. For many years these brave pioneers labored, preaching and teaching amid great perils and strange adventures, but without seeing any converts. Finally, however, their faith was rewarded, for in 1829 the first Bechuana church was formed at Kuruman. There, too, the Bible in the Bechuana tongue was printed in 1857, the translation having been done single-handedly by Moffat. In 1870, enfeebled by age and work, the Moffats returned to England. Mrs. Moffat died the next year, and Mr. Moffat in 1883. During their fifty-three years of heroic service in South Africa they succeeded in turning the murderous savages into Christian people who cultivated the arts and habits of civilized life and had a written language of their own. The mission house and church built by Moffat, still standing on their original site, have been turned over to the government as historic monuments.

An outstanding missionary statesman of that early period was *John Philip*, who for thirty years (1820–50) was superintendent of the London Missionary Society work in South Africa. A great champion of human freedom and a true friend and benefactor of the oppressed Africans, he was ahead of his time in asserting that, given the same training, the Negroes are in no wise inferior to the white people. With characteristic vigor and courage he fought against the white traders in their exploitation of the Africans, and was influential in bringing about the emancipation of the slaves in 1833. A man of strong conviction and forthright speech, he was genuinely hated by the Dutch, who for obvious reasons were in favor of the status quo. With statesmanlike vision, Philip encouraged other societies to send missionaries to South Africa. It was largely through his influence that the *American Board,* the *Paris Mission,* and the *Rhenish Missionary Society* commenced work in this part of the world.

The *Methodist Missionary Society* began its work in South Africa with the arrival of *Barnabas Shaw* in 1816. For ten years he worked among the Namaquas south of the Orange River. The first station north of the river was established in 1834. In 1820 *William Shaw,* a Methodist minister, established a Christian colony at Algoa Bay and began work among the Hottentots who were part of the British garrison at Grahamstown. Three years later a mission was begun among the Kaffirs. By 1831 the Methodists had six stations among the Bantu, stretching 200 miles from Wesleyville to the Natal border. Later the Bible was translated into one of the Kaffir tongues by *John W. Appleyard.* Here as elsewhere the Methodists built up a fine school system. One of their outstanding converts was *John Tengo Jabavu* who, in addition to teaching and preaching, edited a newspaper and generally furthered the cause of African freedom. Today the Methodist Church is the largest group in South Africa with work among the Bantu.

The Methodists were not the only ones to emphasize educational work. All the missions had their schools. As a matter of fact, it was the missions who pioneered in this field. A missionary school begun in 1799 was the first school in the Cape. Likewise in Natal, where the first school was opened in 1835 by Captain Allen Gardiner, who later died a tragic death in attempting to plant the cross in South America. In the Orange Free State the first school was opened by missionaries in 1823. Missionaries began education work in the Transvaal in 1822, and by the turn of the century there were 200 schools. For many decades the missions carried the full burden of education in South Africa. It was not until after the Boer War that the government began to take an interest in the education of Africans, and it was 1924 before an Inspector of Education was appointed. As late as 1946, government schools numbered only 232, while the missions were operating 4,335. As a result of the Bantu Education Act passed in 1953, 5,000 Protestant mission schools were transferred to government control.

Although there were Presbyterian churches in South Africa it remained for the Presbyterian missionaries from Scotland to evangelize the Bantu. Their first missionary arrived in 1818, and was followed three years later by two workers of the *Glasgow Missionary Society*. Their major contribution was in the area of education. Outstanding among their institutions was *Lovedale*. It was founded in 1841 and patterned after Alexander Duff's system of missionary education in India. Its curriculum ranged from primary school to college and included training in theology, agriculture, handicrafts, and other vocational subjects. The second principal of Lovedale was *James Stewart*, who had been a colleague of Livingstone on the Zambezi. Under his principalship (1870–1905) Lovedale became one of the outstanding missionary institutions of the world. With the passing of the Bantu Education Act in 1953 this splendid institution fell into the hands of the government.

At the suggestion of John Philip of the London Missionary Society, the *Paris Evangelical Missionary Society*, organized in 1822, sent its first representatives to South Africa in 1829. One of the original contingent worked for a time among the Hottentots. Two others went to Bechuanaland and established a work near Moffat's station at Kuruman. In 1833 a second party of workers initiated a most successful work among the Basuto whose chief, Moshesh, had asked for missionaries. *François Coillard* spent twenty years in Basutoland before heading up an indigenous mission organized by the Basuto in 1877 to work among the Barotse people in the Rhodesias. The real leader of the Paris Mission after 1860 was *Adolphe Mabille* under whom the Mission greatly expanded all phases of its work.

The Church of England was represented in South Africa by the *Church Missionary Society* and the *Society for the Propagation of the Gospel in Foreign Parts* as early as the 1830's. It was not, however, until the consecration of the first bishop, *Robert Gray*, that aggressive work was undertaken among the non-white population. Then they opened Christian settlements on grants of land obtained from the government for that purpose. By 1914 the Anglicans had missions for the blacks in all four provinces of the Union. The *Church of the Province of South Africa* now has 12 dioceses and a community of 600,000. There are 400,000 white adherents.

The *American Board of Commissioners* has been in South Africa since 1835. Its work has been chiefly among the Zulus in the Durban area; its workers gave the Zulu people the Bible. Its 29 missionaries are strategically located in five main stations centered in and around Durban and Johannesburg. Of its 194 organized churches, 144 are self-supporting. Communicants total 12,000. Its highest educational institution, *Adams College*, went out of existence with the promulgation of the Bantu Education Act.

Two interdenominational faith missions took up work in South Africa in the last decade of the nineteenth century. The *Scandinavian Alliance Mission* (now *The Evangelical Alliance Mission*) entered in 1892 and set up its first station in Swaziland. From there the work gradually expanded to Zululand, Tongoland, Natal, and Transvaal, and more recently to the Orange Free State. Work is also conducted among the Indian population in several areas. Two secondary schools and two Bible institutes represent the extent of the educational work. It operates the *Mosvold Hospital* and has clinics at most of the main stations. South Africa is the most indigenous of TEAM's 22 mission fields; 134 of its 145 organized churches there are fully self-supporting. In 1957 there were 662 new members received by baptism.

In 1894 two infant missions already in the country, the Cape General Mission and the Southeast Africa Evangelistic Mission, united to form the *South Africa General Mission*. *Rev. Andrew Murray* was president and *Spencer Walton* was its first director. Working out from headquarters in Durban, it opened its first station in the wild Zulu country. Podoland was entered in 1895. Work among the Indian population of Natal was undertaken in 1896 but it was not until 1904, when *Mr. and Mrs. Tomlinson,* formerly missionaries to India and familiar with Tamil and Telugu, joined the Mission that real progress was made. The first American workers arrived in 1908. Shortly after World War II it underwent a major reorganization and the missionary staff more than doubled between 1946 and 1955. Its largest field is the Union of South Africa, where it has 293 churches. According to recent statistics this Mission now has a total of 30 main stations: four in Angola, five in Northern Rhodesia, one in Southern Rhodesia, two in Mozambique, two in Nyasaland, and sixteen in South Africa. In 1953 it lost its schools in the Union, but it still has some 125 primary schools in its other fields. Teachers for these schools are furnished by two teacher training institutes, while six Bible institutes help train pastors and evangelists for over 650 congregations.

Continental societies include the *Rhenish Missionary Society* and the *Berlin Missionary Society,* both of which entered the field in the 1830's; the *Norwegian Missionary Society* (1840's); the *Hermannsburg Mission* (1850's); the *Church of Sweden Mission* (1870's); the *Swedish Holiness Union* and the *Norwegian Mission Union* (1880's); and the *Scandinavian Independent Baptist Mission* (1892). Other missions also working here are the *Salvation Army,*

Assemblies of God, Seventh Day Adventists, Mormons, African Methodist Episcopal Church (U.S.A.), and several *Pentecostal* groups whose adherents are said to number 200,000.

No account of Christian work in South Africa would be complete without some reference to the *Bantu Separatist Churches.* Two types are distinguished, the Ethiopian and the Zionist. The former is due in large part to the color bar, and emphasizes the African, or racial, character of the Church. The latter is a much more significant and elaborate expression of the African mind. These Separatist Churches have developed their own form of worship and ritual, which includes hand clapping, dancing, indigenous music, and faith healing. Indeed, in many instances faith healing is the main element of the Christian message as they preach it. The Movement began in the last decade of the nineteenth century and has expanded steadily since that time. In 1904 there were three sectarian bodies with about 25,000 followers. In 1925 the number had increased to 130. According to the latest census figures there are now over 2,000 sects with a following of 1.5 million persons. With segregation so strongly enforced it is not surprising to learn that the South Africans are turning to these sects in ever-increasing numbers. At best they are only semi-Christian; in some instances they are anti-Christian. They are a strange mixture of animism, native customs, and magic, with certain Christian elements added and the whole embellished with the external symbols of Christianity. If the Movement continues to grow at its present pace it will have serious repercussions on the Church.

MALAGASY REPUBLIC
(Madagascar)

Area: 241,000 sq. mi.   Population: 5,000,000
Capital: Tananarive   Religion: Animism
                                               Christianity

THE LAND. It seems most natural that any mention of this island should be made in connection with Africa, because of its close proximity to that continent. Situated about 250 miles off the southeast coast, Madagascar is the third largest island of the globe, being slightly larger than France and Belgium combined.

POLITICAL HISTORY. Madagascar was not discovered by Europeans until the beginning of the sixteenth century. In the eighteenth century it was a center of the infamous slave trade with the West

Indies. The last native sovereign was Queen Rànavàlona III, who came to the throne in 1883. It was a French colony from 1896 until 1958, when it became an independent republic within the French Community and assumed its new name, Malagasy Republic.

THE PEOPLE. Its inhabitants are called Malagasy and are of Malay-Polynesian origin. They are divided into 14 tribes, of which the Hova, or Merina, is much the largest. Prior to the coming of the Christian missionary the people were given over to idolatry of the most degraded kind, and the island was the scene of perpetual war, lust, and superstition. So hopelessly depraved were the people that vices were exalted as virtues, and the French governor of a neighboring island told the first missionaries that they might as well attempt to convert sheep, oxen, and asses. Yet through the wondrous working of divine grace this island has been made famous by the heroic faith of its Christian martyrs.

THE RELIGION. The indigenous religion is animistic. Ancestor worship is common. There is no recognized priesthood but the witch doctor still has considerable influence. Underneath the fetishism is a belief in a supreme deity, the Fragrant One, knowledge of whom is preserved in many proverbs. Since 1895, Christianity, both Roman Catholic and Protestant, has made a great deal of progress, and today it claims about 30 per cent of the population. Islam also is strong; there are about 75 mosques on the island.

EARLY MISSIONS. To the *London Missionary Society* belongs the distinction of being the first Protestant mission to Madagascar. Two Welshmen, *David Jones* and *Thomas Bevan*, landed with their families at Tamatave in 1818. In a few weeks five of the group had died of fever, but Jones declared: "I am determined to continue. Madagascar is a noble field of service." A Christian school was established at Tananarive under the patronage of the beneficent King Radàma; and Jones was joined by Griffiths, Johns, Freeman, Cameron, and others. The Bible was translated, and schools and industries were begun. The work met with such favor and success that by 1833 the Church had 2,000 members and 30,000 Malagasy were able to read.

PERSECUTION. Upon the death of King Radàma in 1828 one of his twelve wives, known to history as Rànavàlona I, seized the throne, murdered all rivals, and began a reign of terror that won for her the name of "Bloody Mary of Madagascar." She was a veritable monster of cruelty, and it is said that hundreds of victims annually fell prey to her atrocious crimes. The wicked Queen soon turned her attention to the Christian Church. Teaching, public worship, and the distribution of the Scriptures were banned. All missionaries except those who were teaching useful crafts were driven from the land. Every conceivable form of torture was employed against the Christians; but they bore the severest suffering, and even death itself, with quiet heroism and unfaltering faith in God. For every one she put to death a score adopted the new faith. For twenty-six years the terror continued, but all to no avail. By the time the Queen died in 1861, the number of Christians had actually multiplied many fold.

THE TURNING OF THE TIDE. Immediately following the proclamation of religious freedom in 1862, the Church came out of hiding, missionaries returned, and Christian work was resumed. In 1868 a wonderful change took place when Rànavàlona II became queen, for soon after her coronation she accepted baptism and became a Christian. Christianity immediately became recognized as the faith of the realm, and people flocked in droves to the Christian banner. The Church was then in greater danger from its friends than it had been from its foes.

PERIOD OF PROSPERITY. For thirty years the Church enjoyed a period of peace and spiritual prosperity. New societies entered Madagascar and took up work in various parts of the country.

The first of these was the *Society for the Propagation of the Gospel* in 1864. In 1866 the *Norwegian Lutherans* sent out *Rev. John Engh* and *Nils Nilsen*. They settled at Betafo in the southern part of Central Province. The following year the number of societies was increased to four by the coming of the *British Friends,* or *Quakers.* Later on two American societies began work in this field, the *Norwegian Lutheran Church of America* (1892) and the *Lutheran Free Church* (1895).

THE SECOND PERIOD OF PERSECUTION. A very sad postscript must be added to the story of missionary progress just sketched. In 1896 Madagascar became a French colony, and a new wave of terror, incited by the Jesuits, swept over the Church. Mission property was confiscated, schools were closed, 700 churches were destroyed, anti-Christian literature was circulated, and pagan customs were revived. For a time it looked as if the missionaries would all have to withdraw. The situation was relieved to some extent by the action of the *Paris Evangelical Society* in coming to the aid of the hard-pressed Protestants.

LATER DEVELOPMENTS. In 1913 the various Protestant missions defined spheres of influence to avoid overlapping and to eliminate competition. As a concession to the newly established mission comity, the London Missionary Society, in a gesture of unusual magnanimity, surrendered to other societies 1,290 schools and 500 of its 700 hard-won churches. Today the London Missionary Society has four main areas of work: Imerina in the Central Province; Betsileo, 250 miles to the south; among the Sihanaka in the north; and among the Marafotsy tribes in the far north. Its 1,200 churches now have a membership of 62,000.

Other missions have experienced comparable growth. The three Lutheran groups united in 1950 to form the *Malagasy Lutheran Church*, the largest Church on the island, with 6 synods and 90,000 members. The *Reformed Church* (French background) reports 1,870 churches. The *Episcopal Diocese* of Madagascar has a resident bishop and indigenous clergy, and a community of approximately 30,000. The *British Friends* have 8,000 members, and the *Seventh Day Adventists* have 2,300. A newcomer to Madagascar is the *Church of the Nazarene*.

XVII

NORTH AFRICA

LIBYA

Area: 680,000 sq. mi.
Capitals: Tripoli and Benghazi

Population: 1,200,000
Religion: Islam

THE LAND. Libya is situated on the southern shore of the Mediterranean Sea between Egypt on the east and Tunisia and Algeria on the west. Her southern neighbors are the two territories formerly known as French West Africa and French Equatorial Africa. The only arable land is a narrow strip of fertile territory along the Mediterranean coast. The remainder of the country—over 90 per cent—is part of the great Sahara Desert.

POLITICAL HISTORY. For four centuries Libya, then known as Tripoli, was under Turkish domination. In 1911 Italy occupied the country and retained control until ousted by the Allies in World War II. Libya became an independent, sovereign, federal kingdom on December 24, 1951. It has a treaty of friendship and alliance with Great Britain. The United States has military bases in the country, and there is an American Point Four program there.

THE PEOPLE. The population is composed mostly of Arabs and Berbers, with a considerable Negroid intermixture. Foreign elements include a dwindling number of Italians (now about 45,000) and small communities of Greeks, Maltese, and Jews. Arabic is the official language.

THE RELIGION. Islam is declared to be the state religion. Religious minorities may practise their religions, but proselytizing is frowned upon. No evangelistic work is possible, not even the distribution of the Scriptures.

MISSIONS. Missionary work in Libya began when the *North Africa Mission*, a British independent faith mission, entered the field in 1888. In spite of much opposition and discouragement, its one missionary, *Mr. William Reid*, persevered in the work. In 1935 he was joined by *Dr. and Mrs. J. A. Liley*, but the following year Mussolini's Ethiopian War occasioned their expulsion. Ten years later they were back at their post in the city of Tripoli. Through the years the witness has necessarily been confined to medical work. Clinics for men, women, and children are held three times weekly. It used to be that the clinic was open from 5:30 A.M. to 11 A.M., and 100 patients constituted a good day. But now they have to close the door at 9 A.M. to keep the crowd down to a manageable 350 patients! Boys and girls gather in classes three afternoons a week; and the lady missionaries have access to the homes of the womenfolk. The task of reaching the men is more difficult owing to the fact that the distribution of Christian literature is forbidden. The permit which for so long authorized the sale of the Scriptures to those who asked for them in person at the Mission Home was withdrawn in 1954. Seven missionaries are now serving in the medical clinic in this strategic city. In spite of all the restrictions placed on Christian work the good seed of the gospel has borne fruit at last. *Dr. Patrick McCarthy*, writing in December, 1957, said: "How we wish you could be here to witness the founding of the Libyan Church. For the first time that we know of in more than a thousand years, Libyans are meeting together as Christians to worship the Lord and study His Word."[1]

Within the last year or two, the *Seventh Day Adventists* have entered Libya and established a 28-bed hospital in the second largest city, Benghazi. One doctor and six nurses carry on a healing ministry there.

TUNISIA

Area: 48,322 sq. mi.   Population: 3,782,000
Capital: Tunis   Religion: Islam

THE LAND. Tunisia is a small country on the Mediterranean Sea wedged in between two much larger countries, Libya on the east and Algeria on the west. On the south it tapers off to a point in the northern part of the Sahara Desert. Situated where the continent of Africa suddenly juts north, about the middle of the Mediterranean Sea, it has a coastline on the east as well as the north. All but the southern tip of the country is fertile land.

[1] *North Africa* (January–February, 1958), p. 5.

POLITICAL HISTORY. Tunisia was a protectorate of France from 1881 until March 20, 1956, when it gained its independence. The monarchy was abolished by the Constituent Assembly on July 25, 1957, and today Tunisia is a sovereign, independent republic. It is basically friendly to the West but understandably sympathetic to the cause of the Algerian rebels.

THE PEOPLE. The Muslim population, numbering about 3,380,000 and divided between Arabs and Berbers, forms the backbone of the country. In addition there are 250,000 Europeans (mostly French and Italian), 60,000 Jews, and 90,000 others. Following Independence, the government greatly accelerated the educational program. The war on illiteracy is making rapid headway and missions are beginning to sense the competition. The new government has outlawed polygamy and abolished the special Muslim courts.

THE RELIGION. The 1956 Constitution recognizes Islam as the state religion. There are about 200,000 Roman Catholics, almost all of whom are Europeans. They are under the supervision of the Archbishop of Carthage. There is also a sprinkling of Greek Orthodox. There are no restrictions on the sale of Bibles or the distribution of Christian literature.

MISSIONS. The *London Jews' Society* began work in Tunisia long before the French took over in 1881. The first missionaries arrived in 1829, and after some interruptions, work has been continued since 1860. Their efforts are centered in Tunis where, in addition to *St. George's Church* and the *Bible Shop*, they maintain a boys' school and a girls' school. All but seven of the 250 students are Jews.

The second mission to enter the field was the *North Africa Mission*. Beginning in 1882, it expanded its work until it occupied seven stations in all parts of the country. In the 1940's lack of workers made it necessary to relinquish five of these stations, leaving only Tunis and Sousse. Originally a British mission, the North Africa Mission set up recruiting offices in the United States and Canada in 1948, and today most of their candidates and a good share of their income derive from North America. Thirteen new workers were added in 1958, and ten more joined the Mission in 1959. With these reinforcements the Mission hopes to reopen some of the closed stations. The Church in Tunis is drawn largely from the European population. The Muslim work in that city centers around the Bible Depot, where a good deal of personal work is done in private conversations.

The *American Methodists* began their work in Tunisia in 1908.

Through the years they have faithfully maintained their one station in Tunis, where at present they have one couple and three single ladies engaged in social and evangelistic work.

No restrictions are placed on the distribution of Christian literature. At the Fifth International Fair in Tunis in October, 1957, two Bible stands, one sponsored by the North Africa Mission and the other by the Bible Society, sold £82 and £96 worth of Bibles respectively.[2] That such witness is abundantly worthwhile is seen from the following incident reported by the Bible Society in its 1959 Report:

> In 1956 a Tunisian Arab bought one of the Bible Society's Gospels in classical Arabic at the Mission stand at the Fair. Not being interested in the book he gave it to his nephew, a student at a college in Tunis. This young man was so impressed by what he read that he sought out the missionaries to learn more. As a result he was gloriously converted, and the following year helped to man the Mission stand at the Fair, where he proclaimed Christ with quite amazing boldness. Before long his roommate was also brought to the Lord, and the two of them are now prominent members of the small Christian community at Tunis.[3]

ALGERIA

Area: 847,500 sq. mi.   Population: 9,350,000
Capital: Algiers   Religion: Islam

THE LAND. Algeria, the largest of the four North African countries, is four times the size of France, to which it belongs. On the north it borders on the Mediterranean Sea. On the west is Morocco, on the east Libya, and on the south the great sprawling territory formerly known as French West Africa. Six-sevenths of Algeria is desert. This leaves only a narrow strip along the Mediterranean shore which is arable. Two-thirds of this belongs to the European *colons* who control the entire wine production, which is the chief product of the country and the basis of its whole economy. Seventy large landowners own no less than 500,000 acres. Between the coastal plain and the Sahara Desert are the Atlas Mountains. Recently the French have struck oil in the southern part of the country. This, too, will be exploited to French advantage.

POLITICAL HISTORY. The French first entered Algeria in 1830, and eighteen years later Algeria became part of metropolitan France. The process of Europeanization has gone on ever since, and Arab

[2] *North Africa* (January–February, 1958), p. 4.
[3] *The Kingdoms Are Moved* (1959), p. 42.

culture has been ploughed under. In 1956 France granted independence to Tunisia and Morocco, but no such plans were in prospect for Algeria, which is not a colony but an integral part of metropolitan France. This, at least, has been France's view of the matter. The Algerian rebels have other ideas on the subject, however, and are demanding independence. The civil war, now entering its sixth year, has already cost France over four billion dollars, but the end is now in sight. The rebels set up a Free Provisional Government in Exile in the fall of 1958, with headquarters in Tunisia. They will probably accept de Gaulle's latest proposal which holds out the promise of eventual independence.

THE PEOPLE. There are more Europeans in Algeria than in any other country of North Africa. Altogether there are 1,200,000 persons of European descent. Most of these, of course, are French, some of whom have been there for four generations. There are also many Spaniards and some Italians. The Jewish community, with full French citizenship since 1870, numbers 130,000. The remainder of the population is made up of Arabs and Berbers. French rule has done little for the Arab population of Algeria, 60 per cent of whom are officially classed as "destitute." Although France has been in charge for 130 years, it was not until 1952 that the government at Paris gave Algeria one penny for Arab education. Not more than 2 per cent of the native population in the bigger towns can read or write. In rural areas it is worse.

THE RELIGION. Islam is the religion of the Arabs and Berbers. The Berbers, however, are not very meticulous in their observance of Islamic law. Islam was imposed on them by their conquerors; consequently they have not taken it too seriously. Moreover, Islam in this part of the world is mixed with animism and other foreign elements. The Europeans are mostly Catholics. The Roman Catholic Church has an archbishop, 2 bishops, and approximately 400 officiating clergy. There are 13 Protestant pastors and 6 Jewish rabbis sharing in government grants.

MISSIONS. Missionary work in Algeria began in 1881 when *Mr. Edward H. Glenny,* founder of the *North Africa Mission,* arrived in Algiers on November 5, 1881. With him were two other men: a Swiss, *Henri Mayor;* and a Druse, *Salim Zeytoun.* These were the first missionaries to set foot in North Africa in modern times. The N.A.M. field in Algeria is divided into two districts, the Arab-speaking area of Cherchell on the Mediterranean coast, and Kabylia, the center of the Berber-speaking people. The Kabylia district has proved to be the most fruitful field in the whole of North Africa, the reason being that the Berbers are a hardy, independent people who have never been completely subjugated by the Muslims. Nominally they are Muslims; but their acceptance of the laws of Islam has never been wholehearted. Consequently they are more open to the gospel. The Mission has work in four centers: Djemaa-Sahridj, Algiers, Cherchell, and Azazga. Four other stations formerly operated are closed, partly because of the civil strife and partly for lack of workers.

The Methodist delegates to the World Sunday School Convention in Rome in May, 1907, stopped off at Algiers. This visit prompted the conviction that the *Methodist Episcopal Church* ought to commence work in North Africa. Under the guidance of Bishop Hartzell, $50,000 was raised and work was opened in Algeria and Tunisia in 1908. Their first missionaries were two English ladies, members of an independent organization, who had been in Algeria since 1891. They joined the Methodist Mission and turned their work over to its care. In 1913 the *North African Mission Conference* was organized. The *Woman's Foreign Missionary Society* sent out as its first missionaries to Algeria *Miss Gwendolyn Narbeth* and *Miss Martha E. Robinson*, who arrived in 1922. Another milestone was reached in 1928 when the *North Africa Provisional Annual Conference*, which includes Algeria and Tunisia, was established. The *American Methodists* have stations in Algiers, Constantine, Fort National, Les Ouadhias, Oran, and Il Maten. On these six stations there are three children's homes, two youth hostels, two dispensaries, one primary school, a social center, and a camp site as well as work in evangelism and literature. Seven churches, most of them rather small, have been organized. The civil war, now in its sixth year, has curtailed the work at Fort National and Les Ouadhias. The Il Maten station was closed temporarily in 1956. One of the 28 Methodist missionaries, *Rev. Lester E. Griffiths, Jr.*, was captured and held for forty-one days by the Algerian rebels in the fall of 1958, but was released unharmed.

Christian Missions in Many Lands has been in Algeria since 1910. Its latest *Prayer List* reports 19 missionaries in 7 stations. Assemblies number 11. The *British and Foreign Bible Society*'s Agency for North Africa is located in Algiers. The whole Bible is available in the Kabyle language.

Other missions in the country are the *Algiers Mission Band, Church Missions to Jews, French Evangelical Missions to the Kabyles,* the *Seventh Day Adventists,* and the *Evangelical Baptist Missions.* This last-mentioned society is an independent mission of

American origin which maintains three stations in Algeria. In the southern part of Algeria, in the heart of the Sahara, is the *Sahara Desert Mission*. Its one station is located at Tamanrasset.

MOROCCO

Area: 174,500 sq. mi.   Population: 9,825,000
Capital: Rabat   Religion: Islam

THE LAND. Morocco is situated at the northwestern tip of the continent of Africa, directly across the Strait of Gibraltar from Spain. On the north is the Mediterranean Sea, on the west the Atlantic Ocean, on the east Algeria, and on the south the Spanish territory of Rio de Oro. In the eastern part of the country are the Atlas Mountains.

POLITICAL HISTORY. From 1912 to 1956 Morocco was a protectorate divided three ways: French Morocco (by far the largest), Spanish Morocco, and the international zone of Tangier. All three were abolished in 1956 when Morocco became a sovereign, independent monarchy.

THE PEOPLE. The native population consists of Arabs and Berbers. Besides these there are about 500,000 Europeans and 200,000 Jews. The number of Jews is diminishing year by year.

THE RELIGION. The Arabs and Berbers are Muslims. The Europeans, mostly of French and Spanish origin, are Roman Catholics under the supervision of the Archbishop of Rabat.

MISSIONS. Here, as in Tunisia, the *London Jews' Society* was the pioneer missionary agency, beginning its work as early as 1875. The *North Africa Mission* followed in 1882. This is the only mission with work in all four of the North African countries. The greater part of its work and the majority of its workers are located in Morocco. The city of Tangier, with Field Headquarters, the *Tulloch Memorial Hospital,* and the *Nurses' Training School,* is the largest N.A.M. center in North Africa. The hospital, one of only two mission hospitals in the whole of North Africa, has 33 beds and handles about 300 patients a year. Its outpatient department treats about 170 patients four days a week. The staff at present consists of three doctors, eight missionary nurses, and an evangelist. Other centers of work are Fez, Tetuan, Alcazar, Rabat, Casablanca, and Settat. Three stations have been vacant for many years for lack of workers.

The *Southern Morocco Mission,* as its name indicates, is the main mission at work in the southern part of the country. A Scottish society founded in 1888, it had at one time a flourishing work. Recent years have seen a decrease in personnel. According to its latest report, it has 15 missionaries, most of them young, stationed in Agadir, Azemmour, Mazagan, Mogador, Safi, and Marrakech. It was at the last-named station that *Dr. Cuthbert Nairn* was fatally stabbed by a fanatic just outside the mission house after fifty-six years of loving service in that city. One lone Danish lady, *Miss Edith Jacobsen,* carries on the dispensary, which attracts 140 patients a day, with only a Moorish helper to render a little nonprofessional assistance.

It is quite possible that the North Africa Mission and the Southern Morocco Mission will merge in the near future. Negotiations to that end are proceeding at the present time.

The *Gospel Missionary Union,* an American faith mission, entered the field in 1894. Some of its workers have directed their efforts to the Europeans and the Jews. One outstanding achievement of this Mission was the translation of the Scriptures into the colloquial Arabic of Morocco. A Bible school for men has been in operation for eight years, and more recently one has been opened for women. There are 6 organized churches with a total membership of 100. The missionary staff numbers 32.

These three are the largest but by no means the only societies working in Morocco. Indeed, Morocco has been blessed with more missionary work than any of the other three countries of North Africa. The *Bible Churchmen's Missionary Society* is working in the central part of the country. It entered the field in 1929 and established two stations; but it did not baptize its first convert until 1940. In 1889 the *Mildmay Mission to the Jews* began its work among the Jewish population. *Christian Missions in Many Lands* has three stations in Morocco. The latest newcomer is the recently formed *Light of Africa Mission.*

RADIO BROADCASTING. Mention should be made of the *Voice of Tangier,* an independent Christian radio station located in Tangier. Now in its sixth year it has broadcast the gospel in many languages to all parts of Europe, North Africa, and the Middle East. Owing to government action prohibiting all private broadcasting in Morocco, the station went off the air for the last time on Dec. 31, 1959. Beginning with the summer of 1960 the Voice of Tangier, now known as Trans World Radio, will be operating a 100,000-watt station in Monte Carlo, the first Christian broadcasting station in Europe.

XVIII

EAST AFRICA

SUDAN

Area: 967,500 sq. mi.   Population: 10,226,000
Capital: Khartoum   Religion: Islam
                                                 Animism

THE LAND. This Sudan must not be confused with the Sudanese Republic, which used to be part of French West Africa. Formerly known as Anglo-Egyptian Sudan, the Sudan is situated directly south of Egypt and extends southwards to Uganda. It is bounded on the west by Chad and the Central African Republic (both formerly part of French Equatorial Africa) and on the east by Ethiopia and the Red Sea. Its main physical feature is the great Nile River, which flows the full length of the country from south to north. The Sahara Desert spreads across the northern one-third of the country.

POLITICAL HISTORY. From 1899 to 1956 the Anglo-Egyptian Sudan was a condominium administered by a governor-general appointed by Egypt with the assent of Great Britain. On January 1, 1956, the Sudan was proclaimed a sovereign, independent republic. The first general elections took place in the spring of 1958. Seven months later a corrupt and ineffective government was ousted by a coup d'état which brought General Abboud to power. Since then missionary activity has been somewhat restricted.

THE PEOPLE. The population of the Sudan falls into two well-defined categories, the Arabs in the north and the Negroes in the south. The former, because of their more advanced state of civilization, dominate both the army and the government, to the deep resentment of the latter.

THE RELIGION. The population of the six northern provinces is almost entirely Muslim, while the majority in the three southern provinces are both primitive and pagan. The Muslims outnumber the pagans at least two to one. There are small Coptic and Greek Orthodox communities. For many years, education was completely in the hands of the missionaries; but in March, 1956, all boys' schools were turned over to the government. Religion is taught in the public schools—Islam to the Muslims, and Christianity to the Christians. The missions have been asked to train persons to teach Christianity in the public schools. In the Teacher Training College in Khartoum there were 80 trainees. A small number of these were Muslims, the remainder about evenly divided between Roman Catholics and Protestants. Girls' schools remain in mission hands. The Constitution guarantees freedom of conscience and religion; nevertheless missionaries are severely restricted in their movements, especially in South Sudan.

MISSIONS. Missionary work in the Sudan began when the *Church Missionary Society* opened its first station at Omdurman in 1899. Khartoum was occupied in 1900, Atbara in 1908, and Wad Medani in 1919. All are in the Muslim area. Work among the pagans in the Nuba Mountains began with the opening of Salara in 1935. In 1939 it was extended to Katcha. The Church Missionary Society work among the pagan tribes of the south began with the opening of Nalek in 1906, additional stations being opened as the work spread. In the initial stages it was exceedingly difficult. The first convert was not baptized until 1916. Since then growth has been rapid, and the number of Christians has increased to tens of thousands. Indeed, the work expanded faster than missionaries could be recruited and the C.M.S. had to accept "missionary associates" on a five-year contract to get enough personnel. Emphasis in South Sudan during the past thirty years has been on evangelism through education, with the government providing the buildings and making subsidies to educational work. Strong and vigorous indigenous churches exist today among six tribes. These churches are under the guidance of their own national pastors, trained at the *Bishop Gwynne College*. All Anglican work in the Sudan was part of the Diocese of Egypt until 1945 when a separate Diocese of the Sudan was created.

Working alongside of and closely associated with the C.M.S. has been the *United Presbyterian Mission*. In 1900 the Mission in Egypt extended its operations into the Sudan. Khartoum was the first and for thirty-eight years the only station in North Sudan. Four more stations were opened in the 1940's. Its most successful work, however, has been in South Sudan, where it is known as the *Upper Nile Mission*. The work began at Doleib Hill in 1902. Today there are nine stations in that area. The United Presbyterian Church there is known as the *Church of Christ in the Upper Nile*. Established in 1956, it consists of one presbytery, has three ordained African pastors and five organized congregations, and covers five language groups. Among a people who only twenty-five years ago were settling intertribal problems with spears, there is today an African Church with an African moderator, African pastors, and African elders.

The *Sudan United Mission* has had workers in the Sudan ever since the first group of Australian and New Zealand missionaries joined the work in 1913. The first station was opened at Melut. They now have 7 dispensaries, 2 Bible schools, and 21 congregations.

Following its expulsion from Ethiopia at the time of the Italian invasion, the *Sudan Interior Mission* moved west, over the border, and opened four stations in the southern part of Sudan. Later, other stations were opened, and at the present time they have 11 centers in the Blue Nile and the Upper Nile Provinces.

The latest arrival is the *Africa Inland Mission* which joined the Sudan work in 1949. *John Boyce,* a veteran of almost fifty years of service, spearheaded the new advance from their main base in Kenya. They now have four stations in Sudan.

The physical needs of the Sudanese are cared for by three hospitals and six dispensaries. The Upper Nile Mission has its own press, *Spearhead Press.* Translators continue to reduce the Scriptures to the vernacular languages. Efforts are also being made to put the vernacular languages into an Arabic script. In 1946 a *Missionary Council* was formed on the initiative of the Church Missionary Society, the United Presbyterian Mission, and the Sudan United Mission.

ETHIOPIA

Area: 395,000 sq. mi.
Capital: Addis Ababa

Population: 18,000,000[1]
Religion: Animism
Christianity
Islam

THE LAND. Ethiopia is located in northeast Africa opposite the Arabian peninsula. It is bounded on the northeast by the Red Sea and British Somaliland, on the west by Sudan, and on the south

[1] The official estimate of the population in 1955 was 18,000,000. Other estimates vary from 12 to 14 million. J. Spencer Trimingham in 1950 placed the figure at 6,972,833. Cf. *The Christian Church and Missions in Ethiopia,* p. 1.

by Kenya and Somalia. On the north it comes to a point where the Sudan touches the Red Sea. A high plateau with a salubrious climate and luxuriant vegetation, Ethiopia has been described as a "mountain garden surrounded by a desert."

POLITICAL HISTORY. After Egypt, Ethiopia is the African country best known to the Bible student. It is mentioned in both the Old and the New Testaments. It is an ancient kingdom with an unbroken dynasty going back hundreds of years before the Christian era. Its present royal family claims descent from King Solomon and the Queen of Sheba. The Emperor, Haile Selassie, has as one of his titles "King of Kings." In the royal coat of arms is the figure of a lion and the motto: "The Lion of the Tribe of Judah Hath Prevailed." Ethiopia was occupied by the Italians from October, 1935, to March, 1941, when the British troops defeated the Italians and Selassie returned to Addis Ababa. In 1950, by action of the United Nations, Eritrea, a former Italian colony on the Red Sea, became an autonomous unit within the Federation of Ethiopia and Eritrea under the Ethiopian Crown.

THE PEOPLE. It is believed that the Ethiopians are of Semitic stock. Certainly they are quite unlike the other inhabitants of Central Africa. Their national language, Amharic, resembles Hebrew and Arabic. There are three important races: the Amharas, who are the ruling and cultured class, nominally Christian; the Gallas, the peasant class, who are Hamitic in origin and are the most numerous; and the Negro races, known as the Shankalla or slave races. There are also 60,000 Jews, called Falashas, who live in the northwestern province of Amhara.

THE RELIGION. The Emperor Menelik once said, "Ethiopia is an island of Christians in a sea of Muslims." The gospel was first taken to Ethiopia by the Ethiopian eunuch baptized by Philip, as recorded in Acts 8. Little is known, however, about the progress of Christianity in Ethiopia until the fourth century, when the country was Christianized by Frumentius. Within ten years of Frumentius' arrival, the King and two-thirds of his people accepted baptism and became Christians. Frumentius was later consecrated first bishop of the Ethiopian Church by Athanasius of Alexandria. The Coptic Church in Ethiopia has close ties with the Coptic Church of Egypt. The Patriarch of Alexandria is head of the Coptic Church of Ethiopia and appoints the bishop, who is head of the Coptic Church in Ethiopia. The present incumbent is the first Ethiopian to hold this office. This state Church is extremely nationalistic and violently opposed to the evangelical movement. Missionaries are restricted to pagan and Muslim areas; they are not permitted to "proselytize" the nominally Christian Copts. To ensure the carrying out of this policy the government has established a Committee of Missions comprising the Ministers of Education, Interior Affairs, and Foreign Affairs; it exercises complete control of all missionary activity. The country is divided into two areas, "Ethiopian Church Areas" and "Open Areas." Missionary work is confined to the Open Areas.

MISSIONS. The *Church Missionary Society* attempted an entrance into Ethiopia as early as 1844, but without success. The first permanent Protestant work began in 1866 when missionaries of the *Swedish Evangelical Mission* landed at Massawa and started a work among the pagan Kunama. In 1870 they extended their work to Monkullo, and later to Geleb among the Mensa. *Carl Cederquist* was permitted to occupy Addis Ababa in 1904. From there, stations were opened among the Shoan and the Leqa Galla. Today they have 44 missionaries on 7 stations. Church members total 6,200, including baptized children.

For almost sixty years this Mission carried on alone; then in 1920 the *United Presbyterians* opened their first station, at Sayo, among the Wallega Galla in western Ethiopia. A second station was established at Goré, and in 1923 the *George Memorial Hospital* was opened in the capital by *Dr. Thomas A. Lambie,* one of their outstanding pioneers. This hospital was expropriated by the Italians during the occupation and is now in government hands. The Mission has another hospital at Sayo. Educational work includes primary schools, village schools, and a fine girls' school in Addis Ababa. The present staff comprises 35 missionaries working in 6 main stations.

The *Sudan Interior Mission,* which has 281 missionaries, 500 churches, and 100,000 church members, is by far the largest Christian work in Ethiopia. It began its work in Ethiopia in 1927 when the *Abyssinian Frontiers Mission,* an independent work founded by Dr. Lambie, merged with the S.I.M. By the time of the Italian occupation in 1935, it had established 14 stations. It recommenced work in 1942, and by 1949 had a staff of over 100. Its latest report indicates 38 main stations in all parts of the country, more than half of which have been opened since 1949. Medical work includes two well-equipped leprosaria, three hospitals, a clinic, and a rest home. The Mission operates many village schools, and there are two Christian academies and nine Bible schools. It also has a press and a school for missionaries' children in Addis Ababa. The Sudan Interior Mission is the largest faith mission in the world. Its total membership is close to 1,300.

The work of the *Bible Churchmen's Missionary Society* in Ethiopia began in 1934. It now has 12 missionaries in 4 stations. Three new missions entered the country in the 1940's, the largest of which is the *Norwegian Mission*, which has expanded its work to 11 centers.

The *Baptist General Conference of America* is one of the larger missions, having 21 workers on the field. It began work in 1950. Other newcomers are the *Finnish Pentecostal Mission*, *Christian Missions in Many Lands*, *Seventh Day Adventists*, and *Mission to Lepers*. The newest member of the missionary community is the *American Lutheran Mission*, which sent its first workers to Ethiopia in 1957.

The *Swedish Evangelical National Missionary Society* has been in Eritrea for almost ninety years. For most of this time it was the only society there. Another Swedish organization, *True Friends of the Bible*, worked for a while in this part of Ethiopia, but it was forced out by the Italians. Since World War II a number of new missions have begun operations in this strategic coastal area. The *Red Sea Mission Team*, an independent faith mission, founded in 1951 by *Dr. Lionel Gurney*, has medical, educational, and evangelistic work in Asmara and Massawa. The *Orthodox Presbyterian Church* has eight missionaries there now. Following its ejection from Egypt in 1956, the *Middle East General Mission* (formerly the Egypt General Mission) transferred some of its workers to Eritrea where they are now working among the Muslims.

Mention should be made of the only work being done among the 60,000 Jews of the country. The *London Jews' Society* began work in Ethiopia in 1860; but it suffered many interruptions through the years, especially during the Italian occupation. In 1948 European workers returned and established a station at Dabat, where they now have a clinic, a school, and a Bible school. A second site, among the half-Jewish Kemant people, has recently been opened.

THE WARTIME REVIVAL. No account of Christian work in Ethiopia would be complete without some reference, however sketchy, to the revival that coincided with the Italian occupation. In spite of the absence of the missionaries and the persecution by the Italian authorities, the infant Church grew by leaps and bounds between 1936 and 1942. Upon its return, the *Hermannsburg Mission* discovered that the Spirit of God had moved so mightily in the hearts of the Galla tribespeople that a mass movement to Christianity had taken place. In the southeast, the Sudan Interior Mission left 59 baptized believers in 3 little assemblies. Seven years later when the missionaries returned there were 18,000 baptized believers in 155 assemblies. The United Presbyterians also found that during their absence the working of God's Spirit in the southwest had brought into existence a body known as the *Bethel Evangelical Church* under the leadership of a blind pastor, *Rev. Gilada Solon.* Several years later, in March, 1947, this group severed its connections with the United Presbyterian Church and became a fully autonomous Church. Today it has a membership of 10,000—five times that of the parent organization.

SCRIPTURE TRANSLATION. The whole Bible is available in Amharic and Tigrinya, the official languages of Ethiopia and Eritrea respectively. The Tigrinya Bible was published in 1957, just a month or two before its translator, *Mrs. Elsie Winquist,* died at the age of ninety-five. The government decree that all teaching must be done in the official languages has discouraged missionaries from undertaking much-needed translation work in the many tribal languages.

SOMALIA

Area: 198,000 sq. mi.   Population: 1,250,000
Capital: Mogadiscio   Religion: Islam

THE LAND. Somalia faces the Indian Ocean and is the most easterly country in Africa. It is located on the spur of the continent that juts out into the Gulf of Aden. It is bounded on the west by Kenya, Ethiopia, and British Somaliland, and on the south it comes to a point where Kenya meets the Indian Ocean.

POLITICAL HISTORY. From 1889 until World War II, Somalia was a protectorate of Italy. During the war this part of Africa was occupied by the British, and remained under military administration until April, 1950, when, with United Nations approval, Italy assumed a ten-year trusteeship of the country. If all goes well, Somalia will become independent July 1, 1960.

THE PEOPLE. There are about 4,500 Europeans in Somalia; all but 150 of them are Italians. The indigenous population is mostly pastoral. Agriculture has been introduced into the south, but as yet only a small percentage of the people are engaged in this pursuit.

THE RELIGION. Islam claims almost 100 per cent of the national population. Since the United Nations trusteeship was established in 1950 there has been freedom of religion.

MISSIONS. Owing to the hostility of the Muslims and the reluctance of the Roman Catholic colonial government to permit Protestant missions to enter the country, Somalia has been sadly neglected by Protestant missions through the years. As early as 1875 the *Evangelical National Missionary Society* of Sweden entered this section of Africa. For sixty years it carried on a heroic work among the Muslims, establishing a program in church, school, and medical work. When Mussolini invaded Ethiopia in 1935 it came to an abrupt end, and the Swedish missionaries, about a dozen in number, were expelled from the country. The Mission was taken over by the Roman Catholics.

During the present decade two missions have entered this neglected area for the first time. The *Eastern Mennonite Board of Missions and Charities* began work in Somalia in 1952. A good beginning has been made in church and evangelistic work, and two dispensaries are operated in the capital city.

In 1954 the *Sudan Interior Mission* was given permission to begin work in Somalia, and that same year it opened its first station in Mogadiscio, where it now has eleven missionaries. Bulo Burti, 150 miles inland, was opened in 1954, and Belet Uen in 1958.

NOTE. There are two other Somalilands, one belonging to France and the other to Great Britain. The Roman Catholics are working in French Somaliland; but there is no Christian work of any kind, Protestant or Catholic, in British Somaliland, owing to the British policy of not alienating the sympathy and support of the Muslim population.

KENYA

Area: 225,000 sq. mi.   Population: 6,240,000
Capital: Nairobi   Religion: Animism

THE LAND. Described by John Gunther as "one of the most fascinating countries in the world," Kenya is an East African colony belonging to Great Britain. It lies south of Ethiopia, east of Uganda, north of Tanganyika, and west of Somalia. The southeast coastal strip borders on the Indian Ocean. There are three main geographical divisions: the hot and humid coastal strip, on which the chief port of Mombasa is located; the Northern Frontier Province (half of the entire country), which is mostly desert wasteland; and the Central

Plateau, known as the White Highlands. With no mineral wealth, no oil, and no waterpower, Kenya is poor even by African standards.

POLITICAL HISTORY. Once part of British East Africa, Kenya became a colony in 1905. The first election in fifty years of British rule was held in March, 1957, at which time eight Africans, six Asiatics, and two Arabs were chosen to serve on the sixty-man Legislative Council of Kenya. Because the white man is outnumbered one hundred to one, the Africans considered their representation on the Council wholly inadequate and to date they have refused to serve. The burning issue in Kenya is land. Four thousand white settlers own 16,000 square miles of the best land in the country, and no African is permitted to buy land in the White Highlands. It was against this injustice that the Mau Mau movement of 1952 was directed. Rehabilitation of the Mau Mau is now completed, Jomo Kenyatta and the last of the 77,000 detainees having been released in April, 1959.

THE PEOPLE. There are three principal groups: Africans (6,000,000), Asiatics (180,000), and Europeans (60,000). Most of the Asiatics are Indians, who are the merchants and shopkeepers. The Africans are divided mainly into three tribes. The largest (1,000,000) and most advanced is the Kikuyu tribe; the others are the Masai and the Kamba.

THE RELIGION. Animism is the religion of the African peoples. The Arabs, of whom there are about 30,000, are Muslims. The Indian population is almost entirely Hindu.

MISSIONS. Mention has already been made of the pioneer efforts in East Africa of such spiritual giants as *John Ludwig Krapf* and *John Rebmann* of the *Church Missionary Society*. Here we shall content ourselves with a brief outline of C.M.S. work in Kenya. It began at the seaport of Mombasa in 1844. Rabai was occupied in 1846, and Frere Town in 1874. In the Taita country, stations were opened at Mbale in 1900 and at Wusi in 1905. In the Giryama country, Kaloleni was opened in 1904. Nairobi, the capital, was reached in 1906. Eight additional stations were occupied in the Central Province between 1900 and 1930. The C.M.S. work, by far the largest in Kenya, is divided into three areas: the coastal district around Mombasa, the Central Province, and the Nyanza district northeast of Lake Victoria. The African Church brought into being by the C.M.S. is known as the *Mombasa Diocese of the Anglican Church of the Province of East Africa*. It has 171 organized churches in the

charge of African pastors trained in St. Paul's United Theological
College at Limuru. The C.M.S. as a missionary organization has an
additional 1,033 places of worship in various stages of development.
During the Mau Mau troubles there was a great falling away. Those
who remained true were the people of the Revival Fellowship. It
is no exaggeration to say that the Church was saved by the members
of this Fellowship, a movement which resulted from a revival which
spread from Uganda to Kenya in 1937.

Protestant work in the interior really began in 1891 when a group
of Christian laymen in the Imperial British East Africa Chartered
Company organized the *East Africa Scottish Mission* under the
leadership of *Rev. Thomas Watson.* In 1900, after the death of Mr.
Watson, the Mission was handed over to the *Church of Scotland,*
which was already working in Nyasaland. A good deal of solid,
constructive work has been done by this Mission over the years. In
1956 the Mission and the Church which it had brought into existence were merged to form the *Presbyterian Church of East Africa.*
Present membership is around 20,000.

The *Africa Inland Mission,* the largest independent faith mission
in East Africa, entered the first of its six African fields in 1895 when
Peter Cameron Scott landed in Mombasa with a party of seven
workers. The first few years of the Mission's history were filled with
disaster and death. Peter Scott lived only fourteen months and then
was translated to higher service. One by one the little band sick-
ened and died, until one lone missionary stood between the Mission
and extinction. Bravely he carried on in the face of overwhelming
difficulties, but eventually he had to give up and return home. A
second venture, under the leadership of *Dr. Charles E. Hurlburt,*
was made a few years later, and this one met with success, Nzawi,
in the Akamba country, was the first station to be opened. A large
party of 23 new workers led by *Lee H. Downing* landed at Mombasa in 1907. After a short stay at Kijabe they divided into two
groups and established work at Kilome among the Masai people
and at Kapropita among the Tugen tribespeople. Today the Africa
Inland Mission has 25 main stations. In 15 of them there are schools
offering training through the eighth grade. Five hundred bush schools
provide education on a lower level for tens of thousands of pupils.
Two hospitals, several leprosaria, and a score of clinics form the
backbone of the medical work. Its 250 organized churches are under
the full-time care of pastors and evangelists supported entirely by
local congregations.

American Friends have been in Kenya since 1902. It is the largest
of their five mission fields, and Kaimosi near Lake Victoria is their

largest station. Here 39 missionaries are carrying on an ambitious program of medical, educational, industrial, agricultural, and evangelistic work. Particular projects include the Bible Institute, Girls' Boarding School, Boys' Boarding School, Junior Missionary School, Industrial Department, Agricultural Department, Men's Teacher Training Center, Women's Teacher Training Center, Press, Work Camp, and Hospital. Besides all this there is an extensive school program on the primary and intermediate levels, which provides education for almost 40,000 children. Bible teaching is given in all schools. The work at Kamusinga, opened in 1957, centers around a secondary school. The Mission has four other stations, two of which are without resident missionaries at present. Monthly Meetings now number 50. Total adherents have climbed to almost 30,000. This is the largest number of Quakers anywhere on the mission field.

The *Church of God* has had missionaries in Kenya since 1919. Its three well-developed stations have been literally carved out of the tropical jungles. Fifty years ago this now densely populated region was inhabited by Africans whose standard of life was exceedingly primitive. Christianity, education, and medical care have improved the lot of these people tremendously. The power of the witch doctor has been broken, and heathen customs are fast disappearing. At its oldest station, Kima, there are the Girls' Secondary School, the Bible Training School, a hospital, a printing press, and a bookstore. The Mission has the Nora Hunter Memorial Hospital and the Teacher Training Center at Mwihila. One of the missionaries, *Calvin Brallier,* is government education supervisor, and as such is in charge of 145 schools of four different missions. One hundred and eighty churches are served by 400 pastors, evangelists, and teachers. The annual budget is over $10,000, all subscribed by the Africans themselves. In June, 1957, Christians of the Church of God who had moved to Nairobi erected a new church in a large government housing project. The building, seating 350 people and costing $10,000, was built and paid for by the African Christians.

The *Seventh Day Adventist* work is divided into four districts. Their 176 churches account for 30,000 of Kenya's Protestants. Besides 200 elementary schools they maintain a college and a hospital.

The *Southern Baptists* entered Kenya in 1956. Other missions with a large following include the *Salvation Army* and the *Pentecostal Assemblies of Canada,* each with approximately 30,000 believers.

One of the most optimistic reports emanating from East Africa in recent years comes from the *Methodist Missionary Society,* which for many years has maintained a work in the Meru area around

Mombasa. During the Mau Mau emergency, church membership fell considerably; but they rose to the occasion and accepted the challenge with courage and vision, actually launching a forward movement. The report says:

Five years ago a small staff was struggling to maintain existing work. Today, an enlarged staff, missionary and African, is coming to grips with opportunities which for years have only been dreams. Four fine young African ministers have completed their training, and are beginning to make their presence felt. For the first time there is a total of ten ordained men from England. In 1958 there were 708 new Full Members; 74 new Local Preachers joined the ranks of voluntary workers. The Church is moving with the times. Eighty-three new churches and preaching places were opened in 1958.[2]

UGANDA

Area: 94,000 sq. mi.
Capital: Entebbe

Population: 6,000,000
Religion: Animism

THE LAND. Uganda is the smallest British possession in East Africa. It is located between Kenya on the east and Belgian Congo on the west. Sudan lies to the north, and Ruanda-Urundi and a small stretch of Tanganyika to the south. Uganda forms the drainage area of the Nile River. Part of Lake Victoria is in the southeast corner of Uganda.

POLITICAL HISTORY. Uganda has been a British protectorate since 1894. It consists of the former kingdoms of Buganfa, Bunyoro, Ankole, and Toro. For present administrative purposes it is divided into four provinces: Eastern, Western, Northern, and Buganda.

THE PEOPLE. The population may be divided into 47 tribes, 13 of which are immigrants from other parts. By far the strongest is the Baganda tribe from which the protectorate took its name. Unlike Kenya, Uganda has only a handful of Europeans. There are 35,000 Indians. Ganda is the main language and is fast displacing the local dialects.

THE RELIGION. The Africans are animists; the Indian population is Hindu. Of all the countries in Africa, Christianity has made its greatest gains in Uganda. More than 50 per cent of the population of Buganda Province are Christians. In the other three provinces the response has not been nearly so great, the Christians forming con-

[2] *The Burning Word, 1958,* p. 29.

siderably less than 10 per cent of the population. Most Christians come from the Bantu tribes; the Nilotic tribes have been much less responsive. Islam is steadily gaining ground and poses a real threat to the Christian Church. Thirty-seven African Sheikhs were created in the Kibali Mosque in Kampala in March, 1957.

MISSIONS. The Church of Jesus Christ in Uganda is unique, not only in the number of converts but also in the social range of the Christian community. Men, women, and children, chiefs as well as peasants, have all received its message; and the influence of Christianity has permeated every phase of national life. All this has come about mainly as the result of the work of one great mission, the *Church Missionary Society*. Its noble missionaries and martyrs left a record of sacrifice and success that has seldom been equaled and never surpassed.

The inspiration for this great missionary venture was furnished in the beginning by *Henry M. Stanley,* who was so profoundly influenced by his intercourse with Livingstone that he resolved to consecrate his life to the continuation of the latter's work. Entering upon his famous journey through the Dark Continent, Stanley sent back to England from Uganda in 1875 his stirring "Challenge to Christendom." *King Mtesa* had asked for missionaries for his people. Would Christians respond to this cry from the heart of Africa? The effect was like magic. Men and means for the projected mission were soon forthcoming, and the next year (1876) saw the first contingent of eight missionaries on their way to Africa under the Church Missionary Society.

Mackay of Uganda, the leading one of these eight, was to become a famous figure in missionary history. Alexander Mackay was a highly educated and gifted young Scottish engineer. "My heart burns for the deliverance of Africa," he wrote the Church Missionary Society, "and if you can send me to any of those regions which Livingstone and Stanley have found to be groaning under the curse of the slave hunter I shall be very glad."

"Mackay's farewell speech to the Board of Directors is characteristic: 'I want to remind the committee that within six months they will probably hear that one of us is dead. Yes, is it at all likely that eight Englishmen should start for Central Africa and all be alive six months after? One of us at least—it may be I—will surely fall before that. When the news comes, do not be cast down, but send someone else immediately to take the vacant place.' "[3]

How sadly prophetic were these words! Within three months one

[3] Wilson Naylor, *Daybreak in the Dark Continent* (Missionary Education Movement, 1912), p. 261.

was dead, within a year five, and in two years Mackay himself was the only survivor. For twelve years he fought on against terrible odds—fever, persecution, the intrigues of Muslim Arab and Roman Catholic priest, and repeated attempts upon his life. The story of his career—his early struggles and later successes, the use of his engineering skill, his keen diplomacy, his tireless energy, his supreme sacrifice for an ungrateful people—reads like a romance. He was finally driven from his field through the subtle influence of Arabs upon *King Mwanga,* and took refuge at the southern end of Victoria Nyanza. There, undaunted, he pursued his labors for three years longer, and then, attacked with fever, he died on February 8, 1890. He had received urgent appeals to give up and come home, but turned a deaf ear and wrote in his last letter: "It is not a time for any one to desert his post. Send us our first twenty men, and I may be tempted to come and help you find the second twenty."

Mackay died facing the foe and without being permitted to see the fruit of his labor. But he and his comrades had laid the foundations of one of the most wonderful missions of modern times.

The transformation wrought by the gospel in Uganda has few parallels in any land. Stanley accurately described these Baganda people, despite their strong physique, expressive features, clean habits, and superiority in many points to the surrounding tribes, as "crafty, deceiving, lying, thieving knaves, taken as a whole." Polygamy, witchcraft, vice, and violence were rife. Human life was held of little account. King Mtesa himself sacrificed 2,000 captives to his dead father's spirit.

The history of the Uganda church is not without its baptism of fire and blood. Under Mtesa's successor a terrible persecution broke out. The missionaries were driven from the country, and many of the native Christians suffered inhuman torture and martyrdom. Their sublime faith shone brightly amidst these fierce testings. Some of the Christian boys actually went to the flames singing the hymns they had been taught. Bishop Hannington was cruelly murdered on his arrival in 1885 by order of the wicked King Mwanga. His last words to his executioners were: "Go tell Mwanga that I die for the Baganda, and that I have purchased the road to Uganda with my life." Such testimony could not fail to bear fruit; before long the missionaries were back again, the tide turned, and the Church entered upon a period of growth.

The greatest gains were made under *Bishop Alfred R. Tucker* between 1890 and 1911. Of rugged physique, unflinching courage, bold initiative, sound judgment, organizational ability, and single-hearted devotion, Tucker made an ideal shepherd, though his flock numbered only 200 when he arrived in Uganda. Before he died, however, church membership had climbed to 65,000. The Cathedral at Kampala, dedicated in 1919, is probably the largest Christian church in Africa. At the opening services the vast building was quickly filled and the throng outside was estimated at 20,000. The following Sunday, 864 communicants partook of the Lord's Supper.

Since then there has been steady growth in all departments of the work. Today the Anglican Church in Uganda has 100,000 members and a community four times that number. Missionaries continue in administrative, educational, and medical work, but the pastoral and evangelistic work is the responsibility of 340 African clergymen who are supported by the many congregations which they serve. In Uganda Province alone there are 5,000 teachers giving Christian instruction in 660 schools; but, unfortunately, not all students turn out to be good Christians. No one is more conscious of this than the Anglicans themselves. The Bishop in a recent report deplores the rapid spread of secularism and he comments on the "lapse of the vast majority of those confirmed every year from school." He continues:

Our chief opportunity and problem is work among children and youth. Sunday Schools are just starting. There is no youth work at all. . . . At present almost all our youth are lost and the worshipping population is getting older and fewer year by year.[4]

Along with the work of the Church Missionary Society should be mentioned the contribution made by the *Bible Churchmen's Missionary Society,* an independent conservative mission within the Anglican Communion. Since 1929 it has been engaged in a small but important work north of the C.M.S. area in the Diocese of the Upper Nile, among the wild and primitive Karamojong, of whom there are over 100,000.

The *Africa Inland Mission* entered Uganda from Kenya in 1918 and in the ensuing forty years has done a fine piece of constructive work. The first station occupied by the Africa Inland Mission was Usambiro, where the famous Alexander Mackay had begun his missionary career many years before. After all five of its missionaries died, the C.M.S. gave up the station and for sixty-three years it lay in ruins until the Africa Inland Mission took over in 1918. The Mission has only three main stations in the northeast part of the country, but it has built up a very large and strong indigenous work around 250 churches and preaching places, all in the charge of African evangelists supported entirely by their own people.

[4] *The Moving Spirit,* p. 67.

The *Seventh Day Adventists* have a hospital at Ankole and a college at Bugema. Elementary schools total 33. There are 3,500 church members organized into 23 churches.

TANGANYIKA

Area: 362,000 sq. mi.	Population: 8,800,000
Capital: Dar es Salaam	Religion: Animism
	Islam

THE LAND. Tanganyika is one of the three countries included in British East Africa. It is a maritime territory facing the Indian Ocean on the east. Kenya is on the north, Lake Tanganyika and Ruanda-Urundi on the west, and Nyasaland and Mozambique on the south. It has three geographical divisions: the coastal plain; the plateau; and the great highlands culminating in Kilimanjaro, the highest peak in Africa.

POLITICAL HISTORY. Once part of German East Africa, Tanganyika has been British territory since World War I. It is now administered under United Nations trusteeship. There is a Legislative Council consisting of a Speaker, 34 governmental and 33 representative members. The first elections were held in 1958.

THE PEOPLE. In addition to the indigenous population there are 20,000 Europeans, 65,000 Indians, and 20,000 Arabs in Tanganyika. The Africans are mostly Bantu in origin. Altogether there are 120 different tribes, but some of them are quite small. The two largest tribes, the Nyamwezi and the Sukuma, account for a million people; they live in the country south of Nyanza. The Arabs and Indians live in the coastal area. Swahili is the trade language.

THE RELIGION. The African tribes are animists, though Islam has won many converts in recent years and now has 1.5 million adherents, 20,000 of whom are Arabs. Hinduism is, of course, the religion of the Indians. The Christian community, Roman Catholic and Protestant, is about 1.2 million. Under British rule the missionaries are free to carry on a full program of Christian work. Seventy-five per cent of the educational program of the country is still in the hands of the missions, all of which receive government subsidies for this phase of their work.

ANGLICAN MISSIONS. Protestant missionary work in Tanganyika began in 1860. The first society to enter this part of Africa was the *Universities' Mission to Central Africa,* one of four missionary organizations which owe their origin to the inspiration of David Livingstone. This particular Mission was the outcome of Livingstone's historic visit to Oxford and Cambridge in 1857. His closing words at Cambridge were simple, direct, and to the point:

> I beg to direct your attention to Africa. I know that in a few years I shall be cut off in that country, which is now open; do not let it shut again. I go back to Africa to try and make an open path for commerce and Christianity; do you carry out the work which I have begun. I leave it with you.[5]

The Universities' Mission to Central Africa is an independent organization of High Churchmen within the Church of England. It now has five dioceses in East Africa. Two of them, in the southern part of Tanganyika, were created in 1952. Medical work centers around two institutions, a hospital at Liuli and a leprosarium at Mngehe. The Mission maintains three middle schools and had hoped to open a fourth in 1957, but the government turned down the offer because they did not have a sufficient number of primary schools to justify the expansion.

After holding the fort alone for sixteen years the U.M.C.A. was joined by a sister organization of the Anglican Communion, the *Church Missionary Society,* which established work at Mpwapwa on the southern shore of Lake Victoria. Two years later a second station was opened at Mamboya. For twenty years these remained their only stations; but a period of expansion began in 1900, and three stations were opened in each of the first three decades of the twentieth century. Today the Church Missionary Society is working in four main areas: East, Central, Southwest, and Northwest. The most striking growth has been in the Central Province where the number of outstations doubled between 1950 and 1954. There has been a speed-up in the work of primary schools, which are being opened at the rate of twenty a year; and hundreds of new bush churches are erected annually. There are 800 African church workers. With a membership of 175,000, the Anglican Church is second only to the Lutherans. Tanganyika has two Anglican theological seminaries, but theological education is still a problem.

There is also a grave shortage of staff capable of giving a full theological education to minds untrained in Western ways of thinking. This requires not only a profound appreciation of Christian theology, but also a thorough knowledge of the Swahili language, a ready and sympa-

[5] *The Unfinished Task—Expanding Frontiers,* U.M.C.A., p. 12.

thetic understanding of Bantu thought and mental attitudes and an ability to enshrine Christian truth in unfamiliar idioms. Assuming that the training staff is European, this is a fairly formidable task.[6]

LUTHERAN MISSIONS. The first Lutheran to establish work in Tanganyika came from Germany. The *Berlin Mission* started work in the coastal area in 1886. Societies from Leipzig and Bethel also sent workers, beginning in the north and northeast in 1892 and 1893. Later on, when these societies had been strengthened by reinforcements from South Africa, they extended their work to the west and south. After World War I, Lutheran Churches in America were asked to care for the "orphaned" Lutheran missions in Tanganyika, the missionaries from Germany having been forced to leave. The *Augustana Lutheran Church* of America began working in the Central Province in 1924 and assisted in the oversight of the orphaned areas as well. The German missionaries were later permitted to return and resume their work.

World War II saw a repetition of this difficulty. The German workers were again expelled, and Lutheran Churches in Europe and America joined forces in the administration of the twice orphaned German missions. Two groups from Sweden, the *Church of Sweden Mission* and the *Swedish Evangelical Mission,* agreed to assume responsibility for the work in the west and south, and sent staff to these districts in 1942.

Three other German missions are now administered by the Department of World Missions Co-operation of the National Lutheran Council, U.S.A. Staff is recruited from several Lutheran bodies in America as well as from Germany, Denmark, Norway, Sweden, and Finland. The *Finnish Missionary Society* and the *Danish Mission* have worked in conjunction with the *Swedish Evangelical Mission* in southern Tanganyika during the past ten years. The *Norwegian Mission* has, during this time, taken over the work begun in 1939 by the Swedish Evangelical Mission in north-central Tanganyika. The seven Lutheran bodies now at work in the country are unified through the *Federation of Lutheran Churches in Tanganyika,* which was formed in 1937. Plans are being laid for the organization of the *Lutheran Church of Tanganyika* in the near future. Church members total 140,000, and the Christian community is estimated at more than twice that number, making Tanganyika the second largest Lutheran field in the world. Only the New Guinea Lutheran Church is larger.

[6] R. T. Jourdain, "The Church in Tanganyika," *East and West Review* (July, 1956).

OTHER SOCIETIES. The *London Missionary Society* maintained a work here for some forty years before turning it over to the *German Moravians* in 1897. When various mission fields were deprived of their German missionaries during World War I, this Mission was taken over temporarily by the *United Free Church of Scotland.* After serving the field faithfully, this Church generously returned the work to the Moravian Mission in 1926. Before the outbreak of World War II, the field was under the administration of the *Herrnhut Mission Board.* When war came the German workers were repatriated by government action. Since then the *British Board of the Moravian Mission* has been responsible for it. The 1958 Report gives these statistics: 300 places of worship; 21,800 communicants; 24 ordained Africans; 761 African workers. The total number of Christians is estimated at 49,300.

The *Africa Inland Mission* entered the country in 1910. It was the second field to be occupied by this Mission. Today, with 316 churches and a Christian community of 40,000, it is the largest of the Africa Inland Mission's six fields.

The *Assemblies of God* sent workers into Tanganyika from Nyasaland in 1953 in response to a call from Pentecostal congregations, which owed their existence to the ministry of an independent missionary, *Paul K. Derr,* in the 1930's. With a nucleus of 15 national workers and about 300 Pentecostal believers, *Wesley R. Hurst* began the task of organizing and consolidating the existing churches on an indigenous basis. The first thing was the establishment of a Bible school. By 1958 there were 48 students in attendance. All but three of their 20 organized churches are in the Southern Highlands.

The *Seventh Day Adventists* have a fine educational work, mostly for the children of their 12,000 Christians. Other missions include the *Salvation Army, Eastern Mennonite Board of Missions, Christian Missions in Many Lands,* and the obscure *Gospel Furthering Fellowship.* The *Southern Baptists* entered in 1956, the latest mission to do so. They plan to open a tuberculosis hospital in Mbeya and a Goodwill Center in the capital.

XIX

CENTRAL AFRICA

CAMEROUN

Area: 200,000 sq. mi.   Population: 4,775,000
Capital: Youande   Religion: Animism

THE LAND. Cameroun is a triangular piece of territory on the bend
of the Gulf of Guinea between Nigeria on the west and Chad and
Central African Republic on the east. Congo Republic and Gabon
are on the south. In the north it comes to a point at Lake Chad. It
belonged to the Germans until 1916, when the French took over
five-sixths, and the British the remaining one-sixth. Both areas have
been under United Nations trusteeship. French Cameroun gained
complete independence January 1, 1960. A United Nations-super-
vised plebiscite in November, 1959, in the British Cameroons
registered a surprising two-to-one vote in favor of continuing trusteeship status under Britain for the time being rather than uniting
with Nigeria.

MISSIONS. In 1841 the *Baptist Missionary Society* of England entered
this part of Africa, the first Protestant mission to do so. Using the
island of Fernando Po as a base, they established their first station
on the mainland in 1848. Led by their great pioneer, *Alfred Saker,*
they reduced languages to writing, translated the Bible, opened
schools, and gathered converts. *George Grenfell* of Congo fame
spent several years in Cameroun in the 1870's. When Germany
assumed control of the area in 1887, the work was turned over to
the *Basel Evangelical Missionary Society.* Shortly after the transfer,
a mass movement set in and several whole tribes asked for Christian instruction. Encouraged by this turn of events, the Basel Mission extended its work inland and by 1914 had established 16 main
stations and 384 schools. When Germany lost Cameroun in 1916
its nationals were expelled from the country, leaving the work in
the hands of the Swiss members of the Mission. The Church that
was built up through the years (present membership is 30,000)
is now part of the larger Presbyterian Church in Cameroun.

The work of the *Presbyterian Church in the U.S.A.* in this part of the world dates back to 1850 when it gained a foothold on the island of Corisco near the mouth of the Gabon River. Later its work was extended to Gabon on the mainland, and in 1871 the two Missions, Corisco and Gabon, were merged. In the 1880's it further extended its work into Cameroun, which later became its only mission field in Africa. The strategy in Cameroun was to establish a few strong central stations from which the surrounding country could be extensively and systematically evangelized. The policy has paid off well. The steady and continuous growth was climaxed in 1957 when the integration of Church and Mission took place and the *Presbyterian Church of Cameroun* came into being. It consisted of three synods and ten presbyteries representing some 83,000 members. The latest Annual Report, however, points out the fallacy of assuming that missionaries are no longer needed. The Church now has full responsibility for seven hospitals, but it does not have one fully qualified African doctor. Some 22,000 children are enrolled in its many schools, but "one can count on the fingers of two hands the Cameroun men and women qualified to take over responsibility for the direction and supervision of the Church's schools."[1]

In 1890, six years after the German occupation of Cameroun, *German Baptists* took an interest in this colony and formed a missionary society. Its first missionary, however, was an American, *August Steffens*, who arrived on the field in 1891. In 1935 this work passed entirely into American hands and is now part of the *American Baptist General Missionary Society*. In 1957 it had 40 workers in 10 stations. Its 250 churches reported a total membership of 15,000. There is a *Bible Training Center* at Ndu and a *Teacher Training Center* at Soppo. It has a hospital at Banso and a leper colony at Mbingo.

The *Sudan United Mission* entered French Cameroun in 1911 and today has ten stations there.

It is necessary to point out that the spectacular growth of the Protestant Church in Cameroun from 1900 to 1940 is reported to have slackened off since then, just at a time when the Roman Catholics are intensifying their efforts to win converts to Catholicism. Roman Catholic priests and teaching fathers outnumber Protestant missionaries four to one.

New stations, well staffed and complete with beautiful churches, schools, and dispensaries, are springing up all over the country even in

[1] *121st Annual Report of the Board of Missions of the Presbyterian Church in U.S.A.* (1958), p. 72.

strong Protestant communities, and the lone African pastor in charge of a lowly bush center, ill-equipped and isolated, suffers in comparison.[2]

Other missions in Cameroun include three *Lutheran Churches* (8,000 members), the *Reformed Evangelical Church* (French background, 80,000 members), and the *Seventh Day Adventists* (3,000 members).

CHAD[3]

Area: 495,000 sq. mi.   Population: 2,620,000

Capital: Fort Lamy   Religion: Islam

                                                               Animism

THE LAND AND THE PEOPLE. Chad is the most northerly of the four provinces which formerly composed French Equatorial Africa. The Central African Republic is on the south, Sudan on the east, Libya on the north, and Niger and Cameroun on the west. In Chad live sedentary and seminomadic tribes of Negroid-Hamitic stock, Fullahs, Saras, and Tibbus. Arab nomads live in the desert. Muslims predominate in the northern part of the country, where the trade language is a corrupt form of Arabic known as Chad Arabic. A number of tribes in central Chad are nominally Muslim but know nothing of the real teaching of the Prophet. The tribes in the south are pagan. There was very little Roman Catholic work here until the middle of the 1930's.

MISSIONS. *Baptist Mid-Missions* began their work here in 1925, making their initial attempt at Fort Archambault among the Sara people. The people were friendly enough; but owing to the determined opposition of the ruling chief, who was also head of the witch doctors, progress was at a standstill for a long time. It was not until his death in 1937 that the break came; then the work grew by leaps and bounds. The first chapel, with a capacity of 400, had to be rebuilt to accommodate 1,200. In 1948 it was enlarged again, this time to

---

[2] *118th Annual Report of Board of Missions of the Presbyterian Church in U.S.A.* (1955), p. 63.

[3] French Equatorial Africa is no longer a political entity. A referendum in September, 1958, completely changed the political status of the four colonies which formerly composed French Equatorial Africa. These four territories are now autonomous republics within the French Community. These republics are Chad, Central African Republic (formerly Ubangi-Shari), Congo (formerly Middle Congo and not to be confused with Belgian Congo), and Gabon.

hold 2,000. Short-term Bible schools were held, leaders were trained, giving was encouraged, and eventually this one church at Fort Archambault was supporting 21 evangelists. In 1952 Communist elements infiltrated the church and caused trouble; and for a time attendance dropped to 200. Two other centers have been occupied, one at Kyabe and the other at Koumra. All three stations are in the south.

There are two other missions in Chad. *Christian Missions in Many Lands* entered the southwest section from its Kano base in Nigeria. *Dr. John R. Olley* began work in Fort Lamy in 1925 and was their outstanding leader for thirty years. He translated the New Testament first into Mbai and later into Kim, and established assemblies in various parts of the country. The present staff of 12 missionaries occupy five main stations. Altogether there are 50 assemblies in the Chad field and approximately 50 more village chapels in which there are regular services, prayer meetings, and daily instruction classes, but no Breaking of Bread.

Canadian workers of the *Sudan United Mission* entered Chad in the 1920's. *Mr. H. C. Wilkinson* opened their first station at Koutou. Through the years their work has grown rapidly. A seminary and three Bible schools ensure a steady supply of adequately trained leaders to man their 300 churches. Medical work is carried on in 5 dispensaries. They have 155 primary schools. The New Testament in Ngambai appeared in 1955.

CENTRAL AFRICAN REPUBLIC
(Ubangi-Shari)

Area: 238,000 sq. mi.   Population: 1,150,000
Capital: Bangui   Religion: Animism

THE LAND AND THE PEOPLE. The Central African Republic is bounded by Congo Republic and Belgian Congo on the south, Sudan on the east, Chad on the north, and Cameroun on the west. There are eight principal tribes: the Manqia, Banda, Zandi, Banziri, Sari, M'Boom, Pambla, and Boonga.

MISSIONS. Protestant missions entered the country in the early 1920's. The *Church of the Brethren* was the first in the field. Four Brethren missionaries reached Brazzaville in 1918, but it was three years later before permission was given for them to enter Ubangi-Shari. In 1922 the first center was established among the Karre people. During the first twelve years three stations serving three different language areas were opened, with 15 missionaries engaged in itineration, translation, and medical work. During the second twelve-year period, missionary personnel doubled and more stations were opened. The postwar decade has witnessed still more centers occupied, bringing the total to 13. There are now 61 missionaries and a baptized membership of 20,660, divided into 388 congregations. Each district has its own elementary Bible school which sends qualified students to the Central Bible Institute, where 60 students are taking the advanced course at present. The Mission also operates one hospital and five dispensaries. A good deal of translation work has been done. The New Testament is available in the Sango, Karre, and Kabba languages. The Old Testament in Sango has just been completed and is ready for publication.

Baptist Mid-Missions has been working in the eastern section of the country. All but one of its eleven main stations have outstations supervised by Bible school graduates. Three small Bible schools furnish a steady supply of students for the Central Bible Institute at Fort Crampel.

Two other missions are at work here, the *Africa Inland Mission* and the *Swedish Baptist Mission*. The Africa Inland Mission entered in 1924 and now has a dozen missionaries in three stations in the eastern part of the country near the Belgian Congo-Sudan border. The Swedish Baptist Mission, located in the southwestern part of the country, also has a small program.

GABON

Area: 103,000 sq. mi.   Population: 410,000
Capital: Libreville   Religion: Animism

THE LAND AND THE PEOPLE. Gabon, located on the Atlantic Ocean, is the smallest of the four provinces which formerly made up French Equatorial Africa. To the north is Cameroun; Congo Republic lies to the east and south. Gabon is essentially forest country. The Omines live on the coast and are the most advanced of all the tribes. The Pahouins are more numerous and have preserved an independent, warlike spirit. They are related to the Badjas of Ubangi. The animists recognize a superior spirit (God) and a host of genii, good and evil. The spirits of the dead are objects of worship. Islam is found in the northern part of the country.

MISSIONS. Initial attempts to evangelize French Equatorial Africa were made in Gabon. As early as 1842 the *American Board of Com-*

missioners, using their base at Cape Palmas (Liberia) as a spring-board, launched the first Protestant missionary effort in Gabon on the lower reaches of the Gabon River. After much discouragement and little progress the enterprise was turned over, in 1870, to the *American Presbyterians,* who twenty years before had established a work on the island of Corisco at the mouth of the river. In 1892 the Presbyterians pulled out and transferred their work to the *Paris Evangelical Missionary Society.* Their work is located on the north side of the Ogooue River and extends north and northwest to the border of Spanish Guinea, including some territory in Cameroun. Church membership in this Mission more than trebled between 1925 and 1950. In 1958 it had 7 stations, 49 missionaries, 420 African helpers, and 175 schools.

The most illustrious member of this Society is the world-famous *Albert Schweitzer,* winner of the Nobel Peace Prize, whose hospital at Lambaréné has become a veritable Mecca for all VIP's visiting Africa. Variously described as the "greatest living Christian," the "Thirteenth Apostle," the "Universal Man," Dr. Schweitzer is with-out doubt one of the truly great men of this century. After a brilliant career in which he achieved fame in three fields of endeavor—philosophy, theology, and music—he decided at the age of thirty to study medicine and devote the rest of his life to missionary work in Africa. Like every genius, he is something of an enigma, even to his admirers. Though he knows Latin, Greek, Hebrew, English, French, and German he does not speak any African dialect. While he is passionately devoted to the brotherhood of man and has served Africa well, he has shown little sympathy for, or understanding of, the greatest force in Africa today, nationalism. Reverence for life, which to him is the essence of religion, he carries almost to Buddhis-tic lengths. Some may hesitate to endorse the statement that he is the greatest missionary of all time, but few will disagree with John Gunther's description of him as a "perfectly enormous personality who has done sublime work."[4] At the age of eighty-five he is still going strong, and any pronouncement he makes on such subjects as disarmament, nuclear fall-out, or the peaceful use of atomic energy will be received with due consideration in the chancelleries of the world.

In the southern part of the country the *Christian and Missionary Alliance* has been at work since 1934 when they entered Gabon from their north Congo field. Bongolo was their first and for some time their only station; but seven additional ones were opened be-tween 1942 and 1958. Educational work includes a Bible school at

[4] John Gunther, *Inside Africa* (New York: Harper, 1955), p. 713.

Bongolo and three primary schools. Certain New Testament books are available in five tribal languages. All the New Testament books except Revelation are now available in mimeograph form in Yipounou. The objective for the next few years is to have a complete translation of the New Testament in the five languages of the area.

REPUBLIC OF THE CONGO
(Middle Congo)

Area: 132,000 sq. mi.	Population: 800,000
Capital: Brazzaville	Religion: Animism

THE LAND AND THE PEOPLE. The Republic of the Congo is bounded by Gabon and Cameroun on the west, Belgian Congo on the east and south, and Central African Republic on the north. In the southwest a narrow strip borders on the Atlantic Ocean. Congo Republic is the home of many tribes, the most important of which are the Bayombi, Bateki, Bakota, and Ubangi. Brazzaville was formerly the capital of French Equatorial Africa.

MISSIONS. Two missions hold the field in this republic. The *Swedish Covenant Mission* has a well-established work in the southern part of the country between Brazzaville and the Gulf of Guinea. It is by far the largest mission in this part of West Africa; it has 60 missionaries and over 400 national workers. Church membership stands at about 45,000. The *Norwegian Missionary Society* has a small work in this area.

BELGIAN CONGO

Area: 900,000 sq. mi.	Population: 13,000,000
Capital: Leopoldville	Religion: Animism

THE LAND. On the map Belgian Congo looks like a small country, but that is because the continent of Africa is so huge. Actually the Congo is seventy times as large as Belgium itself! Located on the equator, it is a hot, steamy, jungle country. On the north it is bounded by the Central African Republic and the Sudan, on the east by Uganda and Tanganyika, on the south by Northern Rhodesia and Angola, and on the west by the Congo Republic. On the west it has a narrow 25-mile-wide neck of land which extends to the Atlantic Ocean. The chief topographical feature is the Congo River, one of the longest in the world, which runs right through Congo, first north, then west, and finally southwest into the Atlantic Ocean. The country is divided into six provinces.

POLITICAL HISTORY. The Berlin Conference recognized King Leopold II of Belgium as the sovereign head of the Congo Free State. Since 1908, when it was officially annexed to Belgium, it has been the sole colony of that country in Africa. During all these years the colonial government has controlled the business as well as the politics of the colony with no thought of preparing the people for eventual self-government. It was not until December 8, 1957, that the first election was held in the Congo; and that was a very modest affair, called a "consultation" rather than an election, which involved eleven townships making up the city of Leopoldville. Nevertheless, this historic event marked a fundamental change from the paternal autocratic policy under which the Belgian Congo has been governed for half a century. Communal riots in the urban centers and unrest and discontent in the rural areas have marked the rather sudden explosion of nationalistic feeling that has swept the colony in the last two years. National elections are to pave the way for representative government by June 30, 1960.

THE PEOPLE. The native population is composed of three ethnic groups: Negroes, Pygmies, and Hamites. These are divided into approximately 200 different tribes, each speaking its own dialect. The European population numbers 110,000, Belgians accounting for 85,000 of that number. There are four main languages: Kingwana in the east, Kiluba in the south, Lingala along the Congo River, and Kikongo in the Lower Congo.

THE RELIGION. Animism is the native religion of the Congoese. Roman Catholic missionaries, of whom there are at present 5,500, have been active in this colony for many decades. As a result, 25 per cent of the population, or 3,000,000 people, are Roman Catholics. Islam is just beginning to invade this part of Africa on its southward march. There are 90,000 Muslims.

EARLY MISSIONS. Following the death of David Livingstone, Henry M. Stanley decided to continue the exploration of Central Africa. In August, 1877, he became the first man to descend the mighty Congo to its mouth. The outcome of his explorations was his *Challenge to Christendom*, which made a tremendous impact on the Christian Church, especially in England. As a result two British societies were prompted to begin work in Congo in 1878. The first was the *Livingstone Inland Mission,* an undenominational mission patterned after the China Inland Mission which had been begun by J. Hudson Taylor in 1865. The first station was opened at Palabala by *Henry Craven* in 1878. The *Baptist Missionary Society,* under which William Carey had gone to India almost one hundred years before, started its work a year later at Banza-Manteke. The pioneers encountered incredible difficulties—geographic, linguistic, and climatic. It is estimated that only one in four survived the first term of service. They made twelve attempts before they finally opened a station at Leopoldville, then called Stanley Pool.

Between 1881 and 1884 the first two mission steamers were launched on the Upper Congo after having been carried in sections by porters 225 miles from the coast. Three outstanding English Baptists of this early period deserve honorable mention. *George Grenfell* stands high on the honor list of African explorers and missionary pioneers. Reaching Africa in 1873, he contributed thirty-three years of splendid service. In his little steamer, *Peace,* he was the first to chart the Congo River and to discover the Ubanga River. The story of his journeys through cannibal tribes and his escapes from showers of spears and poisoned arrows is unsurpassed for exciting interest. *Henry Richards* planted the gospel seed at Banza-Manteke on the Lower Congo in 1879, and after watering it with prayers and tears for seven years he reaped the first ripe sheaf. Thereupon broke out the "Pentecost on the Congo" which swept a thousand souls into the Kingdom. The third great missionary was *Rev. W. Holman Bentley,* who reduced the Kongo language to writing and translated the New Testament.

In 1884 the Belgian Congo became the first of 22 fields now occupied by the small but tremendously virile *Christian and Missionary Alliance.* Thirty years later, after thirty missionary graves had been dug, there were only 800 believers. By 1924 the number had jumped to 4,000. In 1931 its Church in the Congo became self-supporting and self-governing. By 1954, after seventy years of work, church membership had reached 30,000. Converts are being won at the rate of 4,000 a year.

While most of the early pioneers entered via the Congo River, *F. Stanley Arnot,* who had been a playmate of Livingstone's children, entered from the southeast through Angola with Dan Crawford, the well-known author of *Thinking Black.* In 1889 he founded the important work of the *Garanganze Evangelical Mission* in the fabulously wealthy Katanga territory of today. A member of the *Plymouth Brethren,* whose missionary arm is known as *Christian Missions in Many Lands,* Arnot made nine different exploratory trips in Central Africa. The Congo, with 133 missionaries and 26 main stations, is today the second largest mission field of the Plymouth Brethren.

The *Southern Presbyterians* started their work in 1891 at Luebo in the Baluba tribe. One of their outstanding members, *Dr. William Morrison*, reduced the Baluba-Lulua language to writing and translated the Bible. Working among 2,000,000 people all speaking the same language, they have enjoyed great linguistic advantages which they have turned to good account. This is their only field in Africa, and the largest of all their ten mission fields, having 175 missionaries and 12 main stations. In 1957 they reported 70,000 communicants in 1,458 outstations under the supervision of 1,415 evangelistic workers.

In 1899 the *Disciples of Christ* entered the field. Today they have eight stations. In their territory is situated the *Union Training School* in which four missions are co-operating. Another such inter-mission school, reputed to be the finest Protestant teacher training institution in Congo, was founded on the Lower Congo at Kimpese in 1908.

LATER MISSIONS. Between 1900 and 1915 a number of new societies entered the Congo from the United States, Great Britain, Norway, Denmark, and Sweden. Among them were the *Africa Inland Mission* (1912), *Congo Inland Mission* (1911), *Worldwide Evangelization Crusade* (1913), and the *Congo Evangelistic Mission* (1915). When the *American Baptist Mission* opened work in the Kwango district in 1915 the final link in the chain of mission stations from the Atlantic on the west to Tanganyika on the east was completed.

One of the most fruitful fields in the entire Congo is the American Baptist station of Vanga in the Kwango district. Opened in 1915, it produced only ten converts in ten years. The break came with a mass movement in 1946. Since then new converts have been added to the Church at the rate of 2,000 a year. Active membership in 1957 was 30,194, more than one-tenth of the population. Wholly self-supporting, the Vanga Church that same year received four million Congo francs (over $80,000) in contributions. On several occasions it has sent sizable gifts to churches in India, China, and Japan. Today more than 20 per cent of the Vanga staff are serving with Baptist Missions outside their own area. Similar mass movements are taking place in other missions, notably the *Swedish Evangelical Mission* and the *Worldwide Evangelization Crusade*.

The *American Methodist* work in Congo first started with *Bishop William Taylor* in the year 1885, but the venture was short-lived. It was not until 1914 that a permanent mission was established in the area around Elisabethville. Great progress has been made through the years and now the Congo Mission, with its Central and Southern Annual Conferences, is one of the largest Methodist fields in the world. The Central Congo Conference is primarily rural, while the Southern Congo Conference is chiefly urban. In recent years a concerted effort has been made to place the many churches on a completely self-supporting basis. In 1957 the Church in Central Congo was reported to be 76 per cent self-supporting. The Field Committee agreed that this should be raised to 100 per cent by 1959. The Southern Conference is somewhat behind but is moving in the right direction. The Methodist Mission is an active participant in some of the outstanding interdenominational institutions in Congo, such as the *Union Secondary School* at Katubue, the *Union Publishing House* (LECO) in Leopoldville, and the *Union School for Missionary Children* at Lubondai. Full church members number 31,000, with 10,000 more in the process of preparation. Organized churches total 894. There are 80 ordained national preachers assisted by hundreds of evangelists.

Between the two World Wars the number of Protestant missions more than doubled. One of the largest to enter was the *Unevangelized Fields Mission,* which commenced work in the early 1930's in the northeastern part of the country. At present it has 81 missionaries in 6 stations. There are 20,000 believers in 246 outstations. The *Berean Mission,* which began its work in 1938, now has 47 missionaries in 3 stations among the Balega tribe.

RECENT MISSIONS. During the fifteen-year postwar period additional societies, mostly American, have initiated work in the Congo. The *Conservative Baptists* entered in 1946 and within ten years were able to report 65 churches and 900 bush schools taught by 1,600 Congoese teachers. They also had 1,500 preaching centers. In 1957 they baptized 5,000 converts. A newcomer in 1953 was *Baptist Mid-Missions.* It took over 9 stations in the Kwango Province which had formerly constituted the northern district of the Unevangelized Fields Mission. The *Seventh Day Adventists* report 2 hospitals, 2 colleges, and 353 churches, of which 196 are in Ruanda-Urundi.

MEDICAL MISSIONS. Medical work has played an important part in the evangelization of Congo. Today Protestant missions operate 170 major medical institutions, treating one million patients annually. They have a staff of 73 missionary doctors, 200 missionary nurses, and hundreds of well-trained African assistants.

EDUCATIONAL MISSIONS. It was not until 1954 that the first state schools were opened. Before that, education was entirely in the hands of the missionaries, both Protestant and Roman Catholic. Beginning in 1926, Catholic schools received government subsidies; it was not until 1948 that the same treatment was accorded Protestant schools. Education is a watchword today in Congo. Phenomenal progress has been made since the first mission school was opened in 1878 with six pupils. At the present time 12,000 Protestant schools are giving sound Christian education to 350,000 students—28 per cent of the entire student body of Congo.

BIBLE TRANSLATION. Because of the many dialects spoken in Congo, Bible translation has been one of the major concerns of all missions. Commenced by *Nils Westlind* and completed by *Dr. Laman,* the Kongo Fioti Bible, the first complete Bible in Congo, was published by the *British and Foreign Bible Society* in 1905. In eighty years this Bible Society has published more than two million copies of the Scriptures in 62 languages. Included in this figure are 240,000 Bibles and 860,000 New Testaments. The entire Bible is now available in 11 languages, the New Testament in 21, and portions in 30 more. In 1958, Scripture distribution reached an all-time record of 70,000 Bibles, 100,000 New Testaments, and 120,000 portions. Entering Congo in 1958, the *American Bible Society* united with the British and Foreign Bible Society to form a Joint Agency to meet the ever-increasing demands of the Congo field.

SUMMARY. One of the last countries of Africa to be occupied, Congo has attracted more Protestant missions than any other African field. In 1957 there were no fewer than 49 Protestant societies with a total membership of 2,100 missionaries. This means that Belgian Congo, with one-eighteenth of Africa's population, has one-seventh of its Protestant missionaries. All but two or three of the societies are members of the *Congo Protestant Council,* which in 1925 grew out of the Congo Continuation Committee founded in 1911. For many years a member of the International Missionary Council, the Congo Protestant Council withdrew from that body following the Ghana Assembly in January, 1958. Congoese are now members of the Council. Total Protestant church membership is about 800,000, with an additional 300,000 inquirers, which means that one out of every ten persons in the Belgian Congo is directly affiliated with the great and growing Protestant Church. The overall Protestant community is reckoned at 2,000,000—about two-thirds the size of the Roman

Catholic community. There are 10 theological colleges and 39 Bible schools.

RUANDA-URUNDI

Area: 20,910 sq. mi.   Population: 4,500,000
Capital: Usumbura   Religion: Animism

THE LAND. This is a small piece of territory lying immediately east of the Belgian Congo, between Lake Tanganyika and Lake Victoria Nyanza. It is bounded on the north by Uganda and on the south and east by Tanganyika.

POLITICAL HISTORY. Originally part of German East Africa, these two areas were ceded to Belgium by mandate of the League of Nations after World War I. Following the second World War, Belgium's trusteeship of these areas was confirmed by the United Nations. Though not part of Congo, the territory is united with Congo economically and administratively.

THE PEOPLE. Unlike Congo, Ruanda-Urundi is densely populated, so much so that the Belgian government is offering every inducement to the people to emigrate to Congo. There are three principal tribes: the Batutsi, the Bahutu, and the Batwa.

THE RELIGION. Animism is the indigenous religion, but Roman Catholicism is exceedingly strong, the Roman Catholics having been there long before the Protestants were admitted.

MISSIONS. Protestant missions were rather late in coming to this part of Africa. The *Church Missionary Society*, the first and today the largest mission in the territory, opened its first station at Gahini in 1926. Since then other central stations have been opened at Shyira and Kigeme, in 1932; Buhiga and Matana, in 1935; Ibuye, in 1937; and Shyogwe, in 1945. This Mission has developed a well-rounded program of evangelism, education, and medical work. The blessing of God has rested on this work to an unusual degree, and phenomenal progress has been made in three short decades. Evangelistic work is carried on chiefly by local Christian teachers at village churches, of which there are 1,760. Teacher training schools are found at ten main stations, and there are hospitals at all but one of the stations. In 1958 there were 32 African clergymen, 3,477 evangelists, and 1,008 educators. Communicants number 30,000. The C.M.S. field is located in Ruanda.

The *Free Methodists* were the pioneers in Urundi. They opened their first station at Muyebe in 1935. Today they have six stations in Urundi and two in Ruanda. Their fine medical program centers around the hospital at Kibuye, which was opened in 1946. They have several thousand members. The *Seventh Day Adventists* have a large and fast-growing work, including a hospital at Ngoma and a training school with grades one through twelve at Gitwe. In 1957 they reported 196 churches with a total membership of 39,775; 6,452 of those members were added that year.

Other missions include the *Society of Friends*, the *World Gospel Mission*, and *Christian Missions in Many Lands*.

XX

INTRODUCTION TO LATIN AMERICA

LATIN AMERICA

Area: 8,000,000 sq. mi.   Population: 185,000,000

THE AMERICAS. We are accustomed to speak of two Americas—North
and South. Geographically there are in reality four—North, South,
Central, and the Caribbean area. For the sake of convenience, Mexico and the three countries of the Caribbean area are included in
the chapter on Central America. Racially there are two—Anglo-
Saxon America and Latin America. The Rio Grande is the dividing
line, and Latin America stretches south from that line to Cape Horn
and the Antarctic Ocean. It comprises about four-sevenths of the
entire Western Hemisphere, Anglo-Saxon America's area being
7,225,000 square miles against Latin America's 8,000,000 square
miles. In population, however, the ratio is reversed, since Anglo-
Saxon America has 195,000,000 inhabitants against Latin America's
185,000,000.

LATIN AMERICANS. While the inhabitants of Latin America are commonly designated Latin Americans, the truth is that from the racial
point of view only a small proportion—one-fourth at most—can be
properly so called. The foreign blood that is in them is mainly
Latin, and the comparatively small upper class is dominantly of
Latin blood; but the racial basis of the Latin-American peoples as a
whole is Indian, not Latin.

This fact, standing in striking contrast as it does to the case of
Anglo-Saxon Americans, is readily explained by the totally different
nature of European colonization in these two sections of the Western Hemisphere. The early Anglo-Saxon colonists in North America
were actuated largely by religious motives. They came seeking freedom of conscience to worship God, came with their wives and little
ones, came to establish new homes and communities and to settle
down to till the ground and develop the country. They encountered
the Indians, fought and drove them back, but disdained any idea
of intermingling or intermarrying with them.

Not so the Portuguese and Spaniards who first touched the shores of the Southern Continent. These were daring adventurers, lured to the New World by the tales they heard about its fabulous treasures of gold and silver. They came as single men or without their families. Moreover, the first Indians they found were very different from those of North America, for the Incas were civilized, docile, and skilled in agriculture. So while the *Conquistadores* from overseas shamefully mistreated the native races, decimated their numbers, and reduced them to slavery, they did not wipe them out, but mixed freely with them, and thus the surviving Indians furnished the stock upon which the Latin blood from Europe was grafted.

To this day, as the traveler passes from republic to republic of Latin America, he readily observes the varying degree in which Indian blood has been affected by European strain. In Bolivia, Peru, and Ecuador he finds great masses of mixed population in which Indian features and character are dominant; while in Chile and Colombia the mixed populace, although retaining many Indian qualities, is more strongly Spanish in character. The people of Argentina and Uruguay are almost purely European, and constitute nearly one-half of the all-white population of Latin America. In the case of Brazil, and to a much more limited extent Venezuela also, the admixture of blood has become still greater because of the importation by the early colonists of large numbers of African slaves.

NAMES. Miss Lucy Guinness named South America *The Neglected Continent*. Later, Dr. Francis E. Clark called it *The Continent of Opportunity*. Still later, Bishop Stuntz styled it *The Continent of Tomorrow*. All three authors are correct in their designations.

That it has been, and still largely is, "the neglected continent" admits of no argument. The rest of the world has been strangely content to remain in gross ignorance of the geography, the resources, the commercial, educational, and social progress of these growing Latin countries, and to class them all together indiscriminately as illiterate and lawless tropical states—a negligible quantity in world affairs.

But Miss Guinness had chiefly in mind the spiritual neglect of South America, and this is by far the saddest and most serious aspect of the matter. No satisfactory reason can be offered for the aloofness and inaction of centuries on the part of the churches of Protestant lands, and especially North America, toward a continent of 185,-000,000 people lying so close at hand, united to North America by physical bonds and by many common features and interests as well, yet sunk in moral and spiritual degradation.

In recent years a gradually rising tide of interest in our South American neighbors has set in. This is evidenced by more books and magazine articles upon this region, by a new stream of tourist travel in this direction, by strengthened diplomatic relations, and by new and heavy investment of capital in South American enterprises. All this, along with quickened spiritual interest and increased missionary effort, goes to prove that the world has at last discovered in South America "the continent of opportunity," and desires a share in it as "the continent of tomorrow."

THE EARLY RACES. The origin of South America's earliest people is wrapped in mystery. Fragments of earthen pots and crude implements found on the coast of Peru seem to point to a primitive people in the remote past. Following these came a race much more advanced, massive stone relics of whose remarkable civilization are still to be seen near Lake Titicaca in the highlands of Peru and Bolivia. Certain resemblances between these people and the Chinese, Japanese, and Malays have led to theories of their Oriental origin, but where they came from is an unsolved problem.

Of the next succeeding Indian races, most prominent among whom were the *Incas* of Peru, the *Caras* of Ecuador, and the *Aztecs* of Mexico, we have fuller and more reliable knowledge. The Cara kingdom reached its zenith at the end of the fourteenth century, when it was overthrown and partly absorbed by the Incas.

EUROPEAN DISCOVERY AND CONQUEST. *Columbus* himself began the Spanish exploration of South America. On his third voyage, in 1498, he sighted the Venezuelan coast, and in his fourth and last voyage, in 1502, he sailed along the Colombian shore to the Isthmus of Panama.

In 1513 *Balboa* crossed the Isthmus and discovered the Pacific Ocean. The several colonies planted in that region became centers of further exploration north and south. *Cortez* invaded Mexico in 1519, overthrew the Aztec Empire in 1521, and in 1525 extended his conquest for Spain to the territory now comprising Central America. Meanwhile Portuguese navigators had discovered Brazil. The earliest landing there was effected by *Cabral* in 1500, at Bahia. He was succeeded by *Amerigo Vespucci*, whose name was given to the new world, and *de Souza*, who in 1532 founded the first colony at São Vincento, near the present great coffee port of Santos. From this beginning Portuguese colonization spread along the Brazilian coast and to the mountain site of the present city of São Paulo, colonial government was established and the sugar industry begun.

INDIAN POPULATION. It is estimated that the people of pure Indian descent number about 18,000,000. Seven million of these live in the Andean highlands and constitute about half of the population of the three countries of Peru, Bolivia, and Ecuador. Two countries in Central America also have large Indian populations—Mexico and Guatemala. These Indians have never been assimilated by Spanish culture. They retain their own customs, traditions, and languages, and live mainly by agriculture, which they carry on by methods both primitive and unproductive. Illiteracy among them is fearfully high; and medical facilities are practically unknown. Housing is wholly inadequate. Three centuries of Iberian rule, while it brought many material benefits to South America, resulted in untold sufferings to the Indians, sufferings which to this day have not been redressed. Though nominally Roman Catholic they are still more pagan than Christian.

POLITICAL DIVISIONS. Latin America consists of twenty republics, ten of which are north and ten south of Panama. There are other territories belonging to France, Great Britain, Holland, and the United States; but they are not included in this study. In most Latin American countries political colonialism was overthrown 150 years ago. In the twentieth century a kind of economic semi-colonialism has fastened itself on the life of the people. The three South American countries of Venezuela, Colombia, and Argentina are currently struggling with democracy, leaving Paraguay the only military dictatorship. But democracy in this part of the world is not yet on a sure footing. The Latin Americans are a volatile people and this characteristic is reflected in their political life. In former days, governments in Latin America seemed to rise and fall almost with the barometer. Paraguay has been notorious for its revolutions, which have cost her so many men that at one period the female population outnumbered the male five to one. Venezuela had 52 uprisings within a century. Ecuador had 18 presidents in as many years. In one dramatic week in 1955, Brazil had three different presidents. The republics recognized as progressive are Brazil, Argentina, Chile, Uruguay, and Costa Rica. The others are moving in the right direction. Progress is being made and more and more the people are demanding a greater share in government even though politics in some countries is still a dangerous occupation. Spanish, spoken in 18 of the 20 republics, is the lingua franca of Latin America. Portuguese is spoken in Brazil, and French in Haiti. Language, therefore, is no problem for the missionaries except in the case of those working among the Indian tribes.

ROMAN CATHOLICISM. Roman Catholicism is the dominant religion of Latin America. The Roman Catholic Church, which exerted such strong influence in colonial times, is no less a political force in the republics. The Church party constitutes the conservative wing, against which are arrayed the radicals and liberals. The aggressions and political pretensions of the Church are increasingly resented and opposed, not only by the other political parties, but by the public in general. For four centuries she has had an absolutely free hand, without a competitor, and in the main with the substantial backing of the state. Under such conditions she has had the best possible opportunity of showing what she can do to uplift the people. What use has she made of this opportunity, and what results has she to show? Applying the Master's own test, "By their fruits ye shall know them," the following facts speak for themselves:

Romanism has systematically and bitterly opposed every movement toward civil, political, or religious freedom. She has herself been a political rather than a religious power, and her unscrupulous methods have won for her contempt and antagonism in politics.

She set up the infamous Spanish Inquisition in South America, at the hands of which 120,000 people were tortured and 189 were burned at the stake in Lima, and its overthrow was effected only in the teeth of her strenuous resistance.

She has not scrupled to employ the boycott and every form of persecution to intimidate those who have sought peace outside her fold, nor to use violence, imprisonment, and even the assassin's dagger and bomb to despatch heretics.

She has been the inveterate foe of popular education, thereby contributing to the prevailing illiteracy. Her leaders in Argentina persistently fought the Morris Schools, which befriended and educated thousands of homeless waifs in and around Buenos Aires.

She has opposed the translation of the Bible into the vernacular, and its distribution, has forbidden her people to buy or read it, and has publicly burned the Book. Bible colporteurs have been stoned, flogged, imprisoned, and murdered at the instigation of her clergy.

She has defiled herself by becoming a partner in the lottery and other iniquitous practices.[1] She has encouraged Sabbath desecration through the sanction of the use of that day for public games, excur-

---

[1] James H. McLean, the author of *The Living Christ for Latin America* (Philadelphia: Presbyterian Board of Publication, 1916), testifies to having seen over a motion-picture show managed by Franciscan monks the sign "Recreation Hall of the Child Jesus," and more than one wine cellar directly beneath the altar of a church.

sions, feasting, and social merriment, if only early mass has been attended.

But the case against Rome in South America is even yet stronger when her doctrines and morals are examined. Her teaching deserves to be called Mariolatry rather than Christianity, for a godhead of four persons, not three, is recognized, and with Mary the first person. The Jesuits taught their converts to say: "We confess that the Holy Virgin Mary should be held in greater esteem by men and angels than Christ Himself the Son of God."[2]

"On a tablet beside the door of the Jesuit Church in Cuzco, Peru, there is an inscription in Spanish: 'Come to Mary, all ye who are laden with works, and weary beneath the weight of your sins, and she will succor you.' "[3]

Except in the larger coastal cities, where foreign influence is strong, few sermons are ever preached and no prayers offered in any of the churches, in the language of the people. The observance of ritualistic forms and sacraments is made the hollow substitute for repentance and regeneration, as a perusal of the authorized Roman Catholic catechism of Christian doctrine in use will show. And along with these empty ceremonies a whole stock of grossly sacrilegious superstitions are foisted on an ignorant and credulous people.

Little wonder is it that a great proportion of the people, particularly the educated and intelligent classes, have turned in disgust from such a travesty of religion to absolute unbelief, so that the chief task of evangelical missions is not to proselytize from the Roman Church, but to call to a rational faith and a pure and upright life those who have already thrown off this false religion and are drifting toward atheism and moral ruin.

Said an intelligent man in Argentina to a missionary who was endeavoring to awaken in him a concern about spiritual things: "Sir, we have been so miserably deceived and defrauded by this religion, that it will be a long while before we can be expected to take any interest again in anything that bears the name of religion." He spoke with evident heat, and who will blame him? While gratefully recognizing the true Christian faith and character of certain individuals within the Church of Rome, and the heroism and self-sacrifice of some of her early pioneers in this continent, we must solemnly affirm that Romanism in South America stands condemned on its own record, at the bar of God and humanity alike, and is hopelessly impotent to meet the social, moral, and spiritual needs of

[2] Samuel R. Gammon, *The Evangelical Invasion of Brazil* (Richmond: Presbyterian Committee of Publications, 1910), p. 99.
[3] McLean, *The Living Christ for Latin America*, p. 115.

185,000,000 needy souls. After personal contact with South America and most of the great mission fields of Asia and Africa, we share the deep conviction of many other observers that *South America today stands in need of the gospel not one whit less than China, India, Africa, and the Muslim world.*

EARLY ROMAN CATHOLIC MISSIONS. In the discovery and settlement of Latin America the religious motive was not lacking along with the political and commercial, and the very earliest expeditions were accompanied by monks or priests. The first of these were of the Franciscan and Dominican Orders, but the Jesuits who followed were here, as elsewhere, the great missionary agency of Rome.

Some of these were worthy disciples of Loyola and Xavier, and faced hardship, danger, disease, and persecution in a heroic spirit deserving of all praise. They penetrated the continent at many points, and "there was no tropical wilderness too intricate or far-stretching for them to traverse, no water too wide for them to cross, no rock or cave too dangerous for them to climb or enter, no Indian tribe too dull or refractory for them to teach." Yet they were a part of the militant, ecclesiastical, and political system of the times, so that their ardent evangelism and humanitarian service were strangely mingled with cruel slaughter and subjection of the natives, and extortion of their land and wealth. Conversions were often by a wholesale process, and the Church ingeniously adapted its doctrines, rites, and symbols to suit the religious traditions and notions of its pagan "converts."

For the above reasons it is not unfair to say, nor is it surprising, that Roman Catholic missions in Latin America have proved an almost complete failure. The greatest temporary triumphs of the Jesuits were in the interior of southern Brazil and in Uruguay and Paraguay, but later they fell under the suspicion and disfavor of both Portuguese and Spanish governments because of their great accumulation of wealth and assumption of power. In the eighteenth century the Jesuits were expelled, their possessions confiscated, and their work shattered, never to be restored.

ADVANCE OF PROTESTANTISM. Protestant Christianity is on the march throughout Latin America. Nowhere has Christianity grown so rapidly in this twentieth century. In 1900 there were 50,000 Christians in this part of the world; by 1914 the number had risen to 250,000. In 1958 the figure stood at 5,000,000. The most rapid rate of growth is in Brazil where the Methodists are building a new church every twenty days. In 1930 Protestants represented 1.31 per cent of the population in Brazil; in 1940 the percentage was 2.61, and by 1950 it was 3.3 per cent. Eight out of ten of the pastors are nationals. Many of the Christians are intellectuals, teachers, business-men, technicians, politicians, Rotarians, etc. The evangelical com-munity is growing three times as fast as the population; and the population is "exploding" at a rate almost twice that of the rest of the world. Protestant missionaries outnumber Catholic missionaries three to one, and the Roman hierarchy has expressed grave concern over the increasing inroads that Protestantism is making in Latin America. The late Pope Pius declared that the invasion of Protestant-ism into South America was one of "four mortal dangers to the Roman Church."

MISSIONARY OCCUPATION. As might be expected, the preponderance of the 8,000 Protestant missionaries in Latin America are from North America. Moreover, an unusually high percentage of these North American workers are members of the interdenominational faith missions. This is accounted for by the fact that half of the 42 mis-sions which make up the Interdenominational Foreign Mission Asso-ciation of North America have work in Latin America. Some of these missions, such as the *Latin America Mission,* the *Central American Mission,* and the *Bolivian Indian Mission,* have work only in this part of the world. *Wycliffe Bible Translators* has the largest number of missionaries. Seventy-five per cent of its 875 active missionaries are in Latin America.[4]

Here, as in other parts of the world, missionary occupation is not evenly distributed. Brazil with over sixty million people has 980 missionaries, whereas Haiti with about four million has 525 mission-aries. Bolivia has three million people and 522 missionaries, whereas Mexico has ten times the population and only 551 workers. El Salvador has twice the population of Costa Rica but only half as many missionaries. Argentina with 700 missionaries is second only to Brazil. Three countries have fewer than 100 missionaries: Uruguay (79), Nicaragua (65), and El Salvador (55).

Of all the groups working in Latin America the indigenous Pente-costal churches have had the most rapid growth. This is particularly true in Chile, Argentina, and Brazil, where in each case they con-stitute the largest Protestant group in the country. According to reports, there is a definite trend in Latin America to erase the difference between the clergy and the laity. This is especially true of the Pentecostal groups and the independent churches. As a result laymen, as in New Testament times, are playing a major role

[4] *Wycliffe Bible Translators* withdrew from the I.F.M.A. on February 1, 1960.

in the work of evangelism. The Latin American Church today is largely in the hands of volunteers. Every believer is a missionary. It is a truly aggressive Church with a militant witness to the grace of God. Moreover, the strength of the Church is found in the rural areas. When Baptists in Cuba recently held their annual convention in Santiago de Cuba the pastor of the host church prepared for 200 delegates; at the last minute 2,000 believers dropped in from the surrounding countryside to enjoy the fellowship!

MISSIONARY RADIO. Latin America leads the world in this new medium of communication on the mission field. The pioneer station was HCJB in Quito, Ecuador. It began broadcasting on Christmas Day, 1931, and has since become the model for missionary radio throughout the world. Of the 21 radio stations on the mission field today ten are found in Latin America and the Caribbean area.[5]

In March, 1957, ground was broken for the Radio and Audio-Visual Center, CAVE, in Campinas, Brazil. It is now producing daily and weekly broadcasts over 35 stations in Brazil, and films for TV use. In addition programs sponsored by church federations, and even local churches, are to be heard over commercial stations in nearly all the Latin American republics. No other field in the world can compare with Latin America in the matter of Christian broadcasting.

Station HCJB is preparing to introduce missionary television. For three weeks in August, 1959, HCJB-TV programs were televised as part of the National Fair sponsored by the Newspaper Union of Ecuador. The station hopes to go on the air with live telecasts as soon as a permanent permit can be obtained from the government.

FIRST PROTESTANT EFFORTS. The first Protestants to land in South America were a company of French Huguenots sent to Brazil in 1555 by Calvin and Coligny, with the hope of founding a colony for persecuted Protestants. They landed on an island in the Bay of Rio de Janeiro and were reinforced by a second company a year later. But their leader, Villegagnon, turned traitor and abandoned the colony, which was later destroyed by the Portuguese. A few survivors escaped into the interior and attempted work among the Indians, but these were hounded down and put to death by the Jesuits.

In 1624 the Dutch captured Bahia and attempted to plant colonies there and at Pernambuco, with alleged religious as well as commercial ends in view. Religious liberty was decreed and work begun

[5] For a complete list of missionary radio stations consult the chart at the back of the book.

among the Indians, but the Dutch West India Company later decided to withdraw, and so this second missionary attempt was aborted.

Modern evangelical effort may be said to have really begun in 1735, when the Moravians opened work in British Guiana. In 1738 this work was extended to Dutch Guiana.

THE LANCASTRIAN SCHOOLS. The dawn of the era of independence among the South American republics, early in the nineteenth century, coincided with the awakening of the Church in Europe and America to new missionary endeavor, and the formation of societies for the translation and distribution of the Bible. In England a project had been begun by one named Joseph Lancaster for a system of popular schools for children, with the distinctive features that the Bible was the main textbook and that the older scholars were made pupil-teachers of the younger ones. The success of the project at home led to plans for extending its benefits to other lands, and so The English and Foreign School Society was organized. The British and Foreign Bible Society had just begun its great work abroad, and these two societies united in sending *Mr. James Thompson* to South America.

Thompson began his work in Buenos Aires in 1820, only four years after Argentina's declaration of independence. He preached the first Protestant sermon ever preached there. His plans met with immediate success, over one hundred schools were opened in Buenos Aires, and he won the favor and support of the leading statesmen. Uruguay and Chile soon called for his services and initiated his school system under government patronage. Thus he passed from one republic to another, his good work enjoying a temporary triumph which was most gratifying. In Peru, General San Martín turned out the friars of the Convent of St. Thomas and handed the place over for a Lancastrian school. Bibles were everywhere sold in large numbers, and auxiliary Bible Societies were formed in several republics, with the endorsement and support of prominent officials.

But stern reaction soon set in through the secret and powerful tactics of the jealous priesthood. Parents were forced to take their children from the schools, and those who had purchased Bibles were ordered to surrender them to the priests. "Gradually the coils tightened about the evangelical institution and it was strangled by political and clerical pressure. It received a warm welcome because it purported to be educational; it met with a violent death by priestly suffocation because it was evangelical."[6]

[6] McLean, *op. cit.*, p. 115.

Mr. Thompson returned to England in 1826, and the few who followed him grew discouraged under the difficulties which beset them and were compelled to abandon their efforts on these lines.

CAPTAIN ALLEN GARDINER. "The first enduring Protestant Mission to South America began with the sacrifice of Captain Allen Gardiner, who perished of starvation in September, 1851, in Spanish Harbor, Tierra del Fuego."[7]

This noble British naval officer had seen service in many parts of the world, was converted during one of his voyages, and became filled with a passion for Christ and lost souls. He was deeply impressed with the pitiable condition of the aborigines of South America, and made earnest efforts to open work among the Indians of Chile and the region in northern Argentina and western Paraguay known as the *Chaco*. Being persistently balked by the opposition of the priests he turned his attention to Patagonia.

The Indians of that extreme southern tip of the continent and the adjacent island of Tierra del Fuego were among the most degraded people in the world. The eminent naturalist, Charles Darwin, dubbed them "the missing link" between man and monkey, and declared them incapable of moral discernment. Gardiner accepted this challenge and was permitted to labor long enough to convince Darwin of his error.

After some preliminary work among the Patagonians he returned to England in 1843, and effected the formation of the *South American Missionary Society* in 1844. His remaining six or seven years were full of adventure and hardship in his dauntless efforts to plant mission stations in that remote and inclement region and to win the Indians to Christ. Driven from their center at Banner Cove by the truculence and pilfering of the Indians, Gardiner and six companions, who had recently joined him from England, put to sea in their little vessel and took refuge in Spanish Harbor, where they waited and prayed for the coming of the promised supply ship from home. Before it arrived starvation had slowly overtaken every member of the heroic little band, Gardiner himself being the last to succumb. Their bodies and diaries were found to tell the pathetic tale. " 'Poor and weak as we are,' wrote Gardiner, 'our boat is a very Bethel to our souls, for we feel and know that God is here. Asleep or awake, I am, beyond the power of expression, happy.' Instead of repining or lamenting, he left behind only earnest entreaty that the mission

[7] Robert E. Speer, *South American Problems* (New York: Holt, 1914), p. 219.

should not be abandoned, and left a brief plan outlining further operations."[8]

The news stirred the Church of England to its depth and gave new impulse to the work among the Indians. The transformation wrought among the Fuegians as a result of the work begun by Gardiner drew from Darwin a frank testimony of astonishment and appreciation, accompanied by a donation to the Society's funds and a request to be made an honorary member.

[8] Arthur T. Pierson, *The New Acts of the Apostles* (New York: Baker and Taylor, 1894), pp. 111–12.

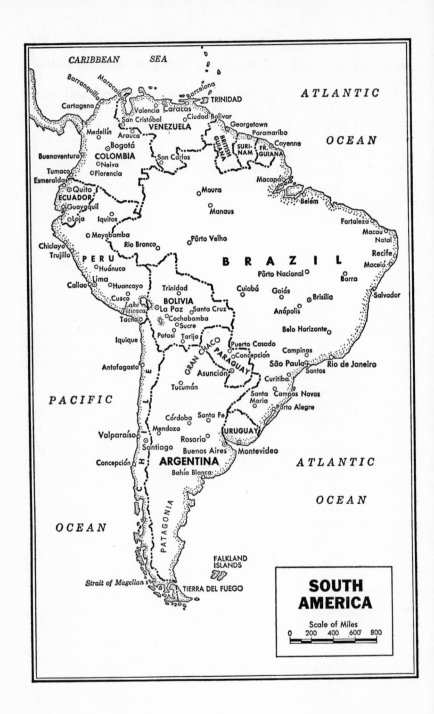

CARIBBEAN SEA

Barranquilla
Maracaibo
Cartagena
Barcelona
Valencia Caracas TRINIDAD
San Cristóbal Ciudad Bolívar
Medellín VENEZUELA
Arauca Georgetown
Bogotá Paramaribo
Buenaventura COLOMBIA BRITISH SURI- FR. Cayenne
Neiva San Carlos GUIANA NAM GUIANA
Tumaco Florencia
Esmeraldas Macapá
Quito Moura
ECUADOR Belém
Guayaquil
Loja Iquitos Manaus
Moyobamba
Chiclayo Rio Branco Pôrto Velho Fortaleza
Trujillo Macau
PERU Natal
Huánuco BRAZIL Recife
Callao Lima Pôrto Nacional Maceió
Huancayo Barra
Cusco Trinidad Cuiabá Goiás Salvador
Lake Titicaca La Paz Brisilia
Tacna BOLIVIA Santa Cruz Anápolis
Cochabamba
Sucre Belo Horizonte
Potosí Tarija
Iquique Puerto Casado Campinas
GRAN CHACO São Paulo Rio de Janeiro
Antofagasta Concepción Santos
PARAGUAY Curitiba
Asunción Santa Campos Novos
Tucumán Maria
Pôrto Alegre
PACIFIC Córdoba Santa Fe
Mendoza URUGUAY
Valparaíso Rosario
Santiago Buenos Aires Montevideo
Concepción ARGENTINA
Bahía Blanca ATLANTIC

OCEAN

ATLANTIC

OCEAN

PATAGONIA

FALKLAND
ISLANDS

OCEAN

Strait of Magellan TIERRA DEL FUEGO

**SOUTH
AMERICA**

Scale of Miles
0   200   400   600   800

XXI

SOUTH AMERICA

BRAZIL

Area: 3,288,050 sq. mi.
Capital: Brasilia

Population: 62,000,000
Religion: Roman
             Catholicism

THE LAND. The country of the "amazing Amazon," Brazil is a land of tremendous proportions. It is the fourth largest country in the world and equal in size to the combined area of all the other South American countries. It stretches for 2,700 miles from north to south and a simliar distance from east to west. With almost 5,000 miles of coastline, it faces the Atlantic Ocean on the east and north. So huge is Brazil that it has contiguous borders with all but two of the countries of South America.

POLITICAL HISTORY. Brazil was discovered by Pedro Alvares Cabral, the Portuguese explorer, who claimed the land in the name of the King and the Pope in 1500. After three centuries of colonization it was declared an independent empire by Don Pedro in 1822. A revolution in 1889 overthrew the empire and the country became a republic under the title of the United States of Brazil. A constitution modelled after that of the United States of America was adopted. It abolished slavery and declared religious liberty. The new capital, known as Brasilia, is now being built in the state of Goias in the interior of the country.

THE PEOPLE. According to the 1950 census, 61.7 per cent of the population is white, 26.5 per cent mulatto, 11 per cent Negro, and the remainder assorted. Indian tribes, many of them savage, inhabit the upper reaches of the Amazon River. Portuguese is the language of the country; but the Indians, of course, speak their own dialects.

THE RELIGION. Roman Catholicism is the dominant religion of the country, holding sway, nominally at least, over the vast majority of the people. Church and State were separated in 1889, reunited in 1934, and separated again by the Constitution of 1946. Religious liberty is guaranteed, and Protestantism is growing by leaps and bounds.

EARLY MISSIONS. The first continuing Protestant work in Brazil was launched by *Dr. Robert Kalley* in Rio de Janeiro in 1855. Opposition from the papal nuncio might have ousted him from the country had it not been for the protection afforded him by the Brazilian government. In spite of all kinds of local persecution Dr. and Mrs. Kalley persevered for twenty years in their efforts to give the gospel to Brazil. The work started by Dr. Kalley was known as *Help for Brazil,* and it co-operated with the handful of Congregational churches in and around Rio de Janeiro. In 1911 this Mission amalgamated with two others, the South American Evangelical Mission and the South American Branch of the Regions Beyond Missionary Union, to form the *Evangelical Union of South America,* the headquarters of which was in London. Later on an American Branch was formed and it became responsible for five states in northeast Brazil. The oldest work is in Paraiba and Pernambuco, where in 1956 there were 25 self-supporting churches under the leadership of national pastors trained in the Bethel Bible Institute in Joao or the seminary in Recife. In the South Brazil field there are 40 missionaries assisted by an equal number of national workers; it is the responsibility of the British Branch of the Mission. The Evangelical Union of South America co-operates on all levels with the *Congregational Christian Union of Brazil,* and all of the 107 churches brought into being by the Mission are members of this autonomous Church, which now represents a Christian community of 20,000.

Of the long-established denominations, the *American Methodists* were the first to enter Brazil. Two abortive attempts were made in the 1830's, one of them by *Rev. Daniel P. Kidder.* He traveled overland and up the great Amazon River, braving hardships, perils, and bitter opposition in his work of distributing the Scriptures for the first time in the vast republic. Twenty-five years later, in 1867, the Southern Methodists sent *Rev. Junius E. Newman* to work among the North American immigrants to Rio de Janeiro. He was followed in 1876 by *Rev. John J. Ransom,* who began a work among the Brazilian population. *Bishop William Taylor* was instrumental in opening a field in the northern part of the country where *Rev. Justus H. Nelson* spent forty-five years, earning his own support by teaching English, German, and Portuguese. The autonomous *Methodist Church of Brazil* was established in 1930. Today it has five Annual Conferences and a rapidly expanding work in nine states. There are 45,000 church members and 333 organized churches, as well as 909 preaching places. The nerve center of the work is located in São Paulo, said to be the most rapidly growing city in the world. Their 53 churches there could be increased to 75 in no time at all if funds and personnel were available. In the same city are the Theological Seminary and the Publishing House, the latter producing huge quantities of religious literature in Portuguese not only for Brazil but also for Portugal, Mozambique, Angola, and the Madeira and Cape Verde Islands.

Presbyterian work in Brazil began with *Rev. Ashbel G. Simonton* whose first audience consisted of two men who were his pupils in English. He was followed by *Rev. George W. Chamberlain,* the great pioneer evangelist who, with his fellow laborer, *Jose Manoel da Conceição,* spent forty remarkable years preaching and organizing churches in the state of São Paulo. In 1888 the churches established by the two Presbyterian Missions (Northern and Southern Boards) united to form the *Presbyterian Church of Brazil.* Around 1894 the Brazilian field was divided into two missions, South and Central. The largest concentration of Presbyterian work in Brazil is in the city of São Paulo. A fine system of schools was established, the capstone of which is *Mackenzie Institute* with its schools of law, medicine, humanities, engineering, and science. This famous institution, with a present enrollment of over 6,000, is now completely self-supporting and is controlled by a national board of directors. Also in São Paulo is the Presbyterian Publishing House. Medical work includes five hospitals which are being staffed increasingly with national personnel. In 1957 the Brazilian Presbyterian Church comprised 9 synods, 45 presbyteries, 637 organized churches, 2,003 congregations and preaching points, and 210,000 members. This includes 25,000 members belonging to the Independent Presbyterian Church, which was formed in 1903. In August, 1959, the World Presbyterian Alliance held its 18th General Conference at São Paulo. The Alliance membership includes 72 national Churches with a world constituency of 45,000,000. This gathering was part of the centennial celebrations of Presbyterian missions in Brazil. So rapidly is the work spreading that the Presbyterian seminaries cannot supply the demand for ministers. A partial solution is found in Bible institutes. The old, well-established churches near the coast are self-supporting and self-governing. Most of the 74 Presbyterian missionaries now in Brazil are in the interior of the country doing evangelistic work. To facilitate travel in this land of great distances, the Mission maintains four planes.

The *Southern Baptists* entered Brazil in 1881. It was their first South American field. They began their work among the North American immigrants in São Paulo in the southern part of the country. The following year they opened a second field in the north. Later on they also began work in the central area. Today they have a flourishing work in all three fields. A strong educational program includes 24 middle schools, 2 women's training schools, and 2 colleges. They have 1,700 Sunday Schools with 160,000 children under instruction. Three seminaries provide a steady flow of 75 new preachers every year. Eighty per cent of their 1,470 churches are self-supporting, and they have almost 4,000 outstations in various stages of development. In 1958, 155,000 members contributed almost half a million dollars.

LATER SOCIETIES. *Pentecostal* missions in Brazil date back to 1910 when *Gunnar Vingren* and *Daniel Berg*, two Swedish ministers from Chicago, settled in Belem near the mouth of the Amazon. Supporting themselves as they preached they soon won a group of zealous converts. With the coming of other Pentecostal missionaries (mostly Scandinavians in the early years) the work spread eastward and southward along the coast into all the major cities. A large number of Brazilians dedicated their lives to the ministry, and they extended the work into the interior. Almost all of the assemblies founded by the nationals were entirely indigenous. Now known as the *Assemblies of God in Brazil*, this fellowship has become the largest evangelical group in the country, with 1,064 ordained ministers and 5,108 lay preachers serving 1,043 organized churches and 5,204 outstations. The total membership is 307,525. Co-operating closely with this Church are two Pentecostal missions, the *Scandinavian Assemblies of God* and the *American Assemblies of God*.

Several societies are working exclusively among the many Indian tribes of Brazil. Space permits the mention of only two of these.

The *Inland South American Missionary Union*, a merger of two small missions, one from Scotland and the other from the United States, began work among the Indians of Brazil in 1919. Two decades later the name was changed to the *South America Indian Mission*. Purposely avoiding the larger centers which offer some of the amenities of civilization, the brave pioneers of the South America Indian Mission penetrated the jungles in search of Indians. This involved perilous journeys in hostile country, long periods of separation from wife and family, frequent exposure to pestilence and disease, and lack of food and medical care. In 1930 *Arthur F. Tylee* and *Mildred Kratz* were killed by the Nhambiquara Indians. Undaunted by the perils and setbacks, the Mission has continued to carry on a program of aggressive evangelism among the Indian tribes of eastern Bolivia, central Brazil, northern Colombia, and eastern Peru. It has its largest work in Brazil where it has over 50 workers in 6 stations.

Brazil was one of the first fields to be entered by the *Unevangelized Fields Mission* founded in 1931. This Mission has assumed responsibility for an area of 850,000 square miles in northeast Brazil, where it has almost 100 missionaries working among ten Indian tribes. Languages have been reduced to writing and Scripture translation is making good progress. Three gospel boats have been pressed into service to facilitate travel between the 13 main stations in the area. Two Bible schools are preparing pastors for a score of organized churches and about 60 outstations.

The *Protestant Episcopal Church* made several unsuccessful attempts to establish a mission in Brazil in the 1850's; but it was not until 1889 that a permanent work was begun in Rio Grande do Sul by *James W. Morris* and *Lucien Kinsolving*. Ten years later Kinsolving was consecrated the first bishop of the Episcopal Church of Brazil. A theological seminary at Pôrto Alegre has for many years supplied the Church in Brazil with its clergy. Until 1949 the Church's work was confined to one missionary jurisdiction, Southern Brazil. When in 1950 the Brazilian mission was divided into three districts with one American and two Brazilian bishops, another great step was taken towards the realization of an independent Church. The present program is designed to strengthen the work of the Church in those places where it has been long established and to extend the work into the northern half of the country. The *National Council of the Episcopal Church of Brazil* is made up of bishops, presbyters, and lay representatives from the three dioceses. This Council coordinates the work of the Church in Brazil and is looking forward to the day when it will become an independent national Church within the Anglican Communion. The measure of self-support is being increased from year to year; for the past ten years the annual grant to the Church in Brazil has been around $200,000. This is over and above the support provided for the dozen missionaries working with the Church. Communicants number about 9,000. The Christian community is estimated at five times that figure.

Though it owes its origin more to European immigration than to missionary endeavor, some reference should be made to the great Lutheran movement in Brazil. In the early 1820's Lutheran immigrants from Europe, particularly Germany, began arriving in large numbers in South America, and many of them settled in Brazil. By the middle of the century Lutherans were present in sufficient numbers to warrant an organized effort to meet their spiritual needs. In 1861 the *Basel Missionary Society* sent its first party of missionaries to Brazil. A synod was organized in 1867. By 1881 ten Basel brothers were at work in the country. During the 1870's the Evangelical Church of Prussia provided financial assistance for the German Protestant churches in Brazil. The *Evangelical Synod of the Rio Grande do Sul* came into being in 1886 and was followed by the formation of the *Lutheran Church in Brazil* in 1895. This group experienced rapid and extensive growth during the first half of the twentieth century. Known today as the *Evangelical Church of Lutheran Confession in Brazil*, it represents a Christian community of some half million people.

In 1889 the *Lutheran Church-Missouri Synod* responded to an appeal for pastors and began a mission in Brazil. It first served the German immigrants but later on began missionary work among the Brazilians. In rapid succession—1911 and 1912—the *Evangelical Synod of Santa Catarina and Parana* and the *Synod of Central Brazil* were formed. In the course of the years more than 100 pastors were sent out. *Concordia Seminary* in Pôrto Alegre has a present enrollment of 100; it furnishes pastors for the Lutheran churches of the country. Now called the *Evangelical Lutheran Church of Brazil*, it has a membership of 80,000.

The *Seventh Day Adventists* entered Brazil in 1894 and began a thriving work. At the present time it is divided into three zones, north, south, and east. Institutional work includes 4 large city hospitals, 200 elementary schools, and 2 colleges. There are 50,000 church members in their 250 churches.

For many decades the Baptists were represented by only one mission in Brazil, the Southern Baptist Convention. More recently other Baptist groups have entered the field. The first of these was *Baptist Mid-Missions*, which began work in the early 1930's. Twenty years later their 70 missionaries had planted 8 main stations across the widest part of the country from Fortaleza on the Atlantic Ocean to Rio Branco near the eastern border of Peru. Their work in Central Amazon Valley is located at Manaus, a city of 120,000 people, where they have a church, a Bible institute, two leper colonies, radio ministry, etc. Two stations, in the extreme northern tip of the country, minister to the Macushi Indians, a small civilized tribe of about 1,500 people. The *Association of Baptists for World Evangelism* took up work in Brazil in 1942. Already it has an expanding work in three districts, south, central, and northwest. In 1959 the missionary staff numbered 54. The *Conservative Baptist Foreign Mission Society* moved into the country in 1946, followed by the *Baptist General Conference of America* in 1955.

The *New Tribes Mission,* which began work in Brazil in 1946, now has 107 missionaries in that country doing evangelistic work among ten different tribes. In three of these tribes there are one or more established churches. *Missionary Aviation Fellowship* inaugurated its Brazilian air service in 1956. Today its four planes are providing swift, safe, and economical transportation for all missions throughout the Amazon jungle area. Other new missions in Brazil include the *Mennonite Brethren Church of North America* (1946), *Free Methodist* (1946), *Independent Board for Presbyterian Foreign Missions* (1948), *Brazil Christian Mission* (1948), *Inter-American Missionary Society* (1950), *Wycliffe Bible Translators* (1956), *Worldwide Evangelization Crusade* (1957), *West Indies Mission* (1957), and *Church of the Nazarene* (1958).

Opportunities for Christian witness in Brazil abound on every hand. Church membership in all denominations increases month by month, and in many instances church accommodation is utterly inadequate to provide seating space, and sometimes even standing room, for those who desire to hear the gospel. Evangelistic fervor continues high among laity and clergy alike. The entire Christian community is keen to share the good things of the gospel with friends and neighbors. Press and radio are also used. Missionaries, still retaining the pioneering spirit of the nineteenth century, are penetrating into the heartland of Brazil and into its vast jungle areas, reaching remote, inaccessible communities by plane, bus, jeep, launch, canoe, horse—and on foot. New communities in the interior are open to the gospel, while in the great cities in the coastal areas Protestant churches are numbered by the hundreds. "There is hardly a town or a village in this vast country which does not have a Protestant church or group. Protestant schools, seminaries, churches, orphanages, publishing houses, and other institutions dot the land from north to south and from east to west."[1]

URUGUAY

Area: 72,172 sq. mi.
Capital: Montevideo

Population: 2,800,000
Religion: Roman
Catholicism

[1] *118th Annual Report of Board of Foreign Missions of the Presbyterian Church in U.S.A.* (1955), p. 72.

THE LAND. Uruguay is the smallest of the South American republics. It is located on the east coast between Brazil on the north and the Rio de la Plata on the south. It is a land of rolling, grassy plains devoted to stock-raising. There is some farming, but not much.

POLITICAL HISTORY. Once a state of Brazil, Uruguay gained its independence in 1825. Through the years it has remained remarkably free from dictatorships. The Colorado party, which has been in power continuously for over 90 years, has a strong tendency to statism and is responsible for the welfare state that exists there today. It is the most progressive of all the South American countries, and is known throughout the continent as a citadel of freedom and a center of culture and education.

THE PEOPLE. More than 90 per cent of the population are Ladinos, most of whom are of Spanish descent. The remaining 10 per cent are Indians, Negroes, etc. Spanish is the official language. Primary education is free and compulsory, and higher education, including college, is also provided free by the welfare state. Illiteracy is almost unknown except among the older people of the rural sections. The standard of living is relatively high.

THE RELIGION. Church and State are separate and there is complete religious liberty. Uruguay is the least Catholic of all the South American countries and can be described as a completely secular state. By government decree Christmas is called "Family Day," and Holy Week is known as "Tourist Week." It is a democratic, open, peaceful nation with strong guarantees of civil rights. The people are largely unchurched and without any religious convictions. Public and private morality is at a low ebb.

MISSIONS. Here as in Argentina and Brazil the *American Methodists* were the first on the field. *Rev. Fountain E. Pitts* and *Rev. John Dempster* each visited Montevideo on his way to Argentina in 1835 and 1838, respectively. The first appointee to Uruguay was *Rev. William H. Norris*, who reached the capital in 1839; but his stay there was short-lived. Owing to unsettled political conditions in Argentina coupled with financial stringency at home, the Mission decided to recall its missionaries from South America. The work was not resumed until 1870 when *Rev. John F. Thomson* returned to the field. The first representative of the Woman's Foreign Missionary Society began work in 1878 by opening an evangelical school for young women. The *Uruguay Provisional Annual Conference* was formed in 1954. Methodist work in Uruguay now embraces 19 organized churches in two districts, and membership is around 2,000. Educational work centers in *Crandon Institute* in Montevideo, now in its seventy-eighth year.

The second North American mission to take up work in Uruguay was the *Southern Baptist Convention*. It moved in in 1911. Almost half a century of work has produced 21 organized churches of which only three are self-supporting at present. In 1958 there were 113 baptisms recorded, bringing the aggregate membership to 1,071. The 14 missionaries there now are engaged in the work of the theological institute, Christian publications, and pastoral work.

The *Assemblies of God* missionaries entered the country in 1946, but the response to their efforts has been small. Uruguay is one of the very few fields in which the Assemblies of God do not have a Bible school. Eight missionaries assisted by two national workers are ministering in four churches. The *Church of God* reports 22 churches with a membership of 1,300.

Another work of about equal size is that of the *Seventh Day Adventists,* who report a membership of 2,200 scattered over some 17 congregations. Educational work is confined to nine elementary schools. There is no medical work.

The *Worldwide Evangelization Crusade* was one of the latest missions to enter Uruguay. *James Finlay,* a Cambridge graduate who had taught in Uruguay in his younger days, returned in 1950 as the Crusade's first missionary to the country. Ten missionaries are at work in the northeastern section where several companies of believers have been won for Christ.

The *Lutheran Church-Missouri Synod* has one church in Montevideo. It was opened in 1936 in response to an appeal from an immigrant family. Uruguay, with three powerful radio stations and complete religious freedom, provides a good base from which to broadcast the *Lutheran Hour* into surrounding countries. The *United Lutheran Church* took up work in Uruguay in 1948, and the *Augustana Lutheran Mission* followed in 1952.

The *Mennonite Board of Missions* began work in the country in 1954. Three couples are there now. Theological training in Uruguay was greatly strengthened by the opening of the *Mennonite Biblical Seminary* in Montevideo in 1956. This seminary trains students of all denominations working in the countries of the River Plate.

The *Waldensians* form the largest Protestant Church in Uruguay with about 10,000 members. They are followers of the pre-Reformation reformer, Peter Waldo, and fled their native hills between

France and Italy to escape the persecution of the Roman Catholic Church.

Other missions include *Christian Missions in Many Lands, New Testament Missionary Union, United Pentecostal Church, Church of the Nazarene,* and the *Salvation Army.*

PARAGUAY

Area: 157,000 sq. mi.	Population: 1,650,000
Capital: Asunción	Religion: Roman Catholicism

THE LAND. Paraguay, one of two completely landlocked South American countries, is bounded on the south and west by Argentina, on the north and northwest by Bolivia, and on the east by Brazil. It is divided into two sections: the Oriente, lying between the Paraguay and Paraná Rivers; and the Chaco, a less densely populated region in the northwest which has been a subject of much dispute with Bolivia.

POLITICAL HISTORY. Paraguay secured its independence from Spain in 1811. This was effected without bloodshed, and the country passed from colonial rule to a dictatorship. Under three dictators it was brought to a place of prosperity and prominence. During the war with Brazil, Argentina, and Uruguay from 1865 to 1870, it lost five-sixths of its entire population. The war with Bolivia in the 1930's was also costly in both men and money.

THE PEOPLE. There were various tribes of the Tupi-Guarani Indians living in Paraguay at the time of the conquest. They intermarried with the Spaniards and from this race amalgamation has come the most distinctive Indian-Spanish group in all of South America. The Paraguayans are bilingual, speaking both Spanish, the official language, and Guarani. There are other smaller Indian tribes which are quite hostile. Primary education is free, and in theory at least, it is compulsory; but a shortage of schools makes it impossible for all children to get an education.

THE RELIGION. Roman Catholicism, which was introduced by the Spaniards, became the official religion of the country; but only a small minority of the population is actively Catholic. The president of the country must belong to the Roman Catholic Church. Other religions are tolerated.

MISSIONS. The work of the *South American Missionary Society* was carried on by others after the tragic death of its founder, *Captain Allen Gardiner*. In 1888 *Adolpho Henricksen* reached the Chaco region, but he lived for only a year. He was followed by *Wilfred B. Grubb*, the first white man to live among the Lengua Indians of Paraguay. For twenty years he labored among these people, engaging in the various types of work peculiar to pioneer fields: reducing languages to writing, translating the Scriptures, preparing grammars, etc. Today the Mission reports only one place of worship, with a Christian community estimated at 800.

The *United Christian Missionary Society* (The Christian Churches) initiated work in Paraguay in 1917. Nineteen missionaries are located in the two main stations of Asunción and Coronel Oviedo where they are carrying on a strong program of evangelism and education. There are five organized churches. The educational work centers around *International College*, which has an enrollment of more than 500.

More recently (1935) the *Mennonite Brethren of North America* opened a mission in the Chaco region and commenced work among the various groups of Mennonites who had fled from Russia, Germany, and Poland after the Bolshevik Revolution of 1917. Later on, this society extended its work to include the Indians in the territory.

The work of the *Assemblies of God* in Paraguay got under way in 1945 when the first missionaries, *Mr. and Mrs. Raymond M. Stawinski*, located in Encarnación to minister to a group of European refugees who had formed a settlement there. With the arrival of another missionary couple, a second station was opened in 1950 in Asunción, the capital. Progress has been slow and the work is still in the pioneer stage. Each new advance has been made in the face of opposition and persecution. Their staff has been augmented by the arrival of two more couples, one going out in 1957, and the other in 1958. There are four organized churches. The primary need is for more national workers who will assume responsibility for the evangelization of their own land. Present plans call for the establishment of a Bible institute to train national preachers, of whom there are now only three.

The *Southern Baptist Convention* has had work in Paraguay since 1945. Compared with other fields, the work in Paraguay is small. Eighteen resident missionaries are located in the capital city where the main body of work is found. Institutional work includes a Bible institute, opened in 1956, the Baptist Hospital, and a school of nursing. Church work includes 6 established churches and 10 chapels. These were organized into the *Paraguay Baptist Convention* in 1956.

Christian Missions in Many Lands has four stations in Paraguay. The *New Tribes Mission,* a comparative newcomer, is already at work among five Indian tribes. There are one or more established churches in two of the tribes.

The *Free Methodists,* the *New Testament Missionary Union,* the *Salvation Army,* and the *Seventh Day Adventists* also have work in Paraguay.

ARGENTINA

Area: 1,084,120 sq. mi.   Population: 19,700,000
Capital: Buenos Aires   Religion: Roman
                                                   Catholicism

THE LAND. The entire 2,300-mile length of this the second largest country in South America is bordered by Chile on the west. The Atlantic Ocean forms the eastern boundary, with Uruguay and Brazil to the northeast, and Paraguay and Bolivia to the north. From north to south there are three topographical and climatic regions: the Gran Chaco, which is tropical and heavily forested; the Pampas, or central plain, which is temperate and largely cattle country; and Patagonia, which is cold steppe-land.

POLITICAL HISTORY. Argentina was discovered by Don Juan Diaz de Solis, who sailed up the Rio de la Plata in 1516. In 1534 the Spanish king sent the first governor, Don Pedro de Mendoza. It was he who founded Buenos Aires. Spanish rule lasted until 1816, when independence was declared. A constitutional government was established in 1853 after almost forty years of anarchy.

THE PEOPLE. Argentina has been called the "melting pot of South America." The population is almost entirely of European origin, with Spanish and Italian strains predominating. About one-third of the people live in or near the capital city. The 40,000 Indians who remain in the country have been neglected and pushed into the border lands. Argentina enjoys the highest rate of literacy in South America, about 85 per cent. A complete school system provides free and compulsory education for all children from six to fourteen years of age, and almost 100,000 students attend the seven universities.

THE RELIGION. Roman Catholicism is supported by the state as the official religion. Until a century ago, laws preventing Protestant teaching and preaching were rigidly enforced; but recently there has been more religious tolerance. The teaching of the Roman Catholic faith is no longer required in primary and secondary schools as it was under the Perón dictatorship only a few years ago. Christian radio broadcasts, suspended for years, have been resumed, and open-air meetings are permitted. While nominally Roman Catholic, the bulk of the population is antichurch, anticlergy, and quite materialistic. One priest for every 9,000 people is evidence of the spiritual neglect of the populace.

MISSIONS. In the Introduction to Latin America mention has already been made of *James Thompson,* who began work in Buenos Aires in 1820, and of *Captain Allen Gardiner,* of the *South American Missionary Society* (missionary arm of the Church of England), who perished of starvation in Spanish Harbor in 1851 after an unsuccessful attempt to start missionary work among the Patagonians. The enterprise, however, was not terminated. Six years later a second expedition was organized on behalf of the benighted people of Patagonia; but again tragedy stalked their efforts and seven of the eight persons in the party were murdered by the aborigines while conducting divine service. Still the Mission did not give up, and courage and perseverance won the day. A work was finally established which has continued to the present. Latest reports from the Missionary Diocese of Argentina, which includes the Falkland Islands, show a baptized membership of 11,000.

James Thompson of Scotland represented the *British and Foreign Bible Society* and the *Lancastrian Educational Society.* Arriving in Buenos Aires in 1820 he received a cordial welcome, was made an honorary citizen of Argentina, and for a brief period achieved an unusual degree of success both in the distribution of the Scriptures and the founding of schools, one hundred of which were located in the city of Buenos Aires.

The *American Methodists* were the first North American group to enter Argentina. *Rev. Fountain E. Pitts* made an exploratory tour of the field in 1835, and the following year permanent work was begun with the arrival of *Rev. Justin Spaulding* and *Rev. John Dempster.* For several decades the work was confined to the many immigrants from Europe. Work among the Spanish-speaking population was begun by *Rev. John F. Thomson,* who is said to have preached the first Spanish sermon in Argentina in 1867. With the coming of two single ladies to the city of Rosario in 1874, the *Woman's Foreign Missionary Society* launched its work in Argentina. The first Protestant periodical in the Spanish language, *El Evan-*

gelista, was published in 1877 by *Dr. Thomas B. Wood.* The *South American Annual Conference* was inaugurated in 1893. In 1954 the Conference was divided into the *Argentina Annual Conference* and the *Uruguay Provisional Annual Conference.* The *Patagonia Provisional Annual Conference* was authorized during the quadrennium 1956–60 by the General Conference. Methodist work in Argentina is centered in the capital. The Publishing House, Ward College, and Union Theological Seminary are located there. The seminary, founded in 1884, is now an interdenominational work carried on in co-operation with the Disciples of Christ, the Presbyterians, and the Waldensians. Methodist membership stands at about 6,400 with almost 1,000 prospective members under instruction. Fifty-two ordained pastors assisted by 21 evangelists shoulder the major responsibility for the work.

In 1897 the *Christian and Missionary Alliance* began work in sections of the country not then occupied by any Protestant mission. The first church was built in La Plata in 1903. It was later turned over to the Baptists, as was also the work in Entre Rios. Owing to financial straits, other sections of the field were transferred at a later date to the Mennonites. Missionary activity reached its peak around 1925 when the Mission had 18 workers on the field. Missionary personnel was depleted, however, by the transferring of workers to other fields when the Mission put into operation a plan to develop indigenous churches along self-supporting lines; and the Depression in the early 1930's still further reduced the work of the Mission in Argentina. In 1946 the *Bible Institute of Buenos Aires* was opened; the Mission's only station is located in that city. Its 24 churches are completely independent.

In 1903 the *Southern Baptists* took over the work that had been carried on for some years by an independent Swiss missionary, *Paul Besson.* Considerable progress has been made in the intervening half century, and at present the Southern Baptists have the largest work in Argentina, with a baptized membership of over 12,000. Buenos Aires is the center of their work. Forty-two of their 170 organized churches are located in that city. In the outlying districts there are 142 chapels and preaching places. Institutions include two goodwill centers in Rosario and Paraná, and a publishing house in the capital. The *International Theological Seminary* in Buenos Aires serves Argentina, Paraguay, Uruguay, Chile, and Bolivia. Eighty-two students from the five countries were in residence in 1959.

Argentina was the first South American country to be entered by the *Salvation Army.* Four officers, who knew no Spanish, established the Army in Buenos Aires in 1890. Operations have since spread to six other countries of South America.

The *Lutheran Church-Missouri Synod* extended its work into Argentina from Brazil in 1905. Special emphasis was placed on a local and bilingual ministry, though the majority of the constituency spoke German. Moreover, self-support was strongly encouraged, with the result that today this Lutheran Synod with a membership of 10,000 and a community of 17,000 is the second largest Protestant Church in the country.

The *United Lutheran Church of America* established a flourishing mission in Buenos Aires in 1919. It also conducts the Women's Bible Training School, the American Evangelical Institute, and a theological seminary there. The *United Evangelical Lutheran Church in Argentina* was organized in 1948, and the American Lutheran Mission is now incorporated in that autonomous United Church, which has 20 congregations and a membership of 3,800.

Several *Pentecostal* groups are at work in the country. The largest of these is the *Church of God,* which reports 46 churches with an aggregate membership of almost 20,000. The *Assemblies of God* have been in Argentina for almost fifty years but their work there has not been large. In 1959 they had six missionaries and 52 ordained national preachers. Sixty congregations account for about 2,000 communicants. The *Church of the Nazarene* has 700 church members. The *Pentecostal Assemblies of Canada* have reported large gains in recent years, with church membership jumping from 400 in 1952 to 5,000 in 1957.

The *Seventh Day Adventists* is one of the few missions in Argentina which has medical and educational work as well as church work. They operate a hospital and a college at Entre Rios. Church membership is around 9,000.

Christian Missions in Many Lands, Evangelical Union of South America, New Testament Missionary Union, United Christian Missionary Union (The Christian Churches), and the *Mennonite Board of Missions* are also working in Argentina.

Newcomers to the country include the *American-European Fellowship* (1940), *Conservative Baptist Foreign Mission Society* (1946), and the *Baptist General Conference of America.*

CHILE

Area: 286,397 sq. mi.
Capital: Santiago

Population: 7,005,000
Religion: Roman
            Catholicism

THE LAND. Known as the "shoestring republic," Chile has the distinction of being the narrowest country in the world for its size. It stretches for 2,600 miles along the coast of South America from Peru to the southern tip of the continent. Its average width is 100 miles. On the east it is bounded by Argentina and Bolivia.

POLITICAL HISTORY. Shortly after Ferdinand Magellan discovered the southern part of South America Spain brought Chile under its control. Spanish colonialism continued until 1810 when Chile declared its independence. The present Constitution, adopted in 1925, resembles closely that of the United States.

THE PEOPLE. The great majority of the people are descendants of the Spanish settlers and the Indians, especially of the Araucan tribe. In the southern part of the country live the descendants of some Germans who located there in the late 1800's. Although they are a small minority group they exert considerable influence in that part of the country. Only a few isolated Indian tribes have remained intact. They have retained their own languages and tribal customs but have added Roman Catholicism to their animism.

THE RELIGION. Over 90 per cent of the people are Roman Catholics, but only 10 per cent of them ever go to mass on Sunday. The country is liberal-minded and there is complete freedom of action. Evangelicals have great opportunities and are making the most of them. There is no official relation between Church and State.

MISSIONS. The first Protestant missionary activities in Chile were started in 1821 by *James Thompson,* an agent of the *British and Foreign Bible Society.* He began his work by establishing schools in which the Bible was the chief textbook. He left the country after a short stay, and the work which he had carried on lapsed.

Protestant missions may be said to have begun with the arrival of *Rev. David Trumbull* at Valparaiso on Christmas Day, 1845. He was sent out by the *Seaman's Friend Society* and the *American and Foreign Christian Union,* both of which are now defunct. Because Protestant work was forbidden, Trumbull began his work among the many sailors aboard the ships which visited Valparaiso. There were about 1,500 annually, coming from some thirty different countries. In 1847 he succeeded in getting permission to organize the Union Church for English-speaking Protestants. A building was erected in 1856—the first Protestant church on the west coast of the Western Hemisphere south of California. In 1873 he transferred the work to the *Presbyterian Board,* which had established its first station in Valparaiso five years before. The Presbyterian Board is, therefore, the oldest mission in Chile. The denominational missions have not found Chile an easy field to work. After 115 years of gospel effort, membership in the Presbyterian Church is less than 2,500. The latest Report states that while the Church grows slowly in numbers it is advancing rapidly in responsibility and is now over 70 per cent self-supporting. Its 16 active pastors serve 25 organized churches and 35 other congregations scattered over 1,500 miles of country. The Board expects the Church to be fully independent by 1960, at which time it plans to withdraw the five fraternal workers now in the country. Institutional work includes the historic *Colegio David Trumbull* in Valparaiso, a maternity hospital, and three dispensaries.

Rev. William Taylor of the *Methodist Church* toured this part of South America in 1877–78. His plan at that time was to establish self-supporting schools in English-speaking communities as a step towards evangelical work among the Latin peoples. In 1884 he was elected missionary bishop for Africa and this work was transferred to the *Transit and Building Fund Society of Bishop Taylor's Self-Supporting Missions,* which was incorporated with the work of the Methodist Board in 1893. In 1904 the *Chile Annual Conference* was founded. Slow but steady progress has been made through the years, and today the Methodist Church, divided into five districts, has an aggregate membership of 4,600, an increase of 51 per cent in twelve years. *Santiago College, Sweet Memorial Institute, Iquique English College,* a student center, a rural life center, and a rural farm project constitute the institutional program.

The *Soldiers' and Gospel Mission,* a faith work operating in Chile, was founded by *William M. Strong* in 1923. Leaving his New York insurance business in the hands of a friend, at forty-five years of age he set out for South America. After two months of travel in Bolivia he proceeded to Chile where an unexpected opening for a gospel service in the regimental barracks in Tacna led to a concerted effort to evangelize the soldiers and sailors of Chile. In 1925 stations were opened in Valparaiso and Concepción, again with soldiers in mind. In 1933 *William M. Strong, Jr.,* joined the Mission and initiated work among the Indian population of the country. Setting up headquarters at Galvarino, he gave himself to the evangelization of 100,000 Mapuche Indians. Additional workers from both America and the British Isles joined the work in the 1930's. In 1956 there were 40 missionaries and 15 stations, all located in central Chile. There were 14 organized churches, 80 per cent of which were self-supporting.

The work of the *Christian and Missionary Alliance* in Chile began in 1898 when the Mission decided to assume the support of two independent missionaries already at work in the country. They were joined by several new workers right after the turn of the century. A Bible institute was opened in 1923. Between 1920 and 1927, fifteen missionaries went out. The three main centers of Alliance work, Temuco, Ancud, and Concepción, are all situated in the central part of Chile. In addition there are 30 self-supporting churches reaching from Santiago in the north to Coyhaigue in the south.

The *Pentecostal* movement in Chile began in 1910 when a Methodist missionary received the baptism of the Holy Spirit and then led the members of his congregation into the same experience. The movement spread rapidly and in a very short time other congregations had followed suit. These churches were organized into what is now known as the *Methodist Pentecostal Church*, an independent, indigenous Church with the largest evangelical constituency in Chile. It is estimated at 250,000.

In 1941 the *Assemblies of God* opened their first station in Santiago. Valparaiso followed in 1945, and Concepción in 1952. Organized in 1950 the *Assemblies of God in Chile* now comprise 14 organized churches and 32 preaching points served by 24 ordained ministers and 8 lay preachers. Almost all of these churches are missionary-minded and are sponsoring branch assemblies in addition to conducting their own church affairs. The *Chilean Bible Institute*, offering a three-year course of study, was established in 1953.

Another Pentecostal group is the *Pentecostal Evangelical Church*, completely indigenous, with about 90,000 members. The Pentecostalists now form the largest group in the country and have more members than all the other Churches combined. They have created what might be termed a "popular religion" among the humble peasants and workers of Chile. They have little institutional work of their own; instead they concentrate their efforts on preaching the gospel and distributing the Scriptures. They conduct no large-scale evangelistic campaigns but go out to the highways and byways, holding open-air services all over the country. They visit hospitals and jails, where they distribute the Scriptures. It was owing largely to their efforts that the Bible Society reported in 1956 the distribution of 23,709 Bibles, 40,109 New Testaments, and 227,-151 Scripture portions.

The *Southern Baptists* launched a mission in Chile in 1917, and now, after more than forty years, they have a solid and flourishing work. Forty-five missionaries man five stations which include, besides churches, a goodwill center, a seminary, a publication board, and the Baptist Academy. There are 75 churches located in nineteen of the twenty-five provinces, and 56 national pastors. Their radio program, known as the *Baptist Hour* and given once a week over seven stations in the principal cities, is the most widely distributed program in the country.

Other missions working in Chile are the *International Church of the Foursquare Gospel, Church of God, Independent Board for Presbyterian Foreign Missions, Association of Baptists for World Evangelism, Christian Missions in Many Lands, Salvation Army, South American Missionary Society*, and *Seventh Day Adventists*.

BOLIVIA

Area: 404,000 sq. mi.	Population: 3,237,000
Capitals: La Paz and	Religion: Roman
Sucre	Catholicism

THE LAND. Bolivia is one of the two completely landlocked countries of South America. Brazil lies to the east and north, Paraguay and Argentina to the south, and Peru and Chile to the west. The primary topographical feature is the high central plateau which averages over 12,000 feet in height. Some mountain peaks rise to 21,000 feet. As one travels east, he descends rapidly into the steaming jungles of the Amazon basin.

POLITICAL HISTORY. Bolivia was part of the famed Inca Empire before the invasion by the Spanish in the early 1500's. Independence was declared in 1825 and the new republic was named after the Latin-American liberator, Simon Bolivar. In a series of wars with each of its five neighbors, Bolivia lost over half of its original territory. The present Constitution, its thirteenth, was adopted in 1947.

THE PEOPLE. The ruling class is of Spanish descent and white in color and comprises only about 13 per cent of the population. Another 25 per cent of the people are of mixed blood; the remainder are Indian. After many years of exploitation and oppression the Indian is coming back into his own. Spanish is the official language, but the Indians speak their own dialects, the two principal ones being Quechua and Aymara. Primary education is free and compulsory, and progress is being made in lowering adult illiteracy, which is estimated at 68 per cent.

THE RELIGION. Roman Catholicism is the recognized state religion, but religious liberty is in effect. Evangelicals are looked upon with favor by the government and have in some cases experienced that favor at the expense of the Catholics.

MISSIONS. Protestant work in Bolivia was started by the *Canadian Baptists* in 1898. They have maintained a strong staff of missionaries through the years, and today the work is established on a firm foundation. In 1959 their field in the southwest part of the country comprised 40 organized churches with a membership of 1,100 under the spiritual care of 17 Bolivian pastors. They operate three clinics. Theological training is prominent in the program, with the *Baptist Seminary* and the *Women's Bible Academy* in Cochabamba, and a Bible school in Guatajata. Educational work is confined to the elementary level. Radio evangelism has been carried on ever since the *Southern Cross Radio Station* in La Paz went on the air in 1949. Its present schedule calls for 30 programs daily.

The *Plymouth Brethren* (Christian Missions in Many Lands) took up work in the country shortly after the Canadian Baptists, and today they have 12 main stations manned by missionaries from New Zealand and the United States of America.

As early as 1878 Rev. William Taylor of the *Methodist Church* began work in Antofagasta, a city on the coast which was later ceded to Chile. Permanent work began in the city of La Paz in 1903. One of the early pioneers was *Rev. Francis M. Harrington,* who started the first Methodist society and founded the *American Institute* in that city. The Woman's Division inaugurated work in Bolivia in 1955. The Conference has about 1,000 members and is divided into two districts, Central and North.

The American Institute of Cochabamba, founded in 1912 as a coeducational school, is one of the outstanding institutions of Bolivia. The President, Dr. Hernán Siles Zuazo, and many other men in prominent places at home and abroad are graduates of this school. Indeed, more than one out of every eight names found in Bolivia's *Who's Who* are graduates of the American Institute. On the fiftieth anniversary of Methodist work in Bolivia it was awarded the government citation of *The Condor of the Andes,* the highest citation in the country. Present enrollment is around 1,000. There is a sister school located in La Paz. Also in La Paz is the *Pfeiffer Memorial Hospital,* the only Methodist hospital in Latin

America. Situated on Lake Titicaca, high up on the western plateau, is the *Rural Reconstruction Center* for the Aymara Indians.

Shortly after the beginning of the century *Mr. George Allen* and five other New Zealanders arrived in Bolivia with a burden for the Quechua and Aymara Indians. At first they co-operated with the Canadian Baptists; but in 1907 Mr. Allen branched out on his own and established the *Bolivian Indian Mission* in San Pedro. Later the Mission transferred its work to Cochabamba, where its headquarters is now located. The Bolivian Indian Mission has concentrated most of its work in the departments of Potosí and Cochabamba. From the beginning the Mission made a special effort to reach the Quechua Indians, into whose language Mr. Allen translated the New Testament. The Bolivian Indian Mission is engaged almost exclusively in evangelistic and church work. One dispensary and a leprosarium in the charge of its only nurse are all it has in the way of medical work. Two primary schools and one middle school represent its contribution to education. The Mission is making every effort to put its 126 congregations, totalling some 5,000 believers, on a thoroughly indigenous basis. With this in view, the two Bible schools are giving high priority to the training of leaders to augment the present staff of 60 national evangelists assisted by 80 missionaries. The Mission operates a plane and several gospel launches.

Founded by *Joseph A. Davis* in 1914 for the purpose of reaching the Indian, the *South America Indian Mission* began work in eastern Bolivia in 1922 at a time when the area was entirely unoccupied by any other society. At the present time the Mission is working among the Ayoreo Indians of the jungle and the assimilated Chiquitano Indians and the mixed-blood peoples found in towns and villages. It has three main stations which are located in Santiago, San Ignacio, and Concepción. There is a Bible institute at Santiago.

Ever since the field was opened by *Rev. Thomas Anderson* in 1931 the *International Church of the Foursquare Gospel* has been working among the Sirionos Indians in the department of Beni.

The *Evangelical Union of South America* extended its work to Bolivia in 1937 and began work in the department of Potosí in the southwest corner of the country. Five stations were opened in this area. The response on the part of the Indians was not encouraging, especially at the beginning. In 1944 the Mission expanded into the lowlands of eastern Bolivia and established a work at Camiri among the Chane Indians, whose response was much better. In 1945 the *Eastern Bolivian Fellowship,* which had been working among the

Chiraguano and Chane Indians, became a part of the Evangelical Union of South America. The Gospels of Mark and Luke have been translated and a dictionary and primer have been prepared.

Bolivia was the first field to be entered by the *New Tribes Mission*, which was founded by Paul W. Fleming in 1942. Today there are 84 New Tribes missionaries in the country, making it the second largest of the 16 fields in which the Mission is working. Among seven primitive tribes the work is still in the pioneer stage; in only one tribe is there a group of believers.

Several missions have entered Bolivia in the postwar period. The first of these was the *Assemblies of God*, which went in in 1946. In the first eighteen months stations were opened at Cochabamba, La Paz, and Santa Cruz. A fourth station was added in 1952 and four new areas were opened up in 1954. Great stress has been laid on the training of national preachers, and three Bible schools are preparing pastors and evangelists for assemblies in all parts of Bolivia. The friendliness of the present government towards evangelicals has provided opportunities for the preaching of the gospel on every hand. In addition to evangelistic meetings, extensive distribution of gospel literature is carried on in all areas. The entire New Testament is available in Quechua and Aymara as well as in some of the languages of the smaller tribes of the eastern lowlands.

The *Church of the Nazarene, Wycliffe Bible Translators, New Testament Missionary Union, Seventh Day Adventists, World Gospel Mission, World Mission Prayer League, United World Mission*, and four groups of the *Friends* are also working in Bolivia.

PERU

Area: 514,059 sq. mi.   Population: 9,950,000
Capital: Lima   Religion: Roman
                                                 Catholicism

THE LAND. Peru has a Pacific coastline of 1,410 miles. It is bordered on the north by Ecuador and Colombia, on the east by Bolivia and Brazil, and on the south by Chile. At its greatest width it is 800 miles across. It boasts seven mountain peaks over 19,000 feet and it is here that the Andes reach their greatest height. The coastal plain is hot and dry, although the wooded uplands are well watered. To the east, Peru slopes down into the Amazon basin with its tropical jungles.

POLITICAL HISTORY. Peru was the center of the ancient Inca Empire and became Spain's chief viceroyalty in South America. It gained its independence in 1824 after three years of war.

THE PEOPLE. Indians make up about 60 per cent of the population; 10 per cent are whites, mostly of Spanish descent; the remaining 30 per cent are chiefly mestizo, with some Negroes and Asiatics included. Primary education is free and compulsory. Since 1946 secondary education has also been free, but as yet it is not too widespread. The five universities have a total enrollment of about 13,000 students. The University of San Marcos, founded in 1551 by Charles V, is said to be the oldest in the Western Hemisphere. Spanish is the official language but many Indians speak Quechua or Aymara. Lima, the capital, has a population of 1,100,000.

THE RELIGION. Roman Catholicism is officially protected by the government; and by a decree in 1929 it is the only religion allowed to be taught in any school, public or private. Religious liberty, while guaranteed by the Constitution, is still somewhat restricted. Open-air services are forbidden but it is now possible to rent public buildings for religious services. Radio evangelism is also permitted and is being used increasingly.

MISSIONS. We have already had occasion to mention the pioneer work of *Mr. James Thompson,* agent of the *British and Foreign Bible Society,* who landed in Argentina in 1820. He then made extensive tours in Chile, Colombia, and Ecuador before going on to Central America. In 1822 he arrived in Peru where, during his two-year stay, he distributed the Scriptures and founded schools.

The work of the *American Bible Society* in Peru dates from 1824. The pioneer agent in this venture was *Rev. Isaac W. Wheelwright* who spent two months in the capital on his first visit. Another agent of the Bible Society, *Francisco G. Penzotti,* gave forty years to colportage work in various parts of South and Central America. He took up residence in Callao, Peru, in 1888, and through the faithful preaching of the gospel and the distribution of the Scriptures he built up a large congregation. He was imprisoned and only after a sensational trial with international overtones was he finally released and permitted to carry on his work. The sub-agency in Lima now employs three full-time colporteurs, and Scripture distribution reached an all-time high of 150,000 copies in 1956.

To the *American Methodists* belongs the distinction of being the first Protestant mission to commence a permanent church work in Peru. Here again we meet with *Rev. William Taylor* who in 1877–

78 started school-church projects at Callao, Lima, Mollendo, and other cities in connection with his self-supporting mission program for South America. Following Bishop Taylor's transfer to Africa in 1885, the mission languished and finally died. Permanent work had to await the arrival of *Rev. Thomas B. Wood* in 1891. From the beginning the Methodists have regarded their school work as basic to their evangelical outreach. In each of their three main centers they have an outstandingly fine educational institution, the largest of which is the *American College of Callao* which offers a coeducational program with primary, secondary, and college-preparatory courses. Graduates from this school occupy important positions in the professional and business life of the country. Fifteen organized churches represent a membership of 1,500.

There was a time when we did not feel that the Church schools could witness openly. . . . We feel that now the institutions of our Church are firmly established and that the time is now ripe for them to include a more definite witness to Jesus Christ in all their programs. . . . The response that we have received to evangelical campaigns in the past year (1957) gives us confidence that in the future hundreds and even thousands of people can be won for Christ. . . . One of the great needs at the present is for more radio evangelism and for more definite relationship of our educational work to the outgoing ministry of the Church.[2]

During the first two decades of the present century several new missions took up work in Peru: the *Holiness Church of California* (1903), *Seventh Day Adventists* (1906), *Salvation Army* (1910), and the *Church of the Nazarene* (1914). The largest and most vigorous program is that of the Seventh Day Adventists. Including their work in the Lake Titicaca region, they reported in 1957 a membership of 17,000 in 62 churches. This is an average of 280 members to a church, an unusually high figure for this part of the world. Their educational work includes 105 elementary schools and 2 colleges. They have 2 clinics, one in Lima and the other in Juliaca.

The *Assemblies of God* is one of the larger missions in the country. Their work began in 1919 and has continued to show steady growth ever since. With a missionary staff of only 15, they have built up a strong indigenous Church. Organized congregations number 134 and outstations are double that figure. The Bible institute in Lima, which has a present enrollment of 65, is largely responsible for the fact that their fine churches are manned by 106 ordained ministers and 77 lay preachers.

The *South America Indian Mission* inaugurated its Peruvian work

[2] *Mission and Witness, 1958,* p. 155.

in 1923. Its field lies east of the towering Andes Mountains. Six of the seven main stations maintain schools, stores, and clinics, Contamana being the only exception; recently a Bible institute was opened there. As its name suggests, the Mission is engaged exclusively in Indian work and at present is working in three different tribes, the Shipibo, Conibo, and Campa Indians.

The *Regions Beyond Missionary Union,* an interdenominational mission founded in 1878 by Dr. Grattan Guinness of London, England, also began work in Peru in 1923. The first missionaries were two young ladies who opened a station at Moyobamba in Indian territory in the northeastern part of the country. The missionary staff, never large, numbers 15, of whom 12 are women.

The *Christian and Missionary Alliance* sent a party of three missionaries to Peru in 1925. The first station was opened in Huanuco among the uncivilized, sun-worshiping Campa Indians. This work was later (1934) turned over to another mission. In 1930 the station at Lima was opened, and for fourteen years the Mission served the entire evangelical cause of Peru through its *Peruvian Bible Institute,* which is now independent. With almost 100 congregations in its four main centers, the Christian and Missionary Alliance is one of the largest missions operating in Peru.

The British branch of the *Evangelical Union of South America* also entered Peru in the 1920's, and since that time has been working in close co-operation with the Christian and Missionary Alliance and the *Peruvian Evangelical Church.* This Church is completely indigenous. It has 309 congregations and is the largest evangelical group in the country.

Peru was one of the first fields entered by the *Independent Board for Presbyterian Foreign Missions.* Its work there began in 1935. Two stations are located at Lima and Huanta, but a January, 1959, report indicates that they now have no resident missionaries in Peru.

The *Wycliffe Bible Translators* entered Peru in 1946. It was the first South American country to be occupied by this Mission. At the end of ten years their linguists were at work in no fewer than 24 different tribes. In 1959 they reported that one tribe has the entire New Testament, now being published by the American Bible Society; two other tribes have two books of the New Testament; and at least one New Testament book has been translated for several other tribes. Altogether, 17 of Peru's jungle languages now possess selected portions of the Word of God while 2 other languages have preliminary drafts. Peru is also the international headquarters for the *Jungle Aviation and Radio Service* operated by Wycliffe Translators.

In recent years three Baptist societies from the United States have taken up work in this country. *Baptist Mid-Missions* has seven main stations, four of which are in the southeastern part of the country in jungle territory not far from the Bolivian border, where conditions are extremely primitive and the work is difficult. The *Association of Baptists for World Evangelism* has 22 missionaries in the country, all but two of them working among the jungle tribes of the Upper Amazon. The *Southern Baptists,* who entered in 1950, are just now getting under way. This society makes no attempt to observe mission comity. In Peru, as in other countries, they have opened churches in the larger cities where Christian work has been established for some time. Their three main centers of missionary residence are Arequipa, Lima, and Trujillo. Special features of the work are two bookstores and a radio ministry.

Other missions working in the country are *Christian Missions in Many Lands,* with resident missionaries in seven centers; the *Free Church of Scotland,* which has a boys' school in Lima; the *Irish Baptists,* whose main concern is the Indian tribes of the Lake Titicaca district; the *Pilgrim Holiness Church,* and the *Church of God.*

ECUADOR

Area: 105,000 sq. mi.   Population: 3,800,000
Capital: Quito   Religion: Roman
                                                    Catholicism

THE LAND. Ecuador borders on only two countries, Colombia on the north and Peru on the east and south. The Pacific Ocean is its western boundary. There are three rather definite geographical areas in Ecuador: the Coasta, or the coastal lowlands; the Sierra, the highlands of the Andes where 60 per cent of the people live; and the Oriente, the low tropical jungles of the Amazon basin lying east of the mountains.

POLITICAL HISTORY. Francisco Pizarro settled the country for Spain in 1532. In 1822 it joined the republic set up by Simon Bolivar in Colombia, but it seceded in 1830 and became an independent republic. Border disputes with Peru have been frequent and costly. In the latest (1942), Ecuador lost over half of its Amazonian territory.

THE PEOPLE. Ecuador is one of three countries in South America where the Indians predominate. The white inhabitants form about 10 per cent of the population, full-blooded Indians 40 per cent, and mestizos 50 per cent. The official language of the country is Spanish. Most of the Indians speak Quechua; but some of the tribes, such as the Jivaro of the Oriente, speak their own languages. Primary education is free and compulsory. Not all Indian children, however, are in school. The result is that about 40 per cent of the people over ten years of age are illiterate.

THE RELIGION. The Roman Catholic Church claims the majority of the people; but in actual fact it has not done much to win the Indians to Christianity. Though Ecuador is a Roman Catholic country there is genuine freedom of religion.

MISSIONS. In Ecuador, as in other countries of South America, *Mr. James Thompson* of the *British and Foreign Bible Society* was the pioneer Protestant missionary. The year was 1824. The place was Guayaquil, where he sold over 700 Bibles in a very short time. From there he went to Quito and thence to Colombia. Sixty years went by before another messenger of the Cross visited this long-neglected land. He was *Mr. Andrew Milne,* of the *American Bible Society,* who in 1886 visited Ecuador on a colportage tour of South America. Today the American Bible Society maintains a sub-agency in Quito with one full-time colporteur. The circulation of the Scriptures in 1958 amounted to 66,256 books.

The first society to undertake a continuing work seems to have been the *Gospel Missionary Union,* which despatched its first missionaries to Ecuador in 1896 just a few months after a revolution opened the country to Protestant missions. This Mission has work in three areas among three different types of people. The white and mixed races live in the lowlands, and many of these have turned to the Lord. In the highlands the Quechua Indians, descendants of the ancient Incas, form a large part of the population. Here little headway has been made and few converts have been won. In 1903 work was begun among the Jivaro Indian head-hunters on the upper reaches of the Amazon River, but for many years it proved to be barren and discouraging work. Only within the last decade has any fruit been seen. Nevertheless, today the Gospel Missionary Union is second only to the Christian and Missionary Alliance in size and strength. Its latest Report indicates 22 organized churches with an aggregate membership of 900 and a Christian community several times as large. Ecuador, with 59 missionaries, is the largest of six fields in which the Gospel Missionary Union is working.

Following hard on the heels of the Gospel Missionary Union was the *Christian and Missionary Alliance,* whose pioneer missionaries settled in Quito and Montecristi in 1897. At first, Roman Catholic persecution was so severe that only the timely intervention of the local police saved the missionaries from a violent death. In the early years the most effective means of spreading the gospel was by Scripture distribution, followed a little later by cottage meetings. It was quite some time before public meetings could be held. Converts were very few during this early period. Beginning about 1925 the work expanded to the mountain Indians, and from that time the Mission began to prosper. Three main stations were opened in the Sierra, and a short time later three additional ones were opened in the Oriente, giving the Mission a strong position in all three regions into which the country is divided. It took twelve years to win the first Jivaro Indian to Christ. Up to 1950, in all the Alliance work among the various Indian tribes there were fewer than 100 persons who had made an open confession of Christ, and most of these were won through school work. The Bible institute opened in Guayaquil in 1928 was moved to Los Cerros in 1947. The sixty or more churches brought into existence by the Christian and Missionary Alliance are all an integral part of the independent *National Confederation of Churches.*

Though the *Seventh Day Adventists* have been in Ecuador since 1906, their work there is much smaller than that in the neighboring country of Peru. Latest reports indicate that in the whole of their Ecuador Mission there are only eight churches. They do, however, make widespread use of literature.

Ecuador is the home of the world-famous radio station HCJB, the *Voice of the Andes,* the first radio station ever erected on the mission field. This independent agency, founded by *Clarence W. Jones* and *Reuben Larsen* and now known as the *World Radio Missionary Fellowship,* began broadcasting from Quito on Christmas Day, 1931. Like most missionary ventures, HCJB began on a modest scale, broadcasting the gospel locally on a 250-watt transmitter. Today it is interdenominational in character and world-wide in scope. Its staff comprises 140 foreign and 130 national workers. Located in Quito high up in the heart of the Andes Mountains, HCJB operates six transmitters on both long and short wave, with a round-the-clock schedule in eight different languages involving more than 2,400 separate broadcasts each month. HCJB has been decorated by the Ecuadorean government with several of its highest honors and has been given a renewed contract which extends to 1980. It has recently installed a 50,000-watt short-wave transmitter for more effective world coverage. The *Bible Institute of the Air,* introduced in 1949, has enrolled more than 25,000 students in 30 different countries on 5 continents. A medical department was added in 1949. The *Harry Rimmer Memorial Hospital* was opened in October, 1955. A second hospital, the *Epp Memorial Hospital,* was opened in May, 1958, at Shell Mera, the gateway to the jungle.

A fine example of interdenominational co-operation is the *United Andean Indian Mission* organized in 1945 by the Evangelical and Reformed Church, the Presbyterian Church, U.S.A., the Presbyterian Church, U.S., and the United Brethren. The Mission established its first station, Picalqui Farm, sixty miles north of Quito, in 1946. It has since established another station at Uyumbicho, sixteen miles south of Quito. By 1954, ten missionaries were attached to these two stations, where a fourfold program of evangelism, education, agriculture, and medicine is carried on.

The *Missionary Aviation Fellowship* has been operating in Ecuador since 1948, making it possible to open new stations in the heart of the jungle. In Amazonia an hour's flying time can save 100 man-hours on the trail. Other missions working in Ecuador are *Christian Missions in Many Lands, Church of the Brethren, Evangelical Mission Covenant Church,* and *World Mission Prayer League.* Several societies have entered during the past decade: the *Southern Baptists* and *Inter-American Missionary Society* (Oriental Missionary Society) in 1950, and *Wycliffe Bible Translators* in 1953.

Mention should be made of the five young men who gave their lives on Sunday, January 8, 1956, in a heroic attempt to take the gospel to the savage Auca Indians on the Curaray River in eastern Ecuador. *E. Edward McCully, Jr., Peter S. Fleming,* and *Philip James Elliot* were affiliated with the Plymouth Brethren (Christian Missions in Many Lands); *Roger Youderian* was a member of the Gospel Missionary Union; and *Nathanael Saint* was a pilot of the Missionary Aviation Fellowship. Their martyrdom, far from being a tragedy, was a triumph of the grace of God. With amazing faith and courage, the widows are carrying on. One of them, *Betty Elliot,* and *Rachel Saint,* sister of Nathanael Saint, have succeeded in making friendly contact with the Aucas who murdered their loved ones. In conditions incredibly primitive, they have lived among the Aucas for several months trying to convey to these savage people some concept of the love of God.

COLOMBIA

Area: 439,520 sq. mi.   Population: 13,700,000
Capital: Bogotá   Religion: Roman
                                              Catholicism

THE LAND. Colombia, situated on the northwest corner of the continent, is bounded by Venezuela and Brazil on the east, Ecuador and Peru on the south, Venezuela and the Caribbean Sea on the north, and the Pacific Ocean on the west.

POLITICAL HISTORY. After three hundred years of Spanish rule, Colombia gained its independence in 1819 under the leadership of Simon Bolivar. The officially constituted state of Greater Colombia included what is now Panama, Venezuela, and Ecuador. Venezuela and Ecuador withdrew in 1830; Panama followed suit in 1903.

THE PEOPLE. Whites and half-castes make up the bulk of the population. There are only 110,000 full-blooded Indians and about twice as many Negroes. Education is free but not compulsory. Most of the secondary schools are controlled by the Catholic Church. At the 1951 census an estimated 37 per cent of the population over seven years of age was illiterate. The language spoken is Spanish.

THE RELIGION. Colombia is a Roman Catholic country. Theoretically there is freedom of religion, but during the past decade the Protestant churches have suffered a great deal of persecution instigated by the Roman Catholic authorities. Between 1948 and 1956, forty-seven churches and chapels were completely destroyed by fire and dynamite, and scores of others were closed; over two hundred primary schools were closed, most of them by government order, the remainder by violence. Altogether, 78 Colombian Protestants, men, women, and children, were killed on account of their faith. Moreover, the government has declared two-thirds of Colombia "mission territories" open only to Roman Catholic missionaries. There is no Protestant radio voice in the country. The downfall of dictator General Pinilla in May, 1957, however, resulted in a decrease in violence against the Evangelicals, though some of the repressive decrees of the former regime remain. In the early part of 1959, Colombia relaxed its ban against new Protestant missionaries entering the country.

MISSIONS. Protestant Christianity was first introduced to Colombia by the *British and Foreign Bible Society* whose ubiquitous agent, *James Thompson*, arrived in Bogotá in 1825. As elsewhere in South America, he was accorded a warm welcome, but not for long. The Roman Catholic authorities turned against him and made it impossible for him to carry on. Some thirty years later, in 1856, the Bible

Society despatched its first permanent agent, *Mr. A. J. Duffield,* to Colombia.

Protestant missionary work began in 1856 with the arrival of *Rev. Henry B. Pratt* of the *Presbyterian Church, U.S.A.,* who was responsible for the translation of the Spanish Moderna Version of the Bible from the original languages, the first edition of which was published in 1893. For the first twenty years, progress was slow, but after that reinforcements arrived and the Mission began to prosper. For a time the Southern Presbyterians maintained a work at Barranquilla but it was turned over to the Presbyterian Church, U.S.A., in 1888. Owing to the discrimination suffered by Protestant children in Catholic schools, it has been necessary for the Presbyterians in Colombia to operate one of the most complete systems of general education to be found among Presbyterians in Latin America. On the primary level they have 17 schools, most of them closely church-related. The apex of their educational work is found in three very fine secondary institutions, the *Colegios Americanos* at Bogatá, Barranquilla, and Girardót, which have a combined enrollment of 1,800. A milestone was reached in July, 1959, when the Mission and the Church became integrated. The Church is now responsible for the entire program in Colombia, including educational, medical, and evangelistic work. The 34 missionaries, now called fraternal workers, are under the supervision of the Synod of the *Presbyterian Church of Colombia.* There are 23 organized churches with an aggregate membership of 1,250.

The *Gospel Missionary Union,* which was the pioneering society in neighboring Ecuador, extended its work to Colombia in 1908. *Charles P. Chapman* and *John Funk* formed the vanguard. For two years they engaged in preaching and colportage work in more than 150 towns and villages; but it was not until 1912 that the Colombia mission was really established. A printing plant was set up and a monthly paper, *El Mensaje,* and other literature were published. A Bible school with a five-year course was opened to train young men and women to be pastors, teachers, and evangelists. Largely through the ministry of these graduates the work has grown until today there are 22 organized churches and 200 preaching chapels in various stages of spiritual development. Baptized church members total almost 4,000. The indigenous Church supports its own missionary program with commendable zeal and not a little success. A hospital and four dispensaries minister to the physical needs of Christians and non-Christians alike. Twenty-one elementary schools and one middle school represent the extent of the educational program.

The Evangelical Alliance Mission enterprise in Colombia was an extension of its larger work in neighboring Venezuela. Pioneers in Colombia were *Mr. and Mrs. John Christiansen,* who began preaching services in rented buildings in Cucuta in 1918. It was not until five years later, when *Mr. and Mrs. Olav Eikland* took up residence in this city, that the work was placed on a permanent basis. Cucuta remains the headquarters of the Mission in Colombia. Three other stations are each occupied by a missionary couple.

The work of the *Christian and Missionary Alliance* in Colombia started as an extension of their fine mission in Ecuador. In 1924 missionaries crossed the border and established the first station in the city of Ipiales. So strong was Roman Catholic opposition that on one occasion it was necessary for the missionaries to take refuge in Ecuador for two weeks until the storm blew over. As the work progressed other areas were opened up, and today the Alliance has work in five departments of the country and the Intendencia de Amazonas. *La Aurora Bookstore* in Cali not only supplies Christian literature for all missions in Colombia but also distributes Alliance literature to more than ten countries in Latin America. The Bible institute at Armenia, opened in 1933, continues to furnish pastors and evangelists for some 24 organized churches, more than 60 other worship centers, and over 150 outstations.

The *Worldwide Evangelization Crusade* has been at work in the Bogotá region since 1932 when Colombia was considered to be the least evangelized of all the South American countries. It was some time before any appreciable progress was made. The work today includes a Bible school, a maternity center, a printing press, and 30 churches, the largest of which is in Bogotá. The churches are completely indigenous.

The *Assemblies of God* opened their first station at Sogamoso in 1932. There they built a church, a mission house, and a school. A Bible school was opened in 1943, and in 1955 a second center was occupied. Owing to the ban on the entrance of new missionaries, the Assemblies of God, like other mission societies, were unable to augment their missionary staff, and the work has lagged. After 25 years of hard work there is only a small nucleus of believers in the charge of a national minister assisted by a lay preacher. The missionary staff consists of five persons.

The *South America Indian Mission* has been working among the Aruac and Goajira Indians in the northern part of the country for twenty-five years. It has also established work among the Colombians. National workers have been trained and given responsibility over local congregations. The Gospel of John has been translated into Goajira. The Mission has four missionaries on the field.

Colombia is the only country in South America in which the *Latin America Mission* has permanent church work. It was begun in 1938. Education and evangelistic work have been the Mission's chief concern. The former embraces 12 primary schools and one middle school. Twenty-six organized churches account for 650 baptized believers. Half of the full-time national workers are engaged in teaching. Other institutions include two dispensaries, a Bible school, and a teacher training institute.

During the last two decades the *Southern Baptist Convention* has opened up a large number of new fields, eight of them in Latin America. The first of these was Colombia, which they entered in 1942. Significant gains have been registered in the urban centers of population. Twenty-four missionaries are divided among four main stations. In Barranquilla, where the work began, are located nine of Colombia's 27 Baptist churches. Medical work revolves around the *Baptist Hospital*, also in Barranquilla. The *International Baptist Theological Seminary* in Cali has 25 students from six countries. Twenty-six elementary schools with a total of 1,500 pupils form the backbone of the educational system. The one middle school is a small one with only 18 students. A well-stocked bookroom in Barranquilla serves the evangelical constituency in the northern half of the country.

The American branch of the *Evangelical Union of South America* entered Colombia in 1942. Since that time it has concentrated all its efforts in the department of Magdalena in the extreme northeast corner of the country bordering on Venezuela. Seven churches and 35 unorganized congregations are ministered to by 19 missionaries and 8 national workers.

When World War II threatened to cut off missionary work in the Far East, the *Oriental Missionary Society,* founded in 1901 for work in Japan, decided to look around for other fields to conquer. In 1943 Colombia became the first of four fields in the southern part of the Western Hemisphere to receive missionaries of the Oriental Missionary Society, known in this part of the world as the *Inter-American Missionary Society.* Its main contribution is by means of the *Christaline Bible Institute* and the *Bible Seminary* in Medellin.

There are seven or eight other societies working in Colombia. The *Wesleyan Methodist Missionary Society* and the *Mennonite Church of North America* have three churches each in Colombia. The *Seventh Day Adventists* are one of the larger missions, having some 6,500 members. The *Association of Baptists for World Evangelism* has one couple on the field at present. The *New Tribes Mission* has work among four tribes with one or more churches in each. Two

Lutheran groups, the *Evangelical Lutheran Church* and the *United Evangelical Lutheran Church,* between them support five missionaries in the country. The *Cumberland Presbyterian Church* reports 25 places of worship. In spite of adverse economic conditions and widespread persecution which included the closing of many churches, Scripture distribution increased almost 50 per cent between 1950 and 1956.

VENEZUELA

Area: 352,000 sq. mi.	Population: 6,130,000
Capital: Caracas	Religion: Roman Catholicism

THE LAND. The Caribbean Sea forms the northern boundary of Venezuela, the northernmost country of South America. British Guiana lies to the east, Brazil to the south, and Colombia to the southwest and west. The land is extremely rich. It is second only to the United States in its production of oil, producing 2,750,000 barrels a day; it abounds in the agricultural resources of coffee, sugar, cacao, balata, hides, and rubber; and it possesses natural resources in the form of diamonds, gold, iron, copper, and coal. Transportation is also good. There are 12,000 miles of roads and it boasts the second largest river system in South America, in the Orinoco River and its tributaries.

POLITICAL HISTORY. Led by Simon Bolivar, Venezuela achieved its independence from Spain about 1821; but it did not become an independent republic until 1830, when it seceded from the Federation of Greater Colombia. The present Constitution, adopted in 1953, guarantees many basic rights such as private property, education, employment, health, and fair labor practices. The iron and oil industries have produced South America's one booming economy. Half of the oil revenue goes to the government to be used for public works and welfare.

THE PEOPLE. Sixty-five per cent of the population is mestizo, 20 per cent white, 8 per cent Negro, and 7 per cent Indian. The Indians are mostly confined to the remote interior sections where they speak their own dialects. Spanish is the language of the country. All education is free, and primary and secondary education is compulsory. Caracas, the capital, has a population of 1,000,000. Of all the countries on the Caribbean, Venezuela received the largest number of

European immigrants both before and after World War II, and a large number of them were professional people such as engineers, doctors, and architects.

THE RELIGION. The majority of the people are Roman Catholics. The government, however, is anticlerical, imposing no restrictions on Protestant work except in the Indian territories, which are under the authority of the Roman Catholic Church.

MISSIONS. *Christian Missions in Many Lands* seems to have been the first Protestant society to take up work in Venezuela. The first missionaries arrived in 1883 and began work in the capital city of Caracas. Their work has continued to the present time, and today they have resident missionaries in seven main centers.

The *Presbyterian Church, U.S.A.* began missionary work in Venezuela in 1897. Its first church in Caracas was built around a nucleus of believers led to Christ by a railroad official who died of tuberculosis at the early age of twenty-four. To date, Presbyterian work has been confined to the small state of Miranda, which includes the Federal District of Caracas. The Presbytery of Venezuela has 9 churches with an average membership of 60 persons each. In Venezuela the Presbyterian Church is largely a city church, centered in Caracas and dominated by the influence of a single congregation, *El Redentor*. Only a few years ago a *Christian Rural Center* was opened at Ocumare in the southern part of the state; already it is becoming a base for training young men who will serve as lay evangelists in the isolated villages of rural Venezuela. Following the pattern used elsewhere, the Presbyterians have built up a strong educational system, the capstone of which is the *Colegio Americano* in Caracas. A sister school of the same name but much smaller is located in Guatire. The Mission is now moving towards integration with the Church and has recently transferred various responsibilities to the Presbytery. The *Evangelical Bookstore* in Caracas is the only one of its kind in the country.

Venezuela was the first South American field to be entered by *The Evangelical Alliance Mission*. The first station was opened at Maracaibo in 1906 by *Mr. and Mrs. T. J. Bach* and *Mr. and Mrs. John Christiansen*. The following year they launched *La Estrella de la Mañana* (The Morning Star), Venezuela's oldest evangelical periodical, a biweekly with a present circulation of 6,000. Maracaibo remains the headquarters of the Mission's work. The second largest station is San Cristóbal, where the Bible school is situated. In addition they have missionaries stationed at 17 other centers. There are

60 churches, most of them self-supporting; and through national leadership they are reaching out in a vigorous effort to win their own people to Christ. Other activities include evangelism, radio, literature, day and normal schools, and an aggressive ministry among children.

In 1915 *Van and Vera Eddings* went out to Venezuela as independent missionaries and began work on the island of Margarita. From there they moved to Carupano on the mainland where they spent the remainder of their first term of service. Upon returning to the United States in 1920, they organized the *Orinoco River Mission.* Back on the field for a second term they found the going rough. They were stoned, mobbed, and plotted against; and on one occasion they saw their chapel destroyed by a mob led by the local priest. But the brave couple carried on and little groups of believers were formed. The first convention of churches was held in 1936 on the island of Margarita with 40 delegates in attendance. Today there are 55 missionaries on 13 stations in five states in eastern Venezuela. Field headquarters is located at Ciudad Bolivar. Three thousand believers are organized into 40 congregations. The Mission has no medical work. A modest educational program includes five schools, one of which is a high school. A Bible institute and a bookstore play an important part in the training of national leaders and the building up of a strong Christian constituency. A gospel launch, acquired in 1952, enables the missionaries to reach many remote and hitherto inaccessible towns and villages along the Orinoco River.

Pentecostal work in Venezuela was started by independent missionaries who went out without the backing of any board. *Mr. and Mrs. Gottfried F. Bender,* first of the group to affiliate with the *Assemblies of God,* had located as early as 1919 in Barquisimeto, where they established the first evangelical work in that city. In the mid-twenties a second station was opened in Coro, where there had been no Protestant work of any kind. An assembly was opened in Caracas in 1940 and in Valencia in 1945, and later on another was begun in Ciudad Bolivar. In 1947 these thriving churches were formally united into a central church organization called the *National Convention of the Assemblies of God in Venezuela.* The following year a Bible school was organized in Barquisimeto. Today the Assemblies of God have a flourishing work in Venezuela where their full-time national workers outnumber the missionaries four to one. There are 45 organized churches and 115 outstations in various stages of spiritual maturity.

Of the five fields worked by the *Evangelical Free Church of America,* Venezuela is the only one in South America. Its work here was inherited from another mission in 1920. After thirty-five years of work they reported 40 congregations in the central part of the country but only 3 full-time national workers. A much-needed Bible institute, opened at Maracay in 1954, will doubtless help to solve their greatest problem, a paucity of national leaders. Present plans call for a high school as soon as funds are available.

The work of *Baptist Mid-Missions* in Venezuela began in 1924 in the mining town of El Callao in the state of Bolivar. After five churches had been established in this area, the Mission in 1940 advanced into the delta region of the Orinoco and established work in the capital of Tucupita. In 1950 they began work among the Guarao Indians in the same region. Several attempts have been made since 1950 to begin work in the Gran Sabana near the borders of Brazil, but Roman Catholic obstructionism closed the doors, and the missionaries had to withdraw.

In 1949 the *Southern Baptist Convention* launched new missions in three countries of Latin America, one of which was Venezuela. During the first decade of this work they have been opening new churches at the rate of one every eight months. As yet there is only one elementary school and no medical work. Evangelistic work centers in four large cities. Institutions include a Bible institute at Caracas and a bookstore in Valencia.

Venezuela is the largest of nine fields in which the *New Tribes Mission* is working. Its sole purpose is to take the gospel to the many isolated, uncivilized tribes often neglected or bypassed by other missions. Its present staff of missionaries in Venezuela numbers 46. They are hard at work in five Indian tribes. They have a small group of believers among the Guajibo; in two other tribes they already have established churches.

Other missions working in Venezuela are *Canadian Brethren, International Church of the Foursquare Gospel, Seventh Day Adventists,* and *United World Mission.*

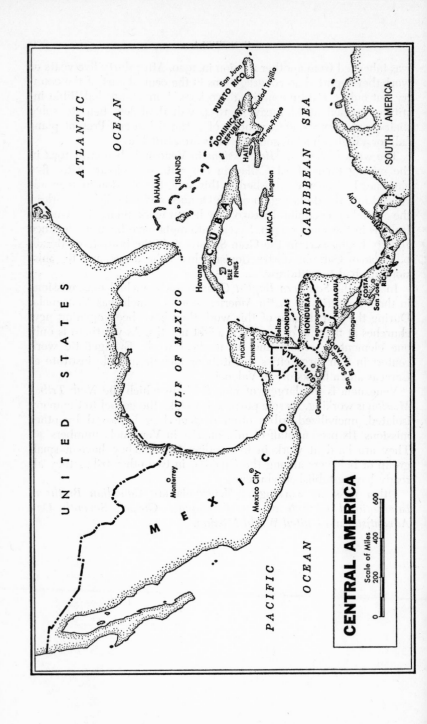

XXII

CENTRAL AMERICA

MEXICO

Area: 760,000 sq. mi.   Population: 31,500,000
Capital: Mexico City   Religion: Roman
                                                         Catholicism

THE LAND. Mexico is our next-door neighbor to the south. It is separated from the United States by the Rio Grande. On the south it
is bounded by Guatemala, on the east by the Caribbean Sea and the
Gulf of Mexico, and on the west by the Pacific Ocean. The interior
is a high plateau averaging 5,000 feet above sea level on which the
principal cities are located. One of them, Mexico City, is said to
be the oldest metropolis on the continent.

POLITICAL HISTORY. Mexico's history may be divided into four periods: the pre-colonial period of Indian rule, of which we know little;
the colonial period under Spanish rule from 1520 to 1810; the period
of nation formation from 1810 to 1910; and the present period which
began with the social revolution of 1911–12.

THE PEOPLE. At least 60 per cent of the population of Mexico is
mestizo. About 30 per cent is pure Indian and the remaining 10 per
cent is of unmixed European descent. Spanish is the official language, but the hundred-odd Indian tribes speak their own languages
and dialects, many of which have not yet been reduced to writing.
More than 700,000 speak the Aztec language, and 300,000 speak
Mayan.

THE RELIGION. Roman Catholicism is the prevailing religion but the
Constitution of 1857 separated the Church from the State. The
governing party came into power over forty years ago as a revolutionary movement. From the beginning it was anticlerical and

401

severely limited the power of the Roman Catholic Church. It seized church property and forbade the wearing of religious garb in public. Today it is more moderate, having lost a good deal of its revolutionary zeal. With the election of President Ruiz Cortinez in July, 1952, Mexico took on a new look. The government returned the land and property it had confiscated in 1934. All such land and property may now be used for educational and medical purposes by Mexican laymen in accordance with Mexican law. All educational work must be secular. Mexican law forbids foreigners to exercise ecclesiastical authority, which means that missionaries cannot hold office in the Church, administer baptism, or conduct Communion services. Radio evangelism is not permitted. Of recent years the Roman Catholic Church has taken advantage of the increasing tolerance of the government to strengthen its position and regain some of its lost prestige. In some rural areas the Evangelicals have been persecuted and some of them have suffered death. Nevertheless, the evangelical constituency continues to grow. There is no restriction on Christian literature, and in 1956 the American Bible Society distributed over half a million copies of the Scriptures in Mexico.

EARLY MISSIONS. The first Protestant thrust into Mexico came in 1826 when the *American Bible Society* sent its first shipment of Bibles to that country. The distribution of the Scriptures was greatly increased during the war between Mexico and the United States in 1846–48. In 1860 the Bible Society despatched an agent to that country. During the Civil War *Rev. James Hickey*, for political reasons, fled from Texas to Mexico. In Monterrey he became an agent for the Bible Society and succeeded in forming a Protestant congregation; but it was not until 1878 that a permanent agency was established. *Arthur Gore* was its first secretary.

To a woman goes the honor of being the first Protestant missionary to Mexico. In 1852, when Mexico was still closed to Protestant work, *Miss Melinda Rankin* opened a school for Mexicans at Brownsville, Texas, on the American side of the Rio Grande. After some years there she moved into Mexico and established a school at Monterrey in 1855. She began as an independent missionary but later affiliated herself with an undenominational organization, the *American and Foreign Christian Union*, whose chief purpose was evangelical work among Roman Catholics. In 1873, because of financial stringency, the Mission turned Miss Rankin's work at Monterrey over to the *American Board of Commissioners for Foreign Missions*.

The American Board began its work in Mexico in 1872. The first two missionaries, *Rev. J. L. Stephens* and *Rev. D. F. Watkins*, organized a church in Guadalajara. Mob violence incited by the local Roman Catholic priest resulted in the death of Mr. Stephens and his Mexican evangelist; but the work prospered in spite of continued persecution. The American Board now has three couples in Mexico making a valuable contribution in the fields of church administration, young people's work, training in stewardship, and education. These missionaries act as a bridge between the substantial American community and the Mexicans. Two fine schools, *Instituto Colon* in Guadalajara and *Colegio El Pacifico* in Mazatlán, have a combined enrollment of 800 and are now firmly under Mexican trusteeship and management.

In 1870 the *American Baptist Home Missionary Society* established a mission in Monterrey. Later on, the work spread to Guadalupe and Mexico City.

Two Presbyterian missions entered Mexico in the 1870's. The *Northern Presbyterians* (now the United Presbyterian Church in the U.S.A.) sent four couples to Mexico City in 1872. A year later the *Southern Presbyterians* opened a field in the southern part of Mexico. After nearly thirty years of work these two groups merged in 1901 to form the Synod of Mexico. In 1947 the General Assembly, comprising 11 presbyteries, was inaugurated. Today, with 80,000 members and a constituency three times that number, the *National Presbyterian Church of Mexico* is the largest Presbyterian Church in Spanish-speaking Latin America. It is almost equal to the Methodist, Baptist, and Congregational Churches combined. All institutions are now under the jurisdiction of the National Church.

Theological training on the less advanced level is conducted in five Bible schools. The *Presbyterian Theological Seminary* in Mexico City is the largest in the Caribbean area, and the president and most of the faculty are Mexicans. There is also a rural seminary in Yucatán which trains leaders for the Mayan churches. Medical work includes three hospitals and a number of dispensaries. The missionaries for the most part are doing evangelistic work in the outlying states of Yucatán, Tabasco, and Oaxaca. The monumental task of translating the New Testament into the Mayan language was completed in 1957. Work is now proceeding on the Zapoteca New Testament. The Gulf Presbytery has few organized churches and fewer ordained ministers, but the amazing number of small congregations served by unordained presbyters makes it one of the strongest presbyteries of the General Assembly. The Mission in 1957 transferred to the General Assembly full administrative responsibility for all mission property in the Federal District. Full integration is impossible at present, "not because the Mission does not desire it, but because much of the leadership of the Church herself seems to be fearful of it."[1]

The *Methodist Episcopal Church* and the *Methodist Episcopal Church, South,* both began work in Mexico in 1873. *Dr. William Butler* pioneered for the former and *Bishop John C. Keener* for the latter. The Southern Church concentrated on the northern section of the country while the Northern Church confined its efforts to the Federal District and nearby states. In 1930 the two constituencies merged to form the completely autonomous *Methodist Church of Mexico.* In recent years progress has been rapid. In a fifteen-year period ending in 1954, 250 new church organizations were added. Church membership doubled during the same period; it now stands at 27,000.

The Methodist work is divided into two Annual Conferences, each with three districts. Forty-four missionaries, most of them from the Woman's Division, are serving in all six districts. Here also the Methodists have built up a fine educational system, including many schools of higher learning. The one hospital, *Sanatorio Palmore* in Chihuahua, is one of the few places in Mexico where Protestant nurses can train in an evangelical atmosphere. The *Union Theological Seminary* in Mexico City is sponsored jointly by the Methodists, Congregationalists, and Disciples. The Methodists also have a large publishing house there.

The *American Episcopal Church* has had a continuing work in Mexico since 1875, when it linked up with an existing group known as the *Church of Jesus,* which had been founded some years before by a converted Dominican friar, *Rev. Manuel Aguas.* Known today as the *Mexican Episcopal Church,* it has 43 churches and a membership of 2,500. At present only one American missionary is serving with this Church, though a good deal of financial aid is still provided.

Mexico was the first of thirteen countries in Latin America to engage the attention of the Southern Baptists. Their first missionary, *John O. Westrupp,* arrived on the field in 1880. Through the years they have maintained a strong staff, with the result that now they have 275 chapels and almost 100 organized churches with a total membership of 8,000. Mexican law prohibits evangelical schools; consequently the Mission has had to resort to student hostels, of which there are six now in operation. They have their own theological seminary in Mexico City, also two bookstores and a print shop. The missionary staff of 44 is divided among eight main stations.

---

[1] *121st Annual Report of Board of Foreign Missions of the Presbyterian Church in U.S.A.* (1958), p. 100.

PENTECOSTAL MISSIONS. All evangelical denominations in Mexico are experiencing rapid growth; but the independent sects, Pentecostal in varying degrees, are growing even more rapidly. These sects are completely indigenous, something that appeals to the Mexican people at this stage of their development.

The emotional, deeply spiritual and basically friendly nature of the Latin, is drawn to the Pentecostal type of worship, to the emphasis on faith healing, and to the warm and intimate fellowship of these sects. Other denominations have much to learn from the sects in the training and use of lay leadership, evangelistic zeal, and faithfulness in prayer.[2]

The first Pentecostal missionary arrived in Mexico in 1915. He was followed by other independent workers, none of whom stayed very long. In 1919 *Cesareo Burciaga,* a Mexican who had been converted to Christ in Houston, Texas, returned to Mexico and settled down in the city of Ciudad Muzquiz, where he founded the first permanent Pentecostal assembly and built the first chapel. With the help of other nationals he organized many other Assemblies of God in Mexico. In 1921, through the ministry of an American missionary, *Mrs. Anna Sanders,* a Pentecostal assembly was started in Mexico City. Ten years later a national organization was formed and registered with the government as *The Assemblies of God in Mexico.* From the beginning, this organization has been in the hands of nationals. The secret of its growth lies, no doubt, in the emphasis on theological training. Five Bible schools are conducted for the training of new workers. They have a total enrollment of 140. It is not surprising to find that according to latest reports the Assemblies of God, with only six missionaries, have 450 organized churches and 300 outstations under the care of 295 ordained ministers and 400 lay workers.

Four other Pentecostal groups are working in Mexico. Two of them have such extensive work that the field is divided into four districts. They are the *Church of the Nazarene* with 191 churches and the *Church of God* with 325 churches. In addition there are the *Pentecostal Holiness Church* and the *International Church of the Foursquare Gospel.* Total Pentecostal adherents in Mexico are estimated at 100,000.

INDIAN MISSIONS. Several societies are working exclusively among the one hundred or more Indian tribes of Mexico. The first of these was the *Mexican Indian Mission* founded by *James Gary Dale,* who had

[2] *117th Annual Report of Board of Foreign Missions of the Presbyterian Church in U.S.A.* (1954), p. 92.

been in Mexico since 1899 and who was released by the Associate Reformed Presbyterian Board to open a faith work among the neglected Indians. In 1931, at sixty years of age, Dr. Dale opened the first station of the new mission in the village of Tamazunchale in the heart of the Huasteca country. Today Tamazunchale, with its dozen or more buildings, is the nerve center of an ever-expanding work which has now reached out into seven of Mexico's twenty-eight states. The Bible school there has graduated more than 60 pastors and evangelists who are caring for the spiritual needs of 12,000 converts scattered over 200 preaching points.

Referring to missions that serve in remote tribes, honorable mention must made of *Wycliffe Bible Translators,* founded in 1934 by *L. L. Legters* and *W. Cameron Townsend.* As its name suggests, this agency is engaged almost exclusively in linguistic and literary work on the mission field and is dedicated to the high task of giving the Word of God to the approximately 2,000 tribes of the world still without a knowledge of God. With modern scientific methods and old-fashioned missionary zeal they believe this can be accomplished in this generation. The unusually rapid growth of this unique society, with its scientific approach to the problem of Bible translation, its many miraculous answers to prayer, the favor it enjoys with foreign governments usually hostile to the evangelical cause, its pioneering spirit, its apostolic zeal and high purpose, is one of the most significant events of the missionary movement in the mid-twentieth century.

Today Wycliffe Bible Translators have 785 active missionaries working among nearly 200 different tribes on eleven mission fields of the world. Already they have translated the Scriptures into 100 languages and dialects. The entire New Testament has been published in seven languages; and at least eight other New Testaments in first draft are undergoing further revision before publication. In addition, the Mission operates 18 aircraft in four countries. Each summer Wycliffe Bible Translators conduct three Summer Institutes of Linguistics in the United States, at the Universities of North Dakota, Oklahoma, and Washington, and a language course in London, England. In 1959 the combined enrollment was 503.

It all began back in 1935 in Mexico. The first missionaries were *Mr. and Mrs. Townsend* and *Kenneth Pike.* For eleven years Mexico was their only field, and it is still their largest, having more workers than any other. It is also the site of the Jungle Training Camp at which all new missionaries get their basic training. At present 218 translators are working in 80 different Indian dialects. Thousands of converts have been made, and a strong indigenous church has been established among the Tzeltal and other tribes.

The *Seventh Day Adventists* have a large and flourishing work in Mexico, where the field is divided into six missions. Almost 200 churches represent a membership of 20,000—and this in spite of the fact that they have very little educational work and only one hospital.

The *American Bible Society* continues its splendid work in Mexico. Besides supplying Scriptures to the many evangelical missions it employs ten full-time colporteurs. In 1956 it established a colportage training school in the capital and called it the *Francisco G. Penzotti Institute*.

The *Missionary Aviation Fellowship* began service in Mexico in 1946 with one airplane and a Christian airman. Two more airplanes and the necessary personnel were added later on as the Fellowship expanded its program of serving other missions. It is now providing air transportation for all evangelical missions in Mexico. In the Tabasco area alone, over thirty Presbyterian churches, isolated by jungle and swamps, have built their own air strips so that the missionary may "drop in" on them for a visit.

Mexico is only one of six fields in which the Missionary Aviation Fellowship is working. With a total staff of 64, it operates 20 airplanes in Mexico, Ecuador, Honduras, Brazil, Sudan, and New Guinea. Scarcely fifteen years old, it has already established branches in London and Melbourne. The Australian branch is responsible for New Guinea, and the British branch is operating in the Sudan.

Missionary Aviation Fellowship grew out of a vision given to several United States airmen in World War II. Soon after his release from the Navy *James C. Truxton* set out to interview mission leaders on the subject of missionary aviation. He was encouraged by their enthusiastic response and immediately laid plans for the formation of a unique missionary agency which would act as an air-arm for evangelical missions working in the jungle areas of Central and South America. Technical standards are set above commercial licensing level for both flying and maintenance, and each pilot is expected to act as his own mechanic. Some formal Bible training is also required. Above all, the Fellowship has made it clear that it does not want adventurers but fully qualified pilots with a passion for missions. To help produce this kind of pilot the *Moody Bible Institute* introduced a Missionary Aviation Course, the only one of its kind in the world.

Other missions in Mexico include the *Associate Reformed Presbyterian Church, Free Methodist Church of North America, Latin*

American Lutheran Mission, Reformed Church in America, World Mission Prayer League, Central American Mission, and *Conservative Baptist Home Mission Society.*

GUATEMALA

Area: 42,000 sq. mi.   Population: 3,350,000
Capital: Guatemala City   Religion: Roman
                                                     Catholicism

THE LAND. Guatemala is located immediately south of Mexico, with El Salvador and Honduras bordering it on the southeast, and British Honduras wedged in between its northeastern border and the Caribbean Sea. Guatemala is a land of mountains and smoking volcanoes, rivers, lakes, and tropical lowlands. Interestingly enough, it is the birthplace of Indian corn.

POLITICAL HISTORY. In pre-colonial days Guatemala was the center of the ancient Mayan Empire, which flourished during the first millennium of the Christian era. Its colonial history began when the Spanish invaders from Mexico subdued the country in 1524 and lasted for three centuries, during which political and economic oppression was the order of the day. The modern period began in 1821 when Guatemala severed connections with Spain. The republic was established in 1839 after having been part of the Confederation of Central America for eighteen years.

THE PEOPLE. Guatemala is more distinctly Indian than any other Central American republic. About 55 per cent of the people are pure Indian and belong to 21 different groups descended from the Maya-Quiché tribe. Ten per cent are full-blooded whites, and the remainder are mostly Ladinos, a mixture of Indian and Spanish blood with the Indian strain predominating.

THE RELIGION. Ninety per cent of the Guatemalans are Roman Catholic, but all other creeds have liberty of worship. The Constitution states that "discrimination by reason of relationship, sex, race, class, religious belief, or political ideas is illegal." The government permits complete freedom of religion, including radio evangelism, the distribution of literature, and public meetings. The Roman Catholic Church has tried hard to get religious instruction into the schools. In 1958 the new government broke a seventy-year separation of

Church and State rule by permitting the teaching of Catholicism in all public schools. Later on the Protestants were given the same privilege. The Catholic Church has almost doubled the number of priests and nuns in the country in recent years.

MISSIONS. Protestant missions in Guatemala began in a rather strange way. In 1881 President Don Justo Rufino Barrios, known as the Lincoln of Guatemala and convinced that the liberating influence of Protestant Christianity would be beneficial to his country, entered into negotiations with the *Presbyterian Board of Foreign Missions* in New York. The following spring, while on a diplomatic mission to Washington, he conferred personally with *Rev. John C. Hill*, a young Presbyterian minister already commissioned for China. So eager was the president to achieve his goal with all haste that he made Mr. Hill a member of his official party and took him back to Guatemala. That was the beginning of Protestant missions in that country. Except for one or two short periods, the Presbyterian Board has maintained a staff in Guatemala for over seventy-five years and is now one of the leading Protestant groups in the country. Its 57 organized churches and 154 unorganized groups represent a Christian community of about 15,000. The Presbyterian Synod is composed of five presbyteries and is the highest judiciary of Presbyterianism in Guatemala. The Church is growing rapidly in strength and numbers. Its forte is its evangelistic spirit and its truly indigenous nature. The *Diamond Jubilee Report* states: "There is no doubt that in Guatemala, taking into account the size of the country, the impact of the Gospel has been as great in proportion as in any other Latin American country."[3] Its medical service is centered in the *American Hospital* in Guatemala City. It has a number of rural schools and two middle schools, one in Quezaltenángo and the other in the capital. Government requirements and the rising standards of public health and education are making it increasingly difficult for institutions of this kind to hold their own. A fruitful form of witness, the only one of its kind in the country, is the *Presbyterian University Center* for the 4,000 university students in the capital. Indian work centers in two institutes, the *Mam Christian Center* and the *Quiché Bible Institute*. The *Primitive Methodists* share in the work of the latter.

The second mission to begin work in Guatemala was the *Central American Mission*, an interdenominational faith mission whose workers are found in all five republics of Central America and in Mexico.

[3] *121st Annual Report of Board of Foreign Missions of the Presbyterian Church in U.S.A.* (1958), p. 96.

Guatemala was the fourth one to be entered. It received its first Central American Mission workers in 1899 when *Mr. A. E. Bishop* and his family moved from Honduras to Guatemala City, where he remained for the forty-five years of his remarkable missionary career of rare achievement. The Mission's largest work is in Guatemala, where it has 55 missionaries and 12 stations. From the beginning it has made every effort to establish strong indigenous churches. Baptized church members total 8,000; in 1955 they gave $109,500 for the support of their own work. Much of the Mission's success along indigenous lines is accounted for by the emphasis placed on the training of national leaders. For this purpose the Mission has maintained two well-established Bible institutes. The smaller and older one is the *Robinson Bible Institute* for dialect-speaking Indians at Panajachel. Its main source of national workers for the Spanish-speaking peoples of all six republics is the *Central American Mission Bible Institute* in Guatemala City. Since its opening in 1929 well over 500 young men and women have studied there. Another area in which this Mission has achieved a good record is in the field of Bible translation. The first work of this kind was the translation of the New Testament into the Cakchiquel dialect. This was undertaken by *Mr. W. Cameron Townsend,* who later became the founder of Wycliffe Bible Translators, and was completed in 1931. In 1938 the New Testament in the Mam dialect was published, a product of collaboration between the Presbyterian Mission and the Central American Mission. The New Testament in the "Conob," or K'anjobal dialect was finished in 1953. The Mission has also done some fine work in radio evangelism. Station TGNA in Guatemala City, which has been on the air since August, 1950, is owned and operated by the Central American Mission.

The first missionaries of the *Assemblies of God* settled in Jutiapa in 1937. There they linked up with several indigenous Pentecostal assemblies already in existence. After a few months they moved to the capital and made it the headquarters of the Mission. From its inception, the work of the Assemblies of God in Guatemala has been carried on by nationals, and at no time has the Mission had more than a dozen missionaries on the field. For several years their national leaders were trained in the Bible school in El Salvador; but since 1950 Guatemala has had its own Bible school. Its current expenses are met largely through the offerings of staple foodstuffs given by the local churches, of which there are almost one hundred. In the Guatemalan Assemblies of God, ordained and licensed ministers outnumber organized churches—a rare phenomenon on the mission field. Other Pentecostal groups working in the country are the *Church of the Nazarene* (66 churches), the *Church of God* (118 churches), and the *International Church of the Foursquare Gospel*, whose work has just begun.

The *Lutheran Church-Missouri Synod* sent its first missionary, *Rev. Robert F. Gussick*, to Guatemala in 1947 in answer to three distinct calls from three different groups speaking three different languages and belonging to three different nationalities. Work is now being done in Guatemala City, Zacapa, Puerto Barrios, and Antigua. In the villages the work is done largely by lay workers who are native Guatemalans. An agricultural evangelist, *Reuben Tafelmeyer*, serves at least a dozen villages in the Zacapa area where he teaches Guatemalan farmers better methods of farming, poultry raising, well digging, etc. A medical mission carried on for some time in a resort hotel was discontinued during the revolution in 1954. The Mission hopes to resume the medical work early in 1960.

The *Southern Baptists* entered Guatemala in 1949. As yet they have no medical or educational work in that country. Church work, however, has made rapid progress; at the end of the first decade they were able to report 19 organized churches and 45 preaching points, none of which is as yet self-supporting. Missionary personnel is confined to the capital where they have a Bible institute, a bookstore, and a student home.

The *California Yearly Meeting of Friends* has had work in Guatemala since 1902, and today reports a Christian community of 12,000. Mention should also be made of a purely indigenous group known as the *Evangelical Church in Guatemala*, whose present membership is around 10,000. The *Primitive Methodists* have been in the country since 1922, and *Wycliffe Bible Translators* since 1952. Other missions having work in the country are the *Seventh Day Adventists*, *United World Mission*, and *Emmanuel Association*.

In May, 1957, the evangelical churches of Guatemala celebrated their Diamond Jubilee. The week-long celebrations, the greatest in the history of the country, culminated in a gigantic parade through the streets of the capital to a large park where 50,000 believers staged a remarkable demonstration of evangelical strength. For hours they marched, led by a band, in groups of uniformed school children from evangelical schools, church groups with flying banners carrying Bible verses, floats, groups on bicycles and motorcycles, and, finally, cars. The paraders represented all types of persons, white collar professionals, artisans, and family groups with the mothers carrying babies on their backs. The city was visibly moved. The local press gave much favorable comment, noting particularly the seriousness of these earnest Christians, their orderly conduct, and the enthusiastic singing. Even the Roman Catholic Church was stirred to urge its faithful to "go and do likewise."

HONDURAS

Area:	43,230 sq. mi.	Population:	1,710,000
Capital:	Tegucigalpa	Religion:	Roman Catholicism

THE LAND. Honduras is the largest of the Central American republics. It is a rugged country bounded on the west and southwest by Guatemala and El Salvador, and on the south by Nicaragua. Broad coastal plains extend inland from the Caribbean Sea for sixty to seventy miles, reaching to the mountain ranges of the south where mountains, jungles, and swamplands merge in the eastern part of the country.

POLITICAL HISTORY. The colonial history of Honduras began with Columbus' fourth and last visit to the New World. By 1544 Spain had completely dominated this part of Central America. Honduras declared its independence from Spain in 1821, and in 1838 became a sovereign independent republic.

THE PEOPLE. Here as elsewhere in Latin America the Spaniards intermarried with the Indian population. The present-day Hondurans are mostly mestizo. In addition there are many Negroes who were brought in, principally from Jamaica, to work on the banana plantations. Spanish is the official language.

THE RELIGION. The vast majority of the people are Roman Catholics. The Constitution guarantees freedom of religion for all.

MISSIONS. The pioneer missionary agency in Honduras was the *Central American Mission*. A party of five missionaries, led by *Mr. A. E. Bishop*, reached Santa Rosa de Copan in western Honduras in 1896. Steady work through the years and a sound emphasis on national leadership have resulted in one of the largest and strongest Protestant churches in the country. The medical work of the Mission is centered in *Hospital Evangelica* in Siguatepeque where 14 of the 40 missionaries are concentrated.

The *California Yearly Meeting of Friends* was the second evangelical mission to enter Honduras; it began its work in 1909. The *Evangelical and Reformed Church* has been working in the three northern departments of the country since 1921. Its work centers in San Pedro Sula, the second largest city in Honduras. This Church is now organized as a national body, the *Synod of Honduras*, and reports a membership of 600. After various visits to the Miskito Indians, permanent work was established by the *Moravians* at Kaurkira in 1930. The missionary staff has never been large; at present it numbers seven. Moderate progress has been made and latest reports indicate 38 preaching places in the charge of 10 unordained ministers and 60 lay assistants. They operate two schools.

The *World Gospel Mission* (National Holiness Missionary Society) entered Honduras in 1943. With headquarters in the capital city of Tegucigalpa, the Mission is responsible for the evangelization of over 300,000 people in the central part of the republic. The work includes a Bible school, printing press, and colportage work.

The *Assemblies of God* launched their missionary work in Honduras, from their base in El Salvador, in 1940 in response to the invitation of three indigenous Pentecostal assemblies which needed outside help. Santa Rosa, not far from the Guatemalan border, was chosen as the best and most central location for their work. A second field was opened later on in the southeastern part of the country, where San Marcos de Colon is the center. The Bible school, opened in 1947 at Santa Rosa, has never had a large enrollment; but it has made a vital contribution to the building up of a strong and indigenous church. There are now 33 national ministers, ordained or licensed, serving 30 organized assemblies and 17 outstations. They have a strong, well-developed Sunday School program, a distinguishing feature of their work in many places.

There are other societies which have been working in Honduras for longer or shorter periods. The *Methodist Missionary Society,* one of two British missions in the country, has established a number of churches on the Bay Islands and on the coast. The *United Brethren in Christ* are responsible for the evangelization of the Miskito Coast where they have fourteen congregations in the charge of six missionaries and five nationals. *Christian Missions in Many Lands* have six main centers of missionary activity. With some two dozen places of worship they are one of the larger missions in Honduras. The *Wesleyan Methodist Missionary Society* also supports work here.

Several mission groups have begun work in Honduras since the end of World War II. The first of these was the *Conservative Baptist Home Mission Society*. The first church was established in the seaport of La Ceiba among the English-speaking Negroes, whose ancestors came from the West Indies. In 1947 the work spread to the Bay Islands 40 miles off the coast, where there are now four organized churches and several outstations. An evangelistic thrust into the interior of the country came in 1958. The missionaries are burdened for the dozens of banana camps owned by the Standard Fruit Company in the Aguan Valley, where as yet there are only five or six preaching places. The Mission has approved the erection of a gospel radio station, the first in Honduras, to be located in the capital city, which has a population of 100,000. Construction will begin as soon as funds are available. Also on the planning board is a Bible training school.

Baptist Mid-Missions entered Honduras in the early 1950's. Their only couple there at present is working among the English-speaking people of the Bay Islands and the north coast. The *Missionary Aviation Fellowship*, with a staff of six, is operating two airplanes in all parts of the republic. In addition to transporting missionaries and supplies, this Mission is carrying on an aerial-ambulance clinic in connection with the *Hospital Evangelica*. Honduras was the last of the Latin American countries to be entered by the *Southern Baptists*. They entered in 1954 and already report 4 organized churches and 13 preaching points. Their work is centered in the capital where they have a small Bible school, an extension of their Guatemala Bible Institute. The bookstore, also in the capital, furnishes evangelical literature to all missions. Radio evangelism is a vital part of their program.

Other missions include the *Seventh Day Adventists, Pioneer Bible Mission,* and *International Church of the Foursquare Gospel.*

EL SALVADOR

Area:	8,250 sq. mi.	Population:	2,275,000
Capital:	San Salvador	Religion:	Roman Catholicism

THE LAND. El Salvador is the smallest and most densely populated of the Central American states. On the south it has a coastline of about 150 miles on the Pacific Ocean. It is bounded on the north and east by Honduras, and on the west by Guatemala.

POLITICAL HISTORY. For 300 years El Salvador was part of Spain's colonial empire in this part of the world. When the Central American Federation was dissolved in 1839, El Salvador became an independent republic.

THE PEOPLE. About 15 per cent of the population of El Salvador is pure Indian. The remainder of the people are Ladinos. Spanish is the official language. Education is free and compulsory, but there is a shortage of both teachers and schools. As recently as 1953 only 20 per cent of the children in the rural areas were in school.

THE RELIGION. Roman Catholicism is the dominant religion. In 1929 the government took control of all schools, private and public, and education was wholly secular. The ban against religious instruction was removed in 1945.

MISSIONS. After six years of work in Costa Rica, in 1894 the *Central American Mission* made plans to enter other nearby fields. The venture ended in disaster when two missionaries en route to El Salvador contracted yellow fever and died within a few days of each other. Two years later a second attempt succeeded, and the first missionary landed in El Salvador. In April of the following year *Mr. Robert H. Bender* began his impressive ministry in this republic. The Mission's work today is centered in San Salvador where there are nine missionaries. Four other stations are occupied. There are 2,300 church members and a Christian community twice that number served at the present time by 50 national workers.

For more than thirty years the Central American Mission was the only evangelical society in the country. It was joined by the *Assemblies of God* in 1929. The work of the Assemblies of God, developed along indigenous lines and supported by many national workers, has made phenomenal progress. Their coeducational Bible institute at Santa Ana, which has a present enrollment of 94, accounts for a good deal of their success. Latest reports indicate 152 organized churches and 426 preaching places, making them by far the largest mission in the country.

Another Pentecostal group is the *Church of God*. It has 37 churches under the care of 30 ordained ministers. There are no missionaries here at present, the work being self-supporting. The *California Yearly Meeting of Friends* has a small work here, and two Baptist groups also are working in this republic. The *American Baptist Home Missionary Society*, with a small staff of missionaries, has built up a fairly strong indigenous work under national leadership. The *National Baptist Convention*, a Negro society which has its headquarters in Philadelphia, reports a Christian community of 2,200 scattered over some 60 places of worship. The *Seventh Day Adventists* have been in El Salvador for some years. There is neither medical nor educational work, however, and no missionaries are here at present.

The most recent mission to enter El Salvador was the *Lutheran*

Church-Missouri Synod in 1956. *Mr. G. E. Kempff* has begun work in a suburb of San Salvador. The other station, in Pasaquina, is in charge of a layman, *Don Ciro Mijia,* who built a small chapel as an addition to his little adobe house.

NICARAGUA

Area: 57,150 sq. mi.   Population: 1,310,000
Capital: Managua   Religion: Roman
                                               Catholicism

THE LAND. Nicaragua is a triangular piece of territory located between Honduras and Costa Rica, with coastlines on both the Pacific Ocean and the Caribbean Sea. It is the most sparsely populated of the Central American countries.

POLITICAL HISTORY. After 300 years of Spanish colonial rule, Nicaragua gained full independence in 1838 with the dissolution of the Central American Federation.

THE PEOPLE. Almost 70 per cent of the people are mestizo. About 15 per cent are pure white; they form the upper classes. A third racial element is the Negro population imported originally to provide labor on the east coast.

THE RELIGION. The prevailing religion is Roman Catholicism, but there is complete freedom of religion.

MISSIONS. Nicaragua was one of the first of the Central American republics to receive Protestant missionaries; and strangely enough, they came not from North America but from Germany. The *German Moravian Church* sent its first missionary to Nicaragua about the middle of the nineteenth century, and for fifty years it was the only Protestant mission in the country. Owing to war conditions, its work was transferred to the management of the *American Moravian Church* in 1914. Sustained work through the years has paid off, and today the Moravians have by far the largest Church in the country. Its membership was 21,500 in 1957. Stations are maintained in 15 centers. The educational program includes 23 primary schools, a Bible institute, and the *Colegio Moravo.* There is a hospital at Bilwaskarma. Particularly strong is the corps of national workers, which includes 84 ministers and 354 assistants, both men and women.

After being the only mission in Nicaragua for fifty years, the Moravians were joined by the *Central American Mission* in 1900. It has a comparatively small missionary staff—about a dozen—located in three main stations. One of these is in the capital. About the same time the *American Baptist Home Missionary Society* began work in the area along the Pacific coast in the well-populated lakes district. It now has a Christian community of about 8,000 and is the second largest group in the country. It has an extensive educational program and a strong emphasis on evangelism.

The *Assemblies of God* took up work in Nicaragua in 1926, building on a foundation laid some years before by independent Pentecostal workers who later affiliated with the General Council. Casualties were high in the beginning, but the Mission persevered and the work was finally established on a solid basis. The main task during the first few years was pioneering in new territory, coupled with the teaching of new converts and the organizing of churches along indigenous lines. From the first they encouraged the local pastors to look to God for the supply of their daily needs. A men's Bible institute was opened in Matagalpa, and later a women's Bible institute was added.

The *Church of the Nazarene* also has work in Nicaragua. The missionary staff in 1959 consisted of 16 missionaries. There are 46 national workers serving in 39 churches and outstations.

The latest Christian radio station in Latin America is small, 500-watt Station YNOL in the capital city of Managua. It is sponsored by a group of local Christians with the help of the Latin America Mission. Its gospel broadcasts began on March 8, 1959.

Other Protestant missions in the country are the *Church of God* and the *Seventh Day Adventists*.

COSTA RICA

Area: 19,690 sq. mi.   Population: 1,050,000
Capital: San José   Religion: Roman
                                             Catholicism

THE LAND. Costa Rica is located between Nicaragua and Panama and is one of the most picturesque and cultured of the Central American countries.

POLITICAL HISTORY. From 1502 to 1821 Costa Rica was a colony of Spain. In 1838, when the Federation of Central America broke up, it became an independent state. Spanish is the official language.

THE PEOPLE. Ninety-five per cent of the population is of Spanish ancestry. Only a few aboriginal Indians remain in the remote sections of the country; a relatively small settlement of Negroes is located on the Caribbean coast.

THE RELIGION. The dominant faith is Roman Catholicism, but there is religious liberty for all.

MISSIONS. This seems to be the logical place to give a thumbnail sketch of the *Central American Mission*, the only interdenominational mission working in all five countries of Central America. It was in the summer of 1888 that *Cyrus Ingerson Scofield,* editor of the widely used Scofield Reference Bible, was made aware of the spiritual destitution of the little country of Costa Rica. Dr. Scofield decided to look into the matter and discovered to his amazement that not only in Costa Rica but in the other republics as well the people, with a few exceptions, were still sitting in darkness and in the shadow of death. The *Moravian Church* had begun work among the Miskito Indians in eastern Nicaragua in 1849, and the *Presbyterian Church, U.S.A.,* had opened a station in Guatemala City in 1882; but that was the extent of missionary work towards the close of the nineteenth century. Upon inquiry Dr. Scofield found that none of the denominational boards was prepared to begin new work in the near future in any of the republics. Realizing that the Christian people of America could no longer bypass the "Samaria" of Central America, he placed the matter before three Christian businessmen in his church (the First Congregational Church of Dallas, Texas), with the result that after much prayer the Central American Mission was formed in November, 1890. Early the following year its first missionaries, *Mr. and Mrs. W. W. McConnell,* embarked for San José to inaugurate the work in Costa Rica.

At the present time the Mission has four stations in Costa Rica in addition to San José, where the Central Language School is located. Some idea of the recent growth of this Mission may be gathered from the fact that in the summer of 1959 there were 19 new missionaries in the language school.

The *American Methodists* began work in Costa Rica in 1918. Their first missionaries, *Mr. and Mrs. C. W. Ports,* located in San José which became the center of their work in that country. For many years progress was slow, due in part to the lack of training facilities. Since the opening of a training school in 1956 at Alajuela, church growth has been accelerated.

Several new chapels have been constructed and many new preaching places have been opened up in the banana section of the country. Costa Rica offers a very splendid opportunity for evangelization. The people are responsive and there are many communities where no evangelistic work of any kind is being conducted. The whole banana zone is open to us. We must soon have three centers instead of two, and at least six pastoral charges instead of three. As we graduate more young people from the training school we should be able to make our work in that zone more effective.[4]

The Methodists have a school and a rural center in San Carlos.

The largest society is the *Latin America Mission,* which has more missionaries in Costa Rica than all ten of the other societies combined. Twenty-five organized churches have an aggregate membership of almost 800.

After eighteen years of successful evangelistic work in Argentina *Harry Strachan* decided to pioneer in the field of mass evangelism in other parts of Latin America. At about the same time God raised up several gifted young nationals who were in love with Christ and had a passion for souls. They were available and overjoyed at the prospect of engaging in a continent-wide ministry of this kind. A survey trip, taken in faith and lasting one year to the day, confirmed the conviction that God was calling them to undertake this type of ministry. Accordingly, in 1921 Harry Strachan, together with a group of Christian brethren in the United States, founded the Latin America Mission (then known as the Latin America Evangelization Campaign) with headquarters in beautiful San José. The purpose of the Mission as stated in its Constitution is "to reach for Christ, by any and all means, in co-operation always with the local missionary organizations, the vast unevangelized masses of Spanish-speaking America."

Large campaigns were held, with the help of local missionaries, in all the major cities of South and Central America. The results were beyond all expectations. Wherever they went, thousands packed the theaters and public halls. Mr. Strachan and his colleagues were not interested in beginning a new mission. They were burdened for the evangelization of Latin America and were content to allow existing missions to absorb their converts. Such largehearted men are rare even in missionary circles. Consequently there is hardly a mission of any size in Latin America which does not count among its members converts won in the many campaigns conducted by the Latin America Mission. For almost forty years the Mission has been carrying on this ministry of mass evangelism in all parts of this vast area.

[4] *Mission and Witness, 1958,* p. 150.

Such outstanding evangelists as Jack Wyrtzen, Anton Marco, Hyman Appelman, and Oswald Smith have ministered in various countries under the auspices of this Mission. Plans are now being made for Billy Graham to tour Latin America in 1961.

The Latin America Mission has established its own churches in only two countries, Costa Rica and Colombia. It also has a hospital and two dispensaries in Costa Rica; in the educational field it maintains two elementary schools, a high school, and a seminary. This Mission pioneered in radio evangelism when Station TIFC went on the air in San José in 1948. It also co-operates with the *World Radio Missionary Fellowship* in the work of Station HOXO in Panama.

The *Assemblies of God* appointed their first missionary to Costa Rica in 1942. From the beginning they have enjoyed considerable success. The *National Conference of the Assemblies of God* comprises 14 churches and 34 preaching places. It is divided into three districts, each with its own presbyter. They have a Bible school in San José.

Southern Baptist work, which began in 1949, is still confined to San José where they have two missionary couples. Their program includes, among other things, radio work and newspaper evangelism. There is a seminary in San José and a day school in Limon.

There are two British missions in Costa Rica, the *Methodist Missionary Society* and the *Society for the Propagation of the Gospel.* The latter has one missionary in the country at present, the other has none.

Pentecostal Churches include the *Church of God, International Church of the Foursquare Gospel,* and the *Pentecostal Holiness Church,* with about a dozen churches among them. The only other mission is the *Seventh Day Adventists,* one of the larger missions, having some 2,500 members.

PANAMA

Area:	28,750 sq. mi.	Population:	950,000
Capital:	Panama City	Religion:	Roman Catholicism

THE LAND. Panama is the narrow strip of territory at the southern tip of Central America, linking Central and South America. It is about 480 miles long, and ranges from 35 to 110 miles in width.

POLITICAL HISTORY. Panama was formerly a department of the Republic of Colombia in South America. It asserted its independence on

November 3, 1903, and ten days later was recognized by the United States. It was not until 1914 that Colombia agreed to recognize the independence of Panama.

THE PEOPLE. About 60 per cent of the population is Ladino. Twenty per cent is Negro, 10 per cent is pure Indian, and the remainder is of European descent. There are four or five Indian tribes, most of them along the Caribbean coast. Spanish is the official language.

THE RELIGION. Over 90 per cent of the people are Roman Catholics. There is religious freedom, and separation of Church and State is maintained.

MISSIONS. For the size of the country, Panama has an unusually large number of Protestant missions. There are almost 200 missionaries, more than half of whom are members of the *International Church of the Foursquare Gospel*. As might be expected, all but one of the missions are from North America. The one exception is the *Methodist Missionary Society* (England) which reported in 1958: "The membership of the Church has been steadily increasing, the finances have improved, and there has been an advance in the sphere of lay leadership."[5]

Shortly after the turn of the century the *Southern Baptist Convention Home Mission Board* began work in Panama. It took over the field once occupied by the *Jamaica Baptist Missionary Society*. The *American Methodists* entered the field in 1905. *Rev. J. C. Elkins* was the pioneer. For eleven years this work was administered as part of the North Andes Mission Conference. Now it is a district in the *Central American Provisional Annual Conference*. There are 9 Methodist congregations with a membership of 600. Most of the 13 missionaries are located in Panama City where the *Pan American Institute* has been maintained since its founding in 1906. About 380 students (half of the student body) at the Institute professed Jesus Christ as Lord and Saviour and asked for baptism after a preaching mission by *Dr. Alfonso Rodriques* of Cuba in 1955.

The two churches with the largest membership are the *International Church of the Foursquare Gospel* (8,100) and the *Protestant Episcopal Church* (7,300). The *Church of God* has 31 churches. Panama was the last of the Central American republics to be entered by the *Central American Mission;* it went in in 1943. Missionaries are located in three centers but to date converts have been comparatively few. The *Gospel Missionary Union* has been at work in

[5] *The Burning Word, 1958*, p. 34.

Panama only since 1953, but they have made remarkable progress. Ten churches served by 21 missionaries have a membership of 500. As yet there are no national workers. The *Latin America Mission* and the *World Radio Missionary Fellowship* are co-sponsors of Station HOXO, which was erected in Panama City in 1949. The *New Tribes Mission* has evangelistic work among three Indian tribes. The *Seventh Day Adventists* have no missionaries in the country at present, but they report 38 churches in charge of nationals. The *Lutheran Church-Missouri Synod* has several mission centers, which are mostly for United States military personnel.

CUBA

Area: 44,200 sq. mi.   Population: 6,410,000
Capital: Havana   Religion: Roman
                                                   Catholicism

THE LAND. Called the "Pearl of the Antilles," Cuba is the largest of the islands of the West Indies. It is located in the Caribbean Sea about 90 miles south of Key West, Florida. It is 730 miles long and 195 miles across at its widest part. Sugar is the big industry, and accounts for 82 per cent of Cuba's exports.

POLITICAL HISTORY. On his first journey to the New World, Columbus landed on Cuba, but exploration and conquest did not begin until 1511. It was a colony of Spain until the close of the Spanish-American War in 1898. The Republic of Cuba was established in 1902. Dictator Batista was toppled from power in 1958 by Fidel Castro, whose present unstable regime is reputed to be infiltrated by Communists. Anti-American sentiment is running high.

THE PEOPLE. The population may be divided into three groups. The descendants of the Spanish colonists represent about 70 per cent. Fifteen to 20 per cent are Negroes, descendants of the slaves who were brought from Africa to work on the sugar plantations. The remaining 15 per cent is almost entirely mulatto. Spanish is the official language.

THE RELIGION. There is no state Church. The dominant religion is Roman Catholicism, but here as in other parts of the West Indies it is mixed with pagan practices introduced from Africa. There is religious liberty, and the Protestant Church, though small, is growing.

MISSIONS. One of the earliest missions in Cuba was the *Southern Baptist Convention*. Its interest in the country was first aroused when a Cuban was led to Christ in Florida by one of its own missionaries. This led to work among the Cubans in Florida and from there the work was extended to Cuba itself. There the Southern Baptists amalgamated with a small independent work which had been established earlier, largely through the efforts of one man, *Alberto J. Diaz,* who had been converted some years before in New York. This field is worked by the Home Mission Board; latest reports indicate a church membership of 8,500 and a Christian community of about 25,000.

The *American Baptist Home Missionary Society,* one of the first boards to enter Cuba after the Spanish-American War, has built up a good strong Church whose membership is slightly less than that of the Southern Baptists. A third Baptist Mission is the *National Association of Free Will Baptists,* which has an estimated membership of 2,000.

As early as 1881 the *Southern Methodists* began sending visiting preachers to Cuba. Settled work began in 1899 when *Rev. George N. MacDonnell* reached Havana. Other centers were opened in rapid succession. The chapel at Matanzas is said to have been the first Protestant church erected on the island. Today the Methodists have a flourishing work in all six of Cuba's provinces. Altogether there are 18 main stations, including one on the Isle of Pines. Some of the finest educational institutions in the country are sponsored by the Methodists. Three colleges in Camaguey, Cienfuegos, and Matanzas have a combined enrollment of almost 1,000. The two colleges in Havana merged in 1957 to form *Candler University,* the only Methodist university in Spanish-speaking Latin America. The Methodists co-operate with the Presbyterians and Episcopalians in the *Union Theological Seminary* founded in 1946 in Matanzas. The Methodist Church is made up mostly of the poor. It has a membership of 10,000, and eight or ten new chapels are being built each year. Much progress in self-support was reported in the last Annual Conference.

Another large Church is the *Protestant Episcopal,* which has the largest Protestant community (60,000) in the island. Early contacts with Cuba reach back to 1871. When a bishop from Florida visited Cuba in 1885 he found 325 candidates for confirmation; but permanent work was not established until 1898. The first resident American bishop arrived in 1904. The Anglicans now have 30 priests, most of whom are Cubans. They have 18 parochial schools, many of which are self-supporting. The Church is now beginning to get second- and third-generation Christians which means, among other things, more suitable candidates for the ministry; but nevertheless the demand continues to outstrip the supply. They have no more clergymen now than they had thirty years ago, but they have three times the amount of work. One hopeful sign is the increasing number of university students and graduates who are being attracted to the Church.

Like the other boards described above, the *American Presbyterians* established tenuous contacts with indigenous Protestant groups in Cuba during the last two decades of the last century; but it was not until after the Spanish-American War that organized work was placed on a permanent basis. For a time both the Northern and the Southern Boards had work here, but in 1919 the Southern Presbyterians pulled out and left the field to the Northern Presbyterians. Today the work is concentrated in the three central provinces where there are 34 organized churches. With the exception of two American teachers, an all-Cuban leadership has been developed. Outstanding among the many educational institutions is *La Progresiva*, founded in Cardenas in 1900. A coeducational school, its enrollment in 1958 was over 1,800, including both day and boarding students coming from all six provinces. The Union Seminary with which the Presbyterians co-operate attracts students from Puerto Rico, Dominican Republic, Venezuela, Colombia, Guatemala, Mexico, and Panama.

The *American Friends* have been at work in Cuba since 1900. Their enterprise was launched by four women. At present they have work in ten main centers, and report a Christian community of about 1,000.

The Pentecostal form of Christianity was introduced to Cuba by missionaries of the *Assemblies of God. Miss May Kelty* arrived in 1920, conducted tent meetings for two years, and then returned to the United States. Nine years later she went back to Cuba, accompanied by other workers, and opened several preaching places. In 1936 the work was organized under the Foreign Missions Department of the Assemblies of God. Today the Mission has centers in the main cities in all parts of Cuba, with 18 missionaries engaged in the work. This is a larger number than the Mission has in any other Latin-American country. There are only 33 organized churches, but evangelistic work is carried on in 260 outstations. The only educational work is the Bible school in Manacas. However, 13,000 children are receiving instruction each week in Sunday School. Three other Pentecostal missions are in Cuba: *Church of God* (Cleveland), *Church of God, Missionary Board,* and the *Church of the Nazarene.*

The *Seventh Day Adventists* have a sizable enterprise in Cuba. It is divided into two Conferences, East and West. Combined membership is in the neighborhood of 5,000. They have 36 primary schools and a college.

The *Mennonite Board of Missions and Charities* has two couples and three single ladies on the field. The work is just now getting under way, having been begun in 1954.

On September 25, 1928, the *Cuba Bible Institute, Los Pinos Nuevos,* opened its doors to 15 eager students. Out of this small beginning grew the *West Indies Mission* which now has 185 missionaries and 350 trained nationals engaged in church and mission work, 6 Bible institutes, 3 printing presses, and 2 bookstores in six countries in the West Indies and two in South America. From the beginning, this Mission has endeavored to operate along strictly indigenous lines. Its consistent strategy has been to train national leaders and send them out to win their own people for Christ. Through the years their main work has been the Cuba Bible Institute, whose graduates now number over 400. There are 28 missionaries and 14 nationals engaged in a fourfold ministry of the Bible institute, the Bible correspondence course school, daily radio broadcasts over a national network, and a gospel press. Graduates from the Bible institute have served about 100 churches besides doing evangelistic work in an equal number of outstations. Other graduates have been called to churches in Ecuador, the Canary Islands, and Algiers in North Africa.

Other missions with work in the country are *Christian Missions in Many Lands, Lutheran Church-Missouri Synod, Open Bible Standard Churches,* and *United World Mission.*

DOMINICAN REPUBLIC

Area: 18,700 sq. mi.
Capital: Ciudad Trujillo
Population: 2,700,000
Religion: Roman Catholicism

THE LAND. The Dominican Republic occupies the eastern two-thirds of the island of Hispaniola, which is located in the northeastern part of the Caribbean Sea, halfway between Puerto Rico and Cuba. The western portion of the island forms the Republic of Haiti.

POLITICAL HISTORY. The Dominican Republic has had a checkered career since 1831 when colonial rule was terminated and a republican form of government was adopted. It was incorporated under the government of Haiti from 1822 to 1844, and was under Spain from 1861 to 1865. To stave off financial disaster, the United States established a provisional government over the Dominican Republic in 1922 which lasted until 1924. The customs receivership was continued until 1941, since which time the country has been completely independent.

THE PEOPLE. Owing to the cruelty and oppression of colonial rule there is practically no trace of the aboriginal Indians left. They were either killed or driven from the island shortly after its conquest by Spain. Negro slaves were imported in large numbers to work on the sugar plantations. Intermarriage between the Spaniards and the Negroes followed, and a mixed race resulted. Today about two-thirds of the population is mixed. Twenty per cent is pure Negro and about 13 per cent is white. Spanish is the official language.

THE RELIGION. Roman Catholicism is the state religion though other faiths are tolerated.

MISSIONS. Protestantism was not introduced into the country until 1889. During that year an independent lay missionary, S. E. Mills of Ohio, began evangelizing in the island. Converts were slow in coming, but the work developed gradually until several small churches were brought into existence. Later, these congregations united to form the *Free Methodist Church of the Dominican Republic*. With a membership of almost 1,000 it is one of the larger Churches in the country.

The *Protestant Episcopal Church* opened its first station in Ciudad Trujillo in 1918. For the first thirty years its work was confined to the English-speaking populace; but beginning in 1948 it branched out into Spanish work as well. It is now divided into two parishes with five mission stations. The Anglican work here is under the American bishop in Haiti.

The *West Indies Mission* entered the Dominican Republic in 1938. *Cecil Samuels*, a native of Jamaica and a graduate of the Cuba Bible Institute, was the pioneer of this Mission. Once settled in La Vega he immediately began house-to-house visitation and open-air meetings. The stolid indifference of the people in general was a discouraging factor. Settled work was established when the missionaries arrived. A special donation of $1,000 made possible the purchase of a farm. Buildings were erected, and in 1942 a Bible school was opened with six students in attendance. Even so, progress has been slow in comparison with Haiti. To date there are eleven organized churches with an aggregate membership of about 300.

The *Assemblies of God* work was begun by a Puerto Rican pastor who, without any visible means of support, went to the Dominican Republic to conduct evangelistic meetings. The first assembly was organized in 1933. It was not until 1941 that American missionaries were appointed to the republic. Four years later a Bible school was established and already it has provided 150 preachers for their 33 organized churches and 250 preaching places.

Baptist Mid-Missions has a small band of missionaries stationed at Hato Mayor and Ciudad Trujillo. Work includes village evangelism, a local church, a Christian day school, a Bible seminary, and a strongly organized youth movement.

Christian Missions in Many Lands, which has 30 assemblies and a membership of 1,400, is one of the larger missions in the country. The *Unevangelized Fields Mission* sent its first workers to the Dominican Republic in 1949. The work is found mainly in the cities of San Pedro de Macoris and La Romano, situated forty miles apart. The *Seventh Day Adventists* are the largest mission. Although they have only 5 American missionaries, national workers number almost 100. More than two dozen churches have a membership of about 3,000. They have 17 elementary schools. The *Dominican Evangelical Church* was founded in 1920 as a union of the Methodist, Presbyterian, and Evangelical United Brethren Churches. This national organization reports 42 places of worship and a membership of 1,500.

Other missions in the country are the *Church of God, Moravian Mission, Missionary Church Association,* and the *African Methodist Episcopal Church.*

HAITI

Area: 10,715 sq. mi.
Capital: Port-au-Prince

Population: 3,400,000
Religion: Roman Catholicism Voodooism

THE LAND. Haiti occupies the western one-third of the island of Hispaniola. Five-sixths of the terrain is mountainous. Coffee and sugar are the chief crops. The southern part of Haiti is densely populated and highly malarial.

POLITICAL HISTORY. The island was discovered by Columbus in 1492 and soon became the base of Spanish operations in the New World.

In 1664 the French West India Company seized control of that part of the island which is now Haiti. The colony finally achieved its independence in 1795, and the republic was set up in 1804.

THE PEOPLE. After the depopulation of the original Indian inhabitants, the Spanish and later the French brought over large numbers of African slaves whose descendants now populate the country. French is the official language. There is a French-speaking élite, but 90 per cent of the peasants are illiterate and speak the Creole dialect. The standard of living is extremely low for this part of the world. Degradation, filth, and ignorance abound on every hand.

THE RELIGION. Since 1865 the Roman Catholic Church has enjoyed the protection of the government. Its clergy is supported with public funds. In 1956 the Jesuits were permitted to return after an enforced absence of two hundred years. There is, however, complete religious liberty; and a strong and growing evangelical church is now reaping the harvest of a century of sowing. Protestant churches without exception are filled to capacity, and sometimes beyond. Protestants now constitute about 10 per cent of the entire population.

Peculiar to Haiti is a religious phenomenon known as Voodooism, which is a weird mixture of African fetishism and Roman Catholicism. When the ex-slaves embraced Christianity they simply grafted Roman Catholic practices onto their paganism without any real change of heart or life. Voodoo is related to the whole broad sweep of Catholic teaching. The *loa* are saints. The "island below the sea" is purgatory. *Paquets* are like Catholic charms and amulets. The *hougan's* temple ceremonies are comparable to the mass; his services for the departed are like the Church's prayers for the dead. The sign of the cross and Voodoo signs are used interchangeably. There is nothing in Catholicism as practised in Haiti that conflicts with Voodoo. An eye-witness described a recent ceremony known as Damballa (snake) Worship:

> The Priestess held her black audience spellbound. . . . Catholic and Voodoo saints were invoked, and Christian and Voodoo blessings were asked for all. . . . She began calling upon Catholic saints and Voodoo *loa*. . . . On a table was a crucifix and several *peirre loa*. . . . A Voodoo altar held a crucifix. . . . The sign of the cross, the kissing of the beads, the chanting of prayers made me wonder where the Mother Church left off and where Voodoo took over.[6]

[6] "Voodooism and Roman Catholicism," *Converted Catholic Magazine*, quoted in Baptist Mid-Missions literature.

MISSIONS. Protestant missions got off to an early start in Haiti. As long ago as 1816 two *Wesleyan Methodists* appeared in Haiti at the invitation of the president of the country. The venture lasted for only two years after which, owing to persecution, the missionaries withdrew, leaving the infant enterprise in the hands of a Haitian pastor.

In 1861 the *Episcopal Church* went to Haiti. *Rev. James T. Holly,* a Negro priest, emigrated with a group of 110 American Negroes in the hope of establishing a colony in that country. Though the colony failed, the Church found fertile soil for its work. In 1874 the national Church was organized as the *Eglise Orthodoxe Apostolique Haitienne,* and that same year Mr. Holly was consecrated its first bishop. In 1913 the Haitian Church was made a missionary district of the Episcopal Church of the United States. The only American clergy at present are the bishop, the dean of the seminary, and the priest in charge of the English-speaking congregation at the Cathedral. There are 20 Haitian clergymen to carry on the work among 46,000 baptized persons and 13,000 communicants. The Church operates about 40 small schools giving primary education to 1,200 children. Progress in the matter of self-support has been slow. The American Episcopal Church continues to subsidize the Haitian Church to the extent of approximately $1,000,000 a year.

For many years Baptists from England maintained a small work in Haiti, but it was transferred to the *American Baptists* upon their arrival in 1924. This enterprise, directed by the Home Missionary Society, has flourished greatly under the impact of a mighty spiritual awakening which has swept thousands into the Kingdom. This society now reports almost 600 churches and preaching places, with an aggregate membership of 25,000 and a Christian community three times as large.

Two Methodist groups are at work in the country. The older of these is the *Methodist Missionary Society* (England) which has been in Haiti for several decades. The missionary staff is reduced to two now, leaving most of the work in the hands of the nationals. The 1958 Report is extremely optimistic:

In the midst of very great problems, God is mightily at work in the Church in Haiti. In comparing the situation now with the scene twenty years ago, one realises what has been achieved. Then there were no Haitian ministers; now there are three. Then there was no way of writing and teaching Creole, the language of most of the people; now over 50,000 Creole Hymn Books have been sold, and a translation of the New Testament and Psalms is about to be printed by the American Bible Society. Then a new Church was needed at Port-au-Prince; now the stately new building has membership training classes attended by over 400 people. Then there were only two adequate school buildings to counteract strong Roman Catholic influence; now it is planned to open a new, well-staffed school in October 1960. Then Jeremie circuit had only one country station; now it has 32 stations and one Christian community of over 4,000 spread over 300 miles. Then the Petit Goave circuit was in danger of disintegrating; now it has 30 country stations, a farming co-operative and a publishing center of the French edition of the *Upper Room.*[7]

The second Methodist society is the *Wesleyan Methodist Missionary Society,* which entered Haiti in 1948.

An interdenominational mission which has done a fine work in Haiti is the *Unevangelized Fields Mission.* Indeed, so responsive have the people been that Haiti has become the largest and most fruitful of the eight fields in which the Mission is working. In 1943 it assumed responsibility for the evangelization of the northwestern part of the country. Tremendous progress has been made in the short span of sixteen years. A staff of 49 missionaries is engaged in the task of building up a strong, spiritual indigenous Church with almost 300 congregations. Institutional work includes a Bible school, two orphanages, a hospital, and a printing press.

Baptist Mid-Missions began work in Haiti when *Rev. and Mrs. Paul Metzler,* veteran missionaries from French Equatorial Africa, visited the country to arrange for the legal transfer to Baptist Mid-Missions of existing Baptist congregations brought into being by *Pasteur Ferrazzini* of Switzerland. *Rev. and Mrs. B. F. Sherwood* were the first couple to be appointed to Haiti, where they had previously served under another board. Immediately the new missionaries began a program of evangelization, education, and medical assistance in the Jacmel district. From the spiritual point of view the greatest problem was overcoming racial prejudice and religious dissension, both of which sprang from the background out of which these independent churches had come. The missionary staff has since been increased to ten. They are located in six main stations.

After seven years in Cuba, its first field, the *West Indies Mission* in 1936 moved into southern Haiti, where it found little groups of believers. Some years before, Haitians had gone to Cuba to work in the sugar mills and while there had heard the gospel from the missionaries. Upon their return home they shared the good news of the gospel with their friends and neighbors. The West Indies Mission work in Haiti began with a Bible school of five men. Today the enrollment in the winter session is around 100, and about the

[7] *The Burning Word,* 1958, p. 34.

same number of women take advantage of the summer course for Biblewomen. Characterized by a zeal for God and a love for souls, and supported generously by the enthusiastic giving of the Haitian churches, the graduates of the Bible institute have reaped an abundant harvest. The missionary staff has grown from three to 32, while the national Church has multiplied from a few hundred to 75,000 believers. In Haiti's southern peninsula there are 210 national workers ministering to 176 congregations and at 266 preaching places. A well-equipped dispensary manned by a competent doctor and five nurses provides a healing ministry to 1,500 outpatients a month. The Mission carries on a fine radio ministry over its own Station 4-VI in Cayes.

The *Church of God* has been at work here since 1937. This Mission likewise has experienced rapid growth. It now has 140 organized churches and 200 outstations with a baptized membership of 10,000. Adherents are estimated at 30,000. An educational system embracing 160 elementary schools is providing schooling for thousands of pupils. Another Pentecostal group is the *Church of the Nazarene*. A handful of missionaries assisted by a national staff five times their number are engaged in church and educational work.

The work of the *Seventh Day Adventists* is now entirely in the hands of national workers. There is no medical work; the only institution is a seminary in Port-au-Prince. They have 21 primary schools. Their 12,500 church members make this one of the largest missions in the country. The *Inter-American Mission* is the most recent newcomer to Haiti; it arrived in 1958. Radio Station 4VEH in Cap Haitien is owned and operated by this Society.

Other missions in Haiti include *East and West Indies Bible Mission, World Evangelization Service, Lott Carey Baptist Foreign Mission Convention,* and *Conservative Baptist Home Mission Society.*

The *Jacmel Baptist Church* is an independent national Church which has no connection at all with any missionary organization. It is a fairly extensive group with over 200 places of worship.

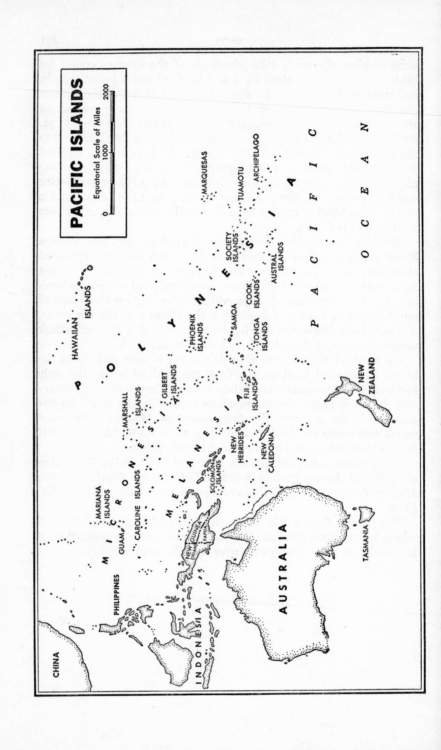

XXIII

PACIFIC ISLANDS

INTRODUCTORY

Area: 383,000 sq. mi.

Population: 3,650,000
Religion: Christianity
Animism

THE LANDS. The Pacific Ocean is the largest body of water in the world, its area being more than a quarter of the earth's surface. Over this vast expanse are scattered some 30 main groups of islands and many lesser groups and separate units. The total number of islands is estimated at 1,500. These islands are usually divided into three major groups:

1. *Polynesia* (Many Islands), which includes the Marquesa, Paumotu, Austral, Society, Cook, Phoenix, Union, Samoa, and Tonga Islands.

2. *Micronesia* (Little Islands), which includes the Gilberts, Marshalls, Marianas, and Carolines.

3. *Melanesia* (Black Islands), which includes such groups as Ellice, Fiji, Santa Cruz, Banks, Loyalty, New Hebrides, New Caledonia, Solomon, Bismarck, and New Guinea.

In formation the islands are of two kinds. Some are coral islands, built up by the slow work of the coral polyp; others are of volcanic origin, the result of upheaval during volcanic eruption. On nearly all of them are extinct craters, and some have active volcanoes.

The beauty of this island world is entrancing. Writers have vied with each other in their glowing descriptions of the wondrous picturesqueness of the scenery, the rugged mountains, deep valleys, and tranquil lagoons; the glistening fringe of sandy beach, the stately trees, feathery palms, and luxuriant creepers; the profusion of bright blossoms, delicious fruits, and gorgeous birds. Such features as these constrained Professor Henry Drummond to call the islands "spots from Paradise."

THE PEOPLE. Whence these island dwellers originally came is still an unsolved problem. It is generally thought that their original home was in Asia, and that in the distant past their forebears were driven by fierce storms across the broad Pacific, until gradually they peopled the various islands. Leading ethnologists trace the main racial stock to the Dravidians of India or to the region of Persia, while the idea of a contributory stream from South America is also entertained.

In general, the islanders may be divided into two racial groups, the Polynesians, who inhabit the eastern islands, and the Papuans, who people the western groups.

The *Polynesians* are fairer, taller, more intelligent, and altogether the finer race. Although they speak many dialects, these all point to a common origin. Their language is soft and melodious, with few consonants.

It is sad, yet true, that where nature has achieved her best, man is often found at his worst. And so these islands of enchanting beauty have been the haunts of the lowest savagery.

"Wars almost exterminated the populations of some of the islands; the immorality was appalling; from one-fourth to two-thirds of the children were buried alive; cannibalism was frequent; the sick and aged were usually killed rather than left to die a natural death."[1]

Of the Fijians, Dr. D. L. Leonard says in part: "Physically and intelligently they rank among the foremost in the South Seas; but before Christianity wrought its astounding miracles of transformation they had no equals for brutality, licentiousness and utter disregard of human life. The world over their name was a synonym for all that is atrocious, inhuman and demoniacal."[2]

Another author writes: "In character they occupied a pre-eminence of degradation unrivaled by that of any other islanders. . . . Cannibalism, occasional on many of the island groups, or reserved for the treatment of conquered foes, was here elevated into a national cult and custom. The man who had eaten the greatest number of human beings was highest in social order. They used to mark these pleasant little achievements by memorial stones. The great chief, Ra Undre-undre, had 872 of these set up to mark his prowess."[3]

[1] Delavan L. Pierson, *The Pacific Islands, from Savages to Saints* (New York: Funk and Wagnalls, 1906), p. 5.
[2] D. L. Leonard, *The Pacific Islanders* (New York: Funk and Wagnalls, 1906), pp. 143–44.
[3] Helen B. Montgomery, *Christus Redemptor* (New York: Macmillan, 1912), pp. 139–40.

THE RELIGION. "In religion they were polytheists almost to the extent of pantheism, for nearly every object in nature was in their eyes a god of good or evil portent. Their religious ceremonies were accompanied with sorcery, human sacrifices, and bestial orgies such as might characterize the infernal regions."[4]

"The spirits of ancestors also were worshiped and their aid sought in battle and in witchcraft. Their crowning superstition was the *tabu*. By this certain articles of food, certain localities or occupations, were forbidden under pain of death. The *tabu* forbade women to eat with men, or to eat pork, fowls, bananas or fish—in fact, most of the choice articles of food."[5]

Yet amidst all this paganism some remnant of man's nobler nature remained and at times asserted itself, and it would be an injustice not to make mention of these better traits to offset in some degree the darkness of the picture.

"In spite of all the cruelty and horror of their lives, these people maintained a sunny brightness of disposition, shared their goods with one another, practised unlimited hospitality, and in their best moments reached out toward something higher and better. Through offerings, sacrifices, charms, and ceremonies beyond number, they sought to bridge the gulf that separated them from God, but because their knowledge of God was so mistaken their lives were lived under shadows that were often black as a starless night."[6]

EUROPEAN EXPLORATION. The first European to look upon the broad waters of the Pacific seems to have been Balboa, who reached its eastern shores across Panama in 1513. Seven years later Magellan sailed the first European ship through the strait which is called after him, and into what he himself named the Pacific Ocean. Other navigators and explorers followed, the most famous being Captain Cook, who was sent out by the British government. The account of his voyages between 1768 and 1778 did much to awaken the interest of the West in this new part of the world.

In the wake of the navigators came whalers, traders, and in the course of time, recruiters of island laborers for work in the plantations and mines of Australia and South and Central America.

While among these Europeans there were some whose lives were irreproachable, for the most part they were dissolute and unprincipled, and left a shameful trail wherever they went. They reveled

---

[4] Pierson, *op. cit.*, p. 5.
[5] Montgomery, *op. cit.*, pp. 7–8.
[6] F. H. L. Paton, *The Kingdom in the Pacific* (London: United Council for Missionary Education, 1912), pp. 15–16.

in the heathen immorality, imported rum wherewith to frenzy the natives, and firearms to add to the horrors of tribal warfare; they deceived and exploited the islanders, and were guilty of the grossest excesses and cruelties. Dr. John G. Paton records how traders deliberately put on shore at different ports of the New Hebrides men ill with measles, in order to diminish the population, and how they met his remonstrance with the scornful words: "Our watchword is, 'Sweep these creatures away and let white men occupy the soil.'"

The traffic in South Sea Island laborers for plantations abroad was very largely slavery in disguise. Natives were kidnaped, seized in open raids, or decoyed on board ship under false pretenses and carried off. Many of them died of starvation on the voyage, or from fever or ill treatment on the unhealthy plantations; others were shot while attempting to escape. Comparatively few ever saw their native land again, and those who did return almost invariably brought back the "civilized" vices, to which they had become addicted, and feelings of intense hatred and revenge toward the race at whose hands they had suffered.

Dr. John G. Paton estimated that 70,000 islanders had thus been taken from their homes by these slave hunters. The fearless fight which this noble missionary and his fellows waged against this iniquitous traffic won for them the sworn enmity of the unscrupulous traders, to whom may be traced most of the libelous tales about missionaries which furnish the stock arguments of critics of foreign missions.

It should further be said that the massacre of John Williams, Bishop Patteson, and other missionaries, as well as inoffensive traders in the South Seas, is directly traceable to the murderous treachery of these white "savages" that produced in the islanders such distrust, hatred, and thirst for revenge.

POLITICAL HISTORY. It is not possible to trace in detail the colonial history of this part of the world; suffice it to say that it was only a matter of time when one by one the European powers took possession of various islands in the Pacific.

In Micronesia the Marianas, the Marshalls, and the Carolines were ruled successively by Spain, Germany, and Japan. The Marshalls and the Carolines are now administered by the United States under a United Nations trusteeship. The Gilbert Islands belong to Great Britain.

In Polynesia the Society, Austral, Marquesa, and Tuamotu Islands are French territories. The Tonga Islands are an independent Polynesian kingdom under British protectorate. Samoa is divided into Eastern and Western Samoa. Eastern Samoa is a United States possession and Western Samoa is administered by New Zealand under a United Nations trusteeship. The latter is slated for independence in 1961.

In Melanesia the Fiji Islands have been a British Crown Colony since 1874. New Caledonia is ruled by France, and the New Hebrides is a condominium administered jointly by Britain and France. New Guinea, the largest island of the entire area, is divided into two sections. The western part is still held by the Netherlands, though Indonesia regards it as being rightfully hers. The eastern part is a United Nations trusteeship mandated to Australia.

SOCIETY ISLANDS

LONDON MISSIONARY SOCIETY PIONEERS. The accounts of Captain Cook's voyages, which were an important factor in shaping William Carey's missionary purpose, aroused extraordinary interest in the South Seas, so that when in 1795 the *London Missionary Society* was formed, it was decided to make these islands its first field of operation. A party of thirty missionaries sailed in September, 1796, in the *Duff*, under Captain Wilson, and in March, 1797, reached *Tahiti*, the largest of some thirteen islands comprising the Society Islands, named in honor of the Royal Geographical Society. Eighteen of the party remained here, ten went on to the Tonga (or Friendly) Islands, and two to the Marquesas. Only one of the latter remained, while those on Tonga suffered severe privations and perils; three of them were martyred and the rest finally escaped.

EARLY HARDSHIPS. The missionaries at Tahiti were at first well received by King Pomare, and glowing reports carried back to England by Captain Wilson called forth fresh enthusiasm and recruits. But the *Duff* on her second voyage was captured by the French, and it was five long years before supplies or communications reached the lonely workers. Meanwhile they had been reduced to sore straits, three were killed, others fled, so that when the nineteenth century dawned but five men and two women were left, the only missionaries in all the vast Pacific.

OPPOSING FORCES. Moral and religious conditions on the island were fearful, and cruel wars were well-nigh incessant. Pomare's treatment of the missionaries fluctuated between courtesy and threats. He was a fickle and brutal king, who during his career offered 2,000 human sacrifices to his gods. He died in 1804, and his son, Pomare

II, who succeeded him, at first walked in his footsteps, until the missionary outlook became as dark as possible.

TURNING OF THE TIDE. Prompted by the grave reports received from the field, a special meeting was called in London in July, 1812, to pray for Pomare's conversion, and in that very month he gave up his idols and asked for baptism. This was the turning point of the work in Tahiti. Idolatry was completely overthrown, the king sent for a printing press to prepare Bibles and hymn books for his people, and at his own expense he built a huge church, where in the presence of 4,000 of his subjects he was baptized. The light spread not only over all Tahiti, but also from island to island of this and other groups, through the efforts of the Tahitian Christians as well as the missionaries, and Tahiti will ever be known as the seed-plot from which the gospel was scattered far and wide over Oceania.

The entire Bible in Tahiti was published in 1838. The first edition was printed in England and a copy was presented to Queen Victoria. In 1843 the London Missionary Society withdrew and handed over its work to the *Paris Evangelical Missionary Society*. Tahiti remains the headquarters of its work in Oceania.

By 1877 heathenism had been completely wiped out. The Christian Church in the Society Islands is today well established along indigenous lines. The work on the various islands includes a leper asylum and a pastors' training school, both of which are maintained by the local churches. The church membership of 4,500 is divided among 80 congregations, large and small. The Christian community, estimated at 34,000, is served by 45 ordained nationals, assisted by 19 missionaries of the Paris Evangelical Missionary Society.

Two other groups are working there at present, the *Anglican Church of New Zealand* and the *Seventh Day Adventists*. The latter reports one church of about a hundred members.

TONGA ISLANDS

MISSIONS. The initial attempt of the *London Missionary Society* to establish work on Tonga proved abortive. Of the ten missionaries who landed there in 1797, three were brutally murdered, one "went native," and the remaining six were picked up by a passing ship and taken to Australia. Two decades later a second attempt was made, this time by the *Methodists* of Australia and New Zealand. Their pioneer, *Walter Lawry* of Australia, arrived in 1822, but ill health cut short his stay. He was followed in 1826 by *John Thomas*, an *English Methodist*, who remained in the Tongas for twenty-five years. By 1850 the entire population of the Tonga Islands had become Christians. To the present time the Methodist churches predominate. Half of the population of 60,000 belongs to the Methodist Church. The *Free Church of Tonga* claims 10,000 communicants and the *Church of Tonga* accounts for another 6,000. The *Anglican Church* and the *Seventh Day Adventists* have a following of about 500 each, and the *Church of the Latter Day Saints* is strong and growing. *Roman Catholics* number 8,000.

SAMOA ISLANDS

MISSIONS. The Samoans first received the gospel from Polynesian teachers from Tahiti in the east and Tonga in the south, not from European missionaries. In 1828 a Samoan visited Tonga, learned the gospel from the Methodists there, became a Christian, and upon his return to Samoa preached the gospel to his own people with such effectiveness that churches sprang up everywhere. In 1830 *John Williams*, of the *London Missionary Society* on Tahiti, paid a visit to Samoa and left behind eight Tahitian teachers trained by the Congregationalists. Five years later, when the first European missionary landed on Samoa, he found a Christian community of over 2,000 meeting in little groups in sixty-five villages. Within twenty months the 2,000 Christians had multiplied to 13,000. In a few years virtually the entire population had embraced Christianity. In two decades the complete Bible had been published in the Samoan tongue. The two missionary societies working in the area decided, in the interests of mission comity, to divide the field between them, assigning Tonga to the Methodists and Samoa to the Congregationalists; but they reckoned without the indigenous churches. The Christians in Samoa, having originally received the gospel from the Methodists in Tonga, were unwilling to relinquish their affiliation with that group to link up with the Congregationalists in Tahiti. The result was that the two missions have continued working side by side, and today both Churches have flourishing communities in the islands. The indigenous population of 50,000 is almost totally Christian, with about three-fifths of them belonging to the Congregational Church. One authority has described the London Missionary Society work in Samoa as "undoubtedly the finest and best-conceived enterprise in the Pacific." Education is almost wholly in the hands of the Church. The Christians in Samoa are among the finest in the world. Through the years they have sent their own missionaries to do pioneer work in Fiji, the New Hebrides, the Solomons, and New Guinea in advance of the European missionaries.

It is doubtful if there is another people on the face of the earth who, in proportion to their numbers have given so many missionaries to the church, or have paid so great a price in sacrifice and martyrdom. At home, not only do they build and maintain their own churches, schools and other institutions, but they sustain their missionary guests as well. They regularly support the worldwide work of their churches. Yes, their philanthropy extends beyond the Church. To Armenian Relief, and the Red Cross, and Dr. Barnardo's Homes and Schools for the Blind in England they sent generous contributions.[7]

The *Assemblies of God* and the *Seventh Day Adventists* both have a small work in Samoa. The latter Mission has seven churches under national leadership serving a Christian community of 1,700.

FIJI ISLANDS

MISSIONS. The story of how the gospel was introduced into the Fiji Islands is a novel one. It came about by means of a curious combination of circumstances which man might regard as pure accident, but which was unmistakably of God's designing. The first ray of light came through converts from the Tonga Islands, 300 miles east, where the *English Wesleyans* had begun work in 1823 and had reaped a rich reward in the conversion of several thousands. Among the Tongans who crossed in their canoes to Lakemba, an eastern island of the Fiji group, for purposes of trade, were some recent Christian converts whose testimony made a deep impression upon the Fijians. This led to the sending of *Rev. William Cross* and *Rev. David Cargill* in 1835. They met with a rough reception, several of their native Christian teachers were killed, and their own lives were in danger. But before long their kindness broke down the hatred and won the good will of the savages. In five months 31 were baptized, and 280 within one year.

But meanwhile by a stranger providence the gospel was finding entrance into Ono, a small island 150 miles south of Lakemba. In 1835 a terrible epidemic raged on this island, and all the efforts of the pagan priests to overcome it by devices to appease the angry gods utterly failed. In this emergency one of the chiefs, crossing to Lakemba, learned from another Fijian chief who had visited Tahiti that the only true God was Jehovah, and that one day in seven should be set apart for His worship. Laying hold of this fragment of truth he and his people set aside the seventh day, and, dressing in their festive attire, attempted to worship this unknown God. While

[7] **Henry** P. Van Dusen, *They Found the Church There* (New York: Charles Scribner's Sons, 1945), p. 94.

they were thus groping their way toward the light, a Christian Tongan teacher visited Ono and told them all he knew of the new faith. Later, other teachers were sent to them from Tonga, and a deep work of grace began. The entire population of this and a neighboring island renounced idolatrous practices. In 1839 *Rev. James Calvert,* who had the previous year reached Lakemba, was sent over to Ono, and within a few months it was given to him to baptize 200 converts.

As yet, however, only the outskirts of the awful realm of darkness in Fiji had been touched. The worst islands lay to the west, whither the missionaries proceeded. A fierce battle lay before them, for they seemed to be attacking the very seat of Satan. Some of the horrors which they were forced to witness—at one time the strangling of the sixteen wives of the king's son who had been drowned, at another the cooking and eating of the bodies of eleven war captives—were almost beyond endurance. For a full decade their faith continued to be sorely tested.

Finally, in 1845, a sweeping revival began. Several influential chiefs—one of them a monster of iniquity—came under pungent conviction of sin and were regenerated by the Spirit, and their people followed in large numbers. From these beginnings such a marvelous work of grace swept the entire islands that sixty years later there were 826 churches and 1,000 points where the gospel was regularly preached. The baptismal font of one fine church, made out of a stone upon which formerly human victims for cannibal feasts were slaughtered, speaks eloquently of what the gospel has done in the Fiji Islands.

Today the indigenous population of almost 200,000 is largely Christian. On the other hand, Christianity has made very little headway among the 160,000 immigrants (Muslims and Hindus) from India. The *Methodist Church* in Fiji represents a Christian community of 130,000. The *Anglican Church* has 3,000 members, and the *Seventh Day Adventists* about half of that number. The *Assemblies of God* also have missionaries in Fiji. The Church in Fiji, like the one in Samoa, has from the beginning been a missionary-minded Church. More than 300 missionaries from Fiji have gone to New Guinea, the Solomons, and the aborigines of northern Australia.

NEW HEBRIDES ISLANDS

MISSIONS. This group, lying to the west of the Fiji Islands, comprises about 70 islands of which 30 are inhabited. The estimated population is 60,000, but among that number 20 different languages are spoken. In connection with the marvelous work of transformation which has taken place among these islanders, three names will always shine with peculiar luster, the names of John Williams, John Geddie, and John G. Paton—"the three epistles of John," as they are sometimes called.

John Williams, the first of the trio and deservedly called "the Apostle of the South Seas," was identified with the New Hebrides in death rather than in life. Born in England in 1796, he was sent out by the London Missionary Society in 1817 to its work in the Society Islands. He was a born leader and a man of unusual resource and action, whose vision for the work reached out far beyond that of the missionaries who preceded him. Declaring that he could not content himself "within the narrow limits of a single reef," he launched a campaign of expansion and began the training of a national agency to augment the missionary force for carrying the gospel to other islands. The result was the extension of missionary effort within a few years to the Austral, Hervey, Samoan, Fiji, and other groups. From first to last five mission ships, purchased or built by himself, were pressed into service by this dauntless apostle, and with such effect that by 1834 "no group of islands, nor single island of importance within 2,000 miles of Tahiti had been left unvisited."[8]

The inception of the work on each new island involved dangers and hardships not a few, but the national workers no less than the English missionaries rose nobly to the task, and they were as nobly backed by the prayers and gifts of the national churches.

Soon after his return from furlough in 1838 he set his heart on a visit to the New Hebrides, and sailed for that group in his new ship Camden, taking with him 12 native teachers as pioneers. On November 20, 1839, he landed on the island of Erromanga with Mr. Harris, a young man sailing in the Camden. All seemed pleasant at first, but suddenly a shout was heard, the natives turned upon them, and before they could make the shore both men were felled by the clubs of savages and then speared to death. Their bodies were dragged into the bush for a horrid cannibal feast.

As the tidings of Williams' martyrdom reached Samoa a wail of profound grief rose from the hearts of thousands of converts. But at once 25 volunteered to take his place, and in six months the Camden was again at Erromanga, where two were landed, but after a year of suffering were forced to withdraw. Continued attempts were made at the cost of a number of lives and much suffering, and by 1852, through the agency of these Samoan teachers and their Erromangan converts, 100 had been won to Christ and two

[8] Arthur T. Pierson, The New Acts of the Apostles (New York: Baker and Taylor, 1894), p. 119.

chapels built. But even after that Erromanga was stained by the blood of many another missionary martyr.

By arrangement during Williams' visit to England, the *London Missionary Society* was to open the New Hebrides work with national workers from other islands, and the field was then to be manned by the Presbyterians of Scotland and Nova Scotia.

John Geddie, "the father of Presbyterian Missions in the South Seas," reached the most southerly island of *Aneityum* in 1848. As a boy in Nova Scotia "little Johnnie Geddie" had pored over the stories of the heroes of the South Seas and longed to become a missionary. Finally his persevering efforts were rewarded and the Nova Scotian churches sent him as their missionary.

It was through many trials and vicissitudes, and by dint of infinite patience and perseverance, that Mr. and Mrs. Geddie won the confidence of the natives and eventually saw the gospel triumph over vile heathen practices and immorality. Mr. Geddie reduced the language of Aneityum to writing, and his translation of the Gospel of Mark was the first completed book published in any language of the western Pacific. He established a printing press and a training school for national workers, and scores of evangelists have gone forth from Aneityum to other islands, supported by the gifts of the national Church.

"On a tablet in the large church, seating 1,000 people, this inscription was placed in memory of John Geddie: 'When he landed in 1848 there were no Christians here; when he left in 1872 there were no heathen.' "[9]

John G. Paton became perhaps the best known of all the missionaries of the last generation, because of the worldwide circulation of his wonderful autobiography. "No narrative of missionary toils and triumphs is either more readable or more romantic, more graphic or pathetic, or more abundant in proofs of supernatural power."[10]

Born in a Scottish highland home, with its plain living and high thinking, Dr. Paton was sent out in 1858 by the Presbyterian Churches of Scotland, Canada, Australia, and New Zealand, and with two associates and their wives settled on the island of *Tanna,* where Messrs. Turner and Nesbit and their wives, missionaries from Samoa, had landed in 1842 and after terrible experiences had been rescued by a passing ship. For four years these new missionaries battled against all the powers of darkness. Their lives constantly threatened by dark foes and in danger of treachery from professed

[9] Montgomery, *op. cit.,* p. 160.
[10] Arthur T. Pierson, *op. cit.,* p. 347.

friends, they went steadily on, teaching, healing, and befriending all whom they could reach. But after they had displayed superhuman courage and overcome tremendous difficulties, the situation grew so grave that nothing remained but flight from the island.

Dr. Paton's subsequent labors were on the small island of *Aniwa*, where, after a series of experiences as thrilling as ever fell to the lot of any missionary, he finally witnessed a marvelous work of grace which changed the whole population from murderers and cannibals into the "most openly and reverently Christian community that he had ever visited." The story of this heroic man "records perhaps fifty cases in which his life was threatened, or death by violence overhung him; yet in marvelous ways deliverance came, so that his preservation seemed like a perpetual miracle."[11]

The Bible translation work begun by John Williams was continued by the Gordon brothers, and by 1870 four groups of islands—Erromanga, Nguna, Tanna, and Futuna—had the Scriptures in their own tongues. By 1901 the Scriptures had been published in no fewer than 22 languages, and in every instance but one the national churches defrayed the cost of printing.

Missionary work in the New Hebrides has been conducted in the face of great obstacles. Nevertheless, much progress has been achieved and today fully half of the population of 60,000 belongs to the Protestant Christian community.

Seven Protestant missions are presently working in the New Hebrides. The largest of these is the *Anglican Church of New Zealand*. Two *Presbyterian* missions, one from Australia and the other from New Zealand, report a combined Christian community of 16,500. The *Australian Churches of Christ* have 11 missionaries assisted by 60 nationals serving 50 churches. The *John G. Paton Mission* combines medical work with evangelistic activities in six islands of the group. The *Seventh Day Adventists* report 12 churches, all under national leadership. The *Apostolic Church Missionary Movement*, a British society, has 10 places of worship.

CAROLINE ISLANDS

MISSIONS. *Kusaie* was discovered by Americans in 1806 and thereafter whaling captains of New England plying the South Pacific made it a port of call. The whalers indulged in wild orgies, abducted Kusaie women, carried off slaves, and left behind a legacy of foreign diseases. As a result the population dwindled from about 2,000 to 200 in fifty or sixty years. The first missionaries to the Carolines were

[11] *Ibid.*, p. 309.

members of the *American Board of Commissioners* who landed in 1852. In the first party were both Americans and Hawaiians. They established stations on Kusaie and *Ponape* and tried to repair some of the damage done by the whalers. Later they were joined by members of the *Hawaiian Evangelical Association*. For a time, during the German occupation of the islands, the work was turned over to the *Liebenzeller Mission*. Following World War II the American Board returned to the Carolines; their 1958 Report indicates that they have eight missionaries on Ponape and two on Kusaie. One hundred and one churches are served by 204 full-time national workers. The German missionaries of the Liebenzeller Mission are located on *Truk, Palau,* and *Yap*. Rev. *Robert W. Logan* translated the New Testament into the Truk language. The transformation effected by the gospel in these islands has been truly remarkable. Once an island dreaded for its savagery and brutality, Kusaie today has no jails, no houses of ill fame, no medicine men, and hardly any disease. Marriage is sacred, and divorce is unknown. Such is the power of the gospel.

SOLOMON ISLANDS

MISSIONS. To *Bishop John Selwyn* of the *Anglican Church of New Zealand* belongs the credit for beginning missionary work in the Solomon Islands. It was he who founded the Melanesian Mission of the Anglican Church of New Zealand. He cruised extensively among the many islands and established a center, first at Auckland, N. Z., and later on Norfolk Island, where promising young men from the different islands were trained to become teachers and evangelists among their own people.

In 1855 Selwyn was joined by *John Coleridge Patteson,* an Oxford graduate of rare gifts and rarer consecration. In 1861 Patteson was made missionary bishop of Melanesia, and thereafter for ten years he directed the work of island evangelization far and near with singular devotion and success. The greatest difficulty he encountered was the wicked work of white traders in carrying off islanders for enforced labor in the plantations of Fiji and Queensland. He fought this fiendish traffic with all his power.

It was in 1871 that with a group of his beloved island workers in the *Southern Cross* he headed for Nikapu, one of the Santa Cruz Islands. Landing alone and without suspecting any harm, he was cruelly murdered and his body placed in a canoe to drift back to the ship. On his breast had been inflicted five wounds covered over with a palm branch tied in five mysterious knots. It was learned later that this signified that the deed was done in revenge for the kidnaping and death of five natives at the hands of white traders some time before.

The Melanesian Mission has through the years maintained an extensive work with great success. Its activities are spread over seven islands and include a training college and an industrial school for the development of native decorative crafts. Medical work is also carried on with national assistance, and successful bush schools have been established under national leadership.

For over half a century the *Plymouth Brethren* of Australia have conducted a very fruitful work in the Solomons. As a young woman *Miss Florence S. H. Young* had worked among immigrants from the Solomons and the New Hebrides. In 1886 her work was organized as the *Queensland Kanaka Mission*. In 1904, after some of her converts had returned to the Solomons, the work was extended to those islands under a new name, the *South Sea Evangelical Mission*. Miss Young was one of the first missionaries to sail under the new Mission. It was with this Mission that *Dr. Northcote Deck* and twelve members of the Deck family served for many years. Three main centers of work are located on Malaita, Guadalcanal, and Makira. In 1957 the Mission had 14 missionaries and hundreds of voluntary pastors and teachers. The Christian community numbered 25,000.

The work commenced in 1902 in the western Solomons by the *Methodist Missionary Society of Australia* is now carried on by the *Methodist Church of New Zealand*, whose 270 churches represent a baptized membership of about 10,000. The missionary staff numbers 36. Educational work includes 88 schools providing elementary education for 3,016 pupils.

The *Seventh Day Adventists* have extensive work throughout many parts of the southwest Pacific. In the Solomon Islands they report 46 churches with an aggregate membership of 3,500.

NEW GUINEA

THE LAND. New Guinea has the distinction of being the second largest island in the world. Its area is 312,000 square miles, or more than the combined area of all the other Pacific islands put together. It is a vast country of high mountains, forest-clad valleys, broad plains, great rivers, and rich resources still largely undeveloped. Indeed, although the island was discovered by the Portuguese in 1511 a great portion remains yet unexplored, owing to the trying climate and the ferocity of the people.

POLITICAL HISTORY. New Guinea is divided into two parts. The eastern half is administered by Australia as a Trust Territory under the United Nations. The western half was retained by the Netherlands when it pulled out of the Dutch East Indies in 1949. This was a disappointment to the Indonesians, who regard it as theirs and show it as such on their maps, calling it Irian. Included in the eastern part of the island is Papua, a non-self-governing possession of Australia.

MISSIONS. Four Protestant Churches have been at work in Papua, each being responsible for the evangelization of a different section of the country. The littoral to the southwest of the Owen Stanley range was assigned to the *Congregationalists* of the London Missionary Society. The *Anglicans* from Australia assumed responsibility for the mainland north and east of the mountains. The Australian *Methodists* occupied the coastal islands to the north and east. German *Lutherans* were active in Papua during the German occupation, but since World War I the Lutheran work has been reinforced by missionaries from Australia and the United States.

The pioneer mission to Papua was the *London Missionary Society*. Its first worker, *Samuel McFarlane,* arrived in 1870 from the Loyalty Islands. Seven years later he was joined by *James Chalmers,* one of the greatest missionaries of the Pacific Southwest. Chalmers, called by Robert Louis Stevenson the "Great Heart of New Guinea," was born in Scotland, and as a boy received the missionary vision through hearing an address on the Fiji Islands. He and his wife were sent out by the London Missionary Society, in 1867, to Raratonga, where they spent ten years.

When Chalmers went to New Guinea in 1877 the work there, already begun by such noble men as Dr. McFarlane and Dr. W. G. Lawes, was in its early pioneer stage. Chalmers with his physical strength, superb courage, quick intuition, tact and resourcefulness, was eminently fitted for pioneering. He pursued a policy of broad exploration and the planting of a chain of stations at intervals along the coast. His career was marked by many thrilling adventures and hairbreadth escapes. His heroic character and splendid achievements were among the foremost influences that changed Stevenson from a prejudiced critic to an enthusiastic friend of missions.

Chalmers twice revisited England, and threw himself with tremendous energy into presenting missions in great meetings throughout the country. His simplicity, fervor, and contagious enthusiasm stirred thousands to new missionary interest.

His thirty-three years of lofty service ended in martyrdom in 1901. Together with a young missionary named Tomkins and several national helpers Chalmers landed on Goaribari Island to make some explorations. Without warning they were set upon by the savages, clubbed to death, and their bodies eaten. The news of Chalmers' death was received with passionate sorrow by the thousands of converts to whom he had been friend and father. Later, a monument to the martyrs was erected on the spot, and a church now stands near the ground where their red blood stained the sands.

The London Missionary Society is now working in 12 language areas involving 200,000 people. Two new stations were opened in the 1940's. In 1954 the missionary staff numbered 36. Ministerial recruitment and training, secondary education, medical work, and Scripture translation have all received much attention, and progress has been made in all these fields. A revision of the Motu New Testament was completed, and the Suau New Testament was published for the first time, by missionaries of the London Missionary Society in 1956. The *Congregational Church of Papua* has 12,000 members and a Christian community twice as large.

The first *Anglican* missionaries waded ashore on the eastern coast of Papua in 1891. They were greeted by a band of warriors, each with a spear in his hand ready for action. One word from their chief and the two missionaries would have been killed, cooked, and consumed all in the one day. Fortunately the chief decided to make friends with the newcomers and sold them land in exchange for 112 pounds of tobacco, ten tomahawks, a bundle of knives, beads and pipes, and a length of Turkey red. This was the beginning of Anglican missions in Papua. Forty years later a cathedral seating 2,000 people was erected on the spot where the work had begun. When the Japanese overran New Guinea in the early days of World War II the British authorities ordered white residents to evacuate to Australia; but many of the missionaries elected to remain to face the dangers and hardships of war with the members of their flock. The Anglican bishop broadcast a message to his staff:

> We must endeavor to carry on our work in all circumstances, no matter what the cost may ultimately be to any of us individually. God expects this of us. The church at home, which sent us out, will surely expect it. The universal church expects it. . . . The people whom we serve expect it of us. We could never hold up our faces again if, for our own safety, we forsook Him and fled when the shadows of the passion began to gather around Him in His spiritual and mystical body, the church in Papua.[12]

The churches of the Pacific Islands suffered greatly during the

[12] Van Dusen, *op. cit.*, p. 94.

Japanese occupation. Many missionaries were captured by the invaders. Some were placed in concentration camps; some were killed, among them the Anglican bishop and eight of his staff. A volcanic eruption of Mt. Lamington in New Guinea in 1951 killed 4,000 people, including English and Papuan clergy and their families. Among others lost were eighteen Papuan teachers, many of them prospective ordinands. So depleted were the ranks that the Anglican Church in 1957 issued an urgent appeal for seven priests and three teachers for Polynesia; three priests, a doctor, a handyman, and five teachers for Melanesia; eight priests, seven teachers, and nine nurses for New Guinea; and one priest, five teachers, and one nurse for Carpentaria. It will be some time before the ravages of World War II are completely repaired. The diocese of New Guinea reports a membership of 20,000 Christians.

Methodist missions in New Guinea date from 1891 when a party of 75 landed on an island off the east coast of Papua. This group was made up of 10 white missionaries and 65 teachers from other parts of the South Sea Islands. Twenty years later not a single member of the original party remained. Some had died of fever; others had returned to their homeland, broken in health. But in spite of all the hardships and privations the work continued to progress and island after island was occupied by missionaries and teachers. *Dr. E. W. Bromilow* translated the entire Bible into what he described as "the language of the worst cannibals in Papua." World War II played havoc with Methodist missionary work in the islands. Most of the white workers complied with government orders to evacuate, leaving the stations in the charge of national teachers. With the return of peace the work of rehabilitation got under way. Today the Methodist Church in New Guinea reports a Christian community of 90,000.

On July 12, 1886, a German missionary, *Rev. John Flierl* of the *Neuendettelsau Missionary Society*, landed at Finschhafen, where he opened a field which was destined to become the largest Protestant mission in the South Pacific. On the field this Mission was known as the Lutheran Mission Finschhafen. Early in 1877 two missionaries of the *Rhenish Missionary Society* of Germany arrived to establish the second Lutheran mission, which became known as the Lutheran Mission Madang. From the beginning the two missions worked together in the most cordial co-operation. Owing to improper food, enervating climate, malaria, and other diseases, however, these missions, especially the Rhenish Mission, suffered staggering losses in the early years; but the missionaries persevered through trial and tribulation, establishing new stations, preaching the gospel, and opening village schools, firmly believing that their labors were not in vain. At last, after thirteen years of work, the Finschhafen Mission baptized its first convert, and four years later the Madang Mission experienced similar encouragement.

In 1908 the infant Church assumed responsibility for the evangelization of its own people and sent four evangelists to the Hube tribe of 8,000 persons. In a short time more than 600 evangelists and teachers were trained and sent to remote areas with remarkable results. Thousands of souls were added to the Church during the early years of the new century. Plantations were acquired. Presses were established. Hospitals were opened. The Christians built their own churches and schools.

During World War I and again in World War II the work of these two German societies was disrupted and only the timely aid of Australian and American Lutheran bodies preserved the continuity of the enterprise. In 1953 the two German missions merged to form the *Lutheran Mission New Guinea*. Also associated with this cooperative effort are the two societies which gave succor during the war years, the *United Evangelical Lutheran Church* in Australia and the *American Lutheran Church*. The Lutheran Mission New Guinea is the largest Protestant mission in the South Pacific, with a staff of 243 commissioned missionaries, of whom 44 per cent are American and Canadian, 21 per cent are Australian, and 35 per cent are German. Over half the staff are lay missionaries engaged in the educational, medical, agricultural, industrial, and administrative phases of the program. The Mission operates two ships, two airplanes, and four plantations. Its medical work includes 5 hospitals, 41 dispensaries, and 2 leper colonies. The *Evangelical Lutheran Church of New Guinea* was organized in February, 1956. Eighty-two ordained pastors and 1,028 full-time evangelists serve 278 organized churches with an aggregate membership of 180,000. Children from Christian homes are educated in 789 elementary schools and 17 secondary schools. Twenty-seven students are enrolled at *Flierl Seminary*.

The *Kwato Mission of Papua* was founded in 1890 by *Rev. Charles W. Abel*, at that time a missionary of the London Missionary Society and for eleven years associated with James Chalmers. After a lifetime of adventure in New Guinea, Mr. Abel was killed in a car accident in London in 1930. The work was continued by the *New Guinea Evangelization Society*, organized in 1923, and the *Kwato Extension Association*, an interdenominational society founded in 1918.

A newcomer to New Guinea in 1940, the *Unevangelized Fields*

Mission has a well-established work in this field. Some 50 missionaries, mostly from Australia, are at work among 20 different tribes in the southwest part of the country. Already considerable translation work has been done in these tribal languages. The Mission also has a small staff of workers in Dutch New Guinea. *

The *Lutheran Church-Missouri Synod* entered the central part of New Guinea in 1948 and now has a fast-growing work among the Enga people in the Western Highlands, of whom there are about 200,000. Fourteen of the Mission's 27 staff members are engaged in direct evangelism and education. In 1957 over 550 persons were baptized and the first hospital was completed. Three new stations were opened the following year.

The western half of New Guinea, sometimes called Irian, was retained by the Netherlands when Indonesia was granted independence in 1949. The population is estimated at 700,000. The State Church was founded and fostered through the years by Dutch missionaries. Today it is said to have 430 places of worship and 30,000 communicant members. The Christian community is estimated at 100,000.

The *Utrecht Missionary Union* sent its first three pioneers to Dutch New Guinea in 1861. The entire venture was fraught with great difficulties and dangers. During one period it was said that in New Guinea there were more missionary graves than Christian converts. After twenty-five years of travail there were only 20 believers. Change came slowly, but in time the people became more friendly. There was a break during the first decade of the present century, and thereafter progress was more rapid. Between 1910 and 1940, the Christian community increased from 500 to 15,000.

The *Christian and Missionary Alliance* initiated work in the Wissel Lakes district in 1939. The vanguard consisted of two missionaries and three national Christians who went in from the coast on foot, reaching the lakes after eighteen strenuous days. The work was just getting under way when the Japanese invasion called a halt to all missionary endeavor and necessitated evacuation to Australia. Work was resumed in October, 1946, and fifteen months later the first converts, 17 in number, were baptized. In June, 1949, the work was extended to the Kemandora Valley, and in 1954 the Baliem Valley was occupied. In 1959 the Mission had 60 workers and 30 national preachers working in 14 main centers. Seven organized churches have a membership of over 1,000 Christians. Hundreds more gather each week in 22 preaching centers. Medical work includes a hospital and four clinics. Teaching, preaching, and Bible translation are going on in nine different tribes. Bible schools are being conducted for the Dani and Uhunduni in the Ilaga Valley, where between 5,000 and 6,000 persons have recently embraced Christianity. Ninety-six students are enrolled in the full-term Bible school for the Kapauku tribe at Enarotalia.

The Evangelical Alliance Mission has been working in New Guinea since 1952, when two pioneer missionaries on an exploratory trip into unknown jungle territory were brutally slain by their native carriers. Undaunted, other missionaries volunteered to take their place. The Mission is working in two districts, Bird's Head in the extreme northwest, and among the cannibals of the South Coast. As yet only three churches have been established.

Wycliffe Bible Translators entered New Guinea in 1956 and established their main base at Aiyura. In September, 1958, the New Guinea jungle camp began operations with eleven candidates on hand. Courses during the ten-week period included language study, orientation, carpentry, mechanics, horseback riding, swimming, hiking, and clinics. Advance has been rapid and already they have translators working in 14 different tribes. Other missions in New Guinea include *New Tribes Mission, Regions Beyond Missionary Union, Church of the Nazarene,* and *Missionary Aviation Fellowship.* This last one is not a missionary society in the strictest sense of the term. Rather it is a service agency which provides air transportation for other missions working in jungle areas where travel is slow and costly.

STATISTICAL CHARTS

STATISTICS ON WORLD RELIGIONS[1]

Christians		
Roman Catholics	500,000,000	
Protestants	275,000,000	
Eastern and Orthodox	200,000,000	
Total		975,000,000
Muslims		400,000,000
Buddhists		350,000,000
Hindus		330,000,000
Confucianists		300,000,000
Taoists		50,000,000
Shintoists		30,000,000
Jews		10,000,000
Animists		185,000,000
Atheists		200,000,000
Others		10,000,000
Total		2,840,000,000

STATISTICS ON MISSIONARY PERSONNEL

Roman Catholic Missionaries		45,000
Protestant Missionaries		
Africa	16,400	
Middle East	900	
South Asia	6,500	
Southeast Asia	3,300	
Far East	4,600	
Pacific Islands	1,200	
Latin America	9,300	
Europe	800	43,000
Total		88,000

[1] Based on *Occasional Bulletin,* Vol. IX, No. 4 (May 6, 1958), Missionary Research Library, New York.

STATISTICS ON
NORTH AMERICAN PROTESTANT MISSIONS

Almost 28,000 of the 43,000 Protestant missionaries in the world are from North America. Altogether there are 271 *sending* organizations and 85 *supporting* agencies, making a grand total of 356 missionary organizations and agencies in North America. These are divided into eight major groups as follows:

Group	Units	Missionaries
1. Division of Foreign Missions of the National Council of Churches	78	10,977
2. Evangelical Foreign Missions Association	49	5,100
3. Interdenominational Foreign Mission Association	42	7,400
4. Associated Mission Agencies of the International Council of Christian Churches	16	851
5. Independent: Denominational	28	2,072
6. Independent: Nondenominational	37	1,695
7. American Branches of International and Interdenominational Agencies	6	207
8. Canadian Boards	15	774
Total	271	29,076
Less duplications		1,343
Actual total		27,733

STATISTICS ON MEDICAL MISSIONS[1]

Area	Hospitals	Dispensaries	Leprosaria	Sanitoria	Doctors	Nurses
Asia	364	192	79	26	485	558
Near East	36	21	6	1	52	73
Africa	305	269	113	1	243	567
Latin America	34	53	6	5	50	85
Caribbean	10	13	—	—	29	41
Pacific Islands	37	17	6	—	24	90
Total	786	565	210	33	883	1,414

[1] Taken from *Directory of Protestant Medical Missions,* compiled by Arthur W. March, Missionary Research Library, New York: 1959.

STATISTICS ON PROTESTANT
THEOLOGICAL SCHOOLS[1]

Area	Number of Schools	Full-time Faculty	Students
Africa	71	219	1,674
Middle East	1	4	12
South Asia	35	167	702
Southeast Asia	32	127	840
Far East	28	221	2,218
Latin America	35	129	748
Total	202	867	6,194

MISSIONARY RADIO STATIONS
OF THE WORLD[2]

Station	Location	Opening Date	Sponsor
HCJB	Quito, Ecuador	1931	World Radio Missionary Fellowship
TIFC	San José, Costa Rica	1948	Latin America Mission
DZAS	Manila, Philippines	1948	Far East Broadcasting Co., Inc.
CP-27	La Paz, Bolivia	1949	Canadian Baptist Foreign Mission Board
HOXO	Panama City	1949	Latin America Mission and World Radio Missionary Fellowship
4VEH	Cap Haitien, Haiti	1950	Oriental Missionary Society
TGNA	Guatemala City	1950	Central American Mission
DYSR	Dumaguete City, P. I.	1950	RAVEMCCO
KAIM	Honolulu, Hawaii	1953	Hawaii Christian Broadcasting Association
ELWA	Monrovia, Liberia	1954	Sudan Interior Mission
Voice of Tangier	Tangier, Morocco	1954	Trans World Radio

[1] Taken from *Occasional Bulletin*, Vol. X, No. 2 (February 16, 1959), Missionary Research Library, New York.
[2] Taken from *Foreign Missionary Radio*, Vol. IV, No. 5 (May 1, 1959).

Station	Location	Opening Date	Sponsor
KSEW	Sitka, Alaska	1954	Board of National Missions of the Presbyterian Church, U.S.A.
HLKY	Seoul, Korea	1954	RAVEMCCO
IBRA	Tangier, Morocco	1955	International Broadcasting Association
WIVV	Vieques, Puerto Rico	1956	Calvary Baptist Mission
HLKX	Inchon, Korea	1956	The Evangelical Alliance Mission
KSAB	Naha, Okinawa	1957	Far East Broadcasting Co., Inc.
PJA6	Aruba, Netherlands Antilles	1958	The Evangelical Alliance Mission
4-VI	Cayes, Haiti	1958	West Indies Mission
YNOL	Managua, Nicaragua	1959	Group of local Christians and the Latin America Mission
HLKT	Taegu, Korea	1959	Churches of Taegu and RAVEMCCO
Voice of Tangier	Monte Carlo, Monaco	1960	Trans World Radio

BIBLIOGRAPHY

Missionary literature has grown to comprise an immense number of books dealing with the various fields and phases of the missionary enterprise. Limitation of space makes possible the mention here of only a very few, and those have been selected which the author thinks may prove most helpful to the student or general reader in amplifying the necessarily brief record of missions contained in the present volume. The selection purposely includes some old standard volumes giving the records of the past as well as more recent books dealing with present-day missions.

The Missionary Research Library, 3041 Broadway, New York City, has the most complete collection of missionary books and magazines on file anywhere in North America, if not in the world, and is prepared to furnish accurate information upon any field or aspect of missions. Its monthly *Book Notes,* furnished on request, is a valuable source of information concerning Christian missions. Another excellent source is the Bibliography at the back of the *International Review of Missions* published quarterly by the International Missionary Council.

Historical and General

Aberly, John. *An Outline of Missions.* Philadelphia: Muhlenberg Press, 1945.

Barnes, L. C. *Two Thousand Years of Missions Before Carey.* Chicago: Christian Culture Press, 1900.

Bliss, E. M. *The Missionary Enterprise.* New York: Revell, 1908.

Boer, Harry R. *The World Missionary Situation Today.* Grand Rapids: Eerdmans, 1958.

Carver, William O. *The Course of Christian Missions.* New York: Revell, 1932.

Dain, A. J. *Mission Fields Today; A Brief World Survey.* Chicago: Inter-Varsity Press, 1956.

Dennis, James S. *Centennial Survey of Foreign Missions.* New York: Revell, 1902.

Edman, V. Raymond. *The Light in Dark Ages.* Wheaton, Ill.: Van Kampen Press, 1949.

Foster, John. *After the Apostles.* London: Student Christian Movement Press, 1951.

——. *Beginning from Jerusalem.* London: Lutterworth Press, 1956.

Gardner, M. T. *Winners of the World During Twenty Centuries.* New York: Revell, 1910.

Hardy, E. R., Jr. *Militant in Earth: Twenty Centuries of the Spread of Christianity.* New York: Oxford University Press, 1940.

Harnack, Adolf. *The Mission and Expression of Christianity in the First Three Centuries.* New York: G. P. Putnam's Sons, 1908.

Henderson, A. *A Historical Survey of Christian Missions from the First Century to the End of the Seventeenth.* London: Faith Press, 1927.

Hutchison, Paul. *The Spread of Christianity.* New York: Abingdon Press, 1922.

Latourette, Kenneth Scott. *A History of Christianity.* New York: Harper & Brothers, 1953.

———. *A History of the Expansion of Christianity,* Vols. I–VII. New York: Harper & Brothers, 1937–1945.

———. *Emergence of a World Christian Community.* New Haven: Yale University Press, 1949.

———. *The Christian World Mission in our Day.* New York: Harper & Brothers, 1954.

Leonard, Delavan L. *A Hundred Years of Missions; Progress Since William Carey.* New York: Funk & Wagnalls, 1913.

Maclear, G. F. *History of Christian Missions During the Middle Ages.* Cambridge: Macmillan, 1863.

Mason, Alfred D. *Outlines of Missionary History.* London: Hodder & Stoughton, 1912.

Mathews, Basil J. *Forward Through the Ages.* New York: Friendship Press, 1951.

McAfee, Cleland B. *Changing Foreign Missions.* New York: Revell, 1927.

Nichols, James H. *History of Christianity 1650–1950.* New York: Ronald, 1956.

Payne, Ernest A. *The Growth of the World Church.* London: Edinburgh House Press, 1955.

Pierson, Arthur T. *The Modern Missionary Century.* New York: Baker & Taylor, 1901.

Robinson, Charles H. *History of Christian Missions.* New York: Scribner, 1915.

Speer, Robert E. *Missions and Modern History.* 2 vols. New York: Revell, 1904.

Thiessen, John C. *A Survey of World Missions.* Chicago: Inter-Varsity Press, 1955.

Thompson, R. W. *British Foreign Missions 1837–1897.* London: Blackie, 1899.

Van Dusen, Henry P. *For the Healing of the Nations.* New York: Scribner, 1940.

———. *World Christianity Yesterday, Today and Tomorrow.* New York: Abingdon-Cokesbury Press, 1947.

Walroud, F. F. *Christian Missions Before the Reformation.* London: Society for the Promotion of Christian Knowledge, n.d.

Warneck, Gustav. *History of Protestant Missions.* New York: Revell, 1904.

Reports, Surveys & Handbooks

Allen, Yorke, Jr. *A Seminary Survey*. New York: Harper & Brothers, 1960.
Bingle, E. J. and Grubb, Kenneth G. (eds.) *World Christian Handbook, 1957*. London: World Dominion Press, 1957.
Christian Handbook of India, 1959. Nagpur: National Christian Council of India, 1959.
Directory of Christian Service in Burma 1956–57. Rangoon: Burma Christian Council, 1958.
Ecumenical Missionary Conference, New York, 1900. 2 vols. New York: American Tract Society, 1900.
Ghana Assembly of the International Missionary Council. London: Edinburgh House Press, 1958.
Goodall, Norman (ed.). *Missions Under the Cross* (Willengen, 1952). New York: Friendship Press, 1953.
Interpretative Statistical Survey of the World Mission of the Christian Church. New York: International Missionary Council, 1938.
Japan Christian Yearbook 1959. Tokyo: Christian Literature Society, 1959.
Jerusalem Meeting of the International Missionary Council, 1928. 8 vols. New York: International Missionary Council, 1928.
Madras Series. 7 vols. New York, London: International Missionary Council, 1939.
Ranson, Charles W. (ed.). *Renewal and Advance* (Whitby, 1947). London: Edinburgh House Press, 1948.
The Christian Prospect in East Asia (Bangkok, 1949). New York: Friendship Press, 1950.
The Common Evangelistic Task (Prapat, 1957). Prapat: East Asia Christian Conference, 1957.
The World Mission of the Church (Madras, 1938). New York: International Missionary Council, 1939.
World Missionary Conference Edinburgh 1910. 9 vols. New York: Revell, 1910.

Bible Basis of Missions

Allen, Geoffrey. *The Theology of Missions*. London: Student Christian Movement Press, 1943.
Andersen, Wilhelm. *Towards a Theology of Missions*. London: Student Christian Movement Press, 1955.
Carver, W. O. *God and Man in Missions*. Nashville: Broadman Press, 1944.
Craig, C. T. *One God, One World, The Bible and our Expanding Faith*. New York: Association Press, 1943.
Glover, Robert Hall. *The Bible Basis of Missions*. Los Angeles: Bible House of Los Angeles, 1946.
Lindsell, Harold. *A Christian Philosophy of Missions*. Wheaton, Ill.: Van Kampen Press, 1949.
Love, James P. *The Missionary Message of the Bible*. New York: Macmillan, 1942.

Neill, Stephen. *The Cross in the Church*. London: Independent Press, 1957.

Soper, E. *The Philosophy of the Christian World Mission*. New York: Abingdon-Cokesbury Press, 1943.

Thompson, James S. *The Divine Mission*. Toronto: Ryerson Press, 1957.

Warren, Max A. C. *The Christian Imperative*. New York: Scribner, 1955.

White, Hugh V. *A Theology for Christian Missions*. Chicago: Willett, Clark, 1937.

Missionary Apologetic

Bavinck, J. H. *The Impact of Christianity on the Non-Christian World*. Grand Rapids: Eerdmans, 1948.

Cragg, Kenneth. *The Call of the Minaret*. New York: Oxford University Press, 1956.

Fraser, Jean M. *Under the Cross*. London: Edinburgh House Press, 1956.

Kraemer, Hendrik. *Religion and the Christian Faith*. Philadelphia: Westminster Press, 1956.

———. *The Christian Message in a Non-Christian World*. New York: Harper & Brothers, 1938.

Latourette, Kenneth Scott. *The Christian World Mission in our Day*. New York: Harper & Brothers, 1954.

McGavran, Donald. *Bridges of God*. New York: Friendship Press, 1955.

Newbigin, J. E. Leslie. *The Household of God*. New York: Friendship Press, 1954.

Warren, Max A. C. *The Christian Mission*. London: Student Christian Movement Press, 1951.

Missionary Strategy

Campbell, J. McLeod. *New Horizons or Christian Strategy in the Making*. London: Church Information Board, 1951.

Chirgwin, Arthur M. *The Decisive Decade*. London: Livingstone Press, 1949.

Davis, J. Merle. *New Buildings on Old Foundations*. New York: International Missionary Council, 1945.

Lamott, Willis C. *Revolution in Missions*. New York: Macmillan, 1954.

Latourette, Kenneth Scott and Hogg, William R. *Tomorrow Is Here*. New York: Friendship Press, 1948.

Leber, Charles T. *World Faith in Action*. Indianapolis: Bobbs-Merrill, 1951.

Mackay, John A. *Christianity on the Frontier*. New York: Macmillan, 1950.

Neill, Stephen. *The Unfinished Task*. London: Lutterworth Press, 1957.

Soltau, T. Stanley. *Missions at the Crossroads*. Wheaton, Ill.: Van Kampen Press, 1954.

Principles and Practice

Allen, Roland. *Educational Principles and Missionary Methods*. London: R. Scott, 1919.

——. *Missionary Methods, St. Paul's or Ours?* (3rd ed.). New York and London: World Dominion Press, 1955.

——. *The Spontaneous Expansion of the Church* (3rd ed.). New York and London: World Dominion Press, 1956.

Brown, Arthur J. *The Foreign Missionary* (rev. ed.). New York: Revell, 1950.

Cable, Mildred and French, Francesca. *Ambassadors for Christ.* Chicago: Moody Press, n.d.

Cook, Harold B. *An Introduction to the Study of Christian Missions.* Chicago: Moody Press, 1954.

——. *Missionary Life and Work.* Chicago: Moody Press, 1959.

Fleming, Daniel J. *Living as Comrades.* New York: Agricultural Missions, 1950.

——. *What Would You Do?* New York: Friendship Press, 1949.

Hodges, Melvin L. *On the Mission Field—The Indigenous Church.* Chicago: Moody Press, 1953.

Kane, J. Herbert. *Twofold Growth.* Philadelphia: China Inland Mission, 1946.

Knight, W. H. *Missions in Principle and Practice.* Nashville: Southern Baptist Convention, 1929.

Ritchie, John. *Indigenous Church Principles in Theory and Practice.* New York: Revell, 1946.

Speer, Robert E. *Missionary Principles and Practice.* New York: Revell, 1902.

Williamson, Mabel. *Have We No Right?* Chicago: Moody Press, 1957.

The Bible and Missions

Broomhall, Marshall. *The Bible in China.* London: China Inland Mission, 1934.

Cable, Mildred and French, Francesca. *The Bible in Mission Lands.* New York: Revell, 1947.

Canton, W. A. *A History of the British and Foreign Bible Society.* 5 vols. London: John Murray, 1904–1910.

Chirgwin, Arthur M. *A Book in His Hand; A Manual of Colportage.* London: United Bible Societies, 1955.

——. *The Bible in World Evangelism.* New York: Friendship Press, 1954.

Dwight, Henry Otis. *Centennial History of the American Bible Society.* New York: Macmillan, 1916.

Edwards, Charles E. *The Romance of the Book.* New York: Revell, 1932.

Kilgour, R. *The Bible Throughout the World.* London: World Dominion Press, 1939.

Nida, Eugene A. *Bible Translating.* New York: American Bible Society, 1947.

——. *God's Word in Man's Language.* New York: Harper & Brothers, 1952.

Niedermeyer, Mabel A. *The Bible Goes Round the World.* New York: Friendship Press, 1947.

North, Eric M. *The Book of a Thousand Tongues.* New York: Harper & Brothers, 1938.

Wallis, Ethel E. *He Purposeth a Crop.* Glendale, Calif.: Wycliffe Bible Translators, 1956.

—— and Bennett, M. A. *Two Thousand Tongues to Go: The Story of Wycliffe Bible Translators.* New York: Harper & Brothers, 1959.

Weed, Violet. *Great is the Company.* New York: Friendship Press, 1947.

Biography—General

Drach, G. *Kingdom Pathfinders.* Philadelphia: Muhlenberg Press, 1942.

Eddy, Sherwood. *Pathfinders of the World Missionary Crusade.* New York: Abingdon-Cokesbury Press, 1945.

Garlick, Phyllis. *Six Great Missionaries.* London: Hamish Hamilton, 1955.

Mathews, Basil J. *John R. Mott, World Citizen.* New York: Harper & Brothers, 1934.

Sinclair, Margaret. *William Paton.* London: Student Christian Movement Press, 1949.

Temple, Helen F. *Declare His Wonders.* Kansas City, Mo.: Beacon Hill Press, 1956.

Weatherspoon, J. B. *M. Theron Rankin: Apostle of Advance.* Nashville: Broadman Press, 1958.

Weinlick, John R. *Count Zinzendorf.* New York: Abingdon-Cokesbury Press, 1956.

Wheeler, W. Reginald. *A Man Sent From God; Biography of Robert E. Speer.* New York: Revell, 1956.

Denominational Missions—General

Arpee, Leon. *A History of Armenian Christianity, from the Beginning to Our Own Time.* New York: Armenian Missionary Association, 1946.

Band, Edward. *Working His Purpose Out; the History of the English Presbyterian Mission 1847–1947.* London: Presbyterian Publishing Office, 1948.

Barclay, Wade C. *History of Methodist Missions.* 3 vols., New York: Board of Missions of the Methodist Church, 1949–1957.

Berry, L. L. *A Century of Missions of the African Methodist Episcopal Church 1840–1940.* New York: Gutenberg, 1942.

Bingham, R. V. *Seven Sevens of Years; the Story of the Sudan Interior Mission.* Toronto: Evangelical Publishers, 1943.

Bronson, Ray T. *Southern Baptists in the Great Adventure.* Nashville: Southern Baptist Convention, 1934.

Brown, Arthur J. *One Hundred Years; the Story of Presbyterian Missions.* New York: Revell, 1937.

Burgess, Andrew S. *Lutheran World Missions.* Minneapolis: Augsburg, 1954.

Canton, W. A. *A History of the British and Foreign Bible Society.* 5 vols. London: John Murray, 1904–1910.

Cole, Marley. *Triumphant Kingdom; Jehovah's Witnesses.* New York: Criterion Books, 1957.

Delong, R. V. and Taylor, M. *Fifty Years of Nazarene Missions.* 3 vols. Kansas City, Mo.: Beacon Hill Press, 1952–1958.

Disciples of Christ. *This Is Missions.* St. Louis: Bethany Press, 1953.

Dwight, Henry Otis. *Centennial History of the American Bible Society.* New York: Macmillan, 1916.

Ekvall, Robert B. *et al. After Fifty Years; a Record of the Christian and Missionary Alliance.* Harrisburg: Christian Publications, 1939.

Emery, Julia C. *A Century of Endeavor 1821–1921.* New York: Department of Missions, Protestant Episcopal Church, 1921.

Findlay, G. G. and Holdsworth, W. W. *The History of the Wesleyan Methodist Missionary Society.* London: Epworth Press, 1921.

Forbes, Jean Gordon. *Wide Windows.* Toronto: United Church of Canada, 1951.

Goodall, Norman. *A History of the London Missionary Society 1895–1945.* London and New York: Oxford University Press, 1954.

Harvey, G. Winfred. *The Story of Baptist Missions in Foreign Lands.* St. Louis: Chancy R. Barns, 1885.

Hooton, W. S. and Wright, J. Stafford. *The Bible Churchmen's Missionary Society.* London: BCMS, 1947.

Hutton, J. E. *A History of Moravian Missions.* London: Moravian Publication Office, 1923.

Kane, J. Herbert. *Faith Mighty Faith.* Handbook of Interdenominational Foreign Mission Association. New York: IFMA, 1956.

Lamson, Byron S. *Lights in the World: Free Methodists at Work.* Winona Lake, Ind.: General Missionary Board, 1951.

Lewis, Barbara H. *Methodist Overseas Missions 1956: Gazetteer and Statistics.* New York: Board of Missions of the Methodist Church, 1956.

Lovett, Richard. *History of the London Missionary Society, 1795–1895.* 2 vols. London: Henry Frowde, 1899.

Maxwell, J. Lowry. *Half a Century of Grace: A Jubilee History of the Sudan United Mission.* London: SUM, n.d.

Medford, Hampton T. *Zion Methodism Abroad.* Washington, D. C., 1937.

Mitchell, David. *Seventh Day Adventists Faith in Action.* New York: Vantage Press, 1958.

Pollock, J. C. *Shadows Fall Apart; the Story of the Zenana Bible and Medical Mission.* London: Hodder & Stoughton, 1958.

Spain, Mildred W. *And in Samaria.* Dallas: Central American Mission, 1940.

Stock, Eugene. *The History of the Church Missionary Society.* 4 vols. London: CMS, 1899–1916.

Strong, William Ellsworth. *The Story of the American Board.* Boston: Pilgrim Press, 1910.

Swanson, J. F. (ed.). *Three Score Years . . . and Then.* Chicago: The Evangelical Alliance Mission, 1950.

Taylor, Dr. and Mrs. Howard. *Hudson Taylor and the China Inland Mission.* London: CIM, 1955.

Thompson, H. P. *Into All Lands: the History of the SPG.* London: Society for the Promotion of Christian Knowledge, 1951.

Torbet, Robert G. *Venture of Faith: the Story of the American Baptist Foreign Mission Society 1814–1954.* Philadelphia: Judson Press, 1955.
Webb, Pauline M. *Women of our Company: Methodist Missions.* London: Cargate Press, 1958.
We Have One Future. New York: United Presbyterian Church in the U.S.A. Commission on Ecumenical Mission and Relations, 1958.

South Asia

Asirvatham, Eddy. *Christianity in the Indian Crucible.* Calcutta: Association Press, 1955.
Carey, S. Pearce. *William Carey, D.D., Fellow of the Linnaean Society.* New York: Doran, 1923.
Davey, Cyril J. *The Yellow Robe.* London: Student Christian Movement Press, 1950.
Ekvall, Robert B. *Gateway to Tibet.* Harrisburg: Christian Publications, 1938.
Emmet, P. B. *Apostle of India: Azariah—Bishop of Dornakal.* London: Student Christian Movement Press, 1949.
French, W. E. *The Gospel in India.* London: Carey Press, 1947.
Higginbottom, Sam. *Sam Higginbottom: Farmer.* New York: Scribner, 1949.
Holcomb, H. H. *Men of Might in India Missions.* New York: Revell, 1901.
Hollister, John W. *The Centenary of the Methodist Church in Southern Asia.* Lucknow: Lucknow Publishing House, 1956.
Houghton, Frank. *Amy Carmichael of Dohnavur.* London: Society for the Promotion of Christian Knowledge, 1953.
Hutton, J. E. *A Story of Moravian Missions* (Section on Western Tibet). London: Moravian Publication Office, 1922.
Lehman, E. Arno. *It Began at Tranquebar.* Madras: Christian Literature Society, 1956.
Macnicol, Nicol. *C. F. Andrews, Friend of India.* London: Clarke, 1945.
Mathews, James K. *South of the Himalayas: One Hundred Years of Methodism in India and Pakistan.* New York: Board of Missions of the Methodist Church, 1955.
McKenzie, John (ed.). *The Christian Task in India.* New York: Macmillan, 1929.
Miller, Basil. *Pandita Ramabai: India's Christian Pilgrim.* Grand Rapids: Zondervan, 1949.
Millham, W. T. T. *Central Asia: The Challenge of Closed Doors* (World Today Survey). London: Mildmay Movement, 1949(?).
Neill, Stephen. *Under Three Flags.* New York: Friendship Press, 1954.
Padwick, Constance. *Henry Martyn, Confessor of the Faith.* London: Inter-Varsity Fellowship, 1954.
Parker, Mrs. Arthur. *Sadhu Sundar Singh.* New York: Revell, 1920.
Paul, Rajaiah D. *The First Decade; An Account of the Church of South India.* Madras: Christian Literature Society, 1958.
Ratzlaff, Mrs. Harold. *Fellowship in the Gospel, India 1900–1950.* Newton, Kansas: Mennonite Publication Office, 1950.

Reformed Church in America. *One Hundred Years With Christ in the Arcot Area: 1853–1953.* Madras: Ahura Press, 1955(?).

Richter, J. *History of Protestant Missions in India.* New York: Revell, 1908.

Robbins, J. C. *Following the Pioneers: A Story of American Baptist Mission Work in India and Burma.* Philadelphia: Judson Press, 1922.

Smith, George. *The Life of Alexander Duff.* New York: American Tract Society, n.d.

Sundkler, Bengt G. M. *The Church of South India; The Movement Toward Union, 1900–1947.* London: Lutterworth Press, 1954.

Swavely, C. H. *The Lutheran Enterprise in India.* Madras: Federation of Evangelical Lutheran Churches of India, 1952.

Taylor, J. T. *Our Share in India; The Story of the Central India Mission of the United Church of Canada.* Toronto: United Church of Canada Board of Foreign Missions, 1931.

Thomas, P. *Christians and Christianity in India and Pakistan.* London: Allen & Unwin, 1954.

Warren, Hugh. *The Christian Handbook of India, 1959.* Nagpur: National Christian Council of India, 1959.

Wells, D. S. (ed.). *Ye Are My Witnesses; One Hundred and Fiftieth Anniversary of the Baptist Missionary Society in India.* Calcutta: Baptist Mission Press, 1942.

Southeast Asia

Anderson, Courtney. *To the Golden Shore; The Life of Adoniram Judson.* Boston: Little, Brown, 1956.

Brown A. J. *The Expectation of Siam.* New York: Woman's Board, Presbyterian Church, 1925.

Carpenter, Kathleen. *Come In.* (Malaya) London: Highway Press, 1957.

Dodd, E. M. *Doctor and Friend; The Story of James W. McKean, M.D., of Thailand.* New York: Association Press, 1954.

Fridell, Elmer A. *Baptists in Thailand and the Philippines.* Philadelphia: Judson Press, 1956.

Hallock, Constance Magee. *West of the Date Line; Christian Pioneering in Southeast Asia.* New York: Friendship Press, 1944.

Howard, Randolph L. *Baptists in Burma.* Philadelphia: Judson Press, 1931.

Hubbard, Ethel Daniels. *Ann of Ava.* New York: Friendship Press, 1941.

Irwin, E. F. *With Christ in Indo-China.* Harrisburg: Christian Publications, 1937.

Kuhn, Isobel. *Ascent to the Tribes; Pioneering in North Thailand.* Chicago: Moody Press, 1956.

Landon, Kenneth P. *Southeast Asia, Crossroads of Religions.* Chicago: University of Chicago Press, 1949.

Manikam, Rajah B. *Christianity and the Asian Revolution.* Madras and New York: Friendship Press, 1954.

—— and Thomas, Winburn T. *The Church in Southeast Asia.* New York: Friendship Press, 1956.

Mathews, Basil J. *Unfolding Drama in Southeast Asia*. New York: Friendship Press, 1944.
McFarland, Bertha. *McFarland of Siam*. New York: Vantage Press, 1958.
McFarland, G. B. (ed.). *Historical Sketch of Protestant Missions in Siam, 1828–1928*. Bangkok: Bangkok Times Press, 1928.
McLeish, Alexander. *Burma: Christian Progress to the Invasion*. London: World Dominion Press, n.d.
Millham, W. T. T. *From Burma to Indonesia: The Dawn of a New Era* (World Today Survey) London: Mildmay Movement, 1949(?).
Nichols, B. L. *Echoes from Indonesia*. Nashville: Convention Press, 1958.
Rattenbury, H. B. *Let My People Know* (Methodists in Burma). London: Cargate Press, 1947.
Robbins, J. C. *Boardman of Burma*. Philadelphia: Judson Press, 1940.
Warneck, J. *The Living Christ and Dying Heathenism* (Indonesia). New York: Revell, 1910.
Wells, Kenneth E. *History of Protestant Work in Thailand 1828–1958*. Bangkok: Church of Christ in Thailand, 1958.

Philippine Islands

A Half Century in the Philippines. New York: National Council Protestant Episcopal Church, 1952.
Barlow, Sanna M. *Mountains Singing*. Chicago: Moody Press, 1952.
Fridell, Elmer A. *Baptists in Thailand and the Philippines*. Philadelphia: Judson Press, 1956.
Hibbard, David S. *Making a Nation: The Changing Philippines*. New York: Board of Foreign Missions of the Presbyterian Church in the U.S.A., 1926.
Higdon, E. K. *From Carabao to Clipper*. New York: Friendship Press, 1941.
Osias, Camilo and Lorenzana, Avelina. *Evangelical Christianity in the Philippines*. Dayton: United Brethren Publishing House, 1931.
Pitts, Joseph S. *Mission to the Philippines*. Kansas City, Mo.: Beacon Hill Press, 1956.
Rodgers, James B. *Forty Years in the Philippines*. New York: Board of Foreign Missions of the Presbyterian Church in the U.S.A., 1940.
Sobrepena, Enrique C. *That They May Be One*. Malate, Manila: United Church of Christ in the Philippines, 1954.
Stevenson, Dwight E. *Christianity in the Philippines*. Lexington, Ky.: The College of the Bible, 1955.
The United Church of Christ in the Philippines. Manila: Federation Press, 1954.

China

Broomhall, Marshall. *Hudson Taylor: The Man Who Believed God*. London: China Inland Mission, 1929.
———. *Robert Morrison: A Master Builder*. New York: Doran, 1924.
Cable, Mildred and French, Francesca. *George Hunter, Apostle of Turkestan*. London: China Inland Mission, 1948.

Canfield, Carolyn L. *One Vision Only; Biography of Isobel Kuhn.* Chicago: Moody Press, 1959.

Cary-Elwes, Columba. *China and the Cross; A Survey of Missionary History.* New York: P. J. Kenedy, 1957.

French, Francesca. *Thomas Cochrane, Pioneer and Missionary Statesman.* London: Hodder & Stoughton, 1956.

Friends, Society of. *Quakers Visit China.* London: Society of Friends, 1955.

Garnier, A. J. *A Maker of Modern China: Timothy Richard.* London: Carey Press, 1945.

Glover, A. E. *A Thousand Miles of Miracle in China.* London: Hodder & Stoughton, 1904.

Goforth, Rosalind. *Goforth of China.* Grand Rapids: Zondervan, 1931.

Hayward, Victor E. *Ears to Hear.* London: Edinburgh House Press, 1955.

Hudspeth, W. H. *The Bible and China.* London: British and Foreign Bible Society, 1952.

Kilen, Juline R. *Forty Years in China; The Lutheran Brethren Mission in China 1902–1942.* Fergus Falls, Minn.: Broderbaandet Publishing Co., 1943(?).

Latourette, Kenneth Scott. *A History of Christian Missions in China.* New York: Macmillan, 1929.

Lyall, Leslie T. *John Sung; Flame for God in the Far East.* London: China Inland Mission, 1954.

MacGillivray, D. (ed.). *A Century of Protestant Missions in China 1807–1907.* New York: American Tract Society, 1907.

Matthews, H. S. *American Board of Commissioners for Foreign Missions: Seventy-five Years of the North China Mission.* Peking: Sheffield Print Shop, Yenching University, 1942.

Mueller, J. Theodore. *Great Missionaries to China.* Grand Rapids: Zondervan, 1947.

Oss, John. *Mission Advance in China.* Nashville: Southern Publishing Association, 1949.

Outerbridge, Leonard M. *The Lost Churches of China.* Philadelphia: Westminster, 1952.

Paton, David M. *Christian Missions and the Judgment of God.* London: Student Christian Movement Press, 1953.

Pollock, J. C. *The Cambridge Seven.* Chicago: Inter-Varsity Press, 1955.

Rattenbury, Harold B. *David Hill, Friend of China.* London: Epworth Press, 1949.

Rose, John. *A Church Born to Suffer; An Account of the First Hundred Years of the Methodist Church in South China 1851–1951.* London: Cargate Press, 1951.

Stauffer, M. T. (ed.). *The Christian Occupation of China.* Shanghai: China Continuation Committee, 1922.

Taylor, Mrs. Howard. *Pastor Hsi; One of China's Scholars.* London: China Inland Mission, 1925.

Thompson, Phyllis. *Desert Pilgrim; The Story of Mildred Cable's Venture for God in Central Asia.* London: China Inland Mission, 1957.

Varg, Paul A. *Missionaries, Chinese and Diplomats. The American Protestant Missionary Movement in China 1890–1952.* Princeton, N. J.: Princeton University Press, 1958.
Williamson, Henry R. *British Baptists in China 1845–1952.* London: Carey Kingsgate Press, 1957.
Young, G. *The Living Christ in Modern China.* London: Carey Press, 1949.

Taiwan

Dickson, Lillian. *These My People.* Grand Rapids: Zondervan, 1958.
Mackay, George L. *From Far Formosa.* New York: Revell, 1895.
MacMillan, Hugh. *Then Till Now in Formosa.* Taipei: English and Canadian Presbyterian Missions in Formosa, 1953.

Japan

Axling, William. *Japan at the Midcentury.* Japan: Protestant Publishing Co., 1955.
———. *This is Japan.* New York: Friendship Press, 1957.
Boxer, Charles R. *The Christian Century in Japan.* Berkeley: University of California Press, 1951.
Cary, Otis. *History of Christianity in Japan.* 2 vols. New York: Revell, 1909.
Clapp, Frances Benton. *Mary Florence Denton and the Doshisha.* Kyoto: Doshisha University Press, 1955.
Cogswell, James A. *Until the Day Dawn.* Nashville: Board of Foreign Missions of the Presbyterian Church in the U.S.A., 1957.
Cowman, Mrs. Charles E. *Charles E. Cowman, Missionary-Warrior.* Los Angeles: Oriental Missionary Society, 1928.
Davis, J. D. *Joseph Hardy Neesima.* New York: Revell, 1894.
Garrott, W. M. *Japan Advances.* Nashville: Convention Press, 1956.
Griffis, W. E. *Verbeck of Japan.* New York: Revell, 1900.
Iglehart, Charles W. *Cross and Crisis in Japan.* New York: Friendship Press, 1957.
Jennings, Raymond P. *Jesus, Japan and Kanzo Uchimura.* Tokyo: Christian Literature Society, 1958.
Johnson, Katherine. *In Our Time 1947–1957.* New York: Interboard Convention for Christian Work in Japan, 1957.
Kerr, William C. *Japan Begins Again.* New York: Friendship Press, 1949.
Lea, Leonora E. *Window on Japan.* Greenwich, Conn.: Seabury Press, 1956.
Mann, J. C. *The Last Fifty Years in Japan.* London: Church Missionary Society, 1948.
Millham, W. T. T. (ed.). *The Changing East: Japan and Her Neighbors.* (World Today Survey). London: Mildmay Movement, 1949(?).
Natori, Junichi. *Historical Stories of Christianity in Japan.* Tokyo: The Hokuseido Press, 1957.
Prichard, Marianna and Prichard, Norman Young. *Ten Against the Storm.* New York: Friendship Press, 1957.

Simon, Charlie May. *A Seed Shall Serve; The Story of Toyohiko Kagawa.* New York: Dutton, 1958.

Society of Friends. *Fifty Years of Quakerism in Japan.* Tokyo: Yearly Meeting of Friends, 1937.

Syrdal, Rolf A. *Mission in Japan; Studies in the Beginning and Development of the Indigenous Lutheran Church in Japan.* Minneapolis: Augsburg Publishing House, 1958.

Tomonobu, Yanagita. *Christianity in Japan.* Sendai: Bible Library Publishers, 1957.

Tucker, Henry St. George. *The History of the Episcopal Church in Japan.* New York: Scribner, 1938.

Verbeck, Guido H. F. *History of Protestant Missions in Japan.* Yokohama: Meiklejohn & Co., 1883.

Whybray, R. N. *The Church Serves Japan.* London: Society for the Propagation of the Gospel, 1956.

Williams, Rev. Philip. *Journey Into Mission.* New York: Friendship Press, 1957.

Young, John M. L. *The Two Empires in Japan.* Tokyo: Bible Times Press, 1958.

Korea

Clark, C. A. *The Korean Church and the Nevius Method.* New York: Revell, 1930.

Griffis, William E. *A Modern Pioneer in Korea; The Life of Henry G. Appenzeller.* New York: Revell, 1912.

Paik, L. George. *The History of Protestant Missions in Korea 1832–1910.* Pyeng Yang: Union Christian College Press, 1929.

Underwood, H. H. *Tragedy and Faith in Korea.* New York: Friendship Press, 1952.

Underwood, Lillias. *Underwood of Korea.* New York: Revell, 1918.

Wasson, A. W. *Church Growth in Korea.* Concord, N. H.: Rumford Press, 1934.

Middle East

Arpee, Leon. *A Century of Armenian Protestantism 1846–1946.* New York: Armenian Missionary Association, 1946.

Baly, Denis. *Multitudes in the Valley; Church and Crisis in the Middle East.* Greenwich, Conn.: Seabury Press, 1957.

Batal, James. *Assignment: Near East.* New York: Friendship Press, 1950.

Bliss, Daniel. *The Reminiscences of Daniel Bliss.* New York: Revell, 1920.

Bridgeman, Charles Thorley. *The Episcopal Church and the Middle East.* New York: Morehouse-Gorham, 1958.

Calvery, Eleanor T., M.D. *My Arabian Days and Nights.* New York: Thomas Y. Crowell Co., 1958.

Gates, Caleb Frank. *Not to Me Only.* Princeton, N. J.: Princeton University Press, 1940.

Greene, Joseph K. *Leavening the Levant.* Boston: Pilgrim Press, 1916.

Hamlin, Cyrus. *My Life and Times* (5th ed.). New York: Revell, 1893.

Harrison, Ann M. *A Tool in His Hand; A Biography of Paul Harrison.*
New York: Friendship Press, 1958.
Jessup, Henry Harris. *Fifty-three Years in Syria.* 2 vols. New York: Revell,
1910.
Milford, C. S. *The Middle East: Bridge or Barrier.* London: Highway
Press, 1956.
Miller, Basil. *Nineteen Missionary Stories from the Middle East.* Grand
Rapids: Zondervan, 1950.
Millham, W. T. T. (ed.). *In and Around Palestine: Lands of the Bible*
(World Today Survey). London: Mildmay Movement, 1949(?).
————. *The Middle East: Lands Under Islam's Sway* (World Today Sur-
vey). London: Mildmay Movement, 1949(?).
Milligan, A. A. Dr. *Henry of Assiut.* Philadelphia: United Presbyterian
Board of Foreign Missions, 1945.
Newton, Frances E. *Fifty Years in Palestine.* London: Coldharbour Press,
1948.
Noshy, Ibrahim. *The Coptic Church: Christianity in Egypt.* Washington,
D. C.: Ruth Sloan Associates, 1955.
Padwick, Constance E. *Call to Istanbul.* London: Longmans, Green, 1958.
————. *Temple Gairdner of Cairo.* London: Society for the Promotion of
Christian Knowledge, 1929.
Penrose, S. *That They May Have Life; The Story of the American Uni-
versity 1866–1941.* New York: Trustees of the American University of
Beirut, 1942.
Rasooli, Jay M. and Allen, Cady H. *The Life Story of Dr. Sa'eed of Iran.*
Grand Rapids: Grand Rapids International Publications, 1957.
Richter, Julius. *A History of Protestant Missions in the Near East.* New
York: Revell, 1910.
Robson, J. *Ion Keith-Falconer of Arabia.* New York: Doran, 1924.
Thompson, A. E. *A Century of Jewish Missions.* New York: Revell, 1902.
Van Ess, Dorothy F. *History of the Arabian Mission 1926–1957.* New
York: Board for the Christian World Mission of the Reformed Church
in America, 1958.
Watson, Charles R. *In the Valley of the Nile.* New York: Revell, 1908.
Wilson, J. Christy. *Apostle to Islam; A Biography of Samuel Zwemer.*
Grand Rapids: Baker Book House, 1952.
Wishard, J. G. *Twenty Years in Persia.* New York: Revell, 1908.
Wysner, Glora M. *The Near East Panorama.* New York: Friendship Press,
1950.
Zwemer, Samuel M. *Across the World of Islam.* New York: Revell, 1929.
————. *A Factual Study of the Moslem World.* New York: Revell, 1946.
————. *The Cross Above the Crescent.* Grand Rapids: Zondervan, 1941.
———— and Cantine, James. *The Golden Milestone.* New York: Revell, 1938.

Africa—General

Anderson, L. K. *Bridge to Africa.* New York: Board of Foreign Missions
of the Presyterian Church in the U.S.A., 1952.

Booth, Newell S. *The Cross Over Africa*. New York: Friendship Press, 1945.
——. *This is Africa South of the Sahara*. New York: Friendship Press, 1959.
Carpenter, G. W. *The Way in Africa*. New York: Friendship Press, 1959.
Fenton, Thomas. *Black Harvest*. London: Cargate, 1956.
Fisher, W. S. and Hoyte, J. *Africa Looks Ahead*. London: Pickering & Inglis, 1948.
Groves, C. P. *The Planting of Christianity in Africa 1840–1954*. 4 vols. London: Lutterworth Press, 1948–1958.
International Missionary Council. *The Church in Changing Africa*. New York: IMC, 1958.
Jester, William L. *Something New*. Nashville: Convention Press, 1957.
Karefa-Smart, John and Rena. *The Halting Kingdom: Christ and the African Revolution*. New York: Friendship Press, 1959.
McConnell, D. *Along the African Path*. New York: Board of Mission and Church Extension, Methodist Church, 1952.
Mueller, J. Theodore. *Great Missionaries to Africa*. Grand Rapids: Zondervan, 1941.
Naylor, W. S. *Daybreak in the Dark Continent*. New York: Young People's Missionary Movement, 1912.
Oliver, Roland A. *How Christian is Africa?* London: Highway Press, 1956.
Patterson, Ira N. *Continent in Commotion*. Nashville: Convention Press, 1957.
Ross, Emory. *African Heritage*. New York: Friendship Press, 1952.
—— and Myrta. *Africa Disturbed*. New York: Friendship Press, 1959.
Society of African Missions. *One Hundred Years of Missionary Achievement 1856–1956*. Cork, Ireland: African Missions, 1956.
Stewart, James. *Dawn in the Dark Continent*. New York: Revell, 1903.
Temple, Merfyn M. *Rain on the Earth*. London: Cargate Press, 1955.
Westermann, Diedrich. *Africa and Christianity*. London: Oxford University Press, 1937.
Wright, Charlotte Crogman. *Beneath the Southern Cross*. New York: Exposition Press, 1955.

West Africa

Birtwhistle, Allen. *Thomas Birch Freeman: West African Pioneer*. London: Cargate Press, 1950.
DeKorne, John C. *To Whom I Now Send Thee: Mission Work of the Christian Reformed Church in Nigeria*. Grand Rapids: Eerdmans, 1945.
Dike, K. O. *Origins of the Niger Mission (CMS) 1841–1891*. Ibadan: Ibadan University Press, 1957.
Helser, Albert D., *The Hand of God in the Sudan*. New York: Revell, 1946.
Maddry, C. *Day Dawn in Yoruba Land*. Nashville: Broadman Press, 1939.
McFarlan, Donald M. *Calabar, The Church of Scotland Missions, 1846–1946*. New York: Nelson, 1946.

Miller, Basil. *Mary Slessor, Heroine of Calabar.* Grand Rapids: Zondervan, 1946.

Miller, W. R. *Yesterday and Tomorrow in Northern Nigeria.* London: Student Christian Movement Press, 1938.

Millham, W. T. T. *West Africa: A Babel of Tongues* (World Today Survey). London: Mildmay Movement, 1949(?).

Nan, Henry. *We Move Into Africa: The Story of the Planting of the Lutheran Church in Southwestern Nigeria.* St. Louis: Concordia, 1945.

Page, Jesse. *The Black Bishop, Samuel Adjai Crowther.* New York: Revell, n.d.

Percy, Douglas C. *Stirrett of the Sudan.* Toronto: Sudan Interior Mission, 1948.

Sadler, George W. *A Century in Nigeria.* Nashville: Broadman Press, 1950.

Schneider, G. *A Graphic Portrayal of a Christian Mission at Work in the Cameroons, West Africa.* Forest Park, Ill.: North America Baptist General Conference, 1957.

Trimingham, J. Spencer. *The Christian Approach to Islam in the Sudan.* New York: Oxford University Press, 1948.

———. *The Christian Church and Islam in West Africa.* London: Student Christian Movement Press, 1955.

Walker, Frank D. *A Hundred Years in Nigeria; The Story of the Methodist Mission in West Nigeria 1842–1942.* London: Cargate Press, 1942.

———. *The Romance of the Black River; The Story of the CMS Nigeria Mission.* London: Church Missionary Society, 1930.

Ward, W. J. *In and Around the Oron Country: The Story of Primitive Methodism in Southern Nigeria.* London: Hammond, n.d.

Whetstone, Harold V. *Lutheran Mission in Liberia.* New York: Board of Foreign Missions of the United Lutheran Church in America, 1955.

Williamson, S. G. and Bardsley, J. *The Gold Coast—What of the Church?* London: Edinburgh House Press, 1953.

South Africa

Blaikie, W. G. *Personal Life of David Livingstone.* New York: Revell, 1903.

Davies, Horton, and Shepherd, R. H. W. *South Africa Missions 1800–1950.* London: Nelson, 1954.

DuPlessis, J. *A History of Christian Missions in South Africa.* New York: Longmans, Green, 1911.

———. *The Evangelization of Pagan Africa.* Capetown: Juta, 1930.

Evans, H. St. J. T. *The Church in Southern Rhodesia.* London: Society for the Propagation of the Gospel, 1945.

Eveleigh, William (ed.). *The Story of a Century 1823–1923.* Capetown: Methodist Publishing House, 1923.

Frame, Hugh F. *Moffat Leads the Way.* London: Livingstone Press, 1949.

Gerdener, G. B. A. *Recent Developments in the South Africa Mission Field.* London: Marshall, Morgan & Scott, 1958.

————. *The Story of Christian Missions in South Africa.* Johannesburg: Linden Christian Church, 1950.

Griffith, Robert. *Madagascar, A Century of Adventure.* London: London Missionary Society, 1919.

Lennox, John. *The Story of Our Missions. South Africa.* Edinburgh: Offices of the United Free Church of Scotland, 1911.

Mathews, Basil. *Livingstone the Pathfinder.* New York: Friendship Press, 1954.

Matthews, F. T. *Thirty Years in Madagascar.* London: Religious Tract Society, 1904.

McMahon, E. O. *Christian Missions in Madagascar.* Westminster: Society for the Propagation of the Gospel, 1914.

Millham, W. T. T. *From the Cape to Angola: Barriers to Unity* (World Today Survey). London: Mildmay Movement, 1949(?).

————. *Zambesi Waterways: On Livingstone's Trail* (World Today Survey). London: Mildmay Movement, 1949(?).

Orchard, R. K. *The High Commission Territories.* London: World Dominion Press, 1951.

Richards, Elizabeth. *Fifty Years in Nyanza 1906–1956.* Maseno, Kenya: Nyanza Jubilee Committee, 1956.

Shank, Ezra A. *Fervent in Spirit; The Biography of Arthur J. Bowen.* Chicago: Moody Press, 1954.

Shepherd, Robert H. W. *Lovedale South Africa.* Lovedale: Lovedale Press, 1941.

Sibree, J. *Fifty Years in Madagascar.* New York: Houghton Mifflin, 1924.

Sundkler, Bengt G. M. *Bantu Prophets.* London: Lutterworth Press, 1948.

Syrdal, Rolf A. *Mission in Madagascar.* Minneapolis: Augsburg, 1957.

Taylor, James Dexter. *The American Board Mission in South Africa.* Durban: John Singleton & Sons, 1911.

Tucker, John T. *Angola, The Land of the Blacksmith Prince.* London: World Dominion Press, 1933.

Wells, James. *Stewart of Lovedale.* New York: Revell, 1909.

Whiteside, J. *History of the Wesleyan Methodist Church of South Africa.* London: Stock, 1906.

North Africa

Campbell, Dugald. *With the Bible in North Africa.* Kilmarnock, Scotland: John Ritchie, 1944.

Kerr, Robert. *Morocco After Twenty-five Years.* London: Murray and Evenden, 1912.

————. *Pioneering in Morocco.* London: Allenson, 1894.

Millham, W. T. T. (ed.). *North Africa, Lands of the Vanished Church* (World Today Survey). London: Mildmay Press, 1949(?).

Warren, T. J. P. *North Africa Today.* Tunis: North Africa Mission, 1947.

East Africa

Barry, W. Grinton. *Bishop Hannington.* London: Religious Tract Society, n.d.

Bernander, Gustaf. *The Rising Tide; Christianity Challenged in East Africa.* Rock Island, Ill.: Augustana Press, 1957.

Cash, W. Wilson. *The Changing Sudan.* London: Church Missionary Society, 1930.

Church of Scotland Foreign Missions Committee. *Kenya 1898–1948; The Jubilee Book of the Church of Scotland Mission, Kenya Colony.* Glasgow: CSFMC, 1948.

Cole, Keith. *Kenya: Hanging in the Middle Way.* London: Highway Press, 1959.

Collister, P. *Pioneers in East Africa.* Nairobi: Eagle Press, 1956.

Dougall, J. W. C. *Building Kenya's Future.* Edinburgh: Church of Scotland, Foreign Mission Committee, 1956.

Grimes, M. S. *Life out of Death; The Story of the Africa Inland Mission.* London: AIM, 1917.

Harford-Battersby, Charles F. *Pilkington of Uganda.* London: Marshall Brothers, n.d.

Kitching, A. L. *From Darkness to Light. A Study of Pioneer Work in the Diocese of the Upper Nile.* London: Society for the Promotion of Christian Knowledge, 1935.

Laws, Robert. *Reminiscences of Livingstone.* Edinburgh: Oliver & Boyd, 1934.

Lloyd, T. E. *African Harvest.* London: Lutterworth Press, 1953.

Oliver, R. A. *The Missionary Factor in East Africa.* London and New York: Longmans, Green, 1952.

Taylor, John V. *The Growth of the Church in Buganda.* London: Student Christian Movement Press, 1958.

Trimingham, J. Spencer. *The Christian Church and Mission in Ethiopia.* London: World Dominion Press, 1950.

———. *The Christian Church in Post-War Sudan.* London: World Dominion Press, 1949.

United Presbyterian Church Board of Foreign Missions. *The Sudan, Its Land and People.* Philadelphia: UPCBFM, 1952.

Wilson, C. J. *Uganda in the Days of Bishop Tucker.* London: Macmillan, 1955.

Wiseman, E. M. *Kikuyu Martyrs.* London: Highway Press, 1958.

Central Africa

Anderson, Erica. *The World of Albert Schweitzer.* New York: Harper & Brothers, 1955.

Anstruther, Ian. *I Presume. Stanley's Triumph and Disaster.* London: Geoffrey Bles, 1956.

Ashmore, Ann L. *The Call of the Congo.* Nashville: Parthenon Press, 1958.

Baker, Ernest. *Life and Explorations of Frederick S. Arnot.* Seeley Service, 1923.

Carpenter, George W. *Highways for God in Congo.* Leopoldville: La Librairie au Congo, 1952.

Crawford, Dan. *Thinking Black.* New York: Doran, 1912.

Grubb, Norman T. *C. T. Studd*. Grand Rapids: Zondervan, 1946.

Hemmens, H. L. *George Grenfell, Pioneer in Congo*. London: Student Christian Movement Press, 1927.

Jobson, Orville D. *Conquering Oubangi-Chari for Christ*. Winona Lake, Ind.: Brethren Missionary Herald, 1957.

Millham, W. T. T. *From the Congo to the Niger: African Jewels* (World Today Survey). London: Mildmay Movement, 1949(?).

Roome, W. J. W. *Through Central Africa*. New York: Revell, 1930.

Shiletto, Edward. *François Coillard, A Wayfaring Man*. New York: Doran, 1923.

Smith, A. C. S. *Road to Revival: The Story of the Ruanda Mission*. London: Church Missionary Society, 1946.

Stanley, Henry M. *Through the Dark Continent*. 2 vols. New York: Harper & Brothers, 1878.

Tilsey, G. E. *Dan Crawford, Missionary and Pioneer*. London: Oliphants, 1929.

Wilson, George Herbert. *The History of the Universities' Mission to Central Africa*. Westminster: UMCA, 1936.

Latin America

Braga, Erasmo and Grubb, Kenneth G. *The Republic of Brazil*. London: World Dominion Press, 1932.

Bratcher, L. M. *The Apostle of the Amazon*. Nashville: Broadman Press, 1951.

Camargo, G. Baez and Grubb, Kenneth G. *Religion in the Republic of Mexico*. London and New York: World Dominion Press, 1935.

Crabtree, Asa R. *Baptists in Brazil*. Rio de Janeiro: Baptist Publishing House of Brazil, 1953.

Davis, J. Merle. *How the Church Grows in Brazil*. New York: International Missionary Council, 1943.

———. *The Cuban Church in a Sugar Economy*. New York: International Missionary Council, 1942.

———. *The Evangelical Church in the River Plate Republics*. New York: International Missionary Council, 1943.

Deter, Arthur B. *Forty Years in the Land of Tomorrow*. Nashville: Broadman Press, 1946.

Easton, Wilfred. *West Indies: What of the Church?* London: Edinburgh House Press, 1956.

Elliot, Elizabeth. *Through Gates of Splendor*. New York: Harper & Brothers, 1957.

Ferger, Henri R. *Flight Over Latin America*. New York: Board of Foreign Missions of the Presbyterian Church in the U.S.A., 1942.

Floyd, O. *Doctora in Mexico*. New York: Putnam, 1944.

Gammon, Samuel R. *The Evangelical Invasion of Brazil*. Richmond: Presbyterian Committee of Publication, 1910.

Gill, Everett, Jr. *Pilgrimage to Spanish America*. Nashville: Broadman Press, 1951.

Graham, Agnes. *Pioneering With Christ in Chile.* Nashville: Broadman Press, 1942.

Grubb, Kenneth G. *An Advancing Church in Latin America.* London: World Dominion Press, 1936.

——. *The Lowland Indians of Amazonia.* London: World Dominion Press, 1927.

——. *The Northern Republics of South America.* London: World Dominion Press, 1931.

Hallock, Constance M. *Looking South.* New York: Friendship Press, 1951.

Hawthorne, Sally R. *Cloud Country Sojourn.* Cochabamba: Bolivian Indian Mission, 1957.

Hay, Alex R. *The Indians of South America and the Gospel.* New York: Revell, 1928.

Herman, Stewart. "Lutherans in Latin America," in *Lutheran Churches of the World.* Minneapolis: Augsburg, 1957.

Howard, George P. *Religious Liberty in Latin America?* Philadelphia: Westminster Press, 1944.

——. *We Americans: North and South.* New York: Friendship Press, 1951.

Hunt, R. J. (ed.). *Among the Araucanians of Southern Chile.* London: South American Missionary Society, 1931.

——. *The Livingstone of South America.* Philadelphia: Lippincott, 1932.

International Missionary Council. *The Listening Isles.* New York and London: IMC, 1957.

Jordan, W. F. *Central American Indians and the Bible.* New York: Revell, 1926.

——. *Crusading in the West Indies.* New York: Revell, 1922.

Lee, Elizabeth M. and Wasson, Alfred W. *The Latin American Circuit.* New York: Board of Missions and Church Extension, the Methodist Church, 1942.

Long, Eula K. *Outlook in Brazil.* New York: Friendship Press, 1942.

Mackay, John A. *Christianity on the Frontier.* New York: Macmillan, 1950.

McNairn, A. Stuart. *Why South America?* London: Evangelical Union of South America, 1936.

Millham, W. T. T. (ed.). *Latin America: Nations in the Making* (World Today Survey). London: Mildmay Movement, 1949(?).

——. *West Indies: Pearls of the Caribbean* (World Today Survey). London: Mildmay Movement, 1949(?).

Montgomery, J. Dexter. *Disciples of Christ in Argentina 1906–1956.* St. Louis: Bethany, 1956.

Moore, R. C. *Piety and Poverty in Chile.* Nashville: Broadman Press, 1946.

Morgan, Carol McAfee. *Rim of the Caribbean.* New York: Friendship Press, 1942.

Quarles, James C. *Christ in the Silver Lands.* Richmond: Foreign Mission Board, Southern Baptist Convention, 1935.

Rembao, Alberto. *Outlook in Mexico.* New York: Friendship Press, 1942.

Rycroft, W. Stanley (ed.). *Indians of the High Andes.* New York: Committee on Co-operation in Latin America, 1946.
——. *On This Foundation.* New York: Friendship Press, 1942.
——. *Religion and Faith in Latin America.* Philadelphia: Westminster Press, 1958.
Trexler, S. *A Pastor Wings Over South America.* Philadelphia: Muhlenberg Press, 1942.
Tucker, Hugh C. *The Bible in Brazil.* New York: Revell, 1902.
Wheeler, W. R. *et al. Modern Missions in Chile and Brazil.* Philadelphia: Westminster Press, 1926.
——. *Modern Missions in Mexico.* Philadelphia: Westminster Press, 1925.
—— and Browning, Webster E. *Modern Missions on the Spanish Main.* Philadelphia: Westminster Press, 1925.
Yoder, Howard W. *Present Limitations on Religious Liberty in Latin America and Their Effects on the Evangelical Communities.* New York: National Council of Churches of Christ in the U.S.A., 1955.
Young, Robert. *From Cape Horn to Panama.* London: South American Missionary Society, 1905.

Pacific Islands

Bell, Ralph, *John G. Paton; Apostle to the New Hebrides.* Butler, Ind.: The Higley Press, 1957.
Burton, J. W. *Missionary Survey of the Pacific Islands.* London: World Dominion Press, 1930.
——. *Modern Missions in the South Pacific.* London: Livingstone Press, 1949.
—— and Deane, Wallace. *A Hundred Years in Fiji.* London: Epworth Press, 1936.
Colwell, James. *A Century in the Pacific.* New York: Kelly, 1915.
Dovey, J. Whitsed. *The Gospel in the South Pacific.* London: World Dominion Press, 1950(?).
Ellis, James J. *John Williams: The Martyr Missionary of Polynesia.* New York: Revell, 1889.
Koskinen, Aarne A. *Missionary Influence as a Political Factor in the Pacific Islands.* Helsinki: Academia Scientiarum Fennicae, 1953.
Mathews, Basil J. *Unfolding Drama in Southeast Asia.* New York: Friendship Press, 1944.
Millham, W. T. T. (ed.). *Gems of the Pacific: A Century of Achievement* (World Today Survey). London: Mildmay Movement, 1949(?).
Murray, A. W. *Forty Years' Mission Work in Polynesia and New Guinea from 1835 to 1875.* London: Nisbet, 1876.
——. *Missions in Western Polynesia. Historical Sketches 1839–1863.* London: John Snow, 1863.
Northcott, C. *John Williams Sails On.* London: Hodder & Stoughton, 1939.
Paton, Frank H. L. *Patteson of Melanesia.* London: Society for the Promotion of Christian Knowledge, 1930.

———. *The Kingdom in the Pacific.* London: London Missionary Society, 1913.

———. *The Triumph of the Gospel in the New Hebrides.* New York: Doran, 1908.

Patterson, George. *Missionary Life Among the Cannibals: The Life of Rev. John Geddie,* D.D. Toronto: James Campbell & Son, 1882.

Pierson, Delavan L. *The Pacific Islanders. From Savages to Saints.* New York: Funk & Wagnalls, 1906.

Shevill, Ian. *Pacific Conquest; The History of 150 Years of Missionary Progress in the South Pacific.* Sydney: Pacific Christian Literature Society, 1949.

Small, Alex. *Chalmers of New Guinea.* New York: Doran, 1924.

Taylor, Richard S. *Our Pacific Outposts; Nazarene Missions.* Kansas City, Mo.: Beacon Hill Press, 1956.

Van Dusen, Henry P. *They Found the Church There.* New York: Scribner, 1945.

Young, F. S. H. *Pearls from the Pacific.* London: Marshall, 1930.

INDEX

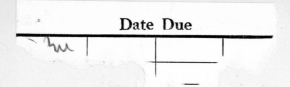

Date Due